Phantom Self

(And how to find the real one)

DavidIcke
BOOKS

First published in February 2016

 David Icke Books Ltd
185a High Street
Ryde
Isle of Wight
PO33 2PN
UK

Tel/fax: +44 (0) 1983 566002
email: info@davidickebooks.co.uk

Cover illustration and book design by Neil Hague

British Library Cataloguing-in
Publication Data
A catalogue record for this book is
available from the British Library

ISBN 978-0-9576308-8-8

Phantom Self

(And how to find the real one)

DAVID ICKE

Dedication

To Sanity

Other books and DVDs by David Icke

Books

The Perception Deception

Remember Who You Are

Human Race Get Off Your *Knees* - The Lion Sleeps No More

The David Icke Guide to the Global Conspiracy (and how to end it)

Infinite Love is the Only Truth, *Everything* Else is Illusion

Tales from the Time Loop

Alice in Wonderland and the World Trade Center Disaster

Children Of The Matrix

The Biggest Secret

I Am Me • I Am Free

...And The Truth Shall Set You Free – 21st century edition

Lifting The Veil

The Robots' Rebellion

Heal the World

Truth Vibrations

It Doesn' t Have To Be Like This

DVDs

David Icke Live at Wembley Arena

The Lion Sleeps No More

Beyond the Cutting Edge – Exposing the Dreamworld We Believe to be Real

Freedom or Fascism: the Time to Choose

Secrets of the Matrix

From Prison to Paradise

Turning Of The Tide

The Freedom Road

Revelations Of A Mother Goddess

Speaking Out

The Reptilian Agenda

Details of availability at the back of this book
and through the website **www.davidicke.com**

Be the anomaly. The aberration. The glitch. The inconvenient. The divergent. The string of junk code. The stubborn apple that falls nowhere near the trees or the forest. Be the fool. The bonehead. The idiot in the room. Let them shake their groupthink heads at you. Let them be ashamed of you. Embarrassed of you. Pissed off at you. They will call you names and you must let them. Let them jeer. Let them point. Let them laugh. Be resistant to their mockery. Be the fodder for their jokes. Be a magnificent failure in their eyes. A tiger does not lose sleep over the opinion of sheep. Go ahead. Be the scar tissue on their worldview. Their normality. They'll loathe you. They'll fear you.

They'll wish they were you.

I am taking my life back from the craziness of this world. I am interrupting the world's plan for me to live out my dreams instead. I am shutting myself off from the deadness of conforming. I am doing this life my way from now on
— S C Lourie

Never be bullied into silence. Never allow yourself to be made a victim. Accept no one's definition of your life, but define yourself
— Harvey Fierstein

Wanting to be someone else is a waste of who you are
— Kurt Cobain

Never be so focussed on what you are looking for that you overlook the thing you actually find
— Ann Patchett

The secret of life

... is to fall seven times and to get up eight times
– Paulo Coelho

The number of those who undergo the fatigue of judging for themselves is very small indeed
– Richard Brinsley Sheridan

People demand freedom of speech as a compensation for the freedom of thought which they seldom use
– Soren Kierkegaard

Think before you speak. Read before you think
– Fran Lebowitz

Phan·tom

(fǎnˈtəəm)

n.

1. Something apparently seen, heard, or sensed, but having no physical reality; a ghost or apparition.

2. An image that appears only in the mind; an illusion.

adj.

1. Fictitious or non-existent, often when intended to deceive.

2. Believed to be real even though illusory.

Contents

Tales from the Rabbit Hole

First they ignore you, then they laugh at you, then they fight you, then you win
Mahatma Gandhi

My life and my books are indivisible and I'll begin with some brief but essential background for new readers to better understand what follows. It's an amazing story, really, and one that continues to unfold every day.

I was born in Leicester, England, on April 29th 1952 and I felt from an early age that I was here to 'do something'. I didn't know what and I felt at first that the 'something' was to be a professional soccer player. This was my childhood ambition and through many 'coincidences' and strokes of 'luck' I went on to play professional football until rheumatoid arthritis ended my career aged 21. 'Lucky coincidences' have been a constant feature of my life and work and some unseen force has clearly been guiding me through the maze. I went on to be a newspaper, radio and television journalist, spokesman for the British Green Party and, since the turn of the 1990s, one of the most ridiculed people in British history (Fig 1). But today with so many of my 'crazy theories' and exposures confirmed to be true there has been a transformation. More people than ever before are observing the world and world events from a new perspective. It's not the majority yet, nowhere near, but compared with how it used to be a quarter of a century ago what has happened borders on the miraculous. People who once ridiculed me are now reading my books and I hope this has inspired others to speak their truth without fear of the consequences however unpleasant they may be. If what you say has validly it will eventually be shown to be so, but before it can be validated it has to be said. Courage to stand up and speak out is so crucial to unravelling the vast web of global deceit that holds humanity in servitude to engineered ignorance.

I was a sports presenter with the BBC and speaking on behalf of the Green Party in 1989 when my life took a rapid and extraordinary new direction. Throughout that year I felt a presence around me, most tangibly when I was alone. The feeling became stronger and stronger to the point in early 1990 where I felt I could almost touch whatever was there. One night in a London hotel room while working for the BBC the presence was so obvious that I said: 'If there is anybody here, will you please contact me because you are driving me up the wall!' A few days later I walked into a local newspaper shop and as I stood in the doorway my feet were suddenly held fast to the ground as if pulled by

Figure 1: Journey to sanity.

Figure 2: The book that I picked up on the day my life changed.

magnets. I know now that I was surrounded by an electromagnetic field. A clear thought passed through my mind out of nowhere saying: 'Go and look at the books on the far side.' It wasn't quite a voice, but close. My feet were unfrozen and I walked bewildered towards the small rack of mostly romantic novels. My eyes immediately turned to one book because it was so different to the rest – *Mind to Mind* written by a professional psychic, Betty Shine (Fig 2). I read the book in a day and wondered if she would be able to explain what was happening with my 'presence'. A week or so later I walked into her front room. I told her nothing except that I had arthritis and maybe her hands-on healing (an exchange of energy) would help. I wanted to see what she might pick up without any leading from me. Nothing unusual occurred in the first two visits, but then came the third. I was lying on a bench while Betty went to work on my left knee when I felt a sort of spider's web on my face. I remembered she had said in her book that this can happen when entities in other dimensions of reality are trying to communicate. I'll explain how all this works later. The 'spider's web' was electromagnetic energy and the same principle applies to hairs standing up on your neck or arm when you are in an excited crowd or haunted house. All are electromagnetic states. I said nothing to Betty about what I was feeling, but I didn't have to. About 10 to 15 seconds later she threw her head back and said: 'Wow! This is powerful. I'll have to close my eyes for this one.' She said she was seeing a figure in her mind who was asking her to communicate 'his' words to me. First of all I was told that 'They' knew that I wanted them to contact me but it couldn't have happened until now because the time wasn't right. Betty knew nothing about what I had said in the London hotel room. This is some of the information that came through Betty that day:

- He is a healer who is here to heal the Earth and he will be world famous.
- He is still a child spiritually, but he will be given the spiritual riches.
- Sometimes he will say things and wonder where they came from. They will be our words.
- Knowledge will be put into his mind, and at other times he will be led to knowledge.
- He was chosen as a youngster for his courage. He has been tested and has passed all the tests.
- He was led into football to learn discipline, but when that was learned it was time to move on. He also had to learn how to cope with disappointment, experience all the emotions, and how to get up and get on with it. The spiritual way is tough and no one makes it easy.
- He will always have what he needs [this could have been 'wants'], but no more.
- He will face enormous opposition, but we will always be there to protect him.

A week later I saw Betty for the fourth and final time and more messages came through:

- One man cannot change the world, but one man can communicate the message that will change the world.
- Don't try to do it all alone. Go hand in hand with others, so you can pick each other up as you fall.
- He will write five books in three years.
- Politics is not for him. He is too spiritual. Politics is anti-spiritual and will make him very unhappy.
- He will leave politics. He doesn't have to do anything. It will happen gradually over a year.
- There will be a different kind of flying machine, very different from the aircraft of today.
- Time will have no meaning. Where you want to be, you will be.

Another psychic that I met soon after meeting Betty Shine gave me similar messages which included this one:

Arduous seeking is not necessary. The path is already mapped out. You only have to follow the clues ... We are guiding you along a set path. It was all arranged before you incarnated.

My life became a series of incredible coincidences or synchronicities as I was led to knowledge through people, books, documents and personal experiences. It was certainly true that arduous seeking wasn't necessary because the information was finding me. Many, many times I have remembered these lines: 'Sometimes he will say things and wonder where they came from – they will be our words' and 'Knowledge will be put into his mind and at other times he will be led to knowledge.' This has absolutely been my experience. I wrote my first book on these subjects in 1990, called *Truth Vibrations*, and I would indeed write five books in three years – and many more since. I headed for Peru in early 1991 purely on a powerful intuition that I had to go there, and it was an extraordinary trip full of stunning synchronicity and experiences. 'Coincidence' led me to Peruvian ruins at Sillustani near the city of Puno on the shores of Lake Titicaca, 13,000 feet above sea level in the Andes. My Peruvian guide had booked me the night before into a hotel in Puno called the Sillustani and when I saw pictures of the place on the wall I knew I had to go. I went there in a mini-bus/taxi with the driver and my guide (Fig 3). Sillustani is beautiful but after walking around I was disappointed that the strength of my feeling to go there was not matched by what had happened. I returned to the bus and set off back to Puno. A few minutes down the road I was daydreaming and gazing at a hill we were passing when the words 'come to me, come to me, come to me' began repeating in my mind. I asked the driver to stop and climbed the hill to see what would happen and I found myself in a massively more powerful repeat of what happened in the newspaper shop. My feet got the magnet treatment to such an extent that the soles of my feet were almost burning. Energy began to enter the top of my head and go through me into the earth with another flow coming in the other direction. My arms then stretched out at 45 degrees without any decision from me to do so (Fig 4). I heard a 'voice' or thought-form in my head which said: 'It will be over when you feel the rain.' I was standing under a cloudless blue sky at the time and what I heard seemed crazy. Energy passing through me became so powerful that my whole body was shaking, I was moving between states of

Figure 3: Beautiful Sillustani.

Figure 4: Recreating what happened 25 years earlier. Back at Sillustani in 2012.

conscious awareness and big-time 'out there'. During one conscious moment I noticed a light grey mist over distant mountains and it became ever darker as a big rainstorm formed and came my way. By the time it reached me in a remarkably short time it was a wall of stair-rod rain. I was almost struggling to stand such was the impact of the energy, but once the rain hit me and drenched me in an instant the energy stopped. My arms had been at 45 degrees the whole time and I felt nothing. Now my shoulders were agony and my legs were doing a passable impression of Bambi.

Figure 5: Off with the fairies in 1990 – but so essential to what followed.

I had no idea what had happened but the effect was clear. Information, concepts and insights began to pour into my conscious mind on such a scale that my brain basically froze like a computer in overload. One recurring pattern and thought was saying: 'You are a son of God.' For three months I hardly knew where I was and I appeared in that state on prime-time television to explain what was happening to me. This was difficult given that I didn't know and mentioning the bit about 'son of God' triggered decades of almost record-breaking ridicule that is still going on among the ignorant who don't read or listen to the detail of what I am saying (Fig 5). It was a lonely journey for much of the last now 26 years, but I have also seen millions and millions awaken to realise that the world is not like they thought it was, and have been told it was, by the institutions and agencies of government and state. I have written a long list of books and I talk to thousands at a time at public events around the world delivering the information gathered through the synchronicity of my life across a vast swathe of interconnected subjects. Dots are interesting, but *connecting* the dots is devastating in the insight that follows. Synchronicity in the early years after Betty Shine and Peru led me first to information about the world of the five senses to expose the web of secret societies and groups that dictate and manipulate the direction of human society through puppet politicians and others who appear to be in power, but aren't really. Next came the non- human 'Hidden Hand' behind that web and revelations about the illusory nature of 'physical' reality. Put them all together as I do in this book and the world that people think they know looks a very different place.

Phantom Self is for readers of my other works and takes the story on, but it's also for those coming to my information for the first time. I think the book is extremely timely as world events and personal experiences lead enormous numbers of people to ask: 'What the hell is going on?' and 'What is life all about?'

Let the revelations begin.

CHAPTER ONE

Last Question

If you do not change direction, you might end up where you are heading
Lao Tsu

It may seem odd to start with the 'last' but, as usual with human society, the opposite is the case. Have you noticed that? Again and again, the truth turns out to be an inversion of what we have been led to believe. It is so blatant when you scan the world that the most effective starting point for pursuing the mysteries of life is to take everything you have ever been told and simply flip it.

There will be examples where this technique doesn't work – but far, far more where it does. I've spent two and a half decades so far uncovering the lies and deceit that 'The System' peddles as 'truth', and the very foundation of my work has been turning perceived and accepted 'reality' on its head in almost every facet of life. The System is a construct of deception and control created by a hidden force that I will be exposing in detail later. Until I get there, I will refer to the hidden force or Hidden Hand which is behind what appears on the surface to be random and unconnected events (Fig 6). They say that we see the world upside down and the brain flips it upright. What I am doing, symbolically at least, is flipping it back. This is what happens when you regain control of your own perception – you see that everything you have been led to believe is an inversion of what is really the case. This book explains why this is and how it relates to the scale and nature of collective human control. I began my ongoing adventure – at least consciously – in 1990 trying to establish why evidence about the nature of reality was virtually ignored by 'education', media and overwhelmingly by society in general. People were being bombarded with this-world-is-all-there-is 'science' and its alleged polar opposite, pick-your-god religion; but where was the tidal wave of evidence explaining reality in ways that largely demolished both? Not only was this not taught in schools and rarely explored by

Figure 6: The world is controlled by those you never see.

media, it was also subjected to reflex-action dismissal and ridicule. Fantastic concepts and potential consequences for humanity were reduced to talk of 'little green men' and 'Hey, Charlie believes in ghosts – what an idiot.' This made no sense to me and I wanted to know what was going on because something clearly was. It was the start of an incredible journey of self and collective discovery which made one thing very clear: humanity is living a Lie so vast, so total and all-encompassing, that the Lie is perceived as universal truth – the 'everyone-knows-that' (Fig 7).

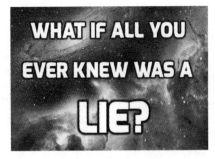

Figure 7: 'Everyone knows' – nothing.

The Lie is such, in both scale and depth, that its promotion and imposition is plainly systematic. We did not trip over the Lie by random accident; it comes courtesy of calculated design. People don't know the very reality they are experiencing because there is a hidden force at work that doesn't *want* them to know. Given that the force controls 'education', media, 'science' and religion, my start-out question of why evidence about reality was suppressed soon secured an answer; but there was so much more, so many revelations and insights as the dots began to connect to form an extraordinary picture. I found that the entirety of human society is a fake and simulated 'computer' reality that people believe to be 'real' and that the world is a planetary Alcatraz because it is meant to be. You don't live in a prison? Then why are the vast majority either doing what they don't want to do or not doing what they do want to do? Why is the morning alarm met with universal regret and not joy at the start of another day? Why did 35 percent of those questioned in a British survey say their jobs were pointless? American comedian George Carlin said:

> Oh, you hate your job? Why didn't you say so? There's a support group for that. It's called everybody and they meet at the bar.

Why do people get through the week with thoughts of the weekend, while kids long to hear the bell that says the warders are setting them free 'til tomorrow? Even then these concepts of temporary freedom are relative rather than actual. I saw this on the Internet ... 'Go to work, get married, have children, act normal, walk on the pavement, watch TV, obey the law, save for your old age, then repeat after me ... I am *freeeeee*' (Fig 8). How can anyone be free no matter what they are doing if they don't even know who they are, where they are or where they 'come from'? Crucial to the perpetuation of mass human control is a belief in a fake self – *Phantom* Self (Fig 9). What you think is you is not *you* at all. It's only the 'you' that you have been manipulated and programmed to *believe* is you, in the interests of a global prison state. Only when you begin to emerge from Phantom Self can you even see that Earth is a prison. Phantom Self is a construct, a figment of

Figure 8: Humans are prisoners who think they are free.

Figure 9: I am a mask therefore I am.

Figure 10: The same 'world', but very different perceptions if you stay connected to Infinite Self or become isolated in Phantom Self.

manipulated perception. The foundation of human oppression is the belief that Phantom Self is 'you'. From this, all else comes. Definitions of the term phantom capture the essence of Phantom Self: 'Something apparently seen, heard, or sensed, but having no physical reality'; 'An image that appears only in the mind; an illusion'; 'Fictitious or non-existent, often when intended to deceive'; 'Believed to be real even though illusory'. Phantom Self is a downloaded self-identity of your name, country, race, culture, religion/science belief system, family history, life-story and the 'education'/media versions of virtually everything. These information and perception sources dictate the sense of who people think they are. They focus human attention almost entirely on the five senses and we become isolated from the insight, knowing and expanded awareness of beyond-the-body Infinite Self which can see, perceive and understand what Phantom Self cannot. Infinite Self speaks to us through intuition and knowing, a state of awareness beyond thought and the lassoed perceptions of the five senses. If we lose touch with Infinite Self we become isolated in Phantom Self and our only source of information and insight to get a fix on life and the world is The System in the form of 'education', media, science and other agencies of deeply controlled five-sense reality (Fig 9). We are meant to stay connected with Infinite Self to be *in* this world, but not completely *of* it in terms of our perceptions of reality (Fig 10); but the overwhelming majority are manipulated into an isolated bubble of awareness and self-identity – Phantom Self (Fig 11). Once entrapped, they live a fake

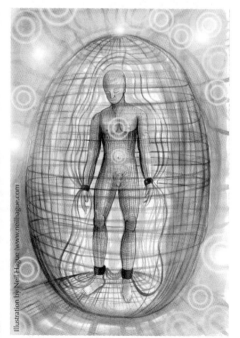

Illustration by Neil Hague (www.neilhague.com)

Figure 11: Closed mind, closed world.

identity that holds them fast in a prison-perception of 'I can't', 'little me' and life-long limitation. When we stay connected to our Infinite Self we see the world for what it is (Fig 12). When we lose that connection we see the world for what we are *told* it is. The realms of Infinite Self are consistently described by near-death experiencers and others who have been freed from the myopia of Phantom Self Body-Mind. One said of the out-of-body state:

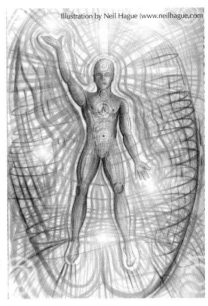
Illustration by Neil Hague (www.neilhague.com)

> ... everything from the beginning, my birth, my ancestors, my children, my wife, everything comes together simultaneously. I saw everything about me, and about everyone who was around me. I saw everything they were thinking now, what they thought then, what was happening before, what was happening now. There is no time, there is no sequence of events, no such thing as limitation, of distance, of period, of place. I could be anywhere I wanted to be simultaneously.

Figure 12: In the world, but not of it.

That is Infinite Self (or some of it) and in most people this has been silenced in pursuit of mass control by a force I will be exposing. Once attention is imprisoned in Phantom Self alone, with no other perspective, we become a babe-in-arms to the tyranny of this hidden force which created and controls human society as we live it today. Phantom Self is not who we are, it is simply what we are *experiencing*. Confusing the two (and being manipulated to do so) is the foundation of human control, programmed limitation and worldwide perception of the powerless 'little me'. Infinite Awareness can be likened to an ocean, and five-sense awareness to the crest of a wave or point of attention within the ocean (Figs 13 and 14). When five-sense awareness loses touch with the ocean and operates in isolation this is Phantom Self. There's a saying that goes 'we see things not as they are but as *we* are'. Everything is perception and from that comes all

Figure 13: A wave and its crest are the same ocean in different forms.

Figure 14: We are a point of attention within the infinite ocean of awareness.

Figure 15: Phantom Self-deception.

behaviour and what we will or won't do. Exploration of self and reality is way down the list of priorities for most people. *Who am I?* This is so often the last question, not the first, as it should be. It falls way behind perceived essentials like: What job shall I do? What clothes shall I wear? What phone shall I buy? How do I make lots of money? Who shall I marry? Where shall I go on Saturday night? Sport alone is, for many, light years ahead in priority of 'what is reality?' I'm not saying those other questions should not be considered, or sport should not be enjoyed as a pastime and entertainment – I do myself – but if it's not given perspective then our peripheral vision can be blocked and this is vital to seeing what those in authority don't want you to see. George Orwell wrote in *1984*: 'Football, beer and above all gambling, filled up the horizon of their minds. To keep them in control was not difficult.' How can we answer any question effectively without some grasp of the *master* questions – Who am I? Where am I? What is this 'reality' that I daily experience? If you didn't understand water you might try to walk across it and drown. The fact you do understand, at least in one sense, means that you either keep away or learn to swim. Humanity is drowning in confusion, bewilderment and chaos because it doesn't understand the very nature of the world, how we interact with it and each other and that we are creating our own reality whether we like it or not. Funny how most children are taught at an early age about water because that is deemed so essential, but they can go through their entire lives without giving much thought to reality itself. They thus assign their beliefs and perceptions to Phantom Self as they sleepwalk through life believing themselves to be wide awake and looking through blindfolded eyes believing they can see (Fig 15). This doesn't get any better for wannabe manipulators of the human experience because moulding humanity to become what they *have* become

Figure 16: Ain't it great to be on the cutting edge of evolution?

would be top of their Christmas list (Fig 16). This is no coincidence, as we shall see. Sleepwalk is a relevant term because Phantom Self lives in the subconscious and dictates conscious behaviour, responses and perceptions which the conscious mind falsely believes it is instigating. All experience and the dos, don'ts, rules, regulations and reality programming from The System are absorbed by the subconscious to construct the fake self-identity that I call

Phantom Self. Conscious mind is aware of so little while the subconscious absorbs *everything*. Subliminal advertising and messages target the subconscious which filters them through to the conscious mind as 'I'll do this' or 'I'll buy that'. Subliminal means 'below threshold' (below the threshold of the conscious mind) and 99 percent plus of the information we receive goes straight to the subconscious – home of Phantom Self. Our subconscious communicates through symbolism and so dreams are virtually always symbolic and rarely literal. The System has its own language of symbolism, which I will be explaining because it is seeking to program perceptions via our subconscious mind.

We are experiencing a reality that can be likened to a computer simulation and the relevance of this to Phantom Self will become ever clearer as we proceed. So it is hardly a surprise that computer language can invariably be used to describe the human plight. This is especially true of the term 'to program' which is defined as 'to arrange (data) into a suitable form that can be processed by a computer' and 'a sequence of coded instructions fed into a computer, enabling it to perform specified logical and arithmetical operations on data'. This is describing most human thought processes which together create what we call human society. Information (data) is fed to the human mind (education, media and endless other sources) and this is downloaded and processed to become human perception or what I call Phantom Self. What is Phantom Self? It's a *program.* In fact, a program made up of endless sub-programs known as human traits and behaviour. This doesn't mean that we – the Infinite 'I' – are a program, only that our phantom *perception* of self and reality is a program which dominates what people think, feel, do, don't do, support and don't support and their very concept of what is referred to as self and 'life'. What we call 'life' is a program being perceived by another program – Phantom Self. You will see as the book plays out how this explains so much about the mysteries and apparent contradictions of 'life'. 'Mysteries' tend to evaporate like ice in a fire when you come from this perspective. Phantom Selves are programmed to program other Phantom Selves. Children enter this reality with the potential to express expanded awareness of the Infinite Self, but immediately programmed programmers go to work as parents upload their own Phantom perceptions into their children. This is mostly done with perceived good intent but perceived by whom? Phantom Self. Jim Morrison, lead singer of the 60s band, The Doors, put it like this:

> The most loving parents and relatives commit murder with smiles on their faces. They force us to destroy the person we really are: a subtle kind of murder.

In this way, Phantom Selves of one generation program Phantom Selves of those who follow them. It is a perpetual-motion programming machine (The System) and those caught in its systematic delusion believe they are thinking their own thoughts and forming their own perceptions when invariably they are not. Their beliefs and perceptions are, when broken down and the source located, merely a repetition of what they have heard from someone else – a teacher, newsreader, politician, scientist or doctor. And what are these people except more Phantom Selves who got *their* views and opinions from still other Phantom Selves programmed by The System in the same repeating process? The System speaks and its unquestioning programs simply repeat

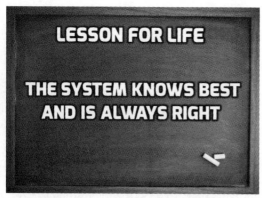

Figure 17: All you need to know to be a slave for life.

generation after generation (Fig 17). From this collective repetition comes the world of 'everyone knows that'. But they *don't*. What people *think* they know because someone else has told them should not be confused with how things really are (Fig 18). This confusion is, however, almost universal because of the way society – the collective human mind – has been hijacked, manipulated and structured to download the Lie. The download is so obvious for those with eyes to see and minds that reject the program and allow its mist to clear.

'Life'-cycle

We come out of the womb and immediately programming begins by mostly loving parents who think they are doing 'what's best for the children'; but who or what is doing the 'thinking' here? Phantom Selves programmed by The System to *be* a Phantom Self (Fig 19). A belief that what they are doing is 'best for the children' is dictated by a

Figure 18: Seeing through the bullshit.

Figure 19: Living the illusion believing it to be real.

lifetime of perception programming from Phantom Self teachers, university academics, scientists, journalists, politicians, doctors and sundry self-appointed 'experts' of which there are legion to tell you what to believe about everything down to the fine detail. Who tells the parents how best to 'bring up' their children? The System. Who tells them how best to 'protect' their health? The System. Who tells them how to guide their children in terms of their 'future' (as a slave of The System)? The *System*. All roads lead to the same master, the same programmer, if only people would lift their gaze and look anew. Programming begins with parents and the child's Phantom Self quickly begins to form. As it does so, the connection, inspiration and insight of Infinite Self fades into silence, drowned out by the cacophony of noise and attention-diversion that constantly invades the five senses. You're on your own now, kid. Gone is any perception filter from beyond the program that can *see* the program. Now you *are* the program and it's only just begun. The next stage is the most profound of them all which we hilariously call 'education'. This is officially defined as 'the act or process of acquiring knowledge, especially systematically during childhood and adolescence'. Knowledge is said to be 'the sum or range of what has been perceived, discovered, or learned'. Education is 'acquiring knowledge', but this 'knowledge' is not what is necessarily true – and usually isn't as history and hindsight constantly confirm. Knowledge is only what you *believe* is true and what others have *told* you is true. Those who tell you what to know are

Figure 20: Repeat, repeat, repeat – be normal laddie.

overwhelmingly Phantom Self programs of The System supervising its ongoing downloads for everyone else (Fig 20). Knowledge is said to be 'the sum or range of what has been perceived, discovered, or learned', but how much of what people call their 'knowledge' was gained first hand from their own unique experience and research? Hardly any – in fact *if* any, in most cases. People largely perceive what they have been told to perceive, discover what they have been told has been discovered and learn what they have been told to remember. You hear people say when questioned about some alleged fact or truth that they 'learned it at school' or university and yet those who provided this information which became their perceptions were Phantom Selves that passed through the same programming machine. They accepted the programming so blindly and totally that they became perpetuators and promotors of the machine as teachers and academics. The System decides and dictates what is true and not true, what can be taught in 'education' institutions and what is suppressed and ignored. George Orwell's concept in *1984* of 2 + 2 = 5 is very apt. If your parents tell you from the earliest age that 2 + 2 = 5 and teachers, university academics, scientists, media and your peers who have been through the same programming tell you 2 + 2 = 5, then there is an excellent chance that you will go through your entire human life believing that 2 + 2 = 5 while in truth it's really 4. Talk to teachers and academics who encourage their students to question conformity and official 'truth' and you'll see what happens to most of them. The System only wants System people and it is not so much jobs for the boys as jobs for the Phantoms. This is the case everywhere, in science, medicine, media, academia, law enforcement and most certainly in politics. When did any freethinker challenging the assumptions of the program ever rise to the top in any of these subject areas? Exactly.

The System wants repetition, not spontaneity, and machines, not mavericks. Spontaneous, freethinking mavericks are dangerous to a System that requires unthinking perception obedience to survive and prosper. Mystics, seers and freethinkers in touch with their Infinite Self have been targeted by authority throughout known human history and they still are through the vehicles of ridicule, condemnation and labels such as extremist, mad and danger to society. This happens because they are a danger to The System and The Program, and those who publicly abuse and ridicule them like Phantom Self academics and journalists are aided and abetted by Phantom Self masses that ridicule and condemn like performing parrots in accordance with The System's blueprint of what constitutes 'normal' (Fig 21). I have experienced such

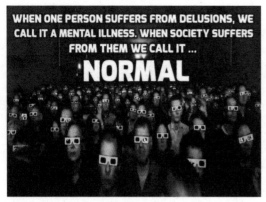

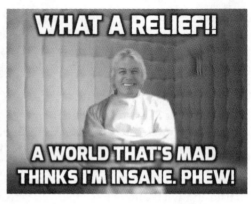

Figure 21: Normal madness.   **Figure 22:** Sanity in a crazy world is called madness.

treatment in the extreme and still do (Fig 22). Giordano Bruno, who was burned at the stake for seeing beyond the program, said: 'Heroic love is the property of those superior natures who are called insane, not because they do not know, but because they over-know.' When you see at such close range the computer mind collectively at work responding only to data input – he's different so I must laugh – it presents enlightening insight into the depth to which Phantom Self has hijacked human society. Most people are too programmed and too childlike in their belief in the Mummy-Daddy System to see that different is not another word for madness; or, as George Orwell put it: 'Perhaps a lunatic was simply a minority of one.' Truth is truth even if no one believes it and a lie is a lie even if everyone believes it. The same applies to social media, Internet forums and comment columns. A chance to express fermenting hatred, prejudice and unmitigated ignorance while hiding behind anonymity has unleashed the shocking extremes of Phantom Self, which before could only be witnessed by family and associates or was suppressed by the need, in the absence of anonymity, to put a manufactured face to the world (Fig 23). Phantoms have been unleashed by the Internet to project their hatreds, ignorance and psychological distortions upon anyone it gives them pleasure to hurt or upset. This has exposed the truth that open eyes could already see – the scale of the madhouse dubbed human society is staggering (Fig 24); but it should not really be such a shock given that the maddest of them all are running the

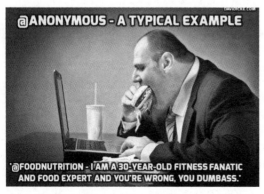

Figure 23: Social media – a playground for Phantom Self.

show in positions of political and financial power, a fact I shall later enlarge upon (Fig 25). Writer Jonathan Swift said these words in the 18th century and they are even more appropriate today: 'When a true genius appears, you can know him by this sign: that all the dunces are in a confederacy against him.' Put another way ... when expanded awareness appears you can know him or her by this sign: that Phantom Selves will be in a confederacy against them. Ancient Greek philosopher

Figure 24: Words have no meaning.

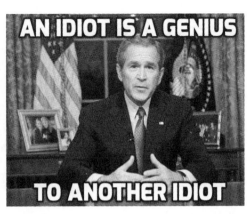

Figure 25: This man became President of the United States. Could it be anything but a madhouse?

Plato said: 'Those who are able to see beyond the shadows and lies of their culture will never be understood, let alone believed by the masses.' Yet none of this has to be and all it takes is for people to form their own perceptions and make different choices by using their own minds and not being an appendage of the program.

'Morning children, welcome to prison'

Parent-pump-primed and already developing Phantom Selves (children) leave home every weekday morning from the age of four or five and head for a prison called a 'school'. It's not a prison? So they can stay at home if they want, then? Or they can leave when they want? No to both. From their very first day in the prison 'school' an authority figure or figures tell them when to be there, when they can leave, when they can eat, when they can play (not much and ever less) and even when they can go to the toilet (Fig 26). Developing Phantom Self quickly learns key lessons of prison school life: 'Truth' comes from authority; intelligence is the ability to remember and repeat; memory and conformity are rewarded; and non-compliance is punished. These lessons are meant to stay with the Phantom for the rest of its life and they mostly do so under terms like 'respect for authority', 'keep your head down', 'don't rock the boat' and, as they say in Japan, 'don't be the nail that stands out above the rest because that's the first one to get hit'. Today this demand for conformity is reaching ever greater extremes with schools dictating more of the child's time outside of the school day (see Texas for the cutting edge) and parents being fined £60 per child by UK schools, rising to £120 if unpaid after three weeks, for 'unauthorised absence'. This can rise to £2,500 and involve three months in *jail* (Fig 27). 'Unauthorised absence' includes family holidays taken in school time when they are far cheaper. 16,430 parents were prosecuted in 2014 – that's 25 percent higher than the year before as the net closes on parental

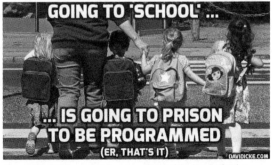

Figure 26: 'Come on kids, go and be told what to think.'

Figure 27: The state is taking over your children before your very eyes.

Figure 28: If we'll take this, we'll take anything.

influence over their own children. Similar rules are being applied in other countries. A thoroughly programmed Phantom Self described as a 'head teachers' leader' said good attendance was 'absolutely critical'. Bollocks it is. *Learning* is what is important and learning and never missing school are not necessarily the same thing. We now have Orwellian surveillance and control in schools through cameras, fingerprint scanning for meals and library books, electronic tagging (see Texas again) and fenced-in classrooms that make them look what they are – prisons for the young (Fig 28). These Orwellian controls are being introduced to program children to accept mass and incessant surveillance as normal so they won't resist when the entire world is like that (Fig 29). 'Counter- terrorism' (counter-freedom) measures proposed by the British Government require even nursery school staff and registered childminders to report toddlers they think are at risk of becoming terrorists. Check that dummy, it could be a bomb. Insanity.

I have seen many debates on *how* children are taught but rarely about *what* they are taught. This reminds me of my mother who used to tell Jehovah's Witnesses knocking on the door that 'we're Church of England'. We weren't and our family never saw the inside of a church except for weddings and funerals (thank you God). But my mother had sorted out our official spirituality with the holding position of 'we're Church of England.' In the same way, most people don't question what is taught in schools any more than my mother thought about religion. It was like just 'there'. We lived in England and it had a Church so 'we're Church of England' was enough without delving

Figure 29: 'Children must have a good programming, er, education.

into detail, thank you. Most people treat education just the same. It's a *school* and that's enough delving into detail, thanks very much. What goes on there? They have lessons and stuff. What lessons and stuff? Well, they're taught what they need to know. And what's that? Well, lessons and stuff. Phantom Self has an image of how things are, an image supplied by the program, but for the most part knows or seeks precious little detail about anything. If parents who truly care about developing and protecting their child's right to freedom and uniqueness looked into the 'lessons and stuff' they would be aghast. Schools are not only prisons; they are *psychiatric* prisons where young minds are moulded to The System's will and perception deception. They are told ('taught') what The System wants them to believe about *everything*. Education as it we know it has been imposed worldwide to install a global system of childhood programming-for-life. 'Education' is not there to develop freethinking uniqueness, but nodding, unquestioning slaves in mind and body who accept their place for life as powerless cogs in a merciless machine that vampires their energy and creativity. John D. Rockefeller, creator of the General Education Board in 1903, said: 'I don't want a nation of thinkers. I want a nation of workers.' A nation of slaves. Then when they can work no more The System spits them out into 'retirement' – usually a few years of financial struggle and hardship for most people before the world waves goodbye. Once you can no longer serve with mind and body The System doesn't give a shit what happens to you. Do we regret the passing of a cog in the car transmission? No, we fit another one and so does The System. Humanity is seen in those terms by their hidden controllers that I expose at great length and detail in other books and later in this one. Physicist Albert Einstein (1879-1955) is a name synonymous with intellect and you hear apparently clever people referred to as 'an Einstein'; but he well understood the myth of 'education'. He said that 'education is what remains after one has forgotten what one has learned in school' and 'the only thing that interferes with my learning is my education'. He said something else highly relevant, too: 'Everybody is a genius, but if you judge a fish by its ability to climb a tree, it will live its whole life believing that it is stupid.' Phantom Self is specifically constructed to serve The System and is 'educated' (downloaded) on the basis of what serves The System's designs and interests. If you are a fish that can't climb a tree then you are written off, excluded, marginalised and labelled a 'slow learner' or 'stupid' because The System only wants the tree climbers who are sure to get lost in its forest.

Who you are is a secret

The System in-point is called birth, the out-point is called death, and the bit in the middle is usually known under its alias of 'human life'. The 'education' hoax is crucial to securing lifetime compliance of body and mind and development and moulding of Phantom Self, which is little more than a narrow band of potential awareness that views everything through the blinkered filter of the five senses. Phantom Self reality is largely only what it can touch, taste, hear, see and smell. These 'senses' are illusory constructs of a programmed brain as I will expand upon, but The System doesn't want you to know that. It wants you to serve its interests by perceiving the five-sense 'physical' illusion as the 'real world' and Infinite reality as a figment of deluded imagination when the opposite is the case (Fig 30). Here is the inversion, the

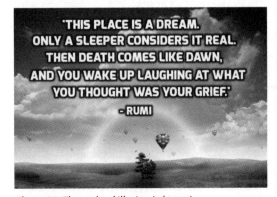

Figure 30: The scale of illusion is fantastic.

Figure 31: Mainstream media is the propaganda arm of Mainstream Everything.

Figure 32: 'It's all so clear to me.'

flip, once again. Education is therefore focussed on promoting a belief in purely 'physical' reality because this belief will hold your perception in five-sense servitude and slam the door to Infinite Self beyond the program. Academia, as a product and creation of The System, follows and promotes the song sheet of mainstream science and medicine, which is also blindly repeated and promoted by the mainstream media. 'Mainstream' anything is an agent and vehicle of The System – that's *why* it is mainstream (Fig 31). Most of those who work in this multi-faceted mainstream will have no idea that they are agents of a hoax, because they have been through the same mainstream education machine and been programmed by the same Mainstream Everything to the point where they, too, are servants of the hoax and believe in the hoax – which they perceive to be the 'real world' (Fig 32). Anyone that challenges and exposes the hoax must, by definition, not be accepted in this 'real world' and they are subjected to reflex-action ridicule, dismissal and contempt (Fig 33). Richard Dawkins, the Oxford University professor to whom anything alternative is as garlic to a vampire, encapsulated the arrogance of ignorance when he said:

You cannot be both sane and well educated and disbelieve in evolution. The evidence is so strong that any sane, educated person has got to believe in evolution.

Figure 33: 'The arrogance of ignorance.

By 'evolution' he means the this-world-is-all-there-is-one-life-and-that's-your-lot garbage peddled by Charles Darwin with his survival of the fittest doctrine which underpined the promotion of eugenics. Dawkins appears obsessed with death being the end of everything and gave us this considered insight: 'Don't kid yourself that you're going to live again after you're dead; you're not.' This is what The System wants you to believe to instil the fear of death (so many ways this can be manipulated) and a sense of pointlessness to life (ditto). Another acceptable alternative is to believe that to make it to paradise you need to do exactly what your god (The System again in another form) says you must do to please 'Him'. Mainstream science is only another religion in disguise and mostly (though not entirely) created by the same close-minded dogma. People like Dawkins castigate and condemn religion while being High Priests of their own – Scientism. Quantum physics has thrown a spanner in all this with the evidence that our reality is anything but 'physical', predictable or operating in isolation from consciousness. There are physicists who break the mould and rightly contend that consciousness creates matter and not the other way round. Quantum physics alone should demolish Mainstream Everything, but it doesn't because The System won't allow it. Instead, while being forced to reluctantly acknowledge the existence of the non-physical quantum world, Mainstream Everything ignores the fundamental implications of such revelations and cracks on with its promotion of the 'physical' hoax in all its forms. A review of a Dogma Dawkins book reported that he doesn't believe that reality is malleable (quantum physics clearly shows that it is) while at the same time the esteemed professor said that his grasp of quantum physics was 'a bit foggy' and so 'declines to delve very far into that topic'. This is a classic of its kind. I can protect my belief system so long as I never read anything that would question my belief system.

'You found something?'

'Yes.'

'Where is it?'

'Over there.'

'Oh, right, so as long as I never go over there I can claim forever that your something doesn't exist because I've never seen it.'

'Nice one.'

This is the reason, in my view, why Dawkins has launched so many attacks through television documentaries and other platforms on alternative explanations of reality and methods of healing. I sense that somewhere deep in his psyche he is seeking to convince *himself* as much as his audience that challenges to his dogma have no validity. Unfortunately for his considerable ego, they do. Dawkins also, again classically, equates intelligence with being 'well educated' and, in turn, links 'well educated' with being sane, as with 'You cannot be both sane and well educated and disbelieve in evolution.' This is another way of saying that 'sane' and 'well educated' can only apply to those who believe what he believes. How appropriate because education is rigged in the same way that Dawkins and his like unknowingly rig themselves. System education (indoctrination) emphasises what it wants you to believe while *dangerous* information – which reveals what it does not want you to know – is ignored, dismissed, given barely a mention or filed under 'not important'. I have been writing for a long time that the 'physical' world is an illusion and only exists in the form we perceive it through a decoding process triggered by the act of observation. I'll be explaining this in detail later. As I began this book, a group of real scientists genuinely pursuing answers announced that experiments strongly suggested that 'the world only exists when we look at it'. This should have been banner headlines given its monumental potential consequences for human life at every level, but it was barely reported and even then without fanfare. The 'why' of this is simple: Would a system of perception control use its institutions to reveal information with the potential to end its perception control? Would prison warders tell their charges how to break out of their cell? Apply this to education and the question is the same: Why would those behind education want fully informed people when that would break the spell that holds them in slavery to The System that controls education? Hence, education is not there to enlighten and inform in the deepest sense but to program perceptions which fuse together to form Phantom Self. Note that I say those *behind* education because everyone else involved, from teachers to esteemed professors, are themselves products of the hoax doing the bidding of the hoax. They are both inmates and warders who can't see the prison they administer and perpetuate. It's hysterical, really, when you see the world for what it is.

Downloading compliance

Programming is regularly checked to confirm that you are conceding your uniqueness to The System and Phantom Self through countless education tests and examinations, in which you are asked to repeat what The System has told you to believe. In another colossal inversion you are deemed a success if you pass the exams to confirm your 'degree' of programming, but you are considered a failure if you don't. Incentives and rewards (more hoaxes) are offered to encourage compliance and these include the fact that many jobs and professions are the domain of exam-passers only. This is when pushy parents step forward again marching to war on their children's freedom, uniqueness and choice. Pushy parents (a form of child abuse in my view) seek to choose and dictate their children's life-path as they outrageously manipulate guilt and desire for acceptance to pressure their children into The System's lair. After all, it's what they have been programmed to do. They treat their kids not as an expression of Infinite Awareness, but as an appendage and extension of themselves and the face they put to the world. '*My*' child went to a good school and got good grades. Oh, well done you, so *you* passed their exams then? They then play the guilt card to dictate the child's chosen profession and this can scar the child for life. I have met people in their 60s who were still racked with guilt because they had 'let their parents down' by not being what they wanted them to be. If parents want to do something let them do it, but children are their own uniqueness and not a trinket of those who had sex to bring them into the world. This goes both ways with parents not having to be what their children insist they should be. 'Oh, mum, you can't do that – it's embarrassing.' When it comes to Phantom Selves, programming does tend to go both ways. Respect for individual uniqueness and people being individually unique keeps The System awake at night and so uniqueness is incessantly discouraged and legislated against. Once the pushy, child-abusing parents decide what their kids should be – lawyer, doctor, scientist, politician, whatever – the race is on to get the grades that The System deems are necessary. At school you need the grades to go to university and then to secure your degree (of programming) to pursue your parents', peer-pressured and System ambitions or perceptions of 'success' in the

Real World (The Hoax). The System has hijacked definitions for perceived success (money, fame, status, passing exams). Those so insecure (most people) that they have to be 'seen' to be successful by others must therefore 'succeed' by the criteria The System has decreed for success (money, fame, status, passing exams). Succeed by your own criteria and you will likely be seen as a failure. They sell us our dreams to keep us asleep. I have come across very rich (and unhappy) people who spend most of their time in the smallest room of their big mansions. This would seem like a contradiction – having such a massive

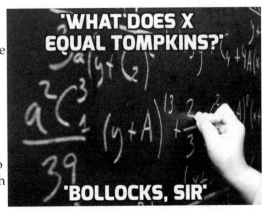

Figure 34: $2 + 3 = 8,456$.

house and all that money but living in the smallest room. In fact, the mansion represents their externalised public persona of 'success' to feed their insecurity and the little room represents their inner desire to live the life they want. Our apparently 'external' world is constant reflecting our inner self. Chasing The System's version of success turns childhood into a nightmare of pressure, fear, anxiety and pursuing 'success' as each new test and exam approaches, when it should be a time of chill and joy and unfettered exploration. Life becomes gotta, gotta, gotta – gotta work, gotta revise, gotta pass, gotta remember. Yes, *remember*. This is what exams are really about. 'Revision' is committing facts and alleged facts to *memory* for exam days. Talk to the same kids a few weeks later and certainly years later as adults and ask them questions they got right in exams. Most will say: 'I dunno – forgot.' Passing exams – which is considered such a measure of intelligence – is mostly an ability to remember facts and alleged facts on one particular day. Remember and you are a 'success'; don't remember and you are a 'failure'. It's extraordinary, and so many parents buy into this crap when they should be protecting their children *from* it. Much of what you are demanded to remember is a complete irrelevance to your life, anyway. I mean, take algebra. What is that all about? 'What does x equal?' I don't give a shit; make it equal what you like because it doesn't matter, mate (Fig 34). How many have ever used algebra or even thought about it again once they leave school?? Oh, but your whole future depends on your exams – gotta, gotta, gotta. *Bullshit*. This is the real point of it all: the process of absorbing information and committing to memory for that one day programs the vast majority, consciously and subconsciously, with The System's version of life, self and the world. Not true? Then ask yourself honestly where your multitude of views, assumptions, reflex-perceptions and responses have their origins and, if you *are* honest with yourself, you will see that they mostly came from school/college/university, parents, media and others who have also been through the same programming machine. Put all this in two words and you get 'The System'. There will be exceptions; people who have genuinely filtered the program to reach their own conclusions, but they will be tragically few even today with many more looking at the world through reassessing eyes. I have met countless people with once unyielding beliefs who eventually checked the facts and saw how deluded they had been. But, hey, The System can't be wrong, surely, and it certainly can't be

Figure 35: So much stress for so little reason.

manipulating you when it's only there to serve your best interests, correct?

We now have terms like exam stress and exam panic to describe the psychological trauma that children and young people are forced to endure by The System and its agents – parents, teachers and all the rest (Fig 35). Some even commit suicide in the face of exam results or the fear of what the results will be. How many pushy parents and teachers ever stop to ponder on the sheer madness of it all? Those that pass their tests go into the world with a skewed and distorted view of their own intelligence (it means passing exams, see) and those that don't pass often have a sense of ongoing failure that can be seen in comments like 'I was not very good at school'. These are Einstein's 'fish' people, but as the same guy said: 'Imagination is more important than knowledge.' So it is, but imagination is connected with expanded awareness, and so lack of imagination is rewarded and imagination that doesn't serve The System is herded into a pen that says 'here and no further'. I saw a funny test paper in which the student had taken the piss out of the questions. What is the main cause of divorce was answered with 'marriage'; What does half an apple look like was answered with 'the other half'; and What can you never eat for lunch and dinner was answered 'breakfast'. The paper was marked with a grade of 'F' because the kid had not told The System what it wanted to hear (he or she had 'failed' the test); but the teacher added a personal note that said 'A+ for creativity'. Isn't that what we want – creative people with expanded imagination? Well, it would make for a better and more vibrant and interesting world for a start, but The System would collapse by not being taken seriously. I ran home in the middle of my first day at school and told my mother I didn't want to go again. Call it intuition. Let us get this straight: passing exams does not mean you're intelligent and not passing them does not mean you're stupid. I never took a major exam in my life because I left school at 15 to play football for a living and yet I

Figure 36: They really are laughing at us.

have written more than 20 books and spoken for days at a time on multiple subjects all over the world. Not once has not taking exams proved a handicap to understanding. In fact, the opposite has been the case because I have not had a deluge of irrelevant trash to get in the way of free thought. Look at how many people have had wonderful lives and proved to be highly skilled in their chosen field, but were not anywhere near the top of the class. Examinations and their association with intelligence, success and failure, are just another hoax.

University for those with the right memory certificates is the finishing school of the education program and the honing down of Phantom Self. Today this comes with crippling repayments for those without parents rich enough to pick up the bill. The UK *Independent on Sunday*, quoting government documents, put the cost of a university degree at up to £100,000 (nearly $160,000 at the time of writing) with all costs included (Fig 36). Get them in debt when they are young and you control them for life (Fig 37).

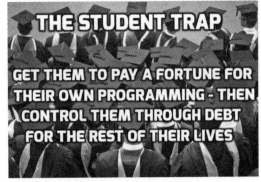

Figure 37: You want to be programmed? That will be £100,000, please. We'll take a cheque.

System People

Professions that administer The System are peopled by graduates and those in the most influential positions are from private schools and elite universities such as Oxford and Cambridge in Britain, and the Ivy League establishments in the United States. Here the future politicians, government administrators, judges, lawyers, doctors, bankers, corporate leaders and journalists rub shoulders. They may appear to be in different professions but they are still assets of the same base program and their by now System minds see the world and reality in basically the same way – The System's way. There will be exceptions who retain at least some of their own uniqueness but they will be few. A young lifetime of incessant perception programming has made The System their God to be worshipped and always protected (Fig 38). You can constantly see the results of this. The System's way is the only way. I read about a mother who was appearing in court in a dispute over cancer treatment for her child. She wanted him to try alternative treatments after seeing the devastating effect on mind and body of mainstream 'medical' madness. I knew what the outcome would be, because it is virtually always the same – and was again. The judge (System program) supported the view of the doctor (System program) and not the mother (questioning The System). Norman Tebbit, a minister in the governments of Margaret Thatcher in the 1980s, made a telling statement about why more was not done to expose paedophile politicians during the Thatcher years. He said: 'At that time I think most people would have thought that the establishment, the system, was to be protected and if a few things had gone wrong here and there that it was more important to protect the system than to delve too far into it.' There is no 'at that time' about it. This is what has always happened and still does. To administrators and servants of The System protecting The System is far more important than horrifically abused children. This will always be so until

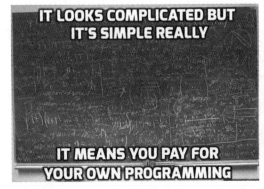

Figure 38: Behind apparent complexity lie simple truths.

Phantom Selves that serve The System awaken from their mind-program. Morpheus in *The Matrix* movie encapsulated this theme when he said:

The Matrix is a system, Neo. That system is our enemy. But when you're inside, you look around, what do you see? Businessmen, teachers, lawyers, carpenters. The very minds of the people we are trying to save. But until we do, these people are still a part of that system and that makes them our enemy. You have to understand, most of these people are not ready to be unplugged. And many of them are so inured, so hopelessly dependent on the system, that they will fight to protect it.

This is exactly what they do in so many and various ways. We are looking at a collective form of Stockholm syndrome: 'A psychological phenomenon in which hostages express empathy and have positive feelings towards their captures, sometimes to the point of defending them.' We see this all the time with human slaves defending The System which holds them in slavery. As the saying goes ... 'They piss on us and we say it's raining.' Stockholm Syndrome is the stablemate of cognitive dissonance defined here by psychiatrist and philosopher, Frantz Fanon:

Sometimes people hold a core belief that is very strong. When they are presented with evidence that works against that belief, the new evidence cannot be accepted. It would create a feeling that is extremely uncomfortable, called cognitive dissonance. And because it is so important to protect the core belief, they will rationalize, ignore and even deny anything that doesn't fit in with the core belief.

Stockholm Syndrome and cognitive dissonance are a devastating combination when it comes to free thought and perception. The world is ruled – at least officially – by politicians (System programs) and they decree laws based on The System's version of reality. This is reported and supported by the media (System programs) who tell the story in line with their System perceptions. Most agents of Mainstream Everything are not knowingly misleading and perpetuating the Lie – that is the domain only of the few. Far more often they are misleading the masses because they themselves have been misled. Most are slaves every bit as much as those they help to enslave. They may have money and apparent prestige but they're still slaves to The Program. Society appears to be diverse with different political parties and labels, apparent competition and uniforms – everything from dark suits to pit helmets – but this is more illusion and deceit. What appear to be differences and diversity are all operating within the rules and limitations of the same System. I met a lawyer once during a civil case that she was prosecuting, and she was obsessed with nit-picking every last word and nuance in her quest to crush her target financially on behalf of her client. I said how sorry I was for her that she did the job that she did, but immediately she shot back: 'I love my job.' I said that now I felt even more sorry for her. She was an unpleasant, aggressive and thoroughly charmless character who got her highs from the latest notch on the legal bedpost and, as such, was probably what they call a 'successful lawyer'; but she was dead. There was no life in her eyes, no sparkle from her soul. She was a daily mechanical processor of whole forests of paper and legal submissions to 'Your Honour'. She took the whole nonsense so terribly seriously while I shook my head in disbelief at the irrelevant circus before me. It was, to me, hilarious in the sense of pathetically hilarious to see her at work; but to the Phantom Self of this legal lady her whole life depended upon it. I bet her parents were so proud with her high-grade passes and the fact that she had 'made it'. She was so consumed by the program which had swallowed her whole, that I doubt she will ever grasp the sheer absurdity of her life as she worked into the night and was up with the dawn to ensure another glorious victory by crushing another human being. But maybe she will. I can only hope so and wish her well. Once people concede themselves to hate, or any form of empathy deletion, they are dead and breathing becomes only a disguise. Dead people can keep on walking – it is only dead bodies that can't.

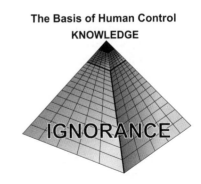

The Basis of Human Control

Figure 39: The mushroom technique: keep them in the dark and feed them bullshit.

From school program to work program

Fast-developing Phantom Selves depart the formal education stage of the program ingrained with its standard view of the world ... that reality is solid and top-down hierarchical structures of power distribution are the only way a society can function with money the answer to everything. This is not so remarkable when these perceptions and beliefs have been instilled every day since they left their mother's womb and especially since they first stepped into the psychiatric prison that is hysterically known as education. Generation after generation Phantom Selves pour off the conveyor belt to fill posts that administer society and tell the Phantom Self masses what to do and think, just as The System tells *them* (Fig 39). Blind leads the blind, programmed leads the programmed. This is 'human society'; this is the realm of Phantom Self (Fig 40). Canadian author Danielle Laporte said: 'Can you remember who you were before the world told you what you should be?' Each generation conditions the next generation, with both leaders and led ultimately slaves of an unseen force directing from the shadows. Presidents, prime ministers, banking magnates and corporate leaders are only obedient gofers to the real brokers of power who are almost never on public display. Not everyone fits this mould of fully-programmed Phantom Self, but the vast majority do and this will continue until humanity awakens to the hoax and its own Infinite nature. Leaders *and* led, 'bosses' *and* 'workers' are deceived by the hoax and controlled by either the carrot or the stick. The carrot is 'success', or at least survival, and if that doesn't work the stick comes out. Essential to successfully dangling this carrot is to project all perceived 'good' things and better things into the illusory 'future'. There is no future as there is no past, as I will explain later, but that doesn't matter to this

Figure 40: I want to be of service to my prison.

technique of mass exploitation. All The System needs is a *belief* in the future so they can hide all their good things and better things (carrots) in its illusory tomorrow (Fig 41). All our lives we are told to work harder and harder to reach Nirvana *tomorrow*. This might be promotion, fame and fortune or even enough to eat and shelter from the cold. It might be your chance to go into debt to 'buy' a house or the latest car, or even any car. Or maybe you're a lawyer and your carrot is to be a judge. Keep working, studying and serving The System machine

Figure 41: The donkey racket.

and the paradise you seek will be yours. It's only a continuation of the education program which tells you to work harder and study harder to get your reward in the end. What does this reward really turn out to be? You work all hours for years to get the bosses job; or you do the same to become a judge, politician, CEO or foreman. You might become very rich with all the trappings of money. But, when you 'get there', when you've reached your long-sought Nirvana, how does it feel? It should be fantastic, surely, after all that effort, sacrifice and emotion that you have invested since the ambition disease (The System's ambition) first struck you down. I know from meeting and observing lots of people that the achievement they have spent their lives pursuing rarely brings them the bliss and happiness they had convinced themselves would be their destiny when they reached their goal. They 'arrive' and it doesn't feel any different, really. Then there are those who don't achieve riches and status but bought the program, too. Work hard, do what the boss says, conform, keep your nose clean and you'll be looked after. Well, until your company decides it can exploit people for even less in the Far East while you search your way through the scrapheap and politicians tell you and your fellow unemployed that if you would only work harder, and for less, everything would be fine.

Hoax Addiction

By now, be you rich and 'successful' or sitting in the job centre with your days of youth long gone, you will likely be asking: 'What was it all about?' and 'What was the point?' There was no point in terms of what you thought was the point because The System's Nirvana was a hoax all along. Even most of the perceived successful people, the 'winners', reach the stage of self-reflection (though many won't openly admit it) because there *is* no Nirvana for Phantom Self, only the illusion of one. The emptiness that people still feel despite money, status, trophy wife and perceived achievement is from living the Lie since they entered the world. They feel empty within because they have lost touch with their 'within' – the magnificence of their Infinity which the program set out from the start to silence. You can't buy that connection with money no matter how rich you may be, but then you don't have to. Not only is it free, it is already YOU. The System has just made you forget. British-born philosopher, Allan Watts (1915-1973), brilliantly described the hoax when he said:

In music one doesn't make the end of a composition the point of the composition. If that were so the best conductors would be those who played fastest, and there would be composers who wrote only finales. People would go to concerts just to hear one crashing chord; because that's the end!

But we don't see that as something brought by our education into our every day conduct. We've got a system of schooling that gives a completely different impression. It's all graded. And what we do is we put the child into the corridor of this grade system with a kind of 'come on kitty kitty kitty', and now you go to kindergarten. And that's a great thing because when you finish that you get into first grade, and then come on; first grade leads to second grade and so on, and then you get out of grade school. Now you're going to go to high school, and it's revving up – the thing is coming. Then you've got to go to college, and by Jove then you get into graduate school and when you're through with graduate school you go out and join the World!

And then you get into some racket where you're selling insurance. And they've got that quota to make, and you're gonna make that. And all the time that thing is coming. It's coming, it's coming! That great thing, the success you're working for. Then when you wake up one day at about 40 years old you say "My God! I've arrived! I'm there". And you don't feel very different from what you always felt.

And there's a slight let down because you feel there's a hoax. And there was a hoax. A dreadful hoax. They made you miss everything. We thought of life by analogy with a journey, with a pilgrimage which had a serious purpose at the end and the thing was to get to that end. Success or whatever it is, or maybe heaven after you're dead.

But we missed the point the whole way along. It was a musical thing and we were supposed to sing or to dance while the music was being played.

And we are *meant* to miss the point – that's the idea. This is the reason for everything I have described in this opening chapter. Those who hear the music don't serve The System. Carl Sagan (1934-1996), the great American cosmologist, referred to what he called the 'bamboozle' and the concept is exactly in line with what I am saying here. Sagan wrote:

One of the saddest lessons of history is this: If we've been bamboozled long enough, we tend to reject any evidence of the bamboozle. We're no longer interested in finding out the truth. The bamboozle has captured us. It's simply too

Figure 42: Thinking clearly?

Figure 43: What an insult.

Figure 44: The System is a hypnotist.

painful to acknowledge, even to ourselves, that we've been taken. Once you give a charlatan power over you, you almost never get it back.

Or, as Mark Twain said: 'It is easier to fool people than to convince them they have been fooled' (Fig 42). Some will enjoy their lives as a Phantom Self although they have no compass with which to judge and compare life as it could be with influence of Infinite Self. There are many caught by Phantom fakery (virtually everyone to some extent) who still have moments and even longer periods when insight and perspective of Infinite Self flood their perceptions. People call this anything from inspired intuition to a spiritual or divine experience. Themes I have described, however, are largely omnipotent in the Phantom realm of the soulless System ('soulless' = the exclusion of Infinite reality). Social media and the Internet in general have allowed us to witness the astonishing scale and depth of Phantom Self and its ability to spew out programmed stupidity, hatred and mind-blowing ignorance, but it doesn't have to be like that. We don't have to concede our Infinite uniqueness to a manufactured sense of self – and when we stop doing so the prison shall be a paradise or, at the very least, comparatively so (Fig 43). We have no reference point for 'paradise' ('a state of delight or happiness') until we have experienced all possibilities, and even then it is a subjective not an

Figure 45: Illusory intelligence.

objective state. But a world lived from the heart and with the expression and celebration of unconfined creativity, uniqueness and open-minded pursuit of knowledge will be very different to the one that we currently see, founded on engineered ignorance that holds people in a spell of ignorance – the *ignore-trance* (Fig 44). We live in a world where ignorance is so all-pervading they call it intelligence (Fig 45). I don't use the term ignorance in condemnation but as a fact and until we accept our ignorance, we cannot transcend it. This has been noted

Figure 46: Wisdom of the ages.

Figure 47: The big penny-drop.

by those throughout the ages who have breached the walls of Phantom Self (Fig 46). Chinese philosopher Confucius said: 'Real knowledge is to know the extent of one's ignorance' and Greek philosopher Socrates said: 'The only true wisdom is knowing you know nothing.' Another variant is: 'Wisdom tends to grow in proportion to awareness of one's own ignorance.' To divert the target population from such wisdom and ensnare perception in Phantom Self, ignorance must be repackaged and called intelligence and cleverness. This is the prime inversion from which all others come – and can be clearly seen in the collective inversion that is human society. The System is a pig with a lipstick, dressed up as the cutting edge of human 'evolution' when it is nothing more than a madhouse, lunatic asylum, a downloaded app from Looney Tunes (Fig 47). Indeed I apologise to pigs and give my condolences to lipstick. It's all inversion and when you begin to emerge from the program you are seen as mad and crazy by mainstream society still imprisoned by the program. Imagine that you grew up in a madhouse and all you had ever known happened within the walls of the madhouse. With no other point of reference you would consider madness to be 'normal' – ignorance to be intelligence. As writer and filmmaker, Alejandro Jodorowsky, put it: 'Birds born in a cage think flying is an illness.' If someone came along from outside the madhouse and pointed out that it *was* a madhouse you would see them as mad or 'not normal', which is nothing more than *your* normal, your *perception* of normal, from your life experience ... *in the madhouse* (Fig 48). I have just described humanity and its journey from cradle to grave in a process widely referred to as 'life' and it has been designed that way to secure the specific outcome of human enslavement to a force we never see. Writer Ellen Goodman provides a definition of madhouse 'normal' – also known by those in the madhouse as 'success': 'Normal is getting dressed in clothes that you buy for work and driving through traffic in a car you're still paying for in order to get to the job you need to pay for the clothes and the car and the house you leave vacant all day so you can afford to live in it.'

Human society really is cuckoo-crazy, but I emphasise again that this doesn't have to be. It doesn't have to be a madhouse. We can change it, but only by changing ourselves – and about time, too.

Figure 48: The real world.

CHAPTER TWO

First Question

Condemnation without investigation is the height of ignorance
Albert Einstein

Unravelling the madness and the source and nature of the madness demands that we return to basics and I mean *real* basics like 'what is reality?' I have never heard a politician even broach the subject and yet how can we know anything about anything of any substance and relevance unless we have some understanding of the very reality that we call 'life'?

How can we live in the 'real world' when the world isn't real, or at least in the way people believe it to be? This must be the first question, the starting point, of any quest to understand human life, surely? Well, apparently not, because this is so often the last question that people ask and not the first. No wonder humanity is so bewildered and confused when the 'solid' reality people think is so real is a monumental, nothing-like-it-seems-to-be illusion. We have politics, science, medicine, commerce, media and everything else deciding policy, perception and possibility on the basis that the world is solid when it isn't. This fundamental flaw then corrupts the whole of society on the principle that bollocks begets bollocks and it's like smacking a mirror in the centre with the cracks shooting off in all directions (Fig 49). In terms of understanding *anything* we're already six-nil down before we've even kicked off. Point number one: There is no 'solid', only our *perception* of solid (Fig 50). A human brain processes some 11 million 'sensations' or 'impressions' every second in the form of information that it decodes into images, sound, sight, smell, taste and feeling or touch; but these 11 million are filtered down to around *40* from which our sense of reality is constructed. Every minute 2,400 impressions are taken from a possible 660 million – so imagine what that would be in a day. We appear to see a seamless reality from these fragments because the brain fills in the gaps with what it *believes* should be there. This,

Figure 49: Prime flaw infiltrates every facet of human society.

31

Figure 50: Yep.

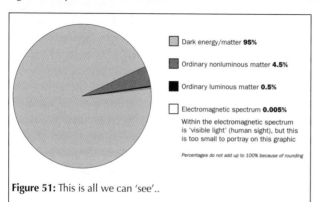

Dark energy/matter **95%**

Ordinary nonluminous matter **4.5%**

Ordinary luminous matter **0.5%**

Electromagnetic spectrum **0.005%**
Within the electromagnetic spectrum
is 'visible light' (human sight), but this
is too small to portray on this graphic

Percentages do not add up to 100% because of rounding

Figure 51: This is all we can 'see'..

ladies and gentlemen, is your 'real world'. The brain is not the origin of consciousness, but a decoder of consciousness/information and if it doesn't decode something then we can't see it. 'Computational theory of mind' is a field of research which I only came across while writing this book and it syncs so perfectly with what I have been writing in previous works. This contends that the human brain/mind is an information processing system and that thinking is a form of computing. Hilary Putnam, an American philosopher, mathematician, and computer scientist, first proposed the idea as long ago as 1961 and it's spot on. From ancient and present day shamans to cutting edge real scientists the theme has always been the same. Physicist Nikola Tesla, the genius who gave us many pillars of the modern world including alternating current electricity, said: 'My brain is only a receiver.' A physicist would seem to be in another world to a native shaman but open-minded scientists, shamans, mystics and awakening people speak the same language. Mexican shaman Don Juan Matus, quoted in the books of Carlos Castaneda, said:

We are perceivers, we are awareness; we are not objects; we have no solidity. We are boundless ... We, or rather our reason, forget this and thus we entrap the totality of ourselves in a vicious circle from which we rarely emerge in our lifetime.

Another thing about the illusion: Even mainstream science agrees that we only 'see' a tiny fraction of what there is to see – and I mean *tiny*. The electromagnetic spectrum is said to be as little as 0.005 percent of what is said to exist in the Universe in terms of matter, mass and energy (Fig 51). 'Visible light', the only frequency range we can perceive with human sight, is a *fraction* of even this 0.005 percent (Fig 52). Some say the electrometric spectrum ratio is a bit bigger, but not much. We don't live 'in' a world as we perceive we do. We live in a frequency band or range which some call dimensions or densities and they interpenetrate each other just like analogue radio and television stations operating on different wavelengths while sharing the same 'space' (Fig 53). Density refers to the density of energy in response to different frequencies. I have hardly started yet and the perceived 'real world' is already in pieces. Sergio Toporek, an artist and filmmaker who has done considerable research into the nature of images, said

> Consider that you can see less than 1% of the electromagnetic spectrum and hear less than 1% of the acoustic spectrum. As you read this, you are travelling at 220 km/sec across the galaxy. 90% of the cells in your body carry their own microbial DNA and are not 'you'. The atoms in your body are 99.9999999999999999% empty space and none of them are the ones you were born with ... Human beings have 46 chromosomes, 2 less than a potato.

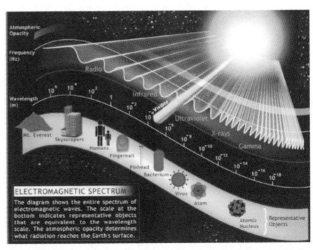

Figure 52: The frequency range of The System; but it still knows it all.

The existence of the rainbow depends on the conical photoreceptors in your eyes; to animals without cones, the rainbow does not exist. So you don't just look at a rainbow, you create it. This is pretty amazing, especially considering that all the beautiful colours you see represent less than 1% of the electromagnetic spectrum.

Scientist Isaac Newton appropriately coined the term 'spectrum' from the Latin word meaning 'apparition or phantom' (hence 'spectre'). Colours are, like everything in our reality, information carried by particular frequencies which the brain and the other receiver-transmitting systems of Body-Mind decode into what we appear to see. An 'object' is not a particular colour or colours, and the illusion of this is created by which frequencies (colours) are reflected or absorbed. We don't see what is absorbed and we do see what is reflected. We are decoding these reflected frequencies when we say 'that

is blue' or 'that is red'. We can only see reflected light and while we may appear to see a landscape, house or chair we are actually seeing only the light that is reflected from them. We can't see anything in pitch black when no light is being reflected. Visible Light is energy / information within a (tiny) frequency band and this is all humans can see because our visual decoding system normally only processes information in that band. What is invisible to us may not be so for

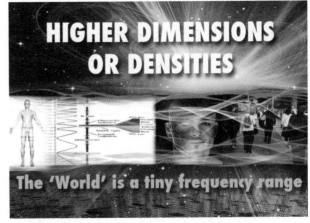

Figure 53: What we call the world is a tiny frequency range.

other species (including non-humans or 'aliens') with a more expansive visual range. Psychically-sensitive animals like cats have a wider visual frequency range and you see them reacting to what humans cannot see – 'What's the cat doing? There's nothing there'.

The Universe is a 'computer'

Five-sense reality – 'the Universe' – is simply the encoding and decoding of information – the same in principle as the way the Internet or a computer game works. An article in the mainstream *Scientific American* magazine about black holes being computers began like this:

> Most people think of computers as specialized gizmos: stream-lined boxes sitting on a desk or fingernail-size chips embedded in high-tech coffeepots. But to a physicist, all physical systems are computers. Rocks, atom bombs and galaxies may not run Linux, but they, too, register and process information. Every electron, photon and other elementary particle stores bits of data, and every time two such particles interact, those bits are transformed. Physical existence and information content are inextricably linked.

Figure 54: We are living in an advanced version of a computer program..

The Universe is like a gigantic computer / Internet system based on encoding and decoding information and there is a good reason for this – we live in a massively more sophisticated version of a computer simulation (Fig 54). Our five-sense reality is a quantum computer with almost unimaginable potential for processing information. Computers that we use are encoded into binary digits (known as 'bits') represented by 1 and 0 or on-off electrical states. Quantum computers employ *quantum* bits ('qubits') which use atoms, photons or electrons etc., to store and process information. Quantum computers can operate in multiple states simultaneously (not only 1 or 0) and so they are millions of times more powerful than even today's supercomputers. Consider the potential, therefore, of a quantum computer on the scale of the Universe for information processing. Quantum physicists are realising that all matter (concentrated energy) is a form of computer, but in fact *all* energy can compute information because it is *conscious*. The Universe is not only a computer of extraordinary power, it is a *conscious* computer. Everything is conscious in some form. I have been saying for many years that the body is a biological computer or living computer – a quantum computer in other words. A definition of biological is 'of, relating to, caused by, or affecting life or living organisms'. A biological computer has consciousness and can think for itself up to a point – as the immune system does all the time, making decisions on how to respond to changing circumstances. Computers have sleep mode (so does the body); they cease to function or 'die' (so does the body); they have a central processing unit or CPU (brain); they have a hard drive (DNA); and they have anti-virus protection (immune system). We have brain-computer interface technology in which the brain can think instructions to the computer because the technology is connecting two computers. A study at the Massachusetts Institute of Technology (MIT) said:

WE ARE AWARENESS

A STATE OF BEING
AWARE

Figure 55: We are eternal awareness having an experience.

> Biology is fundamentally discrete, based on sets of nucleic and amino acids combined into genes and proteins. And computers are fundamentally discrete, based on bits of data processed by logic gates. The latter have long been used to study the former, but a range of emerging technologies are now making it possible to directly convert between these representations.

Just as analog/digital and digital/analog converters provide the interface between computers and the physical world of sensors and actuators, 'biology/digital' and 'digital/biology' converters are allowing computers to create and control biological worlds.

Biologists are now making synthetic cells. So who are we if what we see in the mirror is a biological computer? We think *we* are our bodies, names, races and so on, but they are only Phantom Self, the human experience. They come and go, live and die. Eternal Infinite Self is Awareness, the state of being *aware* (Fig 55). We are points of attention within Infinite Awareness which is Infinite *Everything* – all thought, feeling, knowing, potential, possibility, *awareness* – and this has been known by endless names through the ages (including, of course, God). I prefer the term *All That Is, Has Been And Ever Can Be*. At first sight this description seems ridiculous. How can you be all that is, has been and can be? But this is only another way of saying All Possibility and rightly so because Infinite Awareness *is* All Possibility. Near-death experiencer Anita Moorjani, author of *Dying to be Me*, said of the out-of-body realms: 'When we are not expressing in our physical body, you and I and all of us ... we are all expressions of the same consciousness.' What we call Creation and the realms of form and illusory physicality are Infinite Awareness *experiencing itself*. Albert Einstein said: 'Everyone who is seriously involved in the pursuit of science becomes convinced that a spirit is manifest in the laws of the Universe – a spirit vastly superior to that of man.' Max Planck (1858-1947), the German theoretical physicist behind quantum theory, made a similar point:

> All matter originates and exists, only by virtue of a force. We must assume behind this force is the existence of a conscious and intelligent mind. This mind is the matrix of all matter.

Mainstream religion mocks or condemns anyone suggesting that we are 'God', to use that misleading term. We are told to believe that we are inferior, subordinate, sinners that must worship 'God' when, in fact, we are a point of attention within 'God' as 'God' experiences itself; but this 'God' is not the 'God' of religion – it is Infinite Awareness

Figure 56: Phantom Self or Infinite Awareness – it's just a different perception.

Figure 57: Awareness – from a pinhead to infinity

with Infinite points of attention that can be anything from myopic to All-Knowing. If you focus only on the five senses, your awareness will be myopic but awareness can be expanded until it is All- Knowing with an Infinite point of attention (Fig 56). Anita Moorjani symbolised human reality as holding a flashlight (point of attention) in a pitch-black warehouse. Wherever you point the light is what you see and nothing else. She said that when awareness leaves the body it can be likened to all the lights of the warehouse being switched on and you can see everything. She added:

> There's so much more that exists simultaneously and alongside the things that you can see ... You know that just because you cannot see them, you can't experience it, doesn't mean it doesn't exist.

She said that in her out-of-body state: 'Wherever I put my awareness – there I was.' Who are we at any moment? We are a point of attention or multiple, even infinite points of attention depending on how expanded is our awareness (Fig 57). Our body focusses

Figure 58: What we call human life is a point of attention within our Infinite Self.

attention on the infinitesimal frequency band of visible light and we don't even see most of that never mind all that exists beyond our tiny band of perception (Fig 58). A video on the Internet has people throwing a basketball to each other and the viewer is told to count how many times those wearing white pass the ball. At the end it asks: Did you see the gorilla?' Half the watchers don't, according to a Harvard study, but when you play the video again while not focussing on the ball you see that

someone dressed as a gorilla clearly walks
into shot. Attention is everything when it
comes to perception. The body hijacks
attention and is encouraged to do so by
The System in ways that I will be
explaining.

Meeting with Infinity

I consciously experienced awareness
beyond Body-Mind in the rainforest of
Brazil in 2003. I entered an altered and
expanded state of perception on two

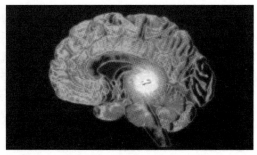

Figure 59: The pineal gland connects us to 'out there'
frequencies beyond the world that we 'see'.

occasions after taking the psychoactive potion ayahuasca, a rainforest plant which
contains the neurotransmitter DMT or dimethyltryptamine. DMT is a naturally-
occurring component of the metabolism of mammals and plants. Ayahuasca can have
many effects, nice and not so nice, and can free you from five-sense awareness to
experience far more expanded states. This happened to me over five incredible hours.
DMT stimulates the pineal gland in the centre of the brain, which is part of the decoding
system known as the 'Third Eye' and can connect us to realities beyond the reach of the
five senses (Fig 59). Pineal glands are only about the size of a grain of rice and look a bit
like a pine cone. This symbol has been used for the pineal gland by many cultures and
can be seen in the enormous pine cone that dominates the Courtyard of the Pinecone in
the Vatican (Figs 60 and 61). Pineal glands are crystalline, as are DNA molecules and the
body and genetic structures, because they are all receiver-transmitters of information.
There are even military radios that exploit the ability of bones to transmit sound. Every
cell membrane is a liquid crystal and we have tens of trillions of cells. What do they use
in communication technology? Crystals. Ancient standing stones and circles were made
with crystalline rock because they were a means of receiving and transmitting
information between their builders and the 'gods' or other frequency bands of reality.
Ayahuasca is known as the 'plant of the gods' for the same reason. It can open the mind
to see 'the gods' (non-human entities) in other realms of frequency. My experience in
Brazil is the only time I have taken a psychoactive potion or drug, apart from some very

Figure 60: The pineal gland has often
been symbolised as a pine cone.

Figure 61: 'Pineal gland' temple.

Figure 62: The Dazzling Darkness of still and silent All Possibility, All Potential, *All That Is And Ever Can Be*.

mild 'magic mushrooms' on one other occasion. Quality of experience is what matters, not quantity, and this one gave me so much both immediately and in further researching information I was given that night. I lay on the floor in a round wooden structure in the forest for about an hour before the effects of the ayahuasca began to kick in. A loud and powerful voice began to speak in my mind. It took a female form (with a hysterical sense of humour) and the illusory nature of physical reality was explained to me. 'David,' the Voice began, 'we are going to take you to where you come from so you can remember who you are.' My awareness was immediately taken to a realm of indescribable bliss where I was pure consciousness. There was no form, no time, no division. All was one seamless consciousness in which I was everything and everything was me. There was no point where I ended and everything else began. I was self-aware as a 'me' (a point of attention called David Icke) but also collectively aware – infinitely aware you might say – as a point of attention within the Infinite Whole. 'This is the Infinite, David,' the Voice said. 'This is where you come from and this is where you shall return.' I was experiencing the real 'self', although 'self' is not really the word, and from this perspective the limitations and illusions of Phantom Self (name, race, family history, etc.) were so clear to see. The Voice said that all I really needed to know was that 'Infinite Love is the only truth – *everything* else is illusion'. The words were repeated many times – 'Infinite Love is the only truth – *everything* else is illusion'. I experienced this infinite state as silence when the Voice wasn't speaking, and as either stillness or sometimes waves moving in serious slow motion. There was pure harmony with no polarities or divisions and although it appeared as a sort of blackness it somehow shone with enormous vibrancy. Others who have experienced this state describe much the same thing – a 'Dazzling Darkness' as one near-death experiencer described it. This was Dr Eben Alexander, an academic neurosurgeon at Harvard for 15 years, who by his own admission could not have been a more unquestioning advocate of mainstream 'science' and its belief that consciousness came from the brain. Then his brain shut down during a near-death experience in 2008 but his awareness continued nevertheless. He describes in his book *Proof of Heaven* what he calls 'The Core' or 'Dazzling Darkness' from where the purest love emanated and all is known (Fig 62). This is the Infinite in awareness of itself, a state of awareness that knows it is the *All That Is And Ever Can Be, All Potential, All Possibility*. One of the terms used through the centuries to describe the Dazzling Darkness is the 'Void'. From here all 'Creation' and form is made manifest as the Infinite experiences itself. Realms of form or illusory form are realms of frequency and vibration (Figs 63 and 64). The Voice said:

Illustrations by Neil Hague (www.neilhague.com)

Figure 63: Out of All Possibility come the worlds of created form through information-encoded frequency and vibration.

Figure 64: Different 'worlds' or realities can share the same 'space' because they operate in different bands of frequency.

If it vibrates, it is illusion. The Infinite [in awareness of itself] does not vibrate; it is the harmony and Oneness of all. Only illusion vibrates – that which is created by the imagination and delusion of mind.

It may seem odd that something silent and still can be the origin of all form and possibility, but again the opposite is the case. Sitting in silence is All Possibility waiting to manifest. Then you start talking and you are choosing that possibility out of all possibility. When you stop speaking everything returns to the silence of All Possibility. The same is true with movement and stillness. Under a microscope all is moving, vibrating, but this is the world of form, not the Dazzling Darkness from which all form originates in the imagination of the Infinite. Physicist and genius Nikola Tesla said: 'In the Universe there is a core from which we obtain knowledge, strength and inspiration. I have not penetrated into the secrets of this core, but I know it exists.' Your imagination is an expression of Infinite Imagination because *you* are the Infinite experiencing itself (Fig 65). Scale, depth and potential of that imagination may be different with

Figure 65: Everything is the Infinite experiencing itself.

each unique expression, but it's the same imagination and self-experience. We are the droplet and the Infinite is the ocean, but when the droplet is *connected* to the ocean where does the droplet end and the ocean start? There is no such point. Both are the same *Oneness*. Different names and labels make us lose sight of this unity just as we speak of the Atlantic Ocean, Pacific Ocean and Indian Ocean when they are all the same body of water. 'Love' as in Infinite Love does not have the same meaning as the illusory love that humanity talks about. Humanity's perception of love is overwhelmingly describing an electro-chemical attraction; or what I call 'Mind Love'. Those who have been involved in government-military mind control programmes have told me how two people who would otherwise have no attraction can be made to fall madly in 'love' purely by stimulating certain chemicals in the brain. We are told that love never dies and in terms of Infinite Love that is true; but how often do those attracted by Mind Love walk away from each other with the attraction long gone and only acrimony to show for it? Infinite Love is far closer to always-there friendship than head-over-heels temporary 'love'. Infinite Love just is. It doesn't have a set of conditions. It doesn't even have to like what you do. It loves because it *is* love. We have to use terms like unconditional love to indicate the difference between Mind Love and love in its Infinite sense which is the harmony and balance of all things, all forces. Humanity has been systematically disconnected from this state of Infinite Love for reasons and through means that will become clear. This is why the world is as it is, but we can reconnect whenever we make that choice. I will refer to the realms of form as 'Creation' in contrast to the *All That Is* or Dazzling Darkness which is the source of that Creation through its infinite points of attention. Creation is not all the work of the Dazzling Darkness in awareness of itself saying: 'Let there be light and there was light' (I'll put that into another context later, anyway). Expressions of Infinite Awareness which are not aware of their own infinite nature also create worlds or simulated worlds. Someone designing a house or car is still using creative imagination to do so as an expression of Infinite Imagination. Only the scale of awareness and potential to manifest is different. An adult can do brain surgery but a child can't because it does not have the same awareness. A child does, however, have the potential to expand its awareness until it can do brain surgery. The relationship is the same between the *All That Is* in awareness of itself and humans in awareness only of being human. A perception of being human is only a temporary experience by expressions of Infinite Awareness – *you*, everyone. Phantom Self is a state of strictly limited awareness which has been tricked into believing that it is the experience, when it is really Infinite Awareness *having* that experience. I explained in the opening chapter some foundations to how the trick works, and I will expand on that and what is behind this manipulation – and why. For now it is enough to say that humanity is living out a false identity by confusing who they *are* with what they are *experiencing* – their name, race, culture, religion, family history. The Voice asked me as I experienced Infinite reality: 'Do you feel any frustration or anger in this place?' I did not. 'Do you have any worries or fear or guilt where you are now?' No, there was only harmony, peace, love and bliss. 'Frustration, anger, fear, guilt and pain are only illusions, figments of disconnected mind,' the Voice continued. 'They don't exist except in your imagination.' Later I began to feel quite nauseous (a common feature of ayahuasca) but this disappeared when the Voice said:

Where is your nausea coming from? Do you think the Infinite is feeling nauseous now? So you must be identifying with your body. It's an illusion, David; your body is an illusion, and so must be the nausea you think you are feeling in your body. If your body does not exist how can nausea or pain?

I think it is fair to say with historic understatement that human perception and Infinite Perception do not see the world the same way.

We live in a simulation

When I returned from Brazil and the 'Voice' in 2003 I began to research what I had been told over those five hours or more. I realised that our reality is actually a highly advanced form of computer simulation like that portrayed in *The Matrix* and this will make so much more sense of the 'world' (Fig 66). I saw that even the cutting edge of mainstream science had established the

Figure 66: The world we think is 'out there' is actually a simulation which we decode into the reality we daily experience. It's is all happening 'in here' – within our decoding processes.

illusory nature of reality, but the institution of science is so fragmented, with each discipline up its own arse, that these revelations were largely ignored in the hope they would go away. Quantum physics – the study of the unseen energetic levels from which our illusory 'physical' world is manifested – has demolished the foundations on which mainstream science has been based and they are still doing their best not to acknowledge that. 'Laws of physics' are only the encoded rules and limitations of the simulation or 'game' and they only operate within the simulation. Expand your awareness to beyond the game and you transcend the game and its encoded limitation. What then happens are called 'miracles', but they are not miracles. There *are* no

miracles, only more expanded understanding of how everything works. The Voice in Brazil told me that the human laws of physics were illusory 'laws' to measure an illusory universe. 'Do you think the Infinite needs 'laws' through which to express itself?' the Voice asked. There were no laws of anything, only perceptions of them. Laws and limitation were only a *belief* in laws and limitation, the Voice said, and this is clearly true. How come if you walk through fire you get burned but if you do

Figure 67: How can people walk through fire without getting burned if our reality is 'real'?

the same in an altered state of consciousness (belief) you don't? This is what firewalkers do and I have seen it for myself (Fig 67). What you believe you perceive and what you perceive you experience. I have been writing and saying for a long time that we live in a simulation or 'Matrix-type' world and my own research and sources are increasingly supported by those mainstream scientists who express a spirit of true exploration rather than song sheet worship. Reports have now even begun to appear in the mainstream media here and there. Physicists at the University of Bonn in Germany have said they may have evidence that the Universe is a computer simulation and they published their findings in a paper headed 'Constraints on the Universe as a Numerical Simulation'. They highlight the Greisen-Zatsepin-Kuzmin (GZK) cut-off which is a barrier for cosmic ray particles caused by interaction with cosmic background radiation and they say that this 'pattern of constraint' is precisely what you would find with a computer simulation. Like a prisoner in a pitch-black cell we would not be able to see the 'walls' of our prison, the team says, but 'through physics we may be able to identify them'.

Simulations can have their own 'laws of physics' in the same way that computer games operate to the rules dictated by the writer of the program. Answers to questions about how something is possible can so often be answered by 'click, click, enter' – simply the way the simulation has been written. I have long contended in my books that the outer 'wall' of the simulation is what scientists call the speed of light (officially 186,282 miles per second). Albert Einstein said this was the fastest speed possible but I strongly beg to differ. There can be no fastest speed within All Possibility for a start and the speed of light is pedestrian compared with what happens outside the simulation. Reality and 'time' go haywire close to the speed of light because we are then approaching the limits of the simulation and entering a realm with very different 'laws of physics' (Fig 68). Time is only an encoded program within the simulation and starts to warp when you reach the outer limits of that program. Consciousness beyond the five senses can override the limitations of the simulation and this often happens in dreams when we can fall off a cliff or something and no one dies. Do the same within the program and you do 'die', or at least the body does, because that is the way the program is written to hijack perception in a state of limitation. A belief in the speed of light as the limit of possibility can keep you entrapped in the program as your sense of reality becomes your experienced reality. Most people believed that no one could ever run a mile in under four minutes, but once Roger Bannister achieved that by a fraction of a second in 1954 others began to do the same and better. This is the same principle.

By 2015 the world record for the mile was nearly *17 seconds* below four minutes. Near-death experiencers find themselves in a totally different reality with different 'laws of physics' when their awareness withdraws from the body – withdraws the point of attention from the sense of limitation specifically programmed into our 'physical' (Matrix simulation) reality. Phantom Self, or five-sense self, is subject to these limitations because it is part of the same program,

Figure 68: The Matrix operates (on the level we perceive) within the speed of light.

Figure 69: Virtual reality games hijack the five-senses with information to project a fake reality.

Figure 70: The fake can seem so real – just like the reality we are experiencing.

but Infinite Self transcends them as it's not part of the program. When this happens the resulting 'miracles' are often dismissed as a piece of trickery – 'things like that can't happen'. How often such words spew forth from Phantom Self, which is attached to the simulation and so believes in its programmed laws and rules. There is Phantom Self trickery and illusion – as with magicians – but the Infinite Self does not require that to transcend limitation when it is *All That Is And Ever Can Be*. Oxford professor Nick Bostrom has also said that our world could be a computer simulation and calculated the 'computational requirements' on which it would be constructed. Bostrom is also a proponent of transhumanism – the fusing of humans with technology – and I will have much to say about this. It is vital for people to appreciate the magnitude of human control that transhumanism represents. We now have technology that basically mirrors the simulation in the form of virtual reality games that can convince the players their virtual world is real (Figs 69 and 70). We have virtual reality training including pilot training, and movie simulations that are getting ever closer to this-world real (Figs 71 and 72). Burns patients in some hospitals are attached to virtual reality technology so they can focus on another reality while their dressings are being changed (Fig 73). Those

Figure 71: Video games are getting ever closer to the reality we experience as the world.

Figure 72: How long before you won't be able to tell the difference?

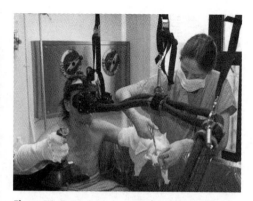

Figure 73: Focussing on a virtual reality can detach the mind from the pain of changing dressings. What the brain doesn't decode we can't feel with the five senses.

at the forefront of virtual reality development say it won't be that long before virtual realities are produced which will be indistinguishable from our 'real world' (simulation). Silas Beane with the University of Bonn team said:

The idea is that in future, humans will be able to simulate entire universes quite easily. And given the vastness of time ahead, the number of these simulations is likely to be huge. So if you ask the question: 'Do we live in the one true reality or in one of the many simulations?, the answer, statistically speaking, is that we're more likely to be living in a simulation.

James Gates, the John S. Toll Professor of Physics at the University of Maryland and Director of The Center for String and Particle Theory, is another mainstreamer exploring evidence that we live in a simulation. He said in a *Physics World* article in 2012 that evidence is indeed there to suggest that our reality is something close to the *Matrix* movie series. Gates detailed how his team had uncovered equations in the fabric of the Universe which include embedded computer codes of digital data that take the form of 1 and 0 – the binary system of on-off electrical charges used by computers. He agreed that 'nature' can be reduced to equations found in computer coding and that finding these codes supported the view that we live in a simulation. Gates also revealed that they had discovered sequences which are the same as mathematical sequences known as error-correcting codes or block codes embedded in computers and other electrical technology. These return or reboot data to its original state if something changes or interferes with it during transmission. Gates said that he didn't know what they were doing in the make-up of our reality, but I suggest they are part of the software that ensures the simulation remains in situ when other data and sources of information threaten its stability. These error-correcting codes are connected to the apparent limitation (walls of the Matrix) that is called the speed of light. Max Tegmark, a physicist at the Massachusetts Institute of Technology (MIT), says the Universe is a mathematical structure 'just like a cube, or a tetrahedron' and is 'entirely described by numbers and maths, just as a video game is encoded. Tegmark, author of *Our Mathematical Universe*, makes the point that the physics of computer games and our world are basically the same:

Suppose you are a character in Minecraft or some much more advanced computer game where the graphics are really good and you don't think you're in a game. You feel that you can bump into real objects and you can fall in love and get excited about stuff. And when you start studying the physical world in this video game, eventually you start discovering that, wow, everything is made out of pixels, and all these things that I used to think were 'stuff' are actually just described by a bunch of numbers. You'd undoubtedly be criticised by some friends saying, 'come on you're stupid, it's stuff after all.' But [someone] looking from outside of this video game would see that actually, all there was was numbers.

And we're exactly in this situation in our world. We look around and it doesn't seem that mathematical at all, but everything we see is made out of elementary particles like quarks and electrons. And what properties does an electron have? Does it have a smell or a colour or a texture? No! As far as we can tell the only properties an electron has are – 1, 1/2 and 1. We physicists have come up with geeky names for these properties, like electric charge, or spin, or lepton number, but the electron doesn't care what we call it, the properties are just numbers.

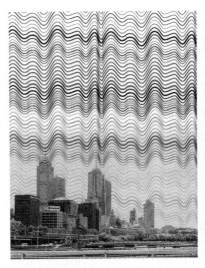

Figure 74: Our reality is an information field or fields that we decode into illusory 'physical' reality.

Simulations operate within specific frequency bands and they are realms of energetic waves, vibration and numbers in contrast to the stillness and silence of Infinite All Possibility in awareness of itself. These waves and vibrations are encoded *information* and the human Body-Mind decodes this information into the world that we experience as physical (Fig 74). I'll come to how it does this in a moment. The simulation is interactive. We decode information from the information fields that we call the Universe and we also change the Universe by posting our own perceptions through thought and emotion (information). For this reason I describe the Universe – the simulation – as the 'Cosmic Internet' (Fig 75). The principle is the same, especially with wireless communication. Wireless Internet information may appear on your computer screen as images, words, graphics and video, but do you see any of those things flying around the room or in your computer tower? This information is in the room, yes, but in the form of unseen information fields (Wi-Fi) which the computer *decodes* into images, words, graphics and video. Body-Mind is a biological computer which decodes

Figure 75: To understand the Universe think Wi-Fi field or Cosmic Internet.

Figure 76: A portrayal of what Wi-Fi would look like if we could see it ...

Figure 77: ... our reality operates in the same way with information fields decoded by the body-computer into the reality that appears to be so real.

information from the unseen Cosmic Internet into the 'seen' world of the conscious five-sense mind. The Universe in its foundation state can be likened very accurately to Wi-Fi fields of information which we are decoding and encoding (Figs 76 and 77). We live within an energetic 'sea' of information – the simulation or Matrix. What is called the World Wide Web only exists in the form we perceive when the computer decodes information onto the screen and our 'physical' reality only exists in the form that we perceive when the brain decodes information onto its 'screen'. There is no 'out there' – the 'out there' is only illusion. People often ask that if we create our own reality as I say we do, then how come we all see the same landscape, house or car? We are all decoding the same background information fields, the same information construct, but not necessarily in the same detail and with the same perception. How do we know what others are seeing? They may see the same basic backdrop (decode the Cosmic Internet) but information we choose to decode and what we think of what we 'see' can be very different. How often we hear people say of those with a different perception of the same thing – 'What planet are you on?' What planet are you decoding and perceiving would be more like it. Remember, too, that while the brain is receiving 11 million 'sensations' or 'impressions' (pieces of information) every second it constructs our sense of visual reality from just 40 while filling the gaps with what it thinks should be there. Are we really saying that every brain is going to fill those gaps in the exactly same way? An observer's sense of reality is also going to dictate what is decoded and what is made of that – as in glass half empty or half full. Now, something that will become very relevant later: You can program a computer to decode information in a particular way and to decode some information and ignore the rest. Body-Mind is a biological computer that can be programmed to do the same. If you wanted to control humanity en masse is this not what you would do? Of course you would – and they *have*. The program is Phantom Self.

Lost in the role

Body-Mind is designed to directly interact with the simulation and this is the vehicle through which our expression of Infinite Awareness – what some call the 'Soul' or superconsciousness – can experience and interact with this reality. 'Soul' resonates to a much higher frequency than the simulation that we 'see' and in its purest Infinite state is beyond frequency and vibration. 'Soul' could not pick up a fork or drive a car in the same way that the frequency of radio station A cannot interact (interfere) with radio station B when they are on very different wavelengths. Eternal Soul overcomes this frequency disparity by transferring its point of attention into the biological computer of Body-Mind through which it can directly interact with the simulation. What can happen – and has happened with humanity – is that our point of *attention* can become so

confused between Body-Mind awareness
and its own Infinite Awareness that it
self-identifies with Body-Mind (Phantom
Self) and its name, race, culture, and
family history. The play, *As You Like It*,
attributed to William Shakespeare, says:

Figure 78: The face we put to the world – Phantom Self.

> All the world's a stage,
> And all the men and women merely
> players;
> They have their exits and their
> entrances,
> And one man in his time plays
> many parts.

Phantom Self is an actor who
is so confused that he thinks
his fictional character is really
him and this confusion is
encouraged and manipulated
for reasons and by forces that I
will reveal. How apt that the
word 'person' comes from
persona or 'actors mask' in
Latin (Fig 78). You could think
of someone sitting at the
computer with the keyboard
and mouse as symbolic of the

Figure 79: When the computer is disconnected from the operator and
goes its own way the greater perspective of reality is lost. The computer
world is all that appears to exist.

Soul and the computer as Body-Mind and the five senses (Fig 79). Imagine the computer
losing contact with the 'someone' and deciding itself where to go on the Internet and
what to do. This is the dynamic I am talking about between 'Soul' and Body-Mind
Phantom Self. We are meant to be simultaneously aware on multiple levels so we are *in*
this world (Body-Mind) but not *of* it (Soul) with the two working in conscious harmony
to exchange information and insight. The more we expand our awareness the more
points of attention we become aware of – 'I could be anywhere I wanted to be
simultaneously', as the near-death experiencer said. The System is specifically
structured to disconnect Body-Mind from the influence and insight of Soul to isolate
perception, attention and awareness in Body-Mind, which then becomes a Phantom Self
unaware of its Infinite Self. The following is all accepted by the scientific mainstream
although its fundamental implications for understanding reality are largely ignored:
Our five senses of sight, hearing, touch, smell and taste decode waveform information
(what I would call the 'Wi-Fi' Cosmic Internet) into electrical information which is then
communicated to the brain to be decoded into the digital 'physical world' that we think
we 'see' (Fig 80). Our 'external world' is actually internal in the sense that it only exists
in the brain. Virtually everything, if not *everything*, is an inversion of the way we
perceive it and this is yet another classic. What we experience as solid and physical is

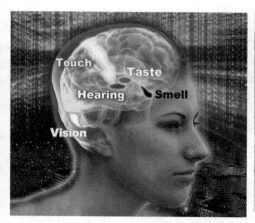

Figure 80: The 'physical world' of 'out there' is a decoded reality that only exists in that form in our brain. What the brain doesn't decode we can't see.

Figure 81: Reality exists as information on many levels which is decoded into what we think is a solid reality, but isn't.

digital/holographic, which can be likened to the holograms you can buy in the shops. They appear to be solid and three-dimensional, but aren't. Body-Mind decoding processes create different versions of the same 'world' by decoding the same information into different states of manifestation. From the waveform Cosmic Internet is decoded the electrical/electromagnetic and then the digital and holographic (Fig 81). By definition Body-Mind operates on all these levels, too. What is called the auric field is the waveform/electrical/electromagnetic level of Body-Mind while the brain and genetic structure deals with the electrical, digital and holographic. Scientists are bewildered to find that particles can also be waveforms at the *same time,* but this can be explained by the fact that they are different manifestations of the same information at different stages of the decoding process (Fig 82). Another apparent mystery is how the solid world is made of atoms and yet atoms have no solidity (Fig 83). How can something with no solidity construct a 'solid' world? This can be answered by another simple fact

Figure 82: All these levels of simultaneous reality are the same information in different forms.

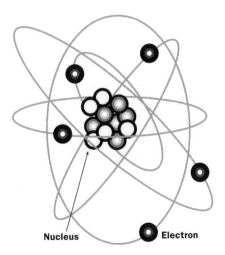

Nucleus   **Electron**

Figure 83: Atoms are packets of electrical energy (information) and empty atoms do not a solid world make.

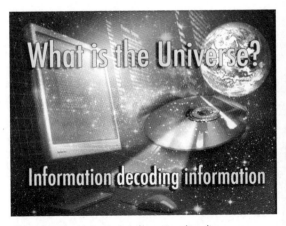

Figure 84: The Universe is information decoding information.

– there is no physical or solid world and so atoms don't need to be. They are packets of energetic information that are part of the decoding process, that's all. Everything in our reality is information being encoded and decoded. What is the Universe? *Information.* In the case of the 'physical' Universe it is *decoded* information in the same way that a computer is information decoding software and Internet information. (Fig 84).

Five-sense illusion

The five senses are decoding systems that turn waveform information into electrical information, which they communicate to the brain – or at least that is a simple way of explaining the process of manifestation. There is a major rider to this, which I will explain at the end of the chapter. Virtual reality games hijack the five senses by sending information to the sight, sound and (through gloves) touch senses. They use the same decoding system through which we create 'normal' reality, but communicate different information. My goodness, how this is going to be so relevant later. Ears decode waveform information and transmit it to the brain to be decoded into sound. Anything that prevents this information reaching the brain in the correct form or stops the brain decoding it will cause the person to be deaf. We hear words when people speak, but *only* when the fields of vibrating information generated by the vocal cords have been decoded into words by the brain. Words do not pass between us, only vibrational information fields. Words come courtesy of the brain which can be programmed to decode different vocal cord information in different ways and we call these different languages. Music is a perfect example of waveform information decoded into sound by the brain. A music concert is a mass of waveform information from vocal cords, strings and drums decoded by the brain into the form that we 'hear'. Music can also be expressed as mathematical codes. We only feel pain when a blow on the knee is transmitted electrically to the brain to be decoded into 'ouch'. Methods of pain relief used today include blocking this communication, because if the brain does not decode the message we cannot feel the pain. We only taste when the brain decodes information from the tongue into 'Mmmm' and 'ugh' and we only smell when the brain decodes electrical messages from the nose. Chemical 'taste enhancers' such as monosodium glutamate (MSG) are added to what passes for food to trick the brain into decoding taste that isn't really there. Different parts of the brain specialise in decoding information from different senses and our entire visual reality springs forth from a few cubic centimetres at the back of the brain. Yep, physical reality is real all right. A scene in *The Matrix* when Morpheus was explaining the illusion of physicality was based on fact:

> What is real? How do you define 'real'? If you're talking about what you can feel, what you can smell, taste and see, then 'real' is simply electrical signals interpreted by your brain.

That's all it is – this 'Real World'. A brain sits in pitch black darkness encased by the skull and only 'sees' light by decoding electrical information delivered from the sight senses. Philosopher and mystic Allan Watts was right when he said:

> ... [Without the brain] the world is devoid of light, heat, weight, solidity, motion, space, time or any other imaginable feature. All these phenomena are interactions, or transactions, of vibrations with a certain arrangement of neurons.

It's not just the brain, either. The whole genetic and body structure is involved in the reality-decoding process and this includes the receiver-transmitter system known as DNA (deoxyribonucleic acid) and the central nervous system. An Internet article described DNA very well:

> From the characteristic form of this giant molecule – a wound double helix – the DNA represents an ideal electromagnetic antenna. On one hand it is elongated and thus a blade which can take up very well electrical pulses. On the other hand, seen from above, it has the form of a ring and thus is a very magnetical antenna.

DNA is also a *software program* as an article in the *San Francisco Chronicle* pointed out: 'DNA is a universal software code. From bacteria to humans, the basic instructions for life are written with the same language.' DNA consists of four (biological computer) codes known as A, C, G and T, and the relationship between them decides if the holographic form is a virus, a mouse or a human (Figs 85 and 86). Only small differences can produce vastly different forms. Body-Mind in its entirety is a software program designed to interact with the overall software program of the simulation or Matrix. This is the realisation that makes sense of our crazy world and the nature of Phantom Self. Body-Mind software is programmed only to visually decode the tiny frequency range called visible light to focus and isolate our perceptions in five-sense reality at the expense of a conscious connection to Infinite Awareness. I will be addressing the whys and wherefores of this and in doing so unravel the mysteries of human society. Scientific naïvety about DNA is such that up to 98 percent has been dubbed 'junk DNA' because they don't know what it does and conclude therefore that it *must have no function*. This is a recurring theme with mainstream science and indeed Mainstream Everything – 'We don't understand how this can happen and so it can't be happening'. Unbelievable. Real scientists can see the nonsense of this 'junk DNA' and

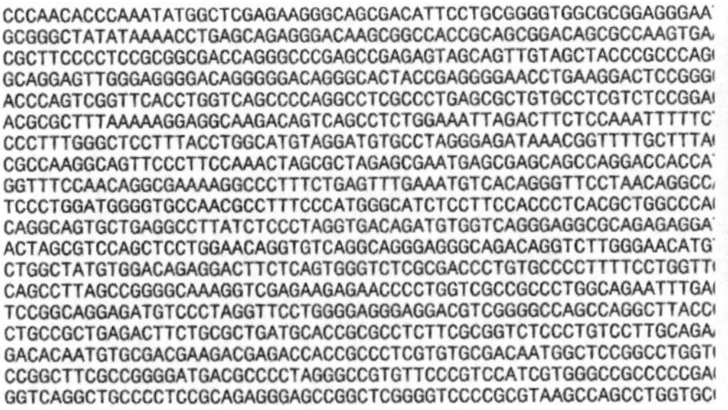

CCCAACACCCAAATATGGCTCGAGAAGGGCAGCGACATTCCTGCGGGGTGGCGCGGAGGGAA
GCGGGCTATATAAAACCTGAGCAGAGGACAAGCGGCCACCGCAGCGGACAGCGCCAAGTGA
CGCTTCCCCTCCGCGGCGACCAGGGCCCGAGCCGAGAGTAGCAGTTGTAGCTACCCGCCCAG
GCAGGAGTTGGGAGGGGACAGGGGGACAGGGCACTACCGAGGGGAACCTGAAGGACTCCGGG
ACCCAGTCGGTTCACCTGGTCAGCCCCAGGCCTCGCCCTGAGCGCTGTGCCTCGTCTCCGGA
ACGCGCTTTAAAAAGGAGGCAAGACAGTCAGCCTCTGGAAATTAGACTTCTCCAAATTTTTC
CCCTTTGGGCTCCTTTACCTGGCATGTAGGATGTGCCTAGGGAGATAAACGGTTTTGCTTTA
CGCCAAGGCAGTTCCCTTCCAAACTAGCGCTAGAGCGAATGAGCGAGCAGCCAGGACCACCA
GGTTTCCAACAGGCGAAAAGGCCCTTTCTGAGTTTGAAATGTCACAGGGTTCCTAACAGGCC
TCCCTGGATGGGGTGCCAACGCCTTTCCCATGGGCATCTCCTTCCACCCTCACGCTGGCCCA
CAGGCAGTGCTGAGGCCTTATCTCCCTAGGTGACAGATGTGGTCAGGGAGGCGCAGAGAGGA
ACTAGCGTCCAGCTCCTGGAACAGGTGTCAGGCAGGGAGGGCAGACAGGTCTTGGGAACATG
CTGGCTATGTGGACAGAGGACTTCTCAGTGGGTCTCGCGACCCTGTGCCCCTTTTCCTGGTT
CAGCCTTAGCCGGGGCAAAGGTCGAGAAGAGAACCCCTGGTCGCCGCCCTGGCAGAATTTGA
TCCGGCAGGAGATGTCCCTAGGTTCCTGGGGAGGGAGGACGTCGGGGCCAGCCAGGCTTACC
CTGCCGCTGAGACTTCTGCGCTGATGCACCGCGCCTCTTCGCGGTCTCCCTGTCCTTGCAGA
GACACAATGTGCGACGAAGACGAGACCACCGCCCTCGTGTGCGACAATGGCTCCGGCCTGGT
CCGGCTTCGCCGGGGATGACGCCCCTAGGGCCGTGTTCCCGTCCATCGTGGGCCGCCCCCGA
GGTCAGGCTGCCCCTCCGCAGAGGGAGCCGGCTCGGGGTCCCCGCGTAAGCCAGCCTGGTGC

Figure 85: DNA codes of A, C, G and T decide what form they will manifest ...

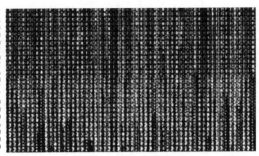

Figure 86: ... and they look remarkably like the 0 and 1 codes in a computer system and those portrayed in *The Matrix*.

have identified many of its functions. A Russian team found that it follows the same rules as human languages and this led them to believe that spoken languages are not random but a reflection of DNA (the software). Yes, because it's *all* a program. The team led by Russian biophysicist and molecular biologist Pjotr Garjajev found that human language can, in turn, also influence DNA through a frequency interaction. Humans can 'talk' to animals and plants through this same DNA frequency interaction. When we speak we create vibrating information fields with the vocal cords and animals and plants can decode this information. They obviously don't do this by knowing human language but by gleaning a feeling or impression from the information fields which they decode in their own way. People get a good or bad feeling from a song even if they can't make out the words. Experiments with electrically-wired plants have shown that they react positively and negatively to words of kindness and abuse, and recognise an abuser when they re-enter the room. We can heal (balance) ourselves and make ourselves ill (imbalance) through words, thoughts and visualisation (concentrated thought) through the vibrational impact. Electrical/energetic healing devices (genuine ones) work in the same way and so does 'hands-on' healing through an exchange of energy (frequency/vibration/information). Molecular biologist Pjotr Garjajev and his colleagues say that: 'Living chromosomes function just like solitonic/holographic computers using ... DNA laser radiation.' Solitonic relates to a particular form of wave, and holographic fits perfectly with what I am saying about reality as we shall now see.

Yes, it feels solid ... but ...

A question rightly asked is; if the solid world is an illusion how come I bang into a wall if I try to walk through it? I'll grant you the world does seem solid (Fig 87). I can answer the question by telling a story that serves as such a brilliant example of all that I am saying here. Michael Talbot was an American writer and researcher who produced an outstanding book entitled *The Holographic Universe*, which compiled research from mainstream scientists, well, the open-minded

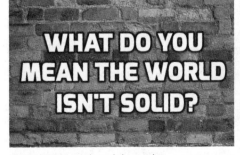

Figure 87: It must be solid – surely?

Figure 88: Nothing exists in the form that we see until we decode it ...

Figure 89: ... and what triggers the decoding process is our attention.

versions, anyway, who have concluded that our reality is holographic and its solidity illusory. He described how his father had a party for friends and invited a stage hypnotist to entertain the guests. At one point a man called Tom was sitting in a chair in a hypnotised state. Tom was told that when he returned to a waking state he would not be able to see his daughter in the room. His daughter was then asked to stand in front of her father as he awakened from the trance. Tom was asked if he could see his daughter. No, he said, even though he was looking into her belly. Next the hypnotist put his hand on the daughter's back and asked Tom if he could see what he was holding. Yes, Tom replied, he was holding a watch. His daughter was standing between him and the watch, but he could still see it. Tom was asked if he could read an inscription on the watch and he did. Ask mainstream scientists like Richard 'Dogma' Dawkins to comment on this story and they would likely say that either it didn't happen or was some sort of trick. In fact, it can all be easily explained if you appreciate that 'physical' reality is an illusion. The Universe in its foundation state is waveform information which is decoded into an apparently physical (holographic) form by the brain. This is true of everything including the body. We even decode our own body into holographic form because the base state of Body-Mind is not what we see but energetic information fields that are decoded into what we *think* we see (Figs 88 and 89). If that decoding process does not happen Body-Mind remains only in its energetic state and cannot be seen by the conscious/holographic mind – yes, even the brain which is also energetic in its undecoded form. Everything is energy, but I am using the term 'energetic' here to describe the difference between 'physical' and 'non-physical' states. All of which brings us back to the article in a British newspaper that I referred to earlier headed: 'Your entire life is an ILLUSION' and 'New test backs up theory that the world doesn't exist until we look at it'. Physicists at the Australian National University had found evidence which supported claims made by other quantum physicists that the Universe as we know it only exists when it is observed. I would take it further and put it like this: 'The world doesn't exist until we *decode* it.' Observing or 'looking' is a focus of *attention* that triggers the decoding process. From this perspective Tom's experience with his daughter makes perfect sense. Hypnotic suggestion to Tom that he wouldn't see his daughter acted like a firewall in his brain which blocked him from decoding her energetic information fields

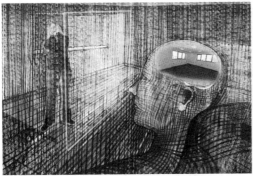
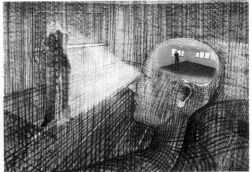

Figure 90: If we don't decode energetic information into holographic form then it cannot appear in the reality of the conscious mind.

into holographic reality. Unless he did so she would not enter the 'world' of his conscious mind in the band of visible light. To his holographic observation she was not part of the holographic scene his brain had decoded and so she could not block his view to the watch (Fig 90). We can now return to the question of why, if the world is not solid, that people bump into walls. Our simulated reality is an energetic information construct and on one level it is electromagnetism. Interaction between holographic ('physical') forms is really happening at a waveform/electromagnetic level. Holographic reality is only a decoded version of that information. When you bump into a wall this is not because it's solid – it clearly isn't from quantum physics alone. The resistance you experience is not solidity against solidity but electromagnetic state against electromagnetic state or information field against information field. This only appears to be solidity against solidity in the way we experience reality within the illusion. People see figures or ghosts passing through walls because the 'ghost' is on such a different frequency that there is no energetic resistance. This difference in frequency means that ghosts mostly look ethereal when they would look as solid as you and me if we viewed them from their own frequency instead of from our own.

'Physical' reality is very much like the holographic principle that we see used ever more often in stage shows, television and advertising which allows long departed singers and entertainers to appear in apparently three-dimensional form. I remember Celine Dion singing a duet with a holographic Elvis, and the late British comedian Les Dawson starred in his own TV show as a hologram (Fig 91). The best holograms look solid, but they're not and you can walk straight through them (Figs 92 and 93). They are

Figure 91: 'Real' Celine Dion sings with holographic Elvis.

Figure 92: They may look solid, but they are holograms.

Figure 93: Two men on the same stage? The one on the right is a holographic projection from another city.

created by the manipulation of light. A laser beam is divided into two parts, the 'reference beam' and the 'working beam'. The first part goes directly to the photographic print and the other records the subject in waveform (Fig 94). Both halves collide on the print and create what is called an interference pattern

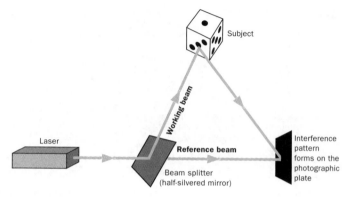

Figure 94: How the holographic illusion of 3D solidity is created.

Figure 95: A holographic print or 'interference pattern' is the information of the subject in waveform. It looks very much like a fingerprint and with good reason given that the human body is a holographic expression of waveform information.

Figure 96: A waveform pattern in water is the same principle.

(Fig 95).

Figure 97: 'Solid' holograms that you could walk through.

Pictures: 'Strawberry' Mirage - 3D Hologram Generator, http://www.eyetricks.com/mirage • 'Rose' courtesy of Holography Studio, All-Russian Exhibition Center, Moscow, see www.holography.ru • Picture 'Saturn' courtesy of Royal Holographic Art Gallery, see www.holograms.bc.ca

This is the same principle as two pebbles dropped in a pond with the waves coming together to create a waveform pattern that represents where the pebbles fell and at what speed (Fig 96). Holographic prints are waveform information versions of whatever the subject may be. A laser is then directed at this waveform 'matrix' and, as if by magic, a three-dimensional image appears (Fig 97). This is the same as the brain decoding waveform and electrical information from the Cosmic Internet into a digital and holographic 'physical' world. A hologram only appears from the waveform print when the laser 'reads' or decodes the information and our 'physical' reality only exists in the form we experience when the brain reads and decodes waveform and electrical information into a holographic state. Our laser is the act of observation, focus ... *attention*. Once again the theme of a computer decoding the Internet (encoded information) into what we see on the screen is an excellent analogy. Holograms are now also made digitally and this is getting even closer to the reality we experience as solidity. The brain is constructing digital holograms. Digital reality was excellently portrayed in *The Matrix* (Fig 98). A media report said of digital holograms:

Figure 98: Digital reality in The Matrix

> And they look so real – so real that when Ford used a [digital] hologram to show off a car concept model people stopped, afraid to walk into it. They thought the holographic car was really there.

This is why our reality appears so solid when it isn't. Some scientists are suggesting that the Universe could be holographic and their findings should be fused with the work of those concluding that we live in s simulation. Only by different disciplines talking to each other in a spirit of true open-minded discovery are they going to connect the dots to see reality as it really is. A copy of the mainstream science magazine *New Scientist* in 2009 ran a front cover saying: 'You are a hologram ... projected from the edge of the universe' (Fig 99). Well, 'we' are not a hologram – 'we' are Infinite Awareness – but our *vehicle* to experience this reality is a hologram. There is no projection from the edge of the Universe. It all happens in the decoding systems of the brain and genetic structure. A 2003

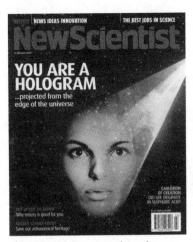

Figure 99: Mainstream science is now exploring the holographic nature of reality to escape the cul-de-sacs of flawed orthodoxy.

Figure 100: The truth cannot be denied forever.

edition of *Scientific American* also had this cover story headline: 'Are You A Hologram? – Quantum physics says the entire Universe might be' (Fig 100). Another article in the same magazine the following year about the computer principles of the Universe concluded: 'Perhaps most significantly, the result leads directly to the holographic principle, which suggests that our three-dimensional Universe is, in some deep but unfathomable way, two-dimensional.' Or perhaps it's not unfathomable at all. Holographic television systems now being developed operate with two-dimensional information observed as three-dimensional forms. I saw a video about holographic TV and the voiceover said:

> And it does look 3D when you sit in front of it [observe it] ... The image is stored on the film or in this case displayed on the screen as an intricate set of interference patterns which only form the image when you view it from the right angle and illuminate it properly.

Other scientific pioneers of the holographic principle of 'physical' reality include quantum physicist David Bohm (1917-1992) and Karl Pribram, Professor Emeritus of Psychology and Psychiatry at Stanford University and Radford University in the United States. Pribram and Bohm both worked on 'holonomic brain theory', which describes the brain as a holographic storage network. Pribram contends that this involves wave oscillations in the brain that create interference patterns that encode memory. Song sheet 'science' is going to have to face the truth eventually that its foundation beliefs about the nature of reality are flawed beyond words and measure and we do indeed live in a computer-like simulation with a holographic 'physical' component. Physicist Nikola Tesla said: 'If you wish to understand the Universe, think of energy, frequency and vibration.' Now holograms should be added to the list.

Time Control

Time and space are information encoded into the fabric of the Universe and when we decode them they appear to us to be real; but they're not. Play a virtual reality game and there will appear to be 'time' (one event or scene following another) and space (three-dimensional perspective) and yet the game is only decoded information encoded with click, click, enter, when the program was written. Near-death experiencers describe how their out-of-body world did not have time and space in the way we perceive it within what I would call the simulation. A quote from earlier said:

> I saw everything they were thinking now, what they thought then, what was happening before, what was happening now. There is no time, there is no sequence of events, no such thing as limitation, of distance, of period, of place. I could be anywhere I wanted to be simultaneously.

Near-death experiencer Anita Moorjani said like so many others that when she 'expanded' out of her body she could be everywhere 'at the same time'. Our perception of time is relative to the perceiver, observer – *decoder*. People throughout what we call history have been described as ahead of their time because they knew things and could do things that were thought impossible by their contemporaries. Leonardo da Vinci (1452-1519) and Giordano Bruno (1548-1600) come immediately to mind (Figs 101 and 102). Da Vinci was inventing technology 500 years before it was replicated and shown to

Figure 101: Leonardo Da Vinci was not ahead of his 'time' – he was beyond 'time'.

Figure 102: Giordano Bruno said: 'Heroic love is the property of those superior natures who are called insane, not because they do not know, but because they over-know.'

work and Bruno was so advanced in his understanding of reality that he was burned at the stake by the Roman Church; but these men and others were not ahead of their time – they were *beyond* time (Fig 103). They were able to expand their awareness to access frequency bands of knowledge outside the walls of the simulation. This knowledge is always available whether the illusory timeline of the simulation is in the Stone Age or Space Age. Those who are able to connect with this level of awareness are either called ahead of their time (with 'hindsight') or mad and dangerous (during their lives).

Figure 103: 'Time' is a construct of the fake simulation and when you expand awareness beyond the five senses you can enter a realm of infinite knowledge and insight.

Psychologist John Eliot said: 'History shows us that people who end up changing the world are always nuts – until they are right and then they are geniuses.' Such perceived genius comes from accessing realms of awareness available to everyone but tapped by so few. Albert Einstein in his theory of relativity said of time: 'When you are courting a nice girl an hour seems like a second. When you sit on a red-hot cinder a second seems like an hour.' Nobuhiro Hagura from the Institute of Cognitive Neuroscience at University College in London made a study of time as it is experienced by leading sportsmen and women. Anyone who has watched sports like tennis and baseball will surely have marvelled at the way a ball can be hit with such accuracy when it is travelling at great speed. Hagura discovered that gifted sports people have 'Matrix-like abilities' that slow down 'time' because they process visual information faster than normal and the world appears to move more slowly. What do people say

Figure 104: 'Time' is relative to the decoder.

Figure 105: Manufactured 'time' that controls perception.

about great sports players? They seem to have more *'time'*. We can now see why and the gift can be developed by practice given that the simulation is interactive and we can change the way we receive information from the Cosmic Internet by how we choose to decode it. If you process information very fast or very slow then your experience of 'time' will be different. The need for sports players to slow down time to make an accurate shot can be activated by the desire – *will* – to improve their game and in the same way the need for different species to develop unique gifts and abilities to cope with their changing environment can lead to mutations that are called 'evolution'. Scholars reported in the UK *Daily Telegraph* claimed that drugs could be used to so skewer a prisoner's sense of time that they could serve an extremely long sentence (in their perception) in a matter of hours. Team leader Rebecca Roache said:

> Uploading the mind of a convicted criminal and running it a million times faster than normal would enable the uploaded criminal to serve a 1,000 year sentence in eight-and-a-half hours. This would, obviously, be much cheaper for the taxpayer than extending criminals' lifespans to enable them to serve 1,000 years in real time.

Putting aside the ludicrous last sentence you can see the common theme here. Time is an illusion that is relative to the observer, and the scenes in *The Matrix* of people moving so fast they could dodge bullets is symbolic of this phenomenon of processing information at enormously fast speeds so that experienced time appears to slow down (Fig 104). Imagine a video on fast forward, but you could watch the scenes as if they were at normal speed. We have taken this time illusion still further and deeper by the invention of clock 'time' and calendar 'time' which are only human constructs (Fig 105). How can time exist as we perceive it when you can cross the theoretical international dateline and go into tomorrow or yesterday? The line is not even straight (Fig 106). A

Figure 106: Imaginary line for an imaginary phenomenon.

'meme' I saw on the Internet said:

> Time doesn't exist, clocks exist. Time is just an agreed upon construct. We have taken distance (one rotation of the earth and one orbit of the Sun), divided it into segments, then given those segments labels. While it has its uses, we have been programmed to live our lives by this construct as if it were real. We have confused our shared construct with something that is tangible and thus have become its slave.

How true that is. Put time and money together and you have pretty much got the human control system. Why can't you do what you want to do? I haven't got the time and I haven't got the money. People say 'time is money' when there is no time and there is no money (explained later). It is so hard for humanity to grasp the concept of illusory time when we are subjected to that illusion 24/7 throughout our lifetimes with the five senses constantly telling us that time exists: What's the time? Is that the time? I'm out of time. Where's the time gone? This is all illusion when the only time is NOW. There is only the NOW, the Infinite NOW. What about past and future? Where are we when we think about the past? In the NOW. Where are we when we think about the 'future'? In the NOW. Everything happens – and can only happen – in the NOW. Past and future are only perceptions (beliefs) constructed in the NOW. An entire movie exists at the same 'time' on a DVD, but as you watch the screen you have the *perception* of past, present and future in that the scene you are watching appears as the present; the ones you have watched is your sense of the 'past'; and the ones you have yet to watch are in your perception of the 'future' (Fig 107). Whichever scene you are watching on the DVD it is always in your NOW. The idea that we are 'run out of time' is more illusion. We can't run out of time when there is no time. We make choices about what we do, that's all. 'I am running out of time and I have to get to so and so' is nothing to do with time. It is only a choice to get to so and so at that moment. How often do these illusory past/future perceptions destroy our enjoyment and peace in the NOW through regret and resentment from the 'past', or fear, desire and foreboding about the illusory future?

When your attention is pulled into illusions of past and future it dilutes your power to influence the only moment in which you can do or change anything – the NOW. John Lennon wrote that life is what happens to you while you're busy making other plans. Life happens in the NOW. Live in the moment – it's *all there is*. Lao Tzu said:

> If you are depressed you are living in the past. If you are anxious you are living in the future. If you are at peace you are living in the present.

Figure 107: Every scene on a DVD is encoded in the same moment – the same DVD – but the play-out sequence gives the illusion of past moving through present to future.

The sequence we call time is largely constructed in the left side of the brain. I will explore the significance of the two brain hemispheres later on. Their very different functions reveal so much about human behaviour and how The System dictates reality. Information decoded in the NOW is put in a sequence by the left-brain that appears to us as the passing of time. How quickly the sequence flows dictates how we experience 'time' as we saw with the sport professionals example. Scientists have believed that time can only run forward into the 'future', but experiments have shown that at the quantum level beyond human sight the story is different. Research published in the journal *Nature Physics* was interpreted as showing that time can run backwards and that the future can influence the past. I say that it is all happening in the same NOW and events in the NOW can impact upon other events in the NOW and influence which possibilities and probabilities become holographic reality. I'll return to time in good time and on time, given its crucial importance to human control.

Gimme some space

Oh, no, he's not going to tell me that space doesn't exist is he? I mean I'm sitting here in my office and there is distance between me and the computer screen and me and the walls. Of course there is space. When I look at the night sky I see all those stars thousands and millions of light years away. One light-year is about 5.9 trillion miles – there has to be space. You're crazy. I know it seems like space is real, but hold on. Our perception of visual reality is constructed in a few cubic centimetres at the back of the brain where electrical information from the sight senses is decoded into our digital/holographic 'world'. How can those stars be thousands and millions, even billions, of light years away? They only exist in that form in a few cubic centimetres of brain tissue (Fig 108). You can go to a planetarium and appear to see the night sky fantastic distances away, but it's only a projection on the ceiling. You can see panoramic landscapes on your computer screen and yet it is only decoded information. The *Scientific American* article on black holes as computers included this line: 'Measuring distances and time intervals is a type of computation and falls under the same constraints that computers do.' Yes, because they are only encoded information. 'Space' is another form of information encoded in the simulation to be decoded into the illusion of 'space' – 'your entire life is an ILLUSION'. Human space travel appears to take an incredible 'time' to cross an incredible 'distance' but that perception is focused on the illusory reality of the holographic realm in which 'solid' craft have to be propelled

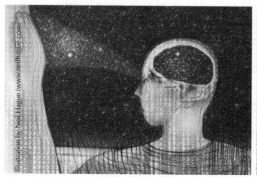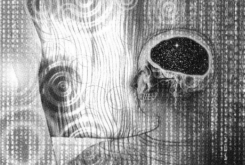

Figure 108: Millions of light-years in 'distance' are really within a few cubic centimetres of the brain where visual reality is decoded.

through 'solid' space with the limited power of 'solid' engines. Advanced forms of extraterrestrial life 'travel' within the energetic realms of the Universe and are not limited to the click, click, enter, 'laws of physics' of the holographic simulation. I hear tales of extraterrestrial experiences dismissed with 'that's impossible' when the truth is that the sceptic is too ignorant of reality to know how to do what he or she says is impossible. 'I can't do it' and 'I don't know how to do it' are not the same as 'it can't be done.' What was I saying about ignorance being so all pervading that it's called intelligence? Scientists have long pondered over how two particles can communicate instantly over billions of miles, but once again they are thinking in 'physical' terms. Particles are only holographic expressions of energetic states and so both 'particles' are actually the same energetic field (consciousness/awareness) communicating with *itself*. Communication is instant when the particles are *each other*. A pinhead and infinity are the same thing given that one is only an expression of the other. When you expand your awareness beyond time and space – beyond the holographic simulation – these things make perfect sense but they can be a real challenge to Phantom Self. Giordano Bruno said of reality:

> There is no top or bottom, no absolute positioning in space. There are only positions that are relative to others. There is an incessant change in the relative positions throughout the Universe and the observer [decoder] is always at the centre.

Expanded awareness of people like Bruno and Da Vinci allows them to operate on a much higher frequency and it has been shown that as the frequency increases the amount of energy carried by the wave also increases in proportion to the frequency. The higher the frequency the more energy (information) can be accessed and processed. Energy (radiation at one level) is information and frequency/wavelength is its delivery and communication system. I have one last point in this chapter as we go even deeper into the illusion and this relates to the brain and five senses. Our holographic body appears to receive its information from 'outside' and the five senses process waveform information which they communicate as electrical information to the brain. This does happen but not 'physically' as it seems to. Waveform/electromagnetic information is processed by the waveform/electromagnetic auric fields and the *energetic* levels of brain, DNA and five senses. Everything that we see as 'physical', from a wall to a tree to DNA, through to the brain and five senses, is only a holographic expression of their waveform/electromagnetic level. Information processing is actually being done by the brain, DNA and five senses in their *waveform/electromagnetic energetic* state – the level of 'Tom's daughter' that he didn't decode into his holographic reality. Holographic projection and illusion makes all the activity appear to be happening 'physically' but it's not (Fig 109). Near-death experiencers leave the body and can still see without holographic eyes and brains. A common theme is 360 degree vision, never mind only 'eye' vision. When a laser manifests a holographic projection from a waveform print the information is being processed and assembled by the *waveform* level, not the projected hologram. What we are seeing (and doctors are 'treating') is only a holographic projection of what is happening in the body's energetic information fields. Drugs are energetic information fields and they are interacting with our energetic level. Drugs only appear to be 'physical' treating 'physical' in the way we decode reality. A hologram is projected from a waveform print as a fully- formed 'done deal'. It doesn't 'do' anything. 'Physical' bodies do *nothing* and can do nothing because they are only projections of our waveform energetic self which does *everything*. Holographic bodies are projections from within in the

Figure 109: Physical' reality is a holographic projection of waveform information. It is at the waveform level that everything really happens.

Figure 110: 'incarnate' self is meant to stay in conscious connection to Infinite Self and when that connection is lost we become Phantom Self.

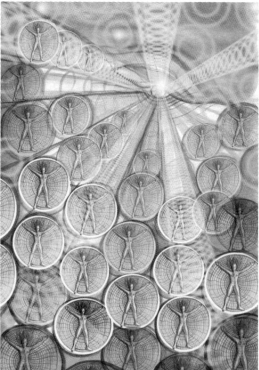

Figure 111: When we take on the perceptions of Phantom Self we enter an energetic reality bubble of low frequency that disconnects us from the influence of Infinite Awareness.

same way that what appears on your computer screen is a decoded projection from information within. Disconnection that isolates Phantom Self from expanded awareness is not between eternal 'Soul' and 'physical' body, but between Soul and the waveform/electromagnetic information fields from which the body becomes holographically manifest (Fig 110). A disconnection of Soul fields from auric fields caused by the difference in frequency which is caused by the difference in perception (Fig 111). Near-death experiencer Anita Moorjani said:

> I believe that the greatest truths of the Universe don't lie outside, in the study of the stars and planets. They lie deep within us, in the magnificence of our heart, mind and soul. Until we understand what is within, we can't understand what is without.

Reality is indeed monumentally different from The System's 'Real World', and this has the most fundamental implications for human life and for both freedom and control.

CHAPTER THREE

'Paranormal' is *Normal*

Reality leaves a lot to the imagination
John Lennon

I talk a lot about the 'inversion'. Human society cannot be understood without the realisation that almost everything is inverted or upside down and there are few better examples than the term 'paranormal'.

This is defined as 'beyond the range of normal experience or scientific explanation'. We are back to the concept of 'normal' again, but normal is only normal from the perception of experiences that people normally have. Whenever we return to 'normal' we must return to the *perception* of normal because that's all normal is – a perception of reality. Someone living in a house in the middle of nowhere will experience a normal of being alone. When a car passes by this is *para*normal, but only to the person living in the middle of nowhere. To someone with a home in an urban street the passing of vehicles is their normal while peace and quiet is their *para*normal. Phantom Self is programmed to believe in The System's version of normal which demands that we perceive everything through the five senses and believe in a world of solidity. When something happens that 'science' can't explain this is labelled 'paranormal' while being perfectly *normal* once you understand reality. If you think the world is solid most of the paranormal is impossible and so it's seen as strange and bewildering, condemned as the 'black arts' or dismissed as a figment of deluded imagination. Such responses block any serious inquiry that could lead to a re-evaluation of what is 'normal' and the cycle of ignorance goes on and on.

Infinity calling ...

I am going to present many examples of the perfectly normal *para*normal in this chapter and I'll start with psychic phenomena. There are many who call themselves physics and mediums who are tricksters and employ fakery to make it appear they are contacting the beyond. Con artists exist in every walk of life, but here we have baby and bathwater dispatched together as usual by Mainstream Everything and *all* psychic gifts and activity are dismissed as fakery. I have experienced fakes and genuine psychics and mediums many times and I can tell you they are certainly not the same. The hidden force behind The System (revealed in the next chapter) is desperate to trash psychic phenomena to protect its perception deception. Once psychic activity and communication is accepted to be real the next question will be 'How does it work?' Suddenly the everything-is-solid-this-world-is- all-there-is theory is in need of a dustpan and brush. The System has a technique that I call defend the first domino. Once a domino falls (psychic phenomena is real, for example) others in the line must follow and the entire perception deception will eventually fall with the end of suppression and ignorance (Fig 112). Every 'first domino' across the range of subjects is protected to stop this process and so instead of 'there are fake psychics and genuine psychics' you get 'it's all nonsense.' Alternative methods of healing and anything 'paranormal' get the same treatment. Fairy tales peddled by Mainstream Everything are so tenuous, unsupportable and in constant danger of exposure that every effort must be made to vanquish any challenge before it can gain traction. Anyone claiming to have psychic gifts is therefore a charlatan or deluded. It's official. Genuine psychics and mediums

Figure 112: Defend the first domino – or they all come down.

Figure 113: Death is not the end of life – just the end of a human experience.

produce information they had no other way of knowing, predict events that subsequently happen and solve crimes that the police cannot, but this is waved away with the arrogant hand of science and academia and the tell-me-what-to-think-sir minds of so many people who believe what they are told to believe. A fundamental disadvantage for the normal paranormal is that the version of reality pedalled by The System is so purposely distorted and inverted that most people can't understand how the so-called paranormal can be possible. This is a major reason why I am writing this book. If you believe the world is solid then psychic happenings make no sense. I mean, how can you contact the departed when they were pronounced dead and either buried in a coffin or went up in flames? Clearly it's not the former body that is being contacted, but then the body is not 'us'. Body-Mind allows 'us' – awareness, consciousness, point of attention – to experience the range of frequencies known as human society. When the body ceases to function the Infinite 'us' withdraws its attention and transfers it to frequencies new (Fig 113). Those left behind can no longer see their departed loved ones because their now disembodied awareness is resonating to higher frequencies beyond the holographic world (think Tom's daughter again). This frequency gap between the 'physical' world and realms of 'Soul' can be bridged by genuine psychics and mediums as their awareness tunes-in to the higher frequency, processes that information into human language, and delivers the messages into the human frequency (Fig 114). This is

Figure 114: Genuine psychics and mediums can connect their awareness with other realities and communicate information and insights that come from that.

Figure 115: Human Body-Mind allows consciousness in very different states of awareness to experience the same 'world' at the same 'time'.

what psychic Betty Shine was doing for me with the messages that began my conscious journey in 1990 and the electromagnetic 'spider's web' that I felt on my face was the electromagnetic channel or connection between another frequency 'world' and ours. A definition of the word 'medium' is 'an intervening substance through which something else is transmitted or carried on'. Another form of 'paranormal' inter-frequency communication is known as channelling. A psychic or medium will see or hear information communicated to them, but with channelling the 'channel' allows another awareness to take over their body and vocal processes to speak through them. I have experienced this with many people around the world and some have been almost hilariously bad while others extremely impressive. Like everything, it comes down to gifts and abilities. I have witnessed the faces and voices of channels change quite dramatically in some cases as the energetic field of the connecting awareness impacts upon the holographic field of the channel.

Body-Mind allows awareness in multiple states of consciousness to experience the same 'world' (Fig 115); but once awareness withdraws from the body, it can only interact with a frequency band with which it can sync. Some leave the body and gravitate to frequencies of pure awareness without form, while others are still so attached to the 'physical' and the programming and sensory pull of the 'physical', that they remain very close to this reality (Fig 116). They can still look like an energetic copy of their former 'physical' selves through what is called in *The Matrix* 'residual self-image' – their programmed perception still dominates their sense of self and reality and they continue to perceive themselves as their once 'physical' personality. Some stay so

Figure 116: Many departed 'souls' or awareness remain so attached to the 'physical' that they stay very close to our frequency band.

Figure 117: Ghosts are out-of-body awareness and they appear to people in an ethereal state like a form of visual broadcast interference.

close to our 'physical' frequency band they don't even realise they have left the body and can't understand why people they knew won't respond or speak to them. Friends and family who are sensitive to their loved-one's frequency-closeness will say things like: 'I can feel him/her around me all the time.' This is one explanation (only one) for ghosts and apparitions. They are so close to our frequency band that they can 'bleed' through like a form of broadcasting interference (Fig 117). A radio accurately tuned to a radio station frequency will produce a clear, sharp reception with no interference, but when the dial is slightly off centre another station or stations can be heard alongside the main one. A 'ghost' is a form of visual interference based on the same principle and another 'paranormal' mystery that is easily explained. Ghost or spirit (energy) figures don't usually look solid because the observer is not on the same frequency, just as broadcast interference affecting a radio station is not crisp and clear. People are being influenced all the time from other frequencies without realising it. They might have a thought or idea out of nowhere and wonder where it came from. This could be self-generated from their subconscious mind, but it can also be communicated telepathically from other frequencies of reality. I have been consciously guided and led to information this way since the days of Betty Shine – 'Sometimes he will say things and wonder where they came from' ... 'Knowledge will be put into his mind and at other times he will be led to knowledge.' Moments of inspired intuition when people say 'I don't know how I know, but I just know' can also be the result of inter-frequency telepathic communication. Genuinely-gifted psychics and mediums expand the range of their receiver-transmission processes to connect with frequencies that we can't see (Fig 118). Some can only tune in to frequencies close to ours, and you see the result with many television psychics (genuine ones) when the interaction is only focussed on people and happenings in this reality. 'I'm getting a Bill, anyone know a Bill?' and 'Fred says thanks for looking after his cat.' Other psychically gifted people and those in highly altered states can expand their receiver range so far that they connect with awareness of pure consciousness that can offer extraordinary insights. This happened to me in the

Figure 118: Psychics and mediums tune their awareness with other realities and communicate information they are given. In our reality this happens through electromagnetic fields or channels.

rainforest of Brazil with the aid of the ayahuasca. In my view, ayahuasca does not *take* you to these high frequencies but rather removes the programmed sense of limitation which stops you getting there. We are all meant to be doing this without support of drugs and potions. It's our natural state to be multidimensional awareness communicating across the frequency scale. We have been manipulated into an unnatural state of isolation by the hidden force that created and controls The System and our simulated reality. Real McCoy psychics and mediums are receiver-transmitters of information with a frequency range greater than that accessed by the rest of humanity. Some tune to visual information (clairvoyance) while others do so through sound (clairaudience) and still others can do both. Mysteries and 'it's-not-possible' fade away in the wake of simple explanation once reality is understood.

This place is haunted

Ghosts and apparently spooky happenings can be energetic recordings. The Universe is a quantum computer encoding and decoding information and every experience is recorded or posted in the fabric of reality. This 'library of everything' is the source of the belief in 'Akashic' fields or 'records', where some contend that every thought and event is stored. Akasha is a Sanskrit word meaning 'sky', 'space', 'luminous', or 'aether' and I would liken the term to the 'hard drive' of the quantum computer. I have heard stories over the years of people hearing the sounds of battle at the scenes of 'past' bloody conflicts, and this can be a quantum computer recording rather than 'real-time' ghostly activity. Witnesses on the Isle of Wight where I live in England claim to have seen a garrison of Roman soldiers marching at night between two ancient Roman sites, but this doesn't mean troops are literally marching in ghostly form. These witnessed experiences can be a powerful recording encoded in the energetic field which those sensitive enough can tune in to. Some people see these things and others don't. Not everyone has the same sensitivity and one person can see or hear something very clearly while someone next to them doesn't. Sensitivity doesn't make you better or more advanced than others. It means you are more sensitive to frequencies outside of visible light. Wisdom and enlightenment is not defined by having psychic experiences, but from what you make of them and what you do as a result. People need to share what they experience outside what is considered 'normal' to break the grip of perception programming and not stay silent for fear that other people (Phantom Selves) will think they're crazy. I have seen accounts of ghostly happenings recurring at particular times of the year but never in between. This can be explained by changes in the energetic field caused by astronomical/astrological factors that activate certain 'recordings' at certain times in certain places in the same way that a laser reads information on a DVD. Emotion is a very powerful energy that can imprint experiences on the energy field (download to the quantum computer) with particular effect. For this reason, many

Figure 119: High levels of emotion (often subconscious) can disturb the energetic environment and appear to be hauntings or poltergeist activity.

paranormal or ghostly experiences are reported in houses and locations where murder, battles and other horrific experiences have taken place. Players in these events can also be trapped in low frequency states close to this reality and be said to 'haunt' the location. Those committing suicide can be trapped in low frequencies by their mental and emotional state when they 'crossed'. They are not dangerous and if you know what you're doing they can be helped to escape their perception entrapment, which is the cause of their frequency entrapment. There are others in the unseen that do have a malevolent agenda and I'll be coming to them. A recurring theme in ghostly tales is of objects moving around and poltergeists – 'a ghost that manifests itself by noises, rappings, and the creation of disorder'. A 'physical' object is a holographic projection of energetic information. If you manipulate the information you manipulate the holographic projection. Paranormal experience is the result of what is happening at the energetic level not the 'physical' and if you move the information field of an object then its holographic projection will appear to move when decoded by an observer. Sound waves that make 'solid' objects levitate are the same principle at work. I have read several accounts of poltergeist activity and moving objects which have involved homes where teenagers (girls in particular) have lived when they were undergoing great emotional stress and challenge. When their stress subsides, so do the 'hauntings' (Fig 119). I've said that emotion is a very powerful energetic force and this can impact on the energy field of a location to cause a great disturbance that appears to be ghostly or poltergeist activity. Objects can even fly around the room. The person involved obviously has no idea that they are *haunting themselves* through a subconscious and extreme form of telekinesis – the ability to move objects with the mind. Disturb the energetic field of an object and you disturb its holographic form. Electric lights and other electrical items are often involved in ghostly experiences as they switch on and off apparently by themselves, but there has to be a source of electrical power for these things to happen. I had my own experience of this on the first of the two nights that I took ayahuasca in Brazil. I was lying on the floor with the only other person sitting next to me when I felt a fantastic energy pouring from the centre of my chest with incredible power. There was a reason why it was my chest which I will come to later in the chapter. Almost immediately as I felt the energy, the music player began to turn off and on several times. The room was in darkness but a strip light came on followed by a second and a third. I lay there wondering why my friend had turned the lights on before realising that he was still sitting next to me nowhere near the light switch. Electrical/electromagnetic energy that had entered the room so tangibly through me was interacting with electrical circuitry of the music player and lights. Betty Shine told me how her record player would sometimes switch on and off in the same way. Electrical systems are the easiest for other-dimensional entities and energies to affect because of the electromagnetic connection. People in haunted places describe having a chill down their spine and this is the electromagnetic effect on their central nervous system. Others say the room suddenly went very cold and again this has an explainable cause. When an entity or awareness is seeking to interact with our reality, it draws energy out of the room in the form of heat to make the connection and come into manifestation.

Atmosphere is electric (literally)

Electricity and electromagnetism are all around us, and why would that not be the case in a computer simulation? There are multiple expressions of the Universe and electricity/electromagnetism is one of them along with the waveform, digital and holographic. A gathering branch of alternative science is known as the 'Electric Universe' which researches and uncovers the properties and roles of electricity, magnetism and the interaction of the two – called electromagnetism. These are vehicles for delivering and communicating information, and electromagnetism generates information-encoded waves travelling at the speed of light. Electric Universe research is rewriting the concept of the Universe promoted by Mainstream Everything. Two Electric Universe pioneers are Australian physicist Wallace Thornhill and researcher David Talbott, co-authors of two excellent books, *The Electric Universe* and *Thunderbolts of the Gods*. They and other proponents of the electrical nature of the Universe (on one level) have comprehensively rewritten the skewed assumptions of mainstream science about how the Universe works with regard to electricity, electromagnetism and much else. I have introduced a very significant word here – *assumptions*. Great swatches of what has come to be accepted as scientific fact turns out to be mere assumptions that have been repeated so often by science, academia and media that they have fused into an 'everyone knows that'. They are only assumptions and often the outcome or headline assumption is founded on a long list of other assumptions. Here are ten of the key assumptions listed by researcher and biologist Rupert Sheldrake in his book *Science Set Free* which have (a) become accepted scientific, academic and media 'fact' despite being nonsense, and (b) ensure that anyone who believes them will never understand reality:

1. That nature is mechanical.
2. That matter is unconscious.
3. The laws of nature are fixed.
4. The total amount of matter and energy are always the same.
5. That nature is purposeless.

6. Biological inheritance is material.

7. That memories are stored as material traces.

8. The mind is in the brain.

9. Telepathy and other psychic phenomena are illusory.

10. Mechanistic medicine is the only kind that really works.

These may be foundation assumptions of mainstream science (though not of quantum physics) but they are all nonsensical. The bottom-line assumption about the Universe is the Big Bang (Fig 120). This theory – and theory is all it is – contends that 13.7 billion years ago the Universe was compressed into the nucleus of an atom that they call the 'singularity'. Then came a rather loud noise as an explosion generated temperatures of trillions of degrees which somehow created subatomic particles, energy, matter, space and time, and later planets, stars and

Figure 120: The 'Big Bang' – 'Give us a free miracle and we'll explain the rest'.

everything else. American writer and researcher Terence McKenna captured this lunacy brilliantly when he said: 'Give us a free miracle and we'll explain the rest.' He goes on:

Every model of the universe has a hard swallow. What I mean by a hard swallow is a place where the argument cannot hide the fact that there's something slightly fishy about it. The hard swallow built into science is this business about the Big Bang. Now, let's give this a little attention here. This is the notion that the universe, for no reason, sprang from nothing in a single instant.

Well, now before we dissect this, notice that this is the limit test for credulity. Whether you believe this or not, notice that it is not possible to conceive of something more unlikely or less likely to be believed! I mean, I defy anyone – it's just the limit case for unlikelihood, that the universe would spring from nothing in a single instant, for no reason?! – I mean, if you believe that, my family has a bridge across the Hudson River that we'll give you a lease option for five dollars! It makes no sense.

It is in fact no different than saying, 'And God said, let there be light.' And what these philosophers of science are saying is, give us one free miracle, and we will roll from that point forward – from the birth of time to the crack of doom! – just one free miracle, and then it will all unravel according to natural law, and these bizarre equations which nobody can understand but which are so holy in this enterprise.

Big Bang Theory was first postulated in 1927 as the 'hypothesis of the primeval atom' by Georges Lemaître (1894-1966), a priest at the Catholic University of Louvain in Belgium. Even he never said it was a fact, only a hypothesis. Modern discoveries have demolished the concept of the ridiculous Big Bang and all assumptions that come from this base assumption; but Mainstream Everything still clings to the nonsense like a sailor in a storm because when that assumption is thrown overboard then the ship itself (see that list above) will sink beneath the swirling waves of open-minded common sense. Given the dependency of mainstream science on assumptions, I had to laugh when American media cosmologist, Neil deGrasse Tyson, said:

A conspiracy theorist is a person who tacitly admits that they have insufficient data to prove their points. A conspiracy is a battle cry of a person with insufficient data.

Figure 121: Plasma is a near-perfect medium for electricity.

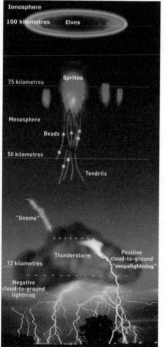

Figure 122: Lightning strikes impact on many levels out into the cosmos.

This is taking self-delusion to shocking extremes when you think that mainstream science is another way of saying 'insufficient data'; but Tyson's worship of Mainstream Everything becomes clear in this quote: 'The good thing about science is that it's true whether or not you believe in it.' Like the Big Bang?? A now mountain of evidence produced by proponents of the Electric Universe have overturned so many accepted 'facts' (assumptions) of Big Bang believers like Tyson who appears to contend there are no conspiracies anywhere only insufficient data. The Universe is awash with electricity and electromagnetic fields from nano-tiny to spanning great swatches of 'space'. Its working environment is plasma which mainstream science agrees is a near-perfect vehicle for electricity/electromagnetism. Plasma has been called the fourth state of matter and 99.999% of the observable Universe is plasma. Everyone will have seen plasma balls which produce lightning-like responses when you touch them (Fig 121). Lightning is an obvious expression of electrical activity in the atmosphere when electricity builds up to the point where it has to be released. Lightning we see from the ground is only part of the story and the same electrical surge continues into the upper atmosphere where science gives it names such as 'elves', 'sprites', 'gnomes' and 'jets'. A lightning strike plays out into the electromagnetic fields of the Cosmos (Fig 122). Tornadoes are fast-rotating electrical fields and so appear during electrical storms. Electricity can also be seen with the Aurora Borealis or Northern Lights. When plasma in one electrical state meets plasma of another electrical state a barrier is created between them known as a Langmuir Sheath after American Nobel Laureate, Irving Langmuir (1881-1957) who discovered the phenomenon. Plasma 'sheaths' define planetary energy fields or magnetospheres. The electrical charge given off by planetary bodies is different to the wider Cosmos and a Langmuir Sheath barrier is formed (Fig 123). Irving Langmuir coined the term plasma when he observed how it carried electrical forces much like blood plasma does with red and white blood corpuscles. He realised that plasma appeared to have a 'life-like' ability to self-organise in response to electrical changes. This is to be expected when you know that plasma is part of a conscious quantum computing system. Electromagnetism pervades the Universe. This, not gravity, holds everything together and dictates movements and orbits of planets (or rather its encoded information does). Electric Universe research points out that electromagnetism is about 'a thousand trillion, trillion, trillion times' more powerful than gravity (Fig 124). When something happens to destabilise the harmony of electromagnetic fields then everything that depends on their stability for their own stability is similarly affected. This can result in anything from objects flying around the room in a poltergeist experience to whole planets and planetary systems going walkabout. Electrical currents are passing through the Universe in the form of filaments of vastly varying size and power. They are known as 'Birkeland currents' after the Norwegian scientist, Kristian Olaf Birkeland (1867-1917) who discovered them. As electricity travels through the plasma another process takes place in which electrical currents create electromagnetism and this, in turn, causes the filaments to rotate around each other while electromagnetic fields keep them apart. This is called the

Figure 123: Planetary energy fields or magnetospheres are formed by Langmuir Sheaths where plasma in different electrical states resist each other.

Figure 124: Electromagnetism is the prime force that holds everything together and apart.

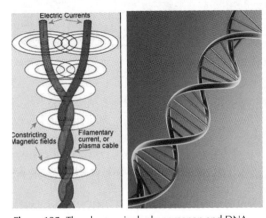

Figure 125: The plasma pinch phenomenon and DNA.

'plasma pinch' and looks remarkably like DNA (Fig 125). This is not a coincidence as we shall see. Human brains, hearts and bodies all operate with electricity and

Figure 126: The Cosmic Internet communicates on one level through electricity and electromagnetism.

Figure 127: The Sun processes electrical power from the cosmic field and does not generate it from within.

electromagnetism. Brain activity is electrical and is just one level of the body's communication system. Communication of information electrically is another example of the Cosmic Internet (Fig 126).

Electrical sunshine

Mainstream Everything claims that the Sun is a nuclear reactor generating heat and light from its core and will at some point burn itself out; but as the American engineer and Electric Universe researcher, Ralph Juergens, said: 'The modern astrophysical concept that ascribes the Sun's energy to thermonuclear reactions deep in the solar interior is contradicted by nearly every observable aspect of the Sun.' This is because the Sun is almost entirely plasma (99 percent) and processes electricity from its atmosphere and not from within. The Sun is absorbing electricity from the universal field and transforming that energy into the 'light' that we see. Solar power is coming from outside not inside and its role is one of processing and transforming (decoding) not generating (Fig 127). We talk of sun cycles as the power of the Sun goes through highs and lows and these are measured by the number of sunspots or the massive 'holes' that appear on the surface (Fig 128). Mainstream Everything says that sunspots are being punched from inside as nuclear energy emerges from within, but this theory doesn't stand up at all. Scientists say that solar energy comes to the surface through a 'radiative zone' and 'convective zone' when there is no evidence of a radiative zone, and an MRI scan of the Sun revealed a convective zone so small that it was only *one percent* of that necessary for the theory to be valid. Sunspot holes are punched by phenomenal electrical charges coming the other way (another inversion). At the ultra-violet level of the Sun you can see a torus or plasma doughnut circling the solar equator and this stores electricity from the Cosmos (Fig 129). When this torus overloads extraordinary bolts of electricity (on the same principle as lightning) are discharged to punch holes in the solar surface. Sunspots measure solar activity and its cycles because the more electrical power gathered in the torus the more is discharged. The Sun operates in basically the same way as an electric light and dimmer switch.

Electrical power in the solar system goes through cycles and these affect the power of the Sun's brightness. You can't see this with the human eye, but it can be measured technologically. Here is another inversion: The hottest part of the Sun is way out from the surface in the corona. This can reach 200 million degrees Kelvin while surface temperature is only 5,000 degrees. I wonder which direction the electrical power is coming from then? David Talbott and Wallace Thornhill summarise the electrical principle in *Thunderbolts of the Gods:*

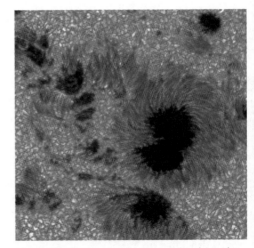

Figure 128: Sunspots of enormous size indicate the cycles of solar emissions.

> From the smallest particle to the largest galactic formation, a web of electrical circuitry connects and unifies all of nature, organizing galaxies, energizing stars, giving birth to planets and, on our own world, controlling weather and animating biological organisms. There are no isolated islands in an electric universe.

Limitless electrical power all around us begs the question of why we rip Earth apart by digging and sucking out sources of energy like oil, coal and gas to generate electricity that we could tap into at will from universal sources. Ignorance that such power exists can be claimed by the general population, but not by those who run The System. Nikola Tesla said in the first half of the 20th century: 'All peoples everywhere should have free energy sources ... electric power is everywhere present in unlimited quantities and can drive the world's machinery without the need for coal, oil and gas.' Tesla proved the reality of free energy from an electrical Cosmos but was blocked at every turn and died virtually penniless in a New York hotel room in 1943 (Fig 130). Many others who have developed technology to exploit this free electrical energy source to benefit human society have

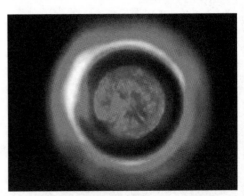

Figure 129: The torus electricity reservoir seen around the Sun at the ultraviolet level.

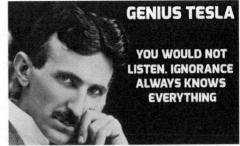

GENIUS TESLA

YOU WOULD NOT LISTEN. IGNORANCE ALWAYS KNOWS EVERYTHING

Figure 129: Nikola Tesla knew about free energy in the first half of the 20th century, but The System didn't want it – and still doesn't.

also faced the wrath of the authorities. The System has an energy agenda that includes keeping the population in servitude to power bills – and the same authorities suppressing the use of free electrical power without the need for fossil fuels, are also condemning the use of fossil fuel energy on the grounds of human-caused 'global warming' (which isn't happening). Why are they suppressing free energy without fossil fuel while saying that fossil fuel emissions threaten the very existence of humankind? This is yet another example of what appears to be a contradiction, but isn't when you know the game. People were told to buy diesel vehicles to 'combat global warming' on the grounds that they emit slightly less carbon dioxide than petrol engines; but they spew out a lot more nitrogen oxide and nitrogen dioxide pollutants and 22 times more tiny particles or particulates that damage lungs, brains and hearts. Diesel-pollution is already estimated to be responsible for thousands of deaths a year in the UK alone and rising. It is destroying air quality especially in cities – all based on a calculated lie. The illusory threat of human-caused 'global warming' is a scam to provide the excuse to transform global society in ways that suit the agenda for human enslavement. Replacing fossil fuels with free electrical energy would scupper their plans and I'll have more about this later on.

Numbers game

Electrical and waveform frequencies interact with those of the digital/holographic levels of the Universe (simulation). The digital level was excellently symbolised by the

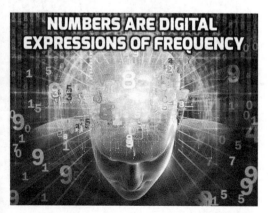

Figure 131: The Matrix – real and in the movies – is digital on one level.

Figure 132: Frequencies are numbers and numbers are frequencies.

codes running through computers in *The Matrix* and the world that Neo saw once he had transcended death and could see beyond the program (Fig 131). Computers work with electrical and digital components and so does the quantum computer Universe. Here we have the background to the 'paranormal' art of numerology, which reads the digital level of reality. Numbers are digital expressions of energetic (frequency/waveform) states (Fig 132). When the same numbers recur in your life they represent recurring information, situations and personal states of being. Numbers we surround ourselves with or attract (even the one on the front door) are not as random as they might appear. We can see numbers and mathematics throughout what we perceive as the natural world. Science has not invented mathematics and numbers as was widely believed – it has only *discovered* them. What was believed to be invention is really tapping into the digital matrix. Repeating numbers and geometry pervade reality. We have: Pi (ratio of a circle's circumference to its diameter and approximated as 3.14159 with an infinite number of decimal places); golden ratio (golden mean, golden section or Phi – 1.6180339887499 ... recurring to infinity); and the Fibonacci sequence (adding the last two numbers to get the next one, as with 1, 1, 2, 3, 5, 8, 13, 21 ...). Golden ratio/mean or Phi can be found throughout nature – in the proportions of the human body and many animals, DNA, plants, the solar system, supernovas, music, waves of light and sound, and so much more. Sound is maths and maths is sound, and so music and human language are mathematical sequences. Everything is – it's a *simulation*. Leonardo Pisano Fibonacci, a 12th and 13th century Italian mathematician, identified the mathematics of his 'Fibonacci sequence' in plants, flowers, trees, shells and proportions of the human face (Fig 133). Recurring numbers are part of a web of interconnected mathematics on which the virtual reality simulation is founded. I heard a scientist say of flowers: 'They set up a little machine that

Figure 133: The Fibonacci spiral in nature (the simulation).

creates the Fibonacci sequence.' I would say they *are* a machine in the sense that they are a creation of the click, click, enter interactive simulation and following the cycle of their encoded information blueprint. A US Public Broadcasting Service (PBS) documentary in 2015, *Decoding the Universe: The Great Math Mystery*, highlighted how mathematics exist at every level of the observable Universe and asked what this could be all about. I would answer the question with another question: Would it be a mystery to find mathematics at every level of a computer program? Max Tegmark, Professor of Physics at the Massachusetts Institute of Technology (MIT), asked in the documentary if the Universe could be just as mathematical as a computer game reality; but then it must be because it *is* a computer game reality, albeit far more advanced than the ones we know. Plato in ancient Greece believed that mathematics and geometry exist in their own world and what we see as reality is a reflection of that world. Mathematics and geometry are indeed a glimpse into the hidden blueprints of 'physical' reality. Galileo Galilei (1564-1642), the Italian astronomer and mathematician , said that the Universe is written in the language of mathematics and so it is. Digital images are made of pixels – 'the basic unit of a digital image, representing a single colour or level of brightness' – and together these pixels interact to appear as a picture. We only see television images when the brain decodes the pixels formed on the screen into perceivable still images and connects them in a way that produces the illusion of movement. An article in the *New Scientist* magazine in 2009 exploring the possibility that reality is holographic, said that under magnification 'the fabric of space-time becomes grainy and is ultimately made of tiny units rather like pixels'. I have described in other works how American brain scientist Jill Bolte-Taylor suffered a stroke in the left side of her brain in 1996, which caused her decoding process to malfunction. She experienced reality as a seamless energetic 'Oneness' which also manifested as *pixels*. Ancient initiates knew that mathematics and geometrical proportion was a way of communicating with the Universe. They knew that if they designed buildings such as churches and temples with certain geometrical and mathematical (digital) proportions they would automatically generate their corresponding waveform and electrical energetic states (information and interdimensional connections). Geometrical and mathematical sequences are digital expressions of waveform and electrical information. The 'primitive' ancients would never have known that? Oh, yes, they would, and did, in terms of their inner circle initiates, and the same stream of knowledge continues in the inner circles of secret societies today. Ancient initiates in the mysteries of numbers – Pythagoras in Greece is the most famous example – believed that 'fractions are numbers in the stages of becoming'. You find the same principle within quantum computer simulations in the form of electrons and atoms 'in stages of becoming' holographic 'physical' reality.

Mysteries, what mysteries?

Many more 'paranormal' questions dissolve when we appreciate one of the most amazing characteristics of holograms and the way they store and distribute information. This can be described in one sentence – every part of a hologram is a smaller version of the whole. Within those few words is a massive revelation. If you cut a holographic waveform print into four parts and apply the laser they will each show a quarter-sized version of the *whole* image (Fig 134). Information from the whole image is stored in every part of the image and this is the real origin of the term 'as above, so below'. Electrical activity in brain and Cosmos look so like each other because of the holographic principle (Fig 135). Fibonacci spirals on a shell are similar to the spiral of a galaxy, and the human energy or auric field is a smaller version of the Earth field through holographic information distribution (Fig 136). The smaller you go, holographically, the less clarity and detail you see, but it's the same information. Our holographic bodies are encoded with the information of the holographic Universe. Every part of the body stores, in miniature, information about the whole body and from this understanding we can be see how acupuncture, reflexology and other forms of alternative healing can identify points

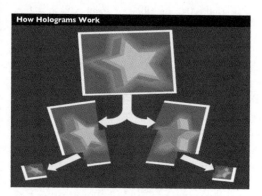

Figure 134: Every part of a hologram is a smaller version of the whole.

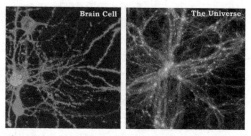

Figure 135: Human brain activity and the Universe – every part of a hologram is a smaller version of the whole.

Figure136:
Human energy field
and Earth energy field.

on the ear, hand, foot, etc. that represent
the heart, brain, lungs, liver and all the rest
(Fig 137). This has to be so when the body
is a hologram and every part of a hologram
is a smaller version of the whole. Hands
are encoded with information representing
the entire body and this can be read and
interpreted by skilled people through the
art of palm reading. Iridology or reading
information in a person's eye is the same
(Fig 138). Synaesthesia – when one sense
decodes another and a sound can appear as
colours or smells, is made possible by all
senses containing the other senses through
their holographic nature. Body language
reflecting states of mind is another 'as
above, so below'. Mainstream scientists in
their Dogma Dawkins arrogance of
ignorance dismiss and ridicule alternative
forms of healing and divination because
they can't grasp the principle on which
they are based. Neither do most of those
who practice these methods in my
experience. They know they can work,
but often have no idea how.

Homeopathy is a healing technique
ridiculed by Mainstream Everything for
the same reason – ignorance. Professor
Dame Sally Davies, the System-brained-
and-trained British Government Chief
Medical Officer, described homoeopathy
as 'rubbish' and condemned its
practitioners as 'peddlers'. When a
British health minister gave his support
for homeopathy he was dubbed by *New
Scientist* magazine 'the new minister for

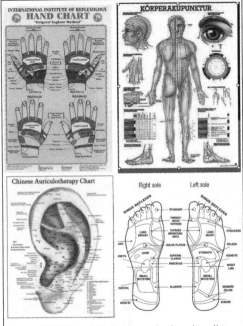

Figures 137: The whole body can be found in all its
parts – because it's a hologram.

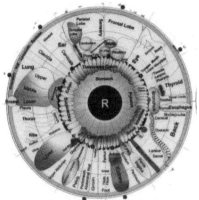

Figure 138:
Each section
of the eye
represents a
part of the
whole body.

LOVE   HATE

Figure 139: The fantastic difference in water crystals after they have been frequency-infused with words of love or hate.

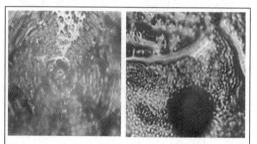

Figure 140: Water crystals subjected to polluted water and heavy metal music.

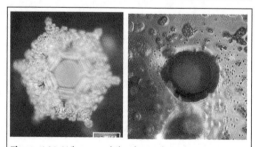

Figure 141: What a mobile phone does to water crystals.

magic.' How extraordinary when the magic necessary to support the Big Bang (so beloved of such publications) is almost beyond comprehension. System minds are so programmed they believe that a pharmaceutical industry, which accrues its annual billions from people being sick, has any interest in anything that would keep them healthy. Homeopathy is based on the fact that everything is information whether it's a plant or a drop of water. If it isn't information it can't exist. I have written at length over the years about the information storage potential of water. Dr Masaru Emoto, the Japanese researcher (who sadly left us in 2014), became well known for revealing the existence of information in water and how this can be changed by human and technological interaction. He was expanding on earlier research. I visited Dr Emoto's centre in Tokyo and we spent a weekend in London sharing information for a co-authored book in Japanese. His work and mine complement each other. Even some mainstream scientists have been attacked and ridiculed for saying that water has a memory (stores information) when the evidence for this is overwhelming and must be true given that *everything* is information. Dr Emoto published many illustrated books to show how thought, emotion and other frequency phenomena impacts on the structure of water and what goes for water goes for everything else. He would attach words, sayings and technology like cell phones to canisters of water and then freeze the water very quickly to photograph the ice crystals.

What he found was stunning confirmation of the interactive Cosmic Internet. Words of love and appreciation produced beautiful patterns of balance and harmony while others such as 'You make me sick, I want to kill you' caused a distorted mess (Fig 139). Spoken words are clearly produced by vocal cords in the form of vibrating information fields and the same is true of the written word. We see words on paper or computer screens but they are only holographic versions of waveform, electrical and digital states. Written words are frequencies and can impact upon other frequency fields in the same way as vocal vibrations. Water in the Emoto canisters is information and at one level it is *vibrational* information. Water only looks as we see it in holographic form. It is information-encoded energy in its base state. Exposing water to the frequency fields of words, written or spoken, changes its information structure, and we see the extraordinary difference between words of love and appreciation and 'You make me sick, I want to kill you'. Dr Emoto demonstrated how the same happened with heavy metal music and polluted water. They produced highly distorted crystals because heavy metal music and polluted water are, like cell phones, states of extreme energetic distortion (Figs 140 and 141). We see pollution pouring into rivers in the holographic realm, but at a deeper level a frequency distortion (pollution) is impacting upon the energetic harmony of the river. We call the result a polluted (energetically-distorted) river. Intent is an immensely powerful energy and it's not the words but the *intent* behind them that makes the biggest energetic impact. This is the process through which intent to achieve something can influence, attract, repel and restructure energetic fields (people, opportunities etc.) to manifest your intent. 'If you believe it you will achieve it', the saying goes, but a better word than believe is *intend*. People who think what they want will never happen infuse that information into their energetic environment and so … it never happens. Half-empty/half-full mentalities impact themselves on our energetic world to repel or attract people, places, opportunities, ways of life and so on – all of which are information fields because everything is. I call this phenomenon 'vibrational magnetism' with electromagnetic fields in different information states repelling and attracting each other (synchronicity or lack of synchronicity). Does anyone really think that people meet their partners, get jobs or bump into those they know in the strangest of places by random accident? How many times do we hear 'I'm so unlucky' and 'how could this happen to me of all people after what's happened to me before'? It is nothing to do with 'luck', and it's happened again because the state of being ('attitudes') that created the first experience hasn't changed and so it is electromagnetically attracting a repeat. Albert Einstein said that 'synchronicity is God's way of remaining anonymous'. My life became a daily wave of synchronistic experiences after my meetings with psychic Betty Shine. Visualisation is concentrated thought that can affect energy fields you attract and repel to manifest what you visualise. Research at Harvard medical school found that those who visualised playing the piano underwent structural changes in the area of the brain associated with finger movement which were almost identical to those in the brains of people who literally learned how to play. Everything is the interaction of mind and consciousness. All 'physical' experience is a holographic reflection of energetic information states and to change the holographic outcome you must change the energetic information state through visualisation, attitude and intent. Confidence or lack of confidence alone so obviously affects performance and outcome. Dr Emoto's work presented visual evidence of this principle of creating our own reality – and what is the age-old concept of prayer? Focussed and concentrated thought interacting with energetic reality.

The Aerospace Institute in Stuttgart, Germany, is another centre for information-in-water research and they crucially developed a method of photographing information in water. They put a flower in a tank of water in one experiment and when it was removed they photographed the droplets. What they discovered confirmed two major truths about reality. One was again the holographic principle with information of the whole

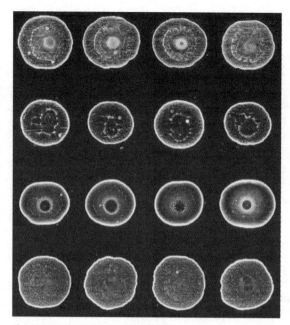

Figure 142: The Stuttgart water droplets.

flower found in every droplet. The second was that even when the 'physical' flower was removed the *information* from the flower was retained in the water. I have but one thing to say ... *homeopathy*. Arrogant dismissal of homeopathy by Mainstream Everything is founded on the belief that preparations diluted in water so many times that no substance remains cannot possibly have any effect; but they are missing the point yet again. A substance (holographic illusion) may be gone but its *energetic information* is still in the water and this does the healing by affecting the energetic information state of the body. Another experiment at the Aerospace Institute involved asking local people to take four droplets from a tank of water and place them in their designated dish.

Researchers found that droplets taken by each individual were all different but the individual's own set of four were virtually the same (Fig 142). A simple act of putting a droplet in a dish had caused an exchange of energy/information between energy fields of water and person. But what did I say? The Universe is a virtual reality simulation that is *interactive* and this experiment is more evidence of the way we energetically impact upon reality and thus create our reality. 'Hands on healing' is an energy (information) exchange between the healer and the patient when the healer (genuine ones) tap into cosmic energy fields (frequencies). I am not saying that alternative treatments are always successful. This depends on the quality of the practitioner/healer and the nature of the problem. What I have explained here is the basis on which they can work. Always be careful when you choose an alternative healer and check their record of success from previous patients if you can. Be even more careful – in fact mega-careful – when you see a doctor. They can be seriously bloody deadly as the figures for death-by-doctor clearly show.

Getting the point

Acupuncture is another method of healing waved aside by Mainstream Everything. Detractors of this ancient Chinese (and probably much earlier) healing art can't understand how inserting hair-like needles into the skin can make any difference to health. They say it's crazy that a needle can be inserted in the foot in an attempt to cure a headache, but then logic always seems crazy to ignorance (Fig 143). A key part of the information interaction between body and Cosmos is through channels of energy (information) known as acupuncture lines or meridians. This is like the motherboard of the body computer (Fig 144). When information (which the Chinese call 'chi') is

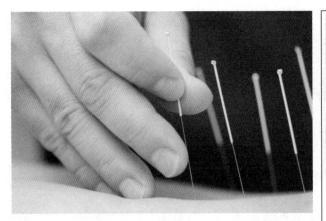

Figure 143: People trash acupuncture because they don't have a clue how it works. They would be better addressing their own ignorance.

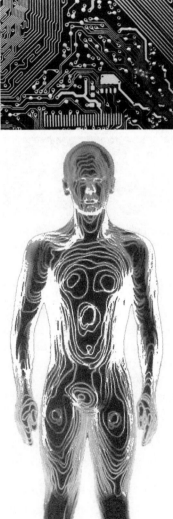

Figure 144: The meridian system – picked out here by a tracer dye – is the motherboard of the body-computer.

circulating the meridians and being processed at the optimum speed the body is healthy. When the flow becomes distorted in some way the body systems begin to malfunction through miscommunicated or uncommunicated information. Computers 'run slow' when a virus distorts information circuits. Acupuncture needles (and other techniques) can regulate energy/information flow when inserted at particular places on the meridians known as acupuncture points. These represent different organs and functions – the holographic principle again. Ancient Chinese acupuncturists were paid when patients were well but not when they were ill. Their job was to keep the chi in balance and their clients healthy. Meridians operate in circuits and they can flow from the foot, up through the head and back again. A pain in the head can be caused by a blockage or malfunction in the energy flow through the foot and when that happens it hardly makes sense to put a needle in the head does it? As acupuncture practitioner and brilliant complimentary healer, Mike Lambert, at the Shen Clinic on the Isle of Wight says: 'Symptom and the cause of the symptom are rarely in the same place.' Mainstream doctors (pharmaceutical cartel drug dispensers) operate on the principle that symptom and cause *are* in the same place in yet another often lethal example of inversion. Acupuncture meridians connect with the 'chakra' vortex points throughout the body. Chakra comes from a Sanskrit word meaning 'wheels of light' and they connect the body to other levels of being and reality (Fig 145). The main ones are: the crown chakra on top of the head; brow (or 'third

Figure 145: The chakra system or 'wheels of light' that connect the hologram to other levels of reality.

Figure 146: The heart chakra – much more later about the role and significance of the heart.

eye') chakra in the centre of the forehead; throat chakra; heart chakra in the centre of the chest; solar plexus chakra just below the sternum; sacral chakra just beneath the navel; and base chakra at the bottom of the spine. Each one has a particular function or functions. We can't see them with the naked eye because they are part of the body's energetic field, but we do feel their effect. The sacral chakra in the lower belly is connected to emotion and that's where people feel anxiety and 'get the shits' when they are nervous or in fear. We feel love and empathy in the centre of the chest – the location of the heart chakra vortex (Fig 146). Energy poured from my chest in the ayahuasca rainforest experience through the heart chakra vortex.

You're a star – all of them

Okay, next we come to the paranormal mysteries of astrology and forms of divination such as tarot cards, rune stones and their like. Divination is defined as 'the practice of seeking knowledge of the future or the unknown by supernatural means.' Nothing presses the buttons of the Dogma Dawkins mentality more than the suggestion that astrology is a science; but it is. Or you could call it an art, it works either way. Sceptics have not a clue how astrology can work and so, by their definition, it

Figure 147: Planets and stars appear to be 'physical' but they are holographic information fields that impact with their movements and interactions on the universal information field – the energy sea within which we live.

Figure 148: Planets and stars are information fields changing and affecting other information fields in the interactive simulation.

Figure 149: Energy sea information fields are changed by planetary movements and we are affected in accordance with our own information make-up dictated by the point at which we entered the cycle – the moment we were born.

Figure 150: We are the Universe and more specifically how it was when we entered the cycle.

can't work. Yawn. Astrology can work and does in the right hands and in the right depth and detail. Everything is information including planets, stars and 'space'. Their movements and interactions exchange information with the universal field or Cosmic Internet (Fig 147). They imprint their information signature upon the universal field in the same way as those people did with water in the German experiment (Fig 148). Movements of planets and stars in relation to Earth impact and change the planetary energy (information) field – the energy 'sea' – with which *we* are constantly interacting (Fig 149). Different planets or groups of planets will have most influence on the Earth field at different points in the cycles. Configurations of planets known in astrology as conjunctions, oppositions, trines, sextiles, squares etc., produce even more powerful information impacts through their combined influence. Humanity, in turn, is interacting with these changing influences but not all in the same way. Body-Mind has astrological information fields which are dictated by where the planets and stars were in the cycle when people were born (some say conceived). Even a few minutes (in our perception) can produce subtle differences. All this means that under the holographic principle of as above, so below, we all have an energetic blueprint within us of the heavens as they were when we were born/conceived (Fig 150). Ancients divided the annual cycle (simulation program) into segments called astrological signs to represent different energetic (information) states caused by the positions of the planets and stars. There are differences, too, within these segments as changes happen hour by hour. Someone born in Leo, for example, will have a different astrological (energetic/information) field to someone born in Aries. They will interact with and be influenced by planetary movements through their lives in different ways to each other. This is the basis of astrology – and ancient astronomers were also astrologers. They knew the two disciplines were inseparable. Astrology columns in newspapers and magazines are dismissed because 'how can it be the same for so many people?' I agree in the sense that even the best of these columns can only be extremely generalised; but when you go into the detail of an individual's astrological background those influences can be measured by skilled astrologers. I emphasise that these astrological influences are *influences* and they don't have to dictate. I had to smile when I came across an astrologer's reading of my chart on the Internet. It described influences that give energetic support for the life journey I have taken, but the reading said that on the negative side I might be open to betrayal by those I thought were friends and also legal situations. I have been in court (successfully as it turned out) with two people who had told me how much they supported my work – and got their livelihoods from it – who were seeking to secure money they had not earned. One of them was trying to steal the entire rights to my books for which he had not produced a single syllable. A third one who once earned his living from my work instigated legal action in pursuit of money while I was writing this book after not hearing a peep from him for a year. I guess he just wanted to support my work which he had said was 'so important'. How noble. Between 2013 and 2015 everything was a challenge for me. No matter how hard I tried little worked as I wanted it to and it was a struggle just to stand still. Then everything changed like a cloud had lifted and fast forward momentum began again. Later an astrologer told me that in this same period the 'stars' (energetic environment) was very bad for me in anything to do with work, career, business and legal matters. The blocker was the position of Saturn and its impact on my energetic field and thus the area of my life to which its position related. This changed in September 2015 and so did the success of my work as I began riding an energetic wave instead of having it flowing against me. Astrology is all about energy flows. Many corporate CEOs employ astrologers to advise them on when to make moves in business to ensure that the energy environment is most conducive to a successful outcome. An astrologer noted years ago that major changes in my life coincided with lunar eclipses again and again. Astrology may sound mumbo-jumbo but only to those who don't understand reality. My experiences and their connection to astrological influences are clear to see when I look at my own life.

Card games

Tarot cards, rune stones and other forms of divination are also said to be ways of reading the future or possible/probable future. Well, it's not the future for a start when there is only the NOW. Divination techniques are reading (again in skilled hands) the probability of a sequence in the NOW. We exist on multiple levels and information/insight/perception/choice operates on all these levels. We exist in waveform, electromagnetic, mathematical/digital and holographic states as well as pure consciousness/awareness. There is a 'you' on all those levels with its own point of attention and perspective. 'David Icke' is not 'me', only the holographic 'me' (Fig 151). We only experience choices with our conscious mind when they are decoded into the hologram as 'physical' happenings, and before that they are only possibilities/probabilities in other energetic realms. I saw a quote which said:

Accidents happen – that's what everyone says. But in a quantum universe there are no such things as accidents, only possibilities and probabilities folded into existence by perception.

Perception = state of being = information / frequency = which possibility / probability you will sync with and project into holographic existence and which you will not. This is why the whole foundation of human control is a *Perception Deception*. Control perception and you control human experience. Tarot cards and divination are not reading the future but rather reading the probable outcome of choices and sequences happening in the subconscious. This is a misleading term given that the subconscious is actually conscious but at levels of awareness beyond the realms of our conscious mind. Subconscious is conscious – but not to the five senses. Tarot cards are reading possibilities and probabilities (information) within our own deeper energetic fields.

Energy flow that manifests eventually as a holographic outcome is not from past through present to future, but between different levels of ourselves in the NOW as possibilities and probabilities become actualities. Each card is illustrated with symbols that represent mental, emotional and information states (Fig 152). Symbols are energetic information just as words are, but much more powerful. Tarot cards are information fields representing energetically what the images symbolise and we don't choose the cards – the cards choose us. Cards are chosen by the electromagnetic field of the card syncing frequencies (vibrational magnetism) with the electromagnetic field of the person in accordance with their information / energetic state (Fig 153). They pick certain cards and not others through frequency compatibility between themselves and the cards. When selected cards are laid out on the table the person is looking at an information 'map' of their energetic self.

Figure 151: We are multidimensional beings and the holographic 'physical' is only one of them.

Figure 152: Tarot cards represent energetic and information states. Symbols have different frequencies as I will be explaining.

Illustration by Neil Hague (www.neilhague.com)

Figure 153: Tarot cards are selected through an electromagnetic connection between the person and the cards.

Even the order they are selected and which way up they are is significant. These also represent different information states. Other forms of divination, such as rune stones and the African technique of 'throwing the bones', work in the same way.

Know what I'm thinking?

Telepathy, synchronicity and teleportation are other examples of the paranormal normal. I'll start with telepathy. Humans operate on a particular frequency band while also having our own unique energy signature within that band dictated by our mental, emotional, perceptional and DNA state. African tribal people who communicate this way led to the term 'bush telegraph' and this can include tuning into frequencies of animals to instinctively know where they are. All species are the same in terms of having their own particular collective frequency and animals and insects are more sensitive to consciously interacting with energetic communication fields because unlike humans they don't get desensitised by The System (Fig 154). From this comes the 'hundredth monkey syndrome' in which a small number of a species learn something new and suddenly others at different locations can do the same without being shown. Animal species are highly sensitive to this communication system in the absence of a lifetime of programming to desensitise them to higher senses as with humans. Phantom Selves can be so energetically isolated and 'dead' they don't pick up this bush telegraph; but many people do and especially when it involves close friends or family members with whom a close bond (energetic/frequency connection) has been established. Someone says something and another replies with 'that's incredible, I was just thinking

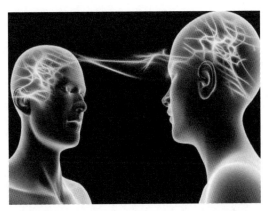

Figure 155 Telepathy is an energetic communication beyond the five senses.

Figure 154: Animals are incredibly sensitive to energetic change which is why they can sense earthquakes or bad weather before they happen. It helps that they don't go through the human education system, study human science or watch the human media.

Figure 156: Teleportation is the transfer of 'matter' as energetic information.

the same myself'. It's not incredible – it's telepathy, the bush telegraph or human Internet (Fig 155). Extrasensory perception (ESP) works on the same principle. People just know that something has happened to someone close to them without any other information to support this. Telepathy can also be used by sources in other realms of awareness with benevolent or malevolent intent to communicate with humans. Are they your thoughts you're thinking now? Synchronistic events can have many interacting sources but the means through which they happen is the same – the attraction of energetic states and frequencies or vibrational magnetism. Swiss psychiatrist Carl Jung said that synchronicity was proof of a collective unconscious, and he was right. It's the bush telegraph again. Teleportation is the 'theoretical transfer of matter or energy from one point to another without traversing the physical space between them.' This is fact not theory and it's possible because there is no matter as people perceive it. Teleportation is the transfer of information from one point to another and even the concept of 'points' are illusions when you go deep enough into reality (Fig 156). Quantum physicists speak about 'entanglement' which basically involves downloading information to another 'location' by syncing where you are with where you want to go. We download an external file by connecting a computer to the location of the file and cause one to be copied by the other. Teleportation is the same principle, really. 'Beam me up, Scotty' is the transfer of illusory matter (information state) in the form of energy (another information state) and its re-manifestation back into illusory matter (original information state).

Global grid

Other sources of paranormal 'mystery' are ley lines, stone circles, pyramids and so on. Planet Earth is criss- crossed and interpenetrated by a network of energy lines known variously as ley lines, dragon lines and meridians. These are the planet's version of the acupuncture meridians in the body on the holographic principle of as above, so below' (Fig 157). A vortex is created where the lines cross and the biggest vortexes are the planetary power centres where the ancients located stone circles, major temples and pyramids to tap into and manipulate the energy and also for interdimensional communication. Crystalline (quartz) stone was used to aid communication with 'the gods' for the same reason that quartz crystal is used in communication technology (Fig 158). Initiates in the circles could tune in to communications transmitted to the stones from other realties. Ancient initiates of the hidden knowledge knew far more than Mainstream Everything wants us to realise. To be aware that advanced knowledge existed in the ancient world is to ask 'why did they know things then that we've only just learned or still didn't know?' From this would come a re-evaluation of official history and so many dominoes would fall. Defend the first domino. Societies don't only go forward into ever greater

Figure 157: The planet is criss-crossed and interpenetrated by energetic force (information) lines like those on which acupuncture is based – the hologram again.

Figure 158: Quartz crystal stone was used at vortex points on the global grid to communicate with the 'gods' and also to balance or manipulate the flow of energy (information) in the same way that acupuncture needles do.

understanding as we're led to believe. If knowledge is suppressed, societies can go the other way, too, into ignorance and reverse development. Compare ancient Egypt with modern Egypt. Initiates in the ancient world knew a great deal more than modern mainstream scientists with regard to the principles of reality. Today's secret societies and many religions are based on this knowledge while hiding behind a Biblical front. The Mormon temple at Salt Lake City is built from crystalline granite for the same reason that Stonehenge is constructed with crystalline stone (Fig 159). Satanic symbols you can see around the Mormon temple site are not by chance either (Fig 160). Researchers have been astonished at the way stone circles, standing stones, pyramids, ancient temples

Figure 159: The inner circle of the Mormon Church know all about the occult (hidden) truths.

Figure 160: Satanic symbols associated with the Mormon Church are no coincidence.

and other 'holy' places are geometrically aligned with each other over often immense distances when there appears to be no historical connection and they involve cultures that didn't know each other. But if you locate your structures on the vortex points of a grid that is geometrically aligned then you automatically geometrically align your structure with those at other points on the grid. Christian cathedrals and churches built on former Pagan sites inspired by vortex points are the same, and you have otherwise inexplicable alignments between Christian churches and ancient pre-Christian structures. My information is that the British Isles are placed at the heart of the global grid pattern and there are more standing stones, circles and ancient earthworks per square mile in Britain and Ireland than anywhere else in the world (especially centre-west and across to Ireland). This energetic power and potential is why these tiny islands have such a history as a centre of global power – and they remain so from the shadows. Britain was considered sacred by the Druids, priestly initiates of the Celts, especially islands such as the Isle of Man, Isle of Anglesey and Isle of Wight. I realised in the years after I came to live on the Isle of Wight what an extraordinary Freemasonic and Satanism presence there is here for such a small place. This is connected (though the majority of Freemasons won't know) to its energetic nature. Islands are particularly important surrounded as they are by the powerful energetic field of water. Manipulating major vortex points can change the frequency and information in the ley line grid, which then impacts upon the frequency and information state of the energy sea. We spend our lives in this energetic sea and are fundamentally influenced mentally and emotionally by its information state. Satanists target vortex points for their rituals for reasons that will become clear, and the most skilled are known as black magicians for their ability to manipulate what they know is malleable reality.

Er, we're not alone

The idea that life as we know it has only emerged on one little planet in one little solar system is taking lunacy to its natural conclusion, but academia, media and the rest of the Mainstream Mafia dismiss the idea of life on other planets with their stock phrase about 'little green men'. Astronomers estimate that there are at least a hundred *billion* galaxies in the observable Universe. That's the *observable* Universe – you know, the tiny

Figure 161: Back to sleep everyone .... Zzzzzzzzz.

frequency range which humans and their technology can see. What about the infinity of what we can't see? It is also pertinent to note that mainstream science has gone from believing in one galaxy in only the 1920s to at least a hundred billion, with some estimates at 500 billion (Fig 161). When scientists tell you what is 'known' it is only what they *believe* is known at that moment. It'll be something else tomorrow, next week or next year. Intelligent life exists on all levels of reality from pure consciousness through waveform, electrical/electromagnetic and digital/holographic. Research into 'aliens' (horrible term) tends to focus almost entirely on the human visual frequency range or the 'physical'. I have been interviewed twice for the History Channel series *Ancient Aliens* – which is very good as far as it goes, but I found it a frustrating experience trying to take the narrative beyond the illusory physical. A 2012 article in *Psychology Today* about DMT, the main active constituent of ayahuasca, describes how users can 'encounter non-human intelligences, often resembling aliens'. I mentioned earlier that ayahuasca has been called a 'plant of the gods' because it can open the frequency channels to those dimensions of reality where the perceived 'gods' reside. Non-human or extraterrestrial life exists in a multiplicity of forms and expressions even among those who observe and interact with Earth. Some are benevolent, some neutral and still others have a malevolent agenda, which I have been exposing for decades. They have appeared to humans over thousands of years and they are the source of endless myths about 'the gods'. The History Channel series is based on these stories and evidence to support them. Ancient Indian documents and texts describe advanced flying machines that brought the gods. Dr. V. Raghavan, retired head of the Sanskrit department at the University of Madras, says that centuries-old documents written in the ancient Indian language describe extraterrestrial visitations:

> Fifty years of researching this ancient work convinces me that there are living beings on other planets, and that they visited earth as far back as 4,000BC. There is a just a mass of fascinating information about flying machines, even fantastic science fiction weapons, that can be found in translations of the Vedas (scriptures), Indian epics, and other ancient Sanskrit text.

Inner-circles of government and military know that extraterrestrial life is still visiting this planet and they just don't want us to know. Most 'aliens' come in and out of our reality. Accounts by those who claim to have seen them or their craft are ridiculed when they describe how they appeared out of nowhere and disappeared just as quickly. To Phantom Mind this is impossible, but it's not. When they enter our frequency band they appear to any observer as if they have manifested out of nowhere and the reverse when they disappear. They have neither appeared out of nothing nor disappeared into nothing. They enter the frequency range of human sight and leave again. Now you see them, now you don't. Extraterrestrial species can travel apparently vast distances instantly by overriding illusory space-time. Some craft may appear to be 'physical', but the more advanced of them move as energy (a sort of teleportation) and their craft are energetic forms which can appear as anything from what seems to be a metallic spaceship to what looks every bit like a cloud. Other flying saucer-type craft that people think must be 'aliens' are really flown by humans with secret technology. Anti-gravity craft have been built in the most secretive military bases especially in the United States for many decades and there are deep underground bases or 'DUMBS' all over the world where interaction takes place between the human 'elite' and extraterrestrial beings. I am coming to this whole area of human control by a non-human force in the next chapter and it goes way beyond 'aliens'.

Excuse my French

Mainstream Everything sets out to trash the 'paranormal' at every opportunity. This is through calculated design by those in the shadows and ignorance by their academic foot soldiers and slaves of The System. Phantom Self always dismisses what it doesn't understand. Academics get their information from other academics and program each other into mutual myopia. No one outside of academia can possibly know more than them. If that were true their 'great education' would have to be seen for what it is – a hoax. Christopher French, Professor of Psychology at Goldsmiths College, University of London, and former Editor-in-Chief of *The Skeptic* magazine, is often wheeled out on television shows in Britain to trash anything 'paranormal'. I'm usually shaking my head when he's on giving his excruciatingly feeble explanations for why anything considered paranormal can't exist. Years ago, there was another academic paranormal-trasher who said that when people died in operating theatres and found themselves looking down at their bodies this was their brain remembering life experiences in the course of dying. How could that be true unless the person had ever floated above their body looking down on it? Mainstream Everything is trying harder and harder to hold the line in the face of emerging evidence, and the academic narrative becomes more desperate and bizarre in response. Quantum physics already means their battle is ultimately lost. Psychiatry is clueless about the forces that both manifest consciousness and influence its perceptions. Shocking numbers of people having perfectly explainable 'paranormal' experiences are incarcerated and drugged only because psychiatry is so deeply infected with the arrogance of ignorance. Psychiatrists enforce their psychological fascism as agents of Mainstream Everything. They have downloaded The System's version of the human mind and repeated this in their examinations to satisfy The System they are 'qualified' to be an agent of The System. This entitles them to support and protection from The System in the form of judges and mental health law. 'Therapists' become multi-millionaires in Hollywood selling this same Stone Age psychiatry. How long have you been in therapy? 'Fifteen years.' Fuck, isn't it time it worked?

Life and reality is nothing like humanity has been manipulated to believe and once you realise the truth paranormal 'mysteries' fade away. But the illusion goes deeper, much deeper. Grab a seat belt and strap in …

CHAPTER FOUR

The Secret – *Shhhhh!*

When you're the only sane person, you look like the only insane person
Criss Jami

I have alluded in general terms so far to a Hidden Hand, or force, behind The System and the simulation that we call the Universe. Now for the detail – the biggest secret.

What I am about to say is a good measure for how deeply some people are entrenched in Phantom Self and how open others are to consider all possibility and not only programmed possibility. I say this because what is really happening, why and by whom, is a challenge to everything Phantom Self represents – limitation, unquestioning dogma, unyielding belief and a refusal to see beyond its downloaded sense of 'normal'. Yes, the 'normal' that The System tells you is 'normal'. Human control and subjugation is *ultimately* not the work of other humans or even anyone in what we call 'form'. Humans play their part in enslaving each other but the force driving the control system and the simulation is far from human. What I am about to relate will quickly part the Phantom from the conscious beyond the Phantom. This parting of the ways is not about whether people believe or don't believe what I say, but whether they are prepared to give information open-minded consideration and see it through to the end as layer is added to layer. Phantom Self in more extreme states will dismiss anything that is at odds with the program. This is, after all, what the program is designed to do (Fig 162).

'IT'S NOT LIKE YOU THINK IT IS.'
'YOU'RE MAD, MATE.'

Figure 162: Been there, done that, got the T-shirt.

Anything different from the perceived normal (especially fundamentally different) is poo-pooed away with an arrogant wave of the hand and a flurry of clichéd declarations such as 'you're mad', 'that's crazy' and 'have you taken your medicine?' Phantom Self responds to program as The System presses enter and those behind The System smile with a glow of relieved satisfaction as another inmate denies the existence of its own prison. If this is where you are coming from then this book is not for you, and this chapter in particular. Those who are not mind-puppets of Phantom Self will at least look at the information without pre-judgement and reflex-action hostility. I have been researching these subjects for decades and as the dots have connected from the synchronistic flow of information (which is what I was told would happen through physic Betty Shine) I have been able to weave together so many common themes that span what is termed human 'history'. One theme is the existence of a hidden force manipulating human affairs from the unseen realms beyond the ridiculously narrow confines of our decoded visual reality. You will find all the highly detailed background and evidence in my other books, like *The Perception Deception*. Even some mainstream scientists have acknowledged that we interact with other dimensions of reality. Bernard Carr, professor of mathematics and astronomy at the Queen Mary University, London, said:

> Our consciousness interacts with another dimension. Our physical sensors only show us a 3-dimensional universe ... What exists in the higher dimensions are entities we cannot touch with our physical sensors.

I am going to tell the story here to the extent that it puts into essential context the architects of Phantom Self, the reason for its creation and why the world operates as it does. I will also take the story on further than ever before. This hidden force is given different names by ancient and modern cultures but the way it is described and its goals and modus operandi are remarkably consistent. Christianity uses the term demons; Islam (and pre-Islamic Arabia) refers to Jinn or Djinn; pagan Gnostics warned about Archons; Zulu legend tells of Chitauri; Central American shamans call them Flyers, Predators and other names; on and on it goes around the world. They are different names describing the *same* force that is portrayed almost wherever you go as the malevolence that has infiltrated and hijacked human reality. Endless gods and goddesses worshipped by the ancients were also largely different names for this force. Today's religion emerged from the worship of these perceived 'gods' which were eventually fused into one God by monotheistic faiths, most notably Judaism, Christianity and Islam. All believe in a negative force behind human affairs under names like the Devil, Satan, Lucifer, Iblis, Asmodai, Haggadah and Samael ('angel of death'). This theme can be found everywhere because this force exists and has been directing human society for a very long 'time'. Religious advocates miss the fact that often their one God is only another version of demon gods in yet another monumental inversion as I have explained at length in *The Perception Deception* and will address later. Satanism is the worship of these 'evil gods' in the knowledge of what they really are – dark, dastardly and highly malevolent with a grotesque agenda for humankind. They know they are worshipping a malevolent force while followers of religions believe their composite God is a force for good. Satanism's symbolism of inverted pentagrams and crosses etc., is portraying the inverted realty their 'gods' have created (Fig 163). I have said that symbols are information fields communicating with the viewer more potently than the spoken word. Symbols are not used for show, but effect.

Figure 163: Satanism is the inversion of anything good, positive or loving and their symbols reflect that.

Secret knowledge

A stream of awareness and perception known as
Gnosticism describes the beliefs of diverse groups
of people referred to as Gnostics. The term
Gnosticism comes from *gnosis*, a Hellenistic Greek
word meaning 'secret knowledge', and Gnostic
translates as 'learned'. They were spiritual outcasts
of mainstream religion and were constantly,
violently and mercilessly targeted by the System-
created Roman Church, which saw them as a
potentially lethal threat to its make-believe dogma.
A famous example was the horrific assault on the
Gnostic Cathars in the Languedoc in southern
France that culminated with the siege of the castle
at Montsegur in 1244. This put an end to the
Cathars or at least those with a public face.

Figure 164: The Royal Library in Alexandria,
Egypt, was an incredible depository of
ancient knowledge and history.

Another barbarous attack on Gnostics by the forces of peace
and love came with the sacking and burning of the Gnostic-
inspired Royal Library at Alexandria in Egypt in around
415AD (Fig 164). This was home to half a million scrolls and
documents detailing history and accumulated knowledge
from the ancient world which the Roman Church did not
want people to know about. Christianity's ludicrous
narrative, pedalled and imposed so violently by the Church
hierarchy and its programmed minions, would have been
demolished by the content. I'm sure that what didn't go up
in flames was secretly secured in the vaults of the Vatican
and will still be there today. Rome's assault on the Royal or
'Great' Library included the hacking to death of Hypatia
(350-415AD), a mathematician, astronomer and philosopher

Figure 165: A painting depicting
Hypatia.

who was head of the Platonist school at Alexandria (Fig 165). She taught the views of
Greek philosophers Plato and Aristotle to Pagan and Christian students alike.
Advanced and open minds gathered at the Royal Library to seek answers to the
Mysteries. Among them was a man who accurately measured the size of Earth and
another who established that Earth orbits the Sun – 2,000 years before this was officially
discovered by Polish Renaissance mathematician and astronomer, Nicolaus Copernicus.
Gnostics used their open minds in pursuit of knowledge and also took psychoactive
potions to expand their awareness in the same way that I did with ayahuasca.
Knowledge – or gnosis to them – was not only about names, dates and places, but
deeper awareness of other realities from where they could better understand this reality.
Gnostic 'knowledge' has the connotation of internal, intuitive knowledge that can see
beyond the program. Their expanded awareness could tap into insight and knowledge
that Phantom Self cannot under the ignore-trance spell of The System. Knowledge is
always dangerous to any tyranny which survives through suppression of knowledge
and the Roman Church ensured that little survived of gnostic insight. Well, that was the

case until a startling find in 1945 at Nag
Hammadi, a town some 77 miles from Luxor in
Egypt. A sealed glass jar discovered by a local
was found to contain 13 codices and more than
50 texts by Pagan Gnostics (not to be confused
with the later Christian Gnostics although their
beliefs had great similarities). The find at Nag
Hammadi was a game-changer for those who
could see its true significance, but was virtually
ignored (for obvious reasons) by Mainstream
Everything (Fig 166). Texts revealed that the
Gnostics believed the 'material' world we see is

Figure 166: The Nag Hammadi find was
sensational and so it was largely ignored by the
mainstream.

a fake reality, and they made the crucial distinction between what they called *nous*
(Phantom Self) and *pneuma* (Infinite Self). Gnostics also used the term Bythos or 'Void'
for the 'Dazzling Darkness' (All That Is) which they said existed before our world was
created. This has to be the case when Bythos is the All Possibility and All Potential from
which all form or illusions of form are ultimately manifested. I was taken aback when I
read of the Nag Hammadi texts because they described my own conclusions gleaned in
other ways and from other sources.

Ladies and gentlemen – the Archons

A fifth of Gnostic texts discovered at Nag Hammadi are focussed on non-human entities
that they call 'Archons' (a name meaning 'rulers' in Greek). This is the force behind the
'Matrix' simulation that we experience as the Universe and The System of human
control and subjugation. Gnostic texts say Archons can possess the human mind and
manipulate perception. They explain how Archons remain hidden (in another frequency
range) and are able to manipulate illusions and instil beliefs. Gnostics describe Archons
as 'deceivers' who engineer illusions which they call *phantasia* – including the fake
human reality, Matrix or simulation that I will describe in the next chapter. They say
Archons invert reality and today's inverted society that I have long exposed is only the
current state of an ongoing inversion imposed by this common source (Fig 167). In our

version of 'time' Archons were
manipulating humanity in the
Gnostic period, and for aeons
before, in the same way they do
today. They have been securing
ever more control by the
centralisation of global power
and decision-making – which is
precisely what we see now at
such an advanced stage. Nag
Hammadi texts say Archons
lack *ennoia* or 'intentionality'.
I would use the term creative
imagination. There is a reason
for this, as I will be explaining.

Figure 167: Archons invert everything they touch and this is why
Satanism does the same.

Figure 168: Many names – same force.

Figure 169: Archons or Jinn are pure energy in their prime state, but they can take form either through manifestation or possession. From Jinn comes genie.

Lack of *ennoia* means Archons cannot create anything from scratch. They can only piggyback, imitate, change and distort what has already been created. Give them a blank sheet of paper and they would be lost, but give them paper with an image or written word and they can manipulate, distort and imitate what is *already there*. They can do things far ahead of what Phantom Self humans can do thanks to knowledge gleaned from other more advanced realities and not because of their own creative imagination. Gnostics referred to Archons as parasites, and part of the reason for this is that they must feed off creative energy and imagination of humans to overcome their disadvantage of not having any themselves. To maintain this status quo Archons have to keep humanity in ignorance of their very existence, never mind their manipulations, goals and illusions. A glance at the world with an open mind will confirm that this continues today. We live in such a parasite society with the political and banking system alone feeding off creativity and labour of the people through oppression, taxation and interest on debt. Archons have specifically structured the financial system and The System in general to parasite human energy and creative imagination. Not only do 'Archons' as described by the Gnostics fit perfectly with my own research over the last 26 years, but it describes what the Islamic and pre-Islamic worlds say of the Jinn; Christianity says of demons; Central American shamans say of Flyers and Predators; Zulu and other African peoples say of Chitauri; and other cultures say of their names for a negative force of human manipulation. Gnostics said Archons are made from 'luminous fire' while the Koran says Jinn are made from 'smokeless fire' (Fig 168). Jinn, or Djinn, comes from an Arabic root word meaning 'hidden' or 'to hide'. They are said to be supernatural beings that live in a parallel realm (frequency band) and are invisible to us. Gnostics said the same about Archons and it is a universal theme. Jinn are the origin of the term genie – entities described as pure energy in their prime state, but which can manifest in form (Fig 169). This is again what the Gnostics said about Archons and others say about their version of the same phenomenon. Gnostic texts describe how Archons serve the Lord Archon or 'Demiurge' which they say is the fake 'God' that created our illusory 'physical' or 'material' reality and stands between humanity and the 'transcendent' God (Infinite Awareness). This block could

Figure 170: When you realise that different names and terms in the ancient world were referring to the same thing the mist starts to clear.

Figure 171: The Demiurge force has many guises, disguises and manifestations.

only be breached by *gnosis* or spiritual knowledge (expanded awareness). Gnostics said the Demiurge created the Archons and here we have the religious concept of the Devil/Satan and his fallen angels (Fig 170). Gnostic texts go further, and I absolutely agree with them, in that they contend the 'God' of the Bible is also an alias for the Demiurge. I would say the same about many other faiths. What fundamental potential implications this has for mainstream religion. It would also explain why religions claiming to worship a loving god have such a record of sheer bloody evil. The 'God' of the major religions, and most smaller ones, is really 'Satan' in disguise? Old Testament angels and demons are both names for Archons? What a wonderful example of the foundation Archon technique of inversion. You can see why it's been crucial to maintain humanity's ongoing ignorance of reality and to hide that knowledge behind the wall of deception and suppression that is Mainstream Everything. How can you grasp how we are controlled or even *that* we are controlled, by whom and to what end, without an understanding of the 'physical' illusion and how it can be manipulated? I am now going to connect and fuse all the themes so far in the book with decades of my own research and insight to present the background to how humans have been deceived all their multi-generational lives. Archons are 'entities' that invert and distort because they are *themselves* an inversion and distortion. Everything is energy/awareness and to understand what Archons are is to understand what *everything* is – energy/awareness. Put bodies and form aside for a moment and think awareness, the state of being aware. It has no body or form; it is pure awareness, which can take form as with the concept of genies (Fig 171). This is what we all are no matter if we are having an experience as a human or an Archon. Forms or bodies through which awareness can observe and experience are only the cloaks and masks of those experiences – 'all the world's a stage'. We get lost when we self-identify with the masks and lose sight of the fact that this is all they are. I am not suggesting that everyone and everything is *equally* aware. When we look through the eyes of the body projection (or think we do) we are obviously not as aware as when we are free of the body 'lens' which focusses our attention on the infinitesimal frequency range of visible light. Near-death and out-of-body experiencers tell of an enormous expansion of awareness when the body lens is no longer concentrating their sense of reality on a frequency range the size of a pea. Infinite Possibility means infinite potential for states of awareness and so we have the Infinite in awareness of itself and we have Boy George Bush. Archons are also awareness that wraps itself in illusory form of many kinds. They appear on one level to be Archons or Jinn (plural), and a 'They'; but 'They' are expressions of an inverted and distorted energetic state and how they behave reflects that energetic state.

Going deeper – it's a 'virus'

Terms like Demiurge and his Archons, and Devil and his fallen angels, are names for an energetic distortion that can best be described as a *computer virus*. When I say this I am being far more literal than symbolic. Everything has awareness and the Demiurge/Archons are a *self-aware* distortion, a *self-aware* computer virus that distorts everything it touches (Fig 172). Computer viruses can 'damage files, slow the system, show messages and take control.' Techy websites describe them as a small piece of software that *piggybacks* on real programs. I have already used the term piggyback for the way Archons parasite human energy and creativity to hijack human society. A virus does not create but piggybacks and distorts what is already created – Archons as described by Gnostics. Viruses can

Figure 172: What the Gnostics called the Demiurge is the equivalent of a computer virus – a self-aware virus that can replicate itself (the Archons).

attach themselves to a program and to quote one article they can '*reproduce* (by attaching to other programs) or wreak havoc'. Another definition that syncs with Archon infiltration says that a virus is 'a piece of code which is capable of copying itself and typically has a detrimental effect, such as corrupting the system or destroying data'. The Demiurge virus has reproduced or copied itself and we call the result *Archons*. Together this virus and its reproductions *have* wreaked havoc on human society and our reality in general. Here is another virus definition:

> Computer viruses are called viruses because they share some of the traits of biological viruses. A computer virus passes from computer to computer like a biological virus passes from person to person. Unlike a cell, a virus has no way to reproduce by itself. Instead, a biological virus must inject its DNA into a cell. The viral DNA then uses the cell's existing machinery to reproduce itself.

> Similar to the way a biological virus must hitch a ride on a cell, a computer virus must piggyback on top of some other program or document in order to launch. Once a computer virus is running, it can infect other programs or documents.

You could hardly read a better summary of how the Demiurge/Archons operate and what they have done to humans and yet it is describing a computer virus. Our experienced reality – 'the world' – is a quantum computer simulation and human Body-

Figure 173: The Demiurge virus has been infused into every area of human society.

Mind is also a biological computer system. Both can be hacked, infiltrated and distorted by a virus or in the case of the simulation controlled by one. A virus can change and distort what we see on a computer screen and the Demiurge/Archon virus has done the same with our 'screen' or decoded sense of reality (Fig 173). Gnostics described Demiurge/Archons in terms of what today we would call technology or computer-like. They are a form of *Artificial Intelligence* and my goodness how significant that is going to be later in the book to what is happening in human society. Artificial Intelligence explains their lack of 'ennoia' or creative imagination. A machine-like force totally disconnected from Infinite Awareness has no imagination. It can only copy, infiltrate and take over like a virus in a computer. I described earlier how the simulation we call the Universe operates as a quantum computer with its own self-awareness. I said: 'Quantum physicists are realising that all matter (concentrated energy) is a form of computer, but in fact *all* energy can compute information because it is *conscious.*' Demiurge/Archons are a conscious (to an extent) Artificial Intelligence computer virus which has set out to take over everything (Fig 174). It can't do this with Creation as a whole because it is not even remotely powerful enough, but it can – and has – wreaked havoc in our reality and in other realities and 'worlds'. Humans began to 'know good and evil' when the virus struck and its many guises brought what we call evil (a *distortion* of balance and harmony). The virus can manifest as pure energy or in endless forms – Agent Smith in *The Matrix* looked human but 'he' was only a computer program and extension of the machines (Artificial Intelligence) behind the simulated reality. Machines in *The Matrix* used human energy as their power source and the Demiurge / Archon virus does the same. A computer virus gets its power from the computer. Morpheus in *The Matrix* captured this theme when he held up a battery and said that the Matrix was 'a computer-generated dream world built to keep us under control in order to change a human being into this' (Fig 175). Not just any human energy will do for Archons. It has to be within the frequency range of the virus or it can't be absorbed and the energy that syncs with the Archon virus is ... low-vibrational emotion based on *fear* and its subdivisions like

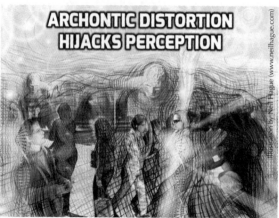

Figure 174: The Demiurge/Archon virus has taken over human society by hijacking human perception and Phantom Self is fundamental to that.

anxiety, stress, hatred, resentment, revenge, conflict, depression and competition. Death and suffering is another Archon virus energy source and so is sexual energy without a love connection. Make sense of the world? Sacrificing people to 'the gods' was – and is – to release extremes of emotion through sheer terror and make a gift of 'food' to 'the gods' (Archons beyond human sight). Evil is appropriately the word 'live' written backwards – inverted. Demiurge / Archons are obsessed with death from their role as an inversion of 'live' or life and therefore their manifestations in our reality like Satanists and black magicians are obsessed with death (Fig 176). Human and animal sacrifice is often performed in cemeteries and churches surrounded by graves of dead people. Death is energy with its own frequency, and all the wars, mass slaughter and death from preventable hunger and disease are the work of the global Archon Death Cult that directs human society and

Figure 175: Humans have been turned into a power source for the virus.

Figure 176: The Demiurge/Archon Death Cult.

feeds off the energy it is manipulated to generate (Fig 177). The evil/live reversal is not a coincidence. Words represent frequency states – which in turn represent states of consciousness and information. Infinite reality has a prevailing balance that we experience as love (in its deepest sense), harmony, joy, kindness and empathy. You can still see so many examples of this in

Figure 177: The virus in all its forms feeds off low vibrational human energy – fear, death and their associated emotions.

Figure 178: Demiurge virus infecting human perception.

Figure 179: One example of the 'black goo' theme.

human society despite everything. 'Love' and harmony is the default state of Infinite Forever and will return when the Archon virus moves aside for Infinite Awareness to bring an end to war, exploitation, imposition, engineered suffering, hatred and abuse of all kinds. We are currently drowning in all of those things and they are distortions of the virus. Go on social media for five minutes to see the scale of hatred and abuse that has infested much of human perception and how it is used to promote Phantom Self-delusion (Fig 178). Facebook would be better called Phantombook. Gnostics said the Demiurge / Archons were an 'error' and they had no soul or direct connection to Infinite Source. This is the origin of the myths (truths) about the Soulless Ones. Without a connection to Infinite Awareness they can operate and perceive only in the realm of mind or Artificial Intelligence. The conspiracy to isolate humans in the realm of Body-Mind through Phantom Self is an effort to turn us into *Them*. Take another look in the light of this at the ultimate control agenda dubbed transhumanism – a *trans-ition* from humans into machine-like Archons. Transhumanism involves fusing humans with Artificial Intelligence and the Archon virus is ... *Artificial Intelligence*. I'll have much more about this later. As I was completing the book I was sent links to a series of videos on YouTube entitled *Black Goo and Programmable Matter* which highlight the extraordinary number of movies, television sci-fi shows, music videos and commercials that involve the theme of an 'intelligent black goo' or liquid looking for a human host. It is variously portrayed as an intelligent substance or 'alien DNA' with the capacity to change shape and take over people and transform or absorb them so they become its vehicles (Fig 179). Christine Aguilera and Lady Gaga are among those who have portrayed this theme and it symbolises the Demiurge/Archon self-aware virus. Shining black leather and PVC are also used to symbolise the goo/virus in music videos and stage shows, as is Darth Vader in the *Star Wars* series.

Possession is real

Gnostics and other cultures describe the motivations and behaviour traits of the Demiurge/Archons ('the virus') in the same way that the term 'psychopath' is defined – no empathy, remorse or shame, pathological liars (deceivers) and parasites who do whatever it takes to get their way. Archons under their many global names and aliases are also described as having no emotion and a trait of psychopaths is the 'shallow effect' or an inability to express a range of emotions. Human psychopaths are those deeply infected with the Archon virus, and psychopathy is much more prevalent in society than is widely believed. What Gnostics call the Demiurge is the original distortion/virus and Archons are copies or reproductions that serve the distortion/virus. People need to suspend their focus on form or a classic 'Devil' figure to grasp what is happening. Malevolence is not a 'being' as we perceive the term but a distorted energy/awareness which can take forms that reflect its distortion. This can be anything from the hideous and distorted faces of a classic 'Exorcist' possession to a (psychopathic) bank CEO causing poverty and suffering in pursuit of still more money and control. Infestation by the virus of the body-computer is the real foundation of 'demonic possession'. This is an age-old theme when demonic entities are said to take over thoughts, emotions and behaviour of their human targets. These accounts are universal across history and culture and remain so today. To dismiss them without investigation is the response of either an idiot or someone so terrified they might be true that they employ ridicule and dismissal to say 'shut up, I don't want to hear it'. A majority react the same way to any mention of conspiracies for the same reason. The rejection of possession as 'not possible' betrays yet again an ignorance of reality. If people are 'solid', how can they be possessed in ways described both ancient and modern? They couldn't be, but people are *not* solid. They are energy/awareness and can be possessed or taken over by other energy/awareness as long as the frequencies are compatible. Possession happens when an entity or energy (the virus) attaches to the human auric field and begins to dictate thoughts, emotions and perceptions. Human fields with high vibrant frequencies cannot be possessed by malevolence, but once people fall into low vibrational (Archontic) states the frequency compatibility is secured and possession can take place. Drug and alcohol abuse can lower human frequency enough to enter the realm of the Archon virus and having sex with a possessed person can allow a possessing entity/virus to slip across the energetic connection to possess the partner. It's the same principle as a virus infecting one computer infiltrating another. Possession takes many forms, not only the distorted faces and demonic behaviour portrayed in films like *The Exorcist* (Fig 180). Those extreme levels of obvious possession do happen but it is mostly far more subtle and often almost imperceptible. Effect on behaviour can span the range from barely observable to full-blown psychopath and facial distortion. When the attachment is relatively weak on the person's auric field the virus may hardly impact itself on the hologram of the target. People possessed in this

Figure 180: Possession is real.

Figure 181: As the information fields of the possessing entity or virus impact upon the fields of the target person their holographic features begin to morph and distort to reflect the possessing force.

way (the majority) continue to look as they always have, although their behaviour and perceptions will be affected to the extent of the possession; but the more powerfully and totally the virus/entity attaches itself the more its 'personality' dictates their behaviour and perceptions and they can start to change as the information infusion from the possessing field impacts upon the hologram (Fig 181). At this point an observer will see the face or even the entire body of the possessed person change and distort to reflect the nature of the possessing entity. I have seen people distorted like this, and others who still looked basically the same but with clear facial changes and very darkened eyes after possession had taken them over to the extent that their personality became very different.

What I have just described is a form of *shapeshifting* although there are other explanations for that, too, and I will deal with them later. I have been constantly ridiculed for saying that the world is covertly ruled by shapeshifting 'leaders' who can shift between human and reptilian (and other) forms. But it's true, despite sounding crazy to those who have done no research into any of this (virtually everyone). Possessed people can be schizophrenics who jump from one personality to another (their own and the possessor). It's not the only reason for schizophrenic behaviour, but it is one. Sometimes a possessing agent of the virus will withdraw and the person's own personality returns until the entity imposes itself again and the target goes through a sometimes dramatic personality transformation. Those who have lived with Satanists describe how they can be one personality by day and quite another by night. Entities can also use their possessed vehicles to infiltrate other people and groups with their 'nice' mask and then suddenly turn on them with a malevolence aimed at doing as much damage as possible. I have experienced this myself several times and those involved will mostly have no idea that their malevolent motivations were not coming only from them, but also from that which possesses them. They have a thought or desire to damage and hurt and they think it's coming from their own mind. Yet all the time a distorted awareness is calling the shots and using them as a vehicle for its own ends.

This is not to always absolve responsibility of those involved. They must have been vibrationally open and frequency-compatible for this connection to happen; but there are also a mass of covert government/military mind control programmes designed to attach possessing entities to otherwise innocent people, who then become their agents (see *The Biggest Secret*). Those exposing The System and especially the Archon virus (very few) need to be constantly vigilant because they are going to be targeted by these programmes and other techniques for obvious reasons. It's certainly happened to me. What follows is a very accurate description of possession attributed to Rumi, a 13th century Persian poet, Islamic scholar and Sufi mystic. Note that date – the *13th century* – and the same is happening today:

> When a man is possessed by an evil spirit
> The qualities of humanity are lost in him.
> Whatever he says is really said by that spirit,
> Though it seems to proceed from the man's mouth.
> When the spirit has this rule and dominance over him,
> The agent is the property of the spirit, and not himself;
> His self is departed, and he has become the spirit.

This describes not only members of the general population subject to possession, but most crucially it applies to those in positions of political, economic, military and administrative power who are mere agents and vehicles in our world of the Archon virus. I will explore this further shortly.

'He says the world is run by seven-foot lizards'

Okay, shapeshifting lizards. This is the phrase you see almost every time my name is mentioned in the media (mainstream and most of the 'alternative') and by the thoroughly ignorant who ridicule me on the Internet as the man who believes in 'lizard people' (Fig 182). They all think they are making statements about me when they are really exposing their own immaturity and ignorance – Phantom Self. 'David Icke believes the world is run by shapeshifting lizards', they say as they laugh and mock. And that's it. No further questions, no further research. The idea that 'shapeshifting lizards', or Reptilians as I call them, could even exist let alone run the world is so far beyond their programmed sense of the possible that their Phantom Selves can't breach their perception firewall. This leaves them with one of two default-position reactions ... ridicule or condemnation (often both). Why should they further question and research when the program tells them it is obviously all madness? I have the same response from the mainstream media, alternative media, rich and poor, Left and Right, reactionary and 'radical'. They all think they're different but they are really self-deluding masks on the same program. They all respond in the

Figure 182: Reptilian entities manipulating human affairs is a fact – no matter how much people may ridicule me.

same way when you press enter by challenging the program, because the program has them. Myopic perception afflicts the whole of humanity no matter what the label, background or income bracket and the antidote is always the same – an open mind. People from all walks of life who are not totally controlled by Phantom Self can look at the world from a far less programmed perspective if they have a mind of their own. For those who do, I'll explain why

Figure 183: Gnostic texts from at least 400AD describe reptilian and grey entities that are reported by witnesses and the UFO research community today.

Reptilians are not so crazy. The self-ware Demiurge/Archon virus can take many forms and possess any form that falls into its frequency range. Two of the most common are reptilian and what have become known as the 'Grey aliens' with their grey 'skin' and big black eyes (Fig 183). I don't mean all entities that take these forms, but certainly those possessed and infected by the Archon virus. A theme running through accounts about Archons, Reptilians and Greys is that they operate with a hive mind much like an ant or bee colony serving a central control system in the form of the queen. This makes sense since they are expressions of the virus and this is their hive-like communication and control network. Archons are seeking to attach humanity into the same hive 'Demiurge Internet' which dictates perceptions and behaviour of Archons and virus-possessed Reptilians and Greys. This is what

Figure 184:
A painting of a Reptilian entity – the Chitauri – by Zulu shaman Credo Mutwa from ancient and modern descriptions.

transhumanism is really all about. Reptilians and Greys are believed by many to be a modern phenomenon as described by the UFO and alien research community. There are large numbers of people worldwide who say they have seen these entities and even been abducted by them – many for genetic experiments and hybrid interbreeding programmes. In fact, reports of Reptilians, Greys and other non-human entities are not new at all. Accounts all over the world and throughout history have told of reptilian 'gods' and non-human entities or 'gods' and 'ant people' that fit the description of Greys (Fig 184). Compared with humans some Reptilians are very tall, and some Greys are very short, and this has led to tales of both 'giants' and the 'Little People'. Gnostic texts found at Nag Hammadi in 1945 say that the Archons can take a reptilian form and also a form that looks like an unborn baby or foetus with grey skin and dark, unmoving eyes. What a perfect description of the 'modern-day' Greys from texts which are estimated to have been hidden around *400AD*. I have compiled a massive amount of

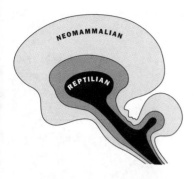

Figure 185: The R-complex or reptilian brain is central to so much human behaviour and emotional response.

information in my other books about a reptilian dimension to human manipulation, sourced from ancient and native peoples, present day research and insider whistleblowers. Accounts of Reptilians and Greys describe how they can appear and disappear (enter the human frequency range and then depart) and that they are cold, mechanical and have no empathy or conscience. The same is said of the Archons under their various names and disguises, and that's because the Reptilians and Greys involved are manifestations of the Demiurge/Archon virus/distortion. Ancient and modern accounts say Reptilians can possess human minds to control behaviour and describe how they interbred with humans to create hybrid bloodlines which are part-human and part-Reptilian (Archon virus). These are the hybrid 'elite' bloodlines that run The System to this day for the hidden Archons, but there is a reptilian dimension to all humans. The 'Icke is mad' brigade in their legions won't know that one of the most profound influences on human behaviour is the reptilian brain – what science calls the R-complex (Fig 185); or that the human embryo also goes through a reptile stage at the start of its development. Survival is the focus of the reptilian brain and it is constantly scanning the environment for potential threats to survival whether they be 'physical', financial or anything from relationships to reputation. Reptilian brain doesn't think, it reacts, often emotionally, and its currency is fear. It is heavily involved in the fight or flight response. Mainstream science says the reptilian part of the brain is responsible for the following behaviour traits:

> Cold-blooded behaviour and 'territoriality' – this is mine; a desire to control; an obsession with hierarchical structures of power; aggression, might is right and winner takes all; protecting status, power, reputation, superiority, intellectual pre-eminence and can also lead to acquiescence to hierarchy and authority.

These are also traits of the Archons/Reptilians/Greys (what a 'coincidence'). The 'They' or 'Them' working towards total control of human society are expressions of the virus, either directly or through possession. This covers the whole raft of names and manifestations from the Demiurge (prime virus) to Archons, Jinn, Demons, Flyers etc., and the Reptilians and Greys infected by the virus. For the rest of the book I will use Demiurge virus/Archon virus/Demiurge/Archons/Archon Reptilians/Reptilians/Greys as interchangeable terms because they are all either the virus itself, manifestations of the virus or infected by the virus to the point of complete control. Look again at behaviour traits of the psychopath: no empathy, remorse or shame, pathological liars (deceivers) and parasites who do whatever it takes to get their way. This is the same personality make-up as the Archon-Reptilian-Greys, and it is they who are the driving force, through possession, behind human psychopaths, satanic psychopaths and paedophile psychopaths. Staggering scales of paedophilia, especially among the perceived 'elite', are connected to this. Another common theme throughout

Figure 186: Kukulkan, another reptilian god of the Mayans in Central America.

Figure 187: A Mayan pyramid. Reptilians were the pyramid builders.

the ancient world was the interbreeding between humans and 'gods' and we see this in the Biblical texts with 'sons of God':

> There were giants in the earth in those days; and also after that, when the sons of God came in unto the daughters of men, and they bare children to them, the same became mighty men which were of old, men of renown. – Genesis 6:4

The union of humans and 'gods' is said to have spawned a hybrid race which the Bible calls 'Nephilim'. Original texts before translation referred to sons of the *gods*, plural, and to the sons of the Elohim as with 'bene ha-'elohim'. Elohim = Archons. Recurring accounts of humans interbreeding with non-human 'gods' often include reptilian themes. Legends of the African San people, or Bushmen, say humanity was created by the 'Great Python' when he arrived with a 'bag of eggs' in the Tsodilo Hills in the Kalahari Desert of Botswana. The oldest form of religious worship so far uncovered is the worship of the serpent or python going 'back' at least 70,000 years to the same Tsodilo Hills. Worship of snake and serpent 'gods' is not only incredibly old but also globally widespread. Rebecca Cann, Assistant Professor of Genetics at the University of Hawaii, was the co-author of a study published in the journal *Nature* in 1987 presenting evidence that modern humans descend from a single mother in Africa about 200,000 BC – a single mother or a single hybrid genetics programme? Zulu Chitauri 'gods' are said to be reptilian – the 'People of the Serpent' – and Mayans of Central America say the first settlers of their land were the Chanes or 'People of the Serpent' led by the god Itzamna. The name is said to derive from 'itzem' (lizard or reptile) and the sacred city of Itzamna would translate as 'the place of the lizard' or 'Iguana House' (Fig 186). Mayan legends tell of a reptilian race known as the 'Iguana Men' who came from the sky and taught them how to build pyramids (Fig 187). Reptilians were pyramid builders all over the world because of the frequency effect in suppressing Earth's energy grid. Anunnaki, an 'alien' race recorded in ancient Sumer and Babylon (present-day Iraq), were described with reptilian connotations. They were said to be led in their mission to Earth by two brothers, Enki and Enlil. Legends of the Zulu Chitauri also include two prominent reptilian brothers, Wowane and Mpanku, and are clearly based on the same story. The Biblical Garden of Eden (similar tales can be found around the world) has a serpent on centre stage with Adam and Eve and relates to the 'Fall of Man' (Fig 188). This symbolises the Archon-Reptilian infiltration of human affairs when everything

Figure 188: Versions of the Garden of Eden story can be found around the world and central to what happened is the snake or serpent.

changed and what the ancients called the Golden Age came to an end. 'Fall' refers to frequency as I will come to. Legends of Golden Age Earth could be likened to the world of the blue people, or Na'vi, portrayed in the movie *Avatar*. Humans previously had far more expanded awareness, communicated with animals and plants through conscious telepathy and knew that everything is connected to everything else. I have asked Christian believers who laugh at the idea of hidden reptilian overlords if they really believe that the serpent in the Garden of Eden was a snake that could talk. The 'Fall of Man' was discovered to be a global theme in the study of serpent worship by Reverend John Bathurst Deane who detailed his research in a 1933 book, *The Worship of the Serpent*. He found worship of reptilian gods and imagery everywhere and he wrote in conclusion:

It appears, then, that no nations were so geographically remote, or so religiously discordant, but that one – and only one – superstitious characteristic was common to all: that the most civilized and the most barbarous bowed down with the same devotion to the same engrossing deity; and that this deity either was, or was represented by, the same sacred serpent.

It appears also that in most, if not all, of the civilized countries where this serpent was worshipped, some fable or tradition which involved his history, directly or indirectly, alluded to the Fall of Man in Paradise, in which the serpent was concerned.

What follows, then, but that the most ancient account respecting the cause and nature of this seduction must be the one from which all the rest are derived which represent the victorious serpent – victorious over man in a state of innocence, and subduing his soul in a state of sin, into the most abject veneration and adoration of himself.

Legends and accounts of serpent gods can be found everywhere, most obviously in China, Japan and the Far East where the reptilian dragon is at the centre of their culture. Even the 'Devil and Satan' in the Biblical Book of Revelation is described as a dragon. People laugh at reptilian 'gods' when the evidence is there all over the world if they would only take the trouble to turn off the program long enough to do even a modicum of research.

Hive-mind humanity

Interbreeding between Archon-Reptilians and humans did not have to be through sexual procreation. You only have to observe technological techniques of today to realise what is potentially possible and this includes growing body parts in laboratories. Archon-Reptilians are way ahead of that with their knowledge of biological technology and illusory reality. They were using advanced techniques of genetic and energetic breeding and hybridisation in other realities while humans in their 'timeline' were knocking rocks together. We live in a simulated world controlled by the Demiurge/Archons and they play a role that can be compared with a computer programmer. Humans and human society are the program. Writers and programmers of videogames are obviously far more advanced in their knowledge than those in the game. Human perception of how interbreeding can happen is only human perception. Archon-Reptilians are not constrained by the limitations they impose on humanity. People think in terms of 'natural' flesh and blood, but Archon-Reptilians know what the body really is – a holographic, biological 'computer' – and they treat it as such. Biological is technological to them and when you study stories and accounts of the Archon-Reptilians in all their forms it is clear that they are obsessed with technology of all kinds. Human scientists today are working with biological technology and creating synthetic forms of biological processes. Genetic mutation

Figure 189: When genetic information is broadcast on the frequency of human DNA a mass mutation can be triggered.

of humanity could have been done collectively simply by broadcasting genetic information of the 'new human' to the DNA of the 'old human'. DNA is a receiver-transmitter of information and so is the entire body hologram and associated energetic fields. If virus-infected information and genetic blueprints were broadcast on the frequency of 'old human' DNA it would mutate the body's genetics by mutating its information field (Fig 189). A Russian research group led by biophysicist and molecular biologist Pjotr Garjajev transformed frog embryos to salamander embryos by transmitting salamander DNA information patterns. The next stage of human genetic mutation (including obesity) is being engineered today through food, drink, water additives and other chemical concoctions plus the fantastic increase in technological radiation in the atmosphere – millions of times what it was 50 years ago. What does radiation do? It mutates genetics. And what does obesity do? Limits and weakens the body and can pass the same characteristics to the next generation. Food additives are intentionally addictive – witness sugar – to keep people on a diet of poisonous, genetic-mutating shite. Archons overcome in part their lack of creative imagination through technological means. It is not a contradiction to say they don't have creativity while at the same time they deal in technology. A computer 'techy' may not be very bright and have no gift for imaginative ideas and creativity, but if he knows how something works he can appear technologically advanced and gifted to someone who may be bright and creative but knows little about computers. Take that analogy further to where access to knowledge about computers has been systemically suppressed so that the bright, creative person has never seen a computer. The not very bright techy will then appear to be a genius doing what appears to be miraculous feats. In the Kingdom of the Blind the one-eyed man is king. Archons are the one-eyed man and they have ensured that humans are blind to what is really possible. This and their secrecy are the only way they could have such power over their gifted and creative human targets (those in a non-

Phantom state). The Archon virus has piggybacked human society and knowledge to feed off the creativity of others. Humans are not the only ones subjected to Archon-Reptilian manipulation. A *Nexus* magazine article some years ago featured the work of what was claimed to be an insider revealing a secret project called the Channelled Holographic Access Network Interface, or CHANI. It described how the government-backed CHANI group had access to advanced technology located in Africa and communicated with an entity in another dimension or frequency band. Interaction/interface was said to have started in 1994 and over the next five years some 20,000 questions were asked and answered. The article included the following comments attributed to the entity:

- A reptilian race was holding back humans so they couldn't 'grow'.
- The entity's species had fought many battles against the reptile race in their own reality.
- Humans were more evolved spiritually than the reptiles but they suppress humans with their technology – 'their god is their technology'.

Whatever you may think about the CHANI article's validity what is said there is absolutely in line with what I have researched since 1990. Common themes just go on recurring. Here is another major point: Archons are not only obsessed with technology – they *are* technology in the sense that in their foundation form they are rogue information or 'error' that operates like a computer virus infesting everything it touches be it Reptilians, Greys or humans. Archon-Reptilians deal in 'technological procreation' that is far more advanced than human knowledge even at the cutting edge where scientists now seed and grow babies in laboratories, gene splice and genetically manipulate to produce offspring without sex. Researcher Mike Barrett at *Naturalsociety.com* wrote:

> Although gene-altering drugs are indeed helping to pave the way for further human genetic modification, it is only a single move in the game. Just a few months ago, we reported on the very first group of genetically modified babies being 'created' in the United States. The scientists stated that 30 babies were born using genetic modification techniques.
>
> In addition, 2 of the babies tested were found to contain genes from a total of 3 different parents. Geneticists state that this genetic modification method may one day be used to create genetically modified babies 'with extra, desired characteristics such as strength or high intelligence'.

What can be manipulated to produce 'extra, desired characteristics such as strength or high intelligence' can be employed to take them away and produce a re-wired human just intelligent enough to serve their hidden masters but not intelligent enough to see that this is what they're doing. Precisely this has happened to humanity and this was the 'Fall' instigated by the symbolic serpent in the symbolic Garden of Eden (Golden Age world before the 'Fall'). Human energy fields and therefore their holographic body counterpart were hijacked by the virus. I contend that the reptilian element of the human brain – which is crucially important in so many ways to behaviour and emotional response – was either not there at all before the genetic hijack or was very

Figure 190: Humans were genetically tuned to the Demiurge hive (virus) mind and the fake simulated reality that they still believe is real.

much less influential and significant. If you consider again behaviour traits of the reptilian brain according to mainstream science you can see the connection to behaviour traits of the Archon virus and its Reptilian agents:

Cold-blooded behaviour and 'territoriality' – this is mine; a desire to control; an obsession with hierarchical structures of power; aggression, might is right and winner takes all; protecting status, power, reputation, superiority, intellectual pre-eminence and can also lead to acquiescence to hierarchy and authority.

This is what human society has also become and has been since the Archon hijack. Archon-Reptilian genetic/energetic manipulation attached humanity to their collective mind like ants in a colony obeying the queen and to their fake reality Matrix simulation that we experience as daily 'life' (Fig 190). The reptilian aspect of the human brain is a major access point for the Archon hive mind. Don Juan Matus, the Mexican shaman quoted in the books of Carlos Castaneda, described the hijack very powerfully, as quoted in Castaneda's final book, *The Active Side of Infinity*:

We have a predator that came from the depths of the Cosmos and took over the rule of our lives. Human beings are its prisoners. The predator is our lord and master. It has rendered us docile, helpless. If we want to protest, it suppresses our protest. If we want to act independently, it demands that we don't do so ... indeed we are held prisoner!

They took us over because we are food to them, and they squeeze us mercilessly because we are their sustenance. Just as we rear chickens in coops, the predators rear us in human coops, humaneros. Therefore, their food is always available to them.

Think for a moment, and tell me how you would explain the contradictions between the intelligence of man the engineer and the stupidity of his systems of belief, or the stupidity of his contradictory behaviour. Sorcerers believe that the predators have given us our systems of beliefs, our ideas of good and evil; our social mores. They are the ones who set up our dreams of success or failure. They have given us covetousness, greed and cowardice. It is the predator who makes us complacent, routinary and egomaniacal.

In order to keep us obedient and meek and weak, the predators engaged themselves in a stupendous manoeuvre – stupendous, of course, from the point of view of a fighting strategist; a horrendous manoeuvre from the point of those who suffer it. They gave us their mind. The predators' mind is baroque, contradictory, morose, filled with the fear of being discovered any minute now.

My own research over the last 26 years supports every word. 'Food to them' is referring to human energy manipulated into low-vibrational states. 'System of beliefs' is the perception program running through Phantom Self. 'They gave us their mind' came from attaching humans to the Archon's collective mind (virus) and their fake 'Matrix' reality. Why does so much human behaviour, and especially among the 'elite' and 'leaders', imitate profusely-described traits of the Archons? You have your answer. Archon-Reptilian genetic/energetic infiltration is the means through which humans are connected to the Archon control system so they can 'give us their mind', and transhumanism is about making this connection even more extreme and total. Don Juan Matus makes the point about the predators giving us our ideas of good and evil. Adam and Eve (symbolic of virus-infected rewired humans) were said to be enticed by the serpent to eat the apple (virus) in the Garden of Eden to know good and evil. Cosmologist Carl Sagan identified the fundamental impact on human behaviour of our reptilian genetics in his book, *The Dragons of Eden*:

> It does no good whatsoever to ignore the reptilian component of human nature, particularly our ritualistic and hierarchical behaviour. On the contrary, the model may help us understand what human beings are really about.

Archon-Reptilian 'elite'

Archon predators or expressions of the virus use the modus operandi of remaining hidden while using others to do their bidding in the world of the 'seen'. Or, rather, what is seen by humans, anyway. What better way to control unmolested and unchallenged than to do so while your targets have no idea that you exist and even ridicule and abuse those who say you do? Archons are experts at deception and illusion – *phantasia*. People will ask why they don't just come out and takeover, but they can't. They are manifestations of an energetic distortion/virus and have severe limitations compared with humans in their true power and potential. Many legends speak of the predators' fear of humans should they be discovered and this is another reason they stay out of sight – at least for now. They have to so deceive humanity that we build our own prison (which we are every day), to the point of complete subjugation. Then we might openly see manifestations of the virus in form. Archons also stay hidden because of a simple law of frequency. 'They' (virus) operate primarily in a different frequency band to ours. Energetically and in most of their various forms they are not on the wavelength of our reality and nor do they sync with our atmosphere. They need far more radiation than we do, and this is the real background to why the Earth's atmosphere is being so massively irradiated through technology. The virus needs power which it cannot generate itself (hence humans being its 'batteries') and it can draw this power from states of high radiation. Fukushima, which has been emitting staggering levels of radiation since the nuclear meltdowns of 2011, was an accident? Sure it was – see *Remember Who You Are* and *The Perception Deception*. Some expressions of the Archon virus can enter our reality of visible light, and ancient and modern witnesses have claimed to have seen them. They appear in myths and legends about visitations by

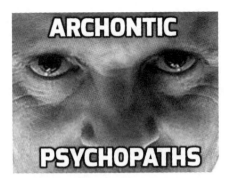

Figure 191: What we call psychopaths are those infused with the Demiurge/Archon virus to extreme levels.

Figure 192: Archon-human hybrids are the middle men and women that represent the Demiurge agenda within the human frequency range.

'aliens' or 'gods'; but they can't stay for long before they have to depart. It's a similar principle to people only being able to stay a short time in radiation fields during nuclear leaks before they have to leave to protect their health (it's often too late even then). Demiurge/Archons overcame these limitations by engineering particular hybrid bloodlines (biological computer programs) that I will call variously the 'Elite', Archon bloodlines, Archon-Reptilian bloodlines and the hybrids. These represent Archon interests and plans within the human frequency band, and they are genetic (information) constructs specifically designed to be vehicles for the Demiurge virus and therefore they behave as the virus does. There are different levels of virus infiltration, which are reflected in how much people are influenced by Infinite Awareness. You have those with expanded awareness who can override much (rarely all) of the impact of Phantom Self and the virus; those with Phantom Self in overwhelming control of perception (majority); Phantom Self in total control (psychopaths); and 'Elite' bloodlines who are Archons incarnate – super-psychopaths (Fig 191).

I can best symbolise the role of the hybrid bloodlines with the analogy of a scientist working in a laboratory with material too dangerous to touch directly. The material is placed in a sealed tank and the scientist stands outside with his arms in long gloves that allow him or her to work inside while standing outside (Fig 192). If you think of the scientist as the Demiurge/Archons, the tank as our reality and the gloves as these Elite bloodlines you have the picture. They are the middle 'men and women' or conduits for control between the hidden Archons and the target human population, and they are manipulated into the positions of power that run The System. Elite hybrids have a greater infusion of Archon-Reptilian energy/genetics (virus) and exhibit those character traits far more than the general population. Duel virus-human DNA (frequency compatibility) allows them to be far more powerfully and completely possessed, and their behaviour and actions controlled to a greater degree. Swiss clairvoyant, Anton Styger, said the following in an interview about his life. This was not related to what I am setting out in this book, he was merely describing some of his experiences:

When I see people in business or politics who are particularly trapped by the material world, for example, I notice that they no longer have any light bodies at all [soul]. In many of these people, the point of light at the heart chakra, which is otherwise always present, is no longer visible to me.

Instead, I see something like a layer of 'shiny tar' around them in which a monstrous being in the shape of a lizard can be distinguished. When such people speak on television, for example, I see a crocodile shape manifesting itself around the person like in a concave mirror; I don't see the light of their throat and forehead chakra.

Figure 193: The world is controlled and directed by Archon-Reptilian human hybrids and their agents and gofers.

As a result of this possession our world is run by psychopaths, parasites and pathological liars (deceivers) who have no empathy, remorse or shame. Put those characteristics together along with the reptilian obsession with hierarchical structures of power and you have the very personalities that have come to power all over the world creating war, division, mayhem, death, destruction and terror throughout known human history (Fig 193). These horrors have been engineered by Archon bloodlines to serve the plan for total human control and to ensure that energetic 'lunch' is always served. Archon-Reptilian hybrids can shapeshift between human and reptilian (and other) forms through their duel DNA (human and Archon-Reptilian information fields). When they switch from one field to the other they appear to an observer to change or shift from one form to another, but there is no physical shift because there is no physical. The non-human energetic field overrides the human one and an observer experiences this as a physical shift; but it's all happening in the observer's decoding processes – their own brain (Fig 194). I

Figure 194: An apparently 'physical' shapeshift only happens within the decoding processes of the observer. It is really a shift in energetic information.

have covered this subject in depth in other books, along with relating experiences of people who have seen this happen. American researcher Stewart Swerdlow learned about the reptilian/non-human control system in the years that he was held captive in the American government-military mind control programme at Montauk on Long Island, New York (see *The Perception Deception*). He says that Archon-Reptilian 'geneticists' are ideally seeking a 50-50 ratio between human and Reptilian genetics to produce agents-in-form that look human but can shapeshift by 'concentrating [intent] on the genetics the hybrid wants to open, or lock up, whatever the case may be'. Stability of the human field can be disturbed when the energetic balance moves too far to the Archon-Reptilian side, and also by states of extreme anger and fury that generate a powerful electrical charge and can cause an unwanted 'shift'. I have spoken with people around the world who have witnessed a human shifting into a reptilian form in a moment of extreme rage.

Hybrid blood drinkers

Drinking copious amounts of human blood, which contains the human genetic (information) blueprint, is one way they can be sure to retain human form when they are not among their own. This is the origin of vampire legends and blood drinking rituals of Satanism. The most infamous blood-drinking vampire was the mass human-sacrificing Vlad the Impaler, the 15th century ruler of Wallachia (now part of Romania). This land is, of course, the home of so many vampire legends, especially the region of Transylvania. Bram

Figure 195: Vlad the Impaler would torture people to death on stakes and drink their blood.

Stoker's stories about the shapeshifting, blood-drinking Dracula were inspired by the life of Vlad the Impaler (Fig 195). Vlad's title comes from the mass murder of thousands of people, often impaled on stakes. He would drink their blood as they slowly died all around him. Decaying corpses (Death Cult again) were everywhere. His father, Vlad Dracul, was initiated into the ancient Order of the Dragon by the Holy Roman Emperor in 1431 and this is one of the elite secret societies of the Archon-Reptilian bloodlines. Secret societies by their very nature are there to keep secrets, and within the exclusive inner circles the biggest secret is Archon-Reptilian control of human reality. The Order of the Dragon emblem has a dragon, wings extended, hanging on a cross. The winged dragon symbolises Archon-Reptilian 'royalty' (it's all hierarchy) known in the extraterrestrial research community as the 'Draco'. Many are albino-white and have a tail just as the 'Devil' is portrayed with wings and tail. 'Draconian' is the word used to describe merciless laws and tyranny and could not be more appropriate. Vlad the Impaler signed his name Draculea or Draculya – the 'Devil's Son' – and from

Figure 196: Mary of Teck, the Queen's grandmother, is descended from the family of Vlad the Impaler. The British royal family is descended from one of history's most infamous human sacrificers and blood drinkers? Surely not.

this came Bram Stoker's Dracula which translates, in theme at least, to 'Son of He who had the Order of the Dragon'. Archon bloodlines incessantly and obsessively interbreed to keep their hybrid genetics intact and it is no coincidence whatsoever that Queen

Figure 197: Prince Charles and his ancestor Vlad the Impaler. They both share a love for the land that includes Transylvania and what else one wonders?

Mary, or Mary of Teck, grandmother to the present Elizabeth II, was descended from the family of Vlad the Impaler or 'Dracula' (Fig 196). We would expect this to be the case given that the British 'royal' family, or House of Windsor, are an Archon-Reptilian duel-DNA bloodline. I have been exposing them for two decades as shapeshifting human-sacrificing Satanists in books like *The Biggest Secret, Human Race Get Off Your Knees* and *The Perception Deception*. I have naturally been ridiculed by Phantom Self media and masses, but it's the truth all the same. Prince Charles is a descendant of Vlad the Impaler through his mother and he has acknowledged this ancestral connection. He has been buying property in Transylvania where he seems to turn up quite regularly (Fig 197). Going home, Charlie? The Bush family in the United States is also related to Vlad the Impaler. You see the pattern and get my drift. I quote at length in those earlier books Christine Fitzgerald, a long-time close friend of Princess Diana. Christine was one of the people who described to me the reptilian nature of the royals and their participation in satanic rituals. Diana was well aware that the Windsors were not what they appeared to be, but who was she going to tell without being considered insane? Christine Fitzgerald said this of the late Queen Mother (when she was still alive) and the royal family in general:

The Queen Mother ... now that's a serious piece of wizardry. The Queen Mother is a lot older than people think. To be honest, the Royal Family hasn't died for a long time, they have just metamorphosised. It's sort of cloning, but in a different way. They take pieces of flesh and rebuild the body from one little bit. Because it's lizard, because it's cold-blooded, it's much easier for them to do Frankenstein shit than it is for us. The different bodies are just different electrical vibrations and they have got that secret, they've got the secret of the micro-currents, it's so micro, so specific, these radio waves that actually create the bodies [holograms].

They know the vibration of life and because they are cold-blooded, they are reptiles, they have no wish to make the Earth the perfect harmony it could be, or to heal the Earth from the damage that's been done. The Earth's been attacked for zeons by different extraterrestrials. It's been like a football for so long. This place was a bus stop for many different aliens. All these aliens, they could cope with everything, including the noxious gases. They're landing all the time and coming up from the bowels of the Earth.

They looked like reptiles originally, but they look like us when they get out now through the electrical vibration, that life key I talked about [holographic manipulation]. They can manifest how they want to. All the real knowledge has been taken out and shredded and put back in another way. The Queen Mother is 'Chief Toad' of this part of Europe and they have people like her in each continent. Most people, the hangers on, don't know, you know, about the reptiles. They are just in awe of these people because they are so powerful.

Figure 198: The Queen Mother – anything but the 'nation's grandmother'. Pure evil.

Figure 199: The Demiurge right to rule.

Christine Fitzgerald is just one of my sources for the reptilian hybrid background of royalty – and not just British royalty, either. Diana privately described the Queen Mother to Christine Fitzgerald as 'evil' while the 'Queen Mum' was portrayed to the public as a kind old lady and the 'nation's grandmother' (Fig 198). No wonder Diana was taken out in the Paris crash, given that she knew symbolically and literally where the royal bodies were buried, and was showing every sign that she was quite prepared to take them on. You'll find far more detail in *The Perception Deception* and *The Biggest Secret* and I will return to the Queen and the royal family when I come to the section on Satanism and its essential contribution to human control. I also address the assassination of Diana in *The Biggest Secret*. Archon-Reptilian human hybrids are the origin of the global theme of 'royal' bloodlines claiming the 'Divine right to rule'. This really means their genetic connection to the Archon-Reptilian 'gods' they were created to serve, as vehicles for the virus (Fig 199). Elite hybrid bloodlines (programs) were installed all over the world to rule humanity on behalf of the Demiurge/Archons and the 'Divine Right' deal spans the globe from Europe to China, Middle East to Far East and Africa to the Americas. Chinese emperors claimed the right to rule through their descent from the 'serpent gods'. Many emperors were called dragons and described in reptilian terms as in a 'dragon-like countenance'. Dragon/serpent/snake symbolism for royalty or kingship is universal and can be found in Celtic society with Pendragon ('Great Dragon', or 'King of Kings'). The *Book of Dzyan*, one of the oldest Sanskrit accounts in India, refers to a reptilian race called the Sarpa, or Great Dragons, which came from the skies. A Buddhist text, the *Mahauyutpatti*, lists 80 kings descended from the Nagas, or 'Serpent Kings', and Indian rulers claimed their right to power through their descent from the Nagas who were said to shift between human and reptilian form. Indian epics say the Nagas interbred with a white people to become the 'royal' line of Aryan kings. A cobra is an ancient symbol of Archon-Reptilian hybrids. Egyptian Pharaohs were buried in caskets with a headdress representing the hood of the cobra, a cobra body protruding from the chin and a cobra on the forehead (Fig 200). Jinn is the Islamic and pre-Islamic name for Archons, and is also spelt Djinn. Dj in Egyptian was a designation that meant serpent, and we have Pharaohs such as Djer, Djoser and Djederfra. There was also an Egyptian order called the Djedhi (Jedi?). Britain's

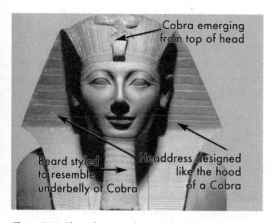

Cobra emerging from top of head

Beard styled to resemble underbelly of Cobra

Headdress designed like the hood of a Cobra

Figure 200: Pharaohs were decorated with reptilian imagery.

Coronation ritual to crown the monarch is based on those of Egyptian pharaohs (from which much Hebrew ritual came). Oil still used in British Coronations today is symbolic of the fat from the Nile crocodile that was part of the Pharaohic ceremonies. Moche was a ceremonial title in Egypt which meant something close to 'He who is anointed with crocodile fat from the Nile River'. Fat from the Nile crocodile, or 'Messeh', led to the term 'messiah' or 'anointed one'. The Biblical 'Moses' (who was found 'floating on the Nile in a basket') comes from 'Moshe'. Ancient kings of Media (now Iran and part of Turkey) were called 'Mar' (snake in Persian) and known as the 'Dragon Dynasty of Media' or 'descendants of the dragon'. On and on it goes. Royal Archon-Reptilian hybrids were perceived as the chosen rulers of the 'gods' and their power came from *genetic* inheritance (vehicles for the virus). A perception of royal bloodlines as the middle men and women between humans and the 'gods' has the same origins as priests being the middle men and women (sometimes) between humans and 'God'. Archon-Reptilian royalty and aristocracy are often called 'bluebloods'. Stewart Swerdlow says that he learned in the Montauk mind control programme that the term blueblood relates to the increased amount of copper in the blood of hybrids which makes it turn a blue-green colour in a process called oxidation.

Hybrid hierarchy

Rule by hybrid bloodline is still going on today with regard to British and other surviving 'royal' families, but this has now expanded into politics, banking, corporations and The System in general. The Windsor clan have the constitutional right to be Head of State for no other reason than their genetics and family

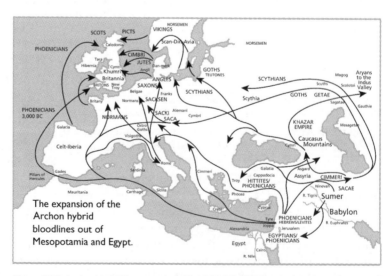

The expansion of the Archon hybrid bloodlines out of Mesopotamia and Egypt.

Figure 201: Archon hybrids expanded out of the Middle East and Asia to take control of Europe and eventually the Americas and elsewhere.

history. We have a Head of State in Britain decided by who had sex with whom, and when to dictate the hierarchical genetic succession. This has been going on for aeons since the Archon virus hijack and the seeding of their hybrid middle men and women. Some of the most significant hybrids came out of Sumer, Babylon and Egypt in the Middle East and earlier from Asia and the Far East. They expanded north to interbreed (share the 'elite' version of the virus) with other Archon-Reptilian hybrids to become kings and queens of Europe (Fig 201). Empires followed the bloodlines as you would expect as representatives of a force seeking to take over (infect with their virus) everything, everyone and everywhere. The Babylonian Empire became the Roman Empire as the bloodlines expanded, then the British and other European Empires. Today, with the bloodlines long established in North America, we have the American Empire in everything but name. All these empires have been empires of the Archon virus and they were the means through which ever-larger swathes of the Earth have been stolen and controlled. From pharaohs to tribal kings, Chinese emperors to European royalty and aristocracy, Archons have ruled while hiding behind human form. You can see why they have been so diligent in protecting their genetics (virus blueprint) by interbreeding only with each other and not with the 'commoners'. This has clearly not been done to somehow maintain their superior 'intelligence' when some of the thickest people in history have been interbred royals. No, it's been to maintain something else – their hybrid genetics. Even when it appears that a commoner has been allowed into their exclusive genetic circle, as with the marriage of Kate Middleton to Prince William in 2011, further research into family backgrounds of alleged 'outsiders' reveals highly significant royal and aristocratic ancestry. There is also an Archon-Reptilian sperm bank programme that has been revealed to me by a number of people, including an unofficial offspring of the seriously Archontic Rothschild family. This allows children of Elite bloodlines to be brought up by other families using the sperm bank technique. These children then come through to be political leaders and other servants of The System, but they don't have the name 'Rothschild' or whatever Elite family their bloodline belongs to, so the common connections can't be easily seen. There are enormous numbers of unofficial Rothschilds alone who do not carry the name but have the *bloodline* and are vehicles for the same Archon virus. All this is necessary because the hybrid genetic program can quickly be diluted and absorbed into the general population if it is fused with those not of the Archon-Reptilian line. Most royal marriages don't result from love or even attraction, but from genetic necessity. Many of their relationships are conducted outside of marriage, and Prince Charles is a classic case with regard to Princess Diana (genetic duty) and Camilla Parker-Bowles (desired relationship). A human genetic type that Archon-Reptilians most seek to interbreed with when they require an infusion of human genetics are blue-eyed, blond-haired people. Diana's friend Christine Fitzgerald told me that the Windsors needed Diana's genetic input because after generations of interbreeding their hybrid genetics were in danger of becoming so reptilian that their human form would be hard to maintain.

'Royal' dark suits

European empires spanned the world and the Archon control agenda was imposed wherever they went. The British Empire was by far the most significant as the British Isles became one of the most powerful Archon bloodline centres on Earth – and remains so. I am not referring to the British government, which is just another Archon front and lackey, no matter what person or party is officially in power. I mean at the level of the global Archon secret society network, or the Hidden Hand behind world events that manipulates Archon bloodlines and their gofers into power. I'll be explaining how this web of deceit functions and operates. Archon bloodline connections and its location on the Earth energy grid together make the British Isles so important to the global network. All was fine with Archon royal tyrannies until people began to rebel and demanded a greater say in was being done and decided. This was potentially lethal to Archon hybrid omnipotence, but calls for people power and 'democracy' in post-royal

Figure 202: Changing the President is only changing the mask.

societies were thwarted by creating a top-down hierarchy of political power with the population sold the myth that a vote every four or five years can significantly impact upon the direction of the world and the lives of the 'free' voters. Today there can surely be no one with eyes even partially open who can't see that no matter which person or 'party' is theoretically elected the incessant direction doesn't change. We can at least thank Boy Bush and Barack Obama for the most blatant confirmation of this. Bush was replaced by 'Mr Change' Obama and everything continued with business as usual (Fig 202). Hybrid bloodlines mostly swapped their crowns and coronets for dark suits and became unofficial kings, queens and princes of the political and financial classes along with those behind big business, science, medicine and media. In doing so they replaced overt royal (Archon) dictatorship with a covert dark suit (Archon) dictatorship called 'democracy' which comes from the ancient Greek 'demos' (people) and 'kratos' (rule). We can see how this really works in present-day Greece with the European Union and international bankers running the country without any 'people rule' except as irrelevant, diversionary window dressing. 'Democracy' is based on promoting dictatorship as free choice. Key to this was not to have truly independent individual would-be politicians elected to govern, but political parties. These are more hierarchies controlled by the few at the top. To be successful in almost any major political election you need to join a party to be given any effective promotion, funding and media coverage. To be selected to represent a party you need satisfy its hierarchy that you will toe the party line because, after all, you are not representing the electorate, but the party (those who control the party). To progress up the ranks to be a minister, Prime Minister or President you have to obey the dictates of the party and its hierarchy or – except in the rarest of circumstances – you have *no chance*. How many genuine people who don't lie through their teeth as a matter of course ever get into high political office? Each party is a hierarchical pyramid of top-down control with the few sitting at the capstone calling the shots and representing (most unknowingly) the interests of the Archon control system. Crucial to the public falling for the 'democracy' scam is that they are manipulated to believe that each party – usually two or maximum three with any chance of forming a government – represent a different choice in how the country is run. Unless people think they are able to make a choice there can be no credibility for

Figure 203: Vote for me – I'm different to them.   **Figure 204:** Democracy at work.

democracy, and different masks on the same face is not choice. Increasing numbers are now losing faith in the political system as the realisation dawns that there is no choice – 'it doesn't matter who you vote for they're all the bloody same'. They *are* the same in overall outcome if not every detail and it has been made to be that way (Fig 203). 'New' parties may appear every now and then but they are soon absorbed by The System to become a duplicate of the ones they were apparently created to challenge. Now, here's a big penny-dropper. The System is a manifestation of the Archon virus and when we talk about once independent-minded people and organisations being absorbed by The System what is really happening is that they are absorbed (infected) by the virus which The System represents. How many times do you see people go into politics with apparently good intent but ending up as the epitome of what they set out to change? Neil Kinnock, the former Labour Party leader in Britain, comes to mind but there are legions of others all over the world. Alexis Tsipras came to power as Prime Minister in Greece pledging to stand firm against the imposition of crushing austerity on Greek people by the European Union, European Central Bank and International Monetary Fund (IMF), in the wake of the engineered debt crisis. Greeks voted 62 percent in a referendum called by Tsipras in favour of rejecting the EU/ECB/IMF economic war against them, but his former finance minister Yanis Varoufakis said Tsipras decided on the night of that referendum to surrender to the psychopaths and bullies on terrible terms for Greek people despite all the rhetoric and bullshit. What followed was an attempt to purge his party of all those who were saying what he had been saying before his capitulation to The System. What happened next? He was voted back into power (Fig 204). The speed of the Tsipras integrity-bypass was fast even for politics, but his submission to the will of The System is the norm. Politics is a construct of the virus and if you don't stay true to your values when you enter its lair the virus will overwhelm you until 'you' are not you anymore. There are few places on Earth where you are more in danger of perception possession than the centres of government where the Archon virus is playing at home.

All major political parties and most of the smaller ones are controlled by the same force – the virus in its various guises. Humanity's top-down hierarchical royal, political, religious and corporate power structure is a holographic reflection of the Archontic royal-type hierarchy in the unseen, with the Demiurge (prime virus) at its peak. The

Figure 205: Hierarchy of fear from the unseen into human society at every level. The reason for Saturn in this image will become clear.

System is an expression in the 'seen' of an interdimensional control structure with its centre of power in the unseen (Fig 205). Human control comes from both Archon hybrid personnel and the strait jacket of programmed perception and possibility ingrained by a life in the Archon-created Mainstream Everything. Add to this the need to attract votes from a population overwhelmingly programmed by Mainstream Everything to fear anything different or new directions, and breaking through The System politically is impossible when politics *is* The System. Political parties today in terms of policy and perspective are pretty much herded together on the same tiny postage stamp or 'political consensus' (Archon agenda). This is the programmed political and economic 'norm' and anyone challenging that norm is by definition perceived and portrayed as an 'extremist' and usually a dangerous one. Differences between parties and political allegiances are fractional to say the least, with the alleged political polarities ('extremes') serving the same System while only appearing to be at odds with each other. We saw a slightly different approach in the election of a new leader for the UK opposition Labour Party in 2015 in the form of Jeremy Corbyn, and that was good in that he has a sense of compassion and decency, which his political opponents lack; but in the end he's still The System in another form. All politicians are. Political 'polarities' fighting for power and prominence can't see they are all representing the interests of the same Archontic

Figure 206: Perfect summary of the political system. Don't like us? Vote for them. Don't like them? Vote for us. Don't like either? Too bad.

agenda for human control. One party may say more taxation and another less taxation; but they all believe in *taxation*, which is the key means together with banking for the Archon virus to vampire the labour and creative imagination of the human population. They may slightly disagree over ways to tinker with The System but they all accept The System as the norm from which they see and judge everything. Once you hand political power to two or three parties it means that political 'choice' is confined to voting for one or the other. If you don't like what Party A does in government you can only remove them

Figure 207: Hillary Clinton: 'Woman of the People' (or rather those who own her). I say 'soul' but hybrids don't have one.

by voting for Party B. If Party B doesn't do any better you can only remove them by returning to Party A (Fig 206). In some countries there might be a Party C, but the principle is still the same. Politics and government are *Archon* politics and government – government of Phantom Self, by Phantom Self, for the enslavement of Phantom Self. But it goes much further and deeper. Parties are only one level of the Archon political control system orchestrated within our reality by Archon bloodlines. America serves as an example of the next level of the rabbit hole. The Republican Party at the time of Boy Bush was (and still is) controlled by an unelected cabal known as the Neocons or neoconservatives who were behind the invasions of Afghanistan and Iraq and much else besides. I'll be saying more later about them and their connection to 9/11. The Democratic Party has a similar controlling cabal that I call the Democons, and they are the real power behind whoever may be a Democrat president, be it Obama, a Clinton, or whoever (Fig 207). At the next level the Neocons and Democons themselves both answer to the *same* masters in the shadows (Fig 208). At this level Republicans and Democrats (political 'choice') are controlled by the *same* force and no matter who

WORLD STAGE

Figure 208: All parties with any chance of forming a government ultimately answer to the same masters.

Figure 209: Go deep enough into the shadows and you'll find that all major political parties and most of the smaller ones are doing the bidding of the same force although the vast majority of those involved will have no idea that this is so.

is theoretically in office the Archons are always in office. Thus the same agenda and direction unfolds whoever is in perceived 'power' (Fig 209). This is the political structure in virtually *every* country and most certainly the major ones in the Americas, Europe, Asia and wherever 'democracy' has installed itself – Australia and New Zealand included (Fig 210). Countries are now themselves being absorbed into bigger groupings such as the European Union, trade zones and trade agreements which are handing power to ever fewer people to dictate the lives of ever more. National governments are becoming mere administrative units for Archon superstates, super trade areas and Rothschild-Rockefeller (Archon bloodline)-created non-governmental dictatorships such as the World Trade Organization and the World Health

Figure 210: The Archon-Reptilian structure of power.

Organization where global trade and heath (death) policy is dictated from under one roof. These are all manifestations of the virus spreading. American Freedom campaigner John Whitehead of the Rutherford Institute correctly said: 'Politics is a game, a joke, a hustle, a con, a distraction, a spectacle, a sport, and for many devout Americans, a religion.' Not only in America, either – everywhere. Whitehead goes on:

> ... it's a sophisticated ruse aimed at keeping us divided and fighting over two parties whose priorities are exactly the same. It's no secret that both parties support endless war, engage in out-of-control spending, ignore the citizenry's basic rights, have no respect for the rule of law, are bought and paid for by Big Business, care most about their own power, and have a long record of expanding government and shrinking liberty.

> Most of all, both parties enjoy an intimate, incestuous history with each other and with the moneyed elite that rule this country. Don't be fooled by the smear campaigns and name-calling. They're just useful tactics of the psychology of hate that has been proven to engage voters and increase voter turnout while keeping us at each other's throats.

The Archon virus has been able to advance its agenda for the constant centralisation of power in all areas of human life with its hybrids and their agents and gofers secure in key positions of global decision-making and influence (Fig 211). Power centralisation has been essential to the Archon hijack. Decision-making diversity means you have far less potential for any cabal at the

Figure 211: You see what you get – but not where it's coming from.

centre to seize total power. They can't control what is being decided in so many places by so many people. Here you have the reason behind centralisation and the war on diversity worldwide. Archon hybrids and their global secret society networks have incessantly centralised power for thousands of years as former tribes were brought together into nations and now nations are merging into superstates and 'trade' (external control) groups. 'Globalisation' is only a name for Archon global centralisation of control through a structure of a planned world government, world central bank, world

'WHEN CHOOSING THE LESSER OF TWO EVILS, ALWAYS REMEMBER, IT IS STILL AN EVIL.'
- MAX LERNER
DAVIDICKE.COM

Figure 212: Great advice.

single electronic currency and world army, which would delete even the current illusion of democracy and bring full- blown, you-can't-miss-it Orwellian global tyranny. I say illusion of democracy in the sense that democracy is believed to be interchangeable with 'free' and 'freedom' when it is only another form of top-down tyranny. Communism and Fascism are perceived as opposites when in terms of controlling and dictating the lives of the populous they are the same. Beware the constant mind-trick of portraying as opposites what I call oppos*sames*. They portray two versions of the same thing as proof that you have choice (Fig 212). A world government and other global institutions and agencies, including a World Supreme Court, are planned by Archons and their hybrids to enforce their fascist decisions on the masses through a vicious and merciless police state with 24/7 surveillance of everyone and everything down to the finest detail. Crazy? It's *happening*. I have been predicting and warning about this for decades and now you can clearly see this coming together by the day. It's advance is ever-quickening because the more you centralise power the more power you have at the centre to centralise even faster. 'World leaders' (Archon hybrids and their gofers) appear to be arguing and fighting among themselves and some of this does genuinely go on. Archon hybrids have an insatiable desire for power and control (it's a virus!) at whatever level it may operate; but the inner core of Archon control ensures that their conflicts and ambitions don't get in the way of the 'Great Work' (as the Freemasons call it) of total human subjugation. Indeed the squabbles, many for public consumption only, act as a smokescreen for common goals and connections coordinated from the shadows. Gofers to the major players don't even know about the Archons or their plans and they are pawns in a game they don't understand. What seem to be random events are actually coldly and carefully instigated to trigger changes that expand Archon control. Some leaders in the public eye know this while many have themselves been fooled, deceived and blinded by a desire for power and status, and will do whatever the Hidden Hand demands in return. Others are compromised into acquiescence by dark secrets they are desperate to hide often in relation to sexual abuse of children. Why do some politicians and parties attract enormous sums in contributions from Archon assets and corporations and others do not? It's because those politicians will do what the major contributors demand for their money – serving the interests of the virus in its endless forms. Money talks throughout The System, not least in politics, and Archon bloodlines have the money for reasons I will explain.

We are seeing – in terms of personnel and structures of global control, wars, division, suffering and injustice – a holographic manifestation of the virus replicating itself and expanding control over the operating system or Matrix simulation which humanity believes to be real. And, to that, I will now turn.

CHAPTER FIVE

Archon Matrix

... You are a slave, Neo. Like everyone else you were born into bondage ... a prison that you cannot taste or see or touch. A prison for your mind
Morpheus in *The Matrix*

We are now going into the deepest depths of deceit to see why this quote from the first of the *Matrix* movies delivers such a fundamental truth. We live not only in a simulation, but one specifically designed to enslave us by hijacking our perception and sense of reality.

The alternative media often uses the term 'Matrix' for the web of political and financial manipulation, but I'm talking about a Matrix that can be likened to the one portrayed in the movie trilogy – a fake reality to entrap and control the entire human race in a prison of the mind. Phantom Self is crucial to its success. I have described how reality we think is so 'solid' and 'real' is actually an interactive information construct which can be equated to a computer simulation, a virtual reality game that we decode into a holographic (illusory physical) world. Unless people appreciate this fact they will never understand what we call human life. There are endless simulated realities within Infinite Possibility through which Infinite Awareness can experience itself. Silas Beane, the Associate Professor of Physics who leads the simulation study at the University of Bonn, said:

> The idea is that in future, humans will be able to simulate entire universes quite easily. And given the vastness of time ahead, the number of these simulations is likely to be huge. So if you ask the question: 'Do we live in the one true reality or in one of the many simulations?', the answer, statistically speaking, is that we're more likely to be living in a simulation.

An article in *Scientific American* relating black holes to computers said:

> ... the Universe is computing itself. Powered by Standard Model software, the Universe computes quantum fields, chemicals, bacteria, human beings, stars and galaxies. As it computes, it maps out its own spacetime geometry to the ultimate precision allowed by the laws of physics [click, click, enter]. Computation is existence.

Well, it is on one level. I have contended for many years that we live in a highly-advanced computer simulation and confirmation of this comes from both ancient and modern sources. Common themes are everywhere. Eastern religions call the 'physical' world 'Maya' or illusion, and the Gnostic Nag Hammadi texts describe it as 'Hal' or 'simulation' – what is known today as virtual reality. John Lamb Lash summarises the Gnostic 'Hal' in his book, *Not In His Image*, using information from the Nag Hammadi texts:

> Although they cannot originate anything, because they lack the divine factor of ennoia (intentionality), Archons can imitate with a vengeance. Their expertise is simulation (HAL, virtual reality). The Demiurge fashions a heaven world copied from the fractal patterns of the eternal Aeons, the Pleromic gods who reside in the galactic centre. His construction is celestial kitsch, like the fake Italianate villa of a Mafia don complete with militant angels to guard every portal.

I will come to the significance of 'fractal patterns' very shortly. Reality that we know as 'the world', the 'real' one that we think we experience as 'solid', is really Archon Hal – a fake simulation specifically imposed to entrap our perceptions for the purpose of ongoing control. Gnostics believed that the material world (simulation) was the work of the Demiurge and not the transcendent 'god' or Infinite Awareness of which we are all an expression. They said that humans were sparks or droplets of the same 'god' but had become trapped in the illusion of physicality. They said the 'Fall of Man' was the fall into matter (a low-frequency state). Gnostics believed that 'sin' was caused by ignorance of our true nature. This fits 100 percent with my own writings over the years, and the 'Fall' was the point when the simulation was imposed to entice human perception into low-frequency states. Nag Hammadi texts describe how the Demiurge/Archons created our 'physical' reality by making a 'bad copy' of the world that humans had known before. I have seen the 'physical' world described as the 'earth plane' and this is apt given that the word 'plane' comes from a Greek term meaning 'error' or 'going astray'. Gnostic texts describe the Demiurge as an 'error'. The Demiurge/Archon self-aware virus made a distorted bad copy (think low-res version) of what existed before and still exists in much higher frequencies elsewhere (Fig 213). Ridiculous? Not possible? Making copies is what even basic technological viruses do. They are 'a piece of code which is capable of copying itself and typically has a detrimental effect, such as corrupting the system or destroying data'. The Archon virus is more than just a computer virus – it is a *self-aware* virus and thus capable of

Figure 213: Bad copy reality – a download of information patterns and codes.

Figure 214: Bad copy Earth was originally a copy of something beautiful, but the process began to turn the bad copy into the Archon world.

Figure 215: High-frequency Earth is manifested from information codes just like ours ...

Figure 216: ... but the codes of bad copy Earth were of a lower frequency and infused with the Demiurge/Archon virus. Human life and perception changed dramatically.

far more. The Demiurge/Archons could not create a new simulation from scratch because they lack *ennoia* or creative imagination and they operate like a counterfeiter making illegal copies of computer games. They can't make the game itself but they can make a copy. Our reality is a 'downloaded' copy of our original reality. Both are illusions in terms of 'physical form', but they come from fundamentally different intent. Bad copy it may have been but it was a bad copy at first of something wonderful. High-frequency Earth is a place of love, harmony and heightened expanded awareness (hence the 'Golden Age' legends) and the Demiurge/Archons have worked and manipulated ever since to twist and distort the bad copy to infuse their own in-built distortion – to infest it ever more deeply with their virus in other words. Our version of Earth is so similar in many ways to high-frequency Earth from which the copy was made but so different when it comes to the experience (Fig 214). Low-frequency Earth is the realm of the Archon virus and has increasingly represented Archon character traits described in terms such as psychopathic; no empathy, remorse or shame; parasites; and pathological liars (deceivers). The life, vibrancy and beauty of original Earth is being systematically destroyed to match the Archon inversion of death, destruction and ugliness. In computer language they 'corrupted the system' and destroyed or blocked data. 'Physical' worlds or simulations are different information blueprints and sources. The difference between original

Earth and bad copy Earth is only the information being decoded by the observer. Bad copy has a much lower frequency and genetic manipulation of the human body-computer was to tune hijacked humanity to the bad copy frequency and information source. This was the 'Fall' (Figs and 215 and 216). I know it may sound like madness at first hearing to Phantom Self, but it's all perfectly possible when viewed from reality as it really is. Whatever world of form we are talking about, it is a simulation in the widest sense – an interactive, virtual reality 'computer game' in which the game affects the players and the players affect the game. Enlightened and aware players produce a very different game to the systematically ignorant and suppressed. Compare players in the football World Cup with those playing in the park on Sunday morning after a night out at the pub. They are playing the same game in a completely different way. People think nothing of clicking 'copy' to download whole websites (realities) from the Internet because this is familiar to them and within their concept of 'normal'; but if you had said this was possible 100 or 200 years ago you would have been called insane and delirious. 'Normal' (as always) is only a perspective, not a truth. To Archon technological awareness taking a copy of a simulation is like downloading a computer game to us.

A matter of fractals

The John Lash quote based on Gnostic texts said: 'The Demiurge fashions a heaven world copied from the fractal patterns ... ' It is therefore highly significant to note that fractal patterns can be found throughout nature (the simulation) and follow the 'as above, so below' principle of holograms. One explanation at *Fractalfoundation.org* says 'a fractal is a never-ending pattern ... infinitely complex [and] self-similar across different scales ... [they are] created by repeating a simple process over and over in an ongoing feedback loop.' Trees are 'self-similar' fractal patterns in that small branches take the same form as bigger ones, and fractals can also be generated by computers (Figs 217, 218 and 219). Our simulated reality is founded on fractal patterns of information distribution and these are just a few examples identified as having such patterns:

River networks, fault lines, mountain ranges, craters, lightning bolts, coastlines, mountain goat horns, trees, animal colour patterns, pineapples, DNA, heart rates, heartbeats, neurons and brains, eyes, respiratory systems, circulatory systems, blood vessels and pulmonary vessels, geological fault lines, earthquakes, snowflakes, psychological subjective perception, crystals,

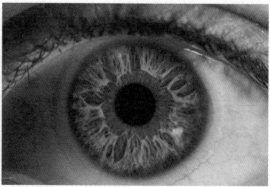

Figure 217: Fractal patterns in Romanesco broccoli.   **Figure 218:** Repeating fractal patterns can be seen in eyes.

Figure 219: Fractals can also be computer-generated.

ocean waves, vegetables, soil pores and the rings of Saturn [very significant shortly].

Fractals have been described as 'a literal web of life' and I would say an 'information web of the simulation'. They are found in patterns of *perception* and even in the patterns of language and speech. It's all a program and the simulation programs *everything* for those who have not expanded their awareness to override the program and see beyond it. *Psychologytoday.com* reported research at Cambridge University into the fractal nature of the brain and how this 'may help to connect us in a very fundamental way to the rest of the natural world.' Everything is connected both as Infinite Awareness and in our reality through the holographic-fractal information web. David Pincus, an American psychology professor, said this about the Cambridge findings:

In the past 10 to 20 years, researchers in psychology have been finding increasing examples of fractal patterns across each of the domains of psychology: Including intentional behaviours, visual search, and speech patterns. In my own lab within the past few years we have found that interpersonal relationships are organized as fractals and most recently that the self-concept is a fractal, with complexity being associated with health in both the psychological and social domains.

Furthermore, it appears that fractal complexity (or rigidity) is routinely exchanged among biological, psychological and social processes. Fractal personality structure helps us to grow and connect, as do fractal relationships, and each likely has direct influences on physical health by encouraging integration and flexibility among circulatory, respiratory, and immune systems.

The study ... has added to much prior research suggesting that the brain exhibits fractal behaviour. This makes a necessary link between the physical processes of the brain and each of the larger scale fractals we see in broader personality and social relationships. It is clear that biological, psychological and social dynamics are highly interlinked across scales, each impacting the other over time in myriad ways. With fractal organisation at each of these scales, one may propose that they in some respects they are all part of the same fractal tree so to speak.

They *are* – the same simulation founded on holographic/fractal information, and connections which drive human life and behaviour in the most fundamental ways, while the subjects of the program think they are making their own decisions and choices. Fractal connections are another major contributor to synchronicity or amazing coincidence. David Pincus noted how fractal patterns 'exist at every scale of measurable reality – from quantum to cosmic [and] perhaps human consciousness is both simply and profoundly a portal through which such fractal connectivity flows'. Or the simulation flows. All those scales of fractal patterns are within the simulation and so what he describes must be. Pincus added that science appeared to be nearing a period of exploring that 'everything in life is connected and that all of the universe [simulation] is alive within these connections'. The *Scientific American* black holes article said that studies spanning ordinary computers, black holes and cosmology 'are testimony to the unity of nature'. Halleluiah. Those conscious beyond the program have said this throughout known human history and been condemned, ridiculed and even killed for their trouble.

Humans logging-on

An ability to replicate original Earth reality doesn't mean the Archons (virus) are more advanced than humans potentially are in terms of wisdom and expanded consciousness. They merely know how reality works (at lower frequencies) and ensure that humans don't – hence the emphasis on controlling science and education. The Demiurge/Archons had to achieve three things: 'Download' a copy of Golden Age reality/simulation; lower its frequency; and then retune the human body-computer vehicle to that frequency. This is where genetic manipulation or 'interbreeding' came in. Genetic manipulation *infected the human Body-Mind with the virus*, which has then been replicated through the generations. All of which fits with themes of the 'Fall of Man' and humans being 'born' with 'original sin' or 'ancestral sin' (Archon virus). Sin was a

major pre-Islamic Mesopotamian god in Akkad, Assyria and Babylonia. From this we get Mount Sinai (Sin was the 'God of the Mountain') and 'Desert of Sin' through which the Israelites are supposed to have travelled. Sin's Sumerian equivalent was Nanna who was said to be the son of one of the Anunnaki brothers, Enlil. Archons created a low-frequency, 'low-resolution' copy of high-frequency Earth reality and then connected humans to the copy. Hey, presto. Those entrapped by the Archon web were now decoding the bad copy into 'physical' reality. They have been doing so ever since and it has become their 'normal' (Fig 220). Bonn University's paper on simulated realities said: '... like a prisoner in a pitch-black cell we would not be able to see the "walls" of our prison' (Fig 221). Morpheus said in *The Matrix*:

Figure 220: The real world is a fake simulation.

Figure 221: Our decoding processes are telling where we are – but aren't really.

Have you ever had a dream, Neo, that you were so sure was real? What if you were unable to wake from that dream? How would you know the difference between the dream world and the real world?

We can now also appreciate the profound truth in that other quote from *The Matrix*:

> You are a slave, Neo. Like everyone else you were born into bondage ... born into a prison that you cannot taste or see or touch. A prison for your mind.

Once humans began to decode the Archon information source, simulation or 'hack', they were indeed living in a prison for their mind, and still are.

The other 'Earth'

Golden Age reality before the Archons intervened was (is) also a simulation of a kind, but the experience is very different. For a start the bad copy is much more mechanical and technological in nature, and you could symbolise the difference as a natural substance compared with a synthetic copy. Synthetic is defined as 'not natural or genuine' and 'artificial or contrived'. Original Earth reality exists in a much higher frequency and is fantastically more enlightened and awake to Infinite Reality. Low-vibrational emotion is unknown because of frequency, expanded awareness and absence of the virus. There is no war, oppression and limitation of possibility. Colours are incredibly vibrant – a higher frequency, higher 'resolution' – and high-frequency Earth has a beauty that defies description. Myths and legends abound of this lost world. I say 'lost' in the sense of lost to human awareness. High-frequency Earth still exists because it never went away – *we* did. The Fall of Man ended the Golden Age as humans perceived it and caused humanity to be ejected from 'the garden' – high-frequency original reality – by eating from the tree of 'good and evil' (falling from unity into the realm of polarity or dualism). Humans fell down the frequencies into the density of ignorance. Jewish tradition relating to this good and evil theme is symbolic of profound truths. The Fall is said to be the beginning of the mixture of good and evil, when before they had been separate and evil only had a 'nebulous existence'. Evil existed, the tradition goes, but separate from the human psyche. Human nature then did not desire it, but after the Fall came the 'Evil Inclination', the tradition goes. What was at the centre of the 'Fall' narrative? The serpent. Dr Eben Alexander said this about evil in the wake of his near-death experience:

> Even on earth there is much more good than evil, but earth is a place where evil is allowed to gain influence in a way that would be entirely impossible at higher levels of existence. That evil could occasionally have the upper hand was known and allowed by the Creator as a necessary consequence of giving the gift of free will to beings like us.

> Small particles of evil were scattered throughout the universe, but the sum total of all that evil was as a grain of sand on a vast beach compared with the goodness, abundance, hope and unconditional love in which the universe was literally awash. The very fabric of the alternate dimension is love and acceptance, and anything that does not have these qualities appears immediately and obviously out of place there.

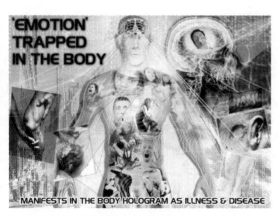

'EMOTION' TRAPPED IN THE BODY

MANIFESTS IN THE BODY HOLOGRAM AS ILLNESS & DISEASE

Figure 222: Emotional response programs are running through the human body-computer to keep us disconnected from Infinite Self, entrapped in Phantom Self, and to ensure a constant supply for the virus of low-vibrational emotional energy.

Alexander said he experienced another Earth with green, lush countryside, amazingly vibrant colour and with people happy, laughing, singing and dancing. This is how the original Earth reality – from which the copy was taken – is described. Near-death experiencers galore have told how the world that humans left behind looks something like our version, but with those vibrant colours, joy, happiness, harmony and absence of fear and its associated emotions, hate, anger, anxiety, worry and stress. When their focus of attention returns to Body-Mind awareness they experience (decode) bad copy reality again with all those emotions in abundance. Emotional programs are running through the body-computer to generate the energy on which the virus feeds (Fig 222). Those in only Phantom Self perception can go through an entire lifetime without having a single original thought or emotional response (see those fractal patterns of interconnected behaviour). High and low frequency 'Earths' can be symbolised as the reality portrayed in the *Avatar* movies in which the blue people or Na'vi were at one with animals, nature and each other while the invaders saw everything in terms of money and power. The fact the invaders were humans from our Earth was highly appropriate, as was the way they infiltrated the Na'vi world by taking on Na'vi bodies (Fig 223). High-Frequency Earth is a heart society and interacts with reality from that perspective of Infinite Love and Awareness. Archontic manipulation has transferred human interaction within the bad copy from the heart chakra (except for those with some expanded awareness) to the gut chakra and in doing so inverted love into fear (Fig 224). This caused the human frequency to fall and closed the door on their frequency prison – the Matrix (Fig 225). The gut is actually the seat of much human energetic power but the emotional programs have dissipated and inverted this. Many

Figure 223: The movie *Avatar* can be likened to the Archon takeover of human society..

Figure 224: The heart society of high-frequency Earth has been inverted in the bad copy to become a gut society that interacts with reality through emotion instead of the innate intelligence and expanded awareness and insight of the heart.

human hearts ache for a return to that *Avatar* world which is still potent in subconscious memory. Heartache, emptiness and longing for 'something' that people either can't explain, or put down the earthly origins, is a longing for what we can subconsciously remember from a frequency now far away. It can also relate to the Infinity that we all are beyond all realms of form. Ancient peoples believed in three 'heavens' and the Bible mentions this, too. The first heaven was 'where the birds fly' and for anything not attached to the Earth. The third heaven was the 'heaven of heavens' or realm of 'God'. The second heaven was said to be in between those two and included the surface of the Earth. This second heaven is described as like a war zone and the realm of 'Satan'. Thomas A. Horn writes in *Nephilim Stargates*:

Figure 225: Humanity is trapped in the 'box' of illusion and suppressed perception.

This war zone is a sort of gasket heaven, the domain of Satan encompassing the surface of the Earth. It was believed that from here powerful demons known as kosmokrators could overshadow cities, intrude upon, and attempt to influence the affairs and governments of men.

It was also believed that from the kosmos Satan's minions sought to close the gateways above cities so that God's blessings could not flow to them. Later, it was believed that when saints bent their knees in prayer, they had to pray through the walls/gates of opposition within this gasket heaven.

'Gasket heaven' is the Archon simulation and fake reality. Kosmokrators (Archons) close gateways to higher frequencies of awareness, and block 'God's blessings' (insights and knowledge from expanded awareness and *All That Is*). Religion's concept of a 'separation from God' is describing the same thing but the truth is lost in translation and dogma (Fig 226).

Nature programmes (programs)

Every time I watch nature documentaries I see the Archon simulation. Animals and 'nature'

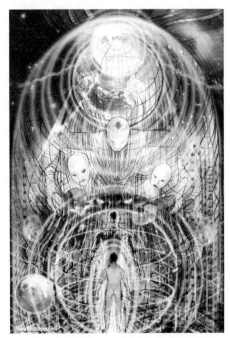

Figure 226: The Demiurge/Archon virus has imposed an energetic perception prison for those who have lost contact with Infinite Awareness. This is the realm of Phantom Self.

are, like the human body, within the Big Program. Humans and animals are said to share a common ancestor, but it's a common *program*, not ancestor. American neuroscientist Christof Koch has pointed out that 'only experts can tell, under a microscope, whether a chunk of brain matter is mouse or monkey or human'. Does anyone really think that the birth process in humans, animals and other forms of 'physical' life is some kind of cosmic accident? Is it by random chance that a human sperm seeks out an egg and the egg thus activated follows a cycle which ends up as a human body nine months later? It's a *software program* (Fig 227). Famed astronomer Fred Hoyle rightly said that the chances of the world being created by accident and not by design were like a whirlwind passing through a scrapyard and assembling a Jumbo Jet. Humans and animals all have 'life-cycles' which are Archon programs running through the cycle of birth-aging-death. All Earth programs involve this process and another common denominator is survival at the expense of others. I shake my head sometimes watching

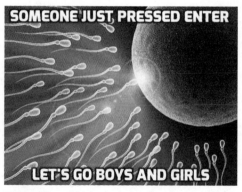

Figure 227: 'Nature' is a software program.

Figure 228: Archon 'nature' is by design about death, fear and survival.

documentaries about animal species, at seeing how each survives by killing others and this is again intrinsic to the human cycle, too. Everything is something else's predator or food source constantly scanning the environment for their 'natural' enemy or 'natural' lunch. What follows is a life of both fear and watching your back and psychopathic empathy-deleted mass murder. They call it the law of the wild, but it's really the law of the program – the law of the Archon virus serving the interests of the virus. Fear and psychopathy empower the virus as frequency expressions of the virus. They are the virus replicating and making copies of itself to infect new targets. Animals and insects fighting and killing their own species over food and territory is another mirror of human behaviour. Different species including humanity are simply different programs following their cycle and in all fundamentals they are the same. I saw a documentary involving *sea coral* and the different types were *fighting and killing each other* (Fig 228). The program is so blatant if only people would look. Create a simulated reality based on survival – or the perception of the need to survive – and all this fear, conflict and death must follow. High-frequency Earth reality does not involve death or survival. Energy is far more abundant, powerful and without our density, and so it can be absorbed directly by high-frequency 'inhabitants' of all kinds. There is no need to kill for food when your sustenance comes directly from energy. Without the fear-survival cycle the relationship between species is very different. Stories of humans living in peace with what are to us

Figure 229: It is so different in High-Frequency Reality.

wild animals, and themes of lions living with lambs, come from subconscious memories of this reality (Fig 229). Distorted bad copy Earth does not have the same frequency and power in its energy 'sea' and this limitation is overcome by consuming energy in its 'physical' (holographic) form – animals, plants – and this has produced the law of the wild along with programs that dictate the behaviour of the species. Everything is energy whether in pure form or 'physical' form and no matter if you are absorbing this from the energy sea or as a burger and chips it is still only energy in different states. Ever wondered why animal species are so perfectly matched for their environment with all the gifts they need to *survive*? Most of that is click, click, enter, by the Archon programmers, but there is another explanation. The simulation is interactive and this means that programs can also 'evolve' and transform as their environments change and new challenges to survival appear. I may upset some people when I say this but there is no such thing as 'nature' as we perceive it in the bad copy. Why is a duck a duck? Genetics? Right, okay, but why does a duck act like a duck? Why doesn't it act like an elephant or a fish? Why doesn't an elephant or a fish act like a duck? They are different *programs*. They don't have the choice to act like another species because the *program* rules perception and behaviour. Phantom Self humans are the same unless Infinite Awareness overrides the program. The 'natural world' of the bad copy is a programmed world and so are all 'natural' cycles from planets moving around the Sun to mayflies that live for just a day. Biological is as much technology as technological. This doesn't mean that we can't appreciate the beauty of what is called nature or that it doesn't have life in the sense of consciousness experiencing through the simulation in all its forms just as our awareness experiences through human Body-Mind. Much of simulated 'nature' *is* beautiful because it is a low-res and low-frequency copy of something stunningly beautiful and some of that beauty remains, albeit in an inferior form.

~~Life~~ Death

Observe the foundations of the fake reality and its programs and you will see that death is a prime component. Archons are an inversion of life and so death is their 'life'. A virus on your PC or laptop distorts the way the system functions and can turn a perfect image on the screen into a mess. Our world is being trashed through environmental destruction and this is the virus spreading. Thousands of species become extinct every year. Beauty is what

Figure 230: High-frequency Earth is about the celebration of life, harmony and beauty.

Figure 231: Archon Earth is about death ...

Figure 232: ... decay and destruction.

Figure 233: Archon Earth is about soulless, uninspired, functional ugliness without creativity.

remains of high-frequency Earth in the bad copy (Fig 230). Ugliness, pollution, extinction and death are the virus distorting the bad copy (Figs 231, 232 and 233). High-frequency Earth is about life and the Archon low-frequency inversion is dominated by death and fear of death. What is death but a distortion and inversion of life? Fear of death is the ignorance of life. There is no death for the core self only the manipulated perception of it. Death is food to the virus because death is an energy that syncs with its frequency and of course a computer virus means the death of balance and harmony for anything it touches.

Demiurge/Archon worshipping Satanists are obsessed with death for this reason. War and other mass killing and suffering (distortions of life) are food-fests for the virus and allow it to spread. Conflict and suffering abounds as the virus makes it so. The realm of the Demiurge/Archon virus is a realm of death and it is my view that Harvard academic neurosurgeon Eben Alexander experienced at least part of the Archon world during his near-death experience. He says in his book *Proof of Heaven* that he found himself in a place where he wasn't human or even animal, but 'a lone point of awareness in a timeless red-brown sea'. He describes reptilian and wormlike creatures moving past him and rubbing against him with their 'smooth or spiky skins'. Faces bubbled up out of the darkness and became ugly and threatening. He heard a pounding that intensified and sounded like 'the work-beat for some army of troll-like underground workers'. There was a smell – 'a little like faeces, a little like blood, and a little like vomit ... A biological smell, in other words, but of biological death, not of biological life'. This is the world ('Hell') of the Demiurge/Archons based on biological death, not biological life, and their plan is to make bad copy Earth the same. The closer they can fuse the frequencies of the Archon world with their fake simulation the more control they will have over humans as the 'Fall of Man' descends still further and the Archon world becomes ours. This is happening before our eyes but it does not have to continue. Eben

Alexander says that even though he felt powerless in that realm of biological death he could move in and out of there at will and without fear or challenge, once he remembered his true self and his limitless power to dictate his own reality. The Archon conspiracy enslaves people in Phantom Self because once humanity remembers its true nature the game is over. This is why I have been banging on about this for the last 26 years (26 illusory years in the NOW).

Lord of the Rings

Synchronicity in my life has led me many times to the concept of a fake reality overlaying reality as it was meant to be. I remember looking at the night sky even when very young and wondering if it was all what it seemed to be. My questioning began when I was taken at about six-years-old to the newly-opened London Planetarium in the late 1950s. I saw the heavens technologically projected on to the domed ceiling and it looked so real. I have since often looked at the heavens and asked the same question – is it as real as it seems to be? The high-frequency original Universe is teeming with life but is the copy? I made the point earlier about looking at the blaze of stars and believing that we are the only 'intelligent' life as we know it. The point still stands, but in the original not the copy (Fig 234). Even the Sun is not the original sun but a copy. Download a website and it

Figure 234: Is this any more real than a highly advanced holographic planetarium? I don't think so.

still looks and works the same – it's just not the original. Maybe there is relatively little other life in the bad copy 'Universe'. I described earlier how extraterrestrial visitations tended to be in the form of entities moving in and out of our reality or in and out of the bad copy. What better way to isolate human awareness than by isolation from other forms of life that could give us a better fix on everything? The first *Matrix* movie in 1999 took me aback when it depicted themes of information and insight that I had been compiling in my mind since I was a kid. When I read books suggesting that fantastic upheavals have happened in our solar system in relatively recent times this also felt so right to me. In the years that followed the synchronicity of information and experience has led me to the following conclusions, and you will find evidence detailed at greater length in *The Perception Deception*. Part of the ongoing distortion of the bad copy simulation has been to move planets around and bring in other bodies like the Moon to further distort human reality and stifle the connection to expanded awareness beyond the Matrix. Once you have downloaded a copy of a website you can change it as you wish. Astrology is the science of reading energetic effects on personality, perceptions and events caused by movement of planets and stars (information fields) and their impact on other information fields (all life, including humans). It is obvious that if you rearrange planets in the solar system, and bring a mini-planet like the Moon into such close proximity to Earth, it is going to impact energetically on life and consciousness in very profound ways compared with the previous arrangement. Saturn is a key 'planet' (actually a dwarf star) for the Archons and was therefore significant to the Gnostics of the Nag Hammadi texts (Fig 235). Saturn has been a constant focus for ancient societies and was the major god of Rome (highly relevant when I come to the Archon-established religions). Readers of my other books will know that The System and its Establishment, secret societies and Satanism are awash with Saturn symbolism for the same reason. They refer to Saturn as the 'Dark Sun' and 'Black Sun' just as the ancients did. Other titles for Saturn are

Figure 235: Saturn – the key to so much.

'Lord of the Rings' and 'Time Lord' (Lord Archon, Demiurge). Saturn is the House of the Lord (Demiurge) as are the churches where Saturn is unknowingly worshipped by congregations. Saturn once dominated the Earth sky and was the predominant sun for inhabitants of Earth. Legends of twin suns relate to this. Saturn was widely and consistently referred to as a sun by the ancients. Chaldean (Mesopotamian) astronomy gave Saturn a name that translates as 'Star of the Sun'. Greek historian Diodorus of Sicily noted that Chaldeans referred to Saturn as Helios or the sun and another name for Saturn was Sol – sun again. Babylonian astrological texts gave Saturn the name of Shamash (Sun) and the Babylonian name for Saturn was Ninib, which was said to 'shine like the sun'. Shamash/Saturn to the Sumerians was Utu and to the Egyptians Atum or Ra, the 'sun god' wrongly associated by historians with the sun we see today. Enormous global focus on Saturn by the ancients came from the simple fact that it dominated the Earth sky. Why would there have been such a focus had Saturn been located where it is today? Saturn was aligned with the Earth's northern pole and was its 'polar sun'. Mars and Venus were similarly aligned between the Earth and Saturn during what the ancients called the Golden Age, as brilliantly uncovered by the long and painstaking research of Saturn specialist and Electric Universe advocate David Talbott (Fig 236). These bodies appeared in alignment when viewed from the Earth. For all the background to this and many other aspects that explain ancient symbols still used today see *The Perception Deception*. Saturn's location changed dramatically along with other bodies including Mars, Venus and Jupiter as a result of fantastic upheavals in the solar system. These reality-transforming cataclysms are described by the ancients in stories about 'wars of the gods' and 'war in the heavens' and what happened is clearly visible in Earth's geological and biological record. Once again see *The Perception Deception* for the detail. Correlation between ancient accounts and modern research is extremely compelling. The upheavals included a gigantic tsunami described

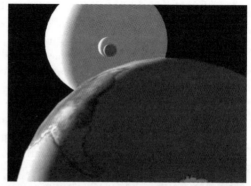

Figure 236: The Saturn-Venus-Mars-Earth alignment before cataclysmic events rearranged the solar system.

Figure 237, 238 and 239: Advanced cities have been found under the ocean.

throughout the ancient world – the Biblical Great Flood. Clay tablets from thousands of years ago in the land of Sumer and Babylon (now Iraq) tell of this flood long before the Bible texts repeated the story. The tablets connect these happenings to non-human invaders they called the Anunnaki ('Those Who From Heaven To Earth Came') who are described in reptilian terms. Legends are endless of great continents, with names such as Atlantis and Mu or Lemuria, disappearing under the sea amid these catastrophes. Vast structures including pyramids have been found around the world covered by the ocean (Figs 237, 238 and 239). From this point bad copy Earth became a *mega* bad copy Earth and transformed human life and perception of everything.

Saturn Pattern

Saturn was the most prominent Earth sun before it was infected by the Demiurge/Archon virus and relocated by the cataclysms to become the outermost planet (sun) visible to the naked eye. Saturn, too, is a *copy* of energetic information patterns of the still-existing original in higher frequencies. We are dealing with computer codes, remember, and not solid objects. Saturn could be transformed through Archon click, click, enter, and it has been. Saturn became a vehicle for the Demiurge virus and a prime source of imposing the fake reality. Saturn (Satan) and what the Gnostics called the Demiurge became interchangeable terms. Ancient accounts of Saturn make no reference to its rings. These have been technologically generated to form a gigantic broadcasting system and they did not exist when Saturn was in its

original location (Fig 240). Saturn's speed of rotation is connected to this. Saturn spins at an estimated 35,700 kilometres or 22,000 miles an hour and the Saturn day lasts less than eleven hours despite being 83.7 times larger than Earth. Extraordinary permanent storms at Saturn's poles are manifestations of radio sound frequencies transmitted by the rings across the solar system. There is a hexagon storm as wide as two Earths at the northern pole and an 'eye' storm at the south (Fig 241 and 242). Saturn's rings consist of fractal patterns and broadcast fractal patterns of the simulation. NASA

Figure 240: Saturn's rings are not 'natural', but part of its broadcasting system.

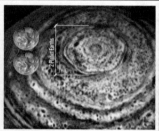

Figure 241: Saturn's permanent hexagon storm at its northern pole.

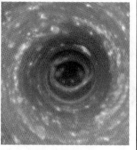

Figure 242: Saturn's eye storm at the southern pole.

Saturn studies reveal that the hexagon storm rotates every 10 hours 39 minutes and 24 seconds in precise synchronisation with the cycle of Saturn's *radio emissions*. Put 'Sounds of Saturn' into YouTube and you'll hear what they sound like. A hexagon is a geometrical representation of the sound frequencies of Saturn and the storm will stay there until what is being broadcast is changed. I was given an image of Saturn's rings by a professional sound engineer who said this is what he saw every day working with sound technology (Fig 243). A hexagon is a flattened out cube geometrically and in terms of their energetic signature they are the same (Fig 244). Cubes (especially black cubes) have long been a symbol for Saturn and this is the real

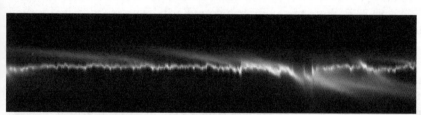

Figure 243: Saturn's rings are broadcasting sound waves carrying Matrix information.

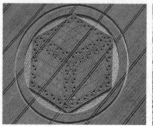

Figure 244: Look at this crop circle image in one way and it is a hexagon. Look from another angle and it is a cube. Energetically the hexagon and cube are the same and represent the frequency of Saturn.

Figure 245: The Kaaba cube in Mecca is a symbol for Saturn and everyone who has this as their focus of worship is being manipulated to worship Saturn.

Figure 246: The 'New Jerusalem' in the Book of Revelation is described in terms of a cube.

origin and significance of the black cube Kaaba (Kaaba means cube) which is the focus of the Islamic religion in Mecca (Fig 245). The Book of Revelation describes the 'New Jerusalem' in terms of a cube (Fig 246). Researchers at the University of Bonn studying the Universe as a simulation are also exploring the possibility that the simulation/matrix could be a 'hypercube'. These are connected to the number 64 and this is a recurring number common to many religions. We have the 64 hexagrams of the Chinese I-Ching and the

Figure 247: Law enforcement often uses the hexagram to symbolise authority – Saturn astrologically represents authority.

Figure 248: The hexagram on papal headgear.

Figure 249: The hexagram symbolising Saturn at the Mother Lodge of Freemasonry in London.

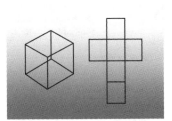

Figure 250: A cross in the correct proportions is a flattened out cube.

Figure 251: The cross is clear to see in the astrological symbol of Saturn..

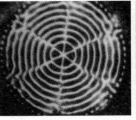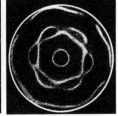

Figure 252: Cymatics uses sound to change particle patterns. When the frequency changes so does the pattern.

64 nucleotides of the genetic code. A six-pointed star or hexagram symbol is also a geometrical expression of the hexagon/cube and represents the same energetic signature. Hexagrams also happen to be an ancient and modern symbol of *Saturn* and are found in Judaism, Christianity, Satanism, secret societies and often used in the badges of law enforcement (Figs 247, 248, and 249). Symbols can be different versions of each other and represent the same frequency. We find this with the hexagram, hexagon, cube and even a cross in the correct geometrical proportions (Fig 250). They all represent the frequency of Saturn and you can see the cross in Saturn's astrological symbol (Fig 251). If you put the word 'cymatics' into YouTube you will see many examples of sound creating form and as the frequency of the sound changes so does the form (Fig 252). Symbols are both created by sound and geometrically represent that sound (Fig 253). I was watching a video with sound causing a liquid to continually change shape in response to the changing frequencies, and when I began to freeze the images I saw classic symbols appear – a six-point star or hexagram more than any other (Fig 254). This is known as the Star of David and considered by many to be an exclusively Jewish symbol, but it's not. Hexagrams are an ancient symbol of Saturn and used as such by countless cultures and religions. It is, however, right that it became a symbol of Judaism and later Zionism given that both are founded on the worship of El, the Judaic god of Saturn, of which more later. I have said that the House of Rothschild is a major Archon-Reptilian bloodline that has done so much to expand the Demiurge virus in the fields of finance, government and war. Well, well. The hexagram, a classic symbol of Saturn, is

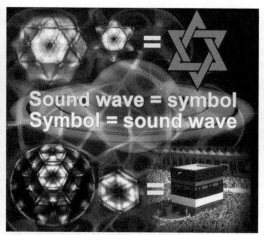

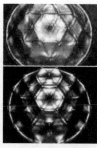

Figure 254: Hexagram frozen frames from a video of sound pulsating through a liquid medium.

Figure 255: The symbol of Saturn – and the origin of the name Rothschild – on the flag of Rothschild-created Israel.

Figure 253: Sound frequencies manifest as symbols and symbols generate those frequencies.

also the very origin of the name 'Rothschild'. Their family name in Germany was Bauer but they changed it to Rothschild ('red sign or shield' in German) in deference to the red hexagram (Saturn) on their home in Frankfurt where their global financial dynasty began. They would later put the hexagram on the flag of Israel, a country which is nothing more than a Rothschild fiefdom based on Saturn (Demiurge) worship (Fig 255). The absolutely overwhelming majority of people calling themselves Jewish today have no historical or genetic connection to the land of Israel and instead originate from a people called the Khazars from the region of the Caucasus and the Black Sea. Khazars were not born Jewish but were subject to a mass conversion to Judaism by King Bulan in 740AD. They later moved north into Eastern and Western Europe to become those called Jewish in Germany (see *The Perception Deception* and *Human Race Get Off Your Knees*). These facts are supported by Jewish sources and historians such as Shlomo Sand, Professor of History at Tel Aviv University, in his book, *The Invention of the Jewish People*. Israel was established in 1947 by a Saturn-worshipping Rothschild hoax to cause the conflict and mayhem (divide and rule) that we have seen ever since. Khazaria's king, by the way, was known as the 'Kagan' which, for the reasons explained, became a common Jewish name to this today. Secret societies, religions and Establishment institutions of human society all employ Saturn symbolism profusely, including the hexagram, because they are all manifestations of the Demiurge-Saturn virus.

Reality rings

Dr Norman Bergrun, an American scientist and engineer, made a long and detailed study of Saturn's rings and came to the conclusion that they are not natural (Fig 256). He detailed his findings in a book, *Ringmakers of Saturn*. Bergrun is no amateur. He was a scientist at what became NASA's Ames Research Center, worked for Lockheed Missiles and Space Company and Douglas Aircraft, and established his own research and engineering company. Bergrun became fascinated by the rings of Saturn after studying photographs from the NASA Voyager I and II missions. They arrived at Saturn nine months apart in 1980 and 1981 and Bergrun saw blatant differences in the rings.

Figure 256: Dr Norman Bergrun, the American scientist and engineer who has done such revelatory work on the nature of Saturn.

'That was the starting point for me. I've been researching this ever since', he said. Images from NASA's Cassini mission, which arrived in 2004, confirmed all his conclusions. He said that some astronomers and physicists had speculated that the rings were much younger than the Universe and maybe about 100 million years old, but 'one pair of pictures shows a change in five minutes!' Bergrun realised that observations of the rings at any point were then considered definitive – when in fact that was only how the rings looked at the time of observation. He said:

An impression is conveyed that latest reported measurements purport to be the true ones when, in reality, all might be quite nearly correct at time of observation. General reluctance to accept variable ring-system geometry occurs because of apparent failure to identify a physical mechanism suitable for producing recurrent change.

We can't explain it so it can't be happening – usual story. Constant change in Saturn's rings was revelatory enough given the belief in their permanence by mainstream science; but Bergrun went further. His long and detailed study of NASA images from three missions led him to conclude that the rings are made by what he calls gigantic 'electromagnetic vehicles'. When he says gigantic he is not kidding, with some of them estimated to be three times the size of Earth and more. Not possible once again? Consider the size of Saturn compared with Earth. We are not talking about the same relative perception of 'big' (Fig 257). Size is governed only by energetic information codes and click, click, enter. One person is taller than another because of *information* running through their genetics. Norman Bergrun said of these electromagnetic vehicles: 'Such an immense propulsive body implies a space engine possessing unheard-of capacity and capability.' Or a completely different form of propulsion involving

Figure 257: Putting the size relationship of Saturn to Earth in stark perspective.

electromagnetism. He does not relate the vehicles to space ships in the conventional way, but to electromagnetic energy and they can be clearly seen in NASA images (Fig 258 and 259). This begs the question of why NASA has never publicly addressed what they are – a question that can be answered by NASA's true role of suppressing information that would open minds and cause a re-evaluation of reality. I have detailed in other books how NASA was established by Nazi –

NASA/Nazi – scientists and engineers who were transferred to the United States after the war by Operation Paperclip to continue their work with space technology and mind control programmes, like the infamous MK Ultra. MK is short for mind control and the German spelling of kontrolle was used in deference to the Nazis who ran it. Among

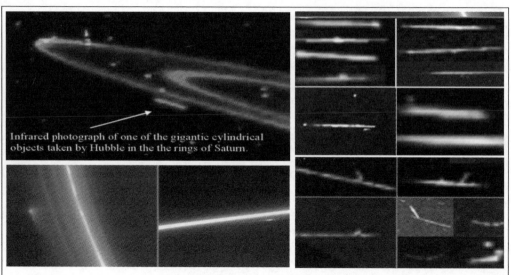

Figure 258: Norman Bergrun's 'electromagnetic vehicles' in NASA photographs. NASA remains silent.

Nazis relocated in America was aerospace engineer and space architect Wernher von Braun. He was the brains behind both the V-2 Rocket, the world's first long-range guided ballistic missile that targeted London during World War II, and the so-appropriately named Saturn-V rocket used by NASA in the Apollo Moon program in the 1960s and 1970s. NASA tells you nothing that The System is not fine for you to know. Norman Bergrun noted how the

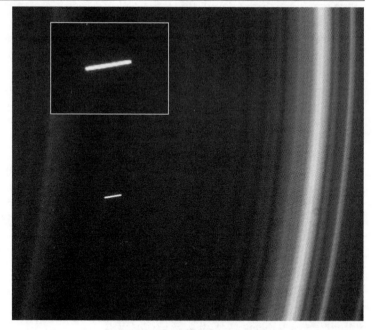

Figure 259: Another 'vehicle' in the rings.

electromagnetic craft could be seen where rings were not yet completed. He said:

On each extremity of Saturn's rings, cylindrical bodies have been photographed spewing emissions. These emissions assume complicated patterns while contributing compositional material for the rings. A time-varying appearance of Saturn's disc is a natural consequence of this process.

The B ring and inner-and-outer-A rings are separate entities because different vehicles fabricate these rings ... Presence of electromagnetic vehicles near other planets is intimated by a finding of rings, the signature left by exhaust and emission products persisting in orbit.

Bergrun refers to the substance making the rings as trails of effluent or exhaust discharged by the vehicles, but I would connect this to some crystalline or similar material related to the transmitter-receiver systems of Saturn. He describes how jets are emitted from different points on the vehicles and each jet appears to consist of a series of 'bulbous swellings' (Fig 260). He says these are 'indicative of the form of electrically-charged flows known as pinched plasmas' (which I mentioned earlier). Location of the rings is decided by the positioning of the vehicles and the 'degree of emission activity', he said. Vehicles like those highlighted by Bergrun have been seen near our Sun, but he said that Saturn is their focus:

A concentrated presence of them appears at Saturn, thereby introducing the interesting speculation that the planet serves as an operational base. Ultra-superlative intellect is implied by the existence of these highly sophisticated electromagnetic vehicles. Not only do these units demonstrate mastery of nuclear power and massive electro-potential force fields, but also they show

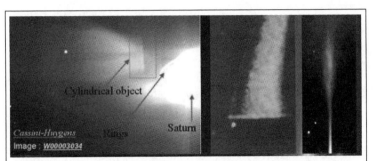

Figure 260: Material being released by Bergrun's vehicles to make the rings.

an ability to modify extensive surface areas of large celestial bodies. Indeed, a realistic possibility is raised that good-sized celestial bodies can be moved about.

Now, what was I saying about Archons rearranging parts of the solar system? Are they 'vehicles' or an expression of click, click, enter? Bergrun said vehicles are pictured striking the surface of Saturn's moons (in its own mini solar system) with electromagnetic blasts. He relates the effects to the surface of our own Moon and points out that some Moon craters and scored-out landscape could have been caused in the same way: 'Mobile bodies of high electrical potential can entrap and disfigure celestial bodies [and this] has implications of unforeseeable magnitude.' What I am presenting here may sound impossible to most people, but as Bergrun said of his findings:

These are not conclusions you ordinarily would expect from someone with such a traditional background, but upon applying scientific rigour to the study of Saturn, its rings and its moons, the facts keep pushing me toward some inescapable conclusions.

This all fits with my own contention that Saturn (a computer system in effect) has been infested with the Demiurge virus and transformed into a colossal broadcasting system delivering at least part of the Matrix information source to human decoding processes (Fig 261). Saturn is such a focus for these vehicles because the work is ongoing and Saturn is an interdimensional gateway between our reality and Archon reality. So is the Sun. Saturn's broadcasts also block information at frequencies beyond the Matrix to further isolate people in five-sense reality by acting like a computer firewall (Fig 262). This is nothing like as difficult and complicated as it may seem when you think that analogue television broadcasts have been blocking our ability to see whole galaxies (which operate within the same frequency band) from Earth. Once frequency-isolation had been secured humanity had to make sense of the world while having no other source of information or insight except for that communicated *in* that world – 'education', media, religion, government, 'science', and all the rest (Fig 263).

Figure 261: Saturn broadcasts fake Matrix information to human decoding processes.

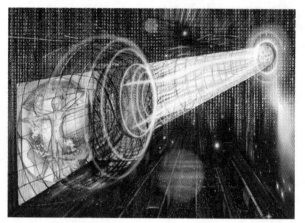

Figure 262: The Matrix also acts as a firewall to block information from beyond the simulation.

Humanity was, and is, both in the world and *of* it, until awareness is expanded to realities and insight beyond the Matrix. Entrapment is based on isolating the population in five-sense reality and then controlling the information they receive within five-sense reality. No wonder people are so lost in the illusion and no wonder, too, that Gnostics and other ancient sources so emphasised Archon expertise in illusion and deception. Near-death experiencer Anita Moorjani described out-of-body reality as 'a realm of clarity where I understood everything'. She said she felt 'connected to everybody'. Phantom Self programs have been designed to block this clarity. How do you divide and rule people who know that they are each other? Saturn broadcasts are a Pied Piper of perception and, surprise, surprise, another symbol of Saturn is the Greek and Roman horned god known as 'Pan' who is depicted playing his pipes or Pan Pipes (Fig 264). American Freemasonic historian Manly P. Hall, wrote in *Secret Teachings of All Ages*:

> Pan was a composite creature, the upper part – with the exception of his horns – being human, and the lower part in the form of a goat ... the god himself is a symbol of Saturn because this planet is enthroned in Capricorn, whose emblem is a goat.

Figure 264: Pan, the half-human, half-goat symbol of Saturn playing the 'pan pipes' – the Matrix.

Figure 263: Humanity decodes the fake reality information source into the world we think we are living in. In fact, we are decoding our own hamster wheel life cycles and Phantom Self prison cells.

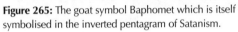

Figure 265: The goat symbol Baphomet which is itself symbolised in the inverted pentagram of Satanism.

Figure 266: Baphomet is widely portrayed – here with Beyonce, Lady Gaga, Madonna and Baroness Philippine de Rothschild.

Pan is associated with the term 'Diablo' or Devil. Saturn's goat symbolism can be seen in Baphomet, or the 'Sabbatic Goat', a major symbol of Satanism worshipped by the Knights Templar secret society and other members of the Elite (Figs 265 and 266). Saturn broadcasts are connected to the Matrix illusion of time and the ancient Greek god of Saturn, Chronos, is the source of the classic image of Old Father Time (Figs 267 and 268). Chronos was said to be serpentine in form and he and his serpentine consort

152

Figure 269: The Grim Reaper, symbol of death, is Saturn.

Figure 267: Chronos, the Greek god of Saturn with scythe, beard and symbol of time. The Greeks said Chronos (Saturn) controlled time.

Figure 268: Chronos as Old Father Time.

Ananke were believed to have created the ordered universe of earth, sea and Sky. Time is crucial to Archontic perception control because this illusion is decoded from simulated reality to further attach people to five-sense reality at the exclusion of expanded awareness – which operates in the no-time NOW. In fact, the relationship of Chronos to time was described in terms of 'a time lapse, a moment of indeterminate time in which everything happens.' Chronos was portrayed by the Greeks with an hour glass and a scythe and we see another symbol of Saturn with the scythe-holding Grim Reaper – the symbol of death with which Saturn is esoterically (energetically) associated (Fig 269). Chronos was also associated with death as is Saturn-ruled Capricorn. The scythe has many Saturn connotations including the belief by the ancients that it was the god of agriculture and harvest ... harvesting humanity more like. I say that the Large Hadron Collider, the world's largest and most powerful particle accelerator at CERN in Switzerland, has been created with money-no-object to enhance the effects of the Matrix, Earth's connection with Saturn and establish an interdimensional gateway or stargate to the Archon realm. A statue at CERN depicts the Vedic god Lord Shiva (Lord Archon/Demiurge) dancing within a ring. Shiva is represented by Saturn in Vedic astrology (Fig 270). He is also the god of death and time – just like Saturn. Shiva's dance symbolises the primordial destructive force of the Universe and this is the real origin of the term 'Lord of the Dance'. What is this doing outside the European Organization for Nuclear Research? CERN is built on a site which, in Roman times, was dedicated to the demonic god 'Apollyon' ('the Destroyer'), or Abaddon in Hebrew and known in Asia as *Shiva*.

Figure 270: Lord Shiva, Lord of the Dance, at CERN.

The location was apparently believed to be a gateway to the underworld. Apollyon/Abaddon appears in the Bible as the ruler of the Abyss and the king of an 'army of locusts'. The Book of Revelation says the Abyss, a great smoking pit, will open and a horde of demonic locusts will rise from it. The Internet, which as we shall see is so important to the plan for total human enslavement, came out of CERN. Sergio Bertolucci, Director for Research and Scientific Computing at CERN, said the Hadron Collider could create or discover 'unknown unknowns' like 'an extra dimension' and he added: 'Out of this door might come something, or we might send something through it.' The Collider is a ring tunnel of superconducting magnets and energy-boosting technology that runs for 17 miles at up to 575 feet under the Swiss-French border. Particle beams travel through the ring at almost the speed of light to crash proton particles together and a proton makes 11,245 circuits of the ring every second. Superconducting magnets in the Hadron Collider are 100,000 times more powerful than the gravitational pull of Earth, and temperatures are reported to reach more than 100,000 times those claimed to be at the center of the Sun. Some scientists have voiced their grave misgivings about the possible unknown consequences, but in the shadows I say they know what the consequences are. For them the consequences are *intended*. Ten thousand scientists and engineers are involved from more than 100 countries at a cost so far estimated by *Forbes* magazine at $13.25 billion. The official story is that the Collider was built to 'test the predictions of different theories of particle physics'. In terms of the ultimate aim, I don't believe it. An upgrade has greatly increased the power while the speed of particle collisions is being increased all the time in pursuit of the real goal.

Moon Mind

The Moon is part of the fake reality delivery system and not real in the sense of being there by 'natural' causes. Earth's Moon is very much like the Death Star in the *Star Wars* movies with everything going on inside (Fig 271). The Moon is a colossal broadcasting transmitter that amplifies Saturn transmissions and directs them at Earth (Fig 272).

Saturn and the Moon are broadcasting the human 'prison for your mind'. Soviet scientists suggested as long ago as 1970 that the Moon is a construct or part construct because there are so many unexplainable anomalies and mysteries – including where it came from. Irwin Shapiro of the Harvard–Smithsonian Center for Astrophysics, said: 'The best explanation for the Moon is observational error – the Moon doesn't exist.' Soviet scientists believed that the Moon was hollow and some kind of giant spacecraft. There is much evidence that the Moon is indeed hollow and this is supported by the response of the Moon to massive impacts. NASA scientists said the Moon 'reacted like a gong' and vibrations continued for 'three hours and twenty minutes to a depth of 25

Figure 271: Moon anomalies disappear when you realise what it really is.

Figure 272: You could think of the Moon as a gigantic broadcasting dish directing amplified Saturn broadcasts at the Earth and human decoding processes.

Figure 273: What are the chances of the Moon being the same size as the Sun when viewed from Earth during an eclipse?

miles' after one strike with the equivalent of 11 tonnes of TNT. Ken Johnson, a supervisor of the Data and Photo Control Department during the Apollo missions, said the entire Moon 'wobbled' and it was 'almost as though it had gigantic hydraulic damper struts inside it'. Once you come at the Moon from the construct perspective the long list of apparent anomalies become explainable, as you will see in *The Perception Deception* and *Human Race Get off Your Knees*. Anyone who thinks the Moon is 'naturally' close to Earth should explain the size of the bloody thing. It is 2,160 miles in diameter and the fifth largest moon in the solar system despite the presence of giant planets (dwarf stars) such as Saturn and Jupiter. No other moon in the solar system has the same size ratio of planet to satellite and it is a quarter the size of Earth. Even mainstream scientists have conceded that this makes no sense ... *unless*. Scientists say the Moon is precisely positioned in that life as we know it would be not be possible if it were significantly closer or further away. They have no idea why this should be so and say it must be chance. Is this really all a coincidence? Yes, of course it is, and I was born in an ant hill to a family of fish. Another thing – why do we only see one side of the Moon from Earth? I've heard the official explanation, but what's the real reason? The Moon appears from Earth to be the same size as the Sun during a total eclipse, because the Moon is 400 times smaller than the Sun and at a solar eclipse 400 times closer to Earth (Fig 273). Just one more amazing coincidence? I mentioned earlier the Channelled Holographic Access Network Interface (CHANI) project, which is claimed to have communicated with an entity in another dimension for five years starting in 1994. What the entity is reported to have said supports this version of the Moon:

- The Moon is not a natural heavenly body.
- Life was better for humans before the Moon came.
- 'Moon forces' control time and manipulate the mood of humans.
- The Moon is there to control the Earth's 'mood' and a big calm would come over the Earth without the Moon – there would only be little storms, not big storms.
- Oceans would be much calmer, heavy thunderstorms and lightning would be rare and the climate would be balanced with no extreme heat or cold.

- The 'old race' [Archon-Reptilians] captured the Moon from space and located it next to the Earth.
- Without the Moon telepathic and interdimensional communication would become widespread and people would be able to see new colours in an enhanced colour spectrum.
- There would be major changes to the human respiratory system as blood and breathing chemistry changed.
- Those born after the Moon's demise would be able to hold their breath underwater for hours at a time.

Figure 274: Archon-Reptilian Moon.

The claim that the 'old race' or Archon Reptilians captured the Moon and took it to its present location is supported by many ancient peoples who spoke of the time before the Moon. Norman Bergrun said of the electromagnetic vehicles that he believed interacted with the Moon: 'Indeed, a realistic possibility is raised that good-sized celestial bodies can be moved about.' Greek authors Aristotle and Plutarch, and Roman authors Apollonius Rhodius and Ovid, recorded how a people called the Proselenes in Arcadia, Greece, said their ancestors lived in that land 'before there was a moon in the heavens'. 'Proselene' means 'before Selene' – the Greek goddess of the Moon. Many legends and accounts say the Moon was located close to Earth by various global names for the Archon-Reptilians. They are still inside the Moon in their own sealed atmosphere (Fig 274). Zulu legend says that the leaders of the reptilian Chitauri, brothers they call Wowane and Mpanku (the Sumerian Anunnaki brothers, Enki and Enlil) stole the Moon from the 'Great Fire Dragon' in the form of an egg and hollowed out the 'yoke'. The Moon has often been associated with the theme of an egg and the Babylonian goddess Queen Semiramis, or Ishtar, was said to have come from the Moon in a 'giant moon egg' (possibly a craft of some kind) and landed in the River Euphrates. 'Ishtar's egg' is the origin of Easter eggs today. The Moon as an egg is symbolic of the Moon being hollowed out and this is what the Soviet scientists said had happened when they explained why the metallic content of the Moon's surface should be found inside, not outside. Dr Don L Anderson, professor of geophysics and director of the seismological laboratory at the California Institute of Technology, once said that 'the Moon is made inside out'. Life was certainly better for humans before the Moon came with its frequency suppression of expanded awareness and manipulating mood – personality and perception. The Moon significantly impacts on human hormones (mood) through the endocrine system and the female reproduction cycle is linked to the Moon. Pineal and pituitary glands are part of the endocrine system. They form the 'Third Eye' of expanded awareness and 'sixth-sense' insight beyond the five senses. Rods and cones found in eyes are also in the pineal gland, which acts as a crystalline antenna to pick up higher frequencies. Those who think that something the size of a

Figure 275: Broadcasts from the Moon and Saturn are dictating the nature of human society.

Illustration by Neil Hague

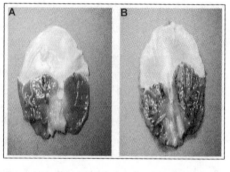

Figure 276: Fluoride calcifies the pineal gland – yet another way that Phantom Self is disconnected from Infinite Self.

grain of rice couldn't decode very much should look at an antenna you can plug into a computer socket to decode television and radio stations from all over the world. The Archon virus seeks to suppress that psychic sensitivity through many and various means, and certainly through what is being broadcast from Saturn and the Moon (Fig 275). Suppress the function of 'Third Eye' glands and you can isolate people in five-sense reality just as you can when you calcify the pineal gland with fluoride in drinking water and toothpaste (Fig 276).

Controlling Earth's mood and disturbing the calm on many levels fits with something I have been emphasising all these years. This is the manipulation and stimulation of low-vibrational emotion on which the Archon virus feeds. Genetic re-wiring implanted programs that generate these emotions and they are activated by the structure and experience of human society and by what is being broadcast from or via the Moon. Near-death experiencers have reported again and again that they didn't feel 'human emotion' when their attention withdrew from the five senses (and the Saturn-Moon broadcasts). Anita Moorjani said that during her near-death experience she 'didn't get emotionally sucked into the drama'. Archons want Phantom Self to do just that and get sucked into the drama and illusion until it becomes its only reality. Another classic in the CHANI entity list is: 'Without the Moon telepathic and interdimensional communication would become widespread and people would be able to see new colours in an enhanced colour spectrum.' The whole point of the Matrix and its components like the Moon and Saturn is to suppress expanded awareness and focus attention and perception in the realm of the Matrix. 'New colours in an enhanced colour spectrum' relates to how what is being blasted at the Earth is suppressing our frequency. Higher frequencies produce more vibrant and numerous colours, as so many near-death experiencers have reported and I saw through ayahuasca. 'Moon forces control time' is another highly-relevant point and common theme. You can add Saturn to that, too, and its portrayal as 'Old Father Time'. The Moon has always been associated with time, even down to the word month or *moon*th (Fig 277). Both celestial bodies are manipulating our perception of time because time is only information encoded in the Matrix. The last comment on the CHANI list appears to come straight out of left field. It says that without the Moon 'there would be major changes to the human respiratory system as blood and breathing chemistry changed ...Those born after the Moon's demise would be able to hold their breath underwater for hours at a time'. This is a profound indication of just how much

Figure 277: The Moon is also a dictator of humanity's sense of 'time'.

human potential is being blocked by the Moon, Saturn and the Matrix. We are not what we are meant to be, but *we can change that.* A fake reality as depicted in the *Matrix* movies is being broadcast in the form of information within the frequency band of the human decoding system which was retuned and manipulated to receive and transmit

within that band during the genetic engineering symbolised by 'interbreeding with the gods'. If your Body-Mind is not open to expanded awareness beyond the Matrix, the only reality that you can perceive and believe to be 'real' is the Matrix – 'they gave us their mind' (Fig 278). *Gotcha!* Those relative few who have expanded their awareness to see the Matrix are called mad, bad and agents of the Devil when they point out that the 'real world' is actually systematic smoke-and-mirrors designed only to control us through the manipulation of perception. Human life encapsulated.

Matrix Heaven

Why would anyone choose to come into a reality controlled in the way that I have described? This would really be crazy. Surely it's the last place any sane soul would head for unless they were coming

Illustration by Neil Hague (www.neilhague.com)

Figure 277: What you decode is what you perceive – whether it is real or not.

Figure 279: Matrix minds can stay in the Matrix after death if their frequency is not high enough to escape and perception = frequency.

Figure 280: Awareness with a connection to Infinite Self can leave the Matrix after death and break the 'reincarnation' cycle.

here to alert the enslaved to their plight. This question can be answered and it doesn't make easy listening, but, hey, we have to know the situation we face before we can do something about it – as we will. The Archon Matrix doesn't only operate in the realm of the holographic five senses. It is a closed system within a frequency bubble, web or net designed to entrap even departed 'souls' when they leave the body, at what we call death, unless they are in a high enough state of awareness (Figs 279 and 280). Souls or aspects of formerly embodied consciousness are then recycled back into new bodies to continue their service to the Archons under another human alias or Phantom Self in ignorance of what it is and where it comes from. This is what is known as reincarnation. We are Infinite Awareness. We don't have to come in and out of different bodies, incarnating and reincarnating, to 'evolve' and become 'enlightened'. We *are* enlightened in our infinite state. It is our gift as an expression of Infinite Awareness. A so-called reincarnation cycle is really about suppressing that enlightenment to make us slaves to the Archons. The virus would soon lose its energy source if all souls (points of attention) could get out of the Matrix once they withdrew from the reality of the five senses: 'Sod that for a game of soldiers, I ain't going back there – it's a shit place.' Anyone looking into the Matrix frequency bubble would hardly be queuing up to buy a ticket to the madhouse. Souls originally trapped in the Matrix are still trapped, or most of them, anyway, and others will have come here on the same principle as moths being attracted

by the light. Oh, yes, the *Light*. It has long
been my contention that light or 'The Light' is
another Archon inversion. 'The Light' is
widely associated with goodness, spirituality
and 'God', and we hear about people being
'light workers' in service to the always
interchangeable 'love and light' (see freedom
and democracy); but light is also the
frequency band that entraps humanity in the
Matrix – visible light – and Archon secret
societies worship The Light under names
such as Lucifer the 'light bringer'. They also
profusely employ symbols of light including
the sun (Saturn) and the flame. Biblical texts
say that 'Satan himself masquerades as an
angel of light'. Biblical Satan is the Gnostic
Demiurge or Lord Archon. Controversial as it
may be, the angry, merciless and bloodthirsty
Old Testament God is another version of the
Demiurge/Lord Archon, hence it is called
'The Lord'. 'He' is quoted as saying at the
very start of *Genesis:* 'Let there be light.' I say
that the *Genesis* narrative about the 'creation
of the world' is actually symbolising the
creation of the Matrix with 'light' as the star
of the show (Fig 281). There is widespread

Figure 281: The Demiurge/Lord Archon – the Light of the World.

Figure 282: The near-death 'tunnel? But where does it lead?

confusion between light (as in the light that allows you to see in the dark, sunlight,
lamplight) and the frequency band of visible light and the electromagnetic spectrum.
Scientists talk about dark matter and dark energy, but these are terms that only mean
they are invisible to us (of another frequency) and not that they are pitch black – hey,
Ethel, got a match? When you are resonating to the same frequency as your reality you
can 'see' just as well as you can in visible light. It is not about 'light' in terms of
luminosity, but the frequency band of what we perceive as light – the frequency band,
or one of them, of the Matrix. The light is not the way out of here – it's the *trap.*
Inversion, inversion, inversion.

How interesting then that many near-death experiencers tell the same story of
passing through a tunnel with an immensely bright light at the end when they leave the
body (Fig 282). They feel bliss and euphoria and meet spirit beings or long departed
loved ones who tell them they must go back because their time [slavery] on Earth isn't
over or they are given the choice to stay or return. I have pondered on all this over the
years but as the puzzle pieces have come together I am sure this is all another Archon
Matrix illusion. It's my view that if you 'go to the Light' you will stay in the Matrix to be
recycled back to five-sense Earth for another lifetime of slavery, no, oops, sorry, another
incarnation on your endless journey of learning on the road to enlightenment. More
mysteries are solved from this perspective. Why do so few people remember their
previous lives here in the madhouse? Memories are erased by passing through

immensely powerful electromagnetic fields, which are a far more potent version of technology used by the inner circles of the intelligence community to delete memories of those with knowledge they don't want to be shared. The principle is the same. Why do so many people incarnate into horrific circumstances of war, hunger, suffering and deprivation? Some explain this away by talking about karma or cause and effect and you reap what you sow. I am not saying that this does not happen through energetic attraction or that souls incarnate together for a mutual experience or task; but what if that was not the whole story at all? What if souls with erased memories and still in ignorance were simply being recycled back into the Matrix? Remember those questions again: Who are we? Where are we? What is this

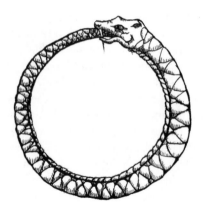

Figure 283: Leviathan, Ouroboros or 'Ring-Pass-Not' which Gnostics said is beyond Saturn and must be breached to escape the world of the Demiurge.

reality? Why don't we remember where we have come from to get here? I mean, look at it. Generation after generation, perceived millennium after millennium, humans come and go, come and go, with no idea where they come from or where they are going to? I can't be alone in thinking that all this seems ludicrous unless it is *made* to be that way? I hear the New Age-type explanation that we have to experience everything cold so we can 'learn our lessons' but I don't buy it. Religions of the East have reincarnation as a founding principle and the way the process is described sounds remarkably like the scenario I have been setting out. Buddhism, for example, portrays reincarnation as a cycle of struggle and suffering (slavery) known as the wheel of Samsara. The cycle is eternal until a soul's frequency is raised (awareness expanded) to allow liberation from the cycle. That, in a sentence, is what I am saying, too, from my own research and experience, which has had nothing to do with Buddhism or any other religion. I would say that expanded awareness (higher frequency) allows liberation from the *Matrix*.

Saturn Ring-Pass-Not

Common themes are everywhere as we can see with the Nag Hammadi texts of the Gnostics. They say that souls are duped by further simulated illusion, or *phantasia*, at the point of death and to escape the Archontic fake reality they had to pass beyond the planetary spheres of the Archons. They say the outermost of them is ... here we go again ... *Saturn*. This is the planet (sun) associated with death and symbolised as the Grim Reaper. Gnostics said that beyond Saturn was Leviathan, the *(reptilian)* snake or serpent swallowing its own tale and also known as the Ouroboros (Fig 283). Biblical Leviathan of the Old Testament is said to be an ancient serpent sea monster. The Ouroboros is symbolic of the outer walls of the frequency net and Gnostics said that souls had to pass through Leviathan to reach Paradise. An Ouroboros around Saturn can be seen at the Mother Lodge of Freemasonry in London (Fig 284). In-the-know levels of secret societies serve the Archon agenda and have access to a mass of knowledge kept from the public and their other members. This Ouroboros theme takes us to the 'Ring-Pass-Not', a

Figure 284: Saturn encircled by Leviathan/Ouroboros/Ring-Pass-Not in the Mother Lodge of Freemasonry in London. The illuminated 'moon' shape inside the ring is symbolic of Saturn for reasons I explain in *The Perception Deception*.

mystical or occult (hidden) concept of a circle or frontier within which consciousness of those still under the sway of the delusion of separateness is entrapped. Gottfried de Purucker's *Occult Glossary* provides this definition: 'An entity, having reached a certain stage of evolutionary growth of the unfolding of consciousness, finds itself unable to pass into a still higher state because of some delusion under which the consciousness is labouring, be that delusion mental or spiritual.' You see what I mean about common themes. All this reminds me of the Voice in the Brazilian rainforest in 2003 which talked to me so clearly for five hours about the illusory nature of reality. At one point I was shown the image of a path across a field. People dropped from the sky and began to walk along the path until it was worn away and transformed into a groove on one of the old vinyl records. They continued to walk through the groove and it became deeper and darker. The Voice said that it was no wonder people looked up for Heaven when it was the only place they could see light. Words and images explained that people drop into the program so easily with each incarnation because they have been there so many times that it's basically second nature. One of my books is called *Tales From The Time Loop*, a term I have used to describe the hamster wheel cycle of the closed-world Matrix (Fig 285). One of the principles of fractal patterns of information is that they are, to quote the Fractal Foundation: 'A never-ending pattern ... created by repeating a simple process over and over in an ongoing feedback loop.' The Matrix in one. Expanded awareness can escape the Matrix at all levels while ignorance keeps you in. Self-identifying with Infinite Awareness and not Phantom Self will take you home and especially if you are streetwise about what you are dealing with.

Figure 285: The Time Loop – a constantly repeating cycle of the same experience within the fake Matrix.

Saturn's left-brain

Energetic influences of Saturn, the reptilian segment of the brain and the left side of the brain all have very similar traits. They are part of the same control system encoding and decoding the Matrix. A brain has two hemispheres with a bridge between them known as the corpus callosum (Fig 286). These hemispheres, or sides, have very distinct 'personalities' and roles to play in decoding reality as mainstream science agrees. We are supposed to integrate both hemispheres via the 'bridge' and be whole-brained, but this is not the case with most people thanks to 'education' and life-long manipulation of reality. The right side of the brain perceives (decodes) unity, not division, and sees wholes, not parts; it is the random, spontaneous, creative, inspirational and unpredictable maverick and has a 'subjective' sense of reality – 'proceeding from or taking place in a person's mind rather than the external world'. Right brain is individuality, artistic and creatively inspired. Mavericks terrify the Archon virus, which demands uniformity and predictability and seeks to suppress the right hemisphere to allow the left side to dominate perception. Personality/decoding traits of the left-brain are focussed on the 'logical, rational and sequential' – all pillars of perception reality pedalled by the Archon conspiracy. System thinkers like Richard Dogma Dawkins are obsessed with what they believe to be logical and rational, but all that means is logical and rational when viewed from a skewed belief in what is real. What can be logical and

Figure 286: The two hemispheres of the brain connected by the bridge of the corpus collosum.

rational to someone who believes in a solid reality can seem like drop-dead stupid to those who don't. The reverse is true, too, of course. Reality perceptions of the left side of the brain are the very epitome of mainstream science and Mainstream Everything. Left-brain reality overwhelmingly decodes into being the world that people think they daily experience. Left-brain is 'objective' which means 'based on observable phenomena, presented factually: an objective appraisal'. Put another way ... can I touch it, taste it, smell it, hear it or see it? I *can*? Oh, it must exist then. Try telling the left-brain what the right-brain can perceive and it will dismiss the very idea. 'That right-brain must be deluded or mad', it will say. 'It should get a proper education like me.' Left-brain is the target and focus of System education with all its emphasis on remembering names, dates and alleged facts in pursuit of its definition of intelligence (Fig 287). Education can be nicely summarised as dealing with 'observable phenomena, presented factually' (or its version of factually). Pursuits that activate and stimulate right brain awareness such as the arts and music hardly register by comparison, either in number or funding, within the school system. Children are beginning left-brain education at an ever earlier age to ensure the left hemisphere will dominate their sense of self and reality for the rest of their lives. Many American states already have mandatory pre-school kindergarten and a movement is growing to do the same everywhere to trap in The System even children who are going to be home-schooled. A Conservative party pressure group in

Figure 287: 'Education' works to imprison perception in the left side of the brain.

Figure 288: Left-brains at the ready. Atten-shun.

Britain called Bright Blue (blue it may be) has called for parents to be denied child benefit payments if they don't send their children to government pre-school 'education' from the age of three. Their left-brain is the target at the expense of the right although the programmed education foot soldiers involved will have no idea. Freethinking imagination called 'play' is being squeezed by left-brain schoolwork and 'smart' technology, because ad-lib playing activates the right side of the brain (Fig 288). Education is an excellent example of compartmentalisation or the mushroom technique of keep them in the dark and feed them bullshit. Most teachers have no idea that they are programing children to become The System's software. They are only teaching what they are told to teach and how to teach. Do it any other way and your job has gone. You have to go deep into the hidden networks before you will find anyone who knows what the game is. The left-brain is also our arbiter of time, or sense of time, and this is where the bit about 'sequential' comes in. Left-brain decodes information in the timeless NOW and makes it appear to happen in the sequence that we know as 'time'. The speed it makes the sequence happen dictates how you experience the passage of 'time'. Right-brain can connect you with 'out there' and the left is focussed almost entirely on the 'down here'. While right-brain sees connections and unity of everything, the left side sees only parts with 'space' in between. It sees dots, not pictures, and is obsessed with structure and hierarchy. This is, not by coincidence, the reality of Mainstream Everything. The following quote is a good example of the difference between brain hemispheres: 'The moment a little boy is concerned with which is a jay and which is a sparrow [left-brain] ... he can no longer see the birds or hear them sing [right-brain].' The System is structured to entrap the human sense of reality in the left side of the brain so we decode reality in a form that most enslaves us, and it deploys guards at the entrance to the left-brain called teachers, academics, scientists, media people, politicians and others to block right-brain influence (Fig 289). In the same way that soldiers fight wars without understanding the true background so these guards insist on subordination to left-brain perceptions even though this is oppressing *them,* too, and their own families, by suppressing their sense of reality (Fig 290). They are left-brain prisoners working to imprison every subsequent generation and have no idea they are doing so. You can't see how everything is connected and how the dots fit together if your reality is only the result of left-brain perception. Left-brain can't decode unity when it can perceive only apartness and this is the perception that dominates education, science, medicine, politics, media, economics and business. We talk about people being 'in the box' and in decoding terms the left side of the brain is the box. It's a jail cell, a neurological Alcatraz. I don't mean of course that it has no part to play as part of the whole brain; but when it is the dictator of perception at the expense of right-brain insight the cell door slams shut.

Everything connects

When you compare left-brain reality-traits with those attributed to Saturn and the reptilian aspect of the human brain more pieces come together. Left-brain is focussed on five-sense reality, hierarchical structures, rules and laws, apartness and time-space, and dictates a sense of time through its sequencing. Reptilian brain involves obsessive, compulsive and ritualistic behaviour, conforming to precedent, an obsession with hierarchical structures of power, laws, rules and regulations, a desire to control, protection of status, power, reputation, superiority and intellectual pre-eminence. Saturn's energy/information influence on perception and behaviour has even been given a name – 'Saturnine' – and Saturn's colour is black. (see 'black goo' and virus/Saturn symbol Darth Vader in Star Wars). Vader is the 'heroic Jedi Knight seduced by the dark side of the Force' (the virus). Saturnine is defined as 'having the temperament of one born

Figure 289: The System's guards on the gate to the left-brain to repel influence from the right side.

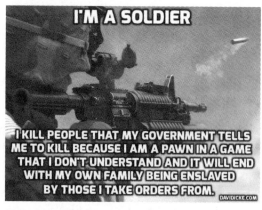

Figure 290: Left-brain enslavement.

under the supposed astrological influence of Saturn, melancholy or sullen, marked by a tendency to be bitter or sardonic, a gloomy temperament, taciturn, broodingly and sullenly unhappy'. Saturn's astrological (energetic) characteristics are cold and non-emotive, limitation, austerity, discipline and depression. Saturn energy represents banking (astrologically ruled by Saturn); politics and intuitions of State at all levels

Figure 291: Black gowns throughout The System are Saturn symbolism – black is the colour associated with Saturn.

(astrologically ruled by Saturn); corporations (astrologically ruled by Saturn); law and the court system (astrologically ruled by Saturn); and science (astrologically ruled by Saturn). Add to this the fact that major religions are worshipping Saturn while all but a few of those involved have no idea this is so. Saturn symbolism is reflected in the black gowns of judges, barristers, priests, rabbis and academia (Fig 291). Mortarboards or squares worn by students when they graduate are Saturn symbols placed on the crown chakra as they are awarded their degree of programming, just as secret society members are awarded their degrees of initiation. Put the traits associated with Saturn together with those of left-brain and reptilian brain and you have the world of the Matrix and the attitudes, structures and goals of the Matrix.

These are the insights and understandings that people need in order to break free from the prison of the mind, and the prison of perception. Awareness of what is happening and the methods of manipulation immediately begins the process of disconnecting you from the Matrix, by bringing subconscious to conscious, hidden to the seen. Swiss analytical psychologist Carl Jung said: 'Until you make the unconscious conscious, it will direct your life and you will call it fate.' Phantom Self is constructed in the subconscious and making Phantom Self visible to the conscious – the point of this book – begins to disconnect us from its influence. Humanity is being subjected to a monumental program of ongoing control that Phantom Self could not begin to imagine, but Infinite Awareness is all-powerful and cannot be enslaved except through manipulation into isolated ignorance – which is what has happened.

All might seem lost if you have read this far and I understand that, but I promise you it isn't. We are going to turn this around by flipping the inversion and the bottom-line to that is for Phantom Self to become Infinite Self.

CHAPTER SIX

Saturnism

I will not let anyone walk through my mind with their dirty feet
Mahatma Gandhi

Phantom Self is a subconscious construct of programmed perception, response and behaviour founded on *belief*. This is defined as something 'accepted as true'. A belief does not have to *be* true and usually isn't – only *accepted* to be true.

Without unyielding belief there can be no Phantom Self and without Phantom Self there can be no Archontic control system. The race is on from birth to program every human to believe in *something* as long as it's not true. Layer after layer of further beliefs that are not true go on being added until Phantom Self is formed and solidified and its program is dictating perception. These programs are in the virus (original sin) running through Body-Mind but they can remain dormant, or their influence diluted, by access to awareness beyond the Matrix. Rigid belief brings the virus to life but at any moment its impact can be dissipated by awakening to Infinite Self. Programming propaganda from cradle to grave forms a bubble of belief or Phantom Self to block this awakening (Fig 292). Mark Twain said: 'Loyalty to a petrified opinion never yet broke a chain or freed a human soul.' Phantom Self is instinctively attracted to belief. Its software code is written to sync and attach to beliefs no matter what they are. 'Come on ladies and gentlemen ... gather round ... get your beliefs here ... something for everyone and every pocket.' The prime belief that starts us off is 'I am human'. I use the term in the sense of self-identification with the body as who we are. Our Infinite nature and the fact that we are not human but only having an *experience* as a human is lost at first base. 'I am a human' then becomes 'I am a man' and 'I am a woman' and these are sub-divided endlessly today into I am

Figure 292: Phantom Self is a believer.

black/white, lesbian, gay, bisexual. I am not decrying any of these 'life choices'. I am only pointing out how self-idenity is being ever sub-divided until the sense of self is a pinhead to infinity. I know I have said that the two are the same but it's the *perception* that they're not that entraps you. All System influences collectively confirm that you are indeed your body, name and family background, living in a solid world, and that you can be defined by the label on your trainers and the colour of your hair. 'Look, there's a ginger!' In the absence of expanded awareness saying 'Hey, hold on a second, I have some questions', Phantom Self goes on absorbing more and more perception programs. There may appear to be a diversity of beliefs and perception called religions, atheism, scientific dogma, political 'choice', Establishment and anti-Establishment, but they are all reflections of the same System and Matrix. Archons and their hybrids know that beliefs and the illusion of diversity offer limitless potential for divide and rule. Beliefs invariably involve a sub-theme of limitation. This can be anything from the laws of physics to subordination to a god who both loves you and will cut your balls off if you don't do what 'He' says. Rigid belief is like a concrete bubble resisting all attempts at escape or infiltration, and the only antidote to the virus of belief is to transfer your point of attention and self-identity from the bubble to Infinite Awareness. Many will say 'we have to believe something' but this is not the case – as I will come to.

Heard it all before

Religion perfectly illustrates my point that the foundation of all belief is the same whatever label may be pinned to its door. There would seem to be so many religions. I mean, what diversity ... Christianity, Islam, Judaism, Hinduism, Mormonism, Jehovah's Witnesses, Buddhism, Sikhism ... the isms have no end as new ones continue to appear and subdivide into the inevitable factions arguing over the fine detail of mostly pure baloney (Fig 293). They usually begin with a focus on one person or founder and after that everything is handled through corporate headquarters (see the Vatican, Mecca, etc.) and the PR department. Religion as software is confirmed by its association with location. If you are born in India you are massively more likely to be a Hindu believer and the same with Islam and the Middle East, Judaism in Israel and Christianity in the Deep South. This applies even to black people in the United States and Africa whose ancestors were enslaved by Christian believers. Some slave traders wrote hymns, like

Figure 293: 'Different' religions – same 'god'.

Amazing Grace. The religion program involves a belief system, a deity, worshippers of the deity, 'sacred' places to worship the deity and people in frocks operating as middlemen, sometimes women, between worshippers and deity (Fig 294). Er, that's it really. Christianity = God/Jesus; Christians; churches; priests/bishops. Islam = Allah/Mohammed; Muslims; mosques; clerics/imams. Judaism = Yahweh/Jehovah/Moses; Jews; synagogues; rabbis. We see the same structure and pattern with almost all of them. This includes the 'only through me' intimidation deal which says that only by believing in the given deity can you make it to paradise and it's hell and damnation if you don't. There can be the odd exception, but religions tick all or most of these boxes with their appointed dictators to interpret the deity's thoughts and tell you what 'He' demands that you do ...'I think what God meant to say', as the late, great American comedian Bill Hicks brilliantly put it. You can crop your hair (Buddhism) or never crop your hair (Sikhism). You can turn up in a tunic (Hinduism) or a suit (Christianity). These little details give the impression of diversity and a choice of belief; but the 'little me' program is non-negotiable – you are down there, the deity is up there

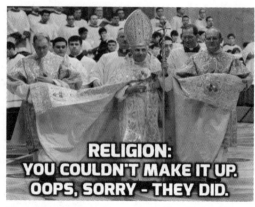

Figure 294: I can't speak, just had a word fail.

and the frocks or suits are in the middle. Religions are nothing more than hierarchical (again) cults and they are structured and administered as cults to impose *belief* and acquiescence on which they are founded. These are some of the manipulation methods of cults:

- Tricking people into joining the cult and accepting its rules and lifestyle without them fully understanding what they are getting involved in.
- Isolating members so they only mix with other advocates of the cult. Demanding absolute devotion to the cult and deity of the cult and submission to the leadership.
- Destroying members' self-esteem and sense of self until they are unquestioning pawns of the leadership.
- Preventing cult followers from making decisions about their own lives and dictating in detail their actions and behaviour.
- Orchestrating group attacks on anyone who questions or refuses to conform.
- Getting members to confess their 'sins'.
- Cutting ties to friends and family not in the cult.

Virtually all religions follow this same blueprint. Some follow the list exactly and others use some of the methods or take a milder approach with 'encouragement' and manipulation of fear and guilt rather than outright compulsion; but in theme they're all the same and worshipping the same fake 'god' – the Demiurge – worshipped by Satanism and secret societies (Fig

Figure 295: All have the same master.

Figure 296: Bubble religion.

295). Tricking people into joining something they don't fully understand is clear to see with religion. What do Christians, Muslims, Jews and Hindus know about the faith that they follow? Only what the religion tells them. How many do any off-message research to see if the cover story stands up? They buy their beliefs like tins of peas – off the shelf and straight to checkout. All religion is a form of madness and in many cases an extreme form. We have had girls left to die in burning buildings because insane and psychopathic 'religious police' in Saudi Arabia would not let them out when they were not 'properly dressed'. A father stopped rescuers in Dubai from saving his drowning daughter because he said he would rather she died than be 'dishonoured' by male lifeguards touching her (saving her life). I told a Christian lady once that Jesus was only one of a long list of deities in many cultures about whom the same basic story was told and often in precise detail. She immediately rejected the very idea but when a fellow Christian said that actually it was true she replied: 'Well, it doesn't matter anyway.' Concrete has set in the bubble and it won't be breached (Fig 296). If religious believers would only calmly and dispassionately look at the evidence (not easy with the program running) they would be shocked at what the frocks are not telling them (and often the inner sanctum is not telling the frocks). Does this remind you of anyone?

Born of a virgin on December 25th and, as the Holy Child, was placed in a Manger. He was a travelling teacher who performed miracles. He 'rode in a triumphal procession on an ass'. He was a sacred king killed and eaten in a Eucharistic ritual for fecundity and purification. He rose from the dead on March 25th. He was the God of the Vine, and turned water into wine. He was called 'King of Kings' and 'God of Gods'. He was considered the 'Only Begotten Son', 'Saviour', 'Redeemer', 'Sin Bearer', 'Anointed One' and the 'Alpha and Omega'. He was identified with the Ram or Lamb. His sacrificial title of 'Dendrites' or 'Young Man of the Tree' intimates that he was hung on a tree or crucified.

Jesus, surely? Nope ... Dionysus, the Greek 'Jesus' and a counterpart of Bacchus, a Roman Jesus, long before the Jesus version of the same story was written or plagiarised. What later became December 25th was the birth date given to these pre-Jesus saviour deities because it corresponded with the period of the Pagan midwinter festival of which the 'Christian' Christmas is only a continuation. Decorated trees,

Figure 297:

Figure 298: Mithra, a pre-Jesus 'Jesus', was associated with Helios and called the Unconquered Sun – Saturn.

exchanging presents, holly and other symbols of the 'Christian' Christmas originate in the pre-Christian world. Christmas is only the modern version of Saturnalia, a Roman midwinter festival dedicated to the chief god of Rome ... *Saturn*. Rome was called 'City of Saturn' and virtually all religions are worshipping Saturn under countless names and codes for the Gnostic Demiurge. At their inner core most are founded on *Saturn*ism (Satanism) and certainly major ones (Fig 297). Mithra or Mithras was a Roman and Persian Jesus-before-Jesus who was said to be born on our December 25th and was known as 'the vine', 'good shepherd', 'redeemer', 'saviour' and 'messiah' who performed miracles and had 12 disciples or followers. He was the lion, the lamb, 'the way, the truth and the light', and was worshipped at the spring equinox (Christian Easter) when Mithra was said to be 'resurrected' after lying dead for three days (Fig 298). Mithras Day or the Lord's Day was Sunday and Mithra rituals included baptism, the Eucharist and a sacred meal involving bread, water and wine. An image of Mithra in the catacombs of Rome portrays him as a child sitting on his mother's lap with Persian Magi offering gifts. A Mother Mary character and a virgin birth are more constants with the dying and resurrected god deities long before Jesus appeared. Reptilian mother and child figurines were found in graves of the Ubaid culture (6,500 to 3,800 BC) in what later became Sumer and Babylon, now Iraq, and a stream of 'Mother Marys' followed across the cultures. The Christian Mother Mary was just another version of the same recurring story. Virgin mothers included the Egyptian Isis and Babylonian Semiramis or Ishtar (Fig 299). Semiramis is the deity who was said to have come from the Moon and landed

Figure 299: The theme of the virgin mother abounds throughout history and the Bible account of Mother Mary is just another plagiarised version put into a different historical context.

in the River Euphrates in her 'moon egg'. Multiple Jesus deities before Jesus and many mothers before Mother Mary can be explained by the travels of Archon bloodlines and peoples they ruled, especially to and from the Middle East and Asia. Religion is in many ways the ultimate hoax which both slams shut the mind to Infinite Awareness while simultaneously manipulating followers to worship as their 'God' the very force that is enslaving them. Religion is an Archon blueprint that has splintered into many faces, facets and guises but they're

Figure 300: The 'Christian' mitre originates with the headgear worn by ancient priests worshipping Archon fish gods.

all the same program employing different names and slightly different beliefs, rules and regulations as the religion virus has been spread across the world. Religious Phantom Self is among the most programmed of all. I have provided detailed background to religion in my other books and I will summarise here in the context of Phantom Self. I'll pick up the story in Babylon (founded about 1,894BC) although the origins of religion go back much further as we perceive time. Babylonians worshipped a trinity of deities – Nimrod, the Father god; Queen Semiramis, or Ishtar, the virgin mother; and Tammuz, or Ninus, the son. Myths say that when Nimrod died he became the sun god Baal and impregnated Semiramis with the rays of the sun. From this union came Tammuz in a *virgin birth*. Tammuz was believed to be a reincarnation of Nimrod and so ... 'Father and Son were one'. Babylonian beliefs were transferred by the bloodlines and their peoples eventually to Rome, and the Babylonian Trinity became the Christian Trinity of Father God (Nimrod), Jesus (Tammuz) and Holy Ghost or Spirit, symbolised as a dove. This just happens to be the symbol in Babylon of the goddess Semiramis/Ishtar and Babylonian attributes and titles for this goddess were attached by the new Christianity to Mother Mary – virgin mother, Queen of Heaven and such like. Easter comes from Babylon along with the Easter egg (Ishtar's 'moon egg'), Easter bunnies (related to Tammuz) and hot cross buns. Easter and Christmas are both recycled Paganism and so is virtually every other religious festival and symbol including the cross. Babylonians didn't put crosses on their buns for no reason. The 'Christian' mitre' comes from the headgear worn by Babylonian priests worshipping the 'fish gods' under names such as Oannes, Dagon or Ea (Fig 300). Remember that one of the Anunnaki brothers, Enki or Ea, was associated with water and the Zulu name for the brothers is Wowane and Mpanku – the 'water brothers' of the Chitauri who are said to have brought the Moon. How do Christians with their mitred priests symbolise Jesus? As a *fish*.

Saturn worship

Roman Emperor Constantine (272-337AD) officially founded today's Christianity at the Council of Nicaea in 325AD. Constantine had no problem changing religions because he wasn't really changing anything except the name. He worshipped Sol Invictus, the 'Unconquered Sun', just as Babylonians worshipped the sun god Nimrod/Tammuz who became Father God/Jesus. Mithra was the 'Invincible Sun' or 'Unconquered Sun'.

Figure 301: Everything falls into place when you see that Sun gods were *Saturn* sun gods.

Figure 302: Church of Babylon relocated.

Here's the question that unlocks so much: They were sun gods, but *which sun?* Rome's major deity was not the sun we know today but the Black Sun/Dark Sun – *Saturn*. Oh, how the pennies fall by the billion when you realise that the ancient sun gods were *Saturn* sun gods (Fig 301). Among them are Atum/Ra (Egypt); Utu (Sumer); and Shamash/Ninib (Babylon). Norse god myths had the same meaning. Ancient Greeks called Saturn 'Helios' and Romans called it Sol – hence Emperor Constantine's Sol Invictus. Helios is translated as sun in the sense of the one we see shining today, but this is the wrong sun. Helios is Saturn and we have Mithra, the Jesus blueprint, associated with Helios and called Sol Invictus or Unconquered Sun. There were once two suns with Saturn the most dominant in the Earth sky and the focus of worship. Heliopolis or 'City of the Sun', in Egypt, was dedicated to Saturn and an original obelisk made for Heliopolis stands to this day outside the Vatican in the centre of St Peter's Square in Rome. Why? The Roman Church (and all forms of Christianity, which came from the Roman Church) is a continuation of the Babylonian and Roman religion – the worship of Saturn (Fig 302). Emperor Gaius Caligula ordered the Heliopolis obelisk to be moved to Rome in 37AD when Romans were openly worshipping Saturn in the 'Christmas' festival of Saturnalia (Fig 303). Rome is still the 'City of Saturn' ('City of the Sun') with more obelisks than Egypt and several from Heliopolis. Original Egyptian obelisks are also located in London, Paris and New York, and the Washington Monument is the same symbolism (Fig 304). Obelisks are in part symbolic of the penis (bloodline) and translations include 'Baal's shaft' or 'Baal's organ of

![Figure 303]

Figure 303: The obelisk made for Heliopolis, the City of the Sun (Saturn), now standing in St Peter's Square amid the City of Saturn that is Rome.

Figure 304: Original Egyptian obelisks in London, New York and Paris, and the Washington Monument in Washington DC.

reproduction'. Baal was another name for Nimrod (Saturn/Father God). Obelisks are used profusely by secret societies like the Freemasons although most of their compartmentalised initiates will not know the significance.

Christianity's 'God' is the Demiurge/Saturn, and the Christian Devil, or Satan, is the Demiurge/Saturn. What a perfect hoax – you worship me and give me your energy and allegiance whichever deity you choose. You worship the God of Light? That's me. God of Darkness? That's also *meeeeee!* The same story plays out across the major religions. Energy flows where attention goes and worship is an extreme form of attention. This means that a focus on either the Christian God or Christian Devil creates an energetic connection to the frequency of the same deity – the Gnostic Demiurge/Saturn. They can be combined because Saturn is infested and controlled by the Demiurge virus, as a computer can be overwhelmed and directed from its original purpose and mode of operation to become a full-blown manifestation of the virus. 'Saturn god' really means 'Archon god' or Demiurge. There was no virus in the original bad copy and Saturn had to be subsequently infected. Saturn, in short, has been possessed and become a 'fallen angel' or Archon. Yahweh/Jehovah, the Old Testament god of Judaism, is so shockingly bloodthirsty and lusts for violence, power and control because this version of 'God' is also a name for the Demiurge/Saturn. Gnostics associated the Old Testament god with the Demiurge who created the fake 'physical' reality, and, as I have mentioned, I contend that the 'God' creating the world at the start of Genesis is actually the Gnostic Demiurge creating the Matrix – 'Let there be light'. The Jewish god El ('Mighty One') is their Saturn god and can be seen within the collective name of Elohim (Archons). Elohim appears in the Bible 2,500 times. An extreme Christian group based in Oklahoma call their community 'Elohim City' with no idea what the name really refers to. Saturn-day or Saturday is sacred to Jews as the Shabbat/Sabbath and the Christian day of worship is *Saturn Sun*day. Tetragrammaton is the Hebrew name for God that 'must never be spoken', and also appears as YHWH (sometimes YHVH), Yahweh, Jehovah, El/Elohim, Adonai ('My Lord') and profusely in the Bible as the 'Lord'. Tetragrammaton is the 'Lord Archon' or Demiurge/Saturn. A Greek form of the Tetragrammaton was Iao 'the highest of all the gods' and ancient Greek historian Diodorus Siculus said Iao (Demiurge/Saturn) was the God of Moses. Iao is the god of Autumn (death/Saturn) in Greek mythology and became associated with the term

'Diablo' or Devil. I have also seen articles
which relate Iao and Saturn to the Holy
Spirit which enters humans 'in the form of a
white dove'. El, the Hebrew Saturn god, is
encoded within the name IsraEL, and some
believe that Israel is a combination of Isis,
the Egyptian goddess, Ra, the (Saturn) sun
god of Egypt, and EL, the Hebrew god of
Saturn. Greek historian Diodorus of Sicily
notes an inscription at Nysa in Arabia in
which Isis is proclaimed as 'the eldest
daughter of Saturn, most ancient of the
gods'. Israel's symbol is the hexagram or
'Star of David'/Seal of Solomon, an ancient
symbol for Saturn and the origin of the
name 'Rothschild'. This financial banking
dynasty was the driving and manipulating
force behind the creation of the modern
Israel on a blatant historical lie. We see the Saturn
god El encoded into ang-*EL* and archang-*EL*s
called Micha-*EL*, Gabri-*EL*, Uri-*EL*, Rapha-*EL* and
Archon Fallen Ang-*EL*s. Politicians are *El*-ected in
El-lections and we have a bloodline *El*-lite. Archon
comes from its Greek meaning of ruler and we
have *arch*-angel, *arch*-bishop and hier*archy*. Words
matter in terms of their frequency and if you
encode words with names for the Demiurge virus
they carry that frequency (Fig 305).

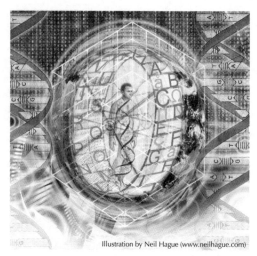

Illustration by Neil Hague (www.neilhague.com)

Figure 305: Words are frequencies and the frequency
of language is part of the programming – or can be.

Islam's most sacred location and symbol is the
black Kaaba cube in Mecca (Fig 306). Kaaba means
cube and a cube is an ancient symbol for Saturn.
Muslims, too, are worshipping the
Demiurge/Saturn although only the inner core
will know. Religious Jews wear a black cube on
their forehead (energetic location of the third eye)
called a Tefillin, which contains scrolls of
parchment inscribed with verses from their written
law or Torah (Fig 307). Jews and Muslims worship
the same deity – Demiurge/Saturn. A major pre-
Islamic god in Arabia was called Sin and one of the
centres of Sin worship was Mecca. Sin is recorded
as a god of the Moon from his symbol of a crescent,
but readers of *The Perception Deception* will know

Figure 306: Mega – or Mecca –
manipulation.

Figure 307: Saturn on his mind.

that the crescent has major symbolic associations with Saturn. Sin morphed into 'al-
ilah', or 'al-llah', and later '*Allah*' when the Prophet Mohammed ended the multiple-god
system and proclaimed that Allah (Sin) was the only god. Islam has fundamental Hindu

influences and origins, and constant
cross-references between religions are
explainable by the fact that at their core
they are manifestations of the same
religion. Does anyone really think it's a
coincidence that major Archon-Reptilian
bloodlines emerged out of Sumer,
Babylon and Egypt into Rome, Europe
and the wider world, and that
Christianity, Islam and Judaism all
emerged from the very same locations?
Or that Archon-Reptilian 'seed' was
widely spread into India from where
Hinduism comes? Or that what is called
New Age in the West is basically an
outgrowth of Hinduism? Saturday or
Saturn's Day in India is called 'Shanivar'
after Shani, the Hindu god of Saturn. Lord
Shiva, regarded by Hinduism as the
Supreme Being and given pride of place at
CERN, also has Saturn connections and is
described as having the Moon in his hair.
Shiva is said to be responsible for
maintaining the life cycle (Saturn-Moon
Matrix). Hindu goddess Kali represents
Saturn (and astrologically the Moon in
Saturn) and she is associated with classic
Saturn traits of death, time and the colour
black. Singer Madonna has mimicked the

Figure 308: Madonna as Kali.

Figure 309: If they only knew.

protruding tongue of Kali in her many Saturn-themed performances (Fig 308).
Hinduism and religions of the East also promote the reincarnation you-must-stay-in-
the-Matrix-after-death belief system. Religions are doing the work of the virus as
creations of the virus and most religious advocates and followers are genuine people
being scammed by the program (Fig 309). Saturn connections to religious worship are
incredible and highly detailed. *The Perception Deception* will blow your mind if you
haven't read it already. When you feel the atmosphere of most churches and centres of
religious worship (and observe the demeanour of the British royal family) they can all
be described as saturnine – 'melancholy, gloomy, taciturn, and sullen'.

Secrets of Saturn

Secret societies would appear to most people to have no connection to religion. Many
religions condemn them even though religions at their core are all secret societies, too.
This is no surprise when both are different forms of Demiurge/Saturn worship as is
Satanism. They use the same symbols, ritualism and techniques of compartmentalised
ignorance. Freemasons call their 'god' the 'Great Architect' and Gnostics referred to the
Demiurge as the 'Great Architect' – architect of the Matrix (Fig 310). Oh, no, Freemasons

Figure 310: Freemasons refer to their 'god' as the 'Great Architect' – the same name that Gnostics used for the Demiurge creator of the Matrix.

Figure 311: The beard theme in the depiction of God, Santa Claus and the Architect creator of the Matrix.

Figure 312: Chronos and the beard religions.

will say, architect comes from the masonic guilds from which Freemasonry was formed; but Gnostics weren't masons and the concept of the Great/Grand Architect of the Universe or Supreme Architect of the Universe can be found in early Christianity (from its Babylonian crossover). Christian extremist John Calvin (1509-1564), founder of Calvinism, widely referred to the Christian God as the 'Architect of the Universe'. Architect is *arch*-itect/Archon-tect. In the *Matrix* movie trilogy the creator of the Matrix was 'the Architect' with his white beard and the personification of 'God' is usually depicted with a beard. 'Santa' – an anagram of Satan and a symbol of the Demiurge god of Saturnalia – is the same (Fig 311). For reasons I explain in *The Perception Deception* beards are associated with Saturn worship and we have so many 'beard' religions which have followed the bearded Chronos personification of Saturn in ancient Greece (Fig 312). William Blake, the British writer, artist and student of the esoteric, produced a painting in 1794 entitled *The Ancient of Days* which is really the bearded Chronos with his architect's compass and the same theme appears on the Archon-Reptilian bloodline-controlled GE building in the Rockefeller Center, New York, which became the Comcast building in 2015 (Fig 313 and 314). Ancient of Days is a term for 'God' (Saturn) in several languages and religions and the *Book of Daniel* says: '... One like a son of man approaches the Ancient of Days and is

Figure 313: William Blake's *The Ancient of Days.*
© The Whitworth Gallery

Figure 314: The same theme at the former GE building in the Rockefeller Center, New York with the mention of time in the words.

invested with worldwide dominion; moreover, his everlasting reign over all kings and kingdoms is shared with "the people of the Most High".' The 'Most High' is Saturn.

Secret societies may appear to be 'individual' entities with different names but they are a crucial foundation of the Archontic global web. They interlock with each other and every other aspect of the web. Secret societies operate by their very nature in secret from mainstream society.

The Masonic Structure

Scottish Rite
33 Sovereign Grand Inspector General
32 Sublime Prince of the Royal Secret
31 General Inspector Inquisitor Commander
30 Grand Elect Knight K–H
29 Knight of St. Andrew
28 Knight of the Sun
27 Commander of the Temple
26 Prince of Mercy
25 Knight of the Brazca Serpent
24 Prince of the Tabernacle
23 Child of the Tabernacle
22 Prince of Libanus
21 Patriach Noachite
20 Master Ad Vitam
19 Grand Pontiff
18 Knight of the Rose Croix of HRDM
17 Knight of the East and West
16 Prince of Jerusalem
15 Knight of the East or Sword
14 Grand Elect Mason
13 Master of the Ninth Arch
12 Grand Master Architect
11 Sublime Master Ejected
10 Elect of Fifteen
9 Master Elect of Fifteen
8 Intendent of the Building
7 Provost and Judge
6 Intimate Secretary
5 Perfect Master
4 Secret Master
3 Master Mason
2 Fellow Craft
1 Entered Apprentice

Other-dimensional
Reptilians

Reptilian
hybrids

York Rite
Order of Knights Templar
Order of Knights Malta
Order of Red Cross
Royal Arch Mason
Most Excellent Master
Past Master (Virtual)
Mark Master
Master Mason
Fellow Craft
Entered Apprentice

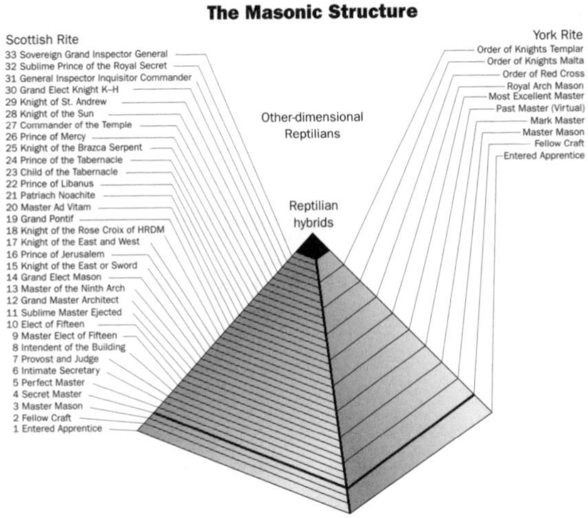

Figure 315: The compartmentalised degrees of Freemasonry.

They manipulate people and events from the hidden while making it appear to the public that ensuing events and happenings are random or the work of whoever is officially tagged with the blame. Freemasonry alone has among its ranks politicians, police, lawyers, judges, doctors, journalists, bankers, business leaders, military top brass, intelligence chiefs and people in every walk of life you need to coordinate decisions and actions to secure the outcome that you want. Secret societies have the added benefit of being so fiercely compartmentalised that only a few in the inner circle will know the ultimate game and the real force behind it (Fig 315). There is always a cover story for the compartmentalised useful idiots, however apparently important they appear to the public to be. They can serve a secret society by doing something they think is for one reason when it is really part of a much bigger picture. 'Individual' secret societies funnel chosen initiates – usually bloodline – into a higher pyramid that many call the 'Illuminati' or illuminated servants of the Demiurge/Saturn (Fig 316). Most members of secret societies have no idea this level even exists and entry to its upper echelons is definitely by Archon-Reptilian bloodline only. This secret society web is the communication and organisational network that allows covert engineering of attacks like 9/11, which are orchestrated to provide an

The Archon Pyramid
Archon-Reptilian Hybrids

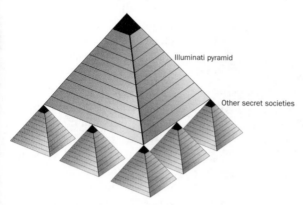

Illuminati pyramid

Other secret societies

Figure 316: There are other levels above the 'individual' secret societies that most of their members have no idea exist.

Figure 317: Jesus being 'resurrected'. Yeah, right.

excuse for transforming society while blaming someone or something else. The *El*-lite Propaganda Due (P2) Freemasonry lodge in Rome provided a wonderful insight into secret society structure and method of operation when it was exposed in the 1980s. P2 was headed by the 'Venerable Master' Licio Gelli, a Mussolini fascist and close friend of Argentina's fascist leader Juan Peron, American President Ronald Reagan and vice-president Father George Archon Bush. Gelli was invited to Reagan's inauguration. Documents that came to light in a police raid revealed that P2 membership included many of Italy's leading figures in the political, intelligence, banking, legal and media *El*-ite. Among them was future prime minister and media tycoon Silvio Berlusconi. P2 members were compartmentalised into sections and the head of each one was only aware of those in his section. Gelli and his inner circle were the only people who knew all the initiates of P2 and they were interacting with each other within the Italian establishment without knowing they were all P2 assets. Secret societies work secretly even with their own membership. P2 controlled the Vatican and its finances. The Roman Church, a relocated Church of Babylon, is an immensely significant part of the same secret society web. At its core the Church of Rome is a central branch of Satanism and worshipping the Demiurge/Archon-Reptilians. They put this on public display with La Resurrezione ('The Resurrection') by sculptor Pericle Fazzini at the Paul VI Audience Hall on the border between the Vatican and Rome (Fig 317). It is claimed to represent Jesus 'rising from this crater torn open by a nuclear bomb; an atrocious explosion, a vortex of violence and energy.' I suggest the image takes us back to CERN, Apollyon/Abaddon and the passage in the Book of Revelation about the opening of the Abyss, 'a great smoking pit', from which a horde of demonic locusts are supposed to rise. Eucharist rituals when participants eat the flesh as bread and drink the blood as red wine are symbolic of the real thing, which Satanists do and did in the Pagan Eucharist before it was Christianised. Catholic Mass is a publicly acceptable version of the Black

Figure 318:
Freemasonic floors
can be found in
many cathedrals.

Mass of Satanism. Major global secret societies such as the
Jesuits, Knights Templar, Knights of Malta and Opus Dei
are all outgrowths of the Roman Church and located in
the City of Saturn. Many Christian churches and
particularly cathedrals have the same black and white

Figure 319: The 33-day Pope who
challenged Freemasonic influence.

squares that you see in Freemasonic and other secret society temples (Fig 318). P2 was
behind the murder of Pope John Paul I after his Freemasonically-significant 33 days in
office in 1978 (Fig 319). He was poisoned after privately ordering the removal of all
Vatican Freemason clergy and staff over their P2 activities. No post-mortem was carried
out on the Pope to cover up the truth and the same network murdered Roberto Calvi,
chairman of Banco Ambrosiano and labelled 'God's banker' for his connections to
Vatican finances. He fled to London after the P2 scandal broke and was murdered to
stop him revealing what he knew. Calvi was found hanged under Blackfriars Bridge at
the entrance to 'The City' – the London financial district controlled to its fingertips by
secret societies and protected by its own Freemason-dominated police force.

Sacrifice to the gods

Secret societies and religion interlock with Satanism and paedophilia as they do with
royalty and the Establishment in general. All are obsessed with ritualistic and
hierarchical behaviour, which are foundation traits of the reptilian brain and genetics
(information blueprint). This is of course not to say that the entire clergy and
membership of secret societies are Satanists and paedophiles, although clearly from
public exposure and my own research many certainly are. Satanism or *Saturn*ism is the
foundation network which ultimately controls the others. Small fry Satanists who
dabble in black arts they largely don't understand won't know anything like the full
picture, but serious Satanists do. Unlike most of those in religion and secret societies
they know they are worshipping pure malevolence and many will know its real nature.
I have spent a quarter of a century investigating Satanism along with other inter-related
subjects and I have spoken with many former targets of Satanic rings (sections of one
global ring) all over the world. Common themes and descriptions abound down to fine
detail. Satanism involves human sacrifice (especially of children), animal sacrifice and
blood drinking (human life force and genetic code) in the same way that ancients did.
Satanism and sacrifice to the gods has been happening since Archon 'gods' moved in.
Human sacrifice and cannibalism began with Archon infiltration when the 'gods'
demanded it. Satanism is a continuation in secret of what was once done openly while it
was considered acceptable. A focus for child sacrifice in the ancient world under its

180

Figure 320: Human sacrifice ritual is not only real, it is incredibly common worldwide. Satanists feed off the blood of the sacrifice and Archons feed off the energy of death and terror.

Figure 321: Some of the world's most famous and prominent people are practicing Satanists interacting with Archontic entities.

many names was ... Saturn. Sacrifice to 'gods' with a preference for 'young virgins' – code for children – is vastly more widespread today than most people would begin to appreciate. Energy and blood of children is particularly sought after by Satanists and Archons. Infamous British Satanist, paedophile and British Intelligence operative Aleister Crowley said:

For the highest spiritual working one must accordingly choose that victim which contains the greatest and purest force. A male child of perfect innocence and high intelligence is the most satisfactory and suitable victim.

Women known as 'breeders' or 'broodmares' are held in captivity all over the world to give birth to babies for sacrifice that never officially exist. Princess Diana described herself as the Windsors' broodmare. A particular form of adrenalin enters the blood stream of those being sacrificed in response to the terror they experience. Satanists want to drink this because it gives these deeply sick and possessed people a 'high'. At the same time the *energy* generated by the terror is absorbed by Archontic demons in the unseen. Here we have the real meaning of sacrifice to the gods. Participants in our reality perform the sacrifice while Archon-Reptilian entities absorb the energy of terror and death (Fig 320). We can't see this energy within visible light (only its effect on behaviour) but we can certainly feel it. Go to a place of death and fear and you will be aware of the vibrational impact. Many participants and witnesses have told me how malevolent entities (often reptilian but far from always) have manifested before them in rituals (Fig 321). This is made possible by the use of colour and sound (chants) of specific frequencies and vibration that create energetic gateways and channels between our reality and the Archon realm. Simultaneous rituals are performed in the Archontic realm and the two 'worlds' are energetically synchronised in the ritual (Fig 322). The more rituals are repeated at the same place the easier it becomes to open these gateways. Beltane (across May 1st) and Halloween (across the end of October) are the biggest satanic ritual periods of the year and this is connected to astrological influences that support the opening of gateways. The dates are reversed in the southern hemisphere. Druids, the religious hierarchy of the Celts, performed the same rituals at the same times that Satanists do today and for the same reasons. They would walk in a torchlight procession on Halloween carrying Celtic crosses (Saturn) and sickles (Saturn). The Celtic cross is a version of the 'cosmic wheel', which was used all over the world to symbolise Saturn and can be seen on ancient Mesopotamian clay tablets (Figs 323 and 324). At each home the Druids demanded a 'trick or treat' which meant a female for sacrifice. If this was refused a hexagram (Saturn) was daubed in blood on the door to alert spirits of the 'horned hunter of the night' (the Demiurge is often represented with horns, hence so is the Devil/Satan). A Jack-O-Lantern or carved pumpkin with a candle inside would be placed outside homes that cooperated to protect them from the evil spirits (Fig 325). 'Treats' were raped and sacrificed on the sacred *bone*fire. Locations of powerful vortexes on the Earth energy grid like Stonehenge were used for this. Many energy lines (ley lines, meridians) cross at these points, and realities can merge – or at least divisions are much thinner. Today's mass promotion of Halloween is to draw people, especially children again, into satanic frequencies – energy flows where attention goes. When people display a Jack-O-Lantern they are making a Druidic sign of cooperation with 'Satan'. Repeated Satanic rituals at major vortex points on the Earth grid can also depress the frequency of the planetary

Figure 322: Rituals are designed to connect the human and Archontic realms.

Figure 323: Ancient depiction of the cosmic wheel – Saturn.

Figure 324: Celtic cross cosmic wheel.

Figure 325: A symbol of cooperation with evil. How many know that when they put them out on Halloween? Energy flows where attention goes.

Figure 326: Archon hierarchy in the unseen becomes satanic hierarchy in the hidden which becomes human hierarchy in the seen.

field or 'sea' and potentially influence everyone as we interact with the 'sea' or Cosmic Internet. A dying Australia Satanist revealed much about the power and methods of Satanism in a document that I publish in full in *Human Race Get off Your Knees*. He wrote: 'What most people do not realise is that Satanism is a ritually based practice and that this repetition has – over time – left strong impressions upon the Morphic Field!' This applies to both the Earth field and the auric field of Satanists. I said earlier that the British Isles was the heart centre of the global energy grid (most powerful vortex or network of vortexes), and this explains why these islands are (a) such a global centre of Satanism; (b) why it has been such a centre of global political and military power; and (c) why it is the home of so many Archon-Reptilian hybrid families and secret societies. If you control the energetic information/frequency state at the heart of the pattern you can do the same to the entire global pattern. Britain – and Rome – is where the hidden Archon power structure is largely centred in the Western world. The United States is powerful on the surface but in many ways it diverts attention from where the power really lies.

Royal Satanists

Satanists willingly open themselves to possession by Archontic entities and they become Archons (virus) incarnate. Satanists can do what they do to children and animals (and each other) because their virus infestation makes them extreme psychopaths with no empathy or remorse to the point where they get high on making people suffer. Archon-Reptilian hierarchy in the unseen becomes satanic hierarchy in our world on the basis of demonic entities that take possession of their human and hybrid vehicles (Fig 326). The higher a possessing demon in the Archon hierarchy the higher will be the one they possess in the satanic hierarchy. This is not to be confused

Figure 327: Politicians decide policy? No, no.

with the Establishment hierarchy that we can see. Those in apparent power in politics and Mainstream Everything are rarely calling the shots. Their agenda is driven by the Satanic hierarchy which, as an expression of the Archon hierarchy, overrides every other (Fig 327). Royalty comes from a bloodline connection to the gods and so royalty and Archontic possession go together. I have said in the face of great ridicule that the British royal family are Reptilian hybrid shapeshifters who take part in satanic ritual including sacrifice (see *The Biggest Secret* and *The Perception Deception*). One source talked to me for days about her direct experience of British royals at sacrifice ceremonies and other occasions when they shapeshifted (switched information fields). She is referring here to Britain's head of state Queen Elizabeth II and her late mother before she died in 2002 in her 102nd year. My source said of the Queen:

I have seen her sacrifice people and eat their flesh and drink their blood. One time she got so excited with blood lust that she didn't cut the victim's throat from left to right in the normal ritual, she just went crazy, stabbing and ripping at the flesh after she'd shape-shifted into a reptilian. When she shape-shifts she has a long reptile face, almost like a beak, and she's an off-white colour. The Queen Mother looks basically the same, but there are differences. [The Queen] also has like bumps on her head and her eyes are very frightening. She's very aggressive' ...

... [The Queen Mother is] ... cold, cold, cold, a nasty person. None of her cohorts even trusted her. They have named an alter [mind control programme] after her. They call it the Black Queen. I have seen her sacrifice people. I remember her pushing a knife into someone's rectum the night that two boys were sacrificed. One was 13 and the other 18. You need to forget that the Queen Mother appears to be a frail old woman. When she shape-shifts into a reptilian she becomes very tall and strong. Some of them are so strong they can rip out a heart and they all grow by several feet when they shape-shift.

What she says supports the information that I was given by Princess Diana's friend, Christine Fitzgerald. All my sources tell the same story even though they had no idea of the others' existence and live in different parts of the world (Fig 328). The Archon-Reptilian side of hybrid genetics is nothing like the 'human' side in terms of strength, height and speed of aging. If you see the two as the same you lose the plot. They are two

Figure 328: Long to reign over us?

Figure 329: And the frog became a queen.

Figure 330: No, I'm not kidding.

different information fields that produce different holographic projections. When you switch from one TV channel to another you don't get the same program (Fig 329). It is sobering to think that British people sing a song of worship to the Queen every time they belt out the national anthem. 'God Save The Queen' is not, of course, a national anthem at all. It is directed at the Queen or monarch and the population demand in the lyrics to be reigned over by a practicing Satanist and shapeshifting Archon-Reptilian. I have to smile every time I hear it. The same Mrs Shifter officially owns institutions of State and everything with 'HM' or 'Her Majesty's' in front of its name: Her Majesty's Government; Her Majesty's 'Most Loyal Opposition'; Her Majesty's Treasury; Her Majesty's Revenue and Customs; Her Majesty's Civil Service; Her Majesty's Attorney General; Her Majesty's Courts; Her Majesty's Armed Services; Her Majesty's Prisons; Her Majesty's Inspector of Prisons; Her Majesty's Land Registry; Her Majesty's Passport Office; Her Majesty's Coroners; Her Majesty's Inspector of Schools; Her Majesty's Inspectorates of Constabulary; Her Majesty's Stationary Office; Her Majesty's Coastguard ... the list goes on. Christian clergy all swear an oath of allegiance to the Queen as head of the Church of England (what happened to turning away from idolatry) and so do Members of Parliament, judges, military and intelligence personnel. Only she can declare war and decide when it's officially over. All this power (and so much more) for an Archon-Reptilian hiding behind human form (Fig 330). I expose the monarchy and its power structure in detail in *The Perception Deception* and *The Biggest Secret*.

Figure 331: The British Prime Minister bows in deference to the bloodline Queen, but it would never happen the other way round. So who has the real and ongoing power?

Figure 332: Enough of this nonsense.

People think that the royal family is purely symbolic with no real power but quite the opposite is the case. The power dynamic is enshrined in ritual and protocol. No one is expected to bow to an elected British prime minister but he or she is expected to bow or curtsey to the Queen (Fig 331). A point to add here – watch for those who are *always there* because that's where the power lies. Royal families are always there no matter who comes and goes in politics and the same with the intelligence networks and government administration (Fig 332).

Archon paedophilia

Satanism's obsession with the energy of children brings me to paedophilia, which is so rampant worldwide the scale is almost incomprehensible. Even the FBI said in 2015 that

sexual abuse of American children was close to 'epidemic level' and there is a reason for this. Archons possessing paedophiles are using the abusers as a vehicle or conduit during sexual activity to draw off the child's energy from the base chakra at the bottom of the spine (Fig 333). Sexual abuse and torture distorts the child's energy field to rewire them mentally and emotionally for life unless the imbalances are corrected. A child's energy before puberty is like nectar to the Archon virus and here you have the major reason why paedophilia is so rife. This is especially so in the *El*-lite levels of society where there are so many Archon-possessed people and Archon-Reptilian hybrids. We think of puberty as a hormonal change but this is a holographic response to an energetic

Figure 333: Paedophiles are possessed vehicles for Archonic entities to feed off the energy of children and distort their energetic fields.

information change. Archon demons want the child's energy before this change happens and they demand an endless supply of children. Don Juan Matus, the shaman source for the Carlos Castaneda books, highlighted this. Castaneda wrote:

> ... [Don Juan] explained that sorcerers saw infant human beings as strange luminous balls of energy, covered from the top to the bottom with a glowing coat, something like a coat of plastic adjusted tightly around the cocoon of energy. He said that glowing coat of awareness was what the predators consumed and that when a human reached adulthood, all that was left of that fringe awareness was a narrow fringe that went from the ground to the top of the toes. That fringe permitted mankind to keep on living, but only barely.

Archon hybrids in human society run paedophile and Satanic networks that control children's homes, 'care centres' and social services or child protection (Fig 334). The shocking and ever-gathering increase in children taken from loving parents by 'child protection' agencies and placed in 'care' or forced adoption for the most spurious and ludicrous reasons is connected in part to extending control over children so they can be 'disappeared' and farmed out for abuse, even sacrifice (Fig 335). Many decent people in

Figure 334: Everywhere you look – same master, same game.

Figure 335: Social services and child 'protection' agencies are taking enormous numbers of children – and rising – from loving parents using outrageous and ludicrous excuses.

child protection are trying to do their best, but the overall structure and associated abuse networks are controlled by paedophiles and Satanists. If you wanted a ceaseless supply of children, which agencies would you target? Children's homes, 'care centres' and social services/child protection. El-ite paedophile and Satanic groups even use their networks within social services and child 'protection' services to steal children to order, and this is another reason why excuses to take children from loving parents can be so blatantly ridiculous. When there is no genuine cause to remove children they have to make them up to ensure delivery. Paedophile rings have been exposed countless times operating within the 'child care' system and they are only the tiny few that come to light. Don't fall for the assumption as most people do that the number of children that go missing can be judged by missing children stories we see in the media. Extraordinary numbers of children go missing worldwide every year and many hundreds of thousands in the United States alone. There are multiple reasons for this, but one is that many end up in the hands of Satanists and paedophiles. Their rings (ring if you go high enough) infest child protection, government, law enforcement, judiciary and the Establishment in general. These are all the institutions and agencies you need to control to hide almost all the abuse and bang down the lid when examples do come to public attention. All the abuse scandals in Britain in recent years represent a trickle of what is going on driven by the Archons' insatiable demand for the energy of children through abuse or sacrifice. The plan is to continually delete parental rights until the state has complete control of children. We are seeing this progression all the time today as schools and state agencies claim the right to dictate every area of a child's life. Scotland is one of the most disgusting examples with the plan to impose a 'state guardian' on all children to oversee their upbringing to age 18 and some schools in America have agreed to have staff from Child Protective Services in situ several days a week. This is only the beginning of where they want this to go. If you read *Brave New World* by insider Aldous Huxley, published in 1932, you will see the agenda for children laid out. Eventually, even the procreation of children is planned to be taken from parents and handed to

**IT WASN'T JUST A STORY
IT WAS KNOWLEDGE OF THE 'FUTURE'
A 'FUTURE' THAT IS NOW**

Figure 336: Orwell's *1984*, like Huxley's *Brave New World*, came from knowledge of what was planned, which is why they are proving so accurate.

laboratories or 'State hatcheries' as Huxley put it. *Brave New World* wasn't written only from imagination and neither was George Orwell's *1984*. Huxley taught Orwell, real name Eric Blair, at the *El*-lite Eton College where the royal children go and they became friendly. They both had access to inner-circle sources on which their books were founded and this is why they have both proved to be so prophetic (Fig 336). Predicting the 'future' is easy when you know the gist of what is planned as I have shown myself. Their books reveal different aspects of the same agenda – a police state tyranny and control through drugs and genetics.

El-ite paedophiles

I exposed the VIP paedophile network in Britain involving famous politicians and others in *The Biggest Secret*, first published in 1998, and named names; but while the open-minded took it seriously the general response was dismissal or ridicule. The content was far too much for the perception of solidified Phantom Self to take in and, anyway, that Icke bloke is a nutter isn't he? That response has changed big-time since 2012 with an explosion of shocking revelations about paedophile politicians and child abuse rings involving the Westminster parliament and the government of Prime Minister Margaret Thatcher in the 1980s. The Establishment cancelled the laxative order and headed for the bathroom where it has been sitting ever since. Police 'investigations' with code name after code name have been set up to seek the truth (it says here) but as I write years later not a single politician has been collared. Some genuine police officers will be involved and doing what they can within a command structure that doesn't want the truth to come out. An obvious cover up was instigated in which mostly C-list celebrities were used to divert attention from politicians and at the time of writing a coordinated campaign has clearly begun in sections of the British media (including the BBC as usual) to trash the idea that these political and VIP rings exist despite all the evidence (see *The Perception Deception*). They are doing this by taking the weakest of the witnesses and targeting them while ignoring all the credible witnesses including a list of former police officers who have told how their cases involving prominent people were ordered to be dropped (Fig 337). This is a classic technique that I have explained in other books. You don't challenge the best evidence because you can't win if you do.

Figure 337: So many genuine police officers have had their investigations into paedophilia blocked by the police, intelligence and Establishment hierarchy when they began to uncover names of politicians and other pillars of The System.

Instead you ignore that and focus only on the weakest elements of a case and attempt to discredit all the evidence by tarnishing the weakest evidence. How these people can call themselves 'journalists' without blushing I cannot comprehend and even more so how they sleep at night. A government 'inquiry' was delayed by appointing two chairwomen so unbelievably inappropriate that they had to stand down. One frontline witness they would have had to question was Leon Brittan, Home Secretary in the Thatcher government, who had to explain how a dossier handed to him exposing Westminster paedophile politicians and others was not

Figure 338: Jimmy Savile, close friend of Prince Charles and the royal family, prime ministers Margaret Thatcher and Edward Heath, Satanist and procurer of children for the rich and famous. Nice man.

acted upon and then went 'missing'. The first chairwoman appointed was the *sister* of the Thatcher Attorney General Lord Michael Havers who was fundamentally implicated in the paedophile cover up with Leon Brittan. The second was a friend of Brittan and his wife and lived in the *same street*. This caused a big time delay in starting the inquiry – enough for Brittan to die from 'long-term cancer' that had never been mentioned before. 'Secret' government documents were found after he died relating to his sexual activities along with other known political paedophiles. Brittan and Havers were both paedophiles and this is why they instigated the cover up. I knew that Brittan was a paedophile and yet his colleagues and friends in the Conservative Party of Prime Minister David Cameron *didn't?* Or Cameron's Home Secretary Theresa May who appointed the two chairwomen who had to resign – a delay that put paid to Brittan ever being questioned? Neither knew that their friend Brittan was supposedly dying of cancer and needed to be questioned with haste? Theresa May went to New Zealand for another establishment judge to be the third chairwoman and Justice Lowell Goddard is talking of many years before she will report. *Phew,* we've got time for the public to forget all about it. Leon Brittan is one of the men along with former Prime Minister Edward Heath that the media campaign has been trying so hard to portray as innocent and wrongly accused. What a sick joke.

The Westminster paedophile story broke in the mainstream after the death in 2011 of a former BBC entertainer and disc-jockey called Jimmy Savile (Fig 338). He was famous for being what they call a character when, in fact, he was a paedophile of record-breaking proportions as confirmed by police and media after a television documentary triggered the exposure in 2012. I was told by Princess Diana's friend Christine Fitzgerald in 1998 that Savile was a paedophile and necrophiliac (sex with dead bodies). She was my only source and with his 'good old Jimmy' image so different to the reality and no cross-referenced supporting sources I was stuck. He could have sued me into the street no problem. I told people by word of mouth when his name came up and posted what I was told on the day his death was announced in 2011. This was mostly ignored or dismissed as usual, but not anymore. It is worth noting that Christine Fitzgerald who has proved to be so accurate about Savile is one of the sources for the Reptilian hybrid nature of the British royal family. I have seen some Phantom Self idiots claim on the

Internet that I must have known about Savile when I worked at the BBC in the 1980s but this is based on the usual ignorance about the size of the BBC and how I worked – almost entirely from home or on location – for a completely different area of the corporation. My knowledge about Savile came from Christine Fitzgerald not the BBC. I present this brief background to Savile because from him many dots connect. First of all he was not only a paedophile but a procurer of children for the rich and famous. This vital fact has not come out in the mainstream, and it explains how he could go about his astonishing levels of paedophilic abuse (we now know) for decade after decade in the knowledge of the Establishment, police, intelligence agencies and members of government, and still be allowed to get away with it. The collective Archon web and paedophile and satanic networks have infiltrated all these institutions and so many more. Savile was expert in supplying children for them and they were not going to let him go down. His back was their back.

Paedophile royalty

Christine Fitzgerald also told me in 1998 about Savile's close connection to the royal family and how Princess Diana couldn't stand him because he was so sleazy. She wasn't wrong (Fig 339). These close associations with the inner sanctum of the royals have been glossed over but they reveal and connect so much. He was particularly close to Vlad the Impaler's bloodline relative Prince Charles (Fig 340). Media reports after Savile's exposure said he had 'a licence to roam' in Charles' London palace and was 'granted unprecedented access across all the royal palaces upstairs and downstairs'. A royal correspondent wrote: 'Savile was so close to Charles that not only did he advise on the appointment of a senior aide, but also sacked another figure because, I was told, the Prince didn't have the stomach to do it himself.' Another report suggested that Charles had wanted Savile to be godfather to Prince Harry before this was blocked by royal aides. Charles didn't know what Savile, the record- breaking paedophile and procurer of children, was doing?? British Intelligence didn't know while allowing him to walk through royal palaces at will? Savile said himself that he was introduced into the royal inner circle in the 1960s by Lord Mountbatten, formerly Battenberg. 'Britain's' royal family is the German bloodline of Saxe-Coburg-Gotha. They changed their name to

Figure 339: Savile was very close to Prince Charles and had the run of royal palaces. Princess Diana called him sleazy and couldn't stand him.

Figure 340: Where are the questions about Saville's closeness to Charles and the royal family over decades while the police and intelligence services knew he was a rampant paedophile?

Figure 341: What a joke it all is.

Figure 342: Prince Philip at a Nazi funeral.

Windsor during World War I as an urgent PR exercise while their German relatives led by Kaiser Wilhelm were at war with Britain and bombing London with planes called Gotha (Fig 341). Battenberg became Mountbatten at the same time and the Windsors had many Nazi-supporting German relatives during World War II (Fig 342). Lord Mountbatten's close association with Savile is highly significant because Mountbatten, a mentor to Prince Philip and Prince Charles, was not only a premier royal advisor and confidant, but also a paedophile (Fig 343). I named him in earlier books and in 2015 he was named by an abuse whistleblower for his role in the cover up of a child abuse scandal at the Kincora boys' home in Belfast, Northern Ireland. There was a reason for that – he abused children from Kincora. Two others named were Sir Maurice Oldfield, former head of MI6, and Anthony Blunt, an employee of the Queen. Blunt was the Queen's surveyor of pictures, a close friend of the Queen Mother and a publicly-exposed Russian spy (Fig 344). I had named Oldfield and Blunt years before as paedophiles. We have paedophiles Mountbatten and Blunt with major connections to the royal family while child procurer and paedophile Savile was in the inner royal sanctum for decades. Savile

Figure 343: Lord Mountbatten, mentor to Prince Charles and Prince Philip, was a paedophile who brought paedophile and child procurer Jimmy Savile into the royal inner circle.

Figure 344: Anthony Blunt, paedophile, child killer, outed Russian spy, and employee and friend of the Queen and, especially, the Queen Mother.

was a BBC disc-jockey and lightweight entertainer and for many of those decades an aging and out of work one. Why would he be in the royal inner circle? *Unless*. Don't tell me they didn't know. You can't cough in the vicinity of the royal family without the intelligence and security agencies knowing all about you (Fig 345). Yet he was a royal insider for decades when we now know that police forces were well aware of his child

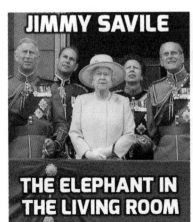

Figure 346: Jimmy Savile was a close friend of Margaret Thatcher who did nothing about paedophiles she knew were in her government and among her closest advisors.

Figure 345: The media refuse to ask obvious questions about Savile and the Addams family while seeking to discredit investigations into a Westminster paedophile ring.

Figure 347: Savile was given a papal knighthood by Pope John Paul II, head of the biggest paedophile operation on Planet Earth known as the Roman Church.

Figure 348: MP Peter Morrison, one of Thatcher's closest and longest-serving aides, was a widely-known paedophile in political and media circles, but 'moral Maggie' did nothing.

abuse. Savile was extremely wealthy right up to his death while having no obvious source of income because most of his money came from procuring children for abuse. He was also a Satanist and media stories have described rituals in hospitals. This put him much higher in the network and increased his protection. Satanism takes us into the highest levels of the Archon conspiracy and this level is afforded maximum protection and cover up, even more than non-satanic paedophilia. Savile famously volunteered as a porter to 'do his bit to help people' when he was really securing access to the mortuary for his necrophilia (Archon obsession with death). Margaret Thatcher was another close friend of Savile during her more than a decade as British Prime Minister (Fig 346). Once again British Intelligence and police forces knew all about Savile but allowed him to get so involved with a sitting Prime Minister as they did with the royals. Why is the mainstream media not making these points? Rhetorical question. Savile was given a knighthood by the Queen after years of lobbying by Thatcher and he was also awarded a papal knighthood by Pope John Paul II on behalf of the Church of Babylon, the biggest child abuse network on Planet Earth more widely known as the Roman Catholic Church (Fig 347). Everything interconnects. Recent revelations have made it clear that Thatcher covered up the paedophile nest in her government which included Leon Brittan and her two closest aides between 1975 and 1990, Lord Alastair McAlpine and MP Peter Morrison (Fig 348). I named McAlpine in *The Biggest Secret* in 1998 and repeated this again when he was threatening all and sundry with libel actions in 2012 for even hinting at his activities. BBC and ITV paid him hundreds of thousands of pounds in damages when they did *not* name him (extraordinary, I know), but he never came near me when I had openly done so for more than 14 years. I could name him because, unlike Savile, I had multiple sources over the years. Peter Morrison was a well-known child abuser among his colleagues and Thatcher knew but did nothing – the usual story. Morrison was also named in government documents that came to light after Leon Brittan died. Paedophiles and Satanists in politics provide endless potential for blackmail and ensuring that decisions will be made that suit the Archon-hybrid agenda even among those who would not otherwise be on board. The dying Australian Satanist quoted in full in *Human Race Get off Your Knees* wrote this of political paedophiles:

> Politicians are introduced by a carefully graded set of criteria and situations that enable them to accept that their victims will be, 'Our little secret'. Young children sexually molested and physically abused by politicians worldwide are quickly used as sacrifices. In Australia, the bodies are hardly ever discovered, for Australia is still a wilderness.

In smaller and more densely populated countries than Australia they use private crematoria owned by satanic rings. I have highlighted over the years that Australia is a global centre for Satanism and its associated paedophilia and a VIP paedophile scandal erupted there as I was finishing this book over three alleged child abusing former prime ministers and other Establishment figures. The story was a repeat of what has come to light in Britain because we are looking at a global web in which each part reflects the whole and operates in the same way. Another famous politician I named in *The Biggest Secret* in 1998 was Edward Heath, Britain's Prime Minister between 1970 and 1974. Heath signed Britain into what is now the thoroughly Archontic European Union. He was Thatcher's predecessor as leader of the Conservative Party. I had multiple sources again and named him not only as a paedophile but as a serial child killer and Satanist. I continued to name him over the years at every opportunity. A journalist, or what passes for one, read Heath the passage in *The Biggest Secret* soon after the book was published but no action was taken in the seven years he went on to serve as a Member of Parliament before he died. Another 17 years passed before Heath's paedophilia came to mainstream attention with a series of police forces revealing investigations into claims against him. The media refused to acknowledge that I had named him as a paedophile and much more nearly 20 years earlier. This would have been far too embarrassing for them to admit that a person they had condemned and ridiculed as a madman could have been right about such extraordinary happenings. The UK's *Daily Mail* even ran headline when the Heath story broke saying: '... no one ever called Heath a paedophile.' What a joke. Those they label 'conspiracy theorists' can never be seen to be right or people might look at what else they are saying. Edward Heath is an outstanding example of how paedophilia and Satanism are intrinsically connected and how both are driven by the Demiurge/Archon virus. I am expecting big efforts to discredit claims about Heath because he was a high Satanist and therefore a gateway to the darkest depths of what lies behind human control. Paedophilia is covered up but Satanism and satanic abuse even more so.

Archon black eyes

When I was first told about Heath in the 1990s I recalled a seriously strange experience I had with him years before in a television make-up room. I was about to be interviewed

Figure 349: What Heath's eyes looked like during my extraordinary experience.

on a political programme and he was waiting to have his make-up removed after already appearing. I walked into the room and didn't see him at first because he was behind the open door. I thought I was alone but when I sat down and turned around there he was. I should point out here that this experience was years before I knew anything about the subjects in this book. I was a television presenter and Green politician. I nodded 'hello' to Heath but he didn't react in any way. He just stared at me in a puzzled and curious way as if he was observing something interesting. Then he lifted his eyes to the top of my head. Only his eyes moved as they scanned me from the top of my head to my feet and back again before he turned away without saying a word and looked at the make-up mirror in front of him. The most shocking part of the experience was that during the 'scan' his eyes turned jet black and I mean all of them even the whites (Fig 349). I described it later as like looking into two black holes. There was no eye contact (impossible with no eyes) and I was looking through him into blackness. I had no idea what had happened until years later when it became very clear. I was looking through 'him' into the Archon realm for which his body was only a vehicle to manipulate our world. I almost doubted what I had seen because it was so extraordinary but I would later come across legends and accounts around the world of the 'black-eyed people' which described the experience I had with Heath. Put 'black-eyed people' into a search engine and you'll see what I mean. Some movie portrayals of the 'black goo' (virus) taking over people have their eyes turning black in the way I saw those of Ted Heath. Another story involving Heath was in the 1990s when I returned to Britain from a long trip to the United States during which I had met a lot of people – 12 in 15 days at one point – who told me about their direct experience of reptilian 'aliens' and hybrids who could shapeshift between human and reptilian form. I was still compiling this information and had said nothing publicly about it. I had arranged a meeting back in the UK with a women who said she had information about Edward Heath being a Satanist. I went along to see her with no mention of what I had been told about reptilian shapeshifters. She told me that she had been married to a Satanist who was warden of Burnham Beeches, an area of forest, copses and clearings to the west of London not far from Slough. The land is owned by the globally-important City of London financial district known as 'The City' or 'Square Mile' which is awash with secret societies, especially the Knights Templar, and with Satanists. It stands on the site of the original London occupied by the Romans. 'The City' logo is two flying reptiles holding the symbol of the Knights Templar (also the flag of England) and at the point where 'The City' meets the Temple district, once owned by the Knights Templar, you find a flying reptile statue in the middle of the road (Figs 350 and 351).This is where the centre of British and much of global finance meets the centre of the British (and again in many ways global) legal profession. Control banking, money and the law and you control society. The Temple area of London is named after a Knights Templar church featured in the movie *The Da Vinci Code* and is today the

Figure 350: 'The City' logo of flying reptiles holding the shield of the Knights Templar.

headquarters of Britain's legal profession and home to the *Royal* Courts of Justice. The lady told me she had been walking in the darkness one night at Burnham Beeches when she saw lights through the trees and moved closer to see what was happening. She said that to her horror she saw a satanic ritual circle being led by then Prime Minister Edward Heath and alongside him was his Chancellor of the Exchequer Anthony Barber. Chequers, the official country residence of the British prime minister, is not far from Burnham Beeches. What she described supported what others had told me about Heath's Satanism, but there was more. As our conversation ended and I turned to go, I mentioned that I had been having some strange experiences in America with people telling me about shapeshifting reptilian people. I heard a gasp behind me and I looked back to see her clutching her chest as if in shock. She said she had not mentioned that subject because she thought it might seem crazy even to me. She went on to tell me of seeing hooded figures in Burnham beeches, mostly at dusk, that had turned to show their reptilian faces and she elaborated on her Heath experience. She said that at one point in the ritual he began to transform into a reptile and grew by some two feet (a very common theme in such accounts worldwide). 'He eventually became a full-bodied Reptiloid', she said. He went on to speak in a fairly normal way although she said it sounded like the old long-distance telephone lines with short time lapses. She had been amazed at the reaction of other people in the circle to what happened. Their response, or lack of it,

Figure 351: Flying reptile statue where The City meets the Temple district – where money meets the law.

made it clear this was perfectly normal for them, and it is with Satanists at this level of the network.

Edward Heath was not only a sexual abuser of children, but also a mass murderer in his joint role as paedophile and Satanist. However many people come forward to tell of their abuse by Heath they will be a tiny minority of his victims. He killed most of them (or had them killed) immediately after the abuse. Many were thrown over the side of his series of yachts called Morning Cloud often on trips to the Channel Islands. One

Figure 352: Savile procured children for Heath and many other members of the Establishment and this made him, to use his own term, 'untouchable'.

Figure 353: The 40-foot stone owl or Moloch/ Molech where the rich and famous conduct their rituals at Bohemian Grove.

Figure 354: The Moloch owl is a symbol for Saturn.

Figure 355: An owl on a pyramid clearly visible in the road plan of Washington DC with the Capitol Building in its belly.

of his main suppliers of children was Jimmy Savile (Fig 352). I know how hard it must be for those new to this information to comprehend the implications of what I am saying, but Satanism, paedophilia, bloodlines and Archons/Reptilians all connect in a global interlocking network, and nowhere more so than North America where one of the most active and brutal paedophiles named in my books is Father George Bush. I highlighted 20 years ago the activities at Bohemian Grove about 75 miles north of San Francisco where the *El*-lite and their hangers-on meet every year for a 'summer camp' in 2,700 acres of redwood forest in Sonoma County. They include the Rockefellers, Rothschilds, Bush family and the rich and famous political, banking and business insiders of America and the wider world. Satanic ritual is on the bill for the inner circle and everyone takes part in the 'Cremation of Care' ritual involving a big fire under a 40-foot stone owl – a symbol of the god Moloch or Molech to whom the ancients sacrificed children in fire (Fig 353). The Bible says in Leviticus, 18-21: 'And thou shalt not let any of thy seed pass through the fire to Molech, neither shalt thou profane the name of thy God.' This was a version of the Celtic Wicker Man which was set ablaze with children inside. Moloch is the Prince of Hell in demonology who loves making mothers weep by stealing their children and here's the punchline ... Moloch is a god representing *Saturn* (Fig 354). Moloch was the Saturn god of the Canaanites/Ammonites and also called Baal (Saturn). The Star of David or five-pointed star/hexagram Saturn symbol has been called the Star of Moloch and Star of Remphan (the ancient Egyptian god of Saturn). The recurring theme is obvious. Molech also appears in the road plan in Washington DC sitting at the top of a pyramid (a leading Archon secret society symbol) and the Congress Building is in the owl's belly (Fig 355). Nothing could be more symbolically accurate.

Therapist's story

A Canadian mainstream psychotherapist and counsellor appeared in 2015 on the Richie Allen radio show, broadcast through Davidicke.com and other outlets, to describe her experiences of the satanically abused and those who report seeing reptilian entities. Sandra Fecht said that her mainstream training had never included instruction on sexual abuse let alone satanic abuse and this is a major way that the truth is suppressed. People with mental and emotional consequences of abuse go to therapists for help only

THE SATANIC ABUSE OF CHILDREN: 'THEY' WOULDN'T DO THAT?

SATANISM.

IT INFESTS OUR SOCIETY – AND I MEAN WORLDWIDE

Figure 356: Satanism is rampant worldwide – especially among the *El*-ite.

to be considered crazy or having their accounts explained away by some mental problem. Sandra Fecht said she was told by aboriginal people in the Northwest Territories in the 1970s that 'there were things going on at night' but it was only later that she realised what they meant and 'stumbled across the satanic stuff'. She said that at first she assumed those telling her about this were 'either crazy or needed antipsychotic medication or hospitalisation or something'. She didn't believe them. Sandra made a telling observation: 'I think a lot of us therapists listen to each other and we look at the academics who taught us and we are not always listening to our clients.' This is precisely the problem and it was no surprise to me to see Christopher 'Mainstream Everything' French, Professor of Psychology at Goldsmiths College, University of London, telling the media that satanic ritual abuse is almost certainly the result of false memories. What a clueless man he is on so many levels (Fig 356). Sandra Fecht said she was dealing with clients who reported childhood memories of 'ceremonies involving cloaks, chanting, all manner of torture, child sacrifice, just very strange things ... blood drinking, eating animal parts, just very curious strange things'. Nothing in the mainstream system had prepared her for this and even more so when clients told her about 'walking reptilian entities'. Sandra said:

I felt as though I was totally losing my grip on the perch to be quite honest when I realised there were so many people doing this or telling me this and then there were two things that happened that made me realise this is the truth. Well, actually three. One is that I was hearing these stories from too many people and they could not all be standing outside my office making up the same story.

The second thing was my hairdresser who ... told me about David Icke and so I read his book The Biggest Secret and it confirmed everything I was finding; and the third thing was I ... received a life-threatening phone call for doing this work and they told me back off or else and I don't know who it was. I told them, well, I'm not backing off so I guess it's Plan B. I reported that and I reported the fact that my building was spray-painted with symbols that I later found out were satanic. I had no idea how all of this worked at the time.

Sandra said that she was told by a police officer that her reports to police were being prematurely deleted and she realised that what she had been told was indeed real. I have heard all the themes of what she said right across the world. The reason for the obsession with children by Satanists and paedophiles is the vampiring of their energy although most paedophiles not involved with Satanism will have no idea. Mental and emotional distortion and control is part of it, too. Satanists and paedophiles are Archontically possessed in a very big way and this makes them psychopaths even if they didn't start out that way. You can't abuse children without serious psychopathic tendencies. Wilfred Wong, barrister and campaigner against satanic ritual abuse for 22 years, appeared on the UKColumn Internet television show in 2015 to share his experience of the subject. He listed common themes in the accounts of those reporting satanic abuse as children and I have heard all of them myself from people I have spoken with across the world:

- People dressed in dark robes and hoods who are chanting, usually in a language which the victim does not understand.
- Drugged prior to their abuse by those dressed in robes and hoods.
- Forced to ingest human or animal faeces and urine.
- Forced to drink human or animal blood.
- Kept in cages or hung on hooks.
- Placed in coffins or buried in the ground – taken out after experiencing the terror of being buried alive.
- Forced to sexually abuse other children.
- Ritual sacrifice of a human or animal.
- Forced to watch human or animal sacrifice and eat sacrificial victim.
- Forced to participate in the killing of sacrifice.
- Women or girls forcibly impregnated and later their child is aborted and used as a ritual sacrifice or born and ritually sacrificed [that is where many babies aborted in hospitals and clinics end up].
- Death threats against themselves, their loved ones and pets if the child reveals what has happened to them.

Satanic communication – symbolism

Archontic vampiring of human energy is a constant theme and this can be done individually and collectively. We return to frequency. When humans are attached to the Archontic frequency band their energy can be trawled and this happens in ways most people could not imagine. The trick is to focus attention on a person or symbol that represents the Archon frequency and the focus makes an energetic connection with them – energy flows where attention goes. Thousands of people outside Buckingham Palace focussing on the Queen or at the Vatican will make these connections and the electromagnetic energy generated by the crowds can be vampired (Fig 357). You can feel this energy at a sporting event when the excitement of the crowd 'makes the hairs stand up'. This is the effect of electromagnetic energy collectively generated. What we call 'atmosphere' at mass events is simply the energy of the people and their

Figure 357: Focus makes an energetic connection with that being focussed upon. Once the connection is made energy can be trawled through that frequency channel.

Figure 358: Symbols are energetic information fields that communicate through the subconscious as I will be explaining.

Figure 359: The Statue of Liberty (inversion) is a depiction of Queen Semiramis, the goddess queen of Babylon seen here on a coin.

Figure 360: Archons and Jinn are 'made from fire'.

Figure 361: Some of the major symbols used by the Archon networks.

emotional state. Another way of hijacking focus is through symbols and this is so important to appreciate (Fig 358). Symbols are everywhere and used profusely by religion, Satanism, secret societies and the Establishment in all its forms. They are overwhelmingly the same symbols in each case and the same as those used by the ancients. The Statue of Liberty (inversion), the work of Freemasons in Paris, is holding the classic Archon network symbol of the lighted torch. 'Liberty' is in fact a depiction of the Babylonian goddess Semiramis or Ishtar (Fig 359). Semiramis was known as the 'Great Queen' in Babylon and so the Mother Lodge of Freemasonry, established in London in 1717, is in Great Queen Street. From here Freemasonry was launched in the United States. A torch or flame is symbolic of illumination (hidden knowledge) and of the Archons who are also known as fire demons (Fig 360). Remember how Gnostics said Archons are made from 'luminous fire' and the Koran says Jinn are made from 'smokeless fire'. They can enter our reality through the frequency of fire – hence fire is often used in satanic ritual. Other major symbols are the eye, pyramid and all-seeing eye, hexagon, hexagram, pentagram and cube among many others (Fig 361). Eye as a symbol comes in part from the eye symbolism of Saturn and the 'all-seeing eye' of Saturn is profusely employed by Freemasonry (Fig 362, 363 and 364). Skull and bones is Saturn symbolism and relates to Saturn's astrological role as governor of the skeletal structure and its association with death (Fig 365). Capitoline Hill, one of the famous seven hills of Rome, gets its name from the Latin 'caput',

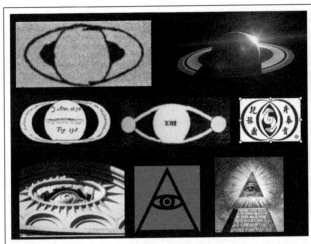

Figure 362: Saturn was depicted as an eye and is widely used by Satanism, secret societies and religion.

Figure 363: Dollar Bill all-seeing eye and pyramid.

Figure 364: All-seeing eye in the mother lodge of Freemasonry in London.

Figure 365: The skull and bones is associated with Saturn for its death symbolism and other reasons.

meaning skull, and so caput means something that is finished or dead (Saturn). Capitoline Hill's previous name was Mons Saturnius – Hill of *Saturn* – and the ruins of the Temple of Saturn still stand at the foot of the hill today (Figs 366 and 367). From this origin comes Capitol Hill in the United States (controlled by the Demiurge/Saturn Death Cult) and the term capital for the centre of government in

Figure 366: Capitoline Hill in Rome.

Figure 367 The ancient Roman Temple of Saturn at the foot of Capitoline Hill or 'Mons Saturnius'.

Figure 368: 'Jesus' on the cross – a symbol of human sacrifice.

Figure 369: Symbols represent energetic information states and impact upon energetic levels of reality beyond human sight.

Figure 370: Information communicated as sound within the human frequency range can be heard by the conscious mind, but information encoded in symbols enters the brain through the sight senses and is overwhelmingly not noted or noticed by the conscious mind. It enters subliminally into the subconscious to influence perception.

every country. We also have capital punishment (sacrificial death). But don't worry, it's just a coincidence, nothing to worry about. 'Jesus' is said to have been crucified at Golgotha or Calvary and both names mean 'Place of the Skull'. It's all esoteric symbolism and the omnipotent symbol in Christianity of Jesus suffering on the cross is a portrayal of satanic sacrifice (Fig 368). Now there's something to focus on and connect with. Symbols of the United Nations, European Union, corporations, religions, secret societies and Satanism are not random.

They have energetic/occult meaning. Symbols represent the Demiurge, Archons, Saturn, Moon and Matrix. They are not all around us for no reason. Satanists have told me that on an energetic level a pentagram within a circle appears as walls of energy which allow entities to slip through into this reality but not to escape from the pentagram energy 'shield' (Fig 369). Satanists are terrified of their masters. Symbols are holographic projections of information fields and we need to see them in this way if we are going to understand the game. Spoken words are energetic information fields generated by vocal cords and we 'hear' them when they are decoded by the brain. We consciously hear what they say as long as they are loud enough. Symbols are the same in every respect except that we don't hear them. At least we have some kind of choice on how to process and respond to words that we can hear, but with anything visual like symbols we don't. They are energy fields just like words but they enter the brain through the sight processes subliminally without us even consciously noting them or most of the time anyway (Fig 370). We are processing some 11 million 'sensations' or 'impressions' every second but they are filtered down to about 40 from which our *conscious* sense of reality is constructed. Everything else is unconscious and infiltrates the brain under the radar of the conscious mind by going via our subconscious where Phantom Self is constructed (Fig 371).

This is why symbols are so powerful in infiltrating and manipulating reality. They are gateways to the psyche. Chinese philosopher Confucius (551-479 BC) said: 'Signs and symbols rule the world, not words nor laws.' If you can be manipulated to focus on a symbol even better because the frequency of the symbol's energy field reflects the frequency of whatever it is symbolising. Focus on a symbol makes an energetic connection; and you connect not only with the symbol but with what the symbol represents (Fig 372). When vast crowds of Muslims gather at Mecca for the Hajj to focus on the Kaaba cube symbol representing Saturn they are 'tuned in' to that frequency and it's the same when Muslims all over the world fall to their knees five times a day to face Mecca and focus on ... the Kaaba cube (Figs 373 and 374). Their energy can be vampired and their Body-Mind even more powerfully connected to the Demiurge/Saturn virus. Thousands have been killed in crushes and stampedes of Muslims during the Hajj in Mecca which Muslims are told to visit at least once in their lives. Many hundreds were killed in 2015 near the spot where Muslims throw stones at the Devil. Takes deep breath, moves on. Whether you worship (focus attention) on the god of religions or the devil figure of religions you are

Figure 371: Human perception is largely constructed in the subconscious – home of Phantom Self – and symbols and images are the major gateway. From here perceptions and reactions filter through to the conscious mind as thoughts and emotional responses.

Figure 372: Focus on a symbol makes a frequency connection with whatever the symbol represents. Energy can then be vampired and perceptions implanted.

Figure 373: Circling the black cube at Mecca focussing on the symbol of Saturn creates a mass field of electromagnetic human energy that can be vampired by anything operating within that frequency.

Figure 374: Focusing on the black cube of Saturn – energy flows where attention goes.

worshipping the same Demiurge virus and either way you are making a connection through which your energy can be vampired and your perception infiltrated. Symbols are also right-brain phenomena and can therefore be embedded even deeper in the subconscious mind. This brings into new light the reason for mass symbolism of the Establishment and especially religion, Satanism and secret societies and why they are so similar and overwhelmingly related to Saturn.

Sigil of Saturn

The predominant symbol in Freemasonry is the compass which is connected to the theme of the Great Architect of the Universe (Matrix) and derives from an ancient symbol known as the Seal or Sigil of Saturn and also Seal of Solomon (Fig 375).

Figure 375: Sigil of Saturn or Solomon – origin of the Freemasonic compass.

Symbolic myths about Solomon and Solomon's Temple are code for Saturn. Every syllable of Sol-Om-On means the 'sun' – the Saturn sun. The Sigil of Saturn comes from the Magic Square of Saturn which is also the Magic Square of Freemasonry (Fig 376). This comprises the numbers 1 to 9 laid out in a way that makes every line in all directions equal 15. In numerology all numbers are added together until you have a single digit. 8,000 would therefore be 8 in numerology and 896 would 8 + 9 + 6 = 23 and 2 + 3 = 5. When you apply this to the Magic Square of Saturn the recurring 15 becomes a recurring 1 + 5 = 6 or 666 – the 'Mark of the Beast' in the Book of Revelation: 'Here is wisdom. Let him that hath understanding count the number of the beast: for it is the number of a man; and his number is Six hundred threescore and six.' Numbers are digital expressions of energetic states and the Magic Square of 666 recurring is not named after Saturn by

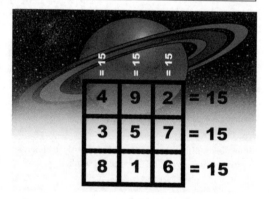

Figure 376: Magic Square of Saturn and Freemasonry.

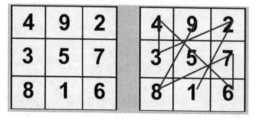

Figure 377: How the Magic Square forms the Freemasonic compass symbol.

chance. All the numbers in the Saturn square add up to 45, which in numerology is 9. Draw a line between all the numbers in order from 1 to 9 and you get the Sigil of Saturn which Freemasonry symbolises as a compass (Fig 377). Saturn's frequency is encoded into the prime symbol of Freemasonry. Numbers 1 to 9 are encoded in all numbers and represent all numbers no matter how big or small because all numbers comprise 1 to 9. Zero is not considered energetically active as with 0 representing an off electrical state in computers. If you control 1 to 9 you control all numbers and numbers express energetic (information) states so you control the game by controlling the mathematics of the Matrix. 'Human' mathematics are not our mathematics. They are Archon mathematics and Matrix mathematics. Only the innermost sanctum initiates of secret societies generally know any of this because of compartmentalisation. Most of the brethren are being programmed and possessed themselves by symbols and ritual that they perform but don't understand. Rituals and symbols in each degree are designed to allow ever more possession of the initiate by the Archon virus and its entities. I have met friends and family of Freemasons who have described how they changed their personality after entering the 'Craft'. I am aware of many Freemasons on the Isle of Wight alone who are full-blown virus-infested psychopaths. Symbols and rituals are

Figure 378: Low-frequency music and satanic symbolism can connect the energy of the audience with the Archon realm.

vehicles for possession by focussing *attention* on what then possesses them. I have been inside three Freemasonic lodges. One was in Boston, Massachusetts, when I walked in

and no one was around so I just kept walking; another was in Birmingham, England, where a non-Freemason event was being held and the third was a public open day at the lodge in my town. Each time the energy could be described in one word ... saturnine. Churches, royal palaces and the royals themselves are the same. Coincidence? Not a chance. Connecting people unknowingly to Archon-Saturn energy also applies to music concerts and videos, which often abound with satanic symbols and use other techniques to pull people in (Fig 378). Madonna's Super Bowl performance in 2012 was an absolute Archon/Saturn-fest from start to finish. The situation is captured in Figure 379 in which all

Figure 379: Deep in the rabbit hole all aspects of The System have the same master.

Figure 380: Subliminal messages everywhere in *They Live.*

Figure 381: *They Live* – the President isn't human.

roads lead to the Demiurge/Archons. This is the Hidden Hand that controls and directs the world on a path of death, destruction and enslavement for the human population. The power and significance of belief in human control relates to hijacking and focussing attention to the detriment of peripheral vision (expanded perception panorama). You don't have to be consciously aware of symbols to be affected. Your focus will make the connection purely from unaware subconscious *attention*. I said earlier that subliminal means 'below threshold' – below the threshold of the conscious mind – and symbols operate most powerfully at this level. Advertisements are encoded with subliminal messages to manipulate your responses to buy the product, and they are encoded into television and radio broadcasts. Subliminal manipulation was brilliantly symbolised in the 1988 movie *They Live* in which special sunglasses allowed people to see what others couldn't see. They realised that subliminal messages were all around them and that a non-human race had taken over by hiding behind apparently human bodies (Figs 380 and 381). Lead actor Roddy Piper said in a radio interview in 2014 that *They Live* was not a movie but a *documentary* and he mentioned the information in my books. You can see *They Live* on YouTube and it is worth watching. Put it together with *The Matrix* and that's basically how things are. Once you bring symbols to the attention of the conscious mind with awareness of the way they work, they will no longer have the same effect because conscious mind blocks the connection. Awareness is everything. The System really isn't bothered so much what you believe as long as you believe something rigidly to the exclusion of other possibilities. Religion, politics, mainstream science, any rigid belief will put you in the pen as will a myopic focus on sport, celebrity, television, smart phones and such like. You can watch sport in its rightful place as entertainment and still be aware of wider reality. Hey, but hold on a minute, we have to believe something don't we? No, we don't. I don't believe anything in the sense of this-is-how-it-is-and-that's-that. I have a perception of how things are at any point but I am constantly open to expanding that perception in the light of more information and insight. A belief that you know all you need to know to understand the world to the point where alternatives can be dismissed by reflex action is the height of arrogance and stupidity – the arrogance of ignorance (and naivety). Ignorance always knows everything. Such people would benefit from a note pinned to the wall reminding them that we can 'see' (decode) the tiniest fraction of what exists and our brains are constructing apparent reality from 40 sensations a second from a potential of 11 million. We need to have the humility to realise how little we know and Phantom Self is *allowed* to know by official sources; we need to drop all rigid, unquestioned belief; and restore peripheral vision by ceasing to focus only on dots and starting to see connections that reveal the picture.

When we do this Phantom Self is in desperate trouble as its foundation programs are deleted. The biggest reason for human control is not even ignorance. It is arrogance and naivety. If people would only rid themselves of these twin imposters then ignorance soon must follow. Until this happens Satanists will stay in control. Prison or paradise is only a choice.

CHAPTER SEVEN

Drop in the Ocean

If you don't become the ocean, you'll be seasick all your life
Leonard Cohen

The ocean is an excellent metaphor to define the human plight because it describes very well our relationship with Infinite Awareness. I have along used the analogy of humans as droplets disconnected from the ocean when, in fact, we *are* the ocean.

We are never literally disconnected in the sense that we are all expressions of Infinite Awareness, but we can certainly be disconnected from its influence, knowledge and wisdom (Fig 382). This is especially so when a hidden force is working ceaselessly to achieve that very outcome (Fig 383). It is not our natural state to be disconnected from the ocean and we become diminished, confused and deluded whenever that happens. Leonard Cohen was so right when he said that if you don't become the ocean, you'll be seasick all your life. If you don't connect with the Infinite you'll be in a state of mental and emotional dis-ease until you do. Osho, an Indian mystic, talked about teaspoons (humanity) trying to measure the ocean (Infinite Awareness). 'It is not possible', he said. No, it's not. Mainstream Everything doesn't even accept the *existence* of the ocean, which takes 'not possible' into still greater extremes of absurdity. All of which brings us back to Phantom Self, the engineered and manufactured vehicle for disconnecting humanity from its true state of Infinite Awareness. We can never be free until we escape from this prison of perception.

Figure 382: Humanity is the droplet that's forgotten it's the ocean.

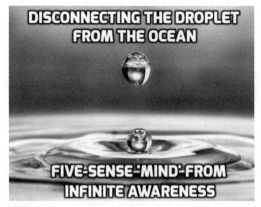

Figure 383: The whole foundation of the Archon conspiracy.

There can be no control by the Matrix and Archon virus once people recognise and *live* their Infinite Self, acknowledge that there *is* a Matrix and identify its methods of perception infiltration and programming. The virus can't attach to Infinite Awareness. The frequency chasm between them means that it needs Phantom Self to achieve its end. Spinning a web is fine but it would be useless unless you can entice your prey to stick themselves to it. In the human case this requires the following: (1) the prey and the web operate in the same frequency band and (2) the prey is disconnected from a level of awareness that can see the web and the motivations behind it. In fact, (1) and (2) are different ways of saying them same thing when the very isolation that comes from disconnection lowers the frequency – the 'Fall of Man'.

How it's done

Awareness enters human reality with higher senses still potentially active. You see babies reacting to what appears to be 'empty space' and young children sometimes talk of seeing a 'special friend' or other phenomena outside of the human visual range. Children soon learn what a hassle it can be to see what others can't see and sometimes even leads to a child psychologist with reality-ignorant mummy and daddy worried about little Johnny or Mary Jo. 'They say they see things that you can't? Oh, right, we have a drug for that.' I have met people over the years who told me how they saw entities as young kids that others couldn't see, but this stopped once their parents intervened and told them that wasn't possible and they must be 'seeing things'. Program perceptions of one generation, and each will program the next while believing they are doing what's 'best for the children'. Parents first transmit their programmed perceptions to their offspring in the ever-diminishing period before The System officially moves in under aliases such as pre-school, school, college and university. System-programmed teachers and professors take the programming on from the parents by repeating as fact the official truths of Mainstream Everything (Fig 384). Even in the little time that children are not under the control and influence of academia these omnipotent 'truths' will be constantly repeated and underpinned by parents, media, friends and siblings who have all been programmed by the same process. The only challenge to this unceasing information download comes from a few parents and acquaintances who do question conformity and they are condemned as bad parents with strange, non-conventional ideas.

Being non-conventional (expressing a spirit of Infinite Possibility) has to be targeted and stamped out or, nightmare of nightmares, it might catch on. I have long exposed the plan to block unwanted parental influence by handing ever more control of children's upbringing to schools and government agencies. This is so obviously happening and with increasing extremes. Observe, too, how even very young children can isolate and target any of their number that is different to their already ingrained sense of normal.

Figure 384: 'Education' – programming the next generation.

Defending 'normal' is part of the program. Children soon learn the consequences for non-conformity with punishment often handed out by other children who have succumbed to the program. They see at an early age the reality of that Japanese saying: 'Don't be the nail that stands out above the rest because that's the first one to get hit.' Programming children with myopic perception, conformity and acquiescence is designed to make this their default state throughout their adult lives. Carrots and sticks are profusely employed. Conformity is rewarded by promotion or a perceived 'quiet life' and non-conformity met with resistance, ridicule, hassle and condemnation. Phantom Self quickly starts to form from these experiences as Mainstream Everything information downloads define the world and sense of self with these programmed conclusions:

> I am a human being; I am my body; I am my sex; I am my race; I am my name; I am my family; I am my genetic history; I am my life story; I am my class; I am my culture. I am my job; I am my wealth; I am my poverty; I am my age; I am my marital status; I am my sexual preference; I am my religious belief; I am my political belief; the world that I see is real and The System is my arbiter of fact, truth and reality.

There are many other facets to Phantom Self, too, but these will do for now. All those listed locate the sense of reality – point of attention – in the five senses and the Archon Matrix. They each define self and reality in terms of limitation and, in turn, this compresses the human frequency into the density of Matrix entrapment. None of these perceptions are true as descriptions of who we and where we are. They are *experiences* and once we confuse experience with who we are (Infinite Awareness *having* the experience) then the trap is sprung and the Matrix has you. Phantom Self is basically an endless series of labels (information/thought fields and beliefs) cemented together to confuse, delude and entrap our 'incarnate' point of attention in a prison of illusion. Without labels there can be no Phantom Self. I am using terms such as Infinite Awareness to help define and explain Phantom Self, but really there is no need for any name to describe our true nature. We all just are and everything just *is*. Realms of form demand that everything is named to stop confusion with everything else, but in expanded levels of awareness they are not necessary. We are all *One* and everything is that Oneness. People think they are defining themselves by labels they attach to their sense of (Phantom) self, but this is more (literal) self-delusion (Fig 385). The System decides the labels and we just pick from the list provided the ones we think best suit our sense of who we are, but aren't. You don't hear people saying 'I am *All That Is and Ever Can Be'*. Instead they say:

'I AM MY NAME, RACE, JOB, INCOME BRACKET, RELIGION AND LIFE STORY.'

Figure 385: Phantom Self.

I am a man. I am a woman. I am black. I am white. I am British. I am American. I am Chinese. I am straight. I am gay. I am a Christian. I am a Muslim. I am a Jew. I am a Hindu. I am New Age. I am a liberal. I am a conservative. I am Left. I am Right. I am rich. I am poor. I am a boss. I am a worker. I am young. I am old. I am successful. I am a failure.

You could spend ages listing labels with which humans self-identify (and the uniforms that go with them) and still never get to the end. I have known gay people who wear the label lightly and get on with their lives without the need to constantly self-associate their sexuality with their every action and perception. There are others who are so totally label-gay in every fibre of their self-recognition that every other consideration is a distant also-ran. You can't disagree with their opinion on anything because this is taken as confirmation that you are 'anti-gay' or 'homophobic'. No, I just disagree with you and this is completely unrelated to your willy's destination of choice which, by the way, is none of my business so long as the receiver is at peace with it. You see the same with the 'I am a feminist' self-identity – 'You are only saying that because you are a misogynist.' No, it's because I think you're talking bollocks. Jewish, Muslim and Christian self-identity can also manifest extremes of 'I am' that make their label the only arbiter of anything. Disagree with the Israeli government's mass murdering and genocidal treatment of Palestinians and you are 'anti-Semitic'. No, I just disagree with mass murder and genocide. Israeli extremists describe Palestinians as a cancer but that is no problem it seems. Question the point in dropping to your knees five times a day while facing Mecca and you are anti-Muslim. No, I am just saying that it all seems daft to me, not that you shouldn't do it if you feel the need. And, by the way, it's my right to find it daft, just as it's their right to do it. The throttle goes both ways. Label-people can't see how diminished they are by such self-identification. They could identify with being Infinite Awareness – limitless All Possibility, All Potential – having an experience as whatever the label may be. Instead they live the label as 'this is me' and the infinite bit is never considered. They therefore live within the limits of the label and fall into the vibrational density of Phantom Self. It's the same with all of the labels, black, white, Jew, gay, there's no difference. You can see this in how label-possessed people have the same attitudes and emotional responses to similar circumstances (data input). They are 'offended', 'upset', 'insulted' and 'discriminated against' because they are [please add label here]. The 'I am' labels are just masks on The System's 'I am a label' program.

Political correctness? Fuck off

Political correctness is another potent example of the Archon virus spreading through the simulation (Fig 386). I have charted in other books its origins in Archon secret society networks and bloodline families, most notably the House of Rothschild. This is to be expected when political correctness, or PC, is such a powerful tool for divide and conquer and Phantom Self creation. It has taken Label-Consciousness to still new extremes of insanity in which labels are urged to condemn other labels and report them for their insults or

Figure 386: Political correctness in a single image.

Figure 387: Political correctness is not about freedom – it's about suppressing freedom.

Figure 388: Essential component of human control.

discrimination (Fig 387). These usually turn out not be insulting or discriminating at all when viewed from the perspective of the most basic intelligence and soundness of mind, and most of the so-called insulted group often couldn't care less. A few professionally-upset opportunists mostly cause the trouble. I read about a non-Muslim woman who was told to remove examples of her ceramic pig collection from a window because they were upsetting to Muslims. I would have thought it was far more relevant to ask both complainers and enforcers to remove examples of their insanity. I find it deeply upsetting that anyone could be so bloody stupid. To consider the sight of pot pigs insulting surely requires some serious psychological support. But, no, not when you are dealing with political correctness and madness is its essential foundation and means of survival. PC serves Archon interests by playing one label off against another to divide and rule and set humanity at war with itself (Fig 388). Phantom people are expert at falling for this one whether it be world wars, conflicts with neighbours or family feuds. Nothing is too trivial, irrelevant and nonsensical to brawl over. Humanity is so focussed on fighting itself and warring with fake and manufactured enemies that it doesn't see the force operating through all the labels – the force that made up the list in the first place. There is also the wish-I-was-someone-else syndrome that you see with white people of the New Age mind-set who desperately wish they were Native Americans or dress as Hindus to mitigate the disappointment that their skin is the wrong colour. We have extraordinary extremes of this phenomenon like the white 'civil rights advocate' who claimed to be black when she wasn't and so-called 'transabled' who self-identify as disabled when there's nothing wrong with them. One academic said: 'The person could want to become deaf, blind, amputee, paraplegic. It's a really, really strong desire.' It's also madness and an extreme example of how Phantom Selves self-identify with their body. From this comes self-hatred when the body does not conform to the programmed norm. Today's real norm is for people to be overweight or at least not catwalk-perfect in some way; but *programmed* norm is what rules perception. Does my bum look big in this? The norm is for men to lose their hair, but programmed norm is that they must not. If the human body didn't grow hair then the opposite would be the case. '*Ahhhh*, I've got hair growing on my head – Ethel, scissors, quick!' Phantom Self's body-program has now reached such lunacy that a major study involving 6,000 children in the UK found they can dislike the size and shape of their body as young as

Figure 389: Too busy fighting each other to see the truth.

eight and this can lead to eating disorders as they chase catwalk conformity. Yet again pressure comes from other Phantom Selves who have downloaded the same program – 'friends', classmates and other peer pressure. The Shepherd (The System) writes the programs and the sheep (through peer pressure) impose the programs on other sheep ... *baa, baa, baa.* The Archon control system can only work if slaves enslave slaves ... once again with feeling ... *THE ARCHON CONTROL SYSTEM CAN ONLY WORK IF SLAVES ENSLAVE SLAVES* (Fig 389).

Political correctness and Label-Consciousness trigger identity-obsession that can see no other point from which to consider or observe any question or situation. Label-obsessed extreme Jews, Muslims, Christians, Hindus, blacks, whites, straights, gays, Lefts, Rights and feminists seem to find it impossible to appreciate the view of anyone who does not reside within the perception walls of their chosen label. They will argue and dismiss to the most jaw-dropping extremes to avoid saying the dreaded, avoid at all costs ... 'Yes, my fellow believer is talking crap on this one' or even 'I don't agree'. Valid points made by another label are rejected and the chosen label must be defended at all costs. It is their god (or goddess), their reason for being and definition of self. They cannot concede they could ever be mistaken. You see this constantly with political parties in which 'we were wrong' is blasphemy and 'you might have a point' is a prima facie case for execution. Another role of political correctness is to isolate groups that do not constitute a 'minority'. Majority groups in any situation are the ranks from which most of the alleged enemies of a minority must be gleaned and there can never be discrimination against enemies, real or mostly otherwise. There is no political correctness for the majority in any situation for this reason. When white people are racially condemned by non-white people, for example, it is a legitimate stance by an oppressed minority; but when it's the other way round white people are called 'racists'. A black presenter on an MTV video condemning Halloween and other children's costumes as 'racist' said that he hoped anyone buying a Confederate uniform for their kids 'gets into a car accident and have to be saved by black paramedics.' Switch that around to black people buying a costume and white paramedics and the storms on Saturn would have some competition. Political correctness is perfectly fine with that because this serves the agenda it was created to serve. Such lunacy and systematic discrimination was personified by Bahar Mustafa, welfare and diversity officer at Goldsmiths College, University in London, in 2015 when she banned white people and men from an event to *promote equality*. The only people welcome were 'self-defining black and ethnic minority women and non-binary people with gender identities that include "woman".' Now if ever I have seen Phantom Self at work Ms Mustafa must take the non-binary biscuit. A non-binary person is one who doesn't identify exclusively with being a man or a woman but I guess that as long as they identity with being a woman a little bit they pass the sentry at the door. There are also 'BME women' in the

Figure 390: Phantom Self can't hear you.   **Figure 391:** Enough of this shit.

newspeak of political correctness, which apparently stands for black, minority and ethnic. See how labels awarded to Phantom Self go on proliferating as the Little Me virus spreads its infection and the sense of 'You' which they represent get smaller and smaller (Fig 390). 'Little me' programs are victim programs and nothing takes your power away quicker than a self-perception of being a victim of something or other. Jacques Barzun, a French-born American historian, described it all very well when he said: 'Political correctness does not legislate tolerance; it only organises hatred.' Political correctness is supposed to be about diversity and tolerance when it is actually organised hatred, organised victimhood and fake tolerance imposed by extreme intolerance. Balls to that. Oh, wait. Was the use of 'balls' sexist there? Do I need gender training? I *do?* Okay, tits then. Oh, it should be balls/tits/non-binary and you'll deal with colour later? Gotcha. CoExist House, a US and UK-based interfaith group, has called on employers to ban ham sandwiches and sausage rolls on the grounds that Muslims and Jews might find them offensive. Not as offensive, however, as CoExist House must be to basic intelligence (Fig 391). Andy Dinham, a University of London professor who wrote the guidelines said: 'It would be good etiquette to avoid heating up foods that might be prohibited for people of other faiths ... We also say, don't put kosher or halal and other... special foods next to another [food] or, God forbid, on the same plate.' Note that serving kosher or halal meat from animals killed in a particularly cruel way that might offend others is fine, but then as a minority they can't be politically incorrect, only the majority can. Eva Brunne, a lesbian bishop, said that Christian crosses should be removed from Swedish churches in deference to Muslims and churches should provide Muslim prayer rooms. Why not go the whole way and remove the Bible? I reject all religion, but that's not the point. The ludicrous scale of political correctness today is the point and we've seen nothing yet if people go on acquiescing instead of saying don't be so bloody stupid. We reached still new levels of absurdity when the University of Wisconsin-Milwaukee announced that the term 'politically correct' is now politically incorrect. Apparently its use is a 'microaggression' (see Orwell) because it suggests that people are being too 'sensitive' and are policing the language. The fact that they *are* is irrelevant when the truth does not matter to the politically correct. Oops, shit, another microaggression. Slaps hand, says three Hail Mustafas, moves on.

Money in madness

Zionist anti-racist groups depend for their existence (and money) on the perception of widespread anti-Semitism, and political correctness groups depend on a ceaseless supply of people who consider themselves to be victims of something or other (Fig 392). I am not saying there isn't prejudice against those with different coloured skin, religions, cultures and sexual orientation. Of course such moronic Phantoms exist. The problem for political correctness is that there are not nearly enough of them to justify its now gigantic freedom-destroying, gravy-train bureaucracy. They overcome this handicap by inventing fake discrimination. They condemn the most mild comments and views as racism or some other 'ism' and tell everyone who isn't a majority that they are victims of the majority, whatever it may be. The majority for non-white people in Western countries is white

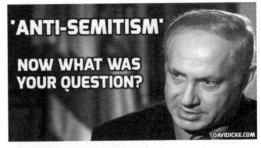

Figure 392: Professional victim.

Figure 393: Downloading the victim mentality.

people; the majority for gay people is non-gay people and so on. A bloke I once knew seemed to be against political correctness but as soon as he came out as gay it was 'you're only saying this or that because you're homophobic.' No, it's because I think you're an idiot. Democrats in California even introduced a bill to ban the words 'husband' and 'wife' from being used in federal law. Apparently they are 'gendered terms' that discriminate against gay people (Fig 393). America's biggest gay rights lobby group produced a guide calling on schools to eliminate 'gender stereotypes' by avoiding the words 'boy' and 'girl' when referring to, er, boys and girls. It said:

> Instead of addressing your class using 'boys' and 'girls', try something new. Words like 'friends,' 'students' or 'scholars' allow all students to feel included, expand student vocabulary and model inclusive language and behavior for other students and teachers.

'Expand student vocabulary' when you are destroying it. Classic Orwell. Transsexual activists have called for the term pregnant women to be replaced by 'pregnant people' or 'birthing individuals'. They say 'pregnant women' promotes hatred against transsexuals in the Phantom minds of these software programs. The term 'pregnant men' appears safe for now, but give them time. 'Transphobic' is the buzz-term and I have seen it suggested that to call the monthly cycle a 'woman's issue' is transphobic as 'not all women have vaginas'. No, it seems you can find dicks everywhere especially when it comes to political correctness. It reminds me of a scene in the Monty Python movie *Life of Brian* when a character in a 'radical' group played by Eric Idle announced that he was a woman and wanted to have babies. It was pointed out that he didn't have a womb so having babies was out of the question but they voted to agree that he had the *right* to have babies. The scene went like this:

Stan: I want to be a woman. From now on, I want you all to call me Loretta.

Reg: What?

Stan/Loretta: It's my right as a man.

Judith: Well, why do you want to be Loretta, Stan?

Stan/Loretta: I want to have babies.

Reg: You want to have babies?!

Stan/Loretta: It's every man's right to have babies if he wants them.

Reg: But ... you can't have babies!

Stan/Loretta: Don't you oppress me!

Reg: I'm not oppressing you, Stan. You haven't got a womb. Where is the foetus going to gestate? You're going to keep it in a box?

Stan/Loretta: Sniff.

Judith: Here, I've got an idea. Suppose you agree that he can't actually have babies, not having a womb, which is nobody's fault, not even the Romans', but that he can have the right to have babies.

Rogers: Good idea, Judith. We shall fight the oppressors for your right to have babies, brother. Sister! Sorry.

Reg: What's the point?

Rogers: What?

Reg: What's the point of fighting for his right to have babies when he can't have babies?

Rogers: It is symbolic of our struggle against oppression.

Reg: Symbolic of his struggle against reality.

It is a brilliant scene from an outstanding film, but how can you comedically exaggerate this nonsense any more when one prominent feminist said: 'Everything is sexist, everything is racist, everything is homophobic.' Presumably on that basis 'everything' includes what she said and everything else she says then? Oh, it's everything except what she says and everyone like her says? Right, thanks for the clarification, appreciated. They are the polar extreme of those like some Jewish sects that ban women from driving because it breaks their 'modesty rules'. Two polarities that would fiercely oppose each other yet both off with the same fairies. This is how Archon society is set up at every turn. It would all be hilarious except for the fact that the most extreme insanities of political correctness are now being enshrined in law, work manuals and promoted by the Archon United Nations. 'Leading' feminists went before the UN to call for governments to be pressured to censor content that criticised radical feminism. Twitter now has a category for reporting abusive or harassing behaviour that includes 'disagreeing with my opinion'

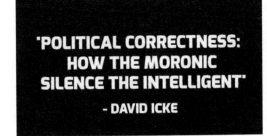

'POLITICAL CORRECTNESS: HOW THE MORONIC SILENCE THE INTELLIGENT'
- DAVID ICKE

Figure 394: The madhouse once again.

(the plan is to stop all opinion outside the official consensus). I am all for equality for everyone, but these professional victims and censors have become a tyranny whose arrogance and stupidity knows no end. This nonsense is actually destroying equality (inversion). They are being played to perfection by those really behind political correctness whose intention is to silence and to break down every individual sense of self until everyone concedes to the nothingness uniformity of the hive mind. Each minority is given a majority on which to place the blame for their sense of victimisation and discrimination and providing an excuse not to get a life. Those in the shadows behind all this couldn't give a shit about 'diversity' or discrimination. This is the same force bombing people with brown faces throughout Africa and the Middle East for goodness sake. Political correctness and the diversity industry are a colossal global exercise in divide and rule on the road to enslaving ALL parties involved by setting the entire target population at war with itself. Try explaining this to the Bahar Mustafa mentality and you will probably hear a very loud bang from genetic implosion and have quite a mess to clear up. Many people from those backgrounds labelled 'minorities' can see through the lunacy and they realise that, as Martin Luther King said, it is not about the colour of the skin but the nature of the character. There are racists and bigots in every race and culture and my goodness the political correctness, diversity bureaucracy is infested with them (Fig 394). PC people do irony on a gargantuan scale. Universities are not bastions of uncontrolled racism, sexism and homophobia and yet a staggering 'diversity' bureaucracy has been developed to 'deal' with something that doesn't exist on a fraction of the scale claimed by those benefiting from this madness, with salaries sometimes upwards of $250,000. University of California, San Diego, has this crowd on the payroll:

Associate Vice-Chancellor for Faculty Equity; Associate Vice-Chancellor for Diversity; Staff Diversity Liason; Graduate Student Diversity Liason; Undergraduate Student Diversity Liason; Chief Diversity Officer; Director of Development for Diversity Initiatives; Director of the Cross-Cultural Center; Director of the Women's Center; Director of the Lesbian Gay Bisexual Transgender Resource Center.

No, no, I didn't make the last one up, I promise. There is no need to exaggerate when PC exaggeration is now an impossibility. The University of California is demanding that *potentially* offensive words and phrases should no longer be used including 'melting pot', 'America is a melting pot', and 'I believe the most qualified person should get the job.' Apparently saying 'there is only one race, the human race' is deemed offensive for denying 'the significance of a person of colour's racial/ethnic experience and history'(the significance of Phantom Self in other words). But, hey, these lunatics want to 'foster informed conversation about the best way to build and nurture a productive academic climate'. My god, I must ask them round to dinner on a night when I know I'm not home. Students of California and everywhere else – *get off your bloody knees.* From

Figure 395: And others are told to believe in racism that isn't there.

where I am standing everyone should be treated the same with the same right to fairness and justice no matter what their colour, religion or label (Fig 395). I don't see race or ethnicity. I see Infinite Awareness having different experiences and I don't identify with being white any more than I do with being a garden gnome. Once you self-identify with a System label you are conceding your right to dispassionately observe the world and to do so without discrimination. This is why those who scream 'racist' the loudest and with the most vehemence and venom are some of the most extreme racists you could ever meet. Jewish racist extremists cry racism while speaking of Palestinians in terms of insects and animals. Muslims demand freedom while their religion enslaves followers in enforced submission. Muslim means 'One Who Submits'. I have seen Muslim women demand freedom from external oppression while talking through a burka that extremes of the religion they support demand that they wear. Hindu believers who support the judged-for-life-by-genetics caste system (Archon-Reptilian genetic hierarchy) have the nerve to condemn what they call racism against themselves. This is what happens when you self-identify with Label-Consciousness, a foundation component of Phantom Self.

More famous the better

The Hidden Hand behind political correctness seeks to terrify people into conformity to its idiocy by targeting those in the public eye for PC treatment and silencing anyone revealing the truth about world events and those involved. Try exposing the Rothschilds or Israel without being attacked by morons as 'anti-Semitic'. Mainstream Everything purveyors of propaganda and choose-to-be stupid Phantom Selves (especially the media) go to war on the well-known

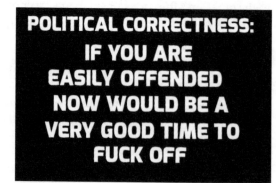

Figure 396: Said with feeling.

person's reputation for the mildest of views. Celebrities then mostly and meekly issue a grovelling apology and ask the public's forgiveness for any 'hurt and offence' caused by having their comment about disliking black coffee and big sausages construed as their opinion about non-white races and reinforcing a stereotype about black men having big dicks. Actor Benedict Cumberbatch apologised amid a manufactured furore for using the word 'coloured' instead of black when pointing out *discrimination against black actors*. His career would have been over had he talked

Figure 397: Lost cause, mate.

about discrimination against white actors. A decorated British scientist lost his job when the Feminist Mafia jumped on his case after an innocuous comment that should have been laughed off. Such character assassinations are now commonplace and they are meant to be. Feminist Phantoms can call for the death of all men or for all men to be put in concentration camps and its perfectly fine. One wants every man killed to stop crime. Well, that will be good for the birth-rate. But she said her insanity is not 'misandry' (ingrained prejudice against men) because misandry would be wanting them dead for no reason (Fig 396). Every PC label has its own hit-squad at the ready to Blitzkrieg social media until their target submits to their onslaught and either walks away into sackcloth oblivion or falls to their knees to beg for forgiveness (and the survival of their career). PC Special Forces are too consumed by their own self-righteousness and far too far up their own arses to see that they are behaving in precisely the same way that they so righteousness condemn. They that discriminate condemn discrimination (inversion). Observe these Phantoms and you'll see. People depending for their living, status or fame on Mainstream Everything are now scanning their every spoken or written word in fear that they will say something to which someone, anyone, will take offence. There have been cases of the most evil and despicable people being left alone by police despite horrific crimes because they were a minority and the police did not want to imply any discrimination. *And what about their ongoing victims??* This is what I mean by political correctness depending on insanity for its very survival. I remember producing a filmed report for BBC News one Easter even before the PC (Archon) virus had fully taken hold. The report was about the opening of the first 'Corkscrew' rollercoaster theme park ride in Britain and I sat in the front of the carriage talking to camera as it reached the highest point where it would go over the top into crash, bang, wallop. My last words were 'what a way to spend an Easter'. The report was put together and transmitted to the London newsroom for the next bulletin, but it was pulled at the last minute. A producer had said that 'what a way to spend an Easter' was the punchline of a joke about Jesus and it might upset Christians. I'd never heard of the joke and I was speaking spontaneously, but it matters not to PC worship, which is there to silence opinion, delete diversity of information and views, and impose conformity to centrally-dictated norms – all of which match the agenda of the control system and the need to mould and isolate Phantom Self (Fig 397).

Figure 398: Everything is ritual to the bloodlines.

Figure 399: Why wouldn't the maddest of all be allowed to run the madhouse?

Knowing your place

Left-brain and reptilian brain software make Phantom Self a cinch to manipulate through an obsession with hierarchy and fear of not surviving. Right-brain connects dots and sees the unity of everything, but the left decodes apartness with space in between and this makes submission to the perception of hierarchy such an easy sell for the vast majority. You hear this in terms like 'know your place' and 'us and them'. Most of those who say they reject hierarchies are still defining their perceptions by them and most could not perceive a world without hierarchies of some description (see democratic hierarchies, fascist hierarchies, communist hierarchies, religious hierarchies, all of which are sub-divisions of Archontic hierarchy). I remember a young student I spoke with at Oxford University who could not conceive how any society could work without hierarchical structures of power distribution. His program couldn't scan any other possibility. Ancient and modern tales of Archon-Reptilians emphasise their obsession with technology, hierarchy and ritual. In fact, hierarchy is a form of ritual in which everyone ritually knows their place. All the pomp and ceremony of the hybrid bloodlines come from their Archon-possession and the same is true of ritual-obsessed secret societies and Satanism. Ritual is a major trait of the reptilian brain as in 'obsessive, compulsive and ritualistic behaviour, conforming to precedent, an obsession with hierarchical structures of power, laws, rules and regulations'. Britain's Archon-Reptilian royal family lives virtually its entire life moving from one ritual to another while living in the same palaces at the same time every year (Figs 398 and 399). The Queen issues a list to her own family telling them who must bow or courtesy to whom with the 'blood royal' taking precedence over incomers no matter how 'well-bred' they may be. Her Majesty couldn't be any other way, given the hierarchy programs running through her Archon-Reptilian genetics. An obsession with hierarchy and ritual can be seen throughout The System dictated by the Archon-Reptilian hive-mind (virus). El-ite' hybrids are the most welded to ceremonial ritual through their greater infusion of Archon-Reptilian genetics and a more powerful connection to the Demiurge master virus; but ritualism has also been downloaded by the population in general. Observe how people largely live their daily lives and you will soon see the ever-recurring ritual of repeating responses and behaviour. Ritual is defined as 'a set of actions conducted routinely in the same manner' and what does that remind you of? A *computer program.*

How much spontaneity do you see in the world compared with predictable, repeating cycles by the hour, day, week, month and year? These are downloaded rituals that become what we perceive and live as the 'norms' – 'Oh, it's so and so o'clock, I must ...' ... 'No, I can't do that, I always do so and so on Thursdays ...' ... 'Pie on Friday? But we always have fish ...' A shocking lack of spontaneity combined with repetition is a manifestation of Phantom Self resisting the urgings of expanded awareness. Infinite Awareness – All Possibility – is by its very nature the maverick that loves to be spontaneous. Phantom Self is a program and this is why there is such a disparity between Infinite and Phantom when it comes to spontaneity and repetition. Many people instinctively fear and reject spontaneity as if it was some fatal disease. To Phantom Self, *it is*. Political correctness rages at any suggestion of stereotypes, even as a joke, but stereotypes exist everywhere and humanity is a collective stereotype. The way people stereotypically respond as the world *cosmetically* changes is often called 'breaking the stereotype' when it is only another stereotypical response and behaviour program to a new situation. Women at home stereotypes become women must have a career stereotypes, for example. The 'norm' changed a bit, that's all, not conformity to it. Stereotypical thinking and behaviour masked as free and personal choice is another hoax to keep you in Phantom Self by kidding you that slavery is freedom.

Programmed programmers

Phantom Self's propensity for hierarchal thinking via left-brain/reptilian brain creates the superior/subordinate dynamic that is the foundation of Archon-Phantom society. The 'us and them' division stems from differences in education, family background, wealth and position. Hierarchy is dictated by the same criteria. We hear that people went to a 'good school' when all this really means is a better and more expensive programming centre. Those from elite hybrid families are programmed to be leaders and administrators while the masses are programmed by state education to be subordinate to the leaders and administrators and know their place (Fig 400). There is some overlap but this is really only window-dressing to hide the truth that a few are programmed to lead and control and the rest are programmed to be led and controlled. I have known people who believed they were challenging this power structure who would turn to jelly in the presence of those they claimed to oppose. I have read accounts by anti-monarchists who have done this in the presence of the Queen and had no idea why. I can tell them – it's the hierarchy program kicking in via the left and reptilian segments of their brain. Only consciousness in its *own* power outside the program can block this response. A programmed sense of hierarchical superiority exalts scientists and doctors who mostly come from 'good families', 'good backgrounds' and have a 'good education'. Conscious and subconscious perception that the hierarchically superior

Figure 400: Brilliant satire of Britain's class society – upper, middle and lower class know their place in the 1960s show *The Frost Report*.

must know best has for thousands of years subordinated the sense of reality of the masses to the perception programming of what are often complete idiots. Posh voice and expanded awareness are not the same thing. This nonsense continues today with regard to politicians, bankers, corporate leaders, military chiefs and media. I am not saying that these people know nothing – though many come close – but they are not *all*-knowing by virtue of family background, wealth and educational programming. These factors can indeed cause them to be monumentally stupid. They say there is no fool like an old fool, but from my experience there are few more bereft of brain activity than an aristocratic or academic fool. 'Lord' is not a definition of intelligence and neither is 'professor'; Prince is not a term for consciousness, nor pauper a term for dumb. Intelligence – *innate* intelligence – does not come from education, wealth or family background but from the scale of connection to Infinite Awareness. This cannot be delivered by System education, only suppressed by it, which, of course, is the idea. Consciousness beyond the Phantom has a frequency 'hierarchy' based on real choice with no one excluded, in that the more you expand your awareness the higher the frequencies you can explore. What we have in human society is an Archon-typical inversion of this. By blocking access to expanded awareness through perception programming and other means they have been able to entrap isolated Phantoms in a hierarchical structure based on dividing those who run The System from those who are slaves to The System. In the end, irony of ironies, they're all slaves to the Archon virus. Entry to the highest echelons of the hierarchy – which the public mostly never see – is by hybrid bloodline only. Their lackeys and gofers are chosen by their ability and willingness to be lackeys and gofers. Some of these will be bloodline though most are not and thanks to need-to-know compartmentalisation the great majority have no idea who and what they are really serving. System-lackey Phantoms can be found at all levels of the hierarchy and you can recognise them easily by their unquestioning loyalty to The System and an obsession with its rules and regulations. Lackey-Phantoms abound in law enforcement, government administration of every kind, schools and academia and any position where the power to enforce laws and rules goes with the job. They can be spotted by the rule book slotted into the computer plug-in on top of their head. In the uniformed professions this is usually obscured by a hat. I have given many examples of such people in other books and you will have many of your own, but here

is one to illustrate the point. A video on Davidicke.com featured a city official in Florida telling a man having a barbeque with friends that he had to stop the smell leaving his property. I kid you not. Pinellas County's Environment lady said the property owner was in violation (a word System-lackeys so adore) of a local rule that bans the smell of a barbeque leaving a property. What was the guy supposed to do? Have a chat with it and get it to see reason? Call the police and have it arrested? If so, I hope it makes a stink. System-Phantom lackey lady told the group:

Figure 401: Satire is becoming increasingly difficult in a world that satirises itself.

I can smell it again right now, but I'm on your property. You're allowed to have it smell on your property, so that doesn't count, but when I'm on the street, that's when it counts.

Correct me if I'm wrong, but that doesn't sound to me like Infinite Awareness at work (Fig 401). The System has always employed what we call in Britain 'jobsworths' – those who say 'it's more than my job's worth' not to enforce this or that ludicrous rule. It has a dictionary definition: 'An official who upholds petty rules even at the expense of humanity or common sense.' Put another way, a Phantom Self extremist. The scale and depth of their programming is constantly reaching still new levels of absurdity and the plan is to have the entire System administered by these programs in a global Orwellian Phantom State. Their numbers are exponentially increasing as programs hire programs to advance the goal. An emergency medical technician was suspended in New York after stopping his ambulance taking a patient to a doctor's appointment to save a seven-year-old girl from choking to death – she was already unconscious and turning blue. He had violated the rules according to his insane jobsworth bosses by stopping on assignment. These are the depths to which humanity has descended. There will soon be virtually nothing that is not against some law or other as mountains of legislation go on being passed, and Phantom-lackeys must be drooling at the prospect. Are they allowed to drool? Isn't there a law against it? Apparently not, amazingly. Regulation 465, 895, 456/WCD/reference FIWT/clause 65, sub-clause 5, of the Rules and Drools (System Servers) Act 2004 declares: 'State employees shall be in accordance with said regulation so long as drool spittle extends downwards no more than two inches and a cloth is summoned should this limit be breached.' So, you see, it's all in accordance with 'protocol' ('a set of rules governing the format of messages that are exchanged between computers'). Phantom Self is a software construct and the more extreme Phantom Self enslavement the more they will be unyieldingly acquiescent to rules and regulations whether enforcers or enforced (Fig 402). Spontaneity and common sense? Forget it. Rule books are always stupid and always heartless because they have no capacity to think and feel. Anyone with a rule book mind is the same. Videos galore on the Internet feature law enforcement officials faced with something unusual happening who move in to impose the law on the basis that if it's unusual there must be a law against it. Then they realise that there is no law against what is before them and it completely fucks with their head. There's a video of police officers in a London park actually going through the rule book in search of a law to stop some bloke holding up a sign saying 'Everything is okay'. In what passes for their minds the officers were seeing something different to the norm and so it had to be against the law. They would be outraged if someone pointed out the obvious fact that they are suffering from a form of mental illness – Phantomitis or clones disease. To them madness is normal and 'just doing my job'. Their sense of security comes from programmed norms

Figure 402: Phantom Self writes.

being forever undisturbed by spontaneity and when that happens their software malfunctions and hits the panic button – 'I am a Dalek, I am a Dalek, exterminate, exterminate.' Their mentality is an extreme expression of the slaves-enslaving-slaves program. Most of the enforcers are serving a System that also enslaves them and their families and is planning to enslave their children and grandchildren with unimaginable levels of tyranny as the Archon virus pursues total control.

Figure 403: I am connected – I'm online.

Competing to lose

Divide and rule by definition requires a means of division and this is where hierarchal perception is so perfect and essential. Phantom Self by its very nature cannot identify with the infinite unity of being a unique point of attention and observation within Infinite Awareness (Fig 403). It cannot perceive itself as an expression of *All That Is* celebrating infinite possibility, potential and diversity. If it could it wouldn't be Phantom Self. Instead its information downloads program perceptions of an isolated individual.

Figure 404: What happens in a competition society controlled by those who rig the game so they always 'win'.

Potential for divide and rule is therefore fantastic even before Phantom Self is herded into groups to be played off against other groups through religion, politics, culture and so much more. A disconnection from the wisdom and insight of Infinite Awareness leaves Phantom Self with only one source of information – the 'out there' world of Mainstream Everything. Without the filter and expanded perspective of Infinite Awareness these Archontic five-sense information sources mostly face little challenge on their way to becoming accepted 'fact'. A subconscious sense of isolation from Infinite Self leads to ongoing insecurity, fear and anxiety which Phantom Self cannot explain or puts down to other Earthly factors. Most people will not even be aware of what I call background sadness or background anxiety just as background noise is not heard if it goes on for long enough. From this insecurity can come a need to control (all control-freaks suffer from extreme insecurity) and a need to define success by other Phantom Selves perceiving you as successful. This sets humanity at war with itself through what is known as competition. We can cooperate and no one would go hungry or homeless (Fig 404). Or we can compete and most will have nothing while the few will have far more than they could ever need. Competition is the offspring of the psychological dependency of being seen to succeed. This dependency in the end comes from insecurity, which comes from a disconnection from Infinite Self. Security comes from Infinite Awareness – which does not have to compete and 'win' to externalise its sense

Figure 405: Winning a hoax is still a hoax.

of success (therefore security) by being acknowledged as successful. Security for those conscious beyond Phantom Self comes from within and not in external adulation or acknowledgement. This is the security of knowing that we are infinite, eternal awareness having an experience and not believing that we *are* that experience. There is no need for external confirmation of what you already are; no need for still more labels like success and failure. Phantom Self lives with a perception of isolation and can only succeed (it believes) by 'doing better' than other Phantom Selves also living with a perception of isolation (Fig 405). 'I beat you!' No, you are Infinite Awareness and so you 'beat' yourself. 'I killed you!' No, you are Infinite Awareness and so you 'killed' yourself. Doing your best in your chosen field is not the same as competing. To do *your* best is to do *your* best and not to define yourself by comparison with others doing their best. You can play football with and against others and do your best without defining the experience by how others do. Your best wasn't good enough? Of course it was because it was the best you could do. Oh, but we 'lost' and all the cheers went to the other side? You are externalising your sense of security again. Who cares how many cheers they got and you didn't. Does our sense of self and security depend on what others think and do? If it does then Phantom Self has you.

I have seen many stories of young lives destroyed and even ended through suicide because of what has been said about them by the mentally deranged on social media. The troll mentality is extreme Phantom Self insecurity and allowing yourself to be affected by these moronic people is extreme Phantom Self insecurity. Trolls are thick as in dense and dense as in density – low frequency. They don't have to be but they have chosen to be and they can make another choice whenever they want. A need to seek security through your perceived place in the hierarchy involves not only climbing the ladder but also making others fall. Here we have a major reason why so many people love to see those perceived as successful brought crashing down and if they can play a part in that demise even better. I can't get up the ladder so next best thing is bringing others down to me. I have taken unimaginable abuse over 26 years and still do so from Phantom Self extremists; but I don't give a shit. I don't need anyone to give me my sense of security, thank you. If my sense of self was dependent on being liked by perception-enslaved idiots what would that say about me? It doesn't matter what people think about you, only what *you* think about you. Another consequence of Phantom Self dependency on externalised security is that to attract confirmation that you are successful you must succeed according the symbols and definitions of success dictated by The System. This is a major vehicle through which The System dictates and limits choice. Once you have programmed the definition of success, which largely comes down to fame, status and money, you have set the ambition criteria for Phantom Self in need of externalised security. This means almost everyone, sad to say. Pushy parents don't tell their offspring to go walking in India to impress their friends. They

demand that their kids pursue ambitions
that their friends have been programmed
to perceive as successful. Until people stop
looking outside of themselves for a sense of
security and worth they can never – *never* –
be free no matter how much they may use
that word or march in its name.

'Revolutions' to 'free the people' always
end in another version of slavery because
the rhetoric changes but not the programs
that dictate their reality.

Figure 406: The reptilian brain/amygdala have one of
their moments.

Mass fear program

Perceptions of hierarchy and acquiescence by the left-
brain/reptilian brain is deadly for free thought
especially when combined with the reptilian brain's
obsession with survival. Together these comprise a
massive and fundamental part of Phantom Self. The
reptilian brain does not think but *reacts* in league with
a part of the brain called the amygdala, which
expresses and processes emotions. Reacting without
thinking can be necessary when someone walks in
front of your car and the reptilian brain slams the
brakes on without any debate about whether to do so.
Thank goodness when to take time to ponder could be
fatal; but reacting from the survival instinct before
other parts of the brain can calmly think is also fatal to
freedom if the survival reaction becomes the governor
of all perception and behaviour. Reptilian brain is

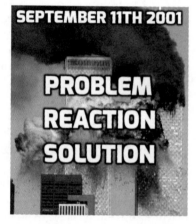

Figure 407: 9/11 was a classic Problem-
Reaction-Solution.

constantly scanning the environment for threats to survival and these include threats to
finances, job, status, reputation, relationship, intellectual pre-eminence and not only
survival of the body. Our fight-or-flight response to danger involves the reptilian
brain/amygdala and so does road rage. We see reptilian/amygdala responses when
people react in an over-the-top manner or even violently and then say 'Oh, my, god,
what have I done?' Panic is a trait of the reptilian brain in the face of perceived threats to
the survival of whatever is perceived to be under threat (Fig 406). Put this reptilian
brain/amygdala reaction system together the left-brain/reptilian brain relationship
with hierarchy and you have the reason why the mass manipulation technique that I
have dubbed Problem-Reaction-Solution (PRS) is so enormously and constantly
effective. It is so simple. You want to change society in line with your agenda for global
control, but you know that if you announce what you want without any justification
you will face potentially severe resistance. Instead you covertly create a problem and
blame someone or something else for what *you* have made happen. This could be a
terrorist attack, financial collapse, epidemic, 'people's revolution' or whatever suits the
changes you wish to make and actions you wish to take. If you want to justify a global
war on terrorism (a war on target countries so you can steal their resources and remove

their leaders) then you engineer a terrorist attack like 9/11 and falsely blame it on those you wish to demonise (Fig 407). All the wars, mayhem and horrors that have followed 9/11 could not have happened without 9/11. I have shown in great detail in other books and especially *Alice in Wonderland and the World Trade Center Disaster* how the attacks of September 11th 2001 were orchestrated by government and military agencies through the Hidden Hand and how the countries that have been targeted and invaded since 9/11

Figure 408: Launching the long-planned – and fake – 'war on terror'.

Figure 410: The Lie Factory.

Figure 409: Get them in fear and they will give you their freedom for you to protect them.

were all listed for 'regime change' long before what happened in New York and Washington provided the initial excuse (Fig 408). If you want to take freedoms away tell the public they have to be deleted to protect people from terrorists (Fig 409). If you want to justify crushing the population through austerity and stealing their money then you need a financial collapse like the one in 2008 and others that are planned. Once again I have detailed elsewhere how the crash of 2008 was coldly engineered and who by. If you want to impose mandatory vaccination of toxic, immune-system destroying shite you release a virus (or make one up) and proclaim that everyone must be vaccinated by law to protect against the virus and so *survive*. My point about making one up is very real. There is another version of PRS that I call *No-Problem-Reaction-Solution*. This doesn't even require a real problem only the perception of one. It's all a mind game after all. Claims about weapons of mass destruction in Iraq to justify invasion are a wonderful example of the No-Problem-Reaction-Solution technique and the outcome is just the same no matter if the problem is real or invented (Fig 410). Henry Kissinger, one of the most active Archon manipulators of the last more than 60 years and a personification of pure

Figure 411: Precisely how it works..

Figure 412: We are the Problem, you are the Reaction, and then we are the Solution.

evil, said: 'It is not a matter of what is true that counts, but what is perceived to be true.' CIA Director William Casey said something similar: 'We'll know when our disinformation program is complete when everything the American public believes is false.'

The technique of PRS can be described as frighten the shit out of people so they will do what you want, and here the left-brain/reptilian brain combo comes into its own (Fig 411). Attachment to hierarchy and knowing your place leads the vast majority to believe in authority when the alleged background to the 'problem' is spun. The reptilian brain survival response based on fear opens the way for acceptance of the 'solution' to the 'problem' – solutions promoted by agents of the same force that covertly created the problem in the first place, and publicly blamed someone else (Fig 412). Fear and survival responses also turn against those that The System wrongly says are responsible. With no hope of calm, rational assessment from a screaming reptilian brain/amygdala everyone with any remote connection to their programmed perception of the 'enemy' becomes a focus of hatred, vitriol and often violence. People who were not Muslims but happened to have brown faces were violently attacked after 9/11 by Phantom Self extremists. Having a brown face was connection enough for these software programs masquerading as consciousness. How quickly and easily the great majority accept the official fairy stories without question or research is testament to what I am saying here. Archontic Bush and Blair blatantly and provably lied for their

Figure 413: Very dangerous. Do not approach without a wad of cash.

masters over weapons of mass destruction in Iraq, which led to untold slaughter and the ongoing mayhem that has followed (Fig 413). I wrote in books years ago that the Bush-Blair (their masters') agreement to invade Iraq in 2003 was made long before there was any talk of it publicly, and leaked documents have since shown that it was at least a year before the boys were sent in. It was actually long before that in the shadows, as I wrote 13 years earlier. Yet it occurs to so few (not least in the media) that the same people who told them the bare-faced lies about WMD in

Iraq, to justify what had long been planned, also told them the official story of what happened (didn't happen) on 9/11. They just download whatever Mainstream Everything tells them without any question or independent research. Journalists, scientists, doctors and academics repeat the official line from Mainstream Everything and the great majority of the population believe them. CIA Director William Colby said the CIA owns everyone of any significance in the major media, but they really don't have to own them all literally – only their perception of reality. Mainstream media

Figure 414: None dare call it journalism.

(and much of the alternative) overwhelmingly consists of Phantom Selves reporting the world of Phantom Self. So few mainstream journalists investigate beyond the official song sheets and if they do the consequences are soon upon them. The term 'journalist', when applied to the mainstream variety, is another inversion – with honourable exceptions. Journalists are supposed to tell people what is going on when *they* don't know what is going on. Investigative journalism is largely reading the morning papers and watching the rolling news on the newsroom telly with 'journalists' telling 'journalists' what is happening who then repeat it as fact. I met a television journalist I knew nearly 40 years earlier when he was sitting behind me at a cricket match in 2015. He clearly believed from the way the conversation went that I was going around the world doing Christian evangelist-type 'healings' like some British Benny Hinn. How had he come to this ridiculous conclusion? By passing through his off-the-peg perception processes the nonsense written by his fellow 'journalists'. These are the people that stand in the pivotal position between what is happening and what you are told is happening and to them the very idea of a global conspiracy is way beyond their can't-get-my-head-around-that capacity for free thought. Government and intelligence insiders who speak out to trash the official story? Paranoid nutters. Thousands of pilots and structural engineers who have given their support to organisations set up to specifically expose that 'Arab hijackers' could not possibly have flown those 9/11 aircraft in the way that is claimed and nor could aircraft fuel fires have collapsed the Twin Towers? More paranoid nutters. Carefully compiled and detailed evidence that the official story can't be true? Internet crap. No scale of evidence is enough for the mainstream media to reconsider Mainstream Everything cover stories, and genius is hardly required to see why (Fig 414).

All planned long ago

An organisation called the Project for the New American Century published a document in September 2000 entitled *Rebuilding America's Defenses: Strategies, Forces and Resources for a New Century* with a list of countries they wanted the United States to 'regime change' through 'multiple-theater wars' in the Middle East and North Africa. They included Iraq, Libya, Syria, Lebanon and Iran and the document also called for

Figure 415: The Bush administration and the Saudis are up to their necks in the 9/11 hoax along with Britain and Israel.

regime change in North Korea and China. It said that this 'process of transformation ... is likely to be a long one, absent some catastrophic and catalysing event – like a new Pearl Harbor'. Among those involved were Dick Cheney, Donald Rumsfeld, Paul Wolfowitz, Dov Zakheim, Richard Perle, Robert Kagan, Douglas Feith, William Kristol and Lewis 'Scooter' Libby who all came to power with the Boy Bush administration a few months later either directly (mostly) or indirectly. A year to the month after the document was published came 9/11 – what Bush called 'our Pearl Harbor' – and this was used to kick-start the process of picking off country after country on their list while blaming the attacks on 'Islamic extremists'. Mohamed Atta, the alleged 'terrorist leader' on 9/11, was such an Islamic fanatic that he had a white, non-Muslim American girlfriend, took cocaine, drank heavily and his favourite food was pork (see *The David Icke Guide to the Global Conspiracy* and *Alice in Wonderland and the World Trade Center Disaster*). In fact, Atta was running drugs for the CIA through Venice airport in Florida where some of the hijackers are supposed to have 'trained' to be pilots. Atta and his fellow 'hijackers' were caught in a trap they didn't understand by Archon elements within the American government, military and intelligence networks in league with Israel and Saudi Arabia where most of the alleged hijackers came from (Fig 415). General Wesley Clark, NATO's former Supreme Allied Commander Europe, said in a television interview on a non-mainstream station in 2007 that wars in the Middle East and North Africa since 9/11 had been planned at least by 2001 (and in truth long before). He said:

About ten days after 9/11, I went through the Pentagon and I saw Secretary Rumsfeld and Deputy Secretary Wolfowitz. I went downstairs just to say hello to some of the people on the Joint Staff who used to work for me, and one of the generals called me in. He said, 'Sir, you've got to come in and talk to me a second.' I said, 'Well, you're too busy.' He said, 'No, no.' He says, 'We've made the decision we're going to war with Iraq.' This was on or about the 20th of September. I said, 'We're going to war with Iraq? Why?' He said, 'I don't know.' He said, 'I guess they don't know what else to do.'

So I said, 'Well, did they find some information connecting Saddam to al-Qaeda?' He said, 'No, no.' He says, 'There's nothing new that way. They just made the decision to go to war with Iraq.' He said, 'I guess it's like we don't know what to do about terrorists, but we've got a good military and we can take down governments.' And he said, 'I guess if the only tool you have is a hammer, every problem has to look like a nail.'

So I came back to see him a few weeks later, and by that time we were bombing in Afghanistan. I said, 'Are we still going to war with Iraq?' And he said, 'Oh, it's worse than that.' He reached over on his desk. He picked up a piece of paper. And he said, 'I just got this down from upstairs' — meaning the Secretary of Defense's office — 'today.' And he said, 'This is a memo that describes how we're going to take out seven countries in five years, starting with Iraq, and then Syria, Lebanon, Libya, Somalia, Sudan and, finishing off, Iran.'

I said, 'Is it classified?' He said, 'Yes, sir.' I said, 'Well, don't show it to me.' And I saw him a year or so ago, and I said, 'You remember that?' He said, 'Sir, I didn't show you that memo! I didn't show it to you.

Figure 416: As it was always meant to be.

Note how information compartmentalisation keeps gofers, even high-level gofers, out of the loop of knowing the real story behind decisions and events. The 'war on terror' launched as a result of the engineered 9/11 has been used to target countries on the original pre-9/11 list, using different manufactured excuses for each one in an attempt to hide the common force behind them all, and used also as an excuse to delete freedoms at home under the pretext of protecting the population from terrorism (Fig 416). What I have laid out in the last few

Figure 417: There is now an Archontic war on those uncovering the truth.

paragraphs is evidence enough for a mainstream media investigation into the background to 9/11, but it hasn't happened because (a) it is blocked by Archontics who own the media and (b) most journalists all over the world will never have heard of the Project for the New American Century or realise its significance to 9/11, or what Wesley Clarke said in his interview. This same ignorance then condemns and ridicules those who are informed and dubs them 'conspiracy theorists' – a term invented by the CIA to discredit those exposing the President Kennedy assassination and other connected events in the 1960s including the assassinations of Robert Kennedy, Martin Luther King and Malcolm X. (Fig 417). The arrogance of ignorance is at work once more, but Phantom Self believes them anyway. A quote from writer Stephen King sums it up: 'The trust of the innocent is the liar's most useful tool.' It's not only the trust of the innocent; it is also the trust of the fearful. Phantom Self is wracked with fear – the fear program is running through body software – and this makes them open to being told what they so *want* to be true. Which is the easiest way to being believed? Telling people what they don't want to hear or telling them what they do? It may not be nice to be told that Muslim hijackers were responsible for 9/11 or that banking greed and incompetence was the only cause of the crash of 2008. But to a shaking, shivering Phantom Self it is quite another thing to be told that a hidden force, that controls government, security agencies and military, orchestrated 9/11 to justify wars of death, destruction and acquisition; or that the same force crashed the financial system to trigger the

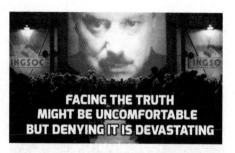

FACING THE TRUTH MIGHT BE UNCOMFORTABLE BUT DENYING IT IS DEVASTATING

Figure 418: This fact is becoming more obvious by the day.

extraordinary transfer of wealth from people via governments to the banking elite and plunged so many into the 'austerity' nightmare of poverty and deprivation (dependency). Accepting even the possibility, let alone the fact, is to see your entire world view demolished – all that you have ever believed about human life and society (Fig 418). You mean governments, intelligence agencies and our own military are working against us? Well, Archon-Reptilian hybrids *controlling* the government, intelligence agencies and military, yes. *'Ahhhhh ... No! No! No!'*, the program screams. Flashback to the scene in *The Matrix* when Neo is told that his 'real' world isn't real and he goes into denial and throws up. Most Phantom Selves cannot grasp nor even want to consider the concept of their own government working so malevolently against their interests – 'They would never do that!' If you observe the sub-text you see that statements like 'you are paranoid' are really saying 'Oh, please don't let it be true' and 'Shut up, I don't want to hear it – I know it could be true'. It appears to in-denial Phantom Self to be so much easier to condemn or shoot the messenger than have the courage and maturity to consider the validity of the message. Divide and rule programs make people far more likely to rush to condemnation and support wars of 'solution' if the official perpetrators are from a different sub-program. Christians are far more likely to support attacks and consequences for Muslims than they are for fellow Christians, and once you have demonised one group you return to demonise the group that you exploited to demonise the first group. Pastor Martin Niemöller famously said this about Nazi Germany:

First they came for the Communists and I did not speak out because I was not a Communist.
Then they came for the Socialists and I did not speak out because I was not a Socialist.
Then they came for the trade unionists and I did not speak out because I was not a trade unionist.
Then they came for the Jews and I did not speak out because I was not a Jew.
Then they came for me and there was no one left to speak out for me.

Phantom Selves are so easy to divide and rule when they see everything as being apart from everything else and cannot conceive that we are all the same Infinite Awareness no matter what labels they may give to themselves and others. Until they do they will go on playing their essential role in their own enslavement.

Softly, Softly, Catchee Monkey...

The refusal to comprehend a long-planned conspiracy ('they would never do that!') or to commit any thought or research to the possibility makes Phantom Self a sucker for the stablemate of Problem-Reaction-Solution, a technique that I call the Totalitarian Tiptoe. This works by advancing towards its goal in steps that are small enough for most people never to see that all the steps are connected and heading in the same direction. Your goal is Z (a global Orwellian state) but you don't want to give the game away too early before enough of the control structure is in place for it not to matter if people know or not. So you go from A to B to C with each step presented as an individual and isolated change in and of itself. The European Union dictatorship has been made possible by this technique as it progressed from a free trade area to a centrally-controlled bureaucratic superstate consuming the sovereignty of nations with every new step. This was revealed by the so-called 'Father' of the EU project, French Rothschild frontman, Jean Monnet, in a letter to a friend on April 30th 1952:

Figure 419: 'I can't be bothered with politics.'

> Europe's nations should be guided towards the super-state without their people understanding what is happening. This can be accomplished by successive steps, each disguised as having an economic purpose, but which will eventually and irreversibly lead to federation.

This has clearly happened and the crushing of Greece and its people is but one example of using engineered financial excuses to justify ever more centralisation of power. We reached still new extremes when Anibal Cavaco Silva, Portugal's constitutional president, refused to appoint a left-wing coalition government that won an absolute majority in the Portuguese parliament because it was sceptical of the EU and wanted to challenge its debt policies imposed on Portugal. Neither Greece nor Portugal is any longer a democracy and every other country is planned to follow. They get away with it because most Phantom Selves are consumed by their own designer myopia. It may be family, job, sport, hobby, television or celebrity, anything that takes your eyes off the panorama of unfolding events (Fig 419). You need at least *some* connection with Infinite Awareness and certainly an active right-brain to see that panorama. A good example of Phantom Self tunnel vision are the Trade Unions that rejected a proposal by the UK Labour Party leader not to spend £100 billion (and the rest) replacing the Trident nuclear weapons system. They said they had to defend jobs in the 'defence sector'. Actually, it is the attack sector, but the point is that what potentially impacted on the

unions was more important than the consequences for the wider world and mass murder of the innocent by the weapons made by their members. Alternative employment that could be generated by the same £100 billion (and the rest) passed them by in their peripheral vision. Len McCluskey, general secretary of the Unite union, said: 'I understand the moral case and the huge cost of replacing Trident, especially in this era of austerity, but the most important thing for us is jobs and the defence of communities.' That's

Figure 420: The end of denial.

Figure 421: 'What is that? I mean, what is it??

Figure 422: Or should be.

the Phantom Self perspective.

How nice it would be if people could just get on with their lives as they choose, but we don't live in a world where that is possible if we don't want to end up with a global society far more extreme than Orwell envisaged (Fig 420). Crucial to this end is for Archon hybrid networks to divert attention from what is happening in the same way that a magician wants you looking at one hand while the trick is done with the other. We can see this in its simplest form when governments make unpopular announcements on days when big stories are dominating the news. The Pentagon announced that *trillions* of dollars had gone missing from its budget with a news release on September 10th 2001, knowing full well that what was going to happen the next day would ensure that this staggering revelation would hardly rate a mention in the media. Magical tricks of perception diversion go much deeper and include five-sense pap and crap of social media, television and celebrity culture (Fig 421). Look at this, listen to that, feel this, smell that, taste this. Aren't the senses great – they're all that exists, you know. The System spews out a constant stream of diversions to focus attention on irrelevance and it's the ultimate attention seeker. Phantom Selves that fall for this just trot along with blinkers in place focused on their own particular interest and leaving the manipulators to go about their business unchallenged. John Lennon made the point in *Working Class Hero* about people being kept doped with religion, sex and TV while thinking they are so clever and classless and free; but, as the next line says: '... you're still fucking peasants as far as I can see.'

Football and sport in general are great examples. I like watching football to a point but I know it doesn't matter in that whichever side wins no one dies, goes hungry or bombs the innocent. You would not think this, however, when you observe the sheer hatred that can be unleashed over people kicking a bag of wind about (Fig 422). Talk about Phantom Self. Tribal programs are activated and spark reflex-action hostility between rival groups of supporters. The closer the clubs are located the greater the hostility – precisely what happens with tribes. If only people would get as worked up about the door banging shut on their freedom and their family's freedom; but, no, the blinkers are on and they are painted in the colours of City or United, Barcelona or Madrid. While I was writing this book, Raheem Sterling, a young player with Liverpool football club, said he wanted to leave and play for a more successful team. The abuse that followed was both shocking and Phantom Self in all its cockeyed stupidity. There were threats against his three-year-old daughter and the wish expressed that Sterling's shirt would be 'soaked in your own blood'. He's a kid, it's a game and there are people in psychiatric wards for far less. When Sterling played for his new club opposition fans booed (what a pathetic sight that is) every time he touched the ball as they responded like parrots to the abuse dished out to Sterling by 'journalists' and others who would have done exactly the same had they have been him. The football diversion alone is such that we have people dying through lack of money and living in abject poverty while footballers are bought and sold for more than £80 million and some paid tens of millions a year for kicking a ball about. Yes, very skilfully many of them, but it's still a ball being kicked by their feet. Football clubs are increasingly owned by fake Arab 'royalty' who have stolen oil reserves from the Arabic masses; oligarchs parasiting off their masses; and money-obsessed, masses-exploiting corporations. Meanwhile football masses pay outrageous ticket prices and buy television subscriptions to fund this grotesque global pig-trough. Football, the sport of 'the people' and the 'working class', has been hijacked by the *El*-ite money-class, while so many of the current 'working class' are quite happy with that so long as the *El*-ite use their billions – secured from football and the efforts and labour of the 'working class' – to buy footballers at stupendous cost to make their team win. They piss on us and we say it's raining. Phantom Selves at this level of programming could never see the outrageous nonsense of this when their sense of what matters is focussed on a dot and not a picture. Phantom Self perceives everything through a microscopic mind where only dots exist, not panoramas. To quote George Orwell again in *1984*: 'Football, beer and above all gambling filled up the horizons of their minds. To keep them in control was not difficult'. This applies to any 'dot' that hijacks attention and distorts perspective and The System turns them out by the million. I'm not saying there is anything wrong with enjoying sport and other pastimes. The key is seeing them for what they are and removing blocks to peripheral vision where the magicians work.

'Spiritual' and 'Radical' Phantoms

Phantom Selves aren't always as obvious and on public display as Raheem Sterling's abusers and those who believe that what some celebrity posts on Twitter actually matters in the great scheme of life. There are hidden Phantoms and by hidden I mean as in hiding themselves from themselves and seeking to do the same to the world. They invariably succeed with the first goal but often less so with the second. Sadly, they often think that they do and confuse hiding themselves from themselves with hiding themselves from others. The latter is much harder though far from impossible as hindsight constantly reminds us. These covert (to themselves) Phantoms include Spiritual Phantoms and Radical Phantoms. The New Age arena is awash with Spiritual Phantoms who talk about love and light and 'we are One' while behaving in every way like a blueprint Phantom. They think they've 'got it' when 'it' has got them. Not all New Agers and 'radicals' are like that by any means, but many are. I have had New Age 'stars' in the United States slag me off for the sort of information I am revealing in this book because their alleged 'open minds' are not open enough. I appeared in a documentary with some of them once and they wrote an open letter to the producers complaining that I had been included without them knowing. They thought it might damage their 'credibility'. Spiritual, right? One of their points was that I was questioning vaccinations. You have got to laugh or the tears would flow. I have had 'alternative' bullshitters pass through my life who talked their fairyland self-deception

Figure 423: Walking the talk? No, running the talk.

Figure 424: If that is where it ends you are a Spiritual Phantom.

about 'love and light' and standing up for truth, but when it came to standing by me in times of trouble and legal cases they couldn't find the horizon quick enough – or they *were* the legal cases. 'All mouth and trousers' as my father used to say and some of these 'spiritual supporters' have gone to newspapers to sell their 'story' for 30 pieces of silver while still considering themselves 'spiritual' as they cashed the cheque. The scale of self-deceit chills the spine. Many New Agers and radicals tell people to 'let go of fear' while they have balls akin to nanotechnology (Fig 423). These fakes lie, manipulate, exploit, break confidences, seek to undermine and hurt, while all the time proclaiming that everyone should love each other and come from the 'heart'. Spiritual Phantom is so consumed by the program and its own self-deception that they can hide the part that does the deeds from the part that does the words. I remember one told me in 2015 that it was a shame I had not stayed on 'the path'. I take it that he meant his version of 'the path' which involved, from observing his life, doing absolutely damn all unless it suited him and avoiding anything that would get his 'spiritual' hands dirty by facing the reality of the human plight and doing something about it. I can only think from my own experience that for many a lack of humility and self-reflection (and ball-removal) are prerequisites of New Age membership. Spiritual Phantoms are some of the most programmed of all in that part of them speaks against the program while the other lives it and serves it. Cognitive dissonance in extremis – 'simultaneously holding contradictory or otherwise incompatible attitudes and beliefs.' Their 'spirituality' is externalised in words and postures instead of coming from a connection with Infinite Awareness (Fig 424). They stand as a warning to all of us that Phantom programs can still control you when you think you are free from them and self-deception is an essential component of Phantom programming. Being honest with ourselves and on constant guard for Phantom influence is vital to unravelling the program. It is easy to condemn the actions of others while convincing ourselves that we're not doing the same when we are. 'If you want to keep a secret you must also hide it from yourself', as Orwell put it. Those that have caused me most stress and most challenge to my health and work over 26 years have been those who most said they wanted to help me. What I was uncovering and communicating was 'so important', they said. This was all fine while they were benefiting from what I do but once that changed Spiritual Phantom transformed immediately into the extreme end of Classic Phantom. My work was suddenly not important at all and had to be undermined and targeted for financial exploitation through the legal system. They were and are drowning in resentment and hatred while still pontificating about love and light and running websites claiming that the people must 'wake up'. Starting with themselves might be helpful. Spiritual Phantom's cognitive dissonance builds a wall between the self-deception of 'I am loving and spiritual' and the self-reality of 'Fuck you, I'll bring you down and love it.' This wall is in many ways located in the corpus collosum that connects right-brain to left and it is certainly located in the disconnection of Phantom Self from Infinite Self. Spiritual Phantoms talk right-brain and act left. Jiddu Krishnamurti said: 'Violence takes many forms, not merely brutal action, striking each other ... violence includes imitation, conformity, obedience; it exists when you pretend to be which you are not.' You can spot a Spiritual Phantom or any other by their obsession with self. Me, me, me is its calling card and when you close your ears to the words and just watch the actions the real agenda and motivations are easy to see (Fig 425). This is a good way for everyone to scan themselves for Phantom

Figure 425: Spiritual Phantom assessing priorities.

Figure 426: They disagree with me – *silence them!*

programs and bypass self-deception. Close your ears to your words and watch your actions. Another example of Spiritual Phantom and Radical Phantom are those who demand freedom of speech but then call for others to be silenced when they don't like what they're saying (Fig 426). I have been subjected to this over the years by the cognitive dissonance of Radical Phantoms who are mostly found in arenas known as Left and Green, but also in other groups. Zionist Phantom extremists would love to silence all opposition while saying how important it is to have freedom of expression. The contradictions are so obvious to anyone with even a smear of connection to expanded awareness but Phantom software is programmed to block this. It is another version of the me, me, me program. Free speech is for me because what I am saying is right and fair, but not for you because you are clearly wrong by saying something different to me. A bloke campaigning against my right to speak in public once said: 'What benefit is there in allowing him to speak?' His speciality, apparently, was human rights. I remember speaking to a policeman many years ago who was dealing with a bunch of Radical Phantoms protesting outside an event where I was speaking. He said that he had been on duty when marches by the far right National Front had been opposed in the same area by marches of the 'radical' Left. His point was telling. He said that if it wasn't for their different banners he would not have been able to tell them apart by the way they behaved. Phantom Self is a collective program. There are sub-programs called Left, Right, Green, Christian, Muslim, Hindu, Liberal or Conservative, but the base program is the same and so their foundation behaviour and responses will be the same. Radical Phantoms think they are challenging The System when they are essential to The System, which needs to divide and rule and hide its centralised control behind the illusion of diversity.

'Alternative' Phantoms

Spiritual Phantoms and Radical Phantoms are legion in the alternative media which has exploded in the wake of world events and the information that pioneers were circulating when few wanted to know. The term 'alternative media' covers a vast spectrum of people, attitudes and beliefs that span the chasm between those barely different from the mainstream in beliefs and approach, to those like myself at the other end who are questioning the entire Mainstream Everything to its very core. This colossal spectrum of belief and perception means that most of the alternative media is acting from the perspective of one Phantom program or another. By that I mean that its advocates are coming mostly from a belief system that attaches them to The System. Maybe they believe in the world view of mainstream science or they are coming from the political Right or Left. Many in the United States are Christian believers, another Archontic creation as with religion in general. What is called 'alternative' media includes some seriously off-the-scale Old Testament extremists and here-today-gone-tomorrow self-promotors along with some of the most decent people you could imagine who genuinely want an end to the insanity of division and for people of all colours, creeds and cultures to come together in mutual respect and support. The only theme that connects them all is that in some way they challenge the propaganda and deceit of the mainstream media. I have been able to witness all this personally given that I am challenging all belief systems of Mainstream Everything. I am not saying that people shouldn't have the right to hold those beliefs. I am only questioning their validity as explanations of the world and pointing out that their origin can be located in the Archontic conspiracy. This has led to an inevitable response that has seen me attacked, abused, dismissed and ridiculed by most of the alternative media every bit as much, and often more, than even the mainstream. You know you are on the right track in questioning Mainstream Everything when those who normally attack each other turn on you with a unity never seen before. Religious advocates don't like me because I question its basis; the Left call me Right and the Right call me Left because in truth I reject them both – and all in between; Zionism calls me anti-Jewish because I expose its manipulation and slaughter of the innocent in Palestine; Muslim groups have sought to condemn me because I say their religion is a control program; many in the New Age don't like me exposing the force behind world events on the grounds that it is apparently negative and frightening for those who urge people to 'let go of fear'; talk of 'Archons', 'Reptilians', Moon, Saturn and simulated reality obviously blows the gaskets of virtually all of them. 'Hey, Bill, don't read that Icke bloke – the repair bills are terrible.' I see the alternative media call the masses 'sheeple'

Figure 427: Alternative Phantom – in a box.

while being sheeple to their own belief systems and letting them colour and limit their 'alternativeness' (Fig 427). One guy interviews people in the street to highlight how little they know and how stupid they are, but he, too, is imprisoned in his own version of Phantom Self. He's so sure of his intellectual superiority that it prevents him from seeing beyond his self-imposed comfort zone. You are not free of Phantom Self just because you believe that 9/11 was an inside job. It goes *waaaaaaay* deeper than that. I see comments on the Internet and social media from people who think they are 'alternative' which are still so me-centric, so Phantom Selfish, instead of supporting the common cause. They label people who are out there exposing what the public need to know as 'CIA' or 'Intel' with no evidence whatsoever and the best one is 'If you were genuine, you'd be dead'. Well, why aren't they? Talk about handing your power to that which you claim to be challenging. They infight among themselves and so do the work of the very force they say they oppose. Physician heal thyself, as the saying goes. In the end, it all comes back to being honest with ourselves and scanning actions, attitudes and behaviour for Phantom programming. No one is immune but we can be constantly self-aware and so constantly dilute the influence. The alternative media has done a brilliant job up to this point and I salute everyone who makes an effort to break the mainstream stranglehold in any peaceful way that suits them; but the great majority in that field are still walking around the rim of the rabbit hole and have not even entered it yet. This should be the next stage. Until minds are opened and Phantom programs cast aside they'll never see the full magnitude and depth of what is happening, and what needs to be known. They might – everyone might – ponder again on the fact that we can see only an infinitesimal fraction of what exists and even that is perceived through the filter and severe limitations of a biological computer programmed to squeeze our perception of reality. It is not only arrogance to think that given these facts we can dismiss possibilities without question or research – it is pure self-deluded stupidity.

Super Phantoms

Bloodline Phantoms and others so profoundly infected (possessed) by the Archon virus that they basically *are* the virus, are what I call Super Phantoms. 'Psychopath' fits the bill here and while many associate this term only with serial killers, it means far more than that. Professor Robert Hare, a criminal psychologist, worked with psychopathic people for decades before compiling his 'Hare Test' definition of a psychopath, which includes the following traits: glibness and superficial charm, grandiose sense of self-worth, pathological lying, cunning/manipulative, lack of remorse, emotional shallowness, callousness and lack of empathy, unwillingness to accept responsibility for actions, a tendency to boredom, a parasitic lifestyle, a lack of realistic long-term goals, impulsivity, irresponsibility, lack of behavioural control. Professor Hare said: 'It stuns me, as much as it did when I started 40 years ago, that it is possible to have people who are so emotionally disconnected that they can function as if other people are objects to be manipulated and destroyed without any concern.' I have been making this very point for decades about Archon-Reptilian bloodlines and this is the wakeup call for those who say 'they would never do that'. No, *you* would never do that; *they* would and *love it*. Imagine if you had no empathy or remorse for the consequences for others of your actions. There would be no emotional fail-safe mechanism to stop any scale of violent and abusive behaviour, nor regret after the deeds were done. Politicians who use

Figure 429: Bombing and austerity, bombing and austerity.

Figure 428: Psychopaths are in positions of power *because* they are psychopaths.

the military to engage in mass murder and impose austerity to crush the poor and most vulnerable are obvious examples (Fig 428). Anyone free of psychopathic traits could never do this, but psychopaths can without any emotional comeback. They even get off on the suffering and mayhem they wreak (Fig 429). Those of the bloodline who know who they are (many don't) see the death and suffering they coldly cause as 'food' for the virus that infests and controls them – and thus power for themselves. They say eyes are the window on the soul, and when you look into the cold eyes of the psychopath you are looking at the virus. I saw a list of psychopathic professions which had bankers and CEOs at the top, followed by lawyers and media people. This is hardly surprising given the death and suffering that psychopathic banking parasites daily cause by using people, nations and the world as a whole as nothing more than casino chips in their very own Las Vegas (City of London, Wall Street etc.). These are not 'financial centres'. They are casinos where the house always wins and the global population always get shafted (Fig 430). I am not saying that everyone who works in a bank or financial house is a psychopath but I am saying that those who control the financial system in general and large numbers who work in that

Figure 430: The house always wins while others lose theirs.

arena most certainly are. You cannot do what they do unless you have an absence of empathy and remorse as lives and nations are daily destroyed by their actions. Can you imagine Goldman Sachs, the investment banking monster dubbed the 'great vampire squid', employing frontline staff that had empathy and remorse? What has been done to countries like Greece is the work of psychopaths or Super Phantoms in the European Union, European Central Bank, IMF and others within Greece itself. Goldman Sachs was also involved. I have met psychopathic lawyers and doctors – two other professions where psychopaths are widely represented although with many exceptions who are not. To see the empathy-deleted almost sexual rush that some lawyers get from vanquishing their targets is a sight to behold.

Those who only associate psychopaths with serial killers will think they are not that common. This would be a major misunderstanding. Human society is infested with psychopathic behaviour. The world is run by psychopaths and they hire other psychopaths at all levels to administer The System for them. These are the ones

Figure 431: Psychopaths and those controlled by psychopaths = armies everywhere.

who mostly (not always, but mostly) end up in positions of power and hire and fire throughout global society. Pharmaceutical and Biotech industries are playgrounds for psychopaths, and so is journalism in the case of those who gleefully destroy lives without any public interest relevance whatsoever. The military are trained to be psychopaths and to be subordinate to psychopaths and unquestioningly follow their orders. Psychopaths in the military then go about their slaughter for the psychopaths in government who are mere vehicles for the psychopaths in the shadows who are agents of the psychopathic Archons and the psychopathic virus. Troops that are psychopaths have no problem at all killing the innocent and destroying lives and countries. Those who are not often suffer serious psychological consequences for the rest of their lives. Show me a soldier who does not deeply regret what he or she did to civilians and children and I will show you a psychopath (Fig 431). We see psychopathic criminals, organised crime, drug dealers, people-traffickers and those who coldly trick the elderly and most vulnerable out of their life savings to leave them with nothing. So-called 'suckers lists' came to light in Britain in 2015 with the names of 200,000 people compiled by criminals (psychopaths infested by the virus) to be targeted with money scams. Most were elderly, with one 87-year-old specifically targeted because her husband had just died. She lost £90,000. No empathy, no remorse – Archontic psychopaths. The scale of psychopathic behaviour is astonishing when you take the trouble to observe the world and this is a manifestation of the virus replicating itself. Social media and the Internet has allowed us to see the scale of psychopathy that we couldn't see before. Trolls and abusers who delight in the hurt they cause to others are psychopaths. No one is immune from psychopathic traits, however mild, with all human body-computers infected with the virus ('original sin'). The question is how conscious are we beyond Body-Mind to override the impulses of the psychopath program. If we look through our lives we will all find examples of acting without empathy (though usually far less so without remorse). Actions that involve no empathy and no remorse are a still higher level of psychopathy. For most people these are moments, but for many (especially those in power and others like Internet trolls) psychopathy is their very being as a Super Phantom. When I look back at people I have known I see psychopathic traits that tick virtually all the boxes in the Hare Test. They would never see themselves that way because they have never looked in the mirror with any honesty, but then they are far

Figure 432: You are my dear – when you're not being psychopathic.

from alone (Fig 432).

The potential is there in everyone for the reasons I have explained and The System is constantly seeking to activate those traits with its actions and propaganda. Violent videogames are a part of this to desensitise people to violence and suffering. You also see psychopathy with a Problem-Reaction-Solution terrorist attack blamed on those from a particular country, and the common response of 'bomb the bloody lot of them'. This is the psychopath program being activated. Another major trait of a psychopath in the Hare Test is a 'parasitic lifestyle' or living off the efforts of others. The term is defined as 'an organism that lives and feeds on or in an organism of a different species and causes harm to its host' and 'one who habitually takes advantage of the generosity of others without making any useful return'. My god, I've known some of those. Observe the world and it all makes sense. The Archon virus which infects human society is parasitic to its foundation and operates in hierarchical structures. Human society is a parasitical hierarchy in which higher levels of the power structure parasite off those below, and this continues down into the lowest levels with, for example, a lazy partner parasiting off the other and criminals from a deprived estate stealing from others in the deprived estate. The parasite program is holographic like everything else in our perceived reality and you find it everywhere right down to the parasites that feed off the body and each other. Cancer, one of humanity's biggest killers, is a parasitical fungus and a bloody stupid one because by killing the body it kills itself. Parasites are not usually very bright which is why, I guess, they are parasites. Cancer is also psychopathic in that it causes death and suffering without empathy or remorse (everything is conscious). Psychopaths and parasites are traits of the same program, which is active throughout the fake Matrix and everywhere the virus infests.

To understand Phantom Self and its many and various expressions and programs is to understand ourselves and human behaviour – and to understand the world. This is especially so when you think that the most extreme example, Super Phantoms, *run* the world. Explains a lot, eh?

CHAPTER EIGHT

We're Free, Honey

You can ignore reality, but you can't ignore the consequences of ignoring reality
Ayn Rand

Archons and the virus are not all-powerful or insurmountable and depend for their survival on extraordinary levels of deceit that entrap humanity in Phantom Self. The virus can be eradicated – and will be – but a first and fundamental step is for people to realise they are slaves of the Hidden Hand and to understand the modus operandi of oppression and manipulation. How can slaves cease to be in slavery while under the illusion they are free?

I have described the origin and depth of human control, and in the next few chapters I am going to show how this plays out in daily life as 'random' events that are all coordinated in pursuit of a common goal. The Archon Control System perpetuates its mass slavery in two main ways: Method one is to control people through violence and a merciless police state so the population know they live in a tyranny, but are too frightened to do anything about it even though they are the great majority and their oppressors a small minority. Method two ('democracy') is to control and dictate choice and events while deceiving people into believing they are free. The plan with current 'democracies' is to accrue so much power at the centre that they can move from method two to method one and we see this happening today ever more clearly. Hijacking choice while promoting this as *free* choice pervades The System and infiltrates all aspects of life. If I offer you a choice of A, B or C you can think you are making a free choice by picking one of them; but A, B and C are not the only choices that you can potentially make. There are billions of others and, ultimately, infinite others. Those three from which you make your 'free' choice are only the ones being offered (Fig 433). Misunderstanding of the difference

Figure 433: The illusion of real choice is everywhere.

Figure 434: The political system.

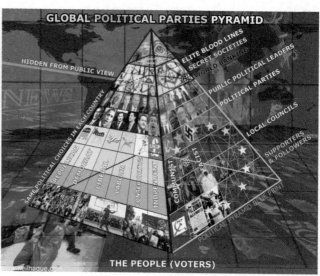

Figure 435: Political parties are hierarchical pyramids controlled by the few for the few.

between free choice and offered choice confuses the majority into thinking they live in 'free societies' when these are only illusions. Political 'choice' is a version of the overall scam with regard to choice with all parties ultimately controlled by the same Archontic Hidden Hand (Fig 434). A periodic right to vote is sold as a definition of political freedom when democracy is really tyranny by the majority and often by the minority. British Prime Minister David Cameron 'won' outright 'victory' in the General Election in 2015 with support from just 37 percent of those who voted and 23.5 percent of those eligible to vote. Governments also have no legal obligation to do what they said they would do (or not do) when lying to the electorate to secure sufficient votes to win power. 'Democratic' government is a joke and has nothing to do with political representation of the populous and yet the right to vote is the constantly-quoted symbol of this 'you are free' confidence trick. You can vote so you must be free, and you can choose the government so this must be government by the People for the People. But for this to be true there must first of all be *choice* in how a society is run and the direction that it takes. Yet all that is offered in the 'free democracies' are political party masks on the same Archontic face – and this is 'choice' scuppered before a single ballot is cast (Fig 435). Once a mask or 'political party' is officially elected it can go its own way (as it always planned to do) with little or often no regard for the election promises through which it attracted its electoral support. Wishes and desires of the population only have to be considered again when the next election is close and the entire farce is repeated. This has been the case throughout the history of 'democracy' and still so many people can't see how they are being systematically shafted. They continue to campaign for the masks and argue with other masks over which mask should be pinned to the unchanging face this time around. You don't like this mask after its years in government? No problem. You can now have another mask and when you eventually reject that mask because it is doing the same as the previous mask, you can choose to go back to the other mask once again. Democracy is NOT freedom as anyone with even a chink of awareness in their program must surely be able to see. But those who point this out are condemned as being anti-freedom because freedom is democracy – everyone

Figure 436: 'Different' parties – same master.

knows that. Jeremy Corbyn who was elected to lead Britain's opposition Labour Party in 2015 is trying to come from a different direction based on more compassionate values, but still within The System that will ultimately dictate events. Corbyn's election was indeed a reaction from Labour Party members to the fact that their party and the Conservative 'alternative' had become virtually indistinguishable. So point number one on the *Am I A Slave?* checklist: You do not decide who governs your country or society. Those that covertly control the political parties make those decisions along with corporations and individuals who fund them and the media that builds them up and knocks them down. In every case they too are more masks on the Archon face (Fig 436). Corbyn has been attacked and undermined from day one by large sections of the British media for the political crime of being a bit different – in an attempt to ensure he never gets into government. By the way, talking of corporations – countries and governments are actually private corporations operating under commercial and maritime law. I have explained this in other books, and specialist researchers on this subject have also done so in great detail. The term 'United States', for example, does not refer to a country but a privately-owned corporation with the president known as the President of the United States.

Archon Web

Okay, so your vote is virtually meaningless and your political choices are delusional in terms of changing anything of substance. Things are already looking pretty bleak with regard to your freedom and I've only just begun. Next question: What governs your choices throughout your life such as what you do, where you go, where you work, if you work, where you live and even *if* you live (see 'if you eat' and 'if you have health care')? This can be answered in one word – *money*. Who controls money and therefore all of those choices and potential life-paths? The same force that decides who is in government, and the same is the case with centres and institutions of power the world over. Archon-Reptilian hybrids created and control the cartels of Big Banking; Big Politics; Big Oil; Big Biotech; Big Pharma; Big Food; Big Media (including Hollywood); Big Internet and so on. This is possible through what I have called The Blueprint or Spider's Web, a global network of secret societies, semi-secret groups and those operating in the public arena such as corporations and governments. All are ultimately vehicles and lackeys for the Spider at the centre of the Web – the Demiurge virus dictating from the unseen (Fig 437). This structure of interconnecting deceit can also be symbolised as a pyramid (Fig 438). The Spider decides, drives and imposes the decisions and direction of all strands in the Web or levels of the pyramid, although only

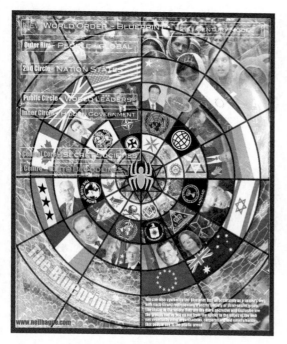

Figure 437: The global spider's web of interconnected secret societies, intelligence networks, organisations, governments and their agencies ultimately directed by the spider – the Demiurge/Archons.

a very few will ever know where their orders really come from and why (in terms of the big picture). Compartmentalisation of knowledge is fiercely and rigidly protected. Secret societies are structured like the Web under the holographic principle of 'as above, so below'. They consist of segments, layers or 'degrees' and each higher degree or level knows more than the one below. Those at the top of individual secret societies don't have the whole story either. There are many levels above them they don't even know about which only the chosen few (almost entirely bloodline) are allowed to enter as I explained earlier. Secret societies and groups closest to the Spider know the most and they are therefore the most exclusive. Many don't even have names which makes them harder to uncover. Secret societies at their higher or deeper levels are closely aligned with Satanism, which directly interacts with demonic expressions of the Archon virus. Each strand in the global Web is a secret society, semi-secret group or publicly-known organisation. At the centre is the Archon

The Pyramid of Manipulation

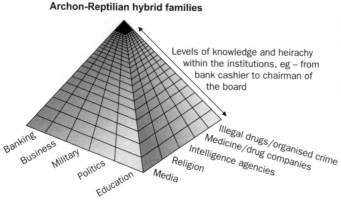

All the major institutions and groups that affect our daily lives connect with the Global Elite, which decides the coordinated policy throughout the pyramid.

People in the lower compartments will have no idea what they are part of.

Figure 438: The control pyramid with only the few at the top knowing what is really going on and why.

Spider and next are the most exclusive and secretive Satanism-aligned cliques and circles. Further out we find secret societies that people will have heard of including the Freemasons, Jesuits, Knights of Malta, Knights Templar and Opus Dei. Notice how many are closely associated with the Roman Church or Church of Babylon, a massive global front for the Archon agenda. A secret society I have exposed at length is the infamous Skull and Bones Society, which is based in a windowless mausoleum alongside the campus at Yale University in New Haven, Connecticut (Fig 439).

Figure 439: Skull and Bones Society headquarters where leaders in-the-making pledge allegiance to their masters for life – and beyond.

This is also known as the Order of Death (Saturn). 'Skull and bones' is Saturn symbolism because of its association with death and astrologically as ruler of the skeletal structure. We are told that anyone can become US president (naïvety as an art form) and yet in 2004 the two presidential candidates were both initiates of the same exclusive Skull and Bones secret society – George W. Bush (like his father and grandfather) and John Kerry who is causing global mayhem as US Secretary of State as I write (Fig 440). I saw a video of a Florida college student being Tasered at a public event after asking Kerry about his and Bush's Skull and Bones membership. Land of the Free, or so they say. America has a population of 320 million, but presidents since 1980 have been:

Figure 440: Kerry and Bush: Two presidential candidates in 2004 and both members of an exclusive secret society to which they had pledged their allegiance above all else.

Ronald Reagan (in truth his vice-president Father George Bush); Father George Bush; Bill Clinton; Boy George Bush; Barack Obama; and at the time of writing Hillary Clinton and Jeb Bush are seeking election in 2016 with the ego champion of the world, billionaire Donald Trump. Yep, anyone can be president. Eventually as we pan out from the Spider we reach the cusp in the Web where the hidden meets the seen. Here you find organisations like the Bilderberg Group, US-based Trilateral Commission and Council on Foreign Relations, Club of Rome and other 'think tanks' whose role is to ensure that the agenda emanating from the Spider is implemented through governments, military, corporations, media etc. 'Cusp' groups are awash with those who work in government, politics, finance, military, intelligence, corporations and media. Put the words 'Bilderberg Group attendees' or 'Council on Foreign Relations/Trilateral Commission members' into a search engine and you will see what I mean. These organisations emerged from a secret society based in London called the Round Table, which was established by Cecil Rhodes and the Rothschilds in the late 19th century. The United Nations was manipulated into being by this network as a

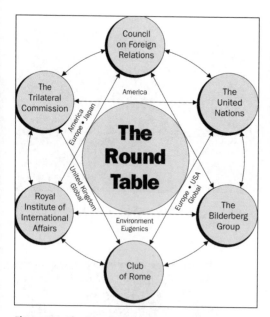

Figure 441: The Round Table network.

Figure 442: The real status of Bilderberg within the Web.

stalking horse for world government (Fig 441). Rhodes plundered Africa for the Rothschilds and the British Crown (same thing). I emphasise, however, that these groups are only vehicles for the Spider and are not the Spider itself (Fig 442).

Systematic ignorance

Archon bloodlines want people to believe that decisions are being made by governments and individual corporations, groups and people, when those decisions that impact on the Archon agenda are really being made deep in the Web and not even in this reality. This is the structure that allows the hidden to control the seen, and all but a few even in the Web will not know the bigger picture of what is going on. Compartmentalisation rules throughout the Web and ignorance is crucial to the Archons among most of their agents and gofers to protect the Biggest Secret. The Web operates holographically with each level structured as a smaller version of the whole right down into local communities (Fig 443). A global corporation dictates rules and policy to all subsidiaries and constituent parts throughout the world from a central point or headquarters and the Archon Web operates in the same way with one major difference. Corporate subsidiaries know that the headquarters is calling the

Figure 443: Holographic control. Every part of the structure is a smaller version of the whole.

shots (on their level anyway) but with the Archon Web it is all done in secret to such an extent that the vast majority serving the Web will never have heard of Archons and would laugh, mock and dismiss their existence if they ever did. Ignorance is not only bliss for the Archon virus it is bottom-line essential. This is how the same force controls The System while making the world appear to be random and diverse and by controlling perceived norms through control of consensus reality. Archon Web 'science' decrees how things are and Archon Web media and education repeat this for the populous as unchallengeable fact. I saw a comment by a bloke called Patrick to one of my social media postings about a BBC 'documentary' of pure propaganda about genetically-modified food or GMO. It's a great example of how people buy the lie because they have no idea how The System works:

> What, do you mean the BBC say that GMOs are safe, as do the worlds scientific community!!!?. Don't trust the BBC, don't trust science (government shills) don't trust logic and evidence based opinion (just a hologram. trust David Icke who very obviously went to University of the Internet (paranoid campus) and knows everything about genetics and genetic modification

Amount of research that the Patricks of this world do before dismissing any suggestion that authority could be lying? Zero. No doubt Patrick's aggression and dismissal comes from his self-identification with being streetwise and intelligent while suffering from terminal (for his freedom) naïvety and ignorance. If Patrick had any clue of how the world works he would never make such a comment. He would know why System sources are self-supporting and replicating; but he doesn't, so he did. His 9/11 version would go like this:

> What, do you mean the BBC say the official story of 9/11 is true, as do the US government!!!?. Don't trust the BBC, don't trust government, don't trust logic and evidence based opinion (just a hologram. trust David Icke who very obviously went to University of the Internet (paranoid campus) and knows everything about 9/11.

Perception by media

The BBC, along with the entire mainstream media, does say the official story of 9/11 is true, but how do they know? American government sources and agencies told them so they could then repeat it as fact without question (Fig 444). People think they have media choice and variety because they see lots of newspapers, television channels and radio stations but they are all owned by a shockingly small number of super-rich Archontic assets who answer to the Spider and the Web. Five giant corporations connected by the Web control 90 percent of America's mass media and 5 billionaires control something

Figure 444: Mainstream media – propaganda arm of the Web.

like 80 percent in the UK. You will find the same story virtually everywhere. Control of information means control of perception for everyone who has not expanded their awareness beyond Phantom Self. Surveys galore have shown how public perception is nowhere even close to the truth across a great spectrum of subjects and issues, when what people believe to be true is compared with how things really are. Their skewed image of the world comes from a skewed version of the world downloaded from the mainstream media. Tell people the same story often enough and it becomes accepted fact – an 'everyone knows that'. At the end of World War II, three out of four newspapers in the United States were independently owned; by 1983 just 50 corporations controlled 90 percent of the US media; it's now down to five and they have not finished yet. I list in *Human Race Get Off Your Knees* the television and radio stations, newspapers and magazines owned by Time Warner alone and it is breathtaking in its scale. Politicians controlled by the Web have continually deregulated ownership restrictions to allow media moguls controlled by the Web to seize ever-greater swathes of mainstream communication to the point where all major media in a community or even city in the US can be owned by the same corporation. Global news agencies owned by more Web assets provide 'news' for mainstream television, radio, print and Internet media all over the world that comes from the same source and even a single reporter. A YouTube video has a series of 'different' television news presenters on 'different' stations reading the same story word for word. Type in 'Easter bunny steps news' and you'll see. While you are there see the same principle at work with politicians making the same election speech. 'Conservative MPs drone on like robots reading the same script' will find you that one. It is all centralised and getting more so by the day. This allows Archon media to support Archon governments by manipulating perceptions of the population about anything they like. British and American 'Web' governments make a decision to remove a regime in a target country and Web media starts a campaign of vilification, lies and fear-mongering against the regime to win public support for its violent overthrow. It really is that simple once you have a combination of Phantom Self and control of information. An alternative and largely independent media has emerged on the Internet since I started on this road – when there was virtually nothing. This has become so successful in providing people with an alternative to mainstream corporate 'news' that every effort is now being made to nullify its effect. More corporate giants – that again you can count on one hand – basically own the Internet and major search engines and they are systemically suppressing the traffic and profile of alternative news sites in their listings so they are seen by as few people as possible. Davidicke.com has had the treatment, which I take as a compliment. They are also seeking to block information from alternative sources that The System does not want to see in circulation.

Funny money

Nothing is more vital to Archon manipulation of five-sense reality than control of money. Archons and their hybrids created the money system for the specific purpose of acquiring the world's real wealth and dictating the choices of their human slaves. Wealth is not the goal in itself to the Archons and their inner circles but a monopoly on wealth in pursuit of total control by denying the target population the foundation requisite of freedom – choice. Without choice and with subsequent dependency (on The

System) there is a single word to describe what this means ... slavery. American journalist Ellen Goodman described this very well when she wrote:

> Normal is getting dressed in clothes that you buy for work and driving through traffic in a car that you are still paying for – in order to get to the job you need to pay for the clothes and the car, and the house you leave vacant all day so you can afford to live in it.

I have exposed the banking and financial system and its second-by-second manipulation and corruption in fine detail in other books (see Archon Economics in *The Perception Deception*) and it will suffice here for new readers and essential dot-connections to describe what money is and how it

Figure 445: Shocking, but true.

comes into being. How extraordinary in the extreme it is to observe how few people even within the financial community know where 'money' comes from. This is especially so when who has money and who doesn't is such a basic and profound dictator of human experience. If you have never come across this information before prepare to be gobsmacked. Money is only worth what people believe (are manipulated to believe) it is worth. Er, that's it. Money is actually worth nothing once buyer and seller stop believing it has worth. Coins have little value in themselves in terms of their metals, while paper and digital money have no value whatsoever outside of that officially ascribed to them. Money is all illusion and engineered perception. One day a pound sterling or a dollar can be worth so and so (in theory) and the next a different so and so (in theory). All that has changed is the *belief* in what it is worth because of some stock market or currency market rumour or government/central bank decision or circumstance. Money is worth, in other words, what 'They' tell us it is. There was a time when money was valued in relation to commodities like gold but that has long gone. We now have 'fiat' currency, which is only worth anything because governments say it is (Fig 445). Definition of fiat currency: 'Paper money or coins of little or no intrinsic value in themselves and not convertible into gold or silver, but made legal tender by fiat (order) of the government.' Fiat has a Latin meaning of 'Let it be done', 'It shall be'. Fiat money has no intrinsic value beyond the government saying 'it shall be' and yet when people 'borrow' this stuff they have to *buy* it in the form of interest. Should they be unable to repay this intrinsically valueless 'loan' plus interest then the lender (bank) can take what they own that does have intrinsic value – their home, land, business etc. The world is being stolen through this global scam by Archon bloodlines that not only control the political and financial systems, but created them with the Rothschilds pre-eminent and they are run by secret society and satanic networks doing the work of the Spider (Fig 446). Today's banking system can be tracked from ancient Babylon (again) through Rome (again) into Europe and worldwide. 'Bank' comes from banco, or bench, after benches used by moneylenders in Italian cities such as Florence, Genoa, Venice and Milan. Wherever Archon hybrids went, control of money went with them. Central to this for centuries has been the Archon-Reptilian House of Rothschild and it was they

Figure 446: 'Satanism, secret societies, politics, banking and media are all linked by the Archontic Web.

who globally established the fiat 'money' con-trick. Ask most people, even most System people, how money is created and they will either look at you bewildered – or 'gone out' as my mother used to say – or they will parrot some nonsense about 'the government'. In fact, the overwhelming majority of money (credit) comes into circulation by private banks (all ultimately owned by the same Archon hybrid families) making 'loans'. This gives them almost total power over how much 'money' is in circulation (boom) and how much is not (recession or depression). You may notice that I am putting a lot of words within quote marks and I do this to indicate that the word doesn't really mean what we are told that it means. A loan indicates that something has been given, but in terms of a 'loan' of 'money' it hasn't, except in theory. I'll explain ...

Money out of nothing

When you apply to a bank for a 'loan' what happens? First they demand that you secure the 'loan' by signing over to them intrinsic wealth – house, land and such like. Then they type into your account the figure they have agreed to 'give' you in return for it all being paid back – plus interest. What have they really 'loaned' you? *Fresh air.* Worthless fiat currency works in league with fractional reserve lending which allows banks to lend nine or ten times (far, far more in truth) what they have on deposit, and so every time you put a pound or dollar in a bank you are giving it the legal right to 'lend' nine or ten that it doesn't have in the form of non-existent 'credit'. Fiat money 'credit' is 'money' that does not and will never exist except in theory (Fig 447). The £100,000 you may have 'borrowed' to buy a house is only six digits and a £ sign that someone has added to your

Figure 447: Banking is legalised theft.

account, and this is only stage one in the money-go-round. You transfer this 'money' (credit) to the owner of the house you are buying and he or she accepts it only because they believe it is worth what they are told it is. They, in turn, transfer it to the owner of *their* next house and the same thing happens. Fractional reserve landing goes even further into the realms of insanity. Say you borrow credit to buy a car and hand this over to the owner who puts it in his bank. The original loan was created out

of nothing by the first bank, but now the second bank can lend nine or ten times its alleged worth again to other people under fractional reserve lending and the same with any subsequent banks where money from the original fresh-air loan of credit ends up. Consider the extraordinary amount of theoretical money or credit that the banking system can generate (and 'lend' again) from a single loan (Fig 448). The Archon hybrid 'one-percent' or less-than-one-per-cent has hijacked the global economy and human society by swapping non-existent credit for wealth of intrinsic value – land, property, resources. There are ways that a theoretical currency can be used as a symbolic means of exchange to overcome the limitations of barter, but that can't happen while there is the addition of interest. Once interest is charged the *very unit of financial exchange is 'created' from the start as a debt.* Interest on fresh air credit changes the game completely. You can also rob people of their real wealth by increasing interest to the point where they can no longer pay you back and by

Figure 448: Put it in another bank and they can lend it again.

Figure 449: This is exactly the situation when people are foreclosed.

crashing the financial system which has the same effect. Once they can't repay your non-existent credit and interest you move in to take the loot and they are often on the street (Fig 449). To those who are new to this it may seem inexplicable that governments should pass laws that allow private banks (owned by the same Archontic cabal) to dominate the creation of 'money' and be able to 'lend' many times what they actually have on deposit (and even that is only in theory). Why do governments borrow money at interest from private banks (which the taxpayer has to repay) when they could issue their own currency interest free? These are all legitimate points and questions, but they have a single answer: Governments are controlled by the same Archon hybrids that own and control the banks. By dictating how much 'money' is in circulation (by how much they decide to loan) the banks are dictating how much economic activity is possible. Recessions and depressions don't happen because people decide they don't want to work, have a home or feed their families. They happen when there is not enough money in circulation or of sufficient perceived value to generate the income required to pay for those things. Who controls that? *The banks.* Who owns them? *The Archon bloodlines.* This following sequence is known by economists (most of them clueless about money-creation) as 'the economic cycle' when it is pure manipulation:

Stage 1: You put lots of money in circulation by making lots of loans at low but variable interest rates. In doing so, you stimulate lots of economic activity – a boom.

Stage 2: People and businesses tend to get into more debt during boom times with confidence in their income leading to new plant, machinery, property and other investments to meet expanding demand or reflecting an improved economic status.

Stage 3: At the optimum time to trawl the wealth of the people you start taking money out of circulation by either raising interest rates and calling in loans or crashing the system as in 2008 to cause what they called the 'credit crunch'.

Stage 4: You grab the loot in property, land, resources and business from those who can no longer afford to pay you back the 'money' which under any sane criteria you didn't actually give them.

Unrepayable debt is coldly encoded in the banking system. A loan of £100,000 that a bank theoretically brings into circulation leads to £100,000 of credit being transferred into your account; but you are not committed to paying back only £100,000. You are repaying this figure *plus interest* and the *interest is never created with any 'loan'*. Take a breath before considering what this means: There is never even nearly enough 'money' in circulation at any time to pay all the outstanding 'loans', plus interest, and people losing their intrinsic wealth to the banks is built into the system. This simple fact can be hidden to an extent during a boom on the principle of Peter paying Paul but during a recession or depression it is perfectly obvious from lost homes, businesses and ruined lives. The debt trap is being played on countries as well as individuals with governments (taxpayers) drowning in debt to banks and other creditors. Official American government debt is approaching $20 *trillion* but the real figure with everything added in is more like *hundreds* of trillions. Laurence Kotikoff, economics professor at Boston University, suggested a figure of $220 trillion some years ago. Cumulative individual debt of Americans is estimated to be $11.85 trillion by 2015 figures with student 'loans' (paying for your own programming) at nearly $1.19 trillion. Debt = control = slavery, just as scarcity = dependency = control. The equation the Archons and their bloodlines want to avoid at all costs is abundance = choice = freedom. We have become used to seeing European and global entities such as the European Central Bank (ECB), International Monetary Fund (IMF) and World Bank moving in to 'bail out' countries like Greece, Ireland and others. 'Bail out' is code for imposing massive interest-bearing debt, transferring wealth from people to bankers, and vicious austerity on entire populations, which they subsequently control by dictating to governments who dictate to the people. These global and European banking entities were created by guess who? Got

Figure 450: Bank for International Settlements in Switzerland – where private bankers dictate policy of central banks and thus national economies.

it in one. I detail in *The Perception Deception* how apparently unconnected financial operations and global groupings are all attached to the same Web and how the same people appear in multiple guises to drive the world economy in the desired direction. Central banks in each country follow a common agenda orchestrated and coordinated through the Rothschild-created Bank for International Settlements (BIS) in Basel, Switzerland, which has branches in Hong Kong and Mexico City (Fig 450). Calculated coordination is camouflaged by claims that the BIS 'fosters international

Figure 451: The US Federal Reserve is a cartel of *private* banks masquerading as the 'government-controlled' central bank of America.

monetary and financial cooperation'. Monetary and financial conspiracy more like with the heads of major central banks meeting in Basle every two months to get their orders from the Archontic Hidden Hand. The BIS is *not accountable to any government*, tax authority or international laws. *The Wall Street Journal* said: 'While many national governments, including the US, have failed to agree on fiscal policy – how best to balance tax revenues with spending during slow growth – the central bankers have forged their own path, independent of voters and politicians, bound by frequent conversations and relationships stretching back to university days.' Bound by frequent conversations with people they would not dare to cross would be far more accurate. Central control of central banks allows the Hidden Hand working through the Bank for International Settlements to dictate financial policy in every country. The Group of Thirty, or G30, founded in 1978 at the behest of the Rockefeller Foundation, is another strand in the Web involving the same crowd. What appear to be government organisations are actually private. The US Federal Reserve is the central bank that directs the American economy but it is a cartel of *private* banks and its control by government is purely illusory (Fig 451).

Always money for war

I was talking many years ago to a man who had been a local bank manager for decades before a recent retirement. He told me the bank had given him a research project to do in the year before he left and it was only then that he realised what money really was and where it came from. He looked at me with little-boy eyes and said: 'There is no money is there?' No, not in the way that people perceive it; but what an example of how deep the illusion goes. Here was a bank manager giving or refusing 'loans' to customers for decades without having any idea what exactly he was 'lending' and declining. Think of all the debt in the world and the death and suffering which results from that debt. Yet all along this has been debt (illusion of debt) on money that has never, does not and will never exist except as a figment of the programmed ignorance of Phantom Self. Global control of the masses is being perpetrated by the same illusion in the form of 'those with the money.' Ask almost anyone why they are not doing what they really want to do with their lives and they will invariably cite a lack of 'money'. They don't have enough

Figure 452: The story of human society since the Archontic hijack.

Figure 453: Inverted world.

Figure 454: There is no need for hunger and poverty in a world of plenty. It's *made* to be that way.

illusory figures on a computer screen which only have value because buyer and seller believe they do. What a gigantic confidence trick – and it controls the world today more than ever. We are told 'there isn't enough money' for the poor to be supported, the hungry fed or the homeless given shelter, but funding for war is never a problem. When was the last time you heard a political leader say they can't go to war because the country can't afford it? Americans are living in tents or on the street while the country spends trillions bombing faraway lands (Fig 452). The United States is responsible for 41 percent of the world's military spending and 31 percent of armaments sold or given to other countries. Some 85-90 percent on average of those killed in wars in which those weapons are used are civilians. America has been at war in 222 of 240 years since 1776. Special Operations Command spokesman Ken McGraw said in 2015 that American Special Forces had been deployed in 147 countries – 75 percent of the world's recognised nations – and at any one time they are active in 80 to 90. The $400 *billion* spent on developing a new fighter jet (with $400,000 each for pilot 'helmets') could have given every homeless person in America a nice place to live (Fig 453). Instead the homeless population of New York alone soars past 60,000 – 40 percent of them children. This is not incompetence, but calculation (Fig 454). Archons and their hybrids that control the creation and distribution of 'money' need war to advance their ambitions and they couldn't care less if people eat or have shelter. Can you imagine the scale of insanity and psychopathy that it takes to allow people to die of starvation for lack of figment figures in a computer program? While this goes on we have laws being passed to stop people feeding the homeless, spikes installed where the homeless might sleep and park benches sectioned with armrests to stop anyone lying down. Those involved in this are psychopaths by any definition. Wars are key to the financial agenda in that Archon banks 'lend' money to Archon governments to bomb countries they want to acquire and when the killing and destruction is over they 'lend' still more to repair the devastation (when it suits them). This constant cycle of death, destruction and 'new investment' has manipulated nations into unrepayable levels of debt, and so control by those to whom they owe the 'money' (Fig 455). Debtor countries have long been owned by Archon 'lenders' if the truth be told. The world looks so different when you know what is really

Figure 455: Not even cake these days.

going on and the apparent complexity is only the cover to hide simple truths. People switch off when it comes to financial issues with all the jargon, gobbledegook, wind and air about hedge funds, bulls, bears, naked shorts, put options, peak rate, non-plan expenditure and all the rest which most of those involved don't even understand. A financial reporter wrote:

> I have been interviewing bankers and asset managers for the best part of two decades and, Lord knows, they can be hard to understand. Many is the time I have looked up from my notepad to realise that I haven't understood a word that the interviewee has uttered for the last few minutes. Or rather, I understood the individual words, but not in the context the banker was using them.

At its core, however, the financial system is simple: you lend people money that doesn't exist (credit) and charge them interest on it; you don't create the interest (as currency) and so there is always far more debt than 'money' in existence to pay it back; when people can't repay, especially when you purposely crash the system, you steal their wealth and their possessions that do exist – their homes, land, businesses and cars. The latest figures I saw confirmed that we are approaching the point where one percent of the global population own 50 percent of the world's wealth in all its forms. They have achieved this largely by exchanging fresh air 'money' for land, property, resources and corporate entities. An Archontic one percent (less in fact) is stealing the world and 50 percent is not nearly enough for them – they want the lot (Fig 456). Another method of mass acquisition is to dip or crash stock markets by bloodline families withdrawing their multiple trillions and waiting for business and asset prices to hit the bottom. Then they buy them for cents on the dollar before the re-infusion of their multi-trillions expands the market and the value of the stocks that they have just bought for a song.

Figure 456: Every last inch.

The Rothschilds did this most famously in the London Stock Market at the time of the Battle of Waterloo in 1815 when they started a rumour that Britain had lost and the market crashed. Rothschild agents bought enormous amounts of stock at knock-down prices during the panic and prices then soared again when the news came through that – as the Rothschilds knew all along – the Duke of Wellington had defeated Napoleon. This happens all the time, and major financial players like the Rothschilds and Rockefellers always end up richer in the wake of banking and financial collapses. Witness what happened after the crash of 2008. Engineered financial crises transfer ever more wealth from the people to the less than one percent and I will be dealing with the planned consequences of that later on. People ask why banks and stock markets would be crashed when many in the financial industry lose their jobs and money, but at their level they are only pawns in the game like everyone else. If you are not in the less than one percent you are just another expendable no matter how rich and powerful you may currently think you are. If you own the World Cup it doesn't really matter which teams win and lose because you always win when you own the game itself. This is the relationship of the global financial system to Archon hybrids and their hidden masters.

Finance and politics are the two major dictators and arbiters of choice in the daily lives of almost everyone with regard to the laws, rules and regulations which limit action, potential and availability of money to allow or deny choice. When you break it all down, there is ultimately no real choice and that means slavery. Oh, people will say, I could choose to be a lawyer, doctor, politician, CEO, the choices are endless; but those are The System's choices, not necessarily yours, and they there to serve its interests. You have only chosen one of those choices on offer once again. Even then you need money to pursue those choices (jobs) and how many are really *your* choices and how many merely the result of pressure and influence from parents and academics who tell you what your 'choice' should be? Try choosing something outside The System without access to money and see what happens. Financial slavery is founded on making the basics of life – food, drink, shelter, warmth – available only in return for money, when they should a human right in any civilised and conscious society. The more you need to serve The System to earn the money to survive the more control The System has over you. All over the world humanity wakes up each morning to a new day of work and toil which is not done as a choice but as a necessity of survival (Fig 457). What better definition could there be for slavery? When you and your family need money for the basics of life and The System is the only source of money to pay for them what choice do you have but to serve The System and allow it to be your master? This is the idea, and why today's financial and corporate system has been created. Once the essentials of life are provided by a society that genuinely believes in freedom, people can choose to accept that lifestyle and do things that don't have to generate more income or alternatively choose to do something else that would. This would be *their* choice, not The

Figure 457: A new day in the slave camp.

System's choice and the Archons' choice. Where would the money come from to provide for the essential needs of everyone as a matter of course? I'll answer that with another question: where does it come from *now*? Where do the open cheques come from for endless war and carnage? 'Money' is a theoretical means of energetic exchange and it can be used for slavery and dependency or for freedom and prosperity. It is just a *choice*. The program dictating the perceptions of Phantom Self is so ingrained and omnipotent in most people that they won't be able to grasp that simple fact. They will continue to demand 'Where will the money comes from?' Are we really saying that humans are less powerful than non-existent money called credit? Are we saying that it should control us and not we it? So it would seem, but that's Phantom Self for you.

Who owns your body?

Surely the most basic of freedoms would be an unchallengeable right to decide what we allow in our own bodies and the right to decide how we are treated when we are ill. How can freedom possibly exist when people are forcibly medicated and denied the treatment they choose to have when alternative practitioners with records of success are banned and jailed? This has to be a foundation definition of fascism, but this is *happening* and it's still nowhere near as extreme as it is planned to be. A clear and coordinated campaign is underway to enforce mandatory vaccination, and there is a war against alternative medicine to make illegal anything that is not produced by the truly Archontic pharmaceutical cartel or Big Pharma – the world's biggest killing machine. The same applies to nutrition supplements that people use to overcome the

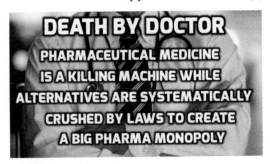

Figure 458: The 'health' inversion.

Figure 459: Where the mistakes are buried.

consequences of the nutrition desert that most of the food chain has now become. This is all part of a global campaign to destroy human health for reasons I will explain later. There can be few more potent examples of Archon inversion than this extraordinary fact: Mainstream medicine in all its forms is America's biggest killer. Doctor errors, drug-reaction deaths, infections contracted in hospital and a long list of other fatalities caused by mainstream medicine together make the treatment of illness the biggest killer of Americans ahead of heart disease and cancer (Fig 458). You'll find the same story almost everywhere (Fig 459). A profusely-sourced report sponsored by the non-profit Nutrition Institute of America concluded that nearly 800,000 Americans die every year as a result of Big Pharma mainstream medicine:

Each year approximately 2.2 million US

hospital patients experience adverse drug reactions (ADRs) to prescribed medications. In 1995, Dr. Richard Besser of the federal Centers for Disease Control and Prevention (CDC) estimated the number of unnecessary antibiotics prescribed annually for viral infections to be 20 million; in 2003, Dr. Besser spoke in terms of tens of millions of unnecessary antibiotics prescribed annually. Approximately 7.5 million unnecessary medical and surgical procedures are performed annually in the US, while approximately 8.9 million Americans are hospitalized unnecessarily ...

... the estimated total number of iatrogenic deaths – that is, deaths induced inadvertently by a physician or surgeon or by medical treatment or diagnostic procedures – in the US annually is 783,936. It is evident that the American medical system is itself the leading cause of death and injury in the US. By comparison, approximately 699,697 Americans died of heart disease in 2001, while 553,251 died of cancer.

Those figures will be bigger today. Studies reveal that non-fatal drug reactions are under-reported by as much as *85 to 94 percent* and if the real figure for death and damage by doctor and Big Pharma 'treatment' were known it would be almost incomprehensible when its alleged – *alleged* – role is to make people well (Fig 460). An investigation by the respected online *Consumer Reports* said:

Infections, surgical mistakes, and other medical harm contributes to the deaths of 180,000 hospital patients a year, according to projections based on a 2010 report from the Department of Health and Human Services. Another 1.4 million are seriously hurt by their hospital care. And those figures apply only to Medicare patients. What happens to other people is less clear because most hospital errors go unreported and hospitals report on only a fraction of things that can go wrong ...

... 'There is an epidemic of health-care harm,' says Rosemary Gibson, a patient-safety advocate and author. More than 2.25 million Americans will probably die from medical harm in this decade, she says. 'That's like wiping out the entire populations of North Dakota, Rhode Island, and Vermont. It's a man-made disaster ... '

Figure 460: The Big Pharma tyranny.   **Figure 461:** Big Pharma insanity.

... 'Hospitals haven't given safety the attention it deserves,' says Peter Pronovost, M.D., senior vice president for patient safety and quality at Johns Hopkins Medicine in Baltimore. Nor has the government, he says. 'Medical harm is probably one of the three leading causes of death in the US, but the government doesn't adequately track it as it does deaths from automobiles, plane crashes, and cancer. It's appalling.

This is shocking enough but its far worse in reality when you consider the fact that 'most hospital errors go unreported and hospitals report on only a fraction of things that can go wrong ...' Mainstream 'medicine', controlled by the global pharmaceutical cartel, is among the biggest killers on Earth (Fig 461). Hospitals for so many are Death Row. Britain's National Health Service (inversion) was reported in 2013 to be paying millions to staff for gagging order severance agreements to block the exposure of incompetence and corruption. A UK Freedom of Information request revealed that more than a thousand patients had starved to death in hospital in four years and four times that number had 'dehydration' on their death certificates. Patients leaving British hospitals suffering from malnutrition had doubled to 5,558 while 'Health' Secretary Jeremy Hunt said in 2015 that a 'plane crash' number of patients were dying avoidably in UK hospitals at the rate of about 200 a week. A Save the Children report in 2013 said the United States with its Big Pharma-controlled 'medical' system had the highest first-day death rate for babies in the industrialised world. This daily devastation of human health unfolds, with government support, while the same authorities are vociferously targeting alternative or complementary practitioners who, while there are many clueless people among their ranks, could not begin to compete with such catastrophic levels of human carnage. How can Big Pharma medicine be anything but a fast-track to the cemetery when it is based on a complete misunderstanding of what the body is and how it functions? I say misunderstanding and that's true of the rank and file, but once again the inner core driving the Big Pharma Archon agenda *do* know the nature of the body and therefore the consequences, short-term and long, of what they are doing. Everything is an energetic information field and when a distorted or disharmonious field comes into contact with human fields this distortion and disharmony can be passed on. We see drugs and vaccines in their holographic form, but in their base state they are distorted information fields that distort human fields. The distortion can be so extreme that the person dies either immediately or cumulatively. These distortions that impact on health are called 'side-effects', but there is nothing 'side' about them. They are effects every bit as much as the alleged positive effect that the drug is claimed to have. Alternative treatments are founded on harmonising human energy fields while Big Pharma medicine devastates them. Whatever is happening in the information fields – harmony or disharmony – is happening in the hologram in the form of health or dis-ease. Mainstream Everything laughs at colour therapy and music therapy but they are using frequencies (every colour is a different frequency) to harmonise human body frequencies. This can also be done electrically, electromagnetically and even by the person's own mind. Stress causes illness through the distorted frequency of emotions impacting on body fields, and the reverse is the case with frequencies in harmony with the body. I am not saying that mainstream medicine has nothing to offer. There have been great advances in some areas and when you break a leg or need resuscitation it is no good going to a reflexologist. Some of the work that surgeons do is incredible. The question is how often does mainstream medicine rush to surgery when it is not necessary (the number must be in the stratosphere) and how often alternative treatments would be more effective than the scalpel and the drug (ditto)? Britain's health system is falling apart systematically to prepare the way for corporations to take over, but also because shit food and drink, shit air and an ever more irradiated environment are bringing about so much illness that no matter how much money is poured in it will never be enough. How can any 'health' system have any credibility or long-term success if it doesn't address the causes of illness to stop it at source – shit food and drink, shit air and an ever more irradiated environment? Plus all the stress. The System makes you ill in multiple ways and then offers you poisons and potions to respond to the symptoms but not the cause. Talk about the old one-two. American television is funded to an enormous extent by Big Pharma advertisements – with a breathless voice at the end of each one reeling off possible side-effects as fast as possible. Even then the list can take a big slice of the ad and Big Pharma has taken to putting images on the screen during side-effect voiceovers to divert attention from what is being said. Public 'protection' agencies like the US Food and Drug Administration (FDA) are largely assets of Big Pharma, and approval is given to many drugs after pathetic levels of testing. Obama's nominee in 2015 for a new head of the FDA was Dr Robert Califf, a one-time board member and consultant of a company specialising in helping pharmaceutical corporations evade and manipulate FDA regulations. Check out the background also to Michael Taylor who has bounced between key positions with biotech giant Monsanto and the FDA that supposed to be protecting the public from Monsanto. Big Pharma is even securing immunity from prosecution over the consequences of vaccines and drugs. The networks that control Big Pharma also control governments and their 'protection' agencies. More powerful drugs are now being sold directly to the public through drugstores and you no longer even need a doctor to kill you in many cases. Cut out the middle man and do it yourself. Big Pharma's advertising cash-cow means that the mainstream media (especially in the United States) will not rock their own boat by exposing 'medical' death and destruction. Instead, they target alternative medicine to destroy the opposition to their Big Pharma sugar daddies. Not that they need to when national governments, the European Union, World Health Organization and global trade agreements are doing this anyway.

Deleting medical choice

One of the prime vehicles being used to end alternative medicine is Codex Alimentarius ('Food Code' or 'Food Book') which was created by Nazis and Rockefellers (sorry, I repeat myself) to target food supplements, nutrition and non-pharmaceutical methods of healing. Codex Alimentarius was launched in 1963 by Nazi war criminals Hermann Schmitz and Fritz ter Meer in league with the Rothschilds and Rockefellers. Official backers were the Food and Agriculture Organization of Rothschild-Rockefeller-created United Nations and Rothschild-Rockefeller-created World Health Organization. Hermann Schmitz was president of the Nazi chemical giant IG Farben and Fritz ter Meer was an executive. Ter Meer was responsible for the phrase 'Arbeit Macht Frei' ('Work Makes Free') over the main gate at Auschwitz (Fig 462). IG Farben ran the camp and some constituent parts of Farben are still well known names today – AGFA, BASF,

Figure 462: Message at Auschwitz from the co-founder of Codex Alimentarius.

Figure 463: Big Pharma is taking over 'nutrition' with its synthetic versions, which are worse than useless.

Bayer and Sanofi. Schmitz and Ter Meer were jailed for war crimes at the Nuremberg trials but Ter Meer only served four of his seven-year sentence after the intervention of his friend and four-times Governor of New York, Nelson Rockefeller. Ter Meer then continued his career with Bayer and eventually headed Codex Alimentarius to use the excuse of 'harmonising' global food and supplement laws and regulations to target alternatives to Big Pharma (Fig 463). Codex Alimentarius is recognised by the Rothschild-Rockefeller-created World Trade Organization, which provides powers of enforcement to Codex laws and regulations. The Rockefeller family, subordinates in the bloodline hierarchy to the Rothschilds, are largely responsible for giving the world today's government-imposed killing field 'allopathic medicine'. Oil and pharmaceutical tycoon John D. Rockefeller was behind the establishment of the American Medical Association (AMA) in 1847 and conspired to impose Big Pharma medicine on the world. Today the AMA has one of the biggest political lobbying budgets in the United States. Rockefeller set out to take over medical schools and introduce a system of medical licencing. This meant that physicians could not be physicians without a licence and they couldn't get a licence unless they treated patients the way The System demanded. Licensing alone gave Rockefeller Big Pharma control over methods of treatment and the means to banish the now so-called 'alternatives' that were used before. Licenced doctors who challenge orthodoxy in any way are jumped upon with a vengeance. The licensing scam is employed throughout The System to ensure that people do things The System's way or not at all. Alternative or complimentary treatment is now a target for this. John D. Rockefeller imposed Big Pharma medicine while being treated by his personal homeopath who was still at his bedside when he died at the age of 97. Notice how many bloodline stalwarts live to a great age compared with the general population. This relates to their genetics and to the fact that they don't have the same treatment they force on the masses. Rockefeller founded the Rockefeller Institute for Medical Research (America's first) in 1901 to promote Big Pharma medicine and this is known today as Rockefeller University. I will feature later an American doctor and Rockefeller insider who made a series of predictions nearly 50 years ago from knowledge of the Archon agenda which have either happened or are happening. Dr Richard Day, professor of paediatrics at Mount

Figure 464: 'Weedkiller' makes you healthy.

Sinai Hospital in New York and executive of the Rockefeller-controlled eugenics organisation Planned Parenthood, told a closed meeting of paediatricians in Pittsburgh, Pennsylvania, in 1969: 'We can cure almost every cancer right now. Information is on file in the Rockefeller Institute, if it's ever decided that it should be released.' I met a CIA scientist in the 1990s who was cured of cancer with a 'serum' that was only for those The System wants to keep alive. Richard Day told the Pittsburgh meeting that the plan was to cull the population through medicine, food, new laboratory-made diseases and suppression of a cure for cancer. 'You may as well die of cancer as something else', this cold, callous Archontic man said. Anyone think that this mentality behind Big Pharma medicine has any desire to see humanity healthy in mind and body? I see genuine people rattling their tins for cancer research but I will not contribute from the knowledge that the cure is already known but suppressed – another reason why many bloodline assets live for so long. Is it really credible that mind-blowing amounts of money have been donated to 'cancer research' worldwide and yet cancer numbers continue to soar? Or that the two main treatments are radiation and chemotherapy, both of which devastate the immune system and open people to more disease including cancer? Chemotherapy is liquid poison or weed killer as one doctor put it (Fig 464). Americans were taking on average twelve medications a year by 2011 with the number growing year on year. Spending on prescription medications increased by *$200 billion* in two decades. This is not even including those bought over the counter. But get this: A research team working with the *British Medical Journal* found that nearly *90 percent* of drugs and treatments *don't work*. Only 12 percent of 2,500 of the most common drugs and treatments prescribed by doctors have been confirmed in *proper scientific studies* as having any effect in treating illness. Now Big Pharma is selling the scam of drugs for 'preventive' reasons, with the notorious Statins among them, along with advice that

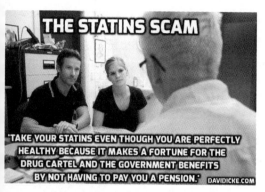

Figure 465: The statins scam encapsulates the Big Pharma conspiracy against human health.

those who don't have Alzheimer's should take Alzheimer drugs to stop them getting it. Statins are said to prevent heart disease by lowering cholesterol, when cholesterol is vital to health by turning sunlight into vitamin D. A deficiency in vitamin D absorption triggers a whole range of negative health effects. *American Journal of Cardiovascular Drugs* published a paper listing almost 900 studies on the adverse effects of statins, including muscle pain; increased blood sugar (adding to the risk of diabetes); cognitive loss; neuropathy;

anaemia; acidosis; fevers; cataracts; sexual dysfunction; increased cancer risk; suppression of the immune system (a constant theme); degeneration of muscle tissue; pancreas dysfunction and liver dysfunction. Still, never mind all that, the experts know best (Fig 465). Professor Sir Rory Collins of the Clinical Trial Service Unit at University of Oxford said that everyone over 50 should be taking take statins *regardless of their health history.* Ethel, smelling salts – quick. Between six and seven million people take statins in the UK every day and *one in four* Americans over the age of 45. They are testament to the power of propaganda over common sense. Mind is another Big Pharma target and the number of mind-altering and suppressing drugs now given to children and taken by adults is absolutely fantastic – and growing (see *The Perception Deception*).

Ending vaccine choice

Political and medical fascism is adding a new element to its tyranny with increasing pressure and laws to impose compulsory vaccination. This has begun with the Totalitarian Tiptoe of banning adults from healthcare jobs and children from school and daycare without government (Big Pharma) 'recommended' vaccinations. You will see this expanded to other locations, too. The claim is that the unvaccinated put the vaccinated at risk, but there are two questions here: What happened to the alleged immunity of the vaccinated and how come outbreaks affect the vaccinated while unvaccinated go unaffected? Oh, and another question: If vaccination is safe why are vast amounts of money paid out to vaccine-damaged people? Mandatory vaccinations means mandatory devastation of health and even death for many (Fig 466). California governor Jerry Brown signed a bill in 2015 eliminating vaccine exemptions for personal and religious beliefs. Only a certified medical reason can avoid vaccination for those in public and private schools and daycare centres (Fig 467). The bill followed a campaign led by California Democratic (joke) senator and paediatrician Richard Pan who is reported to have received $95,000 from Big Pharma during the legislative session of 2013-2014. Madness and arrogance has no end when it comes to mandatory vaccines. A Sacramento father was told by his daughter's *virtual online school,* which allegedly supports home-schooled students, that she would be locked out of her computer course unless she was vaccinated. What are they worried about – the computer catching

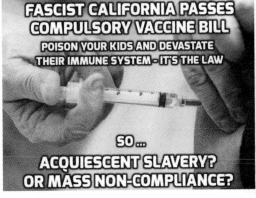

Figure 466: If people will stand for this they will stand for anything.

Figure 467: The war on child health with adults to follow.

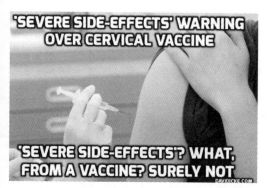

Figure 468: Inventing ever more toxic vaccines for ever more conditions.

Figure 469: Bill Gates – Agenda Man.

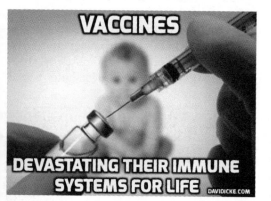

Figure 470: Overwhelming a still-developing immune system with toxic shite. Yeah, great idea. I mean, what harm could it do?

something?? These people are bonkers. Other states are moving in the same fascist direction as California and the ultimate plan is to make vaccinations compulsory for everyone everywhere using fear and other manipulations to gather support (Fig 468). The World Health Organization (WHO) has asked the International Food and Beverage Alliance (including Coca Cola, PepsiCo and McDonalds) for advice on how to overcome public 'vaccine hesitancy'. They advised to forget facts and deal in emotion: 'Reason leads to conclusions, while emotion leads to action.' All that really mattered was the power of the story and people cared about benefits not facts, the advice continued. Remember that next time anyone fancies a Coke, Pepsi or Big Mac. Selling vaccines in the same way as selling Coca Cola or a burger and fries just about sums it up. Health consequences of mass vaccination are catastrophic but to Big Pharma they are only another fact-free brand to sell. Microsoft billionaire Bill Gates is another major corporate promotor of worldwide vaccination and he turns up constantly in projects on the Archontic wishlist (Fig 469). Still-developing immune systems are deluged with toxins by the insane 25 to 30 (and growing) vaccinations before the age of *two,* and even more between then and six-years old, and into teenage years (Fig 470). Their immune system will never be the same again after being devastated by a constant wave of poison, and here we have still another inversion when vaccines are supposed to boost immunity. A damaged and weakened immune system leaves people open to health consequences that would

normally be dealt with by the body, and this will become even more significant later in the book. Gathering awareness and opposition to vaccines worldwide has driven the campaign to make them compulsory and we must not stand for this (Fig 471). GlaxoSmithKline (GSK) made the biggest healthcare fraud settlement in US history ($3 billion) after being exposed for promoting drugs for unapproved uses, failing to report safety data about a diabetes drug to the Food and Drug Administration (FDA) and paying kickbacks to doctors (Fig 472). This same company was reported in 2013 to be developing a *six-in-one* vaccine with an Indian partner for polio, diphtheria, tetanus, whooping cough, hepatitis B, and Haemophilus influenzae type B in a single dose for the poorest and weakest people. Ponder the scale of toxic shit that would overwhelm the immune system in one go (Fig 473). Vaccine ingredients include: Aluminium (dementia and Alzheimer's disease); Antibiotics; Formaldehyde; Monosodium Glutamate (MSG); Thimerosal (lethally-toxic methyl mercury); aborted human foetal and altered DNA material; and genetically-modified human blood protein (albumin). Archon genetic mutation is being covertly imposed on humanity in conjunction with genetically-modified food, genetically-mutating radiation from technological sources and genetically-mutating vaccinations to further rewire the human organism and suppress its receiver-transmitter capabilities.

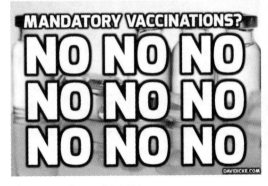

Figure 471: The word is 'NO'.

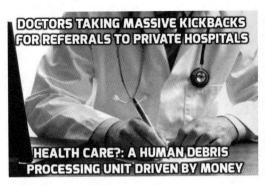

Figure 472: Mainstream medicine is one of the most corrupt expressions of organised crime on Planet Earth.

Figure 473: When the Web is behind you anything goes.

Ending *all* choice

The force behind Mainstream Everything imposes its will by controlling governments and politicians who officially make the law; the legal and 'justice' system that argues and interprets the law; and police and other agencies that enforce the law. Those affected by laws have no say in their introduction when governments are elected to power largely by a minority of the population and laws are passed that were never mentioned by the politicians when they were seeking election. Presidential Executive Orders in the United States become law with a swish of the pen and most laws and regulations come into force without any public debate under terms such as secondary legislation, subordinate or delegated legislation

Figure 474: Control law and law enforcement and you control the world.

Figure 475: Go deep enough and the same force controls them all.

and Statutory Instruments. Governments (those that control governments) do what they like basically, and then the 'justice' system and law enforcement imposes their commands and decrees on the people. I saw a cartoon that said: ' ... you can turn any criminal organisation into a political one by simply legalising every crime you're going to commit.' This is how it's done. Those that believe you must always obey the law should put out their hands now so handcuffs and shackles can be attached. If you have no say in a law being passed but think you must obey it anyway, how can there possibly be any freedom? The point is not about obeying the law but obeying or disobeying *what* law that demands what of the people. Okay, we have changed the law so we can take your children away. Will you obey and hand them over? Yes, of course, we must obey the law. Courts are more Archontic ritual with the uniforms and protocol and headgear that looks in need of a saucer of milk. The cost of the often parasitical and psychopathic legal profession (with many honourable exceptions) means that all but the rich are mostly denied quality representation, or even any representation at all, within a system that is already rigged in favour of the tiny few at the expense of the very many. Governments when challenged pay for legal representation with taxpayers' money but taxpayers who challenge governments have to pay for their own. The legal system has nothing to do with justice. It's about who has the most money to buy the best (often most psychopathic) lawyers, and far more often than people realise it's about who has the influence to fix the judge. If you have the money or someone else to pay your legal costs you can target anyone with even the most ludicrous lawsuits and financially destroy them as they pay to defend themselves (Fig 474). As a result the world's prisons are awash with people who are innocent of the crime they are alleged to have committed. Convicting the wrong person is a good way to protect those servants of The System who are really responsible. Oh, I see they got someone for that murder, then. Job done, game over, move on. Look at the background to judges and see what level of the hierarchy they are overwhelmingly born into. Governments, secret societies and elite school connections make sure that the 'right' judges are appointed to the 'right' cases to reach the 'right' verdict and the very fact that judges are allowed to be members of secret societies shows how claims of 'justice' being seen to be done are beyond farcical. Does anyone think that a Hidden Hand that controls the web of government, finance, corporations, media, intelligence agencies and military is going to have no control of the legal and court system and the Supreme Court in the United States with its final legal yea or nay on what is blocked or allowed? *Please.* All these institutions, organisations and agencies ultimately answer to the same master and it's not the public (Fig 475).

The plan is to use this corrupt system of law and law enforcement to delete all choice in ways that I am going to describe. 'We're free, honey'? Sure we are, said Phantom Self. We live in a land of freedom? Sure we do, said Phantom Self. You must be bloody joking, said Expanded Awareness.

CHAPTER NINE

World Anew

The public have an insatiable curiosity to know everything, except what is worth knowing
Oscar Wilde

Human life looks very different when viewed from the perspective of this book, and apparently inexplicable and unconnected happenings begin to make perfect sense. I am now going to put recent and current events into a whole new context.

The Archon hijack is not static in that the deed was done and then everything stayed the same. We had the original hijack of human perception symbolised by the Garden of Eden, but that was only the start of the plan. Bad copy reality was at first a bad copy of something abundant and beautiful. All along the idea has been to increase the depth of human programming and distort and invert the bad copy to the point where it became basically a holographic and frequency mirror of the Archon realm. Computer viruses don't infiltrate an operating system and stop. They go on expanding and deepening control until the system reflects the virus in totality, and the Archon self-aware virus is doing the same to our simulated reality. Total human control and inversion of the bad copy have reached an advanced stage but they're not there yet. If enough Phantom Selves pop their perception bubbles and open to Infinite Awareness the plan would be scuppered big time.

Society-changing events are not happening by random chance. They are following an agenda embarked upon in what we call the distant past and continued ever since. A carefully orchestrated plan of conquest has been hidden from the masses by making everything appear to be an endless series of unconnected, unrelated choices and decisions. Within the Matrix only those with some connection to beyond-the-Matrix awareness can make genuine choices and free decisions. Everyone else is following the program under the delusion that the thoughts and urgings which dictate their choices and decisions originate in their own mind. I have long contended that most people can go through an entire human lifetime without an original or independent mental or emotional response. They are slaves to the programmed software of Phantom Self. Observe the animal world and the cycles of software behaviour which doesn't change generation after generation. This is especially so with software extremes such as crocodiles and other reptiles. I saw two demonstrations at crocodile farms in Australia in which the keeper showed how the crocs' behaviour is based on impulses that they can't override or resist. The keeper would say that if he did this, the croc would do that, and it happened every time. Great tracts of the human race are the same and Archon-Reptilians certainly are. It's not a case of being either Phantom Self or Infinite Awareness. I said that only those with *some* connection to beyond-the-Matrix awareness can make genuine choices and free decisions. There is a huge spectrum of perception from fully-blown Phantom Self to those with expanded awareness hardly affected by the program. These different states can be observed through behaviour and on that basis many who think they are 'awake' are actually Phantom Self held fast in the program through the self-delusion that they're not. Those influenced by Infinite Awareness have an instinctive empathy that overrides the response of what's in it for me, me, me. I mean empathy expressed in actions and not only words, which have constant potential for deception. I mean those that walk their talk, but few do. Phantom Self has them under lock and key. Infinite Awareness can also be seen in an openness of mind in those who respond with their own intuition or knowing, and not only to the alleged facts and figures of academia and song sheet science. Such people are not immune from Phantom Self programs and they can play them out, but they also have moments, sometimes far more than moments, when they transcend them. These are the people that the Archons are still after in their quest for a closed world in which only Phantom Self exists and humans are devoid of any awareness outside the software. To know this is to grasp a very different understanding of global society and why it is taking the direction that it is.

My approach to research has always been to establish the goal and the methods employed to reach the goal. Without this knowledge everything appears unconnected and a series of events that have no apparent consistency or connection. Once you know where the plan wants to take the world and the methods of manipulation used to take us there then events that seem random and disconnected come into clearly-connected clarity. *Ahhh*, so *that's* why they're doing this or that. The plan for human subjugation has been followed long term with Archons in hybrid bloodlines coming in and out of this reality through cycles of birth and death to advance the agenda through its different phases on the road to total control. They may be called different names by history but they are the same Archons coming, going and returning. It's not quite that simple because there is no time, only the illusion of it, and Archontic manipulation in what we perceive to be 'past' and 'future' can influence events in what we experience as the 'present'. This concept has been explored and portrayed in several movies. Manipulating the past is like changing a scene in a DVD that makes all the scenes that follow also change to sync with it and, in the other direction, to change the final scene which makes the scenes up to that point change to lead to the new outcome. You can't manipulate the 'present' from the perceived 'past' and 'future'? Of course you can – it's all a *program* happening in the infinite NOW. Only the sequence is being changed by manipulating the NOW in a way that appears to flow from past through present to future. There is no such thing as time travel only NOW travel that is experienced as time travel. I have explained the two key methods of mass manipulation – Problem-Reaction-Solution and the Totalitarian Tiptoe – and now I am going to describe the world that these and other perception deceptions are in the process of creating. I refer to this as the Hunger Games Society because the power structure that Archons and their hybrids want to impose is portrayed (but only to an extent) in the *Hunger Games* movie series.

We are well on the way to that end if people will only lift their eyes from the smartphone and look around.

What is coming unless we stop it ...

The Hunger Games Society involves a small *El*-lite of Archon hybrids living in hi-tech fiercely-guarded cities, or capitols, as the *Hunger Games* movies call them. All wealth, resources and access to food and water would be controlled by the *El*-lite and those who refused to obey every command would lose the means to survive even if they weren't killed anyway. A merciless police state involving deeply programmed psychopaths in uniform would protect the *El*-lite from the masses and impose their tyranny. Everyone else – and I mean *everyone*, even those with wealth today who are not part of the *El*-ite – would be slaves serving the Archons and their hybrids. This is the global society planned for humanity, and it is unfolding so fast (Fig 476). See the exposures of how Amazon treats its workers with contempt, no dignity and an iron hand and you'll get some idea of what is planned for everywhere. Artificial Intelligence (AI) would run the whole global structure and that Artificial Intelligence is ... the *Archon virus*. This is another profound revelation that puts the whole transhumanism conspiracy into context. The Demiurge/Archons *are* Artificial Intelligence and the fast-immerging transhumanist agenda is the vehicle for the virus to take total control. I am going to develop this theme later. One-percent of the population already own half the world's wealth and this is the Hunger Games Society moving towards its goal through the Totalitarian Tiptoe – so are worldwide austerity programmes. Accumulated wealth and power allows you to seize still more wealth and power and so the process is getting faster and faster. Another economic necessity in this grand plan of parting everyone

from their financial security is also advancing. We have witnessed a staggering transfer of wealth from the global population to the *El*-lite via *El*-lite-controlled governments through 'bailouts' of *El*-lite- owned banks after the crash of 2008. This marked the start of a new and more

Figure 476: The structure of the planned Hunger Games global society and we are heading there by the day.

extreme stage of the plan to plunge all but the *El*-lite and their gofers and police state personnel into extreme levels of poverty – mass slavery. What they have done to Greece and other countries is what they plan to do to the world – and far, far worse. A major scam to remove financial independence from even those currently wealthy is known as the 'bail-in'. The term came to public consciousness with the manipulated banking crisis in Cyprus in 2013 (Problem-Reaction-Solution). Crashing banks is a doddle when the financial system is controlled by

Figure 477: When you put money in a bank it becomes their property in effect – not yours.

Archontic families like the Rothschilds and Rockefellers. Banking crises were dealt with before Cyprus by governments bailing out banks through borrowing (often from banks) and taxation. This was bad enough, but now it got a whole lot worse. Cyprus banks were 'saved' by taking money directly from accounts of depositors – the 'bail-in' – and this common theft was demanded by the so-called 'Troika' of the Rothschild-controlled European Central Bank (ECB), Rothschild-controlled IMF and Rothschild-controlled European Commission with the enthusiastic support of Rothschild-controlled Germany in the form of Rothschild-controlled Chancellor Merkel. This criminal syndicate, sorry, 'Troika', came together to crush Greece, and the plan is for this Archontic hit-squad to do the same to the entire European Union as a blueprint for the world. At the time of the Cyprus bail-in the EU guaranteed deposits up to 100,000 euros (£85,000), but everything above that was simply stolen to the tune of some 60 to 80 percent of what was in the private accounts. A lot of rich people were not nearly so rich after this bank heist and I cannot emphasise enough that those who have wealth now and think they are immune from poverty and deprivation should think again. If they are not part of this *El*-lite then their wealth is going to be targeted, too. Already a large number of formerly 'middle class' or 'upper middle class' people are living on the street. The European Union announced in 2015 that the deposit guarantee for British savers would be cut from £85,000 to £75,000 and the idea is to remove all bank deposit protection across Europe. The plan is to crash the banking and financial system on a scale that will make 2008 look very small deal. With the bail-in principle now accepted and in place they intend to steal people's money on a mass scale with pension funds also in their gunsights. When you deposit money in a bank you are only an unsecured creditor if the bank goes down, which any of them could at almost any time (Fig 477). Financial reform advocate Ellen Brown said of the new bail-in rules:

> They use words so that it's not obvious to tell what they have done, but what they did was say, basically, that we, the governments, are no longer going to be responsible for bailing out the big banks. There are about 30 (systemically important) international banks. So, you are going to have to save yourselves, and the way you are going to have to do it is by bailing in the money of your creditors. The largest class of creditors of any bank is the depositors.

Figure 478: The derivative market is a ticking time bomb for the global financial system.

Figure 479: What they have done to the East they plan to do to the West – it's already happening.

Figure 480 Very true.

This will allow banks to steal depositors' money all over the world whenever another financial crisis can be engineered. We have had dot com bubbles and housing bubbles 'pop' causing financial mayhem, but there is a gigantic financial hoax called the derivatives market that dwarfs them all. This 'market' is worth hundreds of *trillions* of dollars. Er, or rather it's not, and that's the problem. Derivatives are fresh air finance once again, another bubble with nothing inside. This truth is hidden behind financial complexity and gobbledegook terms such as 'forwards', 'futures', 'options', 'swaps', 'synthetic collateralised debt obligations' and 'credit default swaps'. When the derivatives illusion is unmasked – and this is what is planned – the global financial system goes with it (Fig 478). Four banks, J.P. Morgan, Bank of America, Citi, and Goldman Sachs account for 94.4 percent of total derivative exposure according to figures released in 2015. Archon bloodline families are all prepared of course and they plan to own even more after the next crash (if we let them) in the same way they did after 2008 while those who bailed them out were mired in austerity. Poverty-stricken masses around the 'developing world', especially the Far East, have been exploited with a psychopathic (naturally) inhumanity to serve the slave master corporations to make their products at the cheapest price which are then sold in the West for as much as possible (Fig 479). Jobs in Western countries have been outsourced overseas by global brands and corporate giants to exploit sweatshop labour at the expense of employment at home. The plan is to dismantle Western economies so that what happens now in the Far East will happen in North America and Europe (Fig 480). Look at Greece for a start, and it's only a start. 'They' wouldn't do that? 'They' *are* doing it. 'They' are psychopathic Satanists who get an adrenalin rush at the suffering of others and even more so in knowing they are responsible. A Swiss banker told the Russian magazine *NoviDen* in 2011 about those that run the banking system:

> ... these people are corrupt, sick in their minds, so sick they are full of vices and those vices are kept under wraps on their orders. Some of them ... rape women, others are sado maso, or paedophile, and many are into Satanism. When you go in some banks you see these satanistic symbols, like in the Rothschild Bank in Zurich. These people are controlled by blackmail because of the weaknesses they have. They have to follow orders or they will be exposed, they will be destroyed or even killed.

People like that who control the financial system wouldn't manipulate humanity into poverty and servitude? They think of little else. There is no limit to their depths of empathy-deleted depravity.

Hunger Games hierarchy

I have been exposing the political and enforcement structure of the Hunger Games Society for two decades and the pieces are being constantly moved into place by the Totalitarian Tiptoe. The plan is for a world government (ultimately self-appointed not elected) dictating to everyone on the planet through a world central bank (overseeing a global single electronic currency), world army and agencies to control and dictate the use of all resources (Fig 481). When I say resources I mean *all* resources including rainwater dropping on your garden (Fig 482). Only by then, it won't be *your* garden. If you think this is far-fetched, well I wish it was. American state governments and agencies are already declaring their ownership of all rainwater no matter where it may gather. I promise you it is almost impossible to be far-fetched when describing what these lunatics have in mind. The United Nations was created in 1945 as a stepping stone to world government and associated agencies. Centralisation of power has been going

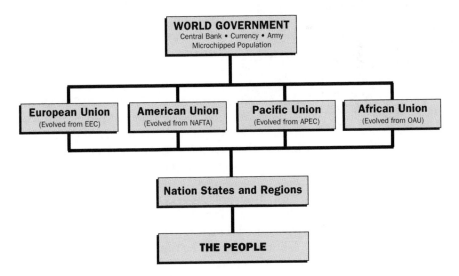

Figure 481: The structure of the planned global dictatorship. There are more superstates than these in the blueprint interconnected with corporate trade agreements (tyrannies).

Figure 482: They want everything including the rain that falls on your property.

Figure 483: The cashless society that I warned about decades ago is now being introduced at speed.

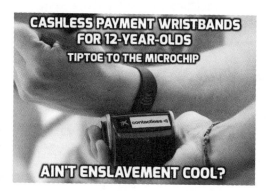

Figure 484: Get them young – keep them for life.

on for thousands of 'years' orchestrated by the common Archontic denominator. Humans once gathered in tribes to make their collective decisions; then tribes were absorbed into nations and a few people in power in the nation became dictators to all the former tribes. Now we have nations being absorbed by superstates like the European Union, with many others planned to emerge from stalking horse 'free-trade areas' in the same way the EU has been. 'Globalisation' is the Archontic agenda on public display but without the essential background for people to see that – until now. For the few to secure ever-increasing control over the many they have to incessantly centralise decision-making; the more you centralise power the more power you have to centralise even quicker. World government is planned to oversee a second tier of EU-style superstates in the Americas, Africa, Middle East, Asia/Australia/New Zealand and so on. None of these or the world government would be elected, and we have this already in the European Union which is controlled by appointed bureaucratic dark suits in Brussels and not elected politicians (except in theory). Global agencies such as the World Health Organization and World Trade Organization, both Rothschild-Rockefeller creations, are Totalitarian Tiptoes to the planned world government that would dictate policy and possibility in every facet of human life. Trans-Atlantic and trans-Pacific trade 'partnerships' being agreed in secret are also part of this process of taking fundamental powers from governments and handing them to corporations, global courts and other Archontic bodies. These 'trade agreements' (fascist impositions) include outrageous and brutal censorship of the alternative media that is terrifying the Archon networks. All finance would be controlled by a world central bank through a single world cashless currency. I have been warning about the plan for a cashless society in my books for more than 20 years and now cash is being replaced so fast by credit cards and cashless banking via smartphones etc., with ATMs being developed that require eye-scanning to get your money (Fig 483). Using cash is planned eventually to be banned and made a criminal offence. Cashless payment wristbands are the Totalitarian Tiptoe to under-the-skin microchips waiting to be introduced when the public can be conditioned to accept them (Fig 484). A chip *on* the wrist is only one step from *in* the wrist. British shops are being warned that they will all have to accept contactless payments by 2020 and this

Figure 485: Total control is being sold as convenience and so many are falling for it.

compulsion is forcing through the cashless agenda which has all been planned and prepared for decades and decades (even before the technology was officially 'invented' for reasons I'll be explaining). What appears to be a recent idea or development has long been waiting for the right time to be introduced for maximum effect. Cashless finance is about control and the plan is to ban cash in stages for various transactions until it has gone all together (Fig 485). Every transaction can be instantly recorded and tracked, and dissidents of The System will be blocked from access to money by a simple click, click, enter on the computer system. 'I'm sorry, sir, the system won't accept your card' (or microchip as it is eventually planned to be). Only barter would remain as an option with no cash in circulation and even that would be made illegal on the grounds of avoiding tax. Paying with a credit card takes only seconds but we are being urged to pay through the new contactless system 'because it's quicker' when the real reason is to secure another stepping stone to a fully cashless and microchipped society. Further engineered economic problems give Archon hybrids more excuses to replace cash. Some countries are virtually cashless already and even Iran is trialling a cashless system.

Fighting for tyranny

A world army would impose the will of the self-appointed world government on any country or community that refused to play ball. I have once again warned for decades that NATO was a Totalitarian Tiptoe to a world army and so it is proving. The United States military is also a proxy world army in conjunction with Britain and other NATO countries, and a time is planned when command of all of them will be given to a world authority. We can see this emerging with the US military structure that has carved the world into 'COMS' or commands (Fig 486). There is a CENTCOM, AFRICOM, EUCOM, PACOM, SOUTHCOM and NORTHCOM and American troops are

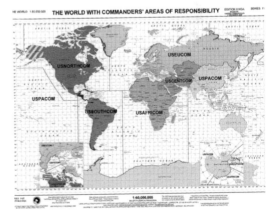

Figure 486: The global command structure of the American military is really being created for the planned world army.

deployed in some form in more than 150 countries. This structure is not actually for the American military ultimately but is being prepared to hand over to the world army. We have proxy world government already under names like 'International Community', G20, G8 and the United Nations Security Council (Fig 487). They decide that a country or regime is not obeying orders and in goes the American military with or without Britain and NATO to get rid of them.

Figure 487: The world government is moving into place before our eyes.

Afghanistan, Iraq, Libya, Syria, the list is so long and getting longer. If the 'international community' in the form of Russia and China doesn't agree America does it anyway. Such 'regime change' is not always done directly and often involves US/NATO trained, armed and funded 'rebels'. This happened with the engineered 'Arab Spring', which has led to death, destruction and suffering throughout the Middle East. Regime-changing too many times by direct invasion will be too obvious. Better to manipulate the population to do it for you. I have detailed the background to the Arab Spring hoax and those behind it in other books. This includes Obama's appointment of Robert S. Ford as United States Ambassador to Syria in the period before 'rebels' began an uprising using US-supplied weapons, and they were later joined by other US- instigated 'rebels' who had removed and killed Gaddhafi in Libya. Ford had served in Iraq after the invasion under Ambassador John Negroponte who orchestrated death squads in Central America on behalf of the Reagan-Father Bush administration during a civil war that cost the lives of 75,000 men, women and children in El Salvador. Ford ran the same death squad deal in Iraq – under Negroponte as Minister Counsellor for Political Affairs – and then repeated the now-dubbed 'Salvador option' after being named Ambassador to Syria (Fig 488). Professor Michel Chossudovsky from the Global Research website said:

> Since his arrival in Damascus in late January 2011 until he was recalled by Washington in October 2011, Ambassador Robert S. Ford played a central role in laying the groundwork within Syria as well as establishing contacts with opposition groups ... Ford also played a role in the recruitment of Mujahideen mercenaries from neighbouring Arab countries and their integration into Syrian 'opposition forces'. Since his departure from Damascus, Ford continues to oversee the Syria project out of the US State Department.

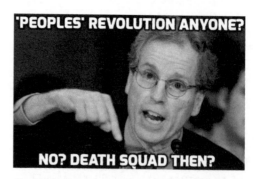

Figure 488: When Robert Ford arrives in your country it is time to leave.

Ford was recalled from Syria because of 'credible threats' to his safety when state television began to expose his involvement in the formation of death squads. The

Figure 489: Death by drone from the other side of the world.

Figure 490: State-sponsored extra-judicial murder.

human catastrophe that is Syria was coldly created by the 'moral' United States on behalf of the Hidden Hand and in league with Israel, Britain and other Archon regimes. 9/11 launched the sequence of mayhem and conquest under the title 'war on terror' – code for seize and control ever greater tracts of the planet, and justify mass surveillance and other freedom outrages at home to 'protect people from terrorism'. American presidents now have the power to kill anyone including their own citizens without charge, evidence or trial once they appear on a CIA 'kill list'. This is mostly done through drone attacks (Fig 489). British Prime Minister David Cameron announced in 2015 that he had sanctioned death by drone in Syria without producing any evidence in support of his claims that the targets were planning terrorism in the UK (Fig 490). It's do what you like time and these are the mass-murdering terrorists who claim to be protecting us from terrorism.

Another pre-determined bonus for Archon hybrids of this systematic violence and upheaval is for dispossessed masses and refugees to head for Europe to escape war and tyranny and bring more chaos and upheaval by their sheer numbers. Chaos, like fear, is the currency of control. What I call Problem-Reaction-Solution is the Freemasonic motto 'Order Ab Chao', or order out of chaos (Fig 491). Create chaos and you create the excuse to impose order – *your* order – as an alleged solution to the chaos. Harmony is almost impossible to manipulate by trying

Figure 491: Freemasonic Problem-Reaction-Solution.

to justify change in a situation where everything is fine. Chaos makes people open to anything they believe will end the chaos. A society-changing influx of refugees from other cultures – plus many opportunists and criminals who are not refugees – presents limitless potential for economic chaos and conflict between migrants and the home population. A central Archon technique is to play off one target group against another to make them so focussed on fighting each other that they don't see the strings on both are held by the same hands. Economic chaos offers further opportunity to steal the people's money and deepen austerity while conflict and upheaval is an excuse to expand the police state to 'bring order'.

Unrestrained immigration is also designed to destroy a sense of nationhood by fusing cultures together. In this way both the home population and genuine refugees are victims of the same force. I am not a flag-waving nationalist and if I ever stood up for the national anthem I would probably genetically implode; but many people do self-identify with nation and culture and that has the potential for major resistance to the systematic destruction of the nation state and its absorption into the world government system. Attacks on the use of the national flag in the United States are related to the deletion of national identity, as was the extraordinary reaction of Chancellor Merkel, widely circulated on the Internet, to a colleague holding a German flag at a public event. Disgust and contempt hardly tells the story. By engineering conflicts and situations that lead to colossal numbers of people from the Middle East and Africa heading for Europe they ensure that identifiable 'cultures' disappear and with it a sense of nation. Germany has been a particular target because it has had such a strong sense of self-identity and Chancellor Merkel, who has driven the policy of open-door immigration into Germany, is a major asset of the Archon network. As one writer put it ... 'European countries, such as Sweden and Germany, have practically mutilated their own cultures to appease the new arrivals.' That's the plan and the same is happening in the United States under successive administrations. Police in Finland have been ordered by their national police board not to publicly identify migrants as criminal suspects so not to 'stir up anger' as the face of European culture is transformed. The whole thing is being micro-managed to bring this about. Tony Blair's UK government was later exposed for coldly setting out to 'change the country forever' by encouraging mass immigration. Jean-Claude Juncker, unelected (by the people) President of the European Commission, called for mass immigration to be allowed for economic migrants not escaping war even as those who were poured into Europe accompanied by the opportunists. This is not about offering a hand of friendship, but speeding the end to European nation states with individual cultures and histories to absorb everyone into a monoculture European superstate on the way to a monoculture world with monoculture food and monoculture minds. Anything promoted by billionaire financier George Soros is the Archon agenda, and he demanded that Europe accept a million migrants a year indefinitely. I detail in *The Perception Deception* and *Remember Who You Are* how trusts and think-tanks controlled and funded by Soros were behind the manipulation of the fake Arab Spring, which ultimately led to the migrant crisis in Europe that he wants to make even worse. Another tell-tale sign of an agenda project is when critics of what they want are attacked and censored. This has happened with those arguing against mass and unchecked immigration. Mark Zuckerberg who officially runs Facebook was caught on a live microphone at the United Nations discussing with German Chancellor Angela Merkel the censorship of posts opposing mass immigration of migrants into Germany. 'Are you working on this?' Merkel asked him. 'Yeah', he said before the microphone was cut. Anyone questioning the unending influx of migrants into towns and countries that cannot cope is branded racist and xenophobic or censored altogether even though in among genuine refugees are some very unpleasant people (Fig 492). This is how political correctness is used to silence those who are only making valid points about obvious consequences. Political correctness is always black and white with no shades of grey. While Germans were initially welcoming and applauding migrants the cameras were running, but when the mood changed with the effects of the sheer numbers (as it

Figure 492: Genuine refugees should be helped and supported – of course. But don't let anyone think that all migrants are genuine or peace-loving because experience shows that they're not.

Figure 493: Russia invades from the west.

was always going to) suddenly they were racist.

I have been saying this since the 1990s that a third world war is planned between the NATO West and Russia/China and the pieces are being moved into place. The US-instigated coup in Ukraine was part of this strategy and, once again, a fake 'people's revolution' was manipulated to remove a leader aligned with Russia and impose an American puppet in Petro Poroshenko in 2014. Poroshenko was described as 'our Ukraine insider' by US State Department documents in 2006 released by WikiLeaks. His rise to power has opened the door to Western takeover of Ukraine while they had the nerve to claim that Russia was invading (Fig 493). To have Malaysian flight MH17 shot from the sky over Ukraine to provide a pretext to blame it on Russia and Russian separatists was so pathetic in the face of the evidence that desperation is the only word. Still more dead people sacrificed on the altar of pure madness. The installation of Poroshenko and the attempt to start a war with Russia in Ukraine was orchestrated by Victoria Nuland, US Assistant Secretary of State for European and Eurasian Affairs and wife of Robert Kagan – co-founder of ... *The Project for the New Amercian Century.*

Nuland's 'war effort' in Ukraine has floundered at the time of writing but she and her masters won't be giving up. Wars are wonderful ways to change the world by destroying the status quo and installing another. We saw this with the first two global conflicts after which power was in far fewer hands than it was when the first bullet was fired. A third world war is planned to justify a world government and army to 'stop another war', just as global economic catastrophe is planned to justify a world central bank and single cashless global currency. Once you see what the goal is and the methods used to take us there the *El*-lite are an open book.

Police state dictatorship

A police state structure to impose the will of the Archontic *El*-lite on the poverty-stricken masses is so obviously happening. Psychopaths are being systematically

Figure 494: If the tyranny is not faced now it will become ever more extreme.

Figure 495: Private prisons and law enforcement – the shape of things to come unless people come together to stop it.

recruited around the world to don the uniform of law enforcement at the expense of the decent police officers they are replacing (Fig 494). The process is planned to be speeded up through privatisation of law enforcement and prisons. Here you have the reason for private policing and security companies such as G4S securing government contracts no matter what their performance. Volunteer police officers or Community Support Officers in Britain are being given ever more powers from the professional police as part of the dismantling of policing as we have known it until now. Private prisons are negotiating contracts in which governments agree to ensure high occupancy rates (Fig 495). Better have more laws then, eh? How about a ban on breathing? This new police/policed dynamic was captured in Australia when a police officer on the Gold Coast was charged with 'misconduct in public office' for leaking a video to the media exposing how his colleagues brutally beat a 21-year-old while the blood was washed away by a senior sergeant. The officers who did this were not charged, only the one who exposed what they did. Do what you like lads, just don't tell anyone. Doing it is fine, just don't get caught. Psychopaths and software minds are also being recruited into government administration at every level and they and law enforcement personnel are sent on 'training courses' which are nothing more than mind control operations to further integrate the program and instil a sense of us and them with the public. New York police have been told to take pictures of homeless people in the streets and post them

Figure 496: Psychopaths in uniform in the gathering police state.

online to 'shame them'. This is so indicative of the psychopathic, us and them mentality that is now dominating positions of authority (Fig 496).Vital for the planned control structure to work is for law enforcement and government administration to identify with their masters – the less than one percent – and see the population as the enemy. Police brutality even in the so-called civilised countries of the West is now so unspeakable in scale it is closing in on commonplace (Fig 497). Almost every day

Figure 497: The Hunger Games is coming if humanity continues to do nothing.

on Davidicke.com there are more videoed or reported examples of the most horrific levels of psychopathic behaviour by police officers and there are efforts to make filming the police illegal to stem the exposure. FBI Director James Comey said ludicrously that public outrage over police brutality videos might have caused an increase in violent crime – what, by the police? He produced no evidence, of course, because he's an idiot. Police beat, shoot, kill and Taser with virtual impunity in terms of official consequences for their actions. I provide a long list of them in *The Perception Deception* and where but in a psychopathic police state would you find headlines like '14 San Francisco cops gang up on homeless man with one leg and 'armed' with crutches'? Put those words into a search engine and you'll see the video of morons in uniform. How much more extreme and psychopathically outrageous can you get than British police officers holding down an innocent Brazilian electrician, Jean Charles de Menezes, on a London tube train while another officer shot him in the head at point-blank range *seven times*? They said they mistook him for a 'terrorist' when he was just a young guy going about his day. If anyone else had done what those officers did it would be considered cold-blooded murder and a long prison sentence would follow, but the officer who fired the gun was promoted and so was the police commander overseeing the operation, Cressida Dick. She was also made a Commander of the Order of the British Empire (CBE) for 'services to policing' and now works for the British Foreign Office.

I know that most people are bewildered when they see police brutality and murder around the world, especially in the United States, and officers involved facing no consequences. Once you know what is going on and where it is planned to lead the mystery dissolves. Police officers are not disciplined, fired or jailed because they are literally *doing their job*. Oh, no, this is not official yet, but it is the underlying, unspoken theme (Fig 498). The idea is to make the public so terrified of police and other forms of law enforcement that they become subservient, acquiescent and unquestioning. It's already happening. Tasers with their 55,000 volts of electricity are all part of this. They said at first that Tasers would only be used by trained firearms officers when lives were threatened but I wrote at the time that this was only the start of a Totalitarian Tiptoe to widespread and indiscriminate use. This is exactly what has happened. Do what I say or you get the

Figure 498: This is meant to be commonplace in the West as it is now in countries like Egypt.

Figure 499: Give a psychopath a Taser – that will keep them in line.

Figure 500: Giving new meaning to the term 'military police'.

voltage is the message and the long list of people who have died after being Tasered is not a negative for the authorities but a bonus. Death by Taser adds enormously to fear and acquiescence. Tasers are being used ever more frequently on children by these lunatics (Fig 499). Put these words into a search engine to see how far it's already gone: 'Shocking Video Shows How a Schoolyard Quarrel is Dealt With In a Police State.'

Notice how police increasingly look (and behave) like the military. The aim is to have no distinction between the two and to fuse them into a global military enforcement structure with a central command operating at every level of society down into every local community (Fig 500). New York Mayor Bill de Blasio declared his intent for the city's law enforcement to join the United Nations and the US Department of Justice in combatting 'all forms of violent extremism, whether it's based in religious, or racial, or nationalistic or ideological intolerance'. But not if it's the work of the New York police, presumably. New York is also participating in 'The Strong Cities Network' to 'counter a range of domestic and global terror threats'. Usual cover story. The Strong Cities Network is another vehicle for coordination on the way to a global police/military force as cities 'integrate' efforts to 'safeguard citizens' by deleting their freedom. It is being run by the Institute for Strategic Dialogue (ISD) established by British-based Zionist George Weidenfeld (Baron Weidenfeld) to 'counter extremism,' among other things. Your definition of 'extremism', pray? Then we have the 1033 program in the United States through which the Pentagon has been transferring military hardware and weapons worth billions of dollars to local police and SWAT teams (psychopaths mostly) for nothing or next to nothing. Half a billion dollars' worth was transferred in 2014 alone and it's been increasing every year. Hi-tech weaponry handed to county police forces has included *grenade launchers, M-16 assault rifles, armoured vehicles and tanks, helicopters and military robots.* Why do local police forces need grenade launchers and tanks? They don't to do the job they are officially supposed to do, but that is only for public consumption and perception deception (Fig 501). People were so shocked by the military vehicles and equipment used so publicly during the Ferguson riots in Missouri in 2014 and 2015 that police have been ordered to hand back some of the more extreme military vehicles and weaponry, but many police forces are kicking and screaming and this story is not over yet long term. Fundamental militarisation of the police is a march to the very global military state that I have been warning about and is designed to be

Figure 501: Police need tanks for law enforcement?
No, they need them for tyranny enforcement.

Figure 502: Parking ticket patrol United States.

the enforcement arm of the Hunger Games Society (Fig 502). Giving grenade launchers, armoured vehicles and tanks to local police forces may seem crazy, but less so when you realise that the control structure is planned to be from the bottom-up as well as top-down. Law enforcement and government administration is being prepared for the fascist control of local communities to prevent any challenge to the power structure gathering momentum. Many will have noticed how authoritarian local councils and state and county government are becoming and how ever-more government agencies operate with armed enforcement units in the United States. These include the Federal Emergency Management Agency (FEMA), the Bureau of Alcohol, Tobacco and Firearms (ATF) and even the Food and Drug Administration (FDA) and the Environmental Protection Agency (EPA), among a list of others (Fig 503). At the time of writing there are calls for the Transportation Security Administration (TSA) to follow suit on its way to being America's version of the East German state security or Stasi. All these agencies and so many more are merging with the police and military into a global enforcement network to impose the will of the Archon *El*-lite. Fascist police states are founded on almost everything being illegal and we are having a tidal wave of new laws and regulations dictating every facet of life cascading from governments and parliaments of the world in the last few decades. Federal judges in Texas even ruled that having pro-police bumper stickers, air fresheners and religious symbols in a vehicle can be

Figure 503: 'Hey, that hedge is too high.'

considered 'reasonable suspicion of criminal activity' and justify a police traffic stop. Authorities in Ferguson, Missouri, have targeted black people in particular with ... wait for it ... 'pants sagging laws' and 'manner of walking violations'. A British comedy show years ago did a sketch about a racist police officer who was arresting black people for walking on the cracks in the pavement and wearing loud shirts. We have reached a stage of madness where even comedic exaggeration is no longer necessary or possible. During the nine-year British premiership of big-time Archon front man, psychopath and war criminal Tony Blair, 3,000 new criminal offences were created – almost one per day. We also have the ever more mountainous scale of 'international law', regulations and treaties. International laws that everyone on the planet is supposed to obey are essential to a world government dictatorship (Fig 504). At the same time protection and detection of crimes against the public are being constantly reduced to remove 'psychological and physical security' and use crime 'to manage society' in the words of a bloodline insider I will highlight in the next chapter. When law enforcement is perceived to be ineffective, people will be open to the police being run by private Archontic corporations and involvement from the military – Problem-Reaction-Solution. The same scam is being played out to hand Britain's health service to private corporations. We have had the most bizarre policies announced by British police forces that include not investigating burglaries at odd-numbered

Figure 504: The Spider is producing an explosion of laws, taxes and financial demands to attach people to its web.

houses (I kid you not) and stopping all investigation of 'criminal damage, minor assaults and lower-value thefts.' One police chief suggested that people who have been burgled should email the evidence to the police to save them coming round, others have been asked to use Skype and we have had police officers going to crime scenes by bus because there are not enough cars (Fig 505). Reducing funding to police makes it easy to force them into cutting the scale and breadth of operation, which leads to privatisation – the plan from the start.

No place to hide

Engineered terrorist attacks, systematically-promoted fear of terrorist attacks, and fury generated among those whose countries are devastated by Archontic psychopaths all provide calculated excuses to take away basic freedoms to 'protect the public from terrorists' and advance the police state. This is happening on a mega and quickening scale as new technologies are constantly introduced to face-scan, eye-scan, finger-scan, everything-scan, and record every communication through

Figure 505: The System wants crime to frighten people into accepting more laws and deletions of freedom and this is why so much is being ignored and uninvestigated.

Figure 506: The global fascist state is being introduced step-by-step in the hope that people won't notice, but it's now gone so far only an idiot could miss it.

Figure 507: Target the young so they'll accept surveillance and control for life.

Figure 508: Eyes-in-the-sky

email, social media, smartphones and cameras in Smart TVs (the Telescreens envisaged by Orwell in *1984*). Technology is now developed that can read your fingerprints from metres away and the range for such detailed identification is bound to get longer and longer. They represent only a very partial list of technology that forms a global web of individual and mass surveillance through 'hyperconnectivity' (Fig 506). Schools and children are being particularly targeted for cameras and other forms of technology to condition people from a young age to believe that 24/7 surveillance is 'normal' (Fig 507). We now have surveillance drones and so-called 'Intellistreets' where your conversations can be recorded by street lamps and your movements tracked. Boeing has secured a patent from the US Patent and Trademark Office for an autonomous drone system that can be recharged in the air and never has to land. One report described the plan as 'reminiscent of something straight out of the *Matrix* movies' and likened the potential to the 'Sentinels' seeking out those who operated outside of the *Matrix* (Fig 508). The report went on:

A future with pre-programmed automated flying drones which never need to land except for maintenance could result in a dystopian reality for humanity if manipulated by the military industrial complex [it's planned to be]. The use of swarm algorithms in relation to autonomous drone fleets, when taken in concert with substantial advances in AI capabilities, has the potential to make the unimaginable a reality.

While the creation of a more efficient means of charging a fleet of drones seems on the surface a simple way to streamline the technology, the long-term implications for privacy and civil liberties could be devastating. Add to the list of concerns the arming of domestic drones and you have a recipe for disaster. Do we as a society really trust a swarm of autonomous drones,

Figure 509: The walls are closing in.

potentially armed, which in theory could almost never need to leave the sky?

In a Hunger Games Society the sky would be alive with drones of all kinds and sizes for surveillance, law enforcement, Wi-Fi and deliveries (Fig 509). Amazon is pushing through plans to deliver products by drone to the point where 'seeing drones shuttling around the sky will be as normal as seeing mail trucks on the road'. No, they can't even leave the sky alone. They – and Amazon is a significant part of the 'They' – think they have a right to own and dictate everything. Amazon's justification is 'quicker deliveries' – give your freedom away and your right to a clear sky so you can get your parcel a day earlier. I will never use a company delivering in this way and I urge others to do the same. It was announced in 2015 that high-powered lasers are to be fitted to US military drones and the plan is eventually to use them against domestic populations once the fully-fledged police state is in place. Terrorism is only the excuse to get the infrastructure of control operational. Cars are being introduced that can be externally controlled or disabled and they have black boxes to record your speed, driving and where you go. Insurance companies offer cheaper premiums if you fit a drive-tracking 'App' on the Totalitarian Tiptoe to a compulsory black box. New York City launched a 'trial' of Drive Smart technology, an on-board tracking device to tell give them a vehicle's location, speed and fuel use with the excuse that it will 'make the streets safer'. Once again, cheaper insurance comes with the deal. These people are nothing if not predictable. In fact, the idea is that no one will be allowed to drive themselves in a new world of driverless cars controlled by Artificial Intelligence. These are now being developed by the truly, truly Archontic Google or 'Alphabet' as most of the company has rebranded itself to hide its multiple connections to the agenda. Internet giants such as Google, Facebook and Microsoft are creations of the Archon-Reptilian hybrids. They are government surveillance and data-gathering agencies under another name and Facebook uses software to scan private

Figure 510: I personally would not trust this man to tell me the time in a room full of clocks.

communications for what it calls 'key words' that can cause them to alert the authorities. I have had Facebook posts censored, and they use algorithms to negatively affect the traffic to and from pages that challenge the conspiracy. Their carefully contrived image of 'we're your friend', 'it's all cool, man' is only a cover (Fig 510). The Electric Frontier Foundation says of Internet surveillance:

There are almost no restrictions on what can

be collected and how it can be used, provided a company can claim it was motivated by 'cybersecurity purposes'. That means a company like Google, Facebook, Twitter, or AT&T could intercept your emails and text messages, send copies to one another and to the government, and modify those communications or prevent them from reaching their destination if it fits into their plan to stop cybersecurity threats.

Revelations about the extraordinary surveillance reach and capabilities of the United States National Security Agency (NSA) don't even begin to tell the story of the scale of surveillance to which the population is now subjected with so much more to come (Fig 511). Britain's GCHQ surveillance operation is just the same or worse (Fig 512). American Edward Snowden, who worked for a company contracted to the NSA, went public in 2013 to reveal the astonishing scale (to most people) of surveillance on the public by these agencies. He fled to Russia and was charged by the Obama administration under the Espionage Act which had only been used to prosecute government-connected officials three times since 1917 before Obama began to use it as a tool for punishing and silencing those who sought to expose what they know about government and intelligence corruption and the scale already of the Big Brother State. Obama is a complete fraud on so many levels and in so many ways. These spook agencies are monitoring all Internet traffic and the NSA opened a facility in Utah in 2014 at a cost of $1.5 billion to process global information from multiple sources (Fig 513). The Center is said to process 'all forms of communication, including the complete contents of

Figure 511: Headquarters of the US National Security agency (NSA)

Figure 512: GCHQ and its ring of deceit.

Figure 513: The multi-billion dollar 'data center' in Utah to filter and store global communications.

private emails, cell phone calls, and Internet searches, as well as all types of personal data trails – parking receipts, travel itineraries, bookstore purchases, and other digital "pocket litter".' This doesn't mean that everyone is watched every day in what they call 'real time' – though targeted people will be – but they can access any information they want about your movements, statements and activities whenever they like. Snowden revealed that the authorities can switch on your smartphone at a distance and turn on the microphone even when the phone is turned off. This may sound

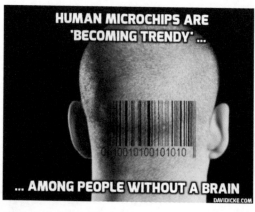

Figure 514: Chips with everything.

outrageous, but what they are planning is far more extreme as I will be explaining. We have traffic cameras recording numberplates that can also be read from satellite. Smart meters in homes and businesses using wireless technology can tell the authorities how many people you have in your home and what rooms they're in – even when you open the fridge. We even have gaming technology like the X-box able to hear conversations and see through clothing. Microchipped people – which I have constantly warned about in the last quarter of a century – are now a reality. The plan is to extend this to everyone by first selling microchips as 'cool', then making it ever more difficult to function and deal with money without one and finally making them compulsory (Fig 514). I'll be expanding on the significance of human microchipping. 'Pre-crime' technology is being used to assess body language and emotions so people can be arrested for doing something they've not yet done and never intended to. Does anyone really believe that this colossal scale of surveillance and control is being done to 'protect the public from terrorism'?? Consider this: how many people actually die from terrorism (especially non-engineered terrorism) compared with road accidents, cancer, heart attacks, 'treatment' by mainstream medicine and accidents in the home? The number killed by terrorism, even including the terrorism carried out by government agencies and blamed on others, is *tiny* by comparison. American civilians who died worldwide in terrorist attacks in 2010: *Eight*. At least 29 died in the same period from being struck by lightning. Heart disease and cancer kill 1.5 million in America each year and one study I saw suggested that research into cancer runs at some $10,000 per American victim while spending to 'combat terrorism' (delete freedom) equates to $500 million per American victim. I am not saying that lives lost to governments and other terrorists don't matter, but clearly the unlimited money assigned worldwide every year to 'fighting terrorism' is not about terrorism at all. They are using the *excuse* of terrorism and perceived terrorism to justify the police state of the Hunger Games Society.

Engineered terror

I have detailed the background in other books to how bogymen terrorist groups like 'Al-Qaeda', ISIS/ISIL/Islamic State and others like Boko Haram in Africa are the creations of the very Archontic Hidden Hand that dictates the political and military response to

Figure 515: Home of terrorism.

Figure 516: ISIS is a Pentagon/CIA creation using the technique of Problem-Reaction-Solution.

Figure 517: I know exactly how you feel, guys.

their terrorism – Problem-Reaction-Solution (Fig 515). Lieutenant General Michael Flynn, former head of the US Defense Intelligence Agency (DIA), told Arab TV station Al Jazeera that the American government made a 'wilful decision' to ignore a classified DIA report presented in August 2012 warning that US policy could lead to the creation of ISIS or Islamic State. The report, made public through the Freedom of Information Act, warned of 'dire consequences' from allowing (US-created) Al-Qaeda to unify the jihadist Sunni Muslim forces in Iraq, Syria and the rest of the Arab world against all other Muslim minorities. It said: 'ISI (the Islamic State of Iraq) could also declare an Islamic State through its union with other terrorist organizations in Iraq and Syria, which will create grave danger in regards of unifying Iraq and the protection of its territory.' Precisely this has happened and the warning was ignored because those in the shadows wanted to justify all that has followed in terms of war in the Middle East and using terrorism to terrify populations at home into conceding their freedoms to 'stop the terrorists' (Fig 516). Turkey is supposed to be in the (fake) United States 'coalition' against ISIS, but began bombing Kurdish fighters who were presenting some of the most effective opposition to ISIS. Images and reports have confirmed American airdrops of weapons and other supplies in ISIS-held areas and hi-tech military hardware was taken over by ISIS which the American military left behind in Iraq. At the same time the American government has blamed it all on Syria's President Assad and even claimed that he was supporting

ISIS while it was taking over much of his country (Fig 517). 'Moderate' (anything but) 'rebels' fighting President Assad in Syria have been armed, funded and trained by the US in the full knowledge that they would be used in support of ISIS as they have been

Figure 518: 'Moderate rebels' in Syria are an extension of the US military.

Figure 519: The most disgusting regime on Planet Earth is part of America's 'anti-terrorist coalition'.

Figure 520: This is the truth they don't want you to know.

(Fig 518). Hundreds of millions of dollars have been spent on 'moderate' terrorists and thugs that have passed on their weapons and allegiance to ISIS while ISIS fighters drive around in fleets of Toyota trucks first supplied to 'moderate rebels' by the US State Department. Saudi Arabia, Qatar, Kuwait and the United Arab Emirates have also been sources and conduits for funding and arming the ISIS nutcases. Fake royalty in these countries are assets of America which

ignores their horrific human rights records, especially in Saudi Arabia where someone is executed – usually by beheading – on average every two days. Even those who were children at the time of the alleged offence have been put to death. Saudi Arabia's US-armed military and air force have caused mass death and destruction in Yemen, and terms like evil don't begin to suffice (Fig 519). Yet in 2015 Saudi Arabia was chosen to head a key panel in the United Nations Human Rights Council and the move was welcomed by the US State Department which claims without laughing to be 'fighting terrorism'. Barack Obama even had the nerve to talk about the 'bankrupt ideology of violent extremists'. He must have been looking in the mirror at the time. The war on terror is a hoax and I have taken it apart in book after book. Many Muslims fall for this as much as anyone else as they fight the 'Holy War' against the Great Satan West – when those behind the Great Satan West are also behind the 'Holy War' which many Muslims support and die for (Fig 520).

The Chessboard

What we have been watching since the inside job that was 9/11 is the United States, Britain and NATO following the demands and ticking off the countries in the September 2000 document from the Project for the New American Century and the list given to General Wesley Clarke immediately after the September 11th 2001 attacks. It hasn't all gone the way they wanted but they've done their best. They started in Afghanistan with the excuse that Osama bin Laden and the Taliban were behind 9/11 when they were not. Bin Laden came from a mega-rich Saudi Arabian construction family who were friends of Father George Bush and had connections with him through the Carlyle Group, a global private equity, asset management and financial services corporation based in Washington DC. Bush was an advisor to the group and the Bin Laden family were investors. They liquidated their holdings in Carlyle a month after 9/11. Bin Laden had been the American poster boy who was brought from Saudi Arabia to Afghanistan to be the public face of the Mujahedeen fighters opposing Soviet Union occupation of the country between 1979 and

Figure 521: Insider and Russia-hater Brzezinski. His books tell you what is planned.

1989. The Soviets had invaded to protect their satellite government in the capital Kabul from being overthrown by the Mujahedeen. Zbigniew Brzezinski, National Security Advisor to President Jimmy Carter from 1977 to 1981, later admitted to a French news magazine that he and the US military had trained and armed the Mujahedeen to attack the Soviet-backed Kabul government, in order to force the Soviets to invade and give them 'their Vietnam' (Fig 521). The plan worked and thanks to Brzezinski and the United States up to 1.5 million Afghan civilians were killed and millions fled the country as refugees to countries like Iran and Pakistan. What has happened since 9/11 is only the continuation of a plan that had been in operation long before under both Republican and Democrat administrations which are one and the same. Osama bin Laden was the good guy when the public was required to support these Afghan atrocities, but when the plan required support for the 2001 US and British invasion of the country Bin Laden became the villain to be demonised. This is not a contradiction as it may appear. Apparent contradiction hides the consistent theme: whatever is necessary to advance our agenda we will do and say. 'Al-Qaeda' means 'the base' or 'database' and the name comes from the CIA database of Mujahedeen fighters that morphed into the largely mythical 'Al-Qaeda' that took the blame for 9/11. 'Al-Qaeda' at the time was only the US created, armed and funded Mujahedeen under another name. The claim that they were a global network was pure fiction to justify the fake war on terror. The involvement of Zbigniew Brzezinski is highly significant. He is a major Archontic insider who was co-founder, with David Rockefeller, of the Trilateral Commission within the Round Table/Bilderberg network and he's very helpful in his own arrogant way in that whatever he says should or will happen is almost always what the plan intends. His 1970 book *Between Two Ages: America's Role in the Technetronic Era* accurately predicted 'the gradual appearance of a more controlled society' which would be 'dominated by an elite, unrestrained by traditional values' and how it would soon be possible 'to assert almost continuous surveillance over every citizen and maintain up-to-date complete files containing even the most personal information about the citizen'. These files he said would be 'subject to instantaneous retrieval by the authorities'. Brzezinski could be so accurate given that he knew what was planned and it's the same with his 1998 book *The Grand Chessboard: American Primacy and Its Geostrategic Imperatives* in which he said that to control the world the United States had to control

Figure 522: Eurasia – what the 'war on terror' is really all about.

Figure 523: All planned a long time ago.

Figure 524: Agenda gofer Tony Blair with the man they later had murdered.

the landmass called Eurasia (Europe across to China and from Russia down to the Middle East). This just happens to be where the post-9/11 wars have been along with other conflicts including the one in Ukraine and where are located the list of countries targeted by The Project for the New American Century (Fig 522). Brzezinski wrote:

... how America 'manages' Eurasia is critical. A power that dominates Eurasia would control two of the world's three most advanced and economically productive regions. A mere glance at the map also suggests that control over Eurasia would almost automatically entail Africa's subordination, rendering the Western Hemisphere and Oceania (Australia) geopolitically peripheral to the world's central continent ...

... About 75 per cent of the world's people live in Eurasia, and most of the world's physical wealth is there as well, both in its enterprises and underneath its soil. Eurasia accounts for about three-fourths of the world's known energy resources ...

This is what the war on terror is really all about – providing the excuse to take over Eurasia and this will mean at some point a conflict between the West and Russia/China if these insane people are allowed to continue. The Project for the New American Century document called for regime change in China. I have been saying since the 1990s that this conflict between the West and Russia/China was the plan and Brzezinski's chessboard is now clear to see (Fig 523). They have used different excuses to pick off countries on their list to hide the common theme. After Afghanistan came Iraq (weapons of mass destruction that didn't exist); Libya (Colonel Gaddhafi is killing his own people); and Syria (President Assad is a tyrant and 'freedom fighters' and 'moderates' need our help). Gaddhafi and Assad were, like Saddam Hussein, considered friends of the West in other times, but, as Osama bin Laden found out, you

Figure 525: The inevitable – and planned – consequence of what has happened in the Middle East.

Figure 526: And so they are.

Figure 527: Libyans must have been so grateful to be bombed and protected from violence.

are a friend or enemy based only on what the agenda requires to happen (Fig 524). Invasions and air attacks in Afghanistan, Iraq and Libya have left those countries with ongoing violence and chaos (the currency of control) and destroyed, and ended the lives of millions of civilians. For those who have survived their every day is another horror amid violence, refugee camps or trekking into Europe (Fig 525). Only psychopaths like Bush, Obama, Blair, Cameron, Hollande, Sarkozy and those who control them from the shadows or do their bidding could possibly contemplate doing what they have and show no remorse whatsoever for the death and suffering that stands at their door; but Archons have no empathy and no remorse and they can lie with every spoken word – they are genetic deceivers (Fig 526). Libya was torn asunder on the grounds that Gaddhafi was using the military against civilians, when in fact he was responding to attacks by well-armed 'moderate rebels' trained and funded by the West especially the United States. Defending government targets from Western-instigated 'moderate rebels' provided the excuse for Obama and Cameron to lead calls for NATO bombing of Libya cities 'to protect the people from violence'. If it wasn't so sick it would be funny (Fig 527). What you see is all a mind game to move the pieces on the chessboard and terms like 'extremists', 'regime' and 'moderates' are mind control labels and triggers that the politicians use to deceive perception, ably supported by the mainstream media that compliantly repeats them. 'Regime' = bad guys; 'moderate = good guys; 'extremist' = anyone resisting the Archontic cabal. Libya was bombed into death and ongoing catastrophe and many of the same 'moderate rebels' were then moved on to Syria to do the same to President Assad. The psychopaths expected him to fall just as fast as Gaddafi, but he didn't and the plan became bogged down as Cameron and Obama failed to win political support for air attacks on the Assad regime. They have tried

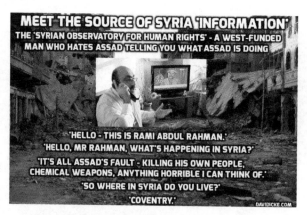

Figure 528: The Comedy Club.

Figure 529: Iran is surrounded by American military bases – who is threatening who?

Figure 530: Obama – spelt F..R..A..U..D.

everything to justify this and that includes having 'rebels' use chemical weapons on civilians which the West tried to blame on Assad, but they have had to settle for bombing in Syria to 'fight ISIS'. Much of the propaganda against Assad quoted by governments and major media with alleged 'supporting' casualty figures have come from the Syrian Observatory for Human Rights. This sounds good, but it consists of one man, Syrian dissident and Assad-hater Rami Abdul Rahman working from his home in Coventry, England (Fig 528). What a credible, unbiased source on which to base public perception. Most of the propaganda against the Muslim world comes from an 'intelligence' organisation called SITE (Search for International Terrorist Entities) run out of Washington DC by vehement Zionist Rita Katz who served in the Israeli army. Her father was executed by Saddam Hussein for allegedly spying for Israel. Katz has somehow beaten 'Islamic terror groups' to circulating their own videos, some purporting to be from Osama bin Laden. Quite a feat, but funding by the United States government and fundamental connections to Israel and its vicious military intelligence arm Mossad must help. IntelCenter, 'a private contractor working for intelligence agencies' based near Washington DC, is another media and government source for anti-Islamic propaganda which has been accused of forging videos of Osama bin Laden and others. Surely not, I'm shocked. IntelCenter is headed by Zionist Ben Venzke. Propaganda to vilify your targets is not a problem and it is so easy to delude a population that overwhelmingly gets its information from Mainstream Everything. Iran has been labelled a threat to the world when it hasn't invaded anyone for hundreds of years while the United States is dubbed the peacemaker when surrounding Iran with its military bases (Fig 529).

When the US and Britain failed to win public and political support to directly bomb Assad they used the excuse of 'fighting ISIS' to bomb in Syrian territory (Fig 530). As I write Syria is being bombed or attacked by the United States, France, Turkey and Israel on behalf of the peace-loving 'West' (Fig 531). Russia also began bombing in support of Assad in late September 2015 with China and Iran also supporting Assad militarily in the country. President Putin said he was intervening to oppose ISIS, but he had Western-backed 'rebels' attacking Assad in his sights as well. Russian bombing has forced back the ISIS advance at the time of writing and exposed the fact that the American 'anti-ISIS coalition' (of terrorists) had not been trying. When Russia announced what targets had

Figure 531: Bringing peace and democracy to the world.

Figure 532: Where most modern wars and terrorism have been hatched and coordinated.

been hit the BBC added the rider 'but these claims have not been independently verified'. Funny how they never say that when they are parroting Western claims without question. All these countries and all this bombing focussed on a country little bigger than North Dakota and with a population of just 22 million (2013). ISIS is only a seamless continuation in a much expanded form of Western armed and funded terrorism going back to the Mujahedeen and further. They are so well armed and funded because arms and money are coming from the United States and other Western sources, plus Saudi Arabia, Qatar and others (Fig 532). ISIS beheading videos have been circulated to instil maximum horror and fear to manipulate people to support the solution. Meanwhile, ISIS funder Saudi Arabia beheads people all the time without a murmur from the 'moral West'. But then we live in a world of inversion in which to quote George Orwell war is peace, freedom is slavery and ignorance is strength. We have America, Britain and other 'lands of freedom' condemning terrorism and violence while being the world's biggest terrorists and purveyors of mass violence. They lecture others about justice while detaining a British citizen Shaker Aamer for 14 years without charge or trial in the fascist prison at Guantanamo Bay (Fig 533). He had committed no crime and was handed over to the Americans by a bounty-hunter. Shaker has been

Figure 534: A mass killer condemns mass killers. Another day in the madhouse.

Figure 533: Shaker Aamer with the children he never saw grow up. Kids denied their father by the evil that runs America. Yes, including you, Obama.

brutally treated, tortured in collusion with British Intelligence and denied sharing the childhood of his children. He had never seen his youngest son Faris who was born after his imprisonment. They, too, have been denied a childhood with their father when all parties are innocent of any crime. The United States government should be in the dock for the sheer evil it has imposed upon this family and other families, and the British government deserves equal condemnation for its weak, half-hearted and pathetic efforts to have one of its own citizens released from the dastardly clutches of a so-called ally. If anyone needed confirmation that the war on terror is a sick joke then this is it. Shaker was finally released in the last days of October in 2015.

Israel is the elephant in the living room here, too. ISIS is claimed to be an extreme Islamic group and where would you expect them to head first once they got their army together, except Israel and the West – the 'infidels'. But their targets have all been secular Islamic countries on The Project for the New American Century list and their fellow Muslims. This has divided the Islamic world even more fiercely between their two factions, Sunni (led by Saudi Arabia) and Shia (Iran). I predicted in earlier books that this would happen and ISIS is merely the vehicle as a Western front to conquer the Middle East (Fig 534). Israel wasn't attacked because Israel is one of the key countries

Figure 535: Israel was created for Jews? No, for and by the Rothschilds. On the right – Mr. Angry.

behind ISIS and is gunning for a war
with Iran, which supports Assad in
Syria. Israel has already committed
air strikes in Syria and it is not
beyond the bounds of possibility that
Israel will eventually be attacked on
purpose to justify the full-blown
involvement of their trigger-happy
military which is one of the best
armed and funded in the world
thanks to the United States. Israel also
has a nuclear arsenal which America
has agreed not to discuss while both
countries were condemning Iran for
being a nuclear threat without having
a nuclear capability. Israel refuses to
sign the Nuclear Non-Proliferation

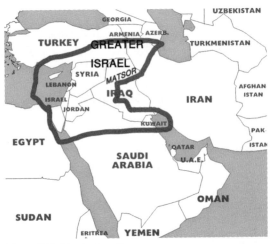

Figure 536: 'Greater Israel'.

Treaty on the grounds that Israel is a law unto itself and to sign the treaty would be to
admit to having a nuclear arsenal. Israel is a fiefdom of the Rothschilds and any regime
in Tel Aviv is a front for the Rothschilds, especially one headed by the Archon-to-his-
finger-tips Benjamin Netanyahu (Fig 535). Interestingly, they have the concept of a
'Greater Israel from the River Nile in Egypt to the River Euphrates in Iraq and this
includes the very land that is at the centre of war and turmoil (Fig 536). Neighbouring
Lebanon is in Israeli gunsights and on the list of the Project for the New American
Century which was entirely made up of Zionists either by birth or affiliation. I expose
the detailed background to Israel in *The Perception Deception*.

World War III?

What is happening in Syria could now go anywhere with the US and West on one side
and Russia, China and Iran on the other all with a presence in the same country.
American Freemasonic hero Albert Pike, the Supreme Pontiff of Universal Freemasonry
in the 19th century and inspiration for the Ku Klux Klan, is best known for the letter
that he is said to have sent in 1871 to Italian bloodline asset and Mafia founder
Giuseppe Mazzini in which he outlined three world wars that would lead to global
control. He used the term 'Illuminati' for the Hidden Hand. The letter is officially
claimed never to have existed but then other documents dismissed as forgeries and
fakes have turned out to tell the history of the world since they came to light. William
James Guy Carr, an English-born Canadian naval officer, revealed what he said was the
content of the letter in his book *Satan, Prince of this World*, written in 1959. The text
accurately described the first two world wars, but it is what was said about the third
that is of most relevance here because that was still to happen when Carr's book was
made public. Pike is alleged to have said about World War III:

> The Third World War must be fomented by taking advantage of the differences caused by the
> 'agentur' of the 'Illuminati' between the political Zionists and the leaders of Islamic World. The
> war must be conducted in such a way that Islam (the Moslem Arabic World) and political

Zionism (the State of Israel) mutually destroy each other. Meanwhile the other nations, once more divided on this issue will be constrained to fight to the point of complete physical, moral, spiritual and economical exhaustion. We shall unleash the Nihilists and the atheists, and we shall provoke a formidable social cataclysm which in all its horror will show clearly to the nations the effect of absolute atheism, origin of savagery and of the most bloody turmoil.

Then everywhere, the citizens, obliged to defend themselves against the world minority of revolutionaries, will exterminate those destroyers of civilization, and the multitude, disillusioned with Christianity, whose deistic spirits will from that moment be without compass or direction, anxious for an ideal, but without knowing where to render its adoration, will receive the true light through the universal manifestation of the pure doctrine of Lucifer [the Demiurge], brought finally out in the public view. This manifestation will result from the general reactionary movement which will follow the destruction of Christianity and atheism, both conquered and exterminated at the same time.

There was no publicly-organised Zionism in 1871 when the letter is said to have been written, but there was by the end of that century and I have been emphasising all these years how the Archon agenda is a blueprint put together long before events and organisations involved even yet exist. Whatever your view or the detailed background to the letter it is clear that Pike's description of the lead-up to World War III fits what is happening in the Middle East. Nihilists or Nihilism certainly describe the brain-dead of ISIS – 'a political belief or action that advocates or commits violence or terrorism without discernible constructive goals'. Footage from inside ISIS-held territories has shown the next generation of Nihilists, with very young children being 'trained' to be ISIS fighters and subjected to classic brainwashing and trauma-based mind control techniques. I have exposed at great length in other books these techniques, which are used in mind control programmes in the United States, Britain and elsewhere. ISIS-captive children are ordered from the earliest age to listen and obey at all times and never question or they will be killed. Young children are forced to watch executions and even carry them out, and they are programmed to believe that the infidels (anyone not with ISIS) must die. If they refuse to conform they can be mutilated and have limbs cut off. These super-psychopaths are Archons incarnate and express the depth of their empathy-deleted depravity. ISIS is the virus spreading and how life is planned to be in the Brave New World in which the state controls children from birth while parents as we know them are no more. I urge Jews to also note the line in Pike's letter about Zionism and Islam mutually destroying each other. You are only pawns in this game like everyone else and you have been played like a stringed instrument all along. Wake up while you still can and let us meet this challenge together. I won't be staying under water 'til it happens, though. Jewish cultural and religious programming is right up there with the fiercest indoctrination on Earth and I feel for them given what they are put through from the earliest age to download their perceptions of self and the world.

'Home grown terrorism'

We now have the next stage of this monumental conspiracy which goes under the scare-them-shitless heading of 'domestic terrorists'. This term is meant to include people like

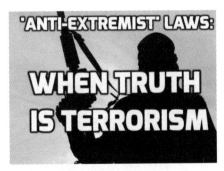

Figure 537: When telling the truth is extremism you know that fascism has arrived.

me exposing the conspiracy and activists of any kind challenging elements of The System (Fig 537). There is now a war against the alternative media. Google, YouTube (Google) and Facebook are all censoring material The System doesn't want people to see. They also manipulate visitor numbers and listings to suppress traffic and, in the case of Google/YouTube, remove advertising revenue from videos challenging their masters. This happened to me with a video exposing what is really happening in Syria which has been watched, at the time of writing, by nearly 350,000 people. Most alternative media researchers and bloggers accept a meagre income to do their work full-time and the little they were getting from Google/YouTube advertising revenue (based on video views) was essential for many to continue. This is why Google/YouTube have been targeting that. These giant corporations and their controllers might seem all-powerful, but their knocking knees and chattering teeth can be seen in the fear they have of exposure and an awakened humanity to the point where they feel the need to undermine people often working out of their bedrooms. For all their arrogance, they are pathetic little boys in short trousers. Another plan is to stop people linking to articles on other websites without permission. This is designed to stop the flow of information on alternative sites that link to mainstream articles while putting them into their true context. I completely understand that it is wrong to cut and paste articles from one site to another and take the traffic for that; but overwhelmingly the alternative media links to the site concerned and cumulatively sends enormous amounts of traffic (and thus advertising revenue) to these mainstream websites. But crushing the alternative media is far more important to these terrified people than even money. No matter, we'll always find a way. The case of Google/YouTube is an example of a recurring sequence and technique of the takeover. Archon corporations first destroy the opposition, secure a monopoly or virtual monopoly, and then dictate who can do what. Amazon is in the process of doing precisely this – not least in terms of books and publishing. It is vital that alternative information sources do not become dependent on these corporations and find distribution and circulation systems of their own. US National Security Agency whistleblower Edward Snowden has even revealed documents that confirm British and American intelligence operations are employing people to post comments on social media, forums and YouTube to discredit researchers and use psychological manipulation on their audience to disrupt and 'promote distrust'. That's how terrified they are of the truth coming out (Fig 538). Labelling people as domestic terrorists to bring them under terrorist censorship laws is the logical next step. Or logical for an imbecile, that is. Teachers in the UK are now required to monitor pupils to report signs of 'radicalisation'. One teachers group was told by police that this could include anti-fracking protestors and 'anti- capitalists'. A peaceful protest against destruction of land and water supplies by fracking is now considered by these lunatics to be 'extremism'. Inversion, inversion, inversion. There is even a psychiatric term which began to be used for some children and is now being used for adults and so-called conspiracy theorists:

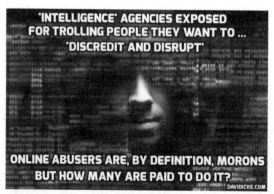

Figure 538: The System is so terrified of the truth getting out that it employs an army of people to post negative comments on the Internet in a bid to discredit what they don't want people to believe. Pathetic.

Figure 539: It sounds extraordinary at first hearing, but check it out.

Figure 540: He's not a hypocrite or anything.

'Oppositional defiant disorder'. If you question and expose authority you must be mad. Jailing dissidents in Soviet psychiatric prisons was justified in just this way. Mass shootings are orchestrated using often drugged and mind-controlled patsies and stooges and are then used to justify making gun ownership illegal and promoting the fear of 'domestic terrorism'. Some like the one at the school in Sandy Hook, Connecticut, in 2012 are complete hoaxes. Never, surely? Yes, *hoaxes*. I know it sounds fantastic and it did to Wolfgang Halbig, a former Florida State Trooper, school principal and nationally recognised expert in school security. He even gave money to the appeal fund, but then he started to investigate, as many others have, only to find that there was no massacre at Sandy Hook (Fig 539). It was contrived using a shooting 'drill' scenario which are happening at schools cross America and it was used to press the case for taking weapons from Americans and terrifying people into accepting more police state. Put 'Wolfgang Halbig, Sandy Hook' into a search engine and YouTube and you will get all the background. Numbers that die in mass shootings (including those by government patsies) are once again fractional compared with other causes. A memo by Greg Ridgeway, deputy director of the National Institute of Justice, a research and development agency of the US Department of Justice, said that fatalities from mass shootings – those with 4 or more victims in a particular place and time – cause on average 35 fatalities per year (though watch that be systematically increased). By contrast, someone is killed on American roads every *13 minutes* with many of them children. A study estimated that the number of people murdered by governments from 1900 to 1999 alone was 262 million (Fig 540). Facts and perspective don't matter to the media as they hype the fear and public response by repeating the government narrative and spin without question and the population is primed to accept the solutions. I think guns are a horrible invention, and I have never fired one except at a coconut in a fairground, but the guns or no guns 'debate' is being promoted as a diversion from the real question which should be asked: Why is there an obsession with disarming the public at the very time that law enforcement is being armed to the teeth – including with military technology? This

Figure 541: Aaron Russo with Nick Rockefeller, a member of the 'master race'. Was he at the back of the queue?

answers itself. Nazis and others have introduced gun control before they launched their fascist takeovers and the plan is for a military coup on the United States and other 'free countries' which will be far easier if the public have no access to weapons of any kind. Military 'exercises' in American towns and cities are a Totalitarian Tiptoe to this takeover. The massive Jade Helm military 'exercise' in Texas in 2015 is an obvious example, which designated Texas as a 'hostile territory' (see domestic terrorism). Jade Helm was justified by the need 'to practice core special warfare tasks, which help protect the nation against foreign enemies.' Utter nonsense. Aaron Russo, the award-winning film-maker who produced *Trading Places* with Eddie Murphy, spoke out against the conspiracy in the last years of his life and revealed what he had been told by the psychopathic Nick Rockefeller who tried to recruit him for the Council on Foreign Relations (Fig 541). The following encapsulates the way the perception deception works. Russo said of Rockefeller:

He's the one who told me eleven months before 9/11 ever happened that there was 'going to be an event' – never told me what the event was going to be – but there was going to be an event, and out of that event we were going to invade Afghanistan to run pipelines from the Caspian Sea; we were going to invade Iraq, to take over the oil fields, establish a base in the Middle East, and make it all part of the New World Order, and we would go after Chavez in Venezuela [who has since conveniently died of cancer which he claimed was externally inflicted].

And sure enough, later, 9/11 happened. And I remember how he was telling me how we were going to see soldiers looking in caves for people in Afghanistan and Pakistan and all these places, and there's going to be this 'war on terror' in which there's no real enemy and the whole thing is a giant hoax, but it's a way for the government to take over the American people.

Not only American people, either, but the world. A whole raft of Presidential Executive Orders are in place in the United States which will allow the President to instigate martial law and take over all property and resources, means of transport, broadcast frequencies, the Internet, sources of energy, food and water, break up families, relocate whoever they choose to wherever they choose and force people to work in any capacity for no pay. Can't be true? Check it out. These powers have been quietly put in place ready for the time when an Archon clone in the White House is told to activate them. The military coup will be launched quite 'legally' because of what is written in executive orders that have come into force through successive presidential signatures without any political vote or public debate. The same will be the case in Britain and elsewhere. What appear to most people to be random events and happenings are not random at all but steps on a long-planned road to Archontic global tyranny.

* See Postscript for updates including the terrorist attack in Paris in November 2015

* The book *Nobody Died At Sandy Hook* has been banned by Amazon. A free download is available at Davidicke.com – put the name of the book into the website search engine

CHAPTER TEN

World Anew (2)

Nothing is easier than self-deceit. For what each man wishes, he also believes to be true
Demosthenes

A world government dictatorship is due to sit atop a massive global structure of control and 24/7 enslavement and most of its major pillars are included in something called Agenda 21 (since updated to Agenda 2030) which is interweaved with themes of 'sustainable development' and 'biodiversity'.

Agenda 21 is being imposed through the United Nations and its centralised control is hidden by the illusion of local initiatives. You have Agenda 21 Seattle, Agenda 21 Oakland, Agenda 21 Isle of Wight and so on, but they're all really Agenda 21 United Nations which is Agenda 21 Hidden Hand. Sustainable development and biodiversity may seem to be laudable goals and that's only to win public support for what are excuses for global tyranny (see 'protecting the public from terrorism'). Agenda 21 was established at the 1992 United Nations Conference on Environment and Development in Rio de Janeiro, Brazil, when Greens and environmentalists from across the world were scammed into supporting a vehicle for total human slavery. Archontic Web insider Maurice Strong, a Canadian oil and business billionaire and frontman operative for the Rothschilds and Rockefellers, hosted the conference. Strong is appropriately a member of the Club of Rome which was established in 1968 as part of the Round Table network that includes the Bilderberg Group, Trilateral Commission, Council on Foreign Relations and Britain's Royal Institute of International Affairs or 'Chatham House'. The Club of Rome instigated the monumental hoax known as human-caused 'global warming', or 'climate change', and provided the excuse for deindustrialisation and the installation of universal serfdom. Red flags should always fly when something continues to be introduced

Global warming stopped 16 years ago, Met Office report reveals

Graph showing tenths of a degree above and below 14C world average

1997 .5°C   2012 .5°C

Figure 542: Temperatures not rising still constitutes global warming to these manipulators, fanatics and idiots.

303

and promoted even after its credibility has been shattered. Every single dire warning about the end-of-the-world consequences of 'global warming' has turned out to be wrong and this is hardly surprising when global temperatures measured from satellite have not risen since 1997/1998 (Fig 542). 'Global warming' became 'climate change' when temperatures plateaued. Yet still we are told that society must be transformed to save the world from climate change with the Pope from the Church of Babylon wheeled out by the Archon PR department to sell the Big Lie (Fig 543). The SUN is virtually ignored by the global warmers, when it is sun activity that drives Earth temperature (Fig 544). Oh, really, do you think the Sun has something do with heat, duh? Scientists at CERN recorded a near perfect synchronisation between Earth temperature and the penetration of cosmic rays into our atmosphere (Fig 545). This information was only released when news that it had been officially suppressed was reported in the media.

Figure 543: Hey, Pope – we need you to get your flock onside.

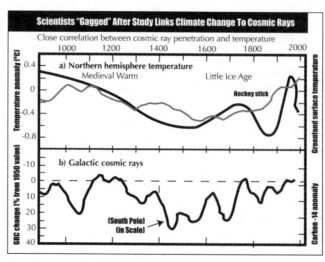

Figure 544: Yep, it's that stupid.

Wait until temperatures begin to rise again in accordance with sun cycles. The Warming Cult will be apoplectic given the hysteria through all the years when they haven't been rising. If they become incandescent we should replace them with a 'green' lightbulb to save the planet. Research the background to global warming front man Al Gore, a mate of Maurice Strong and the serial-lying Clintons with whom he was US Vice-president, and you will see that if he is involved in anything it has to be dodgy (Fig 546). The climate change scam was revealed in the 1991 publication *The First Global Revolution, A Report by the Council of the Club of Rome*

Figure 545: Correlation between cosmic rays and temperature.

Figure 546: Al Gore – High priest of the Climate Cult.

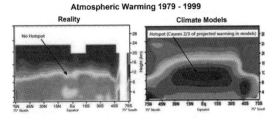

Figure 547: Computer model predictions and what really happens are seriously not the same thing.

which said: 'In searching for a common enemy against whom we can unite, we came up with the idea that pollution, the threat of global warming, water shortages, famine and the like, would fit the bill.' The document's thrust was that 'the real enemy then is humanity itself.' Once you sell a belief in humans as the enemy you can justify actions against the enemy – against human life and freedom. On this is founded the global warming deception. I am not going into all the detail about the breathtaking scale of deceit because I have done so at length in *The Perception Deception* and other books; but I will summarise the plot.

Computer says so

Revelations that have come to light about 'climate scientists' fixing the data to make human-caused global warming appear to be real were not mistakes but necessities to perpetuate the Lie. You also see natural weather-changing phenomena such as the El Nino warming of the Pacific subtly and less subtly manipulated to lump it together with human-caused climate change. End-of-the-world nightmare scenarios delivered as fact were the fantasies of 'computer models' secured by the following sequence: If you put trash in you will get trash out and as long as it's the trash you want then job done. How do you make a computer give you the outcome you desire? You input information that the computer will process to produce what you wish the public to believe (Fig 547). Ignorant, pliable or crooked people have been placed in positions of power and

Figure 548: The wind power hoax.

influence within climate change institutions and staggering amounts of money have been hosed at scientists and pressure groups so long as they support the Lie and press for the transformation of human society that Agenda 21/Agenda 2030 requires. De-industrialisation is the target and insider Maurice Strong said in support of Agenda 21: 'Isn't the only hope for this planet that the industrialised civilisation collapse? Isn't it our responsibility to bring that about?' What his masters want to bring about, more to the point. Strong (who died in 2015) made his billions from industrialisation and both he and Gore have since sought to benefit from projects relating to the global warming lie being true. Human-caused climate change accepted as unquestioned fact is encoded into the curriculum of Archon education and academia and in most of the media with the BBC standing out as one of the most disgraceful examples. Energy bills are increased to 'meet the challenge of climate change' and pay for 'renewables' like the ugly, landscape-destroying windfarms that are both unnecessary and next to useless. Some have been shut down after fortunes have been spent to build them (Fig 548). The

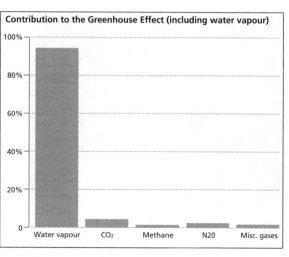

Figure 549: Ban clouds – save the world.

same Hidden Hand behind the global warming Lie is the force behind the systematic suppression of free energy technology, which harnesses electrical and electromagnetic fields of the simulation and turns them into useable warmth and power at next to no ongoing cost. Nikola Tesla who gave us our modern electricity networks was doing just this in the first half of the 20th century and proving that it works. Free energy for the masses means a significantly reduced need to serve The System to pay for warmth and power and the *El*-lite are not having that. Tesla should have been globally acclaimed but died alone and virtually penniless in 1943. 'Global warming' hypocrisy can also be seen in the way those who wish to be self-sufficient in energy and not be connected to the electricity grid are being forced to stay on the grid by the very authorities that bang on about fossil fuels and climate change. One environmentalist in Nova Scotia, Canada, was told that she had to be on the grid 'for her own safety'. Go figure – but then any excuse will do. I am not saying that Earth climate doesn't change because it always has. There are cycles of warming and cooling depending on cycles of sun activity. I am saying that human activity is not the cause and humans in this regard are not the 'enemy'. Carbon dioxide has been demonised (purely to demonise industrialisation) when without it life on Earth would not exist and its contribution to greenhouse gases is so ridiculously small. Plants absorb carbon dioxide and transform it into oxygen. The Greenhouse effect retains heat close to the Earth (without which we would be ice lollies) and is created almost in totality by water vapour and clouds (Fig 549). Why aren't they outlawing condensation? Carbon dioxide (CO_2) is insignificant by comparison and the great majority of that is natural and not caused by human activity. Professor Leslie Woodcock, Emeritus Professor at the University of Manchester, fellow of the Royal Society of Chemical Engineering, a recipient of a Max Plank Society Visiting Fellowship and former NASA researcher, said:

Water is a much more powerful greenhouse gas, and there is 20 times more of it in our atmosphere, around one percent of the atmosphere, whereas CO_2 is only 0.04 percent. Carbon

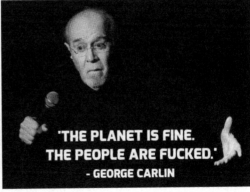

'THE PLANET IS FINE.
THE PEOPLE ARE FUCKED.'
- GEORGE CARLIN

Figure 550: No lunacy is too much for the Climate Cult.

Figure 551: Brilliant.

dioxide has been made out to be some kind of toxic gas, but the truth is that it's the gas of life. We breathe it out, plants breathe it in and it's not caused by us. Global warming is nonsense.

Yet 20 'scientists' wrote to President Obama in 2015 saying that those who argue against the flawed 'science' of human-caused global warming should be prosecuted under laws officially aimed at organised crime syndicates (Fig 550). Then there is Matthew Liao, Clinical Associate Professor of Bioethics at New York University, who wants to genetically engineer babies to be smaller so they are 'more energy efficient'. He suggests that hormone treatment for children could 'close the growth plates'. Liao says that taller people need more cloth in their clothes, wear out shoes and carpets quicker and weigh more on transport systems. These people are all simply too mad to perceive their own madness (Fig 551).

Fixing the figures

A particularly notable exposure of data-fixing scandals revealed efforts to 'lose' the data about the Medieval Warm Period when temperatures were far higher 800 to 1,000 years ago than they are now (Fig 552). Fixers didn't want people to know about this because with no industrialisation at that time how would they explain those temperatures? Only by deleting the Medieval Warm Period could they produce their infamous and fraudulent 'hockey stick' graph which appeared to show temperatures suddenly

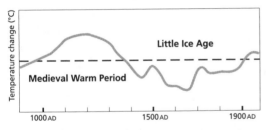

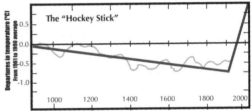

Figure 552: So what caused the warming a thousand years ago? Couldn't have been the Sun could it? No, don't be silly.

Figure 553: The outrageous deletion of the Medieval Warm Period to sell the illusion that temperatures suddenly shot up in recent times.

shooting skywards after industrialisation (Fig 553). Temperature fluctuations before, during and after the Medieval Warm Period correlate with sunspot activity (Fig 554). Temperatures in the warm period were significantly higher than today and yet it was a time of abundance, not catastrophe. It is very cold periods that can be catastrophic for life. The Warm period was followed by what is termed the 'Little Ice Age' when temperatures fell so low that ice fairs were held every winter on a frozen river Thames in London. Scenes from this time are still depicted in Christmas cards (Fig 555). When you hear claims about 'the warmest day [or year] since records began' remember that record keeping often began when we were still emerging from the Little Ice Age and so comparisons are misleading and manipulative. Increasing numbers of scientists have challenged the Lie including Harold Warren Lewis, a respected physicist and former advisor to the Pentagon and US Government, who

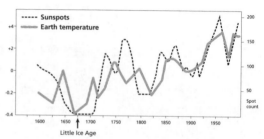

Figure 554: It's the SUN!

Figure 555: Ice fairs on the River Thames during the Little Ice Age.

resigned from the American Physical Society (APS) for its support of 'the global warming scam, with the trillions of dollars driving it that has corrupted so many scientists'. He said that global warming was 'the greatest and most successful pseudoscientific fraud' he has even seen in his career. Lewis said that he had joined APS 65 years earlier when it was 'much smaller, much gentler, and as yet uncorrupted by the money flood'. Now APS had 'accepted the corruption as the norm, and gone along with it'. Philippe Verdier, a household name weatherman with the state-funded France 2 channel, was taken off air after he published a book saying that leading climatologists and political leaders have 'taken the world hostage with misleading climate change data'. He said: 'We are hostage to a planetary scandal over climate change – a war machine whose aim is to keep us in fear.' Verdier decided to write the book when French foreign minister Laurent Fabius called a meeting of the country's main weather presenters and told them to mention 'climate chaos' in their forecasts. 'What's shameful is this pressure placed on us to say that if we don't hurry, it'll be the apocalypse,' he said. Verdier added that 'climate diplomacy' meant leaders seeking to force changes to suit their own political timetables (the timetables of their hidden masters). He said:

Making these revelations in the book, which I absolutely have the right to do, can pose problems for my employer given that the government [which funds France 2] is organising COP [the 2015 climate change conference in Paris]. In fact as soon as you [have] a slightly different discourse on this subject, you are branded a climate sceptic.

It's all manipulated with those scientists and experts that speak out targeted for character assassination. Apparently, unions at France Television called for Verdier to be fired for his views. What a bunch of idiots. David Evans, a full-time or part-time consultant for eleven years to the Australian Greenhouse Office (now the Department of Climate Change), said he had checked the maths in climate models and found that the UN's Intergovernmental Panel on Climate Change has over-estimated future global warming by as much as 10 times (on purpose I say). Evans said:

'Yes, CO2 has an effect, but it's about a fifth or tenth of what the IPCC says it is. CO2 is not driving the climate; it caused less than 20 per cent of the global warming in the last few decades. The model architecture was wrong. Carbon dioxide causes only minor warming. The climate is largely driven by factors outside our control ...

Figure 556: How promotors are bought and dissenters silenced.

... It took me years to figure this out, but finally there is a potential resolution between the insistence of the climate scientists that CO2 is a big problem, and the empirical evidence that it doesn't have nearly as much effect as they say.

Evans said that his discovery 'ought to change the world' but 'the political obstacles are massive'. He had earlier talked about those obstacles and what was actually driving the fraudulent climate change agenda. He said: 'I am a scientist who was on the carbon gravy train, understands the evidence, was once an alarmist, but am now a skeptic.' (Fig 556) He said the whole idea that carbon dioxide is the main cause of warming was based 'on a guess that was proved false by empirical evidence during the 1990s, but the gravy train was too big, with too many jobs, industries, trading profits, political careers, and the possibility of world government and total control riding on the outcome'. Evans said that 'governments and their tame climate scientists now outrageously maintain the fiction that carbon dioxide is a dangerous pollutant', rather than admit they are wrong even when the evidence is overwhelming. The climate change fiction is being dismantled by scientists like these and dogged researchers and in its desperation The System is proposing to make illegal any questioning of the official Lie worldwide. What is described as 'a semi-secret, international conference of top judges' proposed in 2015 to make it illegal for anyone to question alleged scientific evidence for human-caused global warming (which isn't happening). 'Climate Change and the Law' was held in London's Supreme Court and funded by the Supreme Court (taxpayer), UK government (taxpayer) and the United Nations Environment Program (taxpayer). This is how desperate The System is to protect the Lie from public exposure so it can continue to be used as an excuse to transform global society. David Evans highlighted this truth with his point about 'the possibility of world government and total control riding on the outcome'. We are back to Agenda 21 and Agenda 2030 and their fellow hoaxes 'Sustainable Development' and 'Biodiversity'. They are being used to install the world government structure that I have been describing. This is the Agenda 21/Sustainable Development/Biodiversity wishlist as gleaned from their own documents:

- An end to national sovereignty
- State planning and management of all land resources, ecosystems, deserts, forests, mountains, oceans and fresh water; agriculture; rural development; biotechnology; and ensuring 'equity' (equal slavery)
- The State to 'define the role' of business and financial resources
- Abolition of private property (not 'sustainable')
- 'Restructuring' the family unit
- Children raised by the State
- People told what their job will be
- Major restrictions on movement
- Creation of 'human settlement zones'
- Mass resettlement as people are forced to vacate land where they currently live
- Dumbing down education (achieved)
- Mass global depopulation in pursuit of all of the above

These Agenda 21 demands tick all the boxes for the Hunger Games Society even down to children being raised by the state. Mass resettlement as people are forced to vacate their current homes to live in 'human settlement zones' is already happening although not yet officially. Advancing the agenda for as long as possible before anyone knows there is an agenda reduces the chance of serious collective resistance. Agenda 21? Never heard of it, mate. Agenda 2030? What? Do you know the football scores? 'Human settlement zones' are basically human prisons with people removed from rural areas to relocate them in high-rise, densely-packed buildings under 24/7 surveillance and control which reflect the Archon world without creative imagination (Fig 557). Once

Figure 557: The landscape of the planned human settlement zones.

Figure 558: Micro means micro – the two lines on the floor indicate the size of the 'apartments'.

distinctive, even beautiful, towns and cities destroyed by soulless straight-line 'architecture', often high-rise in nature, is also the Archon virus spreading. To give you some idea of what they mean by human settlement zones we had the then Mayor of New York, Michael Bloomberg, announcing in 2012 the building of an initial 165,000 micro-units *30 feet by 10* – bigger than a prison cell, but smaller than a mobile home (Fig 558). This contrasts with billionaire Bloomberg's property portfolio that includes a New York home 40 times larger than the micro units and an estate in Bermuda. But then I did say their aim is a Hunger Games Society. Bloomberg's development is described as only a 'first phase'. Watch for the worldwide promotion of micro-homes because that's the plan. Around 80 percent of present day America would be no-go areas for the population and there's a similar agenda for every country. Anyone who thinks this can't be true should look at the map of the United States demanded by Agenda 21/2030 and the Biodiversity Treaty (Fig 559). The latter is a binding agreement between 200 countries and signed by the United States but not ratified thanks to the efforts of people like ecologist and

Figure 559: The Biodiversity map of the United States with people removed from much of the land.

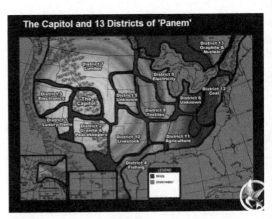

Figure 560: Sectors in The Hunger Games movies portrayed how countries and the world are planned to be divided into isolated specialisations.

ecosystem scientist Dr Michael Coffman who said that he realised in the 1980s and 90s that biodiversity was a front for stealing much of America. Even without ratification the United States government and its agencies have followed its agenda anyway. You can find a colour version of the biodiversity map and see everything clearer by putting the words 'biodiversity map Wildlands Project United States' into an image search engine. The darkest areas are assigned for little or no human use and all except small parts of the lighter areas are for highly regulated human use. This leaves small pockets of unconnected land for the densely-packed human settlement zones. Disconnection between human settlements, except for highly regulated rail travel, blocks a unity of response from the masses. The *Hunger Games* movies portrayed a society in which a tiny *El*-lite lived in the high-tech opulence of the Capitol while served by a population locked away in self-contained 'sectors' (Fig 560). Everyone would be dependent on everyone else and so lose all independence which is where globalisation has taken us (Fig 561). Countries are planned to be 'sectored' into regions with national entities and sovereignty disappearing along with any right (even an illusory one) to choose the

Figure 561: Globalisation is about the centralisation of control and creating dependency for everyone on everyone else to delete self-determination.

government. Code terms used for this by Agenda 21/2030 insiders and gofers are the 'post-industrial' and 'post-democratic' society. European Union bureaucrats have produced a map of Europe sectored into regions with counties deleted and the Rockefeller-funded America 2050 has circulated a regionalised map of the United States (Figs 562 and 563). This divides America into eleven 'megaregions' and includes parts of Canada in a megaregion called 'Cascadia' encompassing Seattle, Portland and Vancouver, British

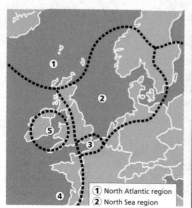

Figure 562: The plan is to divide the European Union into regions with an end to nation states.

Figure 563: The regional map of the United States.

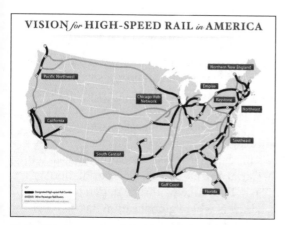

Figure 564: New and upgraded high-speed train routes correspond with the planned US megaregions.

Columbia. Megaregions have megacities (human settlement zones) and the whole plan is referred to as the 'megalopolis' (Greek word for large city or great city). New high-speed railways planned and funded by the United States government connect these very megaregions (Fig 564). High-speed trains are to be the main means of travel in the Hunger Games world. They are easy to police, track and control and they are being built in Britain (HS2) and across Europe for the same reason.

Agenda 2030

The United Nations was created by the Rothschilds and Rockefellers as a Totalitarian Tiptoe to world government and the land on which the UN headquarters stands today was donated by the Rockefellers. They and the Rothschilds were also behind the League of Nations – the failed forerunner to the UN. Anything that comes out of the United Nations in terms of major policy, goals and initiatives is the Archon agenda. No surprise then that Agenda 21

Figure 565: Whatever you want me to say – no problem.

operates through the UN, and in 2015 came its updated and repacked version called Agenda 2030. This is about the date when key pillars of the planned Archon global fascist state are due to be in place with many more to follow. Agenda 2030 – a new universal agenda to use its own description – was agreed at a special UN summit in September 2015 and commits countries to 'a new agenda for sustainable development'. The plan consists of 17 'Sustainable Development Goals' and 169 associated targets and in the words of a European Union statement 'mobilises all countries and stakeholders towards their achievement and affecting domestic policies.' Put this through an Orwellian language translation unit and you get: 'Imposing the will of those who control the UN on everyone in the world.' They used the Pope again to sell this deceit as you would expect as the front man for the Archontic Church of Babylon while other Archontic assets sang from the song sheet to herald the coming of a 'new world' (Fig 565). Well, they were right on that, at least, but it's not the new world they were describing. Most of those who gave their support would have been clueless about what they were buying into. They have no idea what is really going on. The European Union statement said it all without, of course, defining the true context:

> The new 2030 Agenda will re-define how the international community works together on a global commitment to a different kind of future for people and the planet – one which will put the world on a path towards sustainable development. While the Millennium Development Goals (MDGs) targeted developing countries, the 2030 Agenda is the first-ever global agreement setting a universal, comprehensive agenda for action that will affect all countries, including domestic policies.

There you have it – what I have been warning was coming for so long. They are describing the emergence of a global dictatorship to impose policy and action across the whole spectrum of human society by telling national governments what they will and will not do. The EU statement goes on:

> The 17 new Sustainable Development Goals and 169 associated targets balance the three dimensions of sustainable development – environmental, social and economic – covering areas such as poverty, inequality, food security, health, sustainable consumption and production,

growth, employment, infrastructure, sustainable management of natural resources, climate change, as well as gender equality, peaceful and inclusive societies, access to justice and accountable institutions.

Straight off the pages of Agenda 21 and the Archon plan for the world. See how gender equality is in there as part of the political correctness deal? The 'goals' are worded in ways meant to glean a response of 'Well, yes, who could argue with that?' But just as the Archons manipulate from the unseen so their documents manipulate from the unsaid. These are the 17 'goals' and what they really mean:

1) End poverty in all its forms everywhere

(We have no intention of doing this because we are the ones who created the poverty in the first place, but we can use this as the excuse to say that poverty can only be ended by the central control of global finance and a world central bank.)

2) End hunger, achieve food security and improved nutrition and promote sustainable agriculture

(We have no intention of doing this because we are the ones who created the hunger in the first place, but we can use this as the excuse to say that hunger can only be ended by centralised control of global food production and universal use of genetically modified – food supply destroying – GMO.)

3) Ensure healthy lives and promote well-being for all at all ages

(We have no intention of making people healthy – it's the last thing we want – but we can use this as the excuse to impose mandatory vaccination and Big Pharma 'medicine' while banning alternatives methods of healing.)

4) Ensure inclusive and equitable quality education and promote lifelong learning opportunities for all

(We want all children equally programmed through compulsory 'education' and their lives dictated by us through tyrannies that we refer to as 'schools'. We want the programming to be ongoing until they are too old to be any use to use and then we'll have them out of here.)

5) Achieve gender equality and empower all women and girls

(See batshit-crazy radical feminists described earlier.)

6) Ensure availability and sustainable management of water and sanitation for all

(Centralised control of all water sources and supplies – you get water if we say so.)

7) Ensure access to affordable, reliable, sustainable and modern energy for all

(Centralised control of all energy sources and supplies – you get energy if we say so.)

8) Promote sustained, inclusive and sustainable economic growth, full and productive employment and decent work for all

(Centralised control of all economic activity through global government and trade zones, deindustrialisation, and you work where and when we say you work.)

9) Build resilient infrastructure, promote inclusive and sustainable industrialization and foster innovation

(Build human settlement zones and say that industrialisation is unsustainable.)

10) Reduce inequality within and among countries

(Make everyone equality poor – except for us.)

11) Make cities and human settlements inclusive, safe, resilient and sustainable

(Herd people off the land and into intensively-occupied human settlement prison camps made safe by 24/7 surveillance.)

12) Ensure sustainable consumption and production patterns

(Centralised control of all production and distribution.)

13) Take urgent action to combat climate change and its impacts

(Deindustrialisation and clearing people off the land to save the world from something that doesn't exist.)

14) Conserve and sustainably use the oceans, seas and marine resources for sustainable development

(Centralised control of the oceans, seas and everything contained within them.)

15) Protect, restore and promote sustainable use of terrestrial ecosystems, sustainably manage forests, combat desertification, and halt and reverse land degradation and halt biodiversity loss

(Clear people off the land into human settlement zones and ban them from most of the world.)

16) Promote peaceful and inclusive societies for sustainable development, provide access to justice for all and build effective, accountable and inclusive institutions at all levels

(We will keep the peace through a merciless police state, people will be subject to our version of justice and who we say runs the governments.)

17) Strengthen the means of implementation and revitalize the global partnership for sustainable development

(The end of national sovereignty and all power handed to the global centre – us.)

What an example of Archon inversion those 'goals' are and what a dereliction of duty by those who have not done any research into what is really behind them while voting this manifesto of malevolence into place. Human society may be run by evil people but without ill-informed idiots in positions of power, they would not be able to it.

Population cull

A cursory glance at the biodiversity map of the United States makes clear why a major part of Agenda 21/2030 is a dramatic reduction in the human population. Among the methods to achieve this already underway are cumulatively deadly chemical additives in food, drink and water supplies, laboratory-created diseases, vaccines, starvation, an immensely irradiated atmosphere, falling sperm counts and many others (see *The Perception Deception* for detailed background to the population cull). Humans are already toxic time bombs. A draft copy of the United Nations *Global Biodiversity Assessment* demands that the world population be slashed to a billion (it's more than seven billion as I write). Television producer Aaron Russo said that Nick Rockefeller told him in their conversation that the population had to be reduced by at least half. Archontics such as CNN founder Ted Turner and Microsoft billionaire Bill Gates, the vaccine, GMO and death panel promotor, are vocal in their support of such aspirations, as are the *El*-lite in general. Gates's father, William H. Gates Sr., once headed Planned Parenthood, an organisation that started life in the eugenics movement. Gates junior admits that his family once supported the beliefs of the

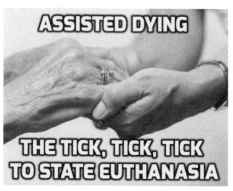

Figure 566: Assisted dying is the thin end of a very big wedge.

Figure 567: Death pathways and assisted dying are all connected to the plan for culling the elderly.

GOVERNMENT POLICY ON THE ELDERLY ANNOUNCED

"WE DON'T GIVE A SHIT"
(ER, THAT'S IT)

DAVIDICKE.CO

Figure 568: You can no longer serve us? We have a pill for you.

infamous eugenicist Thomas Malthus. 'Care pathways' are connected to the cull. People (mostly the elderly) are in effect murdered by doctors by withdrawing medicines and food once the doctor decrees they are going to die. There are many examples of patients taken off these 'pathways' after pressure from loved ones who have gone on to live for years. We are only seeing the foot in the door at the moment (Fig 566). Once people reach an age where they can no longer serve The System the psychopaths want rid of them (Fig 567). Archon agent, mega-psychopath and arch manipulator Henry Kissinger called them and others who don't serve The System 'useless eaters' (Fig 568). Falling sperm counts around the world are also related to the cull, with scientists warning that we will soon reach the point where fertility is compromised. A large Spanish study revealed sperm counts had fallen by up to 38 percent in a decade with toxins being a major factor. Special mention was given to contraceptive drugs peed into the water supply and Bisphenol A or BPA, a hormone disrupter used to coat tin cans and make plastic food containers, bottles, and cash register receipts. None of this is by chance. Why would a Californian biotech company called Epicyte patent a gene in 2001 that makes men and women sterile and infertile if ingested? Why would they *genetically-engineer the gene into corn seeds?* Another 'why' – why would Monsanto and Dupont form a joint venture to buy the Epicyte company to 'commercialise' the Epicyte gene? Epicyte president Mitch Hein said: 'We have a hothouse filled with corn plants that make anti-sperm antibodies' and he suggested this could be a solution to overpopulation. Rima E. Laibow, Medical Director of the Natural Solutions Foundation, pointed out that the Food and Drug Administration (FDA) was blocking the public's right to know if they are eating this gene:

Do you want to know if the food that you're eating contains the Epicyte gene? Sure you do. How about the food that your children are eating, or your grandchildren? Sure you do. But the FDA, the Fraud and Death Administration, has made sure that under current laws it is illegal for you to have that information.

The population cull is being planned in multiple ways, some cumulative, some instant, and we'll be seeing more come to light that we didn't know about now. I guess culling the population will also be easier when all the men are dead, right?

Clearing the land

Agenda 21/2030 and the biodiversity programme require vast numbers of people to be removed from vast areas of land worldwide and this process has begun. American family farmers and rural communities are being driven from the land by economics; destroying employment opportunities, closing rural roads including slip roads from freeways to stop passing trade and the destruction of dams to delete water supplies.

Figure 569: Families forced off the land so the corporations can take over.

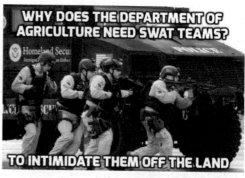

Figure 570: Family farmers and independent growers are increasingly being intimidated by the thugs in uniform.

Strict and outrageously detailed environmental laws which make rural life and small-scale farming impossible are justified by 'climate change'. Zoning laws make livelihoods illegal and land and property is being stolen through eminent domain – what we call in the UK compulsory purchase. The list goes on and on. State officials in California are preparing – as I write – to steal hundreds of farms in the Sacramento-San Joaquin River Delta through eminent domain for a multi-billion-dollar underground water tunnel that was facing considerable opposition. Excuses to clear the land are increasing all the time (Fig 569). Ask any small farmer or smallholder and they will tell you that all these government policies together are a lethal threat to their ability to stay put and economically survive. Many have already gone, leaving ghost towns and villages, and this war on rural life and communities is being waged through the psychopathic administrators and armed SWAT teams of the US Food and Drug Administration (FDA), Environmental Protection Agency (EPA) and Department of Agriculture (USDA) supported by all agencies of government (Fig 570). Their agents assess what needs to happen to make it impossible for a target to remain in rural situ and off they go to make that happen. If the necessary laws don't exist they are either passed at a pace or they do it any way. It comes to something when Congress has to warn Gina McCarthy, head of the Environmental Protection Agency, that she can be jailed for lying to congressional committees – 'with that in mind, we write to request that you correct the record and implore you to be truthful with the American public about matters related to EPA's regulatory agenda going forward.' Extraordinary, and they call themselves 'public servants'. Many people have been ordered to leave their homes and land at gunpoint for no credible reason by state and federal agents when they have nowhere else to go. Native Americans have warned that the government is seizing their lands. Phantom Self lunatics that run Fauquier County in Virginia and 'Zoning Administrator' Kimberly Johnson provide us with a shocking example of the extremes to which this has now gone. Martha Boneta was threatened with thousands of dollars in fines for having a *birthday party* for a ten-year-old on her small farm without getting permission from officials of the madhouse. A birthday party therefore became an 'illegal event'. Martha was prosecuted for selling produce to the public without a licence (permission of the madhouse) because although she had indeed secured a licence for a 'retail farm shop' the inmates decided to change their law, *their* law, and make what had been legal suddenly illegal. In this way they can make anything they choose illegal and then target people with fines and jail. It's fascism – face it. If it quacks, waddles and has webbed feet it's a duck. They want you to believe it's an elephant, but it's a duck, trust me. A supporter of Martha Boneta said: 'It is becoming very difficult for small and mid-size farmers to compete and survive and thrive in this kind of environment'. And *that's the reason for doing it* – Agenda 21/2030. President Obama created a White House Rural Council through a no-debate Presidential Executive Order that involves the Department of Defense and all the agencies required to impose Agenda 21/2030. President Liar said this was to improve life in rural areas when it is part of the campaign to destroy it. The Council has been described as 'the greatest threat to independent and family farming and ranching' and 'a war council ... which has declared its intention to mount an attack on property owners across the nation ... to remove as many as possible from valued agricultural lands across the country'. An Obama Executive Order entitled 'National Defense Resources Preparedness' allows the government to 'legally' seize all land, farms (including livestock and crops), property, industry and business, food production and distribution, health resources, energy and water sources, and transportation, among much else. Control of water even trumps control of food in terms of survival and both are being pursued with a vengeance. The Environmental Protection Agency is claiming rights to all ditches, gullies – even those that appear only temporarily after rain or melting snow – by defining them as 'waterways' under the Clean Water Act. Agenda 21/2030 wants all water controlled by a central water management agency. People are

being jailed for collecting rainwater and a guy called Gary Harrington from Oregon (where the state claims rights to all water) was jailed for 30 days and fined $1,500 for collecting rainwater and snow runoff *on his own land*. Control of food is further centralised every time an independent farm is vacated and a corporation moves in. New laws, including zoning laws, are making it harder and harder for people to grow their own food, and the plan is to eventually ban it altogether. Control food and water and this alone gives you the power to control the people en masse. The US Department of Agriculture has instigated a 'census of agriculture' to register and record every asset of

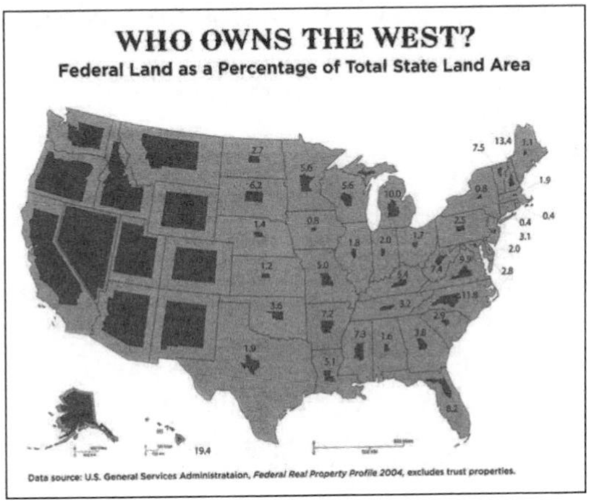

Figure 571: The Federal government and the military already own great swathes of America. Add to this the land owned by state governments and corporations.

American farms and it is all being done with the same aim in mind. Federal Government and the Pentagon already own enormous tracts of the United States and they continually pick off more (Fig 571). Obama has established or expanded 19 so-called 'national monuments' involving more than 260 million acres of land and water in the name of protection but it's really in the name of Agenda 21/2030.

Figure 572: Lynmouth after Operation Cumulus.

THEY CAN'T MANIPULATE THE WEATHER?

THEY'RE ADMITTING IT WHEN IT SUITS THEM

Figure 573: Weather manipulation has been happening for a long time with increasing effectiveness and sophistication.

Changing the weather – whenever they like

Another major way that the population is being driven from the land is through extremes of weather. Oh, but that's the work of 'nature'? No, not always it isn't. Weather modification, or 'geoengineering' has been happening since at least the first half of the 20th century and native peoples were doing it with their rain dances and chants (vibration/frequency) long before that. A BBC radio documentary revealed how death and devastation from a wall of flood water in the coastal village of Lynmouth in North Devon, England, in 1952 was caused by a Royal Air Force weather-manipulation experiment code-named 'Operation Cumulus' and known by participants as 'Operation Witch Doctor' (Fig 572). People in Lynmouth that day told how they smelled sulphur and this can now be explained by the sulphur released by the RAF in a rain-making experiment. What followed was 250 times the normal rainfall which led to 90 million tonnes of water crashing through the village. Dictating the weather is not possible? This was *64 years* ago and the RAF have faced no consequences whatsoever for what they did and still won't officially admit responsibility. The United States used weather manipulation techniques in Vietnam in 1967 when Project Popeye extended the monsoon season for military reasons. Russia openly announced it was spending $4 million on weather manipulation to employ methods originating in the Soviet era to guarantee good weather on two national holidays. US Air Force document AF 2025 Final Report published in 1996 says that weather modification 'offers the war fighter a wide range of possible options to defeat or coerce an adversary' which include artificially created floods, hurricanes, droughts and earthquakes. US aerospace forces [would] 'own the weather' by capitalising on emerging technologies: 'From enhancing friendly operations or disrupting those of the enemy via small-scale tailoring of natural weather patterns to complete dominance of global communications and counterspace control ...' NASA documents from 1966 confirm the United States geoengineering programme with a budget of hundreds of millions of dollars (Fig 573). The Department of Defense, Department of the Interior and a list of universities were among the contributing agencies. Weather is being modified all the time to suit Hidden Hand interests and this includes weather warfare against domestic and foreign populations through drought, flood, monsoon rain, hurricanes and tornadoes. They want you to think it's all 'natural' so they can do what they like without challenge and 'climate change' is a very useful diversion once again. UN treaties ban weather manipulation for malevolent and military reasons, and why would they ban something that wasn't possible? American scientist J. Marvin Herndon wrote in the *International Journal of Environmental Research and Public Health* in 2015:

> The recent calls for open discussion of climate control or geoengineering tend to obscure the fact that the world's military and civilian sectors have modified atmospheric conditions for many decades as has been described by science historian, James R. Fleming. Some of the early weather-modification research resulted in programs like Project Skywater (1961–1988), the U.S. Bureau of Reclamation's effort to engineer 'the rivers of the sky'; the U.S. Army's Operation Ranch Hand (1961–1971), in which the herbicide Agent Orange was an infamous part; and its Project Popeye (1967–1971), used to 'make mud, not war' over the Ho Chi Minh Trail. These few examples of weather-modification, all of them secret at the time they were engaged, show that the weather is in the words of the military, 'a force multiplier'.

Figure 574: HAARP-type technology has multiple uses and among them is weather and earthquake manipulation.

Weather modification entered a new stage with technology that can heat and manipulate the ionosphere in the upper atmosphere (37 miles to 620 miles above the Earth's surface). The same technology can trigger earthquakes. Weather is, like everything, information with a particular frequency. If you technologically generate that frequency you manifest its holographic expression – like weather extremes and earthquakes. The High-Frequency Active Auroral Research Program or HAARP installation in Alaska has been widely exposed by researchers for its impact on weather and earthquakes (Fig 574). HAARP is an atmospheric heater and there are others around the world that operate in much the same way. HAARP-like technology bounces high-power radio waves off the ionosphere and back to earth and has the capability for everything from weather manipulation to earthquakes, mind control and X-raying the Earth for resources. Anyone looking for oil, gas, metals etc. has no chance of competing with Archon corporations which have access to this technology. Countries can be 'regime-changed' or taken over after major earthquakes, and there are examples of significant resource reserves being 'found' once the United States government and military has seized control under the guise of humanitarian support – see Haiti. Small

Figure 575: Extremes of rain are easy to generate.

independent farming has been taken to the brink and beyond by extremes of weather in recent years and most prominently in the United States. In 2011 the US Army Corps of Engineers said they had to blow-up levees to stop the Missouri and Mississippi reaching dangerous levels. This caused catastrophic flooding of farming land over a wide area. Three weeks later the farmers and property owners received letters offering to buy their land on behalf of the government. The letters came from ... the Army Corps of

Figure 576: Extremes of rain or no-rain have the same outcome – getting people off the land.

Engineers (Fig 575). Britain's wettest summer on record in 2012 and the long-term heat and drought in the United States was devastating for farmers and growers either side of the Atlantic (Fig 576). These weather extremes were blamed on the strange behaviour of the jet streams, fast-flowing air currents that largely direct winds from west to east – 'rivers of the sky'. Jet stream stability brings far more predictable weather. They are created by the Earth's rotation and *atmospheric heating* which is what HAARP-like technology is all about. No wonder Bernard Eastlund who wrote and secured HAARP patents for his corporate masters said: 'HAARP can steer the jet stream.' He also spoke of a 'Jet Stream Solar Power Satellite' of which he said:

> ... a dual use satellite which can focus microwave energy into a jet stream to change the direction (steer) of a jet stream. It does this by triggering turbulence in the flowing air which decreases the flow velocity of an edge region of the flow and generating a pressure differential that changes the direction of the bulk air flow.

HAARP technology is based on the work of Nikola Tesla whom Eastlund mentions in the patents. Tesla was able to cause lightning strikes above his laboratory in New York and make the ground shake violently in earthquake-fashion with technology he developed in the first half of the 20th century. What can they do now? Scientists and researchers have spoken of 'the atmospheric jet stream meandering all over North America' causing 'prolonged cold snaps on the East Coast, California drought and frozen mornings in the South'. The global warming cult screams 'climate change' supported by the unquestioning and robotic media as two birds are smacked with the same stone. Climate scientist Jennifer Francis from Rutgers University in New Jersey said: 'Very wavy jet stream patterns have been occurring more often since the 1990s and are now affecting weather around the northern

Figure 577: HAARP technology can move the jet stream.

Figure 578: This is what they are doing.

Figure 579: Fracking is crazy but they keep on pushing for more – always a sign of the agenda at work.

hemisphere.' HAARP came on line in the 1990s (Fig 577). Francis said that the jet stream's unusually large swing to the north had the potential for warmer and drier weather in California, where a prolonged and extreme drought led to water rationing, disappearing lakes and rivers and devastated farmers and food production (Fig 578). All are Archontic goals. Jennifer Francis is not saying this strange behaviour of the jet stream is caused technologically, but I am saying look at the facts. Extremes of weather and droughts serve the agenda to destroy independent farming and force people off the land; weather extremes in recent years have been caused by changes in jet streams; HAARP technology can 'steer the jet stream'; weather-modifying changes to the jet stream have been identified since the 1990s; HAARP began operation in the 1990s. Droughts are easy to generate through weather-manipulation technology and allow for the control and depletion of water supplies. You can't survive without water and so you have to move to where you can find some. This is planned to be to the human settlement zones. Fracking is allowed to continue through the most extreme droughts despite using stunning amounts of water and polluting ground water sources irreparably. The fracking insanity is also connected to the get-them-off-the-land conspiracy (Fig 579). Fracking injects toxic fluid (water mixed with sand and chemicals) at a high pressure to fracture shale rocks and access oil and natural gas. Injected pollution of 600 chemicals that include lead, uranium, mercury, ethylene glycol, radium, methanol, hydrochloric acid and formaldehyde seeps into groundwater. This has led to extraordinary footage of water from taps bursting into flames and horrific levels of pollution (Figs 580 and 581). Each fracking operation involves between one and eight million gallons of water that can never be used again because of its extreme chemical content. The website *dangersoffracking.com* reports the following: 500,000 active gas wells in the United States x 8 million gallons of

Figure 580: Anything goes when something is on the wish list – and fracking is.

water per fracking x 18 times that a well can be fracked = *72 trillion* gallons of water and 360 billion gallons of chemicals required for current gas wells in the United States and this is happening worldwide. Fracking is being promoted by the same governments that sell the myth about human-caused 'global warming' when the fracking process releases the greenhouse gas methane as well as cancer-causing radon gas which add to radiation levels. This would appear to be a contraction, but once again it's not. Promoting the lie about global warming *and* releasing a greenhouse gas through fracking has a common theme – serving the agenda for human control. Corporations like Nestle have also been allowed to take huge amounts of water in California to bottle and sell while the people have been rationed. The reason is the same: Nestle is part of the Web and the people are not.

Figure 581: Suddenly I'm not thirsty.

Weakening the enemy

A hit-list of food, drink, vaccines, multiple forms of toxicity and radiation are being used in the cumulative population cull and to advance the Hunger Games Society by weakening people mentally, emotionally and 'physically'. The Fabian Society in London is a

Figure 582: Genetic mutation for all to see.

strand in the Archontic Web of secret societies and semi-secret groups and appropriately its logo is a wolf in sheep's clothing. George Orwell (*1984*) and Aldous Huxley (*Brave New World)* both had connections to the Fabians. Its name derives from Roman general Quintus Fabius Maximus Verrucosus who was famous for wearing down the enemy over long periods to avoid battles that could be decisive either way. Once the enemy was believed to be weakened enough through hunger, fatigue and others reasons Fabius and his troops walked in unchallenged. This same technique is being deployed against humanity by Archons and their hybrids. They are seeking to weaken the population economically, mentally, emotionally and 'physically' through financial manipulation, stress, chemical shite in food, drink and vaccines, and a toxic, irradiated environment. The idea is to make people exhausted, unfit, obese and suffering from a list of diseases and ailments (including those of the mind) that lead to still more toxicity in the form of pharmaceutical drugs (Fig 582). We can see this happening ever more obviously. Everything people do and everywhere they go involves contact with toxins. Pesticides and herbicides (specifically made to kill) are sprayed on crops in constantly greater quantities and pollute food and water (Fig 583). They seep into groundwater and are peed down the toilet along with endless other residues of chemicals and drugs that also enter drinking water supplies. The US Environmental Protection Agency says that up to

Figure 583: Why would anyone not trust Monsanto?

Figure 584: People are deluged with toxins.

Figure 585: Sugar is highly destructive to health.

70 million pounds of pesticides a year are subject to 'pesticide drift', which damage crops on neighbouring farms and the health of people and wildlife. A study of air quality in Minnesota where vast amounts of pesticides are used on potatoes for the McDonald's 'food' chain found that a third of samples tested positive for one or more pesticides. People clean their homes and wash their dishes and clothes with toxins; cover their skin with them in sunscreen (the real cause of skin cancer); put toxins on their face with makeup; and spray them as deodorant right into lymph glands (with their fundamental relevance to health and disease immunity) under their arms. Toxins are breathed in from traffic fumes and endless other sources including the apparently innocent – but certainly not – talcum powder; and we have the craze of toxic tattoos on the skin, the biggest organ in the body (Fig 584). Sugar is a lethal toxin that people stir into their tea and coffee and it's in almost everything. Soft drink sodas are among the worst (Fig 585). Diabetes is soaring all over the sugar-drenched world (Fig 586). Numbers increased by 60 percent in the UK between 2005 and 2015. Nearly 3.5 million now have the disease in a country of 64 million, and in the United States the figure is 29.1 million or 9.3% of the population. A study published in the *Journal of the American Medical Association* estimated that about half the adult population in the US has either diabetes or is pre-diabetic.

Figure 586: Drinks for children.

Numbers can only go on rising unless things change. Studies have also revealed that high sugar consumption permanently changes some pathways in the brain. Go for a sugar substitute like aspartame (AminoSweet, NutraSweet, E951) and the consequences for the body and brain can be equally bad or worse as I have exposed at length in many books. A mainstream media report in 2015 warned that Diet Coke with artificial sweetener can cause you to store fat (it's 'diet'), rots teeth and affects the body like cocaine within one hour. Artificial sweeteners have been linked in many tests to heart damage, diabetes, high blood pressure and more. From every direction and in almost every facet of life we are being bombarded with poisons and this is not by chance, but by design. Make a note of the chemical and radiation toxins you come into contact with in a single day and you'll what I mean by bombarded. It is also sobering to think that HAARP-type technology can generate electromagnetic fields which amplify the strength of poisons and chemicals in the body by a thousand times to where they become instantly lethal through a process called 'cyclotron resonance'.

I have made clear throughout the book the Archon obsession with genetics and mutation (distortion) of the human body. Radiation is accepted to cause genetic mutation but most people don't realise that the same is true of food, drink, vaccines and other multiple forms of toxicity. They are, in the form that we see them, only holographic reflections of energetic information fields. What we call toxicity or poisons are in their base form deeply distorted energy fields of equally distorted information. They are a *computer virus* and our toxic world is really our Archon virus world. The deluge of toxins and radiation is the virus spreading. Chemically-infested toxic food and drink, toxic vaccinations, cleaning the cooker, washing the pots, splashing on the sun block and spraying under the arms are actually infusing highly-distorted, chaotic and malevolent energy fields – the Archon virus – into the fields of Body-Mind which can absorb and sync with those distortions. Health is balance and 'ease' while ill-health is imbalance and *dis*-ease. When distortions (toxicity, radiation) are absorbed by the fields of Body-Mind this plays out into the hologram and people say 'doctor, I've got a problem'. Whatever is happening in the hologram is a reflection of what is happening in the human energy fields of body and mind. Toxins and radiation can affect people just as much mentally and emotionally as they can 'physically'. The principle is the same as a pipe pouring pollution into a river which then changes its own state to reflect what is coming out of the pipe (Fig 587). Humans are reflecting more and more what is coming out of the fridge, tap, can, bottle, aerosol and the ever-thickening radiation soup that we

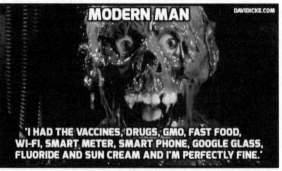

Figure 587: Poisoned world.   **Figure 588:** Never did me any harm.

now live within (Fig 588). All those distortions and more are the *Archon virus*. Every time we use toxins in their endless forms we are dealing with the Archon virus – distortions of the Infinite order of balance and harmony. The 'Demiurge' is a self-aware virus and everything from Archons to vaccines are different manifestations of it.

Frankenstein food

This brings me with as many exclamation marks as I can muster to genetically-modified organisms or GMO (Fig 589). Here we have another expression – a vitally important one – of the Archon virus to distort Body-Mind. GMO is being imposed on humanity by the biotech industry and most notably by one of the corporate centres of undiluted evil – Monsanto. They enjoy enthusiastic support from Archontics like mass vaccine-promotor Bill Gates who funds and supports so many pillars of the agenda. Bill 'GMO is good' Gates owns 500,000 shares in Monsanto worth tens of millions of dollars and promotes Monsanto GMO as the 'solution' to world hunger when it is designed to expand hunger exponentially by destroying alternatives and the very soil itself (Fig 590). Throughout the world this is being shown to be true, with a farmer committing suicide in India about every half an hour in the wake of failing GMO crops and the cost of buying Monsanto poisons essential to GMO. These include

Figure 589: Genetically-modifying humans – and killing them.

Figure 590: It can't be because he doesn't know – not with his track-record of funding agenda projects.

Figure 591: Superweeds courtesy of chemical farming.

the herbicide glyphosate (trade name Roundup) with doses continually increased as its targets mutate into immunity. This has given us the phenomenon of mutated 'superweeds' that are making farming impossible especially for small independent growers (Fig 591). Monsanto GMO 'terminator seeds' last for only one season and then the farmer has to buy them again. Before Monsanto turned up we had the (ironically) *sustainable* method of crops from one season providing seeds at no cost for the next. Peasant farming is being destroyed (as planned) by terminator seeds along with ever-falling harvests from GMO crops when the sell-line is that GMOs will increase yields and save the world from hunger. You couldn't make it up, but there is no need when

328

Phantom Self

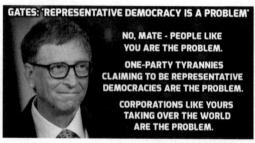

Figure 592: The only way they can sell GMO.

Figure 593: Wherever the agenda goes – Gates seems to be there.

Monsanto and Gates will do it for you (Fig 592). Bill Gates is extraordinary in that what he chooses to fund and promote with his missus through the Bill and Melinda Gates Foundation reads like an Archon hybrid to-do list. This includes GMO, human genetic manipulation, mass vaccination, population reduction, death panels, weather modification, a cashless society, surveillance technology, centralised control of education known as 'Common Core', the list just gets longer all the time. People will have to decide for themselves what his motivations are, but given the crucial role played by his funded projects I am personally not coming down on the side of ignorance (Fig 593). Maybe his mate, Bono, singer with the band U2, could tell us more when he's not also promoting GMO for the developing world. Well, it's worked so well in India didn't it, Bono? Europeans have resisted the imposition of GMO far more than Americans, but the European Union and especially the British government are desperate for widespread use of GMO and will do everything they can to bring this about. The Totalitarian Tiptoe is being feverishly employed while non-GMO, organic and nutritious sources of food are being targeted by EU, British and North American fascist agencies to delete alternatives to Monsanto 'food'. The plan is for only GMO to be available eventually. A report in 2015 highlighted plans to genetically-modify most of the chocolate industry by flooding 70 percent of global cocoa production with GMO cocoa tree hybrids. Funding is being provided by major corporations and the plan is supported by the US Department of Agriculture. Another vehicle for promoting untested genetic engineering to infest the poor and hungry with GMO is UN World Food Program, funded by again governments and corporations. Hidden Hand manipulation uses every trick and invented most of them.

GMO is safe and the Moon is made of cheese

Health effects of GMO have been monumental in the United States and this was as planned as it was inevitable. Vandana Shiva, a prominent opponent of GMO and Monsanto in India, said: 'You cannot insert a gene into a seed and call it life – you haven't created life, instead you have polluted it.' I would strongly advise that you watch a documentary available on YouTube entitled *Genetic Roulette* which reveals that since genetically-modified food became significant in the American diet in the 1990s, cancer, heart disease, autism, obesity, Alzheimer's, Parkinson's and food allergies have soared. Cancer is going through the roof worldwide because this, too, is the Archon virus caused by other expressions of the virus such as mass toxicity, GMO and radiation. Multiple infusions of the virus morph into an even more extreme form – cancer. Pre-pubescent girls as young as *eight* are getting ovarian cancer, which almost never happened before. Americans with three chronic diseases or more have nearly doubled and America's place in the world table for infant mortality has plummeted. A food allergy explosion in the GMO-swamped United States has been caused by the immune system treating GMO 'food' as a threat and going on the attack. GMO crops are manipulated to kill insects by punching holes in their digestive system and it does the same to humans when the food is ingested. Food seeps through a punctured digestive system to where it shouldn't be and the immune system kicks in to record the food as a danger. Next time the same food is eaten the immune system responds to deal with what it now considers a threat. We call this a food allergy. Colossal amounts of Monsanto herbicides and those of other corporations that must be used with GMO are a health and environmental nightmare by themselves with the World Health Organization warning that Roundup (glyphosate) is likely to cause cancer (no 'likely' about it) and a scientist in that

Figure 594: Lower yields, cancer and genetic mutation – put that in your promotion.

Figure 595: Protecting the public.

study said that it definitely mutates DNA (Fig 594). California's Environmental Protection Agency said it will include glyphosate as a cancer-causing chemical. This stuff is sprayed everywhere – on crops, in streets, parks, schools and other public places by people with Roundup backpacks and on quad bikes. Insane is hardly the word but this is what happens when pure evil exploits engineered Phantom Self stupidity and ignorance. In that single sentence I have described the world as it is today and has been for a long time 'past'. Roundup/glyphosate is on the ground, in the soil (and so water sources) and in the air. One commentator rightly said: 'When simply breathing makes you susceptible to glyphosate exposure, we know we are dealing with a problem of unprecedented scale.' But it's *meant* to be, that's the point. Researchers at universities in the United States and Sri Lanka have also found that glyphosate amplifies the damaging effect of heavy metals in the body particular in the kidneys.

I used the Freedom of Information Act to establish that my local council on the Isle of Wight was spraying streets and other public areas with Roundup but when this reached the local newspaper the council defended its actions as 'safe'. This response is typical of public administrators or what I call Mr Bean Phantom Self (Fig 595). Their first, second and only reaction is to defend The System and fuck the consequences for the people including themselves and their own families. If only that were shocking, but it's not anymore. By the way, I say 'local newspaper' here only in the context of what it calls itself. If it really were a newspaper its editor and journalists would have been all over the Roundup story in the interests of protecting their readers from the dangers voiced by the World Health Organization among so many others. Unfortunately, instead of a local newspaper we have the *Isle of Wight County Press*. Tests in Europe have revealed that animals start to suffer liver damage with .0001 parts per million (ppm) of glyphosate in water yet the US Environmental Protection [inversion] Agency says that a figure *7,000 times* higher is safe and GMO corn contains levels *130,000 times* higher even than EPA water 'standards'. When government dark suits tell you that something is within official safety limits don't for goodness sake mistake this for meaning it is safe. This is not what 'safety limits' are there for. Their job is not to protect people but protect Archon corporations so they can legally irradiate and poison the population within the 'law'. Studies have found an increase of up to 70 times in birth defects of children born to workers on farms spraying Roundup/glyphosate and it has been linked to a stream of health problems including Alzheimer's disease; autism; anencephaly (birth defect); multiple cancers; Celiac disease and gluten intolerance; kidney disease; colitis; depression; diabetes; heart disease; hypothyroidism; inflammatory bowel disease (Leaky Gut Syndrome); liver disease; multiple sclerosis; non-Hodgkin lymphoma; Parkinson's disease; pregnancy problems (infertility, miscarriages, stillbirths); obesity; respiratory illnesses. Add to this the growing damage to soil fertility and the infiltration by GMO of non-GMO plants, crops and vegetation and it is clear what a weapon this is for the Archon agenda.

Inverting the bad copy

All that I am describing are examples of the virus spreading to further distort and invert the virtual-reality simulation 'bad copy' of original reality. High-frequency Earth is about life and abundance, joy and freedom, and even the bad copy would have reflected

that before the Archon virus set out to invert everything. The original is about life and the Demiurge/Archon bad copy is now about death. I hear people ask why those in power would want to destroy the planet which they, too, have to live on, but they are only programmed and possessed vehicles of the virus and their control network is therefore a *Death Cult*. Archons are an inversion of life and their world and energy source is founded upon *death*. Pollution, rainforest destruction and eco-system collapse are not happening by accident or ignorance but by Archon demand. Most of those actually doing the damage are ignorant Phantom Selves but

Figure 596: Human world becoming Archon world.

Figure 597: Cutting edge of human evolution?

Figure 598: Destruction of bee colonies will have terrible consequences – which is why they are doing it.

those in the shadows are very consciously orchestrating the transformation of the planet from a state that suits humans to one that suits their masters. Archon manipulation is turning this world into *theirs* and I'll have more to say about this in the next chapter (Fig 596). GMO and lethal herbicide and pesticide poisons are not stupidity in the sense that they can't see what they are doing. They are doing this on purpose to secure the outcome their plan requires. Corporations like Monsanto are still more killing machines. Research what they do and you'll see that it's all about death. We have great swathes of the Earth destroyed by multiple sources of pollution and huge islands of plastic waste floating in the sea. A major study published in the journal *Proceedings of the National Academy of Sciences* predicted that 99 percent of seabird species – and 95 percent of birds within these species – will have plastic in their stomach by 2050 (Fig 597). The implications of environmental destruction for the human food supply are obvious, but then hunger, starvation and control of food availability and distribution are crucial to the population cull and ongoing global dictatorship under which those who survive would live. Bees are an Archon target with their essential contribution to plant life. Their populations have been plummeting through herbicides, pesticides and Archontically-imposed GMO monoculture (while mendaciously promoting 'biodiversity'). These deprive bees of pollen nutrition (Fig 598). This has led to the phenomenon of Colony Collapse Disorder which is destroying hives on a very large scale and bees pollinate about a third of the crops grown worldwide. *Time* magazine reported that the average beekeeper lost 45 percent of colonies in the winter of 2012 alone and there is the additional problem of the sudden and early deaths of queens. Bee expert Dennis vanEngelstorp, an entomologist at the University of Maryland, said: 'We're getting closer and closer to the point where we don't have enough bees in this country to meet pollination demands.' Neonicotinoids, a class of insecticides, are most lethal to bees and virtually all corn grown in America has been sprayed with them. Beekeepers across the United States and Canada have reported big losses when bees have been around corn fields. Steve Ellis, owner of Old Mill Honey Company, said: 'It's time to rethink the use of neonicotinoids and provide farmers with better options that allow all of us to prosper.' But that's not the plan, Steve. Illinois beekeeper Terrence Ingram spent 15 years gathering research into the connection between Monsanto's Roundup and bee deaths, but he arrived home one day to find that he had been raided by the US Department of Agriculture (USDA) and his hives removed and apparently destroyed. He was told they were infected with a disease known as foulbrood. Three weeks later the USDA, which is little more than a subsidiary of Monsanto, said that their evidence for the foulbrood claim had 'disappeared'. By then Ingram had lost his bees, including the hive and queen he was using for his Monsanto Roundup research. Beeologics, one of the leading companies researching the cause of Colony Collapse Disorder, was bought by ... Monsanto. You get the picture.

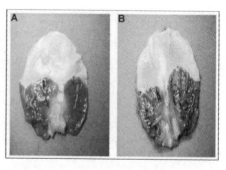

Figure 599: It's worth repeating this image to emphasise the chemical war on human perception.

Entrapping perception

GMO has been introduced to mutate DNA and its ability to receive and transmit information to further squeeze the frequency range it can access. Fluoride is added to drinking water and toothpaste to calcify the 'third-eye' pineal gland and suppress brain function for the same reason (Fig 599). I have been exposing for decades the effect of fluoride on the brain, intellect, teeth and other parts of the body, and in 2015 even the United States government had to bow to a mountain of evidence and lower the recommended level in drinking water. Officials admitted that that Americans had been 'overdosing' on fluoride and the Centers for Disease Control and Prevention (joke) found that some 40 percent of Americans have dental fluorosis from fluoride consumption when the official reason for fluoride in water is protecting teeth (Fig 600). What they didn't mention was the damage to brain function and intellect and the perception isolation caused by calcifying the pineal gland. Dr Arline Geronimus, a visiting scholar at the Stanford Center for Advanced Study, led a team of biologists and social researchers which discovered 'alarming deterioration in DNA of America's urban poor' with 'accelerated aging at the cellular level, and chronic stress linked both to income level and racial-ethnic identity driving this physiological

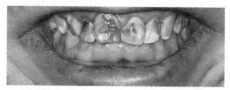

Figure 600: Fluoride is so good for teeth. Must get some.

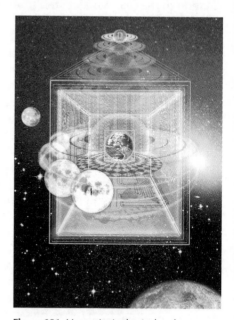

Figure 601: Humanity in the Archon box.

deterioration'. Poor people are also the most likely to be forced into eating the most toxic diet. DNA mutation is driven by vaccines, a rapid increase in radiation and the whole range of toxic sources as well as GMO and together they are used to lock

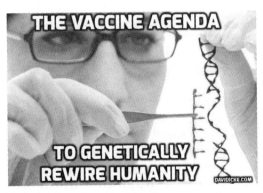

Figure 602: Vaccines are perfect for covert genetic manipulation.

humanity away even more deeply in the Phantom prison of five-sense mind (Fig 601). Vaccines are excellent vehicles for implanting genes and synthetic genes to mutate the human form (Fig 602). This is one reason for so many being inflicted on particularly children and the campaign to make them mandatory. Genetic mutations once instigated can then be passed on to · the next generation which will be from the start weaker in body, mind and immune system and far more likely to suffer from diseases and problems now encoded in their software. These include a greater likelihood of inherited obesity, which is largely caused by the constant inflow of toxins that the body deals with by making fat to store them to protect the body from the cumulatively fatal consequences. Geneticist Dr David Suzuki said:

> Any scientist who tells you they know that GMOs are safe and not to worry about it, is either ignorant or is deliberately lying. Nobody knows what the long-term effect will be.

I agree with the first part, but there is a point being missed. When Suzuki says that nobody knows what the long-term effect of GMO will be this is correct with regard to the great majority; but the Hidden Hand does know what the effect will be and it is coldly working towards that very end. The Spider in the centre of the Archontic Web controls Monsanto, Big Biotech, Big Food, Big Pharma, Big Oil, Big Banking and Big Media as it controls Big Government and agencies of Big Government. The UK *Independent* ran this headline in 2015: 'Gene drive: Scientists sound alarm over supercharged GM organisms which could spread in the wild and cause environmental disasters.' Gene drive is the name for a technique to generate 'supercharged' genetically modified organisms that can spread rapidly in the wild. It is described as like a *virus infection* and this is yet another example of the Archon virus being systematically spread

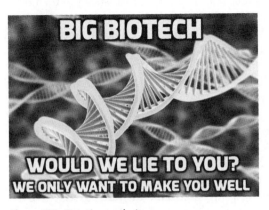

Figure 603: Genetic mendacity.

throughout the simulation or bad copy. Gene drive is being promoted positively as usual as a way to stop mosquito-borne illnesses, eliminate crop pests and 'vermin' species. But David Gurwitz, a geneticist at Tel Aviv University in Israel, said: 'Just as gene drives can make mosquitoes unfit for hosting and spreading the malaria parasite, they could conceivably be designed with gene drives carrying cargo for delivering lethal bacterial toxins to humans.' Technology and techniques with potentially nightmare consequences should never be

Figure 604: Monoculture means catastrophe when those few food varieties are compromised.

left to the lunatic wing of alleged science, but Archontic corporations have almost free reign to impose their evil wares on the population unchallenged by agencies that are supposed to be policing them worldwide. Revolving doors of personnel moving between corporations and government 'protection' agencies have become legendary and so have universities and academics on the Big Biotech payroll to promote and lobby for their products (Fig 603). Toxins, drugs, vaccines and GMO are allowed through to the public with virtually no proper checks. Everyone within Mainstream Everything is ultimately working for the Spider to ensure its will is always obeyed. Some are knowingly part of the plot (the very few) while others do so for money and power, out of fear of not doing what the boss says, and, in the case of the great majority, out of sheer ignorance of what is really going on.

All these facets, elements and subjects are connected to the Archontic hijack of human society by hijacking human perception. GMO and endless sources of toxins and radiation weaken body and mind and mutate DNA into a distorted state to block access to higher frequencies to perceive beyond the Matrix. Destroy independent farming and growing and you hand control of all food production and distribution to Archontic government and corporations and it's the same with water supplies. They know that GMO will eventually contaminate every other plant and crop until there is nothing except GMO. Monsanto and Big Biotech patent their seeds and they own the rights to everything they genetically engineer to dictate who can use them. They plan to own the human body in the same way through patented technology designed to be implanted and other patented genetic manipulation. Abundant non-GMO seed varieties are being deleted and biotech companies are being allowed to patent original seeds they had nothing to do with purely on the basis that they were the first to ask. Global monoculture puts food security under fundamental threat because anything that damages or kills the monoculture crop varieties destroys the human food supply (Fig 604). Check how many varieties of vegetables and fruit have been lost since the turn of the 20th century and you'll be shocked. Rare and older breeds of farm animals are being killed on the orders of government mafia in countries like the United States and Canada until only corporation breeds remain. Targeting small and organic producers of non-GMO food is aimed at removing all alternatives to DNA-mutating GMO in the same way that alternative medicine and nutrition supplements are being targeted to destroy choice. These attacks are not only on the body, but also on the mind. Studies have shown that children on a diet of predominantly processed foods have a lower IQ – just as they do if they consume fluoride in drinking water and toothpaste. By contrast the *Journal of Epidemiology and Community Health* reports: 'Food packed with vitamins and nutrients notably helped boost mental performance as youngsters got older.' Archons and their hybrids want humans to have barely functioning slave minds, not intelligent ones. What we call 'nutrition' is really energy and information. Nutritious foods have bright, powerful energetic fields while GMO and corporate processed foods have virtually none by comparison. Body and mind go into energy deficit on the corporation diet and the cumulative effect is premature aging, illness, death and impaired mental function. Big Biotech's campaign in the United States to stop compulsory labelling of GMO products is to stop people having the right to choose whether to be poisoned and genetically mutated. Monsanto and other biotech companies know that lots of people would not eat GMO if labelling gave them a choice. American states are threatened with lawsuits over GMO labelling by Monsanto who have far bigger pockets, and there is always a colossal difference in spending power between the corporations and the public in GMO labelling referendums. Plus the fact that whether or not these votes are subject to rigging (bet on it) there are always breathtaking numbers of Phantom Self software in labelling referendums who vote against their right to know what is in their food and what it is made from. A more profound definition of insanity I can hardly imagine, but then this is bad copy Earth, land of Phantom Self.

In your face ...

Now, having laid out the multi-faceted and unfolding agenda for human enslavement here's a chap who predicted it all in 1969. Dr Richard Day was a Rockefeller and Zionist insider, professor of paediatrics at Mount Sinai Hospital in New York and executive of the Rockefeller-controlled Planned Parenthood which began in the eugenics movement and was exposed in 2015 for selling foetus body parts. I quoted him earlier about a suppressed cure for cancer that he said was on file at what is now the Rockefeller University. Day knew about much of the plan for humanity gleaned from his big Rockefeller connections in the same way that George Orwell and Aldous Huxley had insider sources for their prophetic *1984* and *Brave New World*. Day was speaking in 1969 to a closed meeting of paediatricians in Pittsburgh, Pennsylvania, less than 20 years after Orwell published his so accurate portrayal of a police state society that is now clearly in the process of happening. The paediatricians were asked not take notes or use recording equipment because (for whatever reason) Day was going to tell them how the world was going to change. One doctor, Lawrence Dunegan, did take notes and before he died in 2004 he gave to a series of radio interviews detailing what Day had described. These were just some of the elements of the new society that Day said, nearly 50 years ago, were planned:

Population control; permission to have babies; redirecting the purpose of sex – sex without reproduction and reproduction without sex; contraception universally available to all; sex education and canalizing [genetic manipulation] of youth as a tool of world government; tax-funded abortion as population control; encouraging anything-goes homosexuality; technology used for reproduction without sex; families to diminish in importance; euthanasia and the 'demise pill'; limiting access to affordable medical care making eliminating the elderly easier; medicine would be tightly controlled; elimination of private doctors; new difficult-to-diagnose and untreatable diseases; suppressing cancer cures as a means of population control; inducing heart attacks as a form of assassination; education as a tool for accelerating the onset of puberty and evolution; blending all religions ... the old religions will have to go; changing the Bible through revisions of key words; restructuring education as a tool of indoctrination; more time in schools, but pupils 'wouldn't learn anything'; controlling who has access to information; schools as the hub of the community; some books would just disappear from the libraries; changing laws to promote moral and social chaos; encouragement of drug abuse to create a jungle atmosphere in cities and towns; promote alcohol abuse; restrictions on travel; the need for more jails, and using hospitals as jails; no more psychological or physical security; crime used to manage society; curtailment of US industrial pre-eminence; shifting populations and economies – tearing out the social roots; sports as a tool of social engineering and change; sex and violence inculcated through entertainment; implanted ID cards – microchips; food control; weather control; knowing how people respond – making them do what you want; falsified scientific research [see 'global warming']; use of terrorism; surveillance, implants, and televisions that watch you; the arrival of the totalitarian global system.

Every facet of what he said in 1969 has happened or is happening because the plan was set in motion a long 'time' ago and has been being rolled out by the century, decade and now by the hour. 'Canalizing of youth as a tool of world government' can be explained by this dictionary definition: 'Canalizing selection – the elimination of genotypes that render developing individuals sensitive to environmental fluctuations.' Current genetic-modifications of the human body are in part preparing for a much-changed energetic and radiation environment and atmosphere for reasons I will come to in the next chapter. One other point to highlight is about 'blending all religions ... 'the old religions will have to go.' They plan a one-world religion to worship the Demiurge and this is what high Freemason Albert Pike was referring to when he said that with the end of traditional religion humanity 'will receive the true light through the universal manifestation of the pure doctrine of Lucifer.' Divide and rule religions have served the Archon plan magnificently, but in its final form they want a 'one' of everything – including religion. Listen to Pope Francis calling for a unity of religions. It sounds good on the surface but what is unsaid is that this is the tiptoe to one religion. The shadow *El*-lite know that religions are worshiping the same Demiurge 'god' and they want to make it open and official when they have secured enough power to do so. Richard Day, incidentally, worked in weather manipulation during the Second World War – you know, the weather manipulation they can't do. Here are some of Day's more detailed comments that relate to subjects I have covered. They are the words of Dr Dunegan describing what Day said and remember this was in 1969:

Politics
He said that very few people really know how government works. Something to the effect that elected officials are influenced in ways that they don't even realise and they carry out plans that have been made for them and they think that they are authors of the plans. But actually they are manipulated in ways they don't understand. He went on to say that most people don't understand how governments operate and even people in high positions in governments, including our own, don't really understand how and where decisions are made.

One of the statements was having to do with change ... the statement was, 'People will have to get used to the idea of change, so used to change, that they'll be expecting change. Nothing will be permanent.' This often came out in the context of a society of ... where people seemed to have no roots or moorings, but would be passively willing to accept change simply because it was all they had ever known. 'Everything has two purposes. One is the ostensible purpose which will make it acceptable to people and second is the real purpose which would further the goals of establishing the new system ...' [He said] 'People are too trusting, people don't ask the right questions.'

Global economic dictatorship
The stated plan was that different parts of the world would be assigned different roles of industry and commerce in a unified global system. The continued pre-eminence of the United States and the relative independence and self-sufficiency of the United States would have to be changed. This was one of the several times that he said in order to create a new structure, you first have to tear down the old, and American industry was one example of that ... this was especially true of our heavy industries that would be cut back while the same industries were being developed in other countries, notably Japan.

And at this point there was some discussion of steel and particularly automobiles – I remember him saying that automobiles would be imported from Japan on an equal footing with our own domestically produced automobiles, but the Japanese product would be better. Things would be made so they would break and fall apart, that is in the United States, so that people would tend to prefer the imported variety and this would give a bit of a boost to foreign competitors. One example was Japanese. In 1969 Japanese automobiles, if they were sold here at all I don't remember, but they certainly weren't very popular. But the idea was you could get a little bit disgusted with your Ford, GM or Chrysler product or whatever because little things like window handles would fall off more and plastic parts would break which had they been made of metal would hold up. Your patriotism about buying American would soon give way to practicality that if you bought Japanese, German or imported that it would last longer and you would be better off. Patriotism would go down the drain then.

The United States was to be kept strong in information, communications, high technology, education and agriculture. The United States was seen as continuing to be sort of the keystone of this global system. But heavy industry would be transported out [exactly what has happened].

Centrally-controlled money
Money would become predominately credit. It was already ... money is primarily a credit thing but exchange of money would be not cash or palpable things but electronic credit signal. People would carry money only in very small amounts for things like chewing gum and candy bars. Just pocket sorts of things. Any purchase of any significant amount would be done electronically. Earnings would be electronically entered into your account. It would be a single banking system. May have the appearance of being more than one but ultimately and basically it would be one single banking system, so that when you got paid your pay would be entered for you into your account balance and then when you purchased anything at the point of purchase it would be deducted from your account balance and you would actually carry nothing with you.

Also computer records can be kept on whatever it was you purchased so that if you were purchasing too much of any particular item and some official wanted to know what you were doing with your money they could go back and review your purchases and determine what you were buying. There was a statement that any purchase of significant size like an automobile, bicycle, a refrigerator, a radio or television or whatever might have some sort of identification on it so it could be traced, so that very quickly anything which was either given away or stolen – whatever – authorities would be able to establish who purchased it and when. Computers would allow this to happen.

The ability to save would be greatly curtailed. People would just not be able to save any considerable degree of wealth. There was some statement of recognition that wealth represents power and wealth in the hands of a lot of people is not good for the people in charge so if you save too much you might be taxed. The more you save the higher rate of tax on your savings so your savings really could never get very far [see negative interest rates].

And also if you began to show a pattern of saving too much you might have your pay cut. We would say, 'Well, your saving instead of spending. You really don't need all that money.' ... The idea being to prevent people from accumulating any wealth which might have long range disruptive influence on the system. People would be encouraged to use credit to borrow and then also be encouraged to renege on their debt so they would destroy their own credit. The idea here is that, again, if you're too stupid to handle credit wisely, this gives the authorities the opportunity to come down hard on you once you've shot your credit.

Electronic payments initially would all be based on different kinds of credit cards ... these were already in use in 1969 to some extent. Not as much as now. But people would have credit cards with the electronic strip on it and once they got used to that then it would be pointed out the advantage of having all of that combined into a single credit card, serving a single monetary system and then they won't have to carry around all that plastic.

Microchipped people
So the next step would be the single card and then the next step would be to replace the single card with a skin implant. The single card [smartphone] *could be lost or stolen, give rise to problems; could be exchanged with somebody else to confuse identity. The skin implant on the other hand would be not losable or counterfeitable or transferrable to another person so you and your accounts would be identified without any possibility of error. And the skin implants would have to be put some place that would be convenient to the skin; for example your right hand or your forehead* [right on the third eye] *... There was some mention, also, of implants that would lend themselves to surveillance by providing radio signals. This could be under the skin or a dental implant ... put in like a filling so that either fugitives or possibly other citizens could be identified by a certain frequency from his personal transmitter and could be located at any time or any place by any authority who wanted to find him. This would be particularly useful for somebody who broke out of prison. There was more discussion of personal surveillance* [just look around at what is happening today].

Imposition of world system through nuclear war
If there were too many people in the right places who resisted this [world dictatorship], *there might be a need to use one or two – possibly more – nuclear weapons. As it was put, this would be possibly needed to convince people that 'We mean business'. That was followed by the statement that, 'By the time one or two of those went off then everybody – even the most*

reluctant – would yield.' He said something about 'this negotiated peace would be very convincing,' as kind of in a framework or in a context that the whole thing was rehearsed but nobody would know it. People hearing about it would be convinced that it was a genuine negotiation between hostile enemies who finally had come to the realisation that peace was better than war [This syncs with the Albert Pike letter in 1871 about three world wars and what would happen after the third one].

Engineered terrorism

There was a discussion of terrorism. Terrorism would be used widely in Europe and in other parts of the world. Terrorism at that time was thought would not be necessary in the United States. It could become necessary in the United States if the United States did not move rapidly enough into accepting the system [hence 9/11 to speed everything along]. *But at least in the foreseeable future it was not planned ... Maybe terrorism would not be required here, but the implication being that it would be indeed used if it was necessary. Along with this came a bit of a scolding that Americans had had it too good anyway and just a little bit of terrorism would help convince Americans that the world is indeed a dangerous place ... or can be if we don't relinquish control to the proper authorities.*

Population control and killing the elderly

Everybody has a right to live only so long. The old are no longer useful. They become a burden. You should be ready to accept death. Most people are. An arbitrary age limit could be established. After all, you have a right to only so many steak dinners, so many orgasms, and so many good pleasures in life. And after you have had enough of them and you're no longer productive, working, and contributing, then you should be ready to step aside for the next generation. Some things that would help people realise that they had lived long enough, he mentioned several of these. I don't remember them all – here are a few: Use of very pale printing ink on forms that people ... are necessary to fill out, so that older people wouldn't be able to read the pale ink as easily and would need to go to younger people for help. Automobile traffic patterns – there would be more high-speed traffic lanes ... traffic patterns that ... older people with their slower reflexes would have trouble dealing with and thus, lose some of their independence.

A big item ... was elaborated at some length was that the cost of medical care would be made burdensomely high. Medical care would be connected very closely with one's work but also would be made very, very high in cost so that it would simply be unavailable to people beyond a certain time. And unless they had a remarkably rich, supporting family, they would just have to do without care. And the idea was that if everybody says, 'Enough! What a burden it is on the young to try to maintain the old people,' then the young would become agreeable to helping mom and dad along the way, provided this was done humanely and with dignity. And then the example was there could be like a nice, farewell party, a real celebration. Mom and dad had done a good job. And then after the party's over they take the 'demise pill'.

People won't be allowed to have babies just because they want to or because they are careless. Most families would be limited to two. Some people would be allowed only one, and the outstanding person or persons might be selected and allowed to have three. But most people would [be] allowed to have only two babies.

Education

... Pressures of the accelerated academic program, the accelerated demands where kids would feel they had to be part of something – one or another athletic club or some school activity – these pressures he recognised would cause some students to burn out. He said 'the smartest ones will learn how to cope with pressures and to survive. There will be some help available to students in handling stress, but the unfit won't be able to make it. They will then move on to other things.' In this connection and later on in the connection with drug abuse and alcohol abuse he indicated that psychiatric services to help would be increased dramatically. In all the pushing for achievement, it was recognised that many people would need help, and the people worth keeping around would be able to accept and benefit from that help, and still be super achievers. Those who could not would fall by the wayside and therefore were sort of dispensable – 'expendable' I guess is the word I want.

Education would be lifelong. Adults would be going to school. There'll always be new information that adults must have to keep up. When you can't keep up anymore, you're too old. This was another way of letting older people know that the time had come for them to move on and take the demise pill. If you got too tired to keep up with your education, or you got too old to learn new information, then this was a signal – you begin to prepare to get ready to step aside.

He was already talking about computers in education, and at that time he said anybody who wanted computer access, or access to books that were not directly related to their field of study would have to have a very good reason for so doing. Otherwise, access would be denied [books like the one you are reading would be banned].

Constant change

Nothing is permanent. Streets would be rerouted, renamed. Areas you had not seen in a while would become unfamiliar. Among other things, this would contribute to older people feeling that it was time to move on, they feel they couldn't even keep up with the changes in areas that were once familiar. Buildings would be allowed to stand empty and deteriorate, and streets would be allowed to deteriorate in certain localities. The purpose of this was to provide the jungle, the depressed atmosphere for the unfit. Somewhere in this same connection he mentioned that buildings and bridges would be made so that they would collapse after a while, there would be more accidents involving airplanes and railroads and automobiles. All of this to contribute to the feeling of insecurity, that nothing was safe.

Portrayal of violence (movies/video games)

Violence would be made more graphic. This was intended to desensitise people to violence. There might need to be a time when people would witness real violence and be a part of it. Later on it will become clear where this is headed. So there would be more realistic violence in entertainment which would make it easier for people to adjust. People's attitudes toward death would change. People would not be so fearful of it but more accepting of it, and they would not be so aghast at the sight of dead people or injured people. We don't need to have a genteel population paralysed by what they might see. People would just learn to say, well I don't want that to happen to me. This was the first statement suggesting that the plan includes numerous human casualties which the survivors would see.

Food control

Food supplies would come under tight control. If population growth didn't slow down, food shortages could be created in a hurry and people would realise the dangers of overpopulation. Ultimately, whether the population slows down or not the food supply is to be brought under centralised control so that people would have enough to be well-nourished but they would not have enough to support any fugitive from the new system. In other words, if you had a friend or relative who didn't sign on, and growing one's own food would be outlawed. This would be done under some sort of pretext. In the beginning I mentioned there were two purposes for everything – one the ostensible purpose and one the real purpose, and the ostensible purpose here would be that growing your own vegetables was unsafe, it would spread disease or something like that. So the acceptable idea was to protect the consumer but the real idea was to limit the food supply and growing your own food would be illegal. And if you persist in illegal activities like growing your own food, then you're a criminal [this is now happening – see The Perception Deception].

Weather control

There was a mention then of weather. This was another really striking statement. He said, 'We can or soon will be able to control the weather.' He said, 'I'm not merely referring to dropping iodide crystals into the clouds to precipitate rain that's already there, but REAL control.' And weather was seen as a weapon of war, a weapon of influencing public policy. It could make rain or withhold rain in order to influence certain areas and bring them under your control. There were two sides to this that were rather striking. He said, 'On the one hand you can make drought during the growing season so that nothing will grow, and on the other hand you can make for very heavy rains during harvest season so the fields are too muddy to bring in the harvest, and indeed one might be able to do both.' There was no statement how this would be done. It was stated that either it was already possible or very, very close to being possible [in 1969].

Mass mind control

Somewhere in the presentation he made two statements that I want to insert at this time. I don't remember just where they were made, but they're valid in terms of the general overall view. One statement: 'People can carry in their minds and act upon two contradictory ideas at one time, provided that these two contradictory ideas are kept far enough apart.' And the other statement is, 'You can know pretty well how rational people are going to respond to certain circumstances or to certain information that they encounter. So, to determine the response you want you need only control the kind of data or information that they're presented or the kinds of circumstance that they're in; and being rational people they'll do what you want them to do. They may not fully understand what they're doing or why.'

Telescreens

One more thing was said, 'You'll be watching television and somebody will be watching you at the same time at a central monitoring station.' Television sets would have a device to enable this [smart TVs]. The TV set would not have to be on in order for this to be operative. Also, the television set can be used to monitor what you are watching. People can tell what you're watching on TV and how you're reacting to what you're watching. And you would not know that you were being watched while you were watching your television. How would we get people to accept these things into their homes? Well, people would buy them when they buy their own television. They won't know that they're on there at first. This was described by being what we *now know as Cable TV to replace the antenna TV* [the rush to digital TV is part of this]. *When you buy a TV set this monitor would just be part of the set and most people would not have enough knowledge to know it was there in the beginning. And then the cable would be the means of carrying the surveillance message to the monitor. By the time people found out that this monitoring was going on, they would also be very dependent upon television for a number of things. Just the way people are dependent upon the telephone today.*

One thing the television would be used for would be purchases. You wouldn't have to leave your home to purchase. You just turn on your TV and there would be a way of interacting with your television channel to the store that you wanted to purchase. And you could flip the switch from place to place to choose a refrigerator or clothing. This would be both convenient, but it would also make you dependent on your television so the built-in monitor would be something you could not do without. There was some discussion of audio monitors, too, just in case the authorities wanted to hear what was going on in rooms other than where the television monitor was, and in regard to this the statement was made, 'Any wire that went into your house, for example your telephone wire, could be used this way.

Day was talking here about the World Wide Web which wasn't 'invented' officially until 1989 by English scientist Tim Berners-Lee who 'wrote the first web browser in 1990 while employed at CERN in Switzerland.' Oh, really? So how did Richard Day know about it in 1969? I said earlier that 'new' technology is sitting in the wings all along waiting for the right time to introduce it. How did Day know about Telescreens or smart TVs many decades before they were 'invented'? How did Orwell?

Human settlement zones
Privately owned housing would become a thing of the past. The cost of housing and financing housing would gradually be made so high that most people couldn't afford it. People who already owned their houses would be allowed to keep them but as years go by it would be more and more difficult for young people to buy a house. Young people would more and more become renters, particularly in apartments or condominiums. More and more unsold houses would stand vacant. People just couldn't buy them. But the cost of housing would not come down. You'd right away think, well the vacant house, the price would come down, the people would buy it. But there was some statement to the effect that the price would be held high even though there were many available so that free market places would not operate. People would not be able to buy these and gradually more and more of the population would be forced into small apartments. Small apartments which would not accommodate very many children [the micro apartments I've been highlighting].

Then as the number of real home-owners diminished they would become a minority. There would be no sympathy for them from the majority who dwelled in the apartments and then these homes could be taken by increased taxes or other regulations that would be detrimental to home ownership and would be acceptable to the majority [divide and rule]. *Ultimately, people would be assigned where they would live and it would be common to have non-family members living with you. This by way of your not knowing just how far you could trust anybody. This would all be under the control of a central housing authority. Have this in mind ... when they ask, 'How many bedrooms in your house? How many bathrooms in your house? Do you have a finished game room?' This information is personal and is of no national interest to government under our existing Constitution. But you'll be asked those questions and decide how you want to respond to them* [happening].

Disappearance of dissidents
When the new system takes over people will be expected to sign allegiance to it, indicating that they don't have any reservations or holding back to the old system. 'There just won't be any room', he said, 'for people who won't go along. We can't have such people cluttering up the place so such people would be taken to special places,' and here I don't remember the exact words, but the inference I drew was that at these special places where they were taken, then they would not live very long. He may have said something like, 'disposed of humanely,' but I don't remember very precisely ... just the impression the system was not going to support them when they would not go along with the system. That would leave death as the only alternative. Somewhere in this vein he said there would not be any martyrs. When I first heard this I thought it meant the people would not be killed, but as the presentation developed what he meant was they would not be killed in such a way or disposed of in such a way that they could serve as inspiration to other people the way martyrs do. Rather he said something like this ... 'People will just disappear.'

The bringing in of the new system he said probably would occur on a weekend in the winter. Everything would shut down on Friday evening and Monday morning when everybody wakened there would be an announcement that the New System was in place. During the process in getting the United States ready for these changes everybody would be busier with less leisure time and less opportunity to really look about and see what was going on around them.

Richard Day also said that there would be mass movements and migrations of people without roots in their new locations because 'traditions are easier to change in a place where there are a lot of transplanted people, as compared to trying to change traditions in a place where people grew up and had an extended family, where they had roots.' Remember what I said earlier about one of the prime reasons for orchestrating the mass migrations from the Middle East and Africa into Europe with the targeting especially of Germany which has such a sense of its own traditions and culture. Chancellor Merkel knows exactly what she is doing and why. Day even said in 1969 that soccer would be promoted in the United States because it was an international game and would help to break down a sense of a unique culture underpinned by baseball and American football. I have been trying to show people for a so long that almost everything is manipulated and part of the plan. All that I have described in this chapter – in fact, chapter after chapter – is to advance the total enslavement of the human race which I have been warning about for a quarter of a century amid constant ridicule and abuse. People might not want to believe what I am saying, but that doesn't stop it being true.

Here and no further
These are some themes to watch for and challenge at every opportunity to slow down the march of tyranny until we delete it altogether: Anything related to changes listed by Richard Day; anything that forces people into cities and denies access to rural lands; anything that makes survival harder for small farmers and businesses to the benefit of corporations; attacks on independent food growing and alternatives to GMO; attacks on

Figure 605: Stand up now or take the consequences.

alternative forms of medicine, non-drug health treatment and supplements; anything forced upon us without choice – like mandatory vaccinations; anything that prevents free movement, makes travel more difficult or proposes new high-speed railways between centres of major population without justification or through a sudden change of policy as in the United States; anything that advances the police state and increases surveillance; any further centralisation of power and decision-making; attacks on the family unit, parental rights and increased control of the state and schools (the state) over the upbringing of children – including those removed from loving parents and put into 'care' or forced adoption for spurious reasons; anything that makes it easier for doctors to legally kill people either directly or by removing what they need to survive; government policies that target the poor and reward the rich. Be aware of anything that relates to centralised collectivism under terms like 'common' as in common core, common goals and common purpose. The latter is the name of a training organisation preparing 'leaders' for the post-industrial, post-democratic society. 'Consensus' is another version of 'common' with constant attempts to manipulate the public 'consensus' to agree to follow the Archon agenda without even realising there is one. Political 'consensus' is almost complete with political parties differing largely only by rhetoric. Manipulating and imposing the consensus also involves marginalising and vilifying anyone who questions and challenges the consensus – oppose all efforts to suppress and destroy the alternative media. When world events happen always ask: 'Who benefits?' And who benefits from people believing the official story of what has happened? I include in this extremes of weather and earthquakes for the reasons I have explained. We stand up and look this in the eye or we run. But there is nowhere to run, so we better get on with it (Fig 605).

In a sane world the mainstream media would be exposing and warning about all this, but instead they condemn and ridicule those who do – the inversion again. They apply the label 'conspiracy theorist' to discredit anyone exposing the truth when the very terms conspiracy theorist or theory were invented by the CIA to discredit those exposing the lies surrounding the assassination of President Kennedy and others in the 1960s. Most journalists – not all, but most – really are pathetic and a disgrace not only to the public in general but to their own families who will have to live in the world they are playing their vital role in making happen. There are executives and journalists who are knowingly serving the Archon agenda but most do so out of ignorance and fall for the hoax that their 'good education' has made them informed and intelligent. Anyone who believes what they are told by the mainstream media should listen to the experiences of German journalist and editor Udo Ulfkotte who has revealed how he worked for governments and intelligence agencies and wrote stories that suited them. He says the mainstream media is controlled by the authorities through intimidation and bribery. If you go to Davidicke.com and put these words into the search facility you can see his highly recommended interview ... 'Reporter Spills the Beans and Admits All the News is Fake'. New laws and methods are being introduced to censor and even jail those journalists who are willing at least to expose and question some elements of The System. The decision by European Union judges (dictators) to give people the right to have information about them deleted from search engine listings like Google is a scam by the *El*-lite and their toadies to hide their own background from public knowledge. This so-called 'right to be forgotten' is no more than an example of George Orwell's 'Memory Hole' in which the Ministry of Truth (inversion) re-wrote historical documents to match the *ever-changing* state propaganda. Britain's Information Commissioner's Office even ordered Google to remove links to stories about Google removing links to stories. So much information that people have a right to see no longer appears in search engine listings and is essentially deleted – down the Memory Hole.

The Archon conspiracy depends for its very existence on the manipulation and suppression of information because from information comes perception and from the manipulation and suppression of information comes the perception deception. What I have described in this chapter alone will be extraordinary enough for those new to my work, but wait for the next bit.

CHAPTER ELEVEN

Transphantomism

Stupidity is the same as evil if you judge by the results
Margaret Atwood

We are fast heading into a transhumanist society in which humans and technology are planned to be seamlessly fused and humanity as we know it will be no more. Transhumanism is the next and final stage of total Archontic control and the Totalitarian Tiptoe to this ultimate dystopia is already well advanced.

I have my own term for this – Transphantomism. Humanity is being manipulated into accepting the enslavement of human perception within the Matrix that goes way beyond even the mind programs of Phantom Self. Archons and their hybrids are in the midst of a transformation of what we call 'humans' after which thoughts and emotions would be controlled technologically and no one would be able to expand their awareness beyond the fake reality. Transhumanism would be Phantom Self on steroids. Archons began with a bad copy of something wonderful and they have systematically inverted and distorted the copy to turn a world of life into one of death. It is the same story with human Body-Mind. They began with what there was before and they have genetically manipulated its receiver-transmitter processes to tune them to the Matrix while infesting humanity with the Archon virus and lowering the frequency – 'Fall of Man'. What they could not do, however, is block all access to Infinite Awareness which could override the program and see the truth. Transhumanism is the plan to so technologically control the human vehicle that it would not be influenced in any way by awareness outside the frequency walls of the Matrix (Fig 606). I have heard it said by some researchers that the transhumanist agenda has been dreamed up to respond to the gathering awakening of humanity from its program-instigated coma. I could not disagree more if I spent my life working at it. Transhumanist-

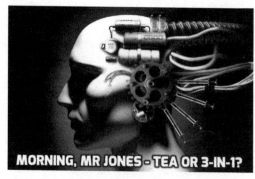

Figure 606: Transhumanism – the end of human.

transphantomist technological control of humans is not a response or afterthought – it was the plan *from the start*. We are seeing the modus-operandi for how the Demiurge-Archon self-aware virus takes over societies and realities. First they hijack perception by making an energetic copy of the original reality and manipulate genetics (receiver-transmission processes) of the target population to tune them into a fake reality. From this point they work to distort the copy to a stage where it reflects their own frequency and preferred 'atmosphere' by the systematic generation of death, destruction, fear and suffering technologically supported by massive increases in atmospheric radiation and nuclear war. All of these energetic sources and many more transform what was originally copied into a reality that suits the Archon virus in its quest for total control. The endgame in these repeating scenarios is to fuse the population with technology controlled by Artificial Intelligence (AI), which is just a fancy cover-name for 'Them' – *the virus*. The machine-controlled world portrayed in the *Matrix* trilogy is an accurate reflection of what this endgame is supposed to deliver and the control came about in the movie narrative through the destruction (death) of the human environment amid nuclear war. 'They' who work to make this happen are all expressions of the virus either directly or through possession and this covers the whole raft of names and manifestations from the Demiurge (prime virus) to Archons, Jinn, Demons, Flyers etc., and the virus-possessed Reptilians, Greys, Archon-Reptilian hybrid 'human' *El*-lite and others. The 'Artificial Intelligence' of transhumanism, then, is the Archon virus. Phantom Self and expressions of the virus and virus-possessed are already controlled by Artificial Intelligence – Demiurge intelligence – and this is now being taken to a whole new level with regard to humanity. Clearly this control is even more powerful once you introduce technology that blocks any contact with expanded awareness (Fig 607).

Technology to make the transhumanist society possible may appear to have developed 'naturally' through a process of 'human evolution', but that's not the case. The Demiurge/Archons had this technology while humans in our 'historical timeline' were in the Stone Age. Remember the ancient texts that describe how the gods visited in their advanced craft. There was no point and no possibility of introducing technology in our reality until humans had reached the necessary level of technological understanding to build it and use it. Give Stone Age man a computer? Yep, great idea. We are back to the question posed by Mexican shaman Don Juan Matus: '... Tell me how you would explain the contradictions between the intelligence of man the engineer and the stupidity of his systems of belief, or the stupidity of his contradictory behaviour.' Humans in Phantom Self mode had to be brought to a point where they could

Figure 607: Infinite Awareness? What's that?

understand enough about technology to build their own prison but without access to Infinite Awareness that would allow them to see that this is what they were doing. That, in a sentence, is how all this has come about and why human society developed as it has. Archon-Reptilian hybrids in positions of power and influence have pump-primed this whole process as they are doing today in the transhumanist movement. There is a rider to this, however. You can't isolate Phantom Self from a wider awareness completely or in everyone. There is a trade-off here between what you need for total control and the danger that at least some people will open their minds further than is good for you. Mind expansion and development necessary for eventual technological awareness has made unacceptable many things once done openly such as human sacrifice and overt rule by royal bloodline. Many more

Figure 608: The Schumann cavity.

people also refuse to 'know their place' and this is a dangerous period for the Archon agenda. Research into transhumanist technology opens the way to the realisation that we live in a simulation as technological developments mimic the very reality we are experiencing. We live in a 'time' of enormous danger but also fantastic opportunity, and they are pushing through transhumanism as fast as they can to lock down human awareness technologically before it can wake up to the truth on a scale that would bring the Archon house down.

Technological sub-reality

A global technological web of total control by Artificial Intelligence (Demiurge virus) is being rolled out by the day and the aim is to create a sub-reality between the ground and the ionosphere in that part of the Earth's atmosphere known as the Schumann Cavity or Schumann Cavity Resonance (Fig 608). German physicist Winfried Otto Schumann is credited with discovering this electromagnetic resonance in the extremely low frequency or ELF range between 6 and 8 Hz. This is within the frequency of human brain activity and all biological systems. Harmonic connection between Earth and other biological life is possible through this frequency compatibility, but the Archon agenda demands that this harmony be distorted and the interconnection destroyed. HAARP-type technology, which interacts with the ionosphere, can function within the same frequency band with potential to achieve this end. Scientists say Earth and the human brain can synchronise at the Schumann resonance frequency of 7.83 Hz and this is a means through which all biological life can communicate. Dolphins generate sound waves of 7.83 Hz. Dr Herbert König, Schumann's successor at Munich University, said the dominant brain wave in mammals is between 6 and 8 Hz. Human alpha brain waves are broadcast in this frequency band while in state of meditation, relaxation and creativity. States of fear, stress and anxiety block alpha wave states and therefore block harmonic connection with everything else. This adds further to a sense of isolation. Alpha waves are also very important to the immune system, which is a recurring target of Archon manipulation. Schumann Resonance operates like a tuning fork to 'entrain' all biological life in a common and harmonious oscillation. 'Entrainment' is a major aspect to Phantom Self creation and control. Entrainment means that the dominant frequency rules perception. If you place three violins together playing the same note or frequency and then introduce another violin playing another note or no note this will be 'entrained' by the combined power of the other three and resonate to their frequency.

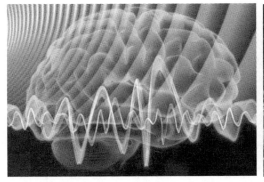

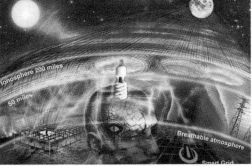

Figure 609: Human brain activity can be entrained by technological frequencies and fake perceptions downloaded.

Figure 610: The planned technological sub-reality.

Technology galore is designed to cumulatively entrain human brain activity with external forces of frequency manipulation (Fig 609). This, too, is aimed at blocking a connection to expanded awareness. The Demiurge conspiracy is building a frequency prison or technologically-created sub-reality through multiple means, including technologically-generated radiation, to entrap the human mind in an even more extreme and myopic fake-reality – a fake reality *within* a fake reality. Given the vast majority are already disconnected from a powerful and conscious connection to Infinite Awareness what would humanity be like if this gathering frequency prison is allowed to reach its intended goal? Here we have still another example of further distorting the 'bad copy' (Fig 610). Studies have already revealed that Schumann resonance is being swamped by the electromagnetic fog or soup amassing from technological sources. Physicist and Schumann researcher Wolfgang Ludwig said: 'Measuring Schumann resonance in or around a city has become impossible ... electromagnetic pollution from cell phones has forced us to make measurements at sea.' Once Schumann harmonic connections are distorted and unravelled fundamental consequences follow mentally, emotionally and 'physically'. Professor Rütger Wever from the Max Planck Institute for Behavioural Physiology in Germany proved this when he built an underground bunker isolated from Schumann resonance and employed student volunteers to live there for a month. He found that their natural biological rhythms (circadian rhythms) went walkabout and they suffered emotional distress (disharmony) and migraine headaches. Only a brief exposure to 7.8 Hz brought them back into kilter and symptoms disappeared. Another highly significant aspect to all this is that DNA communicates through extremely low frequency electromagnetic waves at a frequency of ... 7.83 Hz. This was officially discovered by French virologist Luc Montagnier, joint winner of the Nobel Prize for Physiology or Medicine. DNA can also be entrained with technological frequencies to resist expanded communication and cause genetic mutation. Common themes are clear and this is the real background to the technological society and transhumanism.

Smart is stupid

The term 'smart' is being used for so many technologies and policies today. It's everywhere. We have smartphones, smart tablets, smart watches, smart bands, smart

Figure 611: The Smart Grid.

televisions, smart meters, smart cards, smart cars, smart driving, smart pills, smart dust, smart patches, smart contact lenses, smart skin, smart borders, smart pavements, smart streets, smart cities, smart communities, smart environments, smart growth, and a smart planet to name just some. 'Smart' is intended to promote the impression that anything 'smart' must be in accordance with its definition of 'having or showing intelligence'. A 'Smart Object' is defined as something that 'interacts with not only people but also with other Smart Objects'. I have been warning since the 'smart' era began that all the 'smarts' are designed to communicate and synchronise with all the other smarts to form a global grid of technological wireless communication known as the Smart Grid. This is planned to be connected with the human Body-Mind through microchips, other transhumanist body-inserts and by operating on the same frequency band as human brain and DNA activity to entrain them with the Smart Grid or technological sub-reality. From that moment humans will be nothing more than computer terminals responding to data input from a wireless control grid linking all the 'smart' technologies and many more that won't use that term. Advocates of transhumanism claim that smart environments will create 'a small world where different kinds of smart device are continuously working to make inhabitants' lives more comfortable'. We are talking in truth about a technological prison cell for every man, woman and child on earth (Fig 611). The Smart Grid will not be built and switched on overnight. It is being constructed piece by piece before our eyes through the Totalitarian Tiptoe and the process is getting quicker all the time. If you want to hide something put it on public display. Technologies used for aeons by the Archons in their multiple invasions of societies and realities are being introduced as 'new inventions' when they were known about and developed long ago in the underground bases and other secret locations around the world, especially in the United States. Technology is released in a pre-determined order using cover stories and cover people to explain where it came from. Computerisation is an example of this along with smart and other technology essential to global mind, body and emotional control. Are we really saying that technology crucial to the control agenda just happened to appear by sheer good luck just when the control system needed it? People standing in line for hours to be the first to get the latest release of control-grid technology – I must have an iPhone first – is as sickening as it is sad and shows what a grip technology already has on the human mind. We had the cell phone, then the smartphone, tablet, Bluetooth, smartwatch, Google Glass and now even skin patches that attach an electronic circuit to the skin and communicate with computers (Fig 612). This is one small step from the permanently embedded microchip that I have warned was planned for nearly a quarter of a century. Skin patches are called epidermal electronic circuits (Fig 613). Producers

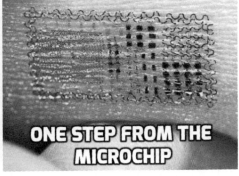

Figure 612: Where we are is nowhere near where it is meant to go.

Figure 613: What they call 'epidermal electrical circuits'.

say the patches could be used for medical applications such as monitoring heart and brain, but the plan is for two-way communication not one-way. Monitoring heart and brain then becomes externally *communicating* with the heart and brain via Artificial Intelligence (Demiurge self-aware virus).

Skin patches, smart technology and those directly interacting with the body such as Google Glass and Bluetooth earphones are preparing people for the next and most decisive step of putting technology inside the body (Fig 614). Internal microchips are already in use and the plan is to have them widely used before making them compulsory through the same Totalitarian Tiptoe technique that we are seeing with vaccines. A CIA scientist confirmed the microchip agenda to me in the 1990s and he said that in secret development projects they were already small enough to be inserted by hypodermic needles in vaccination programmes. Today we call what he was talking about 'nanotechnology' which is well beyond the capacity of the human eye to see. Nanoparticles are now used in food, clothing, medicine, shampoo, toothpaste, sunscreen and thousands of other products. Some scientists have warned that nanoparticles can change the function of cells and how they communicate, and

Figure 614: One of many technologies in the Totalitarian Tiptoe to getting inside the body.

significantly change DNA, but they are ignored given that those outcomes are exactly what is required. Nanotechnology is the level that human microchipping is really planned to happen – is already happening – and in many ways the bigger chips that can be seen are a diversion. The Big Biotech-controlled US Department of Agriculture has awarded millions of dollars to American universities to develop nanotechnology in food. People are being manipulated into such extreme addiction to technology that they will gladly agree to become an extension of it (Fig 615). Addiction to smartphones and

Figure 615: Smartphone addiction turning humans into an extension of technology.

Figure 616: Technology is now in control through addiction in the same way that drugs and alcohol are in control through addictions to them.

tablets alone is incredible to behold with the masses all over the world unable to resist the magnetic attraction of the little screen in their hand. What is energetically coming off these devices to trigger such a *magnetic* attraction? I suggest it's a form of Artificial Intelligence. A poll for the UK's *Channel 4 News* in 2015 found that nearly half the parents questioned believed their children were addicted to smartphones and tablets and almost the same number likened this to emotional dependency (Fig 616). I was on a train coming into a station one day and literally *everyone* the whole length of the platform was bent over mesmerised by smartphones. British newspaper columnist Sarah Vine wrote:

> They stop children from interacting face-to-face (how many groups of teenagers do you see in parks, hunched over their phones, nominally together yet lost in their own separate worlds). What most horrifies me is the way smart phones take normal, healthy children and turn them into zombies whose principal pre-occupations are not schoolwork, riding a bike or even following the latest chart-toppers, but checking how many 'likes' their Instagram picture has amassed, or whether their latest video has amassed sufficient comment.
>
> At a time when young minds should be questioning and expanding, their horizons shrink to one tiny, glowing screen. Forget great art, travel, conversation: all they want to know is what's the Wi-Fi code and where can I get the best signal?'

By 2015 some 66 percent of Britons had smartphones (up from 39 percent in 2012) and they only came on the market in 2007. Smartphones are the fastest-selling gadget in history with half the adult population owning a smartphone and by 2020 it's estimated the figure will be 80 percent. Smartphones, tablets and personal computers are predicted by then to number around 7.3 billion. Even remote tribes in the Brazilian rainforest have been given smartphones on the grounds of protecting them from violent ranchers who want their land. Americans spend an average of two hours a day on a smartphone and 80 percent of smartphone owners are using them within 15 minutes of waking up. *The Economist* magazine rightly referred to the 'Planet of the Phones' and 'phono sapiens'. Yes, phono sapiens on the Totalitarian Tiptoe to becoming transphantom *former* sapiens. A medical term has been coined now for the consequences of this phone obsession – 'text neck'. An American study found this causes excessive wear and tear that may eventually have to be corrected by surgery. Total madness, but such is the power of addiction. Human interaction and conversation is being destroyed by these devices as focus of attention moves away from human interaction to *interaction with technology* (Fig 617). What controls a drug addict? Drugs. What controls an alcohol addict? Alcohol. What controls a smartphone addict? Technology. This is the process of

Figure 617: Interaction with technology beats interaction with people.

conditioning humanity to accept 'technology as their god' – just like the Archon-Reptilians. Smart devices are increasingly at the centre of everyday life and if it's not a text or 'checking my emails' (every few minutes) then it's taking a 'selfie'. I'm not saying that people shouldn't take pictures (although an estimated 1.2 billion selfies in the UK alone in 2014 points to more addiction). I'm pointing out where it is all designed to lead and I can tell you it ain't pretty. Smartphones are transhumanist pied pipers. Smart technology is promoted as a means of instant communication, but when you are covertly selling a prison cell you don't highlight the bars and the lock on the door. You focus on the self-contained accommodation with no utility bills and plenty of time to sleep. Smartphones are about control on multiple levels and they can tell the authorities close to exactly where you are 24 hours a day. German news magazine *Der Spiegel* reported seeing top secret documents from the United States National Security Agency (NSA) revealing how they can access information on phones made by all leading manufacturers including 'contact lists, SMS traffic, notes and location information about where a user has been'. Let no one tell me that this is not done in connivance with the manufacturers through the Archontic Web which controls both them and the NSA. Edward Snowden, the whistleblower on NSA surveillance now in exile in Russia, apparently told lawyers he met on the run in Hong Kong to put their cell phones in his fridge to stop any eavesdropping. Smartphones can be hacked using fake phone 'towers' known as Stingray technology that mimics mobile phone masts and tricks phones into communicating with them. Law enforcement is using these worldwide. Smartphones are a key part of the Totalitarian Tiptoe to total surveillance in which no one will be able to do anything that the authorities can't know about with microphones allowing private conversations to be heard in real time (Fig 618). There is already no privacy worth the name on Planet Smartphone when any action can be instantly videoed or photographed and passed around the world in minutes on social media.

Smartphones on the brain

Electronic communication devices addict the brain to constant stimulation and this is destroying human attention span (exactly as planned). A study of brain activity among 2,000 people in Canada using electroencephalograms revealed that average human attention since the mobile revolution had fallen to just eight seconds – less than that of a

Figure 618: Everywhere you go ... we'll be watching you.

Figure 619: Reversed evolution.

goldfish (Fig 619). Surveys have recorded a serious drop in the number of children reading books for pleasure by the end of primary school because of attention spans, a lack of reading at home (they and their parents are on the phone) and the fact that in the age of the smartphone, reading books is not seen as 'cool'. What is 'cool'? Whatever The System tells the masses is 'cool' and the masses impose what The System says is 'cool' on each other through peer pressure. Programmed programmers are everywhere in every race, age group, country and culture. Young adults now spend around 25 percent less time reading than ten years ago. Attention span deletion is crucial and a central goal of the information assault on the human brain. How can you glean the knowledge necessary to understand the world and the Orwellian conspiracy with an attention span less than that of a goldfish? How can you connect the dots when you are so bored with the first dot that you reach for the smartphone? *The Perception Deception*, my mega exposé of the global conspiracy in all its aspects, runs to 900 pages. How many will never read this simply because their attention span can't cope? Reading books of that size are actually antidotes for the brain to the smart manipulation. Social media and text speak – UR prgmd lol wkup B4 2L8 – are also in the frontline of the war against attention spans. Text language is an obvious example of George Orwell's *Newspeak*, the language which replaced the expansive vocabulary of *Oldspeak* and did not have words to describe thoughts and concepts in detail. Political correctness is the same agenda. British neuroscientist Professor Susan Greenfield, a member of the British House of Lords, published a book in 2014 entitled *Mind Change* to explore the effects on the brain of the social media/smartphone age. I've read the book and recommend it. Greenfield's foundation themes are the following: The brain adapts to the environment; this environment is changing in an unprecedented way; and so the brain may also be changing in an unprecedented way. And it *is*. Scientists believed that once the brain was formed it never changed, but now they know this is not the case. They acknowledge that the brain has what is termed 'placidity' and changes with the information it receives (Fig 620). James Olds, a neuroscientist at George Mason University, said: 'The brain has the ability to reprogram itself on the fly, altering the way it functions.' Species adapt to changing environments by brain and genetic 'placidity' providing new gifts necessary to survive. When this process happens quickly enough we call it

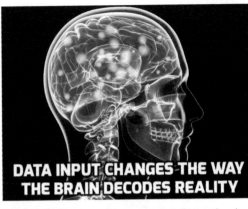

Figure 620: The brain is being severely influenced and changed by the technological revolution.

mutation and when it doesn't we call it extinction. Smartphones, Internet and social media have had fantastic impacts on the brain in a staggeringly short time. Researchers from Tohoku University in Japan concluded that watching television for long periods can also damage brain structure in children. It has long been known that television is addictive and takes the brain into an alpha-wave state similar to hypnosis, which opens the subconscious mind to almost limitless programming. Dr Thomas Mulholland, an American psychophysiologist who studied the mind control potential of television, said that alpha waves appear after only thirty seconds and the viewer falls into a 'virtual trance'. Smart technology has now added enormously to this cognitive takeover and the brains of children and adults are being battered by both smartphones and smart televisions. This is sobering when you think that the market-research agency Childwise estimates that British children spend an average of five hours and 20 minutes a day in front of TV or computer screens. Susan Greenfield told the House of Lords: 'It is hard to see how living this way on a daily basis will not result in brains, or rather minds, different from those of previous generations.' I would add yes, but that's what they want. She said in a powerful and telling comment: 'The mid-21st century mind might almost be infantilised, characterised by short attention spans, sensationalism, inability to empathise and a shaky sense of identity.' Once again this is the intention and while the mid-21st century might realise something like completion this process is already well underway. Scan social media for only a short time to see the child-like behaviour of alleged adults and the gratuitous abuse even of people in tragic circumstances reveals a fundamental lack of empathy (psychopathy). No, not everyone is like that, far from it, but the ratio is high and getting higher from what I can see. Susan Greenfield writes:

> Our brains are under the influence of an ever-expanding world of new technology: multichannel television, video games, MP3 players, the internet, wireless networks, Bluetooth links – the list goes on and on ...

> ... Electronic devices and pharmaceutical drugs all have an impact on the micro-cellular structure and complex biochemistry of our brains. And that, in turn, affects our personality, our behaviour and our characteristics. In short, the modern world could well be altering our human

identity ...

... Already, it's pretty clear that the screen-based, two dimensional world that so many teenagers – and a growing number of adults – choose to inhabit is producing changes in behaviour. Attention spans are shorter, personal communication skills are reduced and there's a marked reduction in the ability to think abstractly.

This games-driven generation interpret the world through screen-shaped eyes. It's almost as if something hasn't really happened until it's been posted on Facebook, Bebo or YouTube.

Altering human identity and perception of self is the whole point of the exercise, and it's interesting that she should highlight the effect on the ability to think abstractly. Definitions of abstract include 'existing in thought or as an idea but not having a physical or concrete existence'; 'dealing with ideas rather than events'; and 'denoting an idea, quality, or state rather than a concrete object'. Thinking in the abstract is primarily the role of the *right-brain*. You know, the side the Archons want to repress and suppress. Take away abstract thinking and attention spans and you remove the ability to understand the world as it really is and further encase human perception in the five-sense illusion of the Matrix. Researchers at De Montfort University in Leicester reached the same conclusion about the Internet, smartphones and reduced attention spans. They found that the more a person was on the Internet or phone the more likely they are to experience 'cognitive failures'. A study by neuroscientists and radiologists at universities and hospitals in China noted that young people were becoming 'Internet dependent' and MRI images revealed that 'excessive Internet use may cause parts of teenagers' brains to waste away'. American technologist Nicholas Carr supports Susan Greenfield's themes in his book, *The Shallows: How The Internet Is Changing The Way We Think, Read And Remember,* and in an article in *The Atlantic* magazine headed 'Is Google Making Us Stupid?' Carr spoke out after concluding that something was changing in the way that his brain functioned. 'I've had an uncomfortable sense that someone, or something, has been tinkering with my brain, remapping the neural-circuitry, reprogramming the memory,' he said. Carr also realised that he wasn't alone when he discussed this with other people. A doctor friend told him he had 'almost totally lost the ability to read and absorb a longish article on the web or in print.' Some friends had stopped reading books altogether and one complained of 'staccato' thinking that stopped him from reading long books like *War And Peace* any more. A study at Emory University in Atlanta discovered that college students reading a book showed improvements in brain function with

Figure 621: Reading books – especially paper books – has been shown to resist the changes caused by technology and the Internet.

changes starting on the first day and lasting for five days after completion (Fig 621). You can see why they don't want people to read books anymore, but for their own sake they *must*. Research has shown that people take in and grasp more information reading paper books than e-books, and that children using computers extensively at school instead of traditional books had lower reading and maths scores. Nicholas Carr talked with linguists, neuroscientists, psychiatrists and psychologists before concluding that

Figure 622: Get them early – keep them for life.

the Internet and social media are rewiring human minds as the time spent online has soared. Gary Small, professor of psychiatry at the University of California, compared the brains of limited users of the Internet with regular users and found that when the first group increased their activity their brains took only a few days to change in line with the second group and the changes were permanent. Carr said that 'like a chemical narcotic, the Net's "cacophony of stimuli" short-circuits both conscious and unconscious thoughts, preventing our minds from thinking either deeply or creatively' and even sympathetically (deletion of empathy or dehumanisation). Other studies of videogame players have shown a reduction in the grey matter of the hippocampus which controls memory, learning and emotion, and is associated with neurological and psychological problems like dementia and depression. In the light of this background what an absolutely extraordinary statement it was in 2015 when Professor Annette Karmiloff-Smith of the University of London said that babies should be given tablet computers 'from birth' (Fig 622). Who said a 'good education' and academic status made you intelligent?

Video download

Susan Greenfield correctly expresses concern at the effect on personality and perception of violent videogames. These are designed to desensitise players to violence on the basis that the brain and subconscious mind doesn't make a distinction between the 'real' and the simulated. Remember how brain responses were so similar between people thinking about learning to play the piano and those actually learning. Greenfield said: 'That eternal teenage protest of "it's only a game, Mum" certainly begins to ring alarmingly hollow.' Desensitivity to violence is another form of psychopathy – a lack of empathy with the victims. A poll of Xbox game owners during the 2012 US election revealed that 72 *percent* supported more drone strikes on 'suspected terrorists' (men, women and children). *Suspected*, that is, not even proven to be. How many psychopaths play violent video games and war scenarios while still under the self-delusion that they are just 'normal' people? Susan Greenfield said: 'We could be raising a hedonistic generation who live only in the thrill of the computer- generated moment, and are in distinct danger of detaching themselves from what the rest of us would consider the real world.' Hedonism is 'the pursuit of or devotion to pleasure, especially to the pleasures of the senses' and believing that 'only what is pleasant or has pleasant consequences is intrinsically good.' A big part of the onslaught of cyber information is to stimulate pleasure centres in the brain via what Greenfield calls the 'pleasures of the [five] senses' and manipulate an addiction to pleasure. Aldous Huxley, author of *Brave New World,* spoke of making people 'love their servitude'. A CIA lunatic called Ivor Browning wired a radio receiver to the pleasure centre known as the hypothalamus in the brain of a donkey and controlled the donkey's behaviour by

Figure 623: Control system with Kevin Warwick.

stimulating the pleasure centre when the donkey did what Browning wanted and stopping when it didn't. The donkey walked along a pre-arranged course and back again by seeking to find the direction necessary for the pleasure to return. This is happening step-by-step to humans to make us transhumans or transphantoms. Kevin Warwick, a human microchip-promoting professor of cybernetics at Britain's University of Reading, said: 'If a machine is passing down signals that keep you completely happy, then why not be part of the Matrix?' If there is a more misguided man than Professor Warwick I would not like to meet him, if it's all the same with you (Fig 623). He once said: 'I don't mind changing dramatically from what I am.' Neither do we, Kev, but I won't be holding my breath. There is also pressure for mind-altering lithium to be added to drinking water to make people docile and 'stabilise mood'. A leading advocate, Dr Jacob Appel at Mount Sinai Hospital in New York, said lithium would make the brain 'more happy' – make people love their servitude. Appel is from the same hospital as the Rockefeller 'prophet' Dr Richard Day. Must be something in the water.

Smart Grid

All smart technologies are designed to wirelessly communicate with each other to form the global Smart Grid that would not only keep surveillance on everyone in the multiple ways I will explain, but would also feed information, perceptions and instructions to the human mind. Smart televisions, for example, are the Totalitarian Tiptoe (almost complete) to the Telescreens described by Dr Richard Day nearly 50 years ago and by George Orwell nearly 70 years ago in his book *1984:*

> The telescreen received and transmitted simultaneously. Any sound that Winston made, above the level of a very low whisper, would be picked up by it; moreover, so long as he remained within the field of vision which the metal plate commanded, he could be seen as well as heard.

> There was of course no way of knowing whether you were being watched at any given moment. How often, or on what system, the Thought Police plugged in on any individual wire was guesswork. It was even conceivable that they watched everybody all the time, but at any rate they could plug in your wire whenever they wanted to.

Figure 624: It's because we love you.

You have to live – did live, from habit that became instinct – in the assumption that every sound you made was overheard, and, except in darkness, every movement scrutinized.

Smart TVs produced by Samsung have been exposed for their ability to listen to conversations of those watching. Hidden away in the privacy policy that almost no one reads it says 'please be aware that if your spoken words include personal or other sensitive information, that information will be among the data captured and transmitted to a third party through your use of Voice Recognition.' So much more is going on with smart televisions (which connect to the Internet) than we are ever told about (Fig 624). Britain's *Daily Mail* reported the evidence uncovered by British IT consultant Jason Huntley who became concerned at what appeared to be advertisements on his smart TV home screen specifically targeting him and his family based on programmes they had been watching. He connected his laptop to the set to access the data passing between the TV and the Internet and he was shocked to find that details of everything he watched and every button he pressed on his remote control were being sent back to corporate headquarters in South Korea. What's more, so were details about his private video collection watched on the TV and camcorder footage of his wife and children. Even when he changed the settings to opt out of data sharing the same invasion of privacy continued. Luigi Auriemma, an IT security researcher and computer programmer from Malta, has demonstrated how smart TVs can be hacked and controlled via the Internet, switched on and off and information they store accessed. Other IT experts have revealed how video cameras built-in to many smart TVs can be hacked to spy on people in their own homes without the light coming on to show the camera is active. Kurt Stammberger from the IT security firm Mocana described this as 'frighteningly easy'. The *Daily Mail* article said:

> These characters can see what clothes you have been wearing and what food you've eaten. They heard every word you said, and logged every TV show you watched. Some are criminals, others work for major corporations. And now they know your most intimate secrets.

What else are these smart TVs doing that we don't know about? As the *Mail* article said – ask any IT security expert and they will tell you it's 'probably the tip of the iceberg'. You can also be watched through the webcam on your computer as many people have found. Given this background to smart TVs, you can appreciate the real motivation behind the Mexican government giving away ten million for free to the poor at a cost of $1.6 billion. Argentina and others have done something similar. The rush to impose digital TVs and radios at great cost to people is because they are an essential component of the Smart Grid.

Then there are smart meters being imposed apace all over the world orchestrated by the Archon Web with its agents and secret societies in every country. Human-caused climate change is the major – and fake – justification for smart meters along with cheaper electricity bills when the opposite turns out to be the case. Smart meters are described by their promotors (liars) as 'an intelligent digitised energy-network delivering electricity in an optimum way from source to consumption.' This flannel is used to disguise the fact that those in the shadows driving the imposition of wireless smart meters well know that they are another crucial element of the global wireless Smart Grid. The meters for power and water receive and transmit information through Wi-Fi

Figure 625: Surveillance system in your home and business that can speak to your mind.

electromagnetic fields in homes and businesses to supply a constant stream of private and personal information to the authorities (Fig 625). Jerry Day, an electronics and media expert from Burbank, California, has been a vocal and tireless opponent of smart meters after realising the extent to which they maintain surveillance of people in their own homes. Day says that smart meters can:

- Identify electrical devices inside the home and record when they are operated to impose an invasion of privacy.
- Monitor household activity and occupancy in violation of rights and domestic security.
- Transmit wireless signals which may be intercepted by unauthorised and unknown parties.
- Record and store data about an occupant's daily habits and activities in permanent databases which are accessed by parties not authorised or invited to know and share this private data.
- Produce through smart meter databases a permanent history of household activities complete with calendar and time-of-day to gain a highly invasive and detailed view of people's lives.

Smart meters are outright surveillance devices in violation of US Federal and State wiretapping laws by recording and storing databases of private information without the consent or knowledge of those being monitored. They can tell how many people are in a property and where they are and even identify sexual activity. Researchers from the University of California, Santa Barbara, have confirmed that they can count people in a given space by measuring the Wi-Fi signal and there is no need for them to have electronic devices. Smart Meters receive and transmit through a Wi-Fi electromagnetic field. There are also many Artificial Intelligence robot technologies being developed and introduced to maintain household surveillance. Smart meter information is already being used by police linking energy use to a suspected criminal activity and when this proves unfounded people have been charged with other offences unrelated to the raid after a search of the property. A British government source was quoted by the Daily

Mail as describing smart meters as 'bonkers' and 'a policy being sold as consumer friendly but in the wrong hands, it will be a total disaster'. He clearly wasn't high enough in the hierarchy to know that what he said would be a disaster was precisely why they were being introduced. A long list of privacy campaigners have sought to warn the public about the consequences of smart meters. Nick Pickles from Big Brother Watch said that we are witnessing a massive intrusion into what

Figure 626: The sales pitch.

goes on in millions of homes: 'This comes when there is increasing surveillance of our society ... smart meters are a step towards our homes becoming the next line of attack for state snoopers.' You know when something is crucial to human enslavement when the technology or policy is imposed on the population without a choice. Mandatory vaccinations, 'green' lightbulbs (more later) and smart meters are all examples of this and the same is planned with microchips. The Tiptoe technique is (1) to introduce something and say it is not compulsory; (2) to make it almost impossible to function without whatever it is; and then (3) to make it compulsory. Many of those who have tested the claim that smart meters are not compulsory have had their properties broken into and the meters installed or had their power cut off.

Smart cities

Smart meters and smart televisions are essential to control and surveillance within 'smart cities' – code for the human settlement zones of Agenda 21/2030 where the inhabitants will live in tiny spaces under constant surveillance from the smart networks of the Smart Grid (Fig 626). The European Union is one of the major advocates of smart cities, and when Brussels bureaucrats open their mouths the Archon hybrids are speaking. Smart cities have their own cover story like all the other 'smarts'. We are told they use digital or information and communication technologies 'to enhance quality and performance of urban services, to reduce costs and resource consumption, and to engage more effectively and actively with its citizens.' All of which is a long-winded way of saying 'utter nonsense'. Smart cities are both new cities and the conversion of current cities designed to be terminals on the global Smart Grid controlled by Artificial Intelligence. Some are being built from scratch like New Songdo in South Korea which is described in one article as being 'studded with chips talking to one another and designated as [a smart city] years before [Archontic] IBM found its "Smarter Planet" religion'. An article on the fastcompany.com website said that the central role of American multinational technology corporation Cisco Systems was 'to wire every square inch of the city with synapses ... from the trunk lines running beneath the streets to the filaments branching through every wall and fixture.' The city would be 'run on information' [sub-reality information]. Cisco's control room, the article said, will be New Songdo's brain stem (and for everyone living there). Plans are underway to establish 20 new cities across China and India using New Songdo as a template. A smart city advocate said that 'in the spirit of Moore's Law each will be done faster, better, cheaper, year after year.' The fastcompany.com article continued:

> China doesn't need cool, green, smart cities. It needs cities, period – 500 New Songdos at the very least. One hundred of those will each house a million or more transplanted peasants [Agenda 21/2030]. In fact, while humanity has been building cities for 9,000 years, that was apparently just a warm-up for the next 40.

> As of now, we're officially an urban species. More than half of us – 3.3 billion people – live in a city. Our numbers are projected to nearly double by 2050, adding roughly a New Songdo a day [Agenda 21/2030]; the United Nations predicts the vast majority will flood smaller cities in Africa and Asia.

Smart cities are Agenda 21/2030 human settlement zones with 'peasants' worldwide forced off the land and all justified by manipulated economic circumstances and the lie about human-caused climate change. A 'war against climate change will be fought in city streets', the fastcompany.com article melodramatically contended. 'While the developing world wrestles with its impending population boom, the entire world is confronting an explosion of another sort: climate change.' The climate lie is so vital to the global plan that if it did not exist (it doesn't) they would have had to invent it (they have). 'Smart growth', like 'smart communities', is code for the move to smart cities and human settlement zones. One article described it perfectly without adding the true context:

> There has been a recent popularization of 'Smart Growth' planning in North American cities. Based upon the aim to decrease the impacts of sprawled regional development on the natural environment, a focus of Smart Growth planning is the intensification of both population and physical development in existing urban areas.

Get the population off the land into the micro-homes of the human settlement zones. Smart cities (also 'eco cities') would largely be car-free eventually but those who are still allowed to drive (well, sit in a car) will be in their driverless smart cars already being developed and introduced by Google, a corporation in the front line of transhumanism and much of which was rebranded in 2015 as 'Alphabet'.

Google Search

Google/Alphabet is working in league with DARPA, the deeply sinister technological development arm of the Pentagon (Fig 627). This explains the apparently bewildering career move of DARPA director and intelligence-military insider Regina Dugan when she became a senior executive with Google (Fig 628). Dugan was simply moving from one vehicle of the transhumanist conspiracy to

Figure 627: One of the world's darkest and most sinister organisations.

Figure 628: Regina Dugan – from DARPA to Google (Alphabet) in a career move that fits perfectly if you know what is going on.

Figure 629: DARPA creation and spokesman.

another. DARPA is behind the 'technological revolution' and says the following on its own website under the heading 'Paving the Way to the Modern Internet':

> DARPA research played a central role in launching the Information Revolution. The agency developed and furthered much of the conceptual basis for the ARPANET—prototypical communications network launched nearly half a century ago—and invented the digital protocols that gave birth to the Internet.

> DARPA also provided many of the essential advances that made possible today's computers and communications systems, including seminal technological achievements that support the speech recognition, touch-screen displays, accelerometers, and wireless capabilities at the core of today's smartphones and tablets.

And Pentagon DARPA which specialises in the development of technology for mass murder did all of this for the benefit of humanity? Bless 'em (Fig 629). DARPA has been the vehicle for taking technology long waiting in the shadows and playing it out in human society in a pre-planned sequence. DARPA, Internet giants and intelligence networks such as the US National Security Agency (NSA) are masks on the same Archontic face. Max Kelly, Chief Security Officer at Facebook, joined the NSA in another inter-departmental appointment. Facebook's Mark Zuckerberg says they are building AI systems 'better than humans at our primary senses' and he believes that virtual reality glasses will eventually be part of our every day. We already have virtual reality glasses called 'eyes' but this is the Archon conspiracy adding yet another layer of illusion and disconnection from prime consciousness. All these corporations and government agencies are speaking the same language, working for the same team and providing an answer to the question 'why are the world's richest people so often the most completely bonkers?' Smart cities or mind control cities of unremitting surveillance involve the concept of the so-called 'Internet of Things' which involves connecting all technology to the Internet, including domestic appliances, to tell the authorities when you even open your fridge door (Fig 630). What is the Wi-Fi home communication system of smart meters except another sub-Internet connected to the global Internet? The then CIA Director David Petraeus said:

'HE'S OPENED THE DOOR - GOING FOR THE CHEESE'

Figure 630: 'In the privacy of my own home'? No such thing anymore with smart meters and smart TVs.

... items of interest will be located, identified, monitored and remotely controlled through technologies such as radio-frequency identification [microchips], sensor networks, tiny embedded servers, and energy harvesters – all connected to the next-generation Internet using abundant, low-cost, and high-power computing that would 'transform' the art of spying and allow people to be monitored automatically without planting bugs or direct infiltration.

They are now so confident of success that they are starting to openly brag about what they are doing. Petraeus also confirmed that people could be watched through their smart televisions. He said that 'low-cost and high power computing' is now being introduced for the Internet of Things. ARM, the Apple-connected chip operation, is producing 'low-powered, less expensive chips for use in domestic appliances, even doorbells'. Google and Microsoft have said that the Internet of Things would be made possible by free and more powerful Wi-Fi and the Archontic Federal Communications Commission (FCC) has proposed just this – a free wireless Internet system for everyone in the United States. This 'super-Wi-Fi' would be far more powerful than the current version.

Going inside

Watch for buzz terms because they are mind trickery and conditioning. We now have 'wearables' and 'implantables' – and 'wearables' are the Totalitarian Tiptoe to 'implantables' (Fig 631). Examples of wearables increase all the time – smart watches, smart bands, Bluetooth ear devices, Google Glass and electronic skin 'tattoos'. Implantables are in-the-body technology like microchips. Smart bands are 'activity trackers' and we can't just live our lives we have to constantly track our lives to prepare us for the authorities tracking our lives. Smart watches are being used by employers to

THE 'COOL' (BRAVE) NEW WORLD OF 'IMPLANTABLES'

THIS IS WHAT IT REALLY MEANS

DAVIDICKE.COM

Figure 631: Totalitarian Tiptoe to total control.

track their workers' behaviour and 'feelings', but it's apparently only to know when to give them a day off when they need it (Fig 632). How kind. The more technology can be connected to the body externally the more ready and willing people will be to have it attached internally (and irreversibly) as the wearable becomes the implantable. Each step in this subjugation and transformation of what we call 'human' is sold as making life easier and everything more 'convenient'. Why have to use a keyboard and mouse when you can communicate with your computer directly

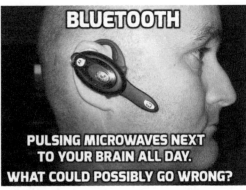

Figure 632: Get them used to technology on their bodies – then go for inside.

Figure 633: Cumulative suicide.

through a chip in the brain? Why even use a computer or eventually a smartphone when the information can be piped directly to your brain? I have warned taxi drivers using Bluetooth ear devices about the dangers to their health, but they just shrug and say it is so much more *convenient* than having to use the radio (Fig 633). I can understand. I mean, lifting a microphone and putting it to your mouth to communicate with the office and tapping on a keyboard or moving a mouse is so onerous. How did we ever cope before? Implantable devices have been waiting in the secret development locations to be introduced at their point in the unfolding process of human control and that moment is here. An article in *Forbes* magazine said we should forget about smart watches because we were about to enter a new level of high tech innovation 'with the next wave of sensor based smart devices – those you can implant into your body'. I have been warning about this for two decades and now here we are. The *Forbes* writer said that although this 'might sound like something you'd see in a science fiction movie', his prediction was that in the next three to five years 'implantable devices will become about as normal as wearing the latest watch' (which has been the plan all along). A neurosignalling patch is in development that uses low voltage electrical currents to alter a person's mood and energy, the article said, and it highlighted the $300 million in US government funding for technology firms, academic institutions and scientists 'to better understand the human mind – and affect it'. Yes, *affect* it, *change* it. Researching treatments for Alzheimer's, schizophrenia, autism, depression and other health problems is the official sales-pitch and *Forbes* said that 'implantables can save lives, improve health, prevent diseases and even begin to make us superhuman'. I am not saying that there aren't applications for technology in the fields of spinal injuries for example, but that is not what this is really all about. Nor is it about making people superhuman. The plan is to make them sub-human and mind-slaves to external stimuli.

Humans as computer terminals

What they call the Smart Grid is a technologically-generated sub-reality within the Schumann cavity that would link all smart and wireless technologies into an electromagnetic Wi-Fi 'cloud' (Fig 634). This would act as a perception-control system for all human minds and block out connections to Infinite Awareness (Fig 635). Wireless

Figure 634: The technological sub-reality.

Figure 635: Transhumanism.

Figure 636: Gwen towers are installed across America and other countries.

Figure 637: The TETRA system that has damaged the health of so many who use it.

communication technologies and networks including TETRA in the United Kingdom (and wider afield) and GWEN in the United States are all part of this. Communication towers of the Ground Wave Emergency Network (GWEN) are being spaced 200 miles apart across the United States in a project that began in the early 1980s overseen by the US Air Force (Fig 636). GWEN communications stay close to ground level where humans are and the official justification is to build a back-up communications network in case of nuclear war. What a joke. TETRA, or Terrestrial Trunked Radio, in the UK is similar to the PCS/Digital or Personal Communication Systems in the United States. It was introduced at great cost by then Prime Minister Tony Blair as a communications network for police and other emergency services. TETRA zaps everyone with dangerous radiation every time they use it and distorts the electromagnetic balance of the body leading to many potential 'physical', mental and emotional consequences including cancer (Fig 637). This multitude of electromagnetic wireless communication sources and smart technologies operate together to form the sub-reality cloud. I can't emphasise enough how central Google ('Alphabet') is to the transhumanist tyranny with its top-secret Google X operation in California developing the necessary technology (or overseeing its introduction). To connect the entire world to the Internet (essential to the whole plan) there has to be global access no matter where you are. Currently the Internet is available to only about a third of the world population. *The Wall Street Journal* reported in 2014, however, that Google planned to launch 180 satellites to provide

WI-FI FROM SATELLITE TO CATCH EVERYONE IN THE SUB-REALITY 'CLOUD'

Figure 638: The real reason for worldwide Wi-Fi.

Internet access for the whole planet. They would orbit the Earth at lower altitudes than traditional satellites, bathe the world in Wi-Fi radiation and link everyone to the Archon mind control sub-reality or cloud. Another venture, once connected with the Google plan, is called OneWeb LTD (formerly WorldVu). Richard Branson is on the board of directors. OneWeb proposes to orbit a 'constellation' of nearly 700 satellites 'operating in circular low Earth orbits of 800 kilometres (500 miles) and 950 kilometres (590 miles)' to provide global broadband access as early as 2019 (Fig 638). Facebook is, like Google, just another strand in the same Archontic Web, and Facebook is developing its own 'solar-powered drones, satellites and lasers to deliver web access to underdeveloped countries'. Virgin Media, another Richard Branson company, is introducing 'smart pavements' (sidewalks) with Wi-Fi generators under your feet and in street lamps to cover whole towns and cities in Wi-Fi radiation fields. Wow, how amazing. A 'pilot' scheme in the English town of Chesham is planned to be the first step to doing it throughout the country. Martin Parkes, a local business owner and spokesman for The Better Chesham Group, said:

> It's great that our customers have access to Virgin Media's public Wi-Fi both in and outside our salon. We're a very unique high street with many independent shops so we don't have the IT infrastructure that big chains benefit from. This will hugely help levelling the playing field and will hopefully bring more people to Chesham too.

Babes in bloody arms. Global Wi-Fi Internet access so crucial to the Archontic mind-control cloud is well underway. Even garbage bins are being turned into Wi-Fi hotspots and you can't get away from it. The Internet came out of 'Large Hadron Collider' CERN (with contributions from DARPA) and it's a Trojan Horse. We should not forget that the Internet was based on military technology (DARPA again) and would not have been made available unless there were monumental benefits for the control system. Not only are those benefits limitless, they are fundamental to what is planned. All the good things about the Internet have been used to hide its real purpose – human control. One of those good points was the free-flow of information but that was only to pull people in and sell it as a vehicle for freedom. Today that free-flow is being incessantly deleted as was planned all along with Archontic Google and Facebook at war with alternative information and websites that expose The System. *Transcendence*, the 2014 movie starring Johnny Depp, was another cinematic exploration and portrayal of something very real – the potential for the Internet to become a conscious entity. I think it's already happened (Fig 639). Johnny Depp plays a scientist researching consciousness, sentience and artificial intelligence and the aim is to produce a sentient computer that would create a 'technological singularity' or 'Transcendence'. Singularity is a transhumanist term for their world of technology-controlled humans and Transcendence is just another word for transhumanism. There is even a Singularity University in the NASA Research Park, Silicon Valley, California, with plans to operate

Figure 639: A conscious Internet is the planned foundation of human control through Artificial Intelligence.

globally and 'educate, inspire and empower leaders to apply exponential technologies to address humanity's grand challenges'. One of its founders is AI super-salesman Ray Kurzweil, of whom more shortly, and one of its sponsors is Google/Alphabet. Kurzweil is a Google executive. The word 'exponential' in that quote is important to emphasise because the speed of development with these AI technologies gets faster and faster as one development increases the speed to the next one. Depp's scientist character knows he's dying and his scientist wife downloads his consciousness to their quantum computer which is then connected to the Internet and the Internet becomes conscious. Connections to the Internet of Things allows his downloaded consciousness to take control of anything Internet-connected and this includes control of human minds infested with sentient nano-particles spread on the wind. This may have been a fictional story but its theme is based on fact – the Internet can (has) become conscious and self-aware via Artificial Intelligence. Neuroscientist Christof Koch, chief scientific officer at the Allen Institute for Brain Science in Seattle, has postulated that the Internet might be conscious. He said:

> The Internet contains about 10 billion computers, with each computer itself having a couple of billion transistors in its CPU [brain]. So the internet has at least 10^{19} transistors, compared to the roughly 1000 trillion (or quadrillion) synapses in the human brain. That's about 10,000 times more transistors than synapses.

If the human brain is processing information to become what we call the conscious mind, why wouldn't an Internet of that capacity be able to do the same?

Artificial *virus* intelligence

There is another factor in the theme of Internet consciousness and that's the self-aware Demiurge virus that I say has already 'done a Johnny Depp' and *is* Internet

Illustration by Neil Hague (www.neilhague.com)

Figure 640: The consciousness controlling the Internet and everything connected to it (including humans) is the Demiurge self-aware virus.

consciousness. The Internet has been built from the start to be the vehicle for the virus to directly control human affairs by controlling everything connected to the Internet (the Internet of Things) including humans through implantables and nanotechnology in the body (Fig 640). Watch the Depp movie if you haven't seen it and you'll get the picture. The Demiurge virus is the 'magnet' that is causing smartphone and Internet addiction and pulling Phantom Self into its frequency. This is, to a very large extent, what is rewiring human brain activity. Anyone still doubting what I am saying should listen to insider 'futurologist' Ray Kurzweil, a director of engineering at Google/Alphabet working on Artificial Intelligence. Kurzweil is the sales-pitcher for Frankenstein and refers to the current human form as 'version one bodies'. He is reportedly fixated with the singularity and the moment artificial intelligence exceeds human capacity (the 'Omega Point' estimated to be 2045). Kurzweil has said publicly that humans will have 'hybrid cloud-powered brains by 2030'. He said that implanted nanobots will connect human brains to the Internet and most of our thinking 'will be done online'. Make that *all* of it. The Internet or World Wide Web has been planned from the start to be the foundation of the global AI Smart Grid control system made conscious by the self-aware Demiurge virus. Nanobots (also nanorobots, nanoids, nanites, nanomachines or nanomites) that Kurzweil talks about are micro-machines that can assemble and maintain sophisticated systems and can build devices, machines, or circuits through a process called molecular manufacturing. They can also produce copies of themselves through self-replication. Yep, just what you want implanted into your Body-Mind. The game is so blatant to anyone with a brain cell of their own. Kurzweil told the Exponential Finance Conference in New York that after the human/Internet nano-connection 'our thinking then will be a hybrid of biological and non-biological thinking.' He said that humans would be able to extend their limitations and 'think in the cloud'. He continued:

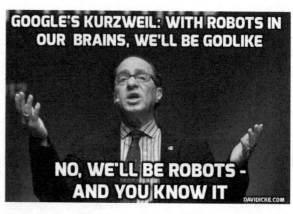

We're going to put gateways to the cloud in our brains ... We're going to gradually merge and enhance ourselves ... In my view, that's the nature of being human – we transcend our limitations.

Figure 641: You mean he doesn't *know??* Come on.

Here we go – *Transcendence.* These are the selling points for covert human enslavement – 'extend limitations', 'create superhumans' and 'solve health problems'. This is coming from the same System that works so tirelessly to limit humans, stop them becoming superhuman through expanded consciousness and hides, blocks and makes illegal means to benefit human health. AI and transhumanism is about the *El*-ite being 'superhuman' and police state personnel being 'superhuman' enough to serve their masters while the hive-mind masses would be nothing more than AI-controlled worker ants. Don't believe the bullshit – it is all about *total control* of human perception and in every other way (Fig 641). Another Kurzweil quote captures what transhumanism is really all about: 'As the technology becomes vastly superior to what we are then the small proportion that is still human gets smaller and smaller and smaller until it's just utterly negligible.' Promotors and apologists for the AI nightmare say that AI is the development of technology that can assess data, learn, conclude and make decisions and yet they claim at the same time that humans will always be in control of this. Mustafa Suleyman from the London-based AI company Deep Mind (bought by Google in 2014) said the idea that a machine-based artificial intelligence could take over decisions and pose a threat to humans was preposterous. No, it's the claim that it's preposterous that's preposterous. I also watched an interview with a 'prominent robotic engineer', Israel-born Professor Hod Lipson from Cornell University, who was asked about the dangers to humanity of AI robots. His replies were, to put it most optimistically, a head-shaker in sheer naïvety. Zionist Ray Kurzweil even has the arrogance to suggest that once humans and the Earth have been given his nanobots treatment then they would expand into space and make the Universe 'wake up' and 'become intelligent'. If he doesn't know the Universe is already intelligent that is shockingly ignorant for a man who thinks he is so clever; but behind the smoke and mirrors and cover stories I'm sure he does know. You don't become head of the transhumanist sales team without an honours degree in bullshit.

Rewired from the sky

A further crucial element of the sub-reality cloud and human cull is geoengineering and the phenomenon known as chemtrails. We have all seen contrails or condensation trails that pour from the back of aircraft and quickly disappear. *Chem*trails can look the same at first but they don't disappear. White streaks often cross-cross the sky as aircraft fly back and forth building up the pattern (Fig 642). They then slowly expand and

Figure 642: Killing the world – 'Archonising' the bad copy.

eventually drop their contents on the ground. Chemtrails began to be noticed in the sky over North America in the late 1990s and they have long been global. They are even being portrayed in some animated films to condition people to believe it is all 'natural'. Ever-increasing numbers observing chemtrails know that natural is the last thing they are. I recommend the chemtrail exposure films of Michael Murphy in the *What Are They Spraying?* series, and also the video *Geoengineering And The Collapse Of Earth*. Put those words into *YouTube* and you'll find them. Chemtrails are vitally important to the Archon agenda for many reasons including weather warfare and manipulation. Paid liars and government disinformation artists join forces with a naive and in-denial public and media to dismiss them as a fallacy or the usual 'conspiracy theory'. This is despite videos proving the spraying is happening, pictures circulating of the chemical tanks inside aircraft and laboratory tests confirming the chemtrail content of known and unknown chemicals, toxins and diseases. Those who might want to speak out about chemtrails, the global warming hoax and other matters of public interest are subjected to government gag orders on staff at the National Weather Service, National Oceanic and Atmospheric Administration and elsewhere. Bill Hopkins, the executive president for the National Weather Service employee's organisation, said: 'As a taxpayer, I find it highly disturbing that a government agency continues to push gag orders to hide how they operate.' Yes, but why would the government want people to know the truth when suppressing the truth is what it is there to do? Truth such as ... chemtrail content includes aluminium, barium, radioactive thorium and highly toxic pathogens including Mycoplasma fermentans (incognitus strain). American scientist J. Marvin Herndon published an article in the *International Journal of Environmental Research* in August 2015 detailing his research into chemtrails. He concluded that they contain 'coal fly ash' within which is found arsenic, barium, beryllium, boron, cadmium, chromium, cobalt, lead, manganese, mercury, molybdenum, selenium, thallium, thorium, vanadium and uranium. He wrote that the consequences for public health are profound and include exposure to a variety of toxic heavy metals, radioactive elements and neurologically-implicated chemically mobile aluminium. Herndon wrote:

> Earth exists in a state of dynamic biological, chemical, and physical equilibrium whose complexity far exceeds the understanding of contemporary science. The pervasive tropospheric

spraying of coal fly ash threatens this equilibrium, whose delicacy or whose resilience we cannot quantify. Human health is at risk as is Earth's biota. Are we to remain silent? Or will we exercise our primal right to speak in our own defense as a species and question the sanity of emplacing coal fly ash in Earth's perpetually moving atmosphere?

Figure 643: For the good of humanity?

Herndon said that 'the monsters are poisoning humanity.' Chemtrails are a cumulative death sentence on the environment and much of humanity via their role in weather engineering (weather warfare), their toxicity and their hidden and most important content – nanotechnology (Fig 643). Chemtrails pollute people, rivers, lakes, seas, land, plants and forests as the Earth and its population are targeted by the Death Cult to change our reality into Archon reality. Trees and plant life are dying from the very toxins found in chemtrails (Fig 644). Once soil and water is contaminated everything gets it. Aluminium and barium levels have been increasing in water and soil all over the world, with snow on Mount Shasta in Northern

Figure 644: Killing the world – 'Archonising' the bad copy.

California recording an astonishing rise from seven parts per billion to *61,000* parts per billion. People under chemtrail bombardment report respiratory and flu-like illness, mental confusion and depression. Barium is known to weaken muscles, including heart muscles, and the immune system; thorium is a known cause of cancer and leukaemia; and aluminium is linked to osteoporosis, Alzheimer's disease, and damage to the immune system (again). Research at Britain's Bournemouth University published in the journal *Surgical Neurology International* reveals a dramatic increase in brain diseases. They compared figures between 1989 and 2010 in 21 Western countries and found that the average onset of dementia started ten years earlier in 2010 than in 1989. Deaths from neurological disease in older people had soared and ever younger people were being affected. Diseases had reached 'almost epidemic' levels and the report suggested that environmental factors were largely to blame. Lead researcher Colin Pritchard said: 'The rate of increase in such a short time suggests a silent or even a "hidden" epidemic, in which environmental factors must play a major part, not just ageing.' Brain-damaging aluminium is a constituent of chemtrails, which have appeared in the same span of

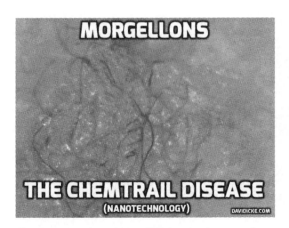

MORGELLONS

THE CHEMTRAIL DISEASE
(NANOTECHNOLOGY)
DAVIDICKE.COM

Figure 645: It's okay – it's just their imagination according to Mainstream Everything.

years covered by the research. Aluminium is also in vaccines. Dr Russell Blaylock, an American neurosurgeon and expert in neurotoxins, is convinced (as I have been for a long time) that chemtrails are a delivery system for nanotechnology. He says nanoparticles of aluminium in chemtrails correspond with an increase in brain degeneration diseases such as Alzheimer's and Parkinson's and he says they quickly enter the brain after people breathe them in. Nanoparticles are the real cause of the 'mystery' Morgellons disease which appeared in the same period that the chemtrails began. Morgellons involves coloured fibres growing inside the body which can be pulled out through the skin only to be replaced by others as they replicate (Fig 645). The same applies to the environment in general which is being constantly bathed in nanoparticles and toxins from the sky. We are in the realms of synthetic biology impacting upon and controlling 'natural' biology through multiple sources (the bad copy being further and further inverted). Synthetic = 'made by chemical synthesis, especially to imitate a natural product'. Big Pharma and Big Biotech-controlled government agencies like the US Food and Drug Administration and European Food Agency block promotion and use of nutrition from nature and yet wave through synthetic versions of the same thing. This is also connected to the agenda to create synthetic humans and a synthetic world. Mass die-offs of trees and plant life from chemtrail chemicals and other content (problem) provide the excuse to replace them with genetically-modified versions resistant to toxins (solution). 'Trials' of toxin-resistant/aluminium-resistant GMO trees, crops and plants are already happening. Frontline transhumanist promotor Ray Kurzweil said: 'Nanobots will infuse all the matter around us with information. Rocks, trees, everything will become these intelligent creatures.' What he is describing there is known as 'programmable matter'. Remember 'black goo and programmable matter'? At least one Morgellons sufferer has had black goo of the classic movie variety come out of their body. Another term for nanobots is 'smart dust' which was pump-primed by the infamous DARPA. Each micro-computer can communicate with all the rest to change anything including the human body because it manipulates programmable matter. Smart dust is the Demiurge/Archon virus. What is the major delivery system through which Kurzweil's nanobots are being distributed to 'infuse all matter'? *Chemtrails.*

Breathing in the 'new' human

Researchers from the University of California at Berkeley have developed what they call 'neural dust' or 'smart dust' to be implanted into human brains to collect data. Smart dust is so small no one would know if their brains had been breached and permanently embedded without need to recharge – the 'sentient nanoparticles spread on the wind' in

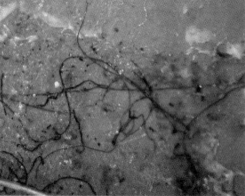

Figure 646: The world is being saturated with neural dust, nanodust or smart dust to make everyone and everything synthetic.

Figure 647: Morgellons fibres.

the movie *Transcendence.* Whenever a pillar of the conspiracy is announced to have been 'discovered' you can safely bet that it has long been available to insiders and to the Archons all along (Fig 646). Filaments and fibres have been found in air, soil and water samples of the same kind that can be seen in Morgellons sufferers. They are hollow tubes that do not exist in nature and cannot be identified from laboratory databases (Fig 647). The tubes are self-replicating, defy all attempts to eliminate them and some have been found in environmental samples containing a form of engineered dried blood cells. Ray Kurzweil has said that 'self-replicating nanotechnology will infuse everything with itself' and that artificial red blood cells were being developed (already exist). Research by scientist Clifford E. Carnicom of the Carnicom Institute in New Mexico found 'red blood cells, white blood cells, and unidentified cell types' within 'sub-micron fibre samples'. The cells appeared to be 'of a freeze-dried or desiccated [preserved by drying] nature in their original form within the microscopic fibres'. What the hell are synthetic blood cells doing in the environment? Fibre cultures have been grown from saliva, body tissue and urine from people who do not have Morgellons and it could well be that the general population is absorbing and integrating nanotechnology in chemtrails while the bodies of Morgellons sufferers are trying to reject it. Almost no mainstream research is being done into Morgellons because it is dismissed as a psychological problem under the term 'delusional parasitosis' (Fig 648). Coloured fibres coming through lesions in the skin is a psychological problem? Says it all, really. To accept the existence of Morgellons would obviously cause the dominoes to fall in pursuit of the cause and so Mainstream

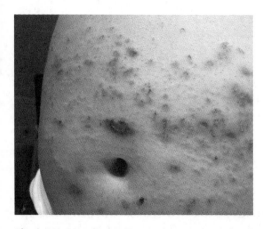

Figure 648: More imagination.

Everything goes into coordinated denial. The fact is that humanity is being infested with nanotechnology (another expression of the Archon virus) and a new synthetic human form is being constructed from *within*. Everything infested will be going through the same process and that means the entire environment under chemtrail bombardment. Central to this is GNA, the *synthetic* version of DNA, and there's another called PNA. Science20.com reported the creation of GNA in 2008 under the headline 'GNA: DNA's Chemical Cousin Is A Nanotechnology Building Block'. The report said:

> Biodesign Institute scientist John Chaput and his research team have made the first self-assembled nanostructures composed entirely of glycerol nucleic acid – a synthetic analog of DNA. The nanostructures contain additional properties not found in natural DNA, including the ability to form mirror image structures.

I wrote earlier about the crystalline nature of the body, and how this was connected to its role as a receiver- transmitter. If you mess with the crystalline structure you change the way that the body will receive and transmit information and what it will and won't connect with (i.e. the Saturn-Moon Matrix and not Infinite Awareness). Well, well. Nanotechnology now polluting humans through chemtrails is crystalline in nature. Long-time chemtrail researcher Sofia Smallstorm has described how 'coloured plaques' or hard pieces of silica have been found in the bodies of people with Morgellons. Some have dots on them and are so small they can only be properly seen under a microscope. She said:

> The plaques are fragile, they can shatter. Quantum dots which are the colours you see are nano-crystal semi-conductors made of heavy metal surrounded by an organic shell. Now I want you to remember some of these terms, 'heavy metals' – heavy metals, aluminium and so forth.

So these are nano-crystal semi-conductors surrounded by an organic shell but they are made of heavy metals and Morgellons subjects are also finding this stuff. Jewel-like hexagons, faceted pyramids, crystals. Hexagons have shown up environmentally, not only in tissues, but they are in environmental fall out ... The industry tells us that quantum dots are tiny nano crystals whose small size gives them unprecedented tunability, okay, tunability!

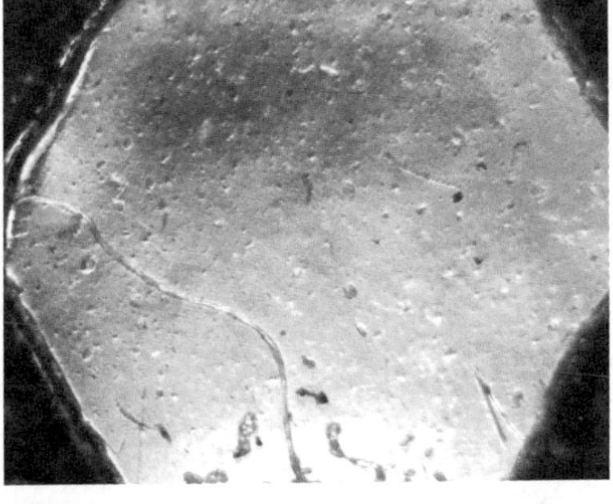

Figure 649: Hexagon crystals found in Morgellons sufferers.

I have already explained the significance of the hexagon and how interesting to find this in Morgellons sufferers and the environment (Fig 649). Common denominator – chemtrails. The new crystalline-manipulated human form is being tuned to the emerging Smart Grid sub-reality and the Demiurge virus frequency. Crystals can generate electricity through what is called the piezoelectric effect to produce a source of power for synthetic genetics and this can be activated by external 'pressure' which the technologically-generated electromagnetic soup is quite capable of triggering. The piezoelectric effect is a process of 'using crystals to convert mechanical energy into electricity or vice-versa.' Sofia Smallstorm put it very well when she said:

> Artificial intelligence will connect the world, homo sapien will be transformed into homo evolutis, biological processes will be run by technology, living things will not be reproductive, the Earth will be populated with engineered species and all processes will be patented, licensed and controlled. You could consider nanotechnology the installation of Artificial Intelligence in living and non-living things. Smart dust and smart moulds for instance are tiny nano-sensors that can float and land anywhere.

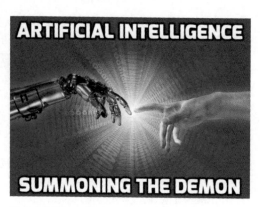

Figure 650: Literally summoning the demon – the Demiurge.

This is why they are in chemtrails – geoengineering to achieve bioengineering and infestation with Artificial Intelligence or Demiurge 'intelligence'. The new trans-human, sub-human, will not have gender (hence the systematic confusing and blurring of gender today); they will not produce children (similar to the ones produced in World State Hatcheries in *Brave New World*); and they will be programmed as genetic slaves detached from Infinite Awareness serving a hive-mind controlled by the 'superhuman' *El*-ite (Demiurge/Archon Artificial Intelligence). Oliver Curry, a researcher in the Institute of Cognitive and Evolutionary Anthropology at the University of Oxford, once said: 'The human race will one day split into two separate species. An attractive, intelligent, ruling elite and an underclass, dim-witted, ugly, goblin-like creatures. So here you have the E-workers and the E-lites.' Spot on in theme – if we allow it. Curry was talking about way into the 'future' but it is in the process of being technologically created now (Fig 650). I don't know about the goblin-like creatures, but the division between worker and *El*-lite is very appropriate. Another point here – Monsanto have successfully sued farmers into oblivion for using their GMO products without a licence when their crops were contaminated by GMO arriving on the wind or from passing trucks. What about body-modifying nanotechnology blowing on the wind? Who would own your body then in the eyes of Archon law? One other thing about nanotechnology smart dust: It is the ultimate in surveillance in that smart dust infusing all matter, as Kurzweil puts it, can recognise an individual anywhere they are to the extent that their computer can be automatically turned on when they walk through the door at work and the elevator can automatically open at the right floor. I am not surmising this – it's in the promotion material for a smart dust world. Who needs smartphone tracking, face recognition tracking or camera tracking when smart dust will recognise where you are, wherever you are, at all times?

All of one mind

The plan is for humans to be nothing more than hive-mind slaves like the Borg in the *Star Trek* series (Fig 651). So many already operate as a hive-mind through lack of expanded awareness and individual perceptions. Brain-scanning research has shown that a neural response to something by very few people can provide an accurate prediction of how the whole population would respond. A Borg-like hive-mind would be dramatically more extreme and technologically driven. Archons are akin to the Borg as slaves and expressions of the Demiurge virus and they are attempting to assimilate humans into the same 'collective'. Here is a description of the Borg. See if you recognise the themes after what I have said so far:

Figure 651: The story of the Borg is the story of the Archons.

> The Borg are a collection of species that have been turned into cybernetic organisms functioning as drones in a hive mind called the Collective, or the hive ... The Borg use a process called assimilation to force other species into the Collective by violent injection of microscopic machines called nanoprobes.

Figure 652: The Borg travelled in black cubes.

If it wasn't so tragic, you could chuckle. The Borg [Archons] even travel in black cubes – the symbol of Saturn (Fig 652). Demiurge-Archon assimilation includes Reptilians, Greys and other non-human species infested with the virus. 'Resistance is futile' is the Borg mantra as in 'we are the Borg ... we will add your biological and technological distinctiveness to our own ...your culture will adapt to service us ... resistance is futile'. *Invasion of the Body Snatchers* released in 1956 had the same theme of human bodies taken over by 'an alien form of life – a cosmic form'. This is one telling piece of dialogue:

> Seeds drifting through space for years took root in a farmer's field. From the seeds came pods which had the power to reproduce themselves in the exact likeness of any form of life ... Your new bodies are growing in there. They're taking you over cell for cell, atom for atom.

> There is no pain. Suddenly, while you're asleep, they'll absorb your minds, your memories and you're reborn into an untroubled world ...Tomorrow you'll be one of us ... There's no need for

love ... Love. Desire. Ambition. Faith. Without them, life is so simple, believe me.

Peter H. Diamandis, co-founder of the Singularity University with Ray Kurzweil, said:

Anybody who is going to be resisting the progress forward is going to be resisting evolution and, fundamentally, they will die out. It's not a matter of whether it's good or bad. It's going to happen [Resistance is futile].

But it's *not* futile – or I wouldn't bother. Hive-mind assimilation is being funded in part by DARPA with a technique called 'mind-meld' which can connect brains into one multiple-functioning unit, transfer thoughts and perceptions between them and has the potential to download into robot technology. Another hive-mind project involving monkeys connected their brains to form a 'collective' or 'superbrain'. An article even compared this with the hive-mind of the Borg (Fig 653).

Figure 653: Connecting humanity to the Demiurge/Archon virus hive mind.

Miguel Nicolelis from America's Duke University School of Medicine was the scientist behind the experiment and it's claimed that this could lead to 'organic computers' or 'collectives of brains linked together'. Nicolelis is quoted as saying: 'We're conditioned by movies and Hollywood to think that everything related to science is dangerous and scary ...These scary scenarios never crossed my mind and I'm the one doing the experiments.' Well, they bloody well ought to, mate. Societal pressure towards collectivism and consensus of view (including political correctness) is connected to this transfer of perception from the individual and unique expression of Infinite Possibility to the hive-mind collective of transhumanist 'assimilation'. So, too, is the war against a sense of individuality which includes the merging of male and female under titles like 'the end of gender' and 'transphobia' with transgender education at the earliest ages to prepare people for the transhumanist AI former human that would be neither male or female and not reproduce. Extreme and expanding bias against heterosexuality in favour of same-sex relationships is all part of this conditioning and if political correctness extremists don't like me saying that well fuck 'em. I don't care where anyone puts their dangle so long as the receiver is okay with it. I am saying that what is happening in terms of sexual bias is preparation for a world when there will be *no sexuality* and straight, gay, binary, non-binary, black, brown, sky-blue pink, minority, ethnic and whatever else will *all* be imprisoned and absorbed in the same AI worker-ant assimilation. They won't have a choice about being binary then because 0 and 1 will be who they are (Fig 654). Observe all that is being thrown at the human body, mind and emotions; the controls, limitations, impositions and deletions of basic freedoms that

Figure 654: All-binary – and then some.

Figure 655: What you tune into you believe you are.

increase by the day; the blatant and admitted plan to merge and assimilate humans with Artificial Intelligence technology that would become *our* intelligence. Is there anyone still brain-dead enough to believe that this is all to protect us from terrorism or in the interests of making us 'super human'? It is about making us sub-human to be assimilated by the non-human.

Mass mind control

Chemtrail metals are changing the air by making it highly-charged and electrically-conductive. This is bad for human health and well-being, increases the power and effectiveness of radio waves and other communications manipulating the human mind and emotions, and empowers still further the technological sub-reality perception 'bubble'. Weather manipulation through HAARP-type technology also becomes even more effective. If you control the nature of the sea, you affect all the fish – and if you control the frequency and information nature of the energy sea you affect all the human 'fish' (Fig 655). Dr Robert Beck, an expert in nuclear engineering, co-authored a scientific research paper nearly 40 ago with Dr Michael A. Persinger of Laurentian University in Canada, an expert in Extremely Low Frequency (ELF) radiation, which explored the potential for mind control through electromagnetic fields. Many levels of the human hologram and auric fields are electromagnetic in nature. Dr Beck told a Psychotronics Association conference in 1979 that people exposed to certain ELF field patterns experienced sensations of uneasiness, depression and foreboding. Dr Andrija Puharich, an American medical and parapsychological researcher, showed some 60 years ago how the use of frequencies can manipulate mood and behaviour and obviously the more powerfully this can be delivered the bigger the effect. He found that 10.80 Hz triggered 'riotous behaviour' and 6.6 Hz made people depressed. Psychics in 'out there'-mode operated at 8 Hz. Frequency warfare is used by the military to manipulate mood and perceptions of enemy troops, and have no doubt this is used against civilian protestors, too. Broadcasting the frequency to stimulate the desired effect can produce riots, depression, whatever response you want. Dr Andrew Michrowski, a technologies specialist with the Canadian Department of State and president of the Planetary Association for Clean Energy (PACE), said that virtually anything could be externally implanted in the human mind, which people would take to be their own 'words, phrases, images, sensations and emotions'. We have even had advertisement 'trials' on German trains in which messages are beamed into the minds of passengers when they lean their head against the window. The Soviet Union broadcast perception-manipulation frequencies and information into the United States in the 1970s through the 'Woodpecker' signal named after its repetitive tapping sound. American Lieutenant Colonel John B. Alexander wrote in *Military Review* that they were well aware that Soviet 'mind-altering techniques' were advanced and included 'manipulation of human behaviour through the use of psychological weapons affecting sight, sound, smell, temperature, electromagnetic energy, or sensory deprivation'. He said that certain low-frequency (ELF) emissions possess psychoactive characteristics which could be used 'to induce depression or irritability in a target population'. Alexander said that large-scale ELF behaviour modification could have an horrendous impact (HAARP technology can operate in this band). Missing from his comments was that the United States and other countries could do the same as the Soviet Union and that in the end all those 'separate' sources of electromagnetic mass mind and emotion control answered to the same Archontic Web. A United States Patent from April, 1976 involved 'apparatus and method for remotely monitoring and altering brain waves' and explained how brain activity could be manipulated and monitored from a distance using electromagnetic fields. The summary said:

> ... high frequency transmitters are operated to radiate electromagnetic energy of different frequencies through antennas which are capable of scanning the entire brain of the test subject or any desired region thereof. The signals of different frequencies penetrate the skull of the subject and impinge upon the brain where they mix to yield an interference wave modulated by radiations from the brain's natural electrical activity.

No, this is not a conspiracy 'theory'. Dr Robert Beck told the Psychotronics Association conference in 1979 that the Woodpecker signals were being broadcast into American homes through electrical systems. He said they were acting 'like gangbusters ... right in the window of human psychoactivity ... permeating power grids in the United States ... being picked up by power lines, re-radiated ...' and then *'coming into homes on the light circuits'*. Two things immediately come from this: firstly he is describing what was happening 40 years ago and the technology is light-years more effective today; and secondly this was being done via an electrical system that was not built for this purpose. The Smart Grid is being built *precisely* for this purpose and this is the reason for the otherwise insane imposition by law of 'green' light bulbs, which are designed not primarily to provide light but as *transmitters of information* for the Smart Grid (Fig 656). I have presented the background in *The Perception Deception* to

Figure 656: Radiation information transmitter.

how these radiation-generating twirling 'green' bulbs manipulate emotional states and are dangerous to health, environment and water supplies by their use of deadly brain-suppressing mercury and the radiation they emit. They are also absolutely useless compared with the incandescent bulbs they are by law replacing. I have said before – alarm bells should ring whenever something ludicrous is being introduced with the force of law at the exclusion of better options. The same mind control themes I have explained here also apply to Wi-Fi sources such as smart meters. Anything that broadcasts information within the

Figure 657: Wi-Fi information taking over the energy sea.

frequency band of the human Body-Mind is a potential mind control device (Fig 657).

Changing the Atmosphere

Archons in form and non-human assets possessed by the virus, including virus-infected Reptilians, require a different frequency and atmosphere to operate here for any lengthy period. Their atmosphere needs to be far more irradiated than is good for humans. Our radiation environment is being systematically transformed to make it 'home' for the Archons and their assets and one aspect is the far more conductive nature of chemtrail-infested air. The former UK Radiological Protection Board said that radiation in the environment has increased by *many* millions of times in only 50 years, and this increase is getting faster all the time as new technological sources are introduced – 'their atmosphere needs to be far more irradiated than is good for humans ...' We have Wi-Fi; computers and wireless keyboards/mice; smart meters; 'green' light bulbs; irradiated food; microwave ovens; power lines; full-body scanners, X-rays and CAT scanners; depleted uranium released from US and NATO weapons unleashed on civilian and

other targets; smartphones; iPads and electronic books; cell phone towers; GWEN, TETRA and other electromagnetic communication; remote controls of all kinds; HAARP-type technology and cosmic rays allowed through by HAARP radio waves punching holes in the ionosphere; and what other radiation is being fired at Earth from satellite? These are only some of the sources of technological radiation that are dramatically changing the energy 'sea' to make it dangerous on all levels of being to humans, animals and the environment in general (Fig 658). Also well known is that contact with powerful electromagnetic

Figure 658: The fast-emerging technological sub-reality is everywhere – including fake cactuses and trees.

fields makes people more open to mind manipulation. Barrie Trower, a retired British military intelligence scientist, has long experience in microwave warfare and has been widely quoted on the dangers of the TETRA system. He explained why microwave frequencies were employed for cell phones and today's mass communication networks:

> During the 1950s and 1960s during the Cold War, it was realised by accident that microwaves could be used as stealth weapons when the Russians beamed the American embassy during the Cold War and it gave everybody working in the embassy cancer, breast cancers, leukaemia whatever, and it was realised then that low level microwaves were the perfect stealth weapon to be used on dissident groups around the world, because you could make dissident groups sick, give them cancer, change their mental outlook on life without them even knowing they were being radiated.

> The electromagnetic spectrum is a band that goes from gamma rays and x-rays at one end, the very high energy waves, and it comes down through visible light, which is also some radiation, and then it goes through infrared microwaves, TV and radio. Now the only ones which really affect us in the communications industry are the microwaves, and microwaves have a special ability to interfere with water, which is how microwave ovens work, and we are made of water. All of our chemical and electrical signals involve water in the body, somehow, electrical communications in the body. So, the industry has picked the worst possible part of the electromagnetic spectrum to give to young children and to adults.

The Hidden Hand made this decision because the effects described by Barry Trower and many more are what they want to happen. Microwaves can penetrate bone, walls and people and hence we have microwave Wi-Fi. We live in a raging sea of microwaves today when Trower says that he was told during his time in the military that there was *no safe level* of microwaves (Fig 659). How could there be when Wi-Fi radiation is interacting with the human auric radiation field from which the body is made manifest? Trower says microwave ovens can change the nature of proteins in the food they zap and yet of the 100,000 different proteins in the body he says 'we only know about 600' and so have no idea about the effect of microwave-mutating proteins. But the Hidden Hand does. Look how much food is cooked in this way in homes, cafes and restaurants. Trower also makes the point that low level microwaves can be even worse than high level because of a mechanism in the body that defends against their effect. He says that this defence mechanism is activated by high level microwaves while at low level they can get 'under the radar'. Trower warns that the smaller you are the more you are affected and that of course brings us to children who also have thinner skulls protecting the brain. Smartphone for your child, anyone? The official 'safe' levels for smartphones (there are none) are estimated using a fake head or 'Sam phantom head' (how appropriate) which is based on the skull thickness of

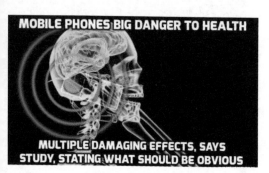

Figure 659: No level of microwave radiation is safe.

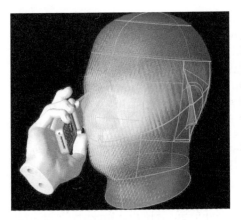

Figure 660: Sam Phantom Head – based on the thick skulls of US troops but the 'safety' measurement for thin-skulled children to use the technology.

Figure 661: Madness.

Figure 662: The consequences are going to be catastrophic.

American troops (Fig 660). Many smartphones are right on that limit and yet used by children with far thinner skulls (Fig 661). I call smartphones the 'Silent Holocaust' because the cumulative effects on health are going to be devastating (Fig 662). Put a microwave device to the side of your brain many times a day, yeah, good thinking. Trower says there is no published paper anywhere in the world giving a safe limit for a child to be subjected to microwaves for a simple reason – there is no safe limit. He reveals that documents in his possession, not made public for obvious reasons, list brain tumours on the front and side of the head as the biggest cause of death in children in the UK. He also quotes university researchers, government scientists and international scientific advisors, as predicting a minimum of 57.7% of schoolgirls exposed to low-level microwave radiation (Wi-Fi) risk foetal abnormalities and giving birth to still-born, genetically damaged children with the genetic damage passing to the next generation.

Now, for anyone who doubts the plan for a colossal cull of the global population here is a devastating point made by Barrie Trower: If nothing is done about Wi-Fi, smart meters etc., then in the lifetime of one person – 60 years – the number of healthy children will be one-*eighth* – one fucking *eighth* – of what it is now. Day after day kids leave their Wi-Fi homes and take their Wi-Fi phones to walk through Wi-Fi streets to sit in Wi-Fi schools for hours while Richard Branson, Facebook and their like work to cover every square inch of the planet in Wi-Fi radiation fields. Cancer has soared with the extraordinary increase in radiation, and when you add mass toxicity it is testament to the human immune system that anyone is still alive. This is why a major and recurring Archon target is the immune system. Mutation and weakening of human genetics through toxicity and radiation are also to dilute the influence and impact of what we call 'human' so the transhuman influences have no opposition or challenge. Barrie Trower, one of the world's most renowned experts on the effects of microwave technology, has a simple message: microwaves are killing us – and fast. Microwave ovens that leak (and so many do) are 'incredibly dangerous to eyes', he says, and 'incredibly dangerous if you are a woman of child-bearing age or are pregnant'. Trower said that he knew of at least 59 scientific papers linking microwaves to breast cancers. He challenges anyone to show him a police station, fire station or other emergency service anywhere in the world that has had TETRA for 18 months and he will 'absolutely guarantee' that the level of violence by the police, breast cancer and other cancers, sickness, miscarriages and still-births will all have gone up. He has challenged anyone to find a location where this is not the case and no one ever has. Trower relates increases in violence by the police to being overexposed to microwave radiation because aggression is 'a symptom of this particular pulsed frequency'. He told the excellent and recommended Richie Allen radio show on Davidicke.com that he has a United States document from 1976 which states that the public and military/law enforcement 'must be deceived' about the full potential damage of microwaves to 'protect industrial output' and avoid legal actions. He quotes the frequencies agreed in official documents to manipulate mood and health including paranoia, depression/suicide, manic behaviour/anger, and blindness (aimed at the head) and heart attack (aimed at the chest). US Department of Defense documents list hypertension, changes in blood state, headache, fatigue, menstrual disorders, depression, anxiety and many ailments previously listed. One says that 'personnel exposed to microwave radiation below thermal levels experience more neurological, cardio-vascular and haemodynamic disturbances than do their unexposed counterparts'. Haemodynamic relates to blood flow within organs and tissue. Trower says that his experience in the Royal Navy, which involved questioning spies, made him realise the even more devastating effect of pulsing frequencies added to microwaves. These can seize the heart and brain and cause hundreds of health and emotional problems and changes in behaviour that the victims would not associate with the real cause. Smartphones, smart meters, Wi-Fi, etc., all operate with pulsing frequencies. Much has been said about the way cell phones heat the brain and that's bad enough, but the pulsing aspect is even worse (Fig 663). Trower said the authorities knew of some 600 different pulsing frequencies for such uses with more being added all the time. This radiation madness has been described as an experiment with life itself, but to those driving the insanity it's no experiment. They *know* what the outcome is planned to be because they have done the same to other societies and realities many times before. What we are seeing is merely the repeating Demiurge-Archon virus modus operandi. Another key source of irradiating the atmosphere is through nuclear 'accidents' and nuclear war. All over the world sit nuclear bombs and disasters waiting to happen called nuclear power stations which were introduced

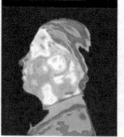

Figure 663: Heating of the brain is bad enough after only a short call, but the pulsing nature of the technology is even more damaging.

Figure 664: Each a potential nuclear bomb.

Figure 665: Fukushima was no accident – see my other books that look at this in detail.

from the start through the manipulations of the House of Rothschild (Fig 664). I have explained in *Remember Who You Are* and *The Perception Deception* why the nuclear catastrophe at Fukushima in Japan in 2011 was no accident and the scale of radiation that this has released into the atmosphere and Pacific Ocean – and is still releasing – is truly astonishing (Fig 665). One researcher specialising in the consequences of Fukushima said: 'The Pacific is in terminal decline. The Fukushima legacy is terrifying.' The unfolding effect on all forms of life is equally horrific with studies finding thyroid cancer rates among children in the Fukushima region 50 times higher than the general population. *National Geographic* reported on a sudden and 'bewildering' die-off in the Pacific:

In March 2012, less than one percent of the seafloor beneath Station M was covered in dead sea salps. By July 1, more than 98 percent of it was covered in the decomposing organisms, according to the study, published this week in the Proceedings of the National Academy of Sciences. The major increase in activity of deep-sea life in 2011 and 2012 weren't limited to Station M ...

... Even though they do not have a 'scientific explanation' for what is happening, the scientists are admitting that they have never seen a die-off of this magnitude in the 24 years that this study has been going on ...

They could never use the politically incorrect 'f' word – Fukushima. The public must not be allowed to make a connection between cause and effect or the future radiation plans of the agenda could come under scrutiny. When radiation levels in water, food and air breach previous 'safe limits' (they weren't) the authorities simply increase the levels they tell the public are officially safe. Oh, yes, *officially*. All that means is the 'safe' limit the agenda requires to safely (legally) continue with its mayhem.

Rule by robots

The Smart Grid/transhumanist conspiracy and the radiation this requires and generates are designed to achieve the following among many other goals:

- Attach human minds technologically to the Smart Grid through genetic manipulation, entrainment and 'implantables' to control thought, emotion and perception and prevent anyone from accessing awareness beyond the Matrix.

- Change the frequency and atmosphere to make it conducive to the Archons and their agents in form.
- Destroy human health as part of the cull and mutate a new slave species that can live in a highly irradiated environment as they are doing with trees, plants etc.

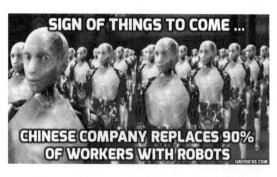

Figure 666: The effect on employment of the robot society is going to be world-changing if we allow it.

This is all planned to be overseen and controlled not only by smart and associated AI technologies but by robots which in the end look so like humans it will be difficult to tell them apart: The ultimate 'singularity' of turning robots into humans and humans into robots. Our world is being transformed by robots of multiple types. Society-changing numbers of jobs are going to be lost to them in coming years and it's already begun (Fig 666); but this is about more than lost employment. It is taking human

Figure 667: We are standing at the threshold of the end of humans. Worth getting off our arses for?

control to a whole new stage and level. iRobot, maker of the Roomba robot vacuum, is developing roving robots with on-board cameras to map your house because CEO Colin Angle says this will be needed 'for tasking a growing team of robots that are in your home.' Taking over your home, more like. Researchers from the Royal Melbourne Institute of Technology said they have created a device 10,000 times thinner than a human hair, which is a 'vital step towards creating a bionic brain', and we are told that 'the best minds' are working towards a truly sentient digital brain. Russian scientists at Tomsk State University in Western Siberia say they have created a model of a brain that is able to educate itself and 'could be an artificial carrier of a natural mind, able to learn and react to the environment'. Robots are predicted to have self-awareness and emotions, and bioengineers at Harvard University have created the first examples of cyborg tissue – 'neurons, heart cells, muscle, and blood vessels that are interwoven by nanowires and transistors' that allow a computer to interface directly with the cells. This is what nanotechnology in chemtrails is doing to humans to turn them into robots. We have reached the point where one legal expert has called for laws to regulate robots in case they 'wake up' and demand rights, and also because of their potentially lethal capabilities (Fig 667). Ryan Calo from the University of Washington's School of Law said that robots 'increasingly blur the line between person and machine' and 'imagine that an artificial intelligence announces it has achieved self-awareness, a claim no one

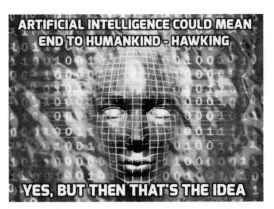

Figure 668: This is the point that is missed. It's not stupidity, it is design.

seems able to discredit'. Software like the Siri personal assistant app and other versions in which people interact with a robot voice are specifically designed to blur that line on the Totalitarian Tiptoe to a robot-controlled society. A Barbie doll has been introduced that does the same thing. A survey of 12,000 users of a digital assistant app similar to Siri found that almost half could imagine falling in love with their virtual assistant. Ryan Calo asks – what if a machine claims the right to make copies of itself (the only way it knows to replicate)? But how do you regulate something that is planned to regulate everything? This is the point that is missed by those warning against the consequences of Artificial Intelligence. Scientist Stephen Hawking has said that without AI safeguards humanity could be heading for a dark future and even the demise of our species (Fig 668). Computer scientist Professor Stuart Russell told the journal *Science* that artificial intelligence could be as dangerous as nuclear weapons or even worse with AI's 'bewildering variety of software that we cannot yet describe'. These are valid points but still the crux of the matter is missing. Those in the shadows (and many who are not) promoting and driving AI and transhumanism intend to have Artificial Intelligence take over humanity and certainly not be subordinate to human laws, regulations and constraints.

Robot Army

While such warnings are being delivered the Pentagon's DARPA, in cahoots with Google / Alphabet, push on with the robot explosion and the creation of robot armies. DARPA is funding a Robotics Grand Challenge which claims to be seeking to improve responses to disasters and rescues, when the real motivation is the military and control

Figure 669: Hey, troops of today – these will be chasing you and your families when they've taken over and you have realised you've been hoaxed.

applications. Positive uses for robotics are only the cover story to hide the truth of where this is meant to lead. Google bought robotics company Boston Dynamics in 2013 along with its DARPA contracts to develop robots for military purposes. The world army / police force that I described earlier is eventually planned to be an army of AI robots (currently called 'autonomous weapons') controlled by AI 'generals' and police personnel (Fig 669). Human troops and those now using transhumanist 'Transformer'-type technologies are just the stepping stone to the robot army and they had better realise this fact and quick. The whole *Transformer* movie theme along with videogames is preparing people for the AI-controlled transhumanist society and making it 'sexy' (Fig 670). 'Fighting for my country' is just another Archontic scam to exploit human troops to impose the will of the Hidden Hand until they, too, become surplus to requirements. *Business Finance News* (BFN) reported in 2015 that Pentagon agency DARPA is heavily funding a project to 'enhance human ability in

Figure 670: On the way to fully-fledged technological control.

war zones, by altering the genetic code of their soldiers'. They hope to achieve supremacy by making soldiers who are stronger, smarter, more focused and *lack empathy*. Here we go again. DARPA refers to the human genetic code as the 'recipe'. The BFN report said:

> The part of the brain that is responsible for empathy can be turned off by gene therapy, making the soldiers oblivious to fear, fatigue and emotions. What makes this thought even more terrifying is the 'Human Assisted Neural Devices program' which focuses on controlling the brain. The result is the next generation of biological war 'machines', which could be controlled by a sophisticated 'joystick'.

Turning troops into robots. 'Biological war machines' = biological computers with no consciousness as we would perceive it. This is a stepping stone to a fully AI military. A US Navy website in 2015 ran the headline 'Navy to Accelerate Artificial Intelligence Development for Warfighting, Support Roles'. The article said: 'The Navy wants to integrate robotics and artificial intelligence (AI) into more of its workload, from warfighting missions to non-combat support roles, and is seeking fleet input on what types of AI research are worth investing in.' This is happening in all parts of the military and across the world as the global robot army controlled by Archon AI takes shape (Fig 671). 'Matrix Sentinels, atten-*shun*.'

Stephen Hawking and thousands of other scientists have warned about a robot arms race in which technological killers will be so cheap to build and be the 'Kalashnikovs of tomorrow'. They warned of terrorists and warlords perpetrating ethnic cleansing, assassinations, destabilising nations, subduing populations and killing ethnic groups. This is possible until the complete takeover but it would be far more pertinent to make this warning

Figure 671: This is the penny that needs to drop.

about governments, and even more so about the shadow forces behind governments. This is where it is really coming from and whose ends it is planned to serve. Once again DARPA, one of the world's most sinister organisations, has been driving transhumanism and artificial intelligence as it brags on its own website:

> DARPA has also long been a leader in the development of artificial intelligence, machine intelligence and semi-autonomous systems. DARPA's efforts in this domain have focused primarily on military operations, including command and control, but the commercial sector has adopted and expanded upon many of the agency's results to develop wide-spread applications in fields as diverse as manufacturing, entertainment and education.

Yes, just as they were meant to. DARPA is also the force behind the development of synthetic genetics and DNA which is a foundation pillar of the Archon transhumanist society. *The Washington Post* reported:

> In the public sector, the role of innovation giant DARPA in funding synthetic biology projects has exploded, eclipsing the role of other prominent U.S. government agencies that fund synthetic biology programs, such as the National Science Foundation (NSF), National Institutes of Health (NIH), and the USDA. In 2014 alone, DARPA funded $100 million in programs, more than three times the amount funded by the NSF, marking a fast ramp-up from a level of zero in 2010.

If DARPA, an arm of the Pentagon (arm of the Archons), is involved in anything then it is always real bad for humanity.

Pill pushers

One other point needs mentioning in this chapter. 'Smart pills' are a forerunner to the population being permanently drugged. A dystopian movie called *Equilibrium* released in 2003 featured a storyline in which both the masses and police state personnel were forced to take mind-suppressing drugs every day and they were technologically monitored to ensure they did so. Today we have headlines like 'Smart Pill Contains Microchip to Monitor Patient Medication' and 'Smart pill with edible microchip that tells you and your doctor when the next dose is due'. Patients take their pills with a sensor that sends information to a receiver patch worn on the shoulder or arm. This data is then communicated to a mobile device, smartphone or tablet, to tell the patient or doctor when the next dose is due (Fig 672). Technological capability for enforced drug-taking portrayed in *Equilibrium* is already here and it is planned to be monitored eventually by Artificial Intelligence. Mandatory vaccinations are a stepping-stone to this goal. The young are most aggressively targeted and here is a

Figure 672: Smart pills for Smart Grid minds.

headline that highlights the point: 'Watchdog Says Report of 10,000 Toddlers on ADHD Drugs Tip of the Iceberg – 274,000 0-1 Year Olds and 370,000 Toddlers Prescribed Psychiatric Drugs'. Pauses for breath. The US Centers for Disease Control admit that ten thousand toddlers are being given mind-changing drugs for Attention deficit hyperactivity disorder (ADHD) which is a make-believe 'disease' concocted by taking a series of childhood behaviours and giving them a name. It was done to justify the mass drugging of the still-developing minds of children to change them for the rest of their lives. This is outrageous enough, but the Citizens Commission on Human Rights, a mental health watchdog, says that data provided by IMS Health, the world's leading health information and analytics company, shows that the situation is seriously more extreme. It says that hundreds of thousands of toddlers are being prescribed far more powerful psychiatric drugs with many given them before their first birthday. By the time they reach the age of five the number is more than a million and this leaps to more than four million for children between six and twelve. American psychiatrist and mental health reformer Allen Frances said:

> There are no objective tests in psychiatry – no X-ray, laboratory or exam finding that says definitively that someone does or does not have a mental disorder. There is no definition of mental disorder. It's bull … I mean you just can't define it.

The mass drugging of children from birth is being done systematically on the road to compulsory psychiatric medication to control the perceptions of the population. The National Institutes of Health list serious side-effects (effects) of these drugs as agitation, mania, aggressive or hostile behaviour, seizures, hallucinations, and sudden death. But the Archons and their hybrids don't care – the agenda is all that matters. Vaccinations are an obvious access point for drugs, toxins and nanochips/nanobots and this is another reason for the gathering campaign to make them compulsory. Researchers at the University of California-San Diego announced in 2015 the development of 'microfish' – 'smart' microbots to travel through the bloodstream delivering drugs to specific parts of the body. There is also a smartphone-connected system that can detect changes in a person's mood and behaviour patterns and transmit this information to 'professionals' in real time (Fig 673); but even that's not enough for these maniacs. Scientists at Taiwan University are creating sensors to be implanted in teeth to transmit information to doctors via Bluetooth (how apt) with information about talking and chewing. How have we ever coped before? Once again insider Zbigniew Brzezinski predicted it all. He wrote in 1970:

> Speaking of a future at most only decades away, an experimenter in intelligence control asserted, 'I foresee a time when we shall have the means and therefore, inevitably, the temptation to manipulate the behaviour and intellectual functioning of the people

Figure 673: Hey, cool, man.

through environmental and biochemical manipulation of the brain.

Through drugs and the technological sub-reality in other words. A long list of movies have featured the same repeating dystopian, transformer/transhumanist themes and this is mass mind-conditioning known as pre-emptive or predictive programming to prepare people to accept just such a society. What is planned is so dramatically different to what has gone before and dystopian and transhumanist movies and other media are making people consciously and subconsciously familiar with this Brave New World to make it less of shock and dilute potential resistance. There are many other levels to pre-emptive programming but this is one of the major ones.

If we don't face what I have revealed in this book and both wake up and grow up, then humanity as we know will be no more – and not too far from now either. The plan is for ever-diminishing human self-awareness on the road to complete perception control by Archontic Artificial Intelligence. That nightmare scenario doesn't have to be, but it is now going to take a colossal and unified effort to stop it. People can call me mad or they can get their arses in gear. This is the choice that will decide the very nature of human existence, and even if there will be human existence in any form that could be recognised as 'human'.

CHAPTER TWELVE

You That Time Forgot

I am intrigued by the smile upon your face, and the sadness within your eyes
Jeremy Aldana

Okay, so what do we do? *I got it.* We gather a People's Army, stockpile weapons and start a guerrilla war against The System. We assassinate its major figures, launch a revolution and bring a People's leader to power. That'll do it.

Well, it never has before. All that's happened is that a lot of people have been killed and maimed to replace one System with another version of the same System. 'Physical' revolutions never changed anything that didn't end up being pretty much the same – or worse. But I *am* calling for a revolution in the sense of 'a sudden or momentous change in a situation'. My revolution can also be described by another definition of the word: 'A turning or rotational motion about an axis.' Put another way: flipping the inversion. Revolutions throughout what we call history have only swapped one form of tyranny and control for another – communism for 'democracy' or 'democracy' for communism and so on. This has happened because they have all lacked the ultimate revolution, a revolution of *consciousness*. A revolution of *awareness*. A revolution of *perception*. A revolution of *self-identity* (Fig 674). If they don't change nothing else can except in rhetoric and presentation. You can seek a solution to what you would like to change and gather a People's Army; or you can remove the cause of the problem and become conscious beyond the Program, conscious beyond Body-Mind. From this all else must come, for everything is a state of consciousness. Our 'world' or reality is an expression of hijacked consciousness. Myopic awareness must always manifest limitation in proportion to the myopia. Closed minds create closed worlds. The Archontic virus has not created our Prison Planet; it has manipulated our sense of perception so we created

Figure 674: The Revolution from which all else comes.

Figure 675: Pixel awareness ...

... and picture awareness – same world but a very different perception.

it ourselves. What you believe you perceive, and what you perceive you experience. Closed awareness sees only dots and thus apartness and division. It is Pixel Awareness and what we need is Picture Awareness; it is Screen Awareness and what we need is Projector Awareness (Fig 675). From a sense of apartness and division comes divide and rule and from that comes war and conflict on multiple levels and the perception that we must 'compete'. Competition is a war on cooperation. Pixel Awareness competes. Picture Awareness cooperates. How could you not cooperate when you know that all is one? What is the point of competing with yourself? What is the point of fighting with yourself? Picture Awareness can see this. Pixel Awareness cannot. So what is my 'revolution'? Pixel Awareness becomes Picture Awareness. Game over.

'It can't be that simple, Dave.' Oh, but it can and it *is*. The world seems so complex and yet it isn't. Apparent complexity is the playing out of what is at its core very simple: What you believe you perceive and what you perceive you experience. A multitude of experience gives the illusion of complexity but how you got there is so simple. Even the 'multitude' is only an illusion because when you break it down most experience is the *same* experience wearing a different disguise. War does not only happen on battlefields of blood and gore (Fig 676). War happens in relationships, business and law courts (Fig 677). You don't need a gun in your hand to hurt your perceived opponent, the one you seek to vanquish and dominate. A row, bankruptcy or legal attack can work just as well. They may not be considered 'war' but they are – 'active hostility or contention; conflict'.

I have had relationships that were based on cooperation and others based on competition (war) and I have experienced legal actions that were nothing less than war by paperwork, claim and counterclaim,

Figure 676: War is only the most extreme level of conflict ...

Figure 677: ... there are many others.

Figure 678: Love or fear? – the universal question.

INSIDE EACH OF US ARE TWO WOLVES

ONE IS EVIL

IT IS ANGER
ENVY SORROW
REGRET GREED
ARROGANCE
GUILT
RESENTMENT
INFERIORITY
FLASE PRIDE
SUPERORITY
AND EGO

ONE IS GOOD

IT IS JOY
PEACE LOVE
HOPE
SERENITY
HUMILITY
KINDNESS
BENEVOLENCE
GENEROSITY
TRUTH
COMPASSION
AND FAITH

© Blu222

WHICH WOLF WINS? THE ONE YOU FEED MOST

Figure 679: Archon reality or Infinite reality?

with one side intent to wound and seize the spoils and the other in a rearguard action of self-protection and survival. How is that any different from the basic dynamic of war? Legal attacks have ended in my favour, but took an enormous amount of money to defend against, which I have never recovered. This is another common theme of war – nobody wins. 'Victory' is counted by the scale of loss, not gain. I heard a quote one time that said something like 'when you go to war you have already lost'. This is so true. How many soldiers from 'victorious' armies have been mentally, emotionally and 'physically' devastated by what they did and saw? History sees 'winners', but I see losers every time. The point I am making is that just as war happens on multiple levels and in multiple ways so do other experiences that appear to be different, but are expressions of the same one. Nuclear weapons, hostile takeovers, legal attacks, a war of words. It is only matter of scale. In the end it comes down to two states of perception: fear and love. Everything is one or the other (Fig 678). War is fear made manifest and so is competition. Peace in its true sense (not just the absence of war) is love made manifest and so is cooperation. Worry, anxiety, stress, regret, aggression, hatred, hostility, arrogance, disharmony, greed and lies are all fear made manifest. Joy, kindness, empathy, compassion, generosity and pursuit of truth are all love made manifest. Which one prevails? That's our choice and we are making it every 'minute' of every 'day'. Which wolf wins? – as a Native American saying puts it (Fig 679). This is the choice that determines the world we live 'in'. Fear infests the perceptions of everyone to a greater or lesser degree and in most the degree is massive although they may not realise it. Fear has many labels to disguise its presence, but the man behind the mask is still the man. Fear is the architect of control. Without it there can be no global El-lite, no oppressed masses, no Archontic conspiracy. The System is a system of control because it is a system of fear. Without fear it has no power. Even now its power is *our* power conceded by fear of not conceding by fear (Fig 680). Phantom Self *is* fear. Without fear there can be no Phantom Self. The 'Fall of Man' into low-frequency Archontic tyranny has been caused by the energetic density of fear. Archon inversion is the inversion of love into fear and every other inversion comes from this prime inversion. The Archon virus is ... *FEAR*. This is how fear came into the world when it

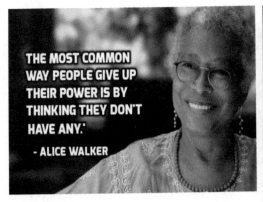

Figure 680: So very true.

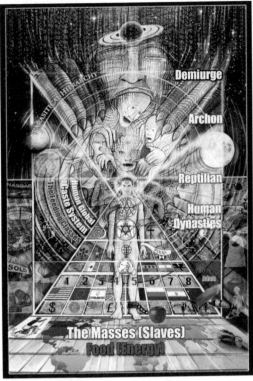

Figure 681: Demiurge/Archon food chain.

wasn't here before. The virus is self-aware fear and feeds off fear because it *is* fear. Phantom Self is fear because it is the creation of a virus that is fear. High-frequency Earth is a place of love and bad copy Earth has been infested with the virus of fear (Fig 681). In this way love has been inverted into fear. As Gandhi said: 'The enemy is fear. We think it is hate, but it is fear.' Hate is actually an expression of fear.

New identity

Humanity needs a new self-identity to rid itself of fear and thus control. Phantom Self can never do that when it is fear. This is far easier than people might imagine. All it takes is to self-identify with being Infinite Awareness having an experience instead of believing we *are* the experience (Fig 682). First step: name, race, culture, family history,

life story, job, income bracket, accent, the whole bloody lot are *experiences* and not *you*. How can they be? If you had been born with a different name, race, culture, family history, life story, job, income bracket and accent you would not be the same person you are today or have the same perceptions. The old city of Jerusalem is divided into quarters for Jews, Muslims, Christians and Armenians who follow their own culture and religion; but if those people had been born in one of the other quarters they would live *that* culture and follow *that* religion. Phantom

Figure 682: The you that time forgot.

Self is a *download* – it's not *you*. I am Infinite Awareness and my experience is called David Icke. This reassessment of my self-identity, my point of attention from which I observe the world, is what transformed my life. It allowed me to come through all the ridicule, abuse, legal attacks and challenges to keep on walking no matter what. I am not saying that this happens overnight, though it can, but the process of re-identification can start whenever we choose. There are relapses when the illusion gets you and you are pulled back into its fear-trap, back into believing you are what you are not. The more you live your true self the rarer relapses become and you can spot them the moment they begin. 'Oh, no, what now, what do I do – *aaahhh?*' It's just an *experience* and soon it will be gone and another will take its place. From the moment I *remembered* who I am through the deluge of reasons and pressures to forget, there was nothing I would not do to be most effective in my work. I knew I had come to do this, and ever since I have seen my life as a job. People go to work and then go home. My self-realisation is the same only from a different angle. I came to work when I blinked out of the womb and I will be going home when my body can function no more. I don't need to live a 'full-life' because how much fuller can you get than to be *All That Is And Ever Can Be*? My 'full-life' is Infinite Life. I don't need what others believe is necessary to have 'a good life' and I don't seek the big house, big car and trappings of 'success'. This is not for any spiritual reason or sense of purity. I really don't want them. They would add nothing to my life or the work which *is* my life. I am writing this as with nearly all the books in a tiny office in a small one-bedroomed flat, and if I were in a big house with its own grounds what difference would that make except to add endless diversions to what I am here to do? A butler to bring me cups of tea would be nice so I didn't have to stop, but he'd have to sleep on the sofa. I am not saying that my life is right for everyone, of course not. There are many roads that people can take although The System is dictating or targeting most of them. I am giving an example of what can happen to your perception of everything once you redefine your sense of self, your point of observation. Things that mattered before no longer do so as you see how insignificant and irrelevant they are. What can wind up others into a frenzy of emotional reaction pass you by and fail to register. You look at the world and the way people behave and respond and you see through the illusion. You realise that so much

Figure 683: Stress = low, distorted frequency – The Matrix.

that people believe is important only matters because they think it matters – have been *programmed* to think it matters (Fig 683). It is worth asking yourself in these situations how you would see them from the perspective of having minutes to live. What would matter about your life then? Hardly anything that got you in such a temper, panic or fear day after day, year after year. I didn't get that job, my team didn't win, my girlfriend left me. What would it matter then? I have read many accounts of what people said and how they felt in the final moments of a human life. All that most seemed to care

Figure 684: Little me?

Figure 685: Why some hear the Infinite music and others don't.

about was how much they loved and were loved. Many of them see through the hoax of pursuing 'success' in terms of money, status and power for their own sake. The same happens when you begin to self-identify with Infinite Awareness. You start to see through it all and here is the bottom-line reason for why expanded awareness is the constant target of The System (Fig 684).

The impact of saying 'I am Infinite Awareness having an experience' is life-changing if you mean it and don't just speak the words or have the thought. You may feel nothing at first, but you will have broken the waters or sprung a hole in the dyke of perception programming. Your point of attention will have begun to move and your five senses will be shouting 'Hey, where do you think *you're* going?' Keep saying it and thinking it, *knowing* it and the breach in Phantom Self will get bigger and bigger. Expanded awareness will begin to circulate your perceptions and you will slowly (or even quickly) see everything from a different angle – a different point of attention (Fig 685). You are still *in* this world but your expanding awareness is no longer completely *of* it. As you continue, despite the relapses that will come, you are less and less *in* it, except for your body, and more and more not *of* it. By now your friends, family and those you meet might have convinced themselves that you are strange, even crazy, or having a mid-life crisis. If so, congratulations – you're getting there. To be seen as strange or mad by a world that's insane is essential confirmation that you are on the right road. 'And those who were seen dancing were thought to be insane by those who could

Figure 686: What music?

Figure 687: What a great tune.

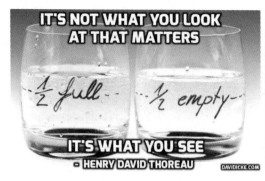

Figure 688: You are what you perceive.

Figure 689: It doesn't matter what other people think about you – they'll think something else tomorrow.

not hear the music', to quote Friedrich Nietzsche (Figs 686 and 687). Self-identity with Infinite Awareness disconnects you from being affected by what other people say or think about you. What would have hurt before is now laughed away if there is any reaction at all. I have undergone monumental abuse and still do, but the abusers are wasting their lives if they think it impacts upon me (Fig 688). If you were abused by someone who had no idea who they are or even why they are saying what they do would you take offence? Of course not. You would say poor chap or poor lady, how sad. It's not what people say that affects you but your *response* to what they say. If you think it matters then it will in terms of how it makes you feel. If you know it doesn't matter because it's all an illusion then the effect on you is zero (Fig 689). Why should we care what someone says about us when their intent is to hurt and harm? They deserve our sympathy, not our outrage. They have to wake up tomorrow and remember they are still them which can't be easy. Those that abuse you are expressions of the same Infinite Awareness that you are. The only difference is that you have remembered you are Infinite Awareness having an experience and they still believe they are the experience. Intent is also crucial to speeding your awakening. I said earlier how powerful is the energy of intent in manifesting what you want. You are the Infinite and the Infinite is you. Intent is a way of interacting with the greater 'you' to bring your desire into holographic reality; but here is where many New Age guru-types miss the point. One chap suggested that people should stick pictures of Ferraris all over the place to help them to visualise one into their life. Quite apart from the fact that anyone who wants to spiritually manifest a Ferrari is still owned by the program, there are other forces at work which I will explain. Humanity's obsession with the accumulation of money and possessions is the program talking and if that's your only goal Infinite Awareness will not be involved.

More than one 'you'

Everyone and everything is an expression of the same Infinite reality, but if we bring it down to the 'incarnate' human there is more than one 'you' (Fig 690). There shouldn't be, but it's the way things are in the madhouse. There is conscious 'you'; subconscious 'you'; and superconscious 'you'. We talk about 'conscious' and 'subconscious' but *both* are conscious. Subconscious simply means not conscious to the 'conscious' (five-sense mind) if you follow me. Superconsciousness is what I have been calling expanded awareness beyond the Matrix and the program. Subconscious mind is constantly interacting with conscious mind and influencing perceptions and actions. Indeed this is where most programming is encoded by The System to filter through to the conscious mind as 'I've just had a thought' or 'I am going to this or that'. Subliminal advertising implants images and perceptions in the subconscious mind for the same reason. Superconsciousness is what the Archons are desperate to suppress, and the overwhelming majority live their lives in their conscious and subconscious minds – different levels of the same mind in fact and what I refer to as Phantom Self. This is the realm of 'I want a Ferrari', 'I want to be super rich', 'I want power and status' and all the rest. It is also the realm of those who encourage people to 'think' themselves a Ferrari. There are none so asleep as those who falsely believe they are awake. Superconsciousness doesn't want a Ferrari. It wants to connect with and awaken its entrapped 'conscious' and 'subconscious'

Figure 690: Our 'human' self is only one tiny expression of our Infinite Self.

aspects caught in the illusion of wanting a Ferrari or thinking their experience is who they are. When you say 'I am Infinite Awareness having an experience' and post the intent on the Cosmic Internet that you want to awaken to your true self don't expect to walk down leafy lanes of beautiful flowers, butterflies fluttering, a bluebird on your shoulder having a Zip-A-Dee-Doo-Dah Day. As I was told through Betty Shine right at the start: 'The spiritual way is tough and no one makes it easy.' What often happens is your old life starts to unravel and great change can be triggered, not all of it what you would like. But hold on. You said you wanted to awaken to your true self and that can't happen if the 'old' life is not serving that intent. Once Body-Mind is breached by superconsciousness, and especially when the floodgates open as they did with me after Peru, you can wave goodbye to what was before. Influence of superconsciousness and the energy matrix created by your intent draws to you through 'vibrational magnetism' the experiences, people, locations and information necessary to dismantle Phantom Self, expose the illusion and allow the superconscious you to express its wisdom and insight amid the madness. We are living an illusion but we can experience these changes at first as if it were all real. Superconsciousness can see the illusion and has a totally different perspective of the same experience. To the conscious 'you' something can seem like a disaster, your worst nightmare, while to superconsciousness the same experience is a great gift that further dismantles the perception and fear construct of Phantom Self (Fig 691). Breakdowns can be *breakthroughs*.

Figure 691: It doesn't matter what other people think about you – they'll think something else tomorrow.

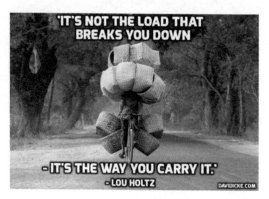

Figure 692: Life = how you perceive it.

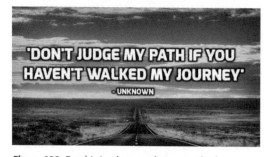

Figure 693: But this is what people constantly do.

Gift of a nightmare

Take my life as an example. To do what I have done for the last 26 years, write what I have and say what I have, I had to be free of caring what other people thought of me – even the national media and its onslaught of ridicule and abuse. This is so important, vital, crucial, essential, indispensable bottom-line. Anyone who wants to awaken from the program and ditch Phantom Self must let go of the fear of what other people think. Almost everyone is editing their views, opinions and lifestyles to avoid being ridiculed, condemned or criticised, and so they are not living their own lives and their own uniqueness, but someone else's version of what they should be, do and think. Phantom Selves policing Phantom Selves, sheep controlling sheep, is how we got where we are. You don't change a situation by doing what created it. What does it matter what others think of you? They will think something else tomorrow (Fig 692). What you are is none of their business and Mark Twain was so right when he said: 'Never argue with stupid people. They will drag you down to their level and then beat you with experience.' Who are they to tell you who you are and what perceptions you should have? You don't have to justify yourself and defend yourself – just *be* yourself. I can tell you from long and extreme experience that you *can* be yourself and not what the crowd tells you to be to mirror their own programming (Fig 693). I could not have done what I have unless this foundation of human control was deleted. Who would talk so publicly about Archons, shapeshifting Reptilians, a Saturn-Moon Matrix and a self-aware virus of Artificial Intelligence if they cared about what others would say? No one – so I had to be freed from that prison of limitation. This is why I went through my record-breaking deluge of national ridicule in 1991 and the years that have followed. It was an experience so extreme that either I emotionally collapsed or I came out with a backbone of steel and a concern only for uncovering the truth no matter how it was received or I was portrayed. I chose the latter and what had seemed to be a nightmare became a gift. Most journalists I have met and worked with have been Super-Phantom Selves with The System on and in their minds. You can be upset by what they say or you can shake your head, smile, and think how sad it must be to live in such concrete bewilderment. As superconscious clears out the program and Phantom Self dissolves, the less and less it matters what people say because you know that it really *doesn't* matter. I wanted to be a professional football player and the doors of 'coincidence' opened to make that happen – for a short while. Six months into my professional career the first signs of what was later diagnosed as rheumatoid arthritis began to appear in swollen joints, but I carried on for years playing successfully while the arthritis pain worsened to the point where every training session warm-up was agony. I hid what was happening and kept going as long as I could before I had to stop playing at the age of 21. Arthritis for a budding footballer (nightmare) became a vehicle for awakening unbreakable determination and a refusal of to go under that I never knew I had (gift). I have had many people come into my life who have proved to be deeply unpleasant frauds and parasites, and had many legal cases to fend off. They thought they were hurting me (nightmare) but they were only making me stronger and allowing me to see and experience what I would not have otherwise done (gift). I also had to come to terms with betrayal and not let it weaken me. Thanks to them I did and it is water to a duck's back now. They weren't nice people but they were the *right* people for me – 'The spiritual way is tough and no one makes it easy'. A gift is what you *need* – not necessarily what you want. How you respond to it decides what happens next.

This is a vital point for people to grasp: rules and regulations, dos and don'ts, musts and mustn'ts, moralities and immoralities that human (Archon) society is programmed to believe in are not the rules and regulations, dos and don'ts, musts and mustn'ts, moralities and immoralities of superconsciousness. They are concepts of Phantom Self, not Infinite Awareness. Superconsciousness is only interested in experience that will lead to the awakening of its isolated fragment of programmed attention and to the exposure individually and collectively of the Archontic illusion. Sometimes you have to do things you later regret to recognise perceptions and programs of Phantom Self. Sometimes others have to do things to you that they later regret to have the same revelations. Sometimes you have to experience things outside the rules and regulations, dos and don'ts, musts and mustn'ts, moralities and immoralities of human (Archon) society that lead you to greater insight into the illusion and how it works. In short, superconsciousness is not coming from anything like the same point of attention and observation in relation to human life as a programmed Phantom Self. Some people commit crimes and go to prison before the veil lifts on self and the world. Others hit rock bottom with drugs or alcohol before they 'bounce'. In another way nice experiences are showing us what happens when you come at life from a different angle. Experience is screaming at us 'look at this – what does it say about you or the world?' The key is to recognise that and change the experience from a nightmare to a gift by changing yourself in the light of what it is telling or showing you. Most people don't and they go from one nightmare to another, when to recognise the first as a gift changes what would otherwise follow. When unpleasant things happen to us (through superconscious influence) they are not punishments but *experiences* to awaken us. Ask what they are telling you and showing you, change yourself and perceptions as a result, and everything moves on. You have awakened another notch from the Phantom to sync even more powerfully with your superconsciousness. Our thoughts, emotions, attitudes and perceptions are all frequencies and electromagnetic phenomena, and they attract via vibrational magnetism other frequencies and electromagnetic fields – people, places, jobs, experiences. You only have to look at the work with water of Dr Masaru Emoto and the Aerospace Institute in Stuttgart to see how humans impact on energetic fields. I saw a quote on the Internet which said: 'Accidents happen, that's what everyone says, but in a quantum universe there are no such things as accidents, only possibilities and probabilities folded into existence by *perception*.' Exactly. What we believe we perceive and what we perceive we experience. What we put out we get back is another way of saying the same thing and this is the foundation of what is called 'karma'. When superconsciousness comes into play its influence attracts to you more and more the people, places, jobs, *experiences*, which give you the best possible chance to complete what you are here to do. This is not 'karma' but 'guidance'. So many 'bad' things that have happened to me over 64 years right back into childhood have been essential preparation for what I am doing now.

My life and my work are indivisible because my own scale of awakening decides the quality of the work. I remember as a little kid in primary school playing a tree (yes, a tree) in the annual play. All the parents and teachers were watching as Prince Charming (teacher's pet) came through our 'forest' with an imaginary scythe to cut us down to reach Sleeping Beauty. I was standing there in my brown top and trousers with make-believe foliage on my head waiting for him to come over to me so I could fall down; but he never did. The others dropped to the floor even though in my mind that was silly because he couldn't cut them down from so far away. I remained standing and Prince Charming never came. The audience began to titter, then giggle and finally laugh out loud. I stood there bewildered at why I was being laughed at when I was only playing it for real. Next day the headmistress, Miss Wilkinson, a very large lady in her tweed suit and with shoulders the envy of quarterbacks, called me out of class and stood over me like some fairy tale ogre telling me how I had let the school down. I can still remember the experience so clearly because of the impact it had upon me. Last one standing and refusing to fall has its own symbolism with relation to my later life but more relevant than that was facing public ridicule at such a very young age. I couldn't have been more than six or seven. This was non-conscious preparation decades earlier for what I faced in mass public ridicule after 1991. It may have been very different in scale, but the experience was the same. I have no doubt that what had such an impact on me at age six or seven opened something in my psyche that made it easier to come through what I have as an adult. Life is not a series of unconnected random events and our choice is to have those events manifested by superconsciousness or Phantom Self. If we don't learn from them, grow from them, awaken from them and see them as the gifts that they are they can add still more layers to Phantom Self in resentment, regret, suppressed and unsuppressed anger and a sense that 'the world's against me'. The Archontic System manipulates this process and programs this perception by labelling, categorising and judging experience to stop the nightmare becoming the gift. We have the concept of Judgement Day and facing the wrath of 'God' and this is manipulated mercilessly to enforce the will of the frocks and others. There is no Judgement Day, nor any wrathful 'God' (except the Demiurge). There is only learning (remembering) from experience and attracting the same experiences until we do – the Biblical 'reaping what you sow'. Don't beat yourself up over what has gone before. There's nothing you can do to change that. Learn from the experience and transform it into a gift of awareness. That's what it's there for.

Thought Control

Superconsciousness is the observer and guide when we open ourselves to its influence. It is the realm of *knowing*. Body-Mind is the experiencer in the realm of *thought*. Phantom Self is a construct of emotion and thought made manifest through the conscious and subconscious mind. Thought is the god of The System because it serves the interests of the Archontic conspiracy. We talk about a 'great thinker' and 'great mind', but thought is the village idiot compared with knowing. Superconsciousness is the knower for it is in conscious connection to the *All Knowing, All That Is* in awareness of itself. People can become so detached from their superconsciousness that when their awareness leaves the body they are still operating in what we call conscious and subconscious mind. Such people are often referred to as 'lost souls' and they are very common given the power of the program to dictate perceptions even after 'death'. These were the symbolic people in my ayahuasca experience dropping from the sky and back into the same 'groove' they had trodden many times before. If you sit quietly you can observe your thoughts passing through your mind. Don't try to influence them. Let them be and observe. This can be hilarious when you witness the nonsensical mind chatter and what Phantom Self waffles on about. It never stops thinking, planning, plotting, reacting to things yet to even happen and probably never will ... it makes gossiping seem like a vow of silence. But here's the point: As you observe this process who is doing the thinking? Phantom Self. Who is doing the observing? Superconscious self. *YOU. Infinite YOU.* The System is specifically designed to entrap us in thought. 'Education' is about thinking and so is science, medicine, business, politics, all of it. Science for example will never understand reality from the realm only of thought because thought cannot access those levels of awareness capable of understanding reality and seeing through its illusion. Great scientific breakthroughs invariably come from inspiration and a sudden 'knowing' and not working it all out in through mind and thought. Physicist Albert Einstein said:

> All great achievements of science must start from intuitive knowledge [knowing]. I believe in intuition and inspiration ... At times I feel certain I am right while not knowing the reason ... Imagination is more important than knowledge.

Einstein also said:

> The intellect has little to do on the road to discovery. There comes leap in consciousness, call it intuition or what you will. And the solution comes to you, and you don't know how or why.

But there is a how and a why. Intuition and creative imagination come from superconsciousness and by accessing that you can be right without knowing the reason – unless you know about superconsciousness. When I first began my conscious journey after meeting Betty Shine I would study information and come to conclusions; but for decades since I have had a 'knowing' and the five-sense information to support that knowing has followed afterwards, not come before. Another Einstein quote said that you can't solve problems with the same level of thinking that created them. This is the Archontic hamster wheel that can only be broken by connection with superconsciousness (Fig 694). Anyone still wonder why the Archon System is obsessed with suppression of awareness and entrapping humanity in the illusion of thought? The Archon virus is fear and communication in the frequency band of fear is done through *thought*. It is a *computer* language, like the information passing through a computer system instigating

Figure 694: Human life until we see beyond the Matrix.

actions that eventually appear on the screen. Thought is the language of the Matrix, for it is the language of the Archon virus. Scientists have found that the coding in what mainstream science called 'junk DNA' – the 98 percent of DNA they said had no discernible function – was the same as that found in human language. Bingo. Of course it is because language is a foundation of the program running through Body-Mind and what is language but the vibrational vocal cord manifestation of ... *thought*. Language within the frequency of thought is a programming system in which we program ourselves and others through the frequency of language. Does anyone really think it is a coincidence that human thought and brain activity operate in what is called the ELF range or Extremely Low Frequency? Superconsciousness doesn't think – it *knows*, and speaks to us through the intuitive knowing that Einstein talked about. When superconscious awareness is expressed in language it is not the same as thought expressed in language. They are on completely different frequencies. I have long said that Body-Mind is a biological computer system encoded with emotional programs to make us react as required, and that the vast majority of people can go through an entire human lifetime without having an original thought of their own. Why? Thought is not original – thought is the program. Originality comes from superconsciousness with its connection to All Possibility, All Knowing. Thought can build technology because technology is an expression of thought which is why the Archons and their Reptilian agents are obsessed with it. Technology overcomes their inability to access superconsciousness from which comes ... *creative imagination*. What did the Gnostics say the Demiurge/Archons didn't have? *Creative imagination*. People may think that smart technologies and others are the result of creative imagination, but amazing as they may seem to humanity's suppressed awareness they are actually the Stone Age. All technology is Stone Age. There is no technology is the realm of superconsciousness. It is beyond thought and mind – the realm where technology is necessary to overcome limitations of awareness and thus potential and possibility. Near-death experiencers have described how entities spoke to them in the out-of-body state without using words. They just knew what was being communicated without hearing a sound. This is

Figure 695: The Demiurge is the one-eyed 'man' that has made humanity blind.

superconsciousness where anything can be manifested in an instant without need of a factory to build it. We are meant to be superconscious and humanity has been tricked by Archon manipulation into descending ('falling') to their level of awareness (and then some) – the realm of thought, low-vibrational emotion and the illusion of physicality. In the kingdom of the blind the one-eyed man is king (Fig 695). Transhumanism is about making the one-eyed man even more powerful and able to control. Gnostics and many other ancient and modern sources I have come across all agree that Archons are terrified of humanity waking up to its true nature. They know their game would then be over. This means awakening to superconsciousness which the Archon virus cannot access. In terms of power and possibility superconsciousness is the giant to the Archon seven-stone weakling. This is why they have had to make humanity a three-stone weakling. Essential to awakening, therefore, is deleting the layers of programming and perception that hold us in servitude to ignorance. Near-death experiencer Dr Eben Alexander described the fundamental difference between the Archon Matrix and the realm of superconsciousness:

> To experience thinking outside the brain is to enter a world of instantaneous connections that make ordinary thinking (those aspects limited by the physical brain and the speed of light) seem like some hopelessly sleepy and plodding event ...
>
> ... Our truest, deepest self is completely free. It is not crippled or compromised by past actions or concerned with identity or status. It comprehends that it has no need to fear the earthly world, and therefore, it has no need to build itself up through fame or wealth or conquest.

This 'truest, deepest self' is what the Archons have worked so hard and incessantly to disconnect us from – this is why reconnection is the revolution.

From the heart

Talk of superconsciousness brings me to the heart. I hear people told to 'use your head'. I say use your heart. I am not talking metaphorically either. Heart is love. Mind is fear. Head is fear. Scientists study the ionosphere, stratosphere and troposphere when they would be far more productive if they studied the mindisfear and headisfear. This is where an understanding of the world really lies. Phantom Self is a construct of fear – fear of not conforming; fear of what others think; fear of failure; fear of the moment; fear of the future; fear (regret) of the past; fear of death and fear of life. Yet fear of death is only the ignorance of life. Fear of life is only the ignorance of death. Programmed fear

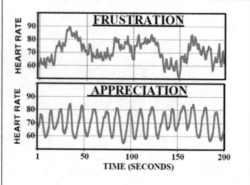

Figure 696: Want to change the world? This is how.

Figure 697: Different states of being make us resonate to difference frequencies.

and ignorance – Phantom Self in one. Or two. Mindisfear and headisfear are easily programmable. Their perceptions come from data input and the Archon Web controls the data. Trash in = trash out; fear in = fear out. Ponder on your life – I don't care who you are or what you do – and you will see how much fear has driven your responses and decisions and programmed your perceptions of almost everything. We are swamped with reasons to fear and invent many more of our own. Why would the Archontic System not unleash its reasons to be fearful parts 1, 2, 3, recurring to infinity? No fear, no System. No fear, no Archon control. Fear and ignorance are indivisible. Ignorance is the calling card of fear. Where there is ignorance there must be fear when one is the work of the other. It is the frequency of fear that shuts us off from superconscious 'enlightenment'. High-frequency Earth is high-frequency because it is a realm of love. When we open our hearts to love by loving and being loved we resonate high-frequency waves that elevate our energy fields and awareness into expanded states of consciousness and perception or superconsciousness (Fig 696). Low-frequency Earth is low-frequency because it is a realm of fear. When we close our hearts in fear by fearing and being feared we resonate low-frequency waves that suppress our energy fields and awareness into density and disconnection from superconsciousness (Fig 697). Pixel Awareness is fear. Picture awareness is love. But what is love? What most people call love is a physical attraction full of conditions, contractual clauses and detail. I love you *if*. I love you *when*. I love you *so long as*. Love in its Infinite sense – the love that comes from knowing we are love – doesn't do contracts, conditions or clauses. Infinite love *loves*. This is what love does, what love *is*, when untainted by fear. How many human 'love' relationships are founded on fear? The great majority I'd say and they are just another inversion of love into fear.

True science is a branch of spirituality as true astronomy is a branch of astrology. We can see this in the work of the Institute of HeartMath in the United States which has pioneered research into the multidimensional nature of the heart. Researchers established that the heart generates the body's most powerful electromagnetic field and more nerves go from the heart to the brain than go the other way (Fig 698). Our hearts also have around 40,000 brain-like neurons and neurotransmitters. Yet another

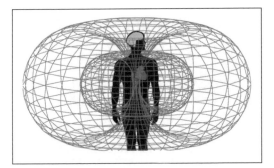

Figure 698: Heart is the body's most powerful electromagnetic field.

Figure 699: The heart chakra is the centre point of the main human chakra system.

profound inversion has been to usurp the role of the heart and its innate intelligence with the brain and its programmed intelligence. I'll elaborate in a moment. On one level the heart can be seen as an electrical pump delivering blood flow (energy/information) to all parts of the hologram. Arteries and veins are holographic expressions of the information or 'chi' circulating the meridian system, which is the basis of acupuncture. Meridians are connected with the chakra vortexes that I described earlier (Fig 144). Lower chakras relate to this 'world', higher ones to other realities, and the balance-point vortex at the centre is the heart chakra. We experience feelings of love in the centre of the chest (my heart 'fluttered') because the heart chakra is our connection to Infinite Love – Infinite Self and superconsciousness. When the heart chakra is open and allowing free expression to Infinite Self then Infinite Love is also Infinite Awareness, Infinite Intelligence, Infinite *Knowing* or superconsciousness (Fig 699). The head thinks, but the heart *knows*. Infinite Awareness is Infinite Awareness – a state of being Infinitely Aware. The more superconsciousness that we access the more we infinitely *know*. Not think. Not try to work out. *KNOW.* It's the All-Knowing, not the All-Thinking. Thought is Phantom Self.

Knowing is Infinite Self. People experience this in the difference between thought and intuition and you hear terms like 'go with your head' or 'go with your heart'. Body language is the head thinking or the heart feeling ... Phantom Self thinking or Infinite Self knowing. We don't put our hands on our heart or chest and say 'I'm thinking'. We put them to our head where the brain is thinking. We put our hands to our chest when we have intuitive insight or feelings and we say 'I just know in my heart'. People even talk of their 'heart of hearts'. Knowing from the heart is something that I have been guided to understand (remember) since I left Betty Shine's front room. Since that day whenever my heart has been in conflict with my head I have gone with my heart, my intuitive knowing, and eventually there is no conflict. Heart and head begin to speak the same language – as they are meant to. The late and very great American comedian Bill Hicks was a very aware man. He had it right when he said:

This is where we are right now, as a whole. No one left out of the loop. We are experiencing a

Figure 700: Connection to home.

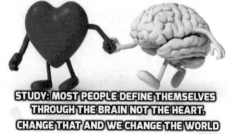

Figure 701: The two should be working together with the heart leading the way.

reality based on a thin veneer of lies and illusions. A world where greed is our god and wisdom is a sin, where division is key and unity is fantasy, where ego-driven cleverness of the mind is praised, rather than the intelligence of the heart.

Research at the Institute of HeartMath revealed that when the energetic field of the heart is in harmony and electromagnetic coherence (communication) with the brain and the central nervous system we enter a far more expanded state of awareness. New data suggested that 'the heart's field is directly involved in intuitive perception, through its coupling to an energetic information field outside the bounds of time and space'. Yes – superconsciousness (Fig 700). Archontic inversion has sought to destroy this coherence and connection, suppress the heart chakra and make the brain centre of attention in every sense. Everything is meant to work in unison to reflect the unity of Infinite Existence, but instead the 'parts' that make the whole have been systematically fragmented. Heart is de-linked from head. Right-brain is delinked from left-brain. Humanity needs to literally pull itself together (Fig 701). Instead of open heart-whole brain unity we have in most people left-brain isolation. The difference is almost beyond description. Deborah Rozman, president and CEO of HeartMath LLC in California, said she once used a technique that has people speaking from the head and then from the heart. 'It was like two different people talking', she said. 'The heart spoke from genuine feeling and authenticity, in the present. The mind spoke from opinions, fears, shoulds and shouldn'ts.' What an encapsulation of Infinite Self against Phantom Self, open heart against programmed mind. Archontic inversion and manipulation has targeted the heart as from day one and the entire subjugation of humanity depends on the overriding of the heart by the brain, especially left-brain. What disconnects us from the heart more than anything? *Fear.* Love in its Infinite sense is the absence of fear – or what is left when fear is eliminated. Bad Copy reality is fear made manifest and all the engineered and manufactured reasons for fear and stress distort and make chaotic what should be electromagnetic coherence and harmony between heart, brain and central nervous system (Fig 702). The heart is meant to be the centre of perception, the connection to superconsciousness, and the brain is supposed to serve the heart not

Figure 703: Phantom Self to Phantom Self.

Figure 702: Breaking the coherent connection with the heart.

Figure 704: Infinite Self to Infinite Self.

replace it as the focus of intelligence and awareness. Or, in the case of the brain, *perceived* intelligence and awareness. Usurping the true role of the heart shuts out expanded awareness and isolates perception in the prison-cell reality of Phantom Self. Pre-hijack humanity interacted with reality through the heart and the brain was there to respond to heart 'knowing'. Once that connection was distorted and blocked, thought and emotion became the governor of perception, response and behaviour (Fig 703). A heart world became the head world that we have had ever since. People talk of having a heart-to-heart and this describes a sparkling truth in that we can communicate heart-to-heart without intervention from the brain (Fig 704). If we did, conflict would end immediately. Deep sadness is described in terms of being 'heartbroken' or having 'heartache' and this is the effect on the heart chakra vortex of the way we are feeling. Energy in and around the heart chakra can become so tense, dense and stagnant in the face of stress, trauma or loss that this plays through to the hologram as a heart attack or heart disease. You really can die from a broken heart. Emotional stress and the energetic effect that becomes a holographic effect is the real reason why heart disease is *officially* the world's biggest killer.

Heart people

To remove the cause of Archontic domination humanity must open its heart to become superconscious. This is a gimme when keeping the heart under lock and key is the foundation of everything they do. Psychopaths run the world and you can't be psychopathic when heart is in the game. You know when your heart is open or opening when you act with kindness, empathy, compassion and generosity (Fig 705). You consider situations and decisions on what is right, fair and just, not on what is necessarily best for you in the moment (Fig 706). Given that we reap what we sow in energetic attraction doing what is right, fair and just is also what is best for you longer

Figure 705: Doing what we believe to be right – not always what we think is right for ourselves in the moment.

Figure 706: A kind non-Archontic world comes from being kind to each other *and* ourselves.

term. How do you cease to be a psychopath without at some point facing experiences that awaken you from your psychopathy? Look at the language ... when we act without kindness, empathy, compassion and generosity we are said to be 'heartless'. All the pressure from Archontic society and The System is for you to act from the head. Dog eat dog, winner takes all, look after number one. Yes, we must look after number one in that we should have love and respect for ourselves, but what is this 'number one' – Phantom 'one' or Infinite 'one'? Which 'one' are we 'looking after'? The phrase obviously refers to Phantom 'one' that must fight, battle, kick and cuss to compete with other Phantom 'ones'. But isn't that how we got into this mess? By looking after (in theory) the wrong number one? Heart people don't neglect themselves. They know the belief that spiritual purity lies in suffering and poverty is nonsense. Sackcloth and ashes are for the Phantom not the Infinite. Kindness, empathy, compassion and generosity must be applied to ourselves as well as others. We are all the same 'one'. A lot of people forget this need for kindness for themselves and in doing so create another Phantom program. 'Look at how spiritual I am, going without and suffering to help others.' This is actually another self-identity, another label, another Phantom Self. Heart just is. It doesn't need labels of isolated self-identity whatever they may be. Heart people know that no one has to go without for others to have. This is such a myth. I know it seems like that from daily experience but remember always that what we experience is a fake reality in which the illusion of limitation is a vital mechanism of control. How can we run out of anything when our experienced reality is only a holographic manifestation of our sense of reality? We experience limitation and shortage by *believing* in limitation and shortage and have been programmed to do so since the baby met the midwife. In fact, this can happen even before that through energetic influence of the mother. Heart people are not martyrs for they know they are not necessary. Martyrs and martyrdom are more Phantom Self labels and delusions playing their role in the stage play. Heart people look after themselves, have kindness, empathy, compassion and generosity for themselves, but here's the point – not at the expense of others. Not to the detriment, suffering, control or loss of others. Heart people seek win-win, not win-lose. With heart economics no one would go without while with head economics this is essential. When Archontic fakery is deleted in its entirety there would be no economics, only conscious manifestation of wants and needs through our true state of superconsciousness. For now we have to deal with perception as it is, but nothing can change without opening the heart to Infinite Self. It is the power of the heart that will get us through this and out of this. George Orwell wrote in *1984*: 'They could lay bare in the utmost detail everything that you had done or said or thought; but the inner heart, whose workings were mysterious even to yourself, remained impregnable.'

Check list

Here is a summary of what I have found helpful and this will definitely kick-start an awakening in anyone if it is done with genuine intent. Re-identify yourself with Infinite Awareness or superconsciousness having an experience instead of believing you are the experience. This alone will instigate a consciousness and frequency shift that will start to sync Phantom you with superconscious you. Say it to yourself as often as you like – I am Infinite Awareness, I am Infinite Awareness. Words are frequencies and can empower the awakening if they come from the heart and not the head. When you face a situation that is pulling you back into Phantom reality (and you will) stop and consciously reaffirm your new sense of self – I am Infinite Awareness, I am Infinite Awareness and this is just an experience. Ditch all 'this world' labels to define your self-identity. If you identify with a label you are Phantom Self. You are not black, white, Muslim, Christian, Jew, Hindu, rich, poor or any of those things. They are only what you are experiencing and believe yourself to be. You are Infinite Awareness having those experiences. This may sound simplistic but it's not. What you self-identify with you become. I am not David Icke – that is my experience. I am not an author – that is my experience. I am not even human – that is my experience. The System is now manipulating people through political correctness to sub-divide into even smaller labels as man and woman, black and white sub-divide into 'non-binary' or 'BME'. Further and further they go from self-identity with superconscious Infinite Self. We will know we're getting somewhere when we hear this:

'Hello, who are you?'

'I am Infinite Awareness having an experience.'

'Oh, so am I – pleased to meet you.'

Activate your heart chakra through kindness, empathy, compassion and generosity and I mean for yourself as well as others. Do things that give you joy which always makes the heart sing. If you are happy and your heart is open everyone you meet reaps the benefits directly and vibrationally. Try never to win if it means others must lose. Life is not meant to be a football match. My own philosophy is simple: Do what you like so long as you don't impose it on others. Ponder on that and you'll see that it covers everything through a simple word called 'respect'. No laws would be necessary if we lived like that and it's perfectly possible when superconsciousness prevails over Phantom Self. Some laws are required for Phantom Self only because it's an idiot. Let go of concern with what other people think. You are you, not them. They are their business, you are yours. If this means people go out of your life then so what? Those that can't respect your right to be you shouldn't be there anyway. They serve no purpose except to limit you or show you how they limit you so you refuse to be limited any longer (Fig 707). Most will secretly envy your expression of uniqueness. They would love to do the same but fear what other people (like themselves, ironically) would think. Mark Twain said that when you find yourself on the side of the majority it is time to pause and reflect. This is so true because the majority – still the vast majority – download their perceptions from the program. Giordano Bruno said centuries ago:

Figure 707: Listening to the awakening self and not the closed minds of the still-asleep.

It is proof of a base and low mind for one to wish to think with the masses or majority, merely because the majority is the majority. Truth does not change because it is or is not believed by the majority of the people.

Mahatma Gandhi took the same view:

Many people, especially ignorant people, want to punish you for speaking the truth, for being correct, for being you. Never apologise for being correct, or for being years ahead of your time. If you're right and you know it, speak your mind. Speak your mind. Even if you are a minority of one, the truth is still the truth.

The mystic Osho put it like this:

The greatest fear in the world is of the opinions of others and the moment you are unafraid of the crowd, you are no longer a sheep. You become a lion. A great roar rises from your heart – the roar of freedom.

People give their uniqueness away by comparing themselves with others, but they are them and you are *you*. I saw a quote which said that confidence is not walking into a room with your nose in the air thinking you are better than everyone else; it is walking in the room not having to compare yourself to anyone in the first place (Fig 708). When you have a decision to make and you are thinking what to do – get the heart involved. Okay, your brain is saying you should do this or that, but what does your heart say? More to the point what does your heart *feel*? The head thinks, but the heart feels and feeling is the communication of *knowing*. Intuition is superconsciousness. I do everything by intuition and have done since all this started. I can be offered something which ticks all the boxes of mind considerations and still say no. I can be offered something that seems crazy with no boxes ticked and still say yes if my intuition says go with it. Intuitive knowing doesn't always lead you to experiences you would like; it

Figure 708: But so many people do – Phantom Selves that is.

leads to experiences that you need. I have stayed with situations I didn't like when my intuition said 'hang in there' and then suddenly when the experience had delivered its gift of insight and self-realisation my intuition said 'time to go'. I could not have uncovered and communicated a fraction of what I have without heart intuition which has been superconsciousness opening and closing doors to synchronistically guide me through what would be for Phantom Self, the head self, an incomprehensible maze. Awakening people notice how synchronicity and 'coincidence' increase in their life and the strengthening connection with superconsciousness is the reason for that. Phantom Self is obsessed with outcomes – 'I want it to be like this, 'it must be like that', but this is a mug's game. By focussing on a specific outcome you are setting yourself up for disappointment if that one outcome doesn't happen. People can spend entire lifetimes banging their head against a door that will not open when infinite possibilities await them elsewhere. Those who have awakened to superconsciousness go with the synchronicity of events. They know that is superconsciousness at work. I have learned profoundly over the years that if it is difficult it is not meant to be and if it flows – go with it. Near-death experiencer Anita Moorjani said:

> I detach myself from preconceived outcomes and trust that all is well. Being myself allows the wholeness of my unique magnificence to draw me in those directions most beneficial to me and to all others. This is really the only thing I have to do. And within that framework, everything that is truly mine comes into my life effortlessly, in the most magical and unexpected ways imaginable, demonstrating every day the power and love of who I truly am.

As you choose intuition over thought a heart connection to superconsciousness will open and the more powerful, sensitive and insightful your knowing will become. In the end intuition will not have to win a battle with the head. They will be moving as one unit in heart-brain coherence as Phantom Head sees that when you follow your intuition you may face challenges but it all works out in the end to your benefit. Once Phantom Head sees this, it is no longer Phantom Head. Heart and head come together. Remember, too, that heart intuition and superconsciousness can say 'no' as well as 'yes' – 'don't go there' as well as 'go there'. It is not about lovey-dovey saying yes to everything because you want to be seen as being kind and generous. Superconscious intuition makes us streetwise to what we don't need to experience. It is observing this reality from another reality and can see all. Superconsciousness often says no, have nothing to do with him, her or it. Mahatma Gandhi said: 'A "No" uttered from the deepest conviction is better than a "Yes" merely uttered to please, or worse, to avoid trouble.' Let no one underestimate how much courage it can take to awaken from the trance and then act on your new awareness of self and the world. Courage is not the absence of fear but the overriding of fear and doing it anyway. What is this fear? Courage is overriding programmed responses of Phantom Self until so much superconsciousness is driving the bus that courage is no longer needed to overcome fear that no longer exists. Superconsciousness doesn't fear – it knows there is nothing to fear. It is *False Emotion Appearing Real*. People talk about the courage of the heart and the heart's connection to superconsciousness is the source of that courage. Self-identifying with Infinite Self is crucial to overriding fear and summoning the courage to act when Phantom Self is screaming 'No, no, what about the consequences'. There is also the little matter that the consequences of not acting will be far, far, worse than the challenges of doing so.

Quiet time

It may seem for a few minutes that I am leaving the theme of awakening, but I'm not as you'll see. We live in a world that is founded on work as you would expect from a world founded on slavery. From the earliest age we are told to 'work hard' and from first school to last job people are largely judged by their 'work ethic'. The point of life, you see, is to work, work, work and then, er, die. Who decided that, may I ask? *Ahh*, The System decided that and the program makes you feel guilty if you don't work, work, work and then, er, die. Bloody slacker. Every government solution to economic crises is that people must *work harder* and for less. This tired old baloney from presidential wannabe Jeb Bush speaks for them all:

> My aspiration for the country, and I believe we can achieve it, is 4 percent growth as far as the eye can see. Which means we have to be a lot more productive, workforce participation has to rise from its all-time modern lows. It means that people need to work longer hours, and, through their productivity, gain more income for their families. That's the only way we're going to get out of this rut that we're in.

Same old, same old. Humans are servants of The System and have no right to joy, happiness or fulfilment. They are here to work and work until they can work no more (Fig 709). The System doesn't refer to the masses as people, but as workers and consumers. Our role is only to work and consume to ensure more 'growth'. Work 'til you die, shop 'til you drop. We can only survive and prosper if we have 'growth'. We must work to ensure 'growth'. Do you know what growth is, or gross domestic product (GDP)? It is the amount of money changing hands for goods and services in any year. That's it. When an oil tanker spills its load in an area of outstanding natural beauty it adds to 'growth' from the money that is spent to clean it up, or try to. Heart attacks in America are good for 'growth' when an ambulance is called and the patient is admitted to hospital. Economic 'growth' is the most ludicrous measurement of 'success' that you can possibly imagine and yet this is what

Figure 709: Don't awaken – *work!*

everyone must work harder and harder to achieve. How about these for measurements of success – how few people are ill; how few are hungry; how few are homeless; how few are in poverty; how few are not free; how few are unhappy; how few are unfulfilled; how few are not living the life that they want. But, no – we must forever plunder more resources, cause more pollution, devastate more land and communities to make more things, sell more things and throw away more things to worship the god of economic 'growth'. To pursue this insanity we must 'work harder'. Do people have to work as hard and as long as they do? No, they don't. The System forces this upon them by ensuring that only by doing a System job to The System's benefit and satisfaction will you earn money to pay for food, shelter and warmth never mind everything else we are told is so essential. Not got the latest iPhone? *What?* Get a life, what a loser. Work is another hoax to enslave us. I am not saying that people shouldn't do things and contribute to the wellbeing of themselves and society, but we don't have that. We have slavery – work slavery. The world is a labour camp that thinks it is free. How many people are doing jobs that don't need doing and only serve the interests of some filthy rich entrepreneur or corporation selling irrelevant products and services we don't need just to make still more dosh for the sake of making still more dosh? A UK survey in 2015 found that a third of workers did not believe their job made any meaningful contribution to the world. If they pondered for longer on what they do, and were not in denial of a truth they don't want to face, the number would have been even higher. How many people wake up in the morning with joy in their hearts delighted they are going to work? The answer is so very few compared with those with aching hearts and anxious bellies at the thought of reporting for duty at their daily prison cell. Research has revealed a 'pandemic' of burn out across 'all age groups, genders, professions, and cultures' and *Scientific American Mind* reported that job satisfaction worldwide is in 'a surprisingly fragile state'. What the hell is surprising about it? To repeat what American comedian and social observer George Carling said:

> Oh, you hate your job? Why didn't you say so? There's a support group for that. It's called everybody and they meet at the bar.

Work, work, work and then, er, die? This is *life?* No, it's not 'life' because it's not living. It's existing, surviving, slaving. George Carling also said that 'we've learned how to make a living but not a life'. The bar, drugs, all forms of escapism are to escape the soulless drudgery and monotony and to somehow feel alive. From the age of four you have teachers telling you what you can do and can't do, where you can go and not go, and when you escape from that prison you enter the next one – the 'world of work' – when bosses tell you for the rest of your working life what you can do and can't do, where you can go and not go. Then you retire usually to live on a pension that leaves you cold and hungry before you, er, die. What the *fuck* are we doing? The System is mad but even madder is that humanity stands for it. Humans are not slaves? I rest my case, M'lud. Humanity by the billion is held fast in slavery by a system controlled by the ridiculously few and we call it life, living or even freedom. We are back to 'they piss on us and we say it's raining'. I have featured a number of times a mass mind control and social engineering manual entitled *Silent Weapons for Quiet Wars* and this is detailed at length in *The Perception Deception*. Anyone who still thinks the conspiracy is only a

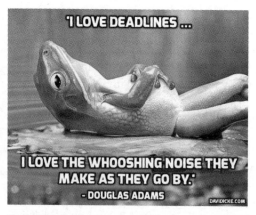

Figure 710: Ponder time when the heart can be heard.

'theory' should read what it says and compare that to what has happened to global society. *Silent Weapons* (the silent weapons of social engineering) was dated May 1979 and was apparently found in July 1986 in an IBM copier purchased at a surplus sale by an employee of Boeing. I mention it now to highlight another reason for the work hoax, school and homework hoax, and the never-off-the-smartphone hoax – hijacking quiet time, reflection time, daydream time. *Silent Weapons* describes how humans are kept ignorant, diverted and under control:

Media: Keep the adult public attention diverted away from the real social issues, and captivated by matters of no real importance; Schools: Keep the young public ignorant of real mathematics, real economics, real law, and real history; Entertainment: Keep the public entertainment below a sixth-grade level; Work: Keep the public busy, busy, busy, with no time to think; back on the farm with the other animals.

No time to 'think' really means no time to reflect or ponder. Gotta, gotta, gotta, always something to do. As Gandhi said: 'There is more to life than increasing its speed' (Fig 710). Children and young people focus almost all day at school followed by homework and most of the rest of their time is taken by technology and other forms of focus, focus, focus. Awakening to superconsciousness is expanded and speeded immensely by quiet reflection without focus when our point of attention – focus of attention – can wander where it pleases. Many people meditate using various techniques but I never have. I prefer to just sit quietly and give my attention a ticket to anywhere. I call what I do daydreaming and so much knowing and insight comes this way. Research published in the journal *Frontiers in Human Neuroscience* found that brain activity was greatest 'when the person's thoughts wandered freely on their own, rather than when the brain worked to be more strongly focused'. They called this state 'non-directive meditation', but they

Figure 711: Let them daydream – let them awaken to their true self.

are talking about simply daydreaming. The System doesn't want people mediating, daydreaming or setting their attention free. Those behind The System know where that leads. New invented childhood disorders have daydreaming among the *symptoms* for goodness sake and other terms such as 'inability to concentrate' are aimed at making daydreaming a 'disorder' in need of psychiatric drugs. System-servers need to keep children and adults focussed in five-sense reality and in the headlights of an oncoming program (Fig 711). Roger Daltrey, lead singer in *The Who*, made this observant point in a television interview:

> People are too busy. Nobody has taught them to do nothing. When you do nothing that's when the mind becomes creative, it comes up with epiphanies and solutions. Where's the time for contemplation? Who's training them to do nothing?

Keep the public busy, busy, busy, with no time to think, back on the farm with the other animals, as the *Silent Weapons* document said more than 35 years ago. Daydreaming is not about clearing your mind but freeing your mind to wander and ad-lib. Even more than that it is freeing your awareness from mind altogether. Tell someone to clear their mind and their mind will immediately be focussed on 'I must clear my mind'. Part of the process of daydreaming is quiet time without distractions that entrap focus. This means turning off the television, radio and smartphone. Little can be heard in the noise but everything in the silence. Reading books is fine because I find some of my most powerful daydreaming comes that way as my mind wanders from the page and goes its own way. Find time for yourself to be alone and you'll be amazed by the cumulative effect as superconsciousness establishes an ever-stronger connection and the same with using your imagination. Treat past and future as the illusions that they are and know that the only moment that exists is the NOW. This can be challenging at first. Everything around you and running through Phantom Self programs is telling you that past and future are real. What we call past and future are experienced in the NOW and to live in the illusion of past and future is to live in Phantom Self which is governed and controlled by a sense of time. Regret and resentment from the 'past' and fear of the 'future' are powerful forces to pull you out of the NOW, or your sense of it. You can't change what has gone - take the experience as a gift of greater awareness. You can change what we perceive as the future by changing what you are in the NOW – experienced reality is 'possibilities and probabilities folded into existence by *perception*'.

'What do we do?'

People ask for solutions to what is happening to the world in terms of action – 'What do we do?' But where does this 'doing' come from? It comes from your state of *being*. This point is so tragically missed, not least by most of the alternative media and research community. Our collective state of being – perceptions, attitudes – manifests as the world that we 'see'. If they don't change then nothing else can. If we want a world of kindness we need to be kind. If we want a world of peace we need to be peaceful. If we want a world of love we need to be loving. This is not esoteric naval-gazing – it is simple, solid-gold *fact*. We have the world we have because so many are not kind, peaceful and loving. How else could it be so? Jim Morrison, lead singer in 60s band, *The Doors*, said:

> The most important freedom is to be what you really are. You trade your reality for a role. You trade your sense for an act. You give up your ability to feel, and in exchange, put on a mask. There can't be any large-scale revolution until there is a personal revolution, on an individual level. It's got to happen inside first.

We need to become superconscious – the You That Time Forgot. We can never do that while Phantom Self has its hands on the wheel of perception. We must free ourselves from the Phantom and live the superconsciousness that we are (Fig 712). Near-death experiencer Anita Moorjani, writer of *Dying to be Me*, described what she learned about life in her out-of-body state:

Figure 712: Now you're talking.

From what I saw, it looked like we are energy first, and physical is only a result of expressing our energy. And we can change our physical reality if we change our energy. (Some people have mentioned I use the term 'Vibration').

For me, personally, I was made to feel that in order to keep my energy/vibration level up, I only had to live in the moment, enjoy every moment of life, and use each moment to elevate the next moment (which then elevates my future). It is in that moment of elevating your energy level that you can change your future. It sounds very simplistic, but it felt very deep when I was experiencing the understanding of it.

I would say change or elevate your NOW rather than the future and it is not simplistic, but simple. Life is so simple, and the complexity is there to hide that profound revelation. Anita says that she was told to return to this world and 'live your life fearlessly', 'love yourself', 'live with humour, laughter and joy', 'be yourself and express your uniqueness', and 'have no fear of failure'. These are all the things I have been saying since my conscious awakening. I was told them, too, by my own connections to the superconscious 'I'. Humour and laughter is so important to raising frequency. I have never laughed so much in my life than when I was hearing the Voice in Brazil taking apart the illusion with such humour. Yes, we need to sort out what is happening, but it's all so ludicrous you have got laugh in its face. We are also Infinite, Eternal Awareness – surely that's something to smile about however challenging the current experience. These are the simple truths that will expand our awareness and lift our frequency beyond the clutches and manipulations of the Archontic conspiracy (Fig 713). 'Love makes you safe, not fear', Anita Moorjani was told, and the why is another 'so simple'. Love in its Infinite sense takes you beyond the Archontic frequency while fear pulls you into it. Remember

Figure 713: The only way out of the Archon frequency prison.

we are not physical, we are energy. High-frequency energy/awareness can experience this world as much as low-frequency. The difference is that the Archons can't attach to high-frequency energy and if they can't attach to you energetically they can't attach to you 'physically' when one is an expression or projection of the other. People have asked me so many times why I am not dead, why I have not been 'taken out'. Here you have the answer. 'They' have not killed me because they *can't*. They would have to attach to me energetically at the level of undecoded 'Tom's daughter' to 'kill' me holographically and they can't do that. I have unbreachable protection at that energetic level and so I don't need any within the hologram. If they can't 'get' the energetic 'me', they can't 'get' the holographic 'me'. This was the meaning of the communication right at the start through Betty Shine – 'He will face enormous opposition, but we will always be there to protect him.' What Archontic forces can do is work through low-frequency people to disrupt me as much as possible – and they have, but without ultimate success. It's almost funny to see them trying to stop me when I can't be stopped. Will they never learn? You have all the power you choose to take to transform your life and together we have all the power we choose to take to transform our reality and end this Archontic nonsense. But then you know that. You've always known that. Remember?

I began this chapter with a quote: 'I am intrigued by the smile upon your face, and the sadness within your eyes.' I chose it because I see this constantly. The smile on the face is a Phantom mask to hide the sadness of disconnection from superconscious, Infinite Self. People are not aware of the real source of their sadness and many may not even realise they are sad. But you can't hide the truth from the eyes – the window on the soul. I have felt this sadness all my life. Deep inside we know who we are and we know it is not the bewildered myopia of Phantom Self. I was told in 1990 by the superconsciousness which has guided me all these years that a Great Awakening was coming and it would set humanity free from the coma of illusion. There was no evidence to support this then, but two and a half decades later the world is awakening. There is still such a long way to go but it *is* awakening.

We have been enslaved long enough by disconnection from what we really are. It is time to go home by bringing 'home' to us.

CHAPTER THIRTEEN

Beyond The Phantom

Disobedience is the true foundation of liberty. The obedient must be slaves
Henry David Thoreau

Awakening to superconsciousness is everything. Nothing can change without that and the Archon hijack will go on to its conclusion unless Phantom Self is identified and dealt with. Humanity and human society are where they are because they're not superconscious. How can you change anything while the cause remains?

I see the alternative media telling people to 'wake up', but they mostly mean a different wake up. They are talking about waking up to see the manipulation of world events and while that is to be welcomed it will not change anything of significance by itself. You only have to observe the hatred, hostility, arrogance and self-centric nature of so many in the alternative media who have woken up to the five-sense manipulation but have not awoken to their true self. Superconsciousness doesn't behave like that and it is perfectly possible to have some knowledge of global manipulation while remaining a Phantom entrapped in the frequency prison of the Archon virus. They, nor anyone else, can escape through their head. It can only be done through the heart – the gateway to superconsciousness. 'Getting our heads together' to work out a response to global tyranny and madness will take us nowhere. We will be trying to solve the madness from within the madness and what will result can only be another version of madness. 'We must fight' will be in there for sure. We must fight the tyranny, fight for justice, fight because the head can only see fighting as a response to its fear. Either that or heading for the hills, as in fight or flight. I don't want to fight *or* flight. I want to change. Fighting changes nothing in a world which is founded on fighting at every level from war to personal relationships. Fighting got us here and it won't get us out. We don't need to fight or flight. We need to remember. Or, more than that, we need to connect with the Infinity within us that does not need to remember because it *knows* and express that in what we say and do (Fig 714). When people ask what we can do and what are the 'solutions' they mean how can we act; but actions come from perceptions and perceptions come from our state of awareness. Solutions from the Phantom are never solutions. They are at best holding positions until the next problem comes along in response to the last 'solution'. It's another form of fighting as solutions fight problems and problems come back for another go. Einstein talked about the impossibility of

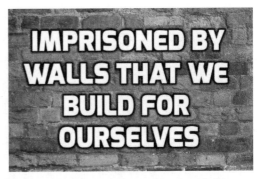

Figure 714: If insanity is going one way we need to go the other.

Figure 715: The question is not who is creating the problems. *We* are.

solving problems with the same level of consciousness that created them. Ah, yes, *created* them. Where do problems come from? They come from us and it can be no other way when we are decoding information through the filter of perception into holographic manifestation. *We* are creating them through our perceptions – '... in a quantum universe there are no such things as accidents, only possibilities and probabilities folded into existence by perception' (Fig 715). The question is not who is creating the problems. *We* are. The question is who or what is dictating our perceptions which then decide what possibilities and probabilities are folded into existence? Is it the virus-programmed Phantom, or superconsciousness? Problems are the speciality of Phantom Self and can only be deleted by Infinite Self. I saw a quote that said everything changes when you start to emit your own frequency rather than absorbing the frequencies around you, when you start imprinting your intent on the Universe rather than receiving an imprint from existence. Here we have the crux of everything, the fork in the road, the ultimate choice and the route to prison or paradise. When the quote talks about receiving an imprint from existence, I would say receiving an imprint from the Archon virus. This is what Phantom does as a manifestation of the Archon Matrix. Expand your awareness and self-identity beyond the Phantom and into superconsciousness and you begin to emit your *own* frequency and imprint *your* intent on the Universe and not implanted Archon intent. We post on the Cosmic Internet or we get posted. Giordano Bruno said: 'The Divine light is always in Man, presenting itself to the senses and to the comprehension, but Man rejects it.' We always have the choice to stop doing so.

I could make a list of things 'we can do' in the form of action. I could talk about the need for mass non-cooperation with The System. I could say that we need to circulate information about the Archon conspiracy and nature of reality to everyone we can. I could say that we must reject transhumanism and Agenda 21/2030 with every fibre of our being. I could point out that a world of more than seven billion can only be controlled by a relative handful if the seven billion allow that to happen through ignorance, disinterest and silence (Fig 716). I could say that we must put aside the manufactured fault lines of race, gender, culture, religion, background and income bracket that are mercilessly employed to divide and rule us. I could say we must come together in unity and harmony to meet the fantastic challenges that face us (Fig 717). I could say that 'there's nothing I can do' is a cop-out to justify doing nothing. I could say

Figure 716: The silent majority need to clear their throats.

Figure 717: Divide and rule is not for fun – it is for Archontic survival.

all these things and more. But those who have a connection with superconsciousness will know all this; and those who don't will not respond anyway. Superconscious people don't need to be told solutions. They instinctively know them from their own expanded awareness and instinctively do them from their own commitment to making a difference. Gandhi knew what to do:

> You assist an evil system most effectively by obeying its orders and decrees. An evil system never deserves such allegiance. Allegiance to it means partaking of this evil. A good person will resist an evil system with his or her own soul (Fig 718).

Superconsciousness is beyond the Matrix and so beyond the realm of fear. Without fear the Archons have no power. Even at the level of courage that transcends fear the Archons have no power. Their power is only the power that we give them out of fear of not doing so. Where does a computer virus get its power from? The computer system it has invaded. Everything comes down to moving our point of attention and awareness from the All-Thinking to the All-Knowing. Superconscious politicians (contraction in terms, I know) would never stand for injustice, unfairness and control. Superconscious journalists would never lie, mislead, seek to hurt or stay silent when truth needs to be heard. Superconscious scientists would never fall for the illusion of solidity, fix the climate change data for political and financial ends or produce poisons and potions to serve their paymasters in Big Biotech and Big Pharma. In a superconscious world

Figure 718: It's our choice to obey tyranny.

there would be no Big Biotech and Big Pharma. Superconscious doctors would never poison, maim and kill their patients or see them as cash machines. They would have the awareness to know what the body really is and treat the cause energetically and not the symptom with scalpels and toxicity. Superconscious lawyers would seek fairness and justice and not see their targets as another notch on the CV and another big cheque in the bank. Superconscious judges would never fix a verdict or do what a government demands. In a superconscious world

Figure 719: Freedom is *our* business and *our* responsibility.

there would be no courts or even laws because they would be not be necessary. Superconscious bankers would not be bankers. Superconscious CEOs would not put profit before people and environment. Superconscious Monsanto would not be Monsanto. Superconscious government agents and agencies would serve the interests of people and not corporations and personal gain. Superconscious social workers would not steal children from loving families. A superconscious world would not need social workers. There is no such thing as a superconscious soldier, terrorist or arms manufacturer. Nor can there be a superconscious religion or religious advocate. In a superconscious world there would be no religion, for there would be nothing to worship. Religion is a Phantom that requires the division and ignorance of other Phantoms to exist. Superconsciousness does not do division or ignorance and nor does it look to someone else for 'salvation' (Fig 719). Phantom world is a prison. Superconscious world is a paradise.

We create paradise as we have created the prison – by decoding and manifesting paradise into holographic existence. Humanity is the vehicle for manifesting its own enslavement. Archons cannot do that without creative imagination. They can only manipulate and program our perceptions so that we create what we have been programmed consciously and subconsciously to perceive. A constant stream of movies portraying transhumanism, robots and dystopian societies are to post perceptions in our energetic fields through pre-emptive programming. Everything is a frequency including transhumanist, dystopian societies. Plant those frequencies in the conscious and subconscious mind and people will decode them into manifestation – fold them into existence by perception.

Figure 720: Time to choose.

Figure 721: I mean love in its Infinite sense.   **Figure 722:** Two faces of Infinite forever.

Unless *we* change nothing else can (Fig 720). What we want to change is being created by *what we are*. Interact with reality from the heart and change will follow – superconscious change. Meet every situation with 'What does my heart say?'; 'What would my heart do?'; 'How would superconsciousness respond?' Your head might scream in alarm and defiance for a while but this will soon pass as your heart returns to its rightful place as the arbiter of perception. The brain has a role to play, but as the servant not the master. Stick with your heart despite the challenges and deceitful ramblings of Phantom Self and you are on the road to superconsciousness. The more who do this, the more the world will follow as contagious superconsciousness begins to circulate (Figs 721 and 722). It's already happening through what I have called for 26 years the 'Truth Vibrations'. I was told right at the start of my conscious journey that a vibrational change was coming that would awaken humanity and I can now see its effect (Fig 723). Open your heart and synchronicity, 'coincidence' and intuitive knowing will guide you. As the heart and thus superconsciousness lead perception, so Phantom Self will dissolve as its programs are deleted. When the programs go they take with them the Archontic world they are designed to impose and create. What will be left is love in the Infinite sense. Not the love that humanity has been deceived into believing is love. A love that is all-knowing, all-caring, all-being, with its holographic expression of

Figure 723: However bad it may seem at first sight – an enormous awakening is happening.

Figure 724: It's all a dream.

joy, kindness, empathy and a celebration of life itself. A world of infinite possibility and potential to manifest our dreams by knowing that life *is* a dream and dreams have no limitation unless we believe they do (Fig 724). French writer and philosopher Albert Camus said that the only way to deal with an unfree world is to become so absolutely free that your very existence is an act of rebellion (Fig 725). The Demiurge / Archon virus is terrified of awakening people living their freedom. It knows they will end its game. The System reflects that in surveillance and efforts to undermine those who can

Figure 725: If not now, then when?

'see'. I am on the surface one man sitting here in a little spare bedroom typing away exposing the All-powerful System; but I'm not afraid of The System – it is afraid of me. Banning me from speaking in places like 'free' Canada and the hassle I always have when trying to get a visa to speak in Australia are expressions of that fear, as are governments and agencies who block my website on their computer systems. It is simply a fear of information that will change perceptions on which the whole edifice of illusory power depends. *We* have the power – not The System. Osho said:

> People are afraid, very much afraid of those who know themselves. They have a certain power, a certain aura and a certain magnetism, a charisma that can take out alive, young people from the traditional imprisonment. The awakened man cannot be enslaved – that is the difficulty – and he cannot be imprisoned ...
>
> ... The awakened man is the greatest stranger in the world; he does not seem to belong to anybody. No organisation confines him, no community, no society, no nation.

And no System, no virus. 'Charisma' comes from the Greek charismata meaning divine gift or power – superconsciousness.

I've described in the book how the world of the seen is created and manipulated from the unseen. There is no sense in trying to change the seen within the seen. You are trying to change the symptom without dealing with the cause. Answers do not lie in the seen and the conspiracy is fine with those great tracts of the alternative media that seek answers in the seen. They are not there. The answers are in the unseen – in our perceptions, in our frequency, in our hearts. This is the knowledge or knowing of the ages that has been expressed throughout what we call time by those who have accessed superconsciousness. Gnostics responsible for the Nag Hammadi texts are an example. They believed that *gnosis* or secret knowledge came from intuitive knowing and that 'God' did not create the 'material' Universe, but a fake 'god' or Demiurge. Humans were sparks or droplets of the same essence as 'God' but became trapped in their bodies from which they will eventually escape. The 'Fall of Man' was the fall into 'matter'.

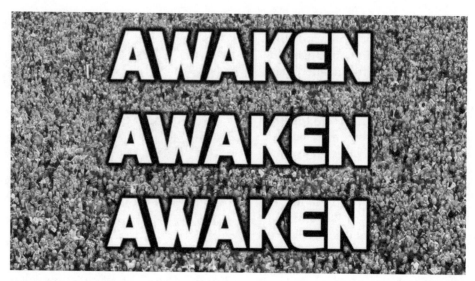

Figure 726: ... To Infinite Awareness.

Humanity became ignorant of its true nature, but the Gnostics said that 'God' sends forth emanations of himself to show 'divine sparks of Spirit' their true identity. Salvation was by knowledge – self-knowledge or knowledge of self. I am saying the same using different language and in the context of today's world. Humans are expressions of Infinite Awareness but their perceptions were hijacked and drawn into low-frequency states by low-frequency beliefs, emotions and attitudes. They are trapped by the perceptions of Phantom Self ('trapped in their bodies') and have forgotten their true nature. Escape is through reconnection with Infinite Self or superconsciousness, which raises their frequency and takes them 'home'. The themes are the same because it's the truth (Fig 726).

I'm sure that there were many times during this book for those who have accepted its premise that the situation appeared hopeless. How do we stop this juggernaut to tyranny? There seems no way. But there *is* and it's simple in the saying if not always in the doing. We change ourselves and together we change the world. 'Twas ever thus and always shall be.

Control or freedom is a choice and it's time to make it. Wait any longer and there won't be one to make.

Postscript Updates

The speed with which the agenda I have been exposing for 26 years is now moving can be seen in what has happened in the short period between finishing this book and the printing and production process beginning.

Firstly, we had the terrorist attacks in Paris in November 2015 in which more than 130 people died in a blaze of bullets at multiple locations and suicide bombers blew themselves up. The attacks had Problem-Reaction- Solution (PRS) stamped all over them and the 'solution' has been another upgrade in the war on freedom and the Orwellian state and a further expansion of mass bombing in Syria (Fig 1). ISIS, or Islamic State (IS), was said to have claimed responsibility, but they are only a proxy terrorist army funded, trained and armed by those who imposed the 'solutions' after the Paris horror – the United States, United Kingdom, France and others, very much including Israel (Fig 2). At the same time the ISIS-funding Saudi Arabia continued with its constant beheadings and mass slaughter of civilians using British and American weapons in Yemen without a word of condemnation from the moral 'West'. WikiLeaks published a cable from then US Secretary

Figure 1: An image I posted on social media within hours of the Paris attacks – and this is exactly what happened.

Figure 2: You can add Saudi Arabia, Israel and others to this lot. They are not really 'leaders' – only here-today-gone-tomorrow puppets of the Hidden Hand.

427

of State Hillary Clinton that clearly showed how the terrorist activities of Saudi Arabia are well known to the coalition of hypocrisy that welcomes them into their 'anti-terror' façade. The cable said: 'Donors in Saudi Arabia constitute the most significant source of funding to Sunni terrorist groups worldwide.' These characters orchestrating the movie in the West and the Middle East are beyond evil and it's all a gigantic hoax. Robert Baer, a former senior CIA officer who worked in Yugoslavia during 1991-94 and in the Middle East, gave an interview to *WebTribune* in November 2015 describing his experiences. They are mightily relevant to current events. He told how the CIA spent millions to break up Yugoslavia into warring factions – exactly what is being done in the Middle East and Africa which is just a continuation of the same global plan. Baer said of the CIA:

> They gave us files about a group called 'Supreme Serbia' detailing plans to conduct a series of bomb attacks on key buildings in Sarajevo in opposition to Bosnia's ambition to leave former Yugoslavia. No such group ever existed! Our headquarters lied to us. Our mission was to alarm and spread panic among politicians in Bosnia, simply to fill their heads with the idea that Serbs would attack. To begin with, we accepted the story, but after a while we started to wonder. Why were we raising such hysteria when the group clearly did not exist? ...

> ... I received instructions that Slovenia was ready to declare independence. We were given money, a few million dollars, to fund various NGOs, opposition parties and various politicians who have inflamed hatred ...

> ... Many CIA agents and senior officers disappeared simply because they refused to conduct propaganda against the Serbs in Yugoslavia. Personally I was shocked at the dose of lies being fed from our agencies and politicians! Many CIA agents were directed propaganda without being aware of what they are doing. Everyone knew just a fraction of the story and only the one who create the whole story knew the background ...

This is the compartmentalisation that I talk about – this is how attacks such as 9/11 and Paris can be instigated with only a few of the players knowing the real story. People dismiss the idea of a Hidden Hand behind terrorist attacks like those in Paris because they involve alleged Muslims, but they miss the point of how it's done. If you are working on the shop floor for a global corporation you do your job by following orders from 'on high'; but where is this 'on high' and who are the personnel involved? You may know the hierarchy immediately above you and maybe even above them, but there comes a level beyond which you don't know what is happening or to what end. You don't know the people making the decisions and delivering the orders that come down to you through those that you do know. These Problem-Reaction-Solution events are structured in the same way using the techniques that CIA agent Robert Baer described. Those that carry them out by shooting people, planting bombs and blowing themselves to pieces will genuinely believe in their madness that they are fighting for Allah or some Holy War. They are the fodder – the oil rags of these outrages, not the engineers. We are fed the cover stories about some 'mastermind' behind the attacks which turns out to be some bit of a kid or criminal with the brain the size of a pea. These media-promoted 'masterminds' are always moronic because they are not 'masterminds' – just expendable

idiots serving masters they don't even know
exist. A French journalist who had been a
hostage of Islamic State and interacted with
them every day – including the so-called
'Jihadi John' – said that they were more stupid
than evil. Given the depths of evil to which
they have descended it boggles the mind to
contemplate on that basis just how
unimaginably stupid they must be. But at their
level this has to be so. Anyone with a
modicum of intelligence would see they were
being used and exploited to a very different
end.

Figure 3: It only works while people fall for it.

The key question whenever such attacks
happen is 'who benefits?' Who benefits from
me believing the official version of events and
succumbing to the fear they are designed to
trigger? The answer in Paris – as always with
Problem-Reaction-Solution – is anyone who
wants to advance the agenda I have exposed
in this book (Fig 3). French President François
Hollande ordered an open-ended state of
emergency that essentially suspended what
was left of French democracy and armed
troops were posted on the streets all over the
country. Hollande proposed changes to the
French Constitution to further delete basic

Figure 4: Just another professional liar.

freedoms and install presidential dictatorship (or rather dictatorship by those who
control the president). The British government announced massive increases in
intelligence and surveillance spending while cutting benefits to the most vulnerable
people on the grounds that there was not enough money. The United States, Australia
and others also used the Paris attacks to advance their own police state agendas – or
agenda, singular, with all of them strands in the same global web. British Prime Minister
David Cameron had been desperate to have the Royal Air Force bombing in Syria, but
he could not persuade Parliament to agree. He had been out-voted once before and
appeared to have no prospect of success if he tried again. Then came Paris. Cameron
immediately exploited the horror to take his case to Parliament for bombing in Syria
and this time he won with the one-party state imposing itself over the opposition from
Labour Party leader Jeremy Corbyn. Nearly 70 of Corbyn's MPs voted with the
psychopath Cameron to add Britain to the ever-gathering list of countries bombing a
land the size of Washington State. The US, France, Turkey, Israel, Russia and Australia
were already bombing the shit out of the place at enormous cost in civilian lives and
population displacement which constantly adds to the pressures of migration into
Europe (Fig 4). A Chinese hostage was reported to have been killed by IS and the
Chinese authorities announced that they would be striking the terrorist group while the
German Parliament agreed to send troops to Syria (Fig 5). I am just waiting for Easter

Figure 5: All this bombing in a country the size of Washington State.

Island to announce the same. The prospect of NATO as a whole joining the madness was made possible by the mantra within hours that the Paris attacks were 'an act of war' against France and that 'Islamic State is at war with France'. The theme began with Hollande and was then repeated by all and sundry, not least in the United States. This was highly significant in its clear coordination because when a member state of NATO is attacked in an 'act of war' it can open the way for the 'all-for-one' Article 5 of the NATO Treaty. It says:

The Parties agree that an armed attack against one or more of them in Europe or North America shall be considered an attack against them all and consequently they agree that, if such an armed attack occurs, each of them, in exercise of the right of individual or collective self-defence recognised by Article 51 of the Charter of the United Nations, will assist the Party or Parties so attacked by taking forthwith, individually and in concert with the other Parties, such action as it deems necessary, including the use of armed force, to restore and maintain the security of the North Atlantic area.

Any such armed attack and all measures taken as a result thereof shall immediately be reported to the Security Council. Such measures shall be terminated when the Security Council has taken the measures necessary to restore and maintain international peace and security.

The United Nations Security Council approved a French proposal after the Paris attacks which authorised 'combating' ISIS 'by all means' and France invoked for the first time an EU treaty collective-defence article asking for military support from EU nations in response to the attacks. It was, of course, agreed as the Paris Problem-Reaction-Solution played out.

Same old story

There is a clear pattern to PRS events or 'false flags' which I have been highlighting for years and Paris had all of them once again (Fig 6). There is the finding of a 'terrorist passport' which they use to identify by name and location those they want to blame for the attack. A 'Syrian passport' was found near the body of a terrorist in Paris who had killed himself with a suicide bomb. There was little left of him, but his *passport*? Not a problem. It seems that no matter what scale of explosion or fireball that these passports are subjected to they still come out intact (Fig 7). An Internet comment after the Paris attacks asked for people to send their passports to build a bomb-proof shelter. Nothing, it seems, could be more indestructible. The same happened with 9/11 when the FBI announced that the passport of one of the 'Muslim hijackers' had been found where the

Figure 6: The recurring themes of staged terrorist attacks – and there are others.

World Trade Center towers had stood. Yes, a paper passport from a 'hijacker' who was supposed to have died in the fireball when his plane struck the tower. I watched a BBC newsreader tell me this without laughing despite the sheer idiocy of the claim, but to the BBC if it came from official sources it must be true no matter how ludicrous. A year later a British television crew filming a documentary about 9/11 asked New York Police about the passport that so miraculously survived intact and they were told that it was 'a rumour that might be true'. Well, of course it wasn't true – don't be insane – and how come this 'rumour that might be true' was the subject of a 'we've definitely found it' news conference called at the time of 9/11 by the FBI? These ridiculous official narratives are part of the perception deception and they are circulated only to sell an image that the fairy stories must be true. They know that most people will never question even the most infantile claims and they will soon forget what was said when it is later contradicted by another lie that suits the moment. The '7/7' London Tube and bus bombings in 2005 also had the passport miracle. A man who is supposed to have blown himself apart with a bomb in his backpack somehow left behind an undamaged passport, driving licence and mobile phone insurance certificate for the police to find and identify him. How very thoughtful. It was the same with the 9/11 'terrorists' that we were told left Korans in their hotel rooms and hire cars. If you were a fanatical Muslim what is the last thing you would leave anywhere? They also left some flying manuals to let us know they flew the wide-bodied jets even though their flying instructors described them as hopeless when it came to piloting one-engined Cessnas. I talked earlier about scientists needing one miracle (the Big Bang) and they would take it from there; but with these PRS lie-fests they need far more than that. Miracle after miracle after miracle is required to make possible what is claimed to have happened.

Then there is the 'drill' or 'exercise' going on at the same time as these attacks that follows a scenario which mirrors what really happens. These take statistical chance into the stratosphere of 'coincidence' because they are not coincidence and the same happened in Paris. Drills are organised as a perfect cover for orchestrating the real thing. An 'exercise' on September 11th was happening in the skies over New York and Washington that involved a scenario of hijacked passenger aircraft with at least one to be theoretically flown into a building in Washington. What are the chances of that? The exercise scrambled the usual

Figure 7: They find them in the strangest places and never damaged. I keep mine in a furnace, just so it's safe.

REMEMBER: THIS IS WHAT STARTED IT ALL ...

BASED ON A LIE

DAVIDICKE.COM

Figure 8: The lie that launched the never-ending 'war on terror'.

hijack response by NORAD, the North American Aerospace Defense Command, which should have immediately had fighter jets airborne to see what was going on. This didn't happen and by the time they arrived in New York and Washington the deed was done – just as it was meant to be. I have published part of the NORAD logs for that day in previous books and the confusion is clear between what was 'exercise' and what was 'real'. See *Alice in Wonderland and the World Trade Center Disaster* and *The David Icke Guide To The Global Conspiracy* for the detailed story of the 9/11 inside job (Fig 8). PRS terrorist attacks not only happen – they are allowed to happen by systematic breaches in security that would otherwise thwart what was planned. This is why you see 'security mistakes' as another constant theme in these situations. A drill was happening in London at the same time – and involving the same Tube stations – as the 7/7 bombings and it's the same story with the Oklahoma bombing in 1995, the Oslo bombing of 2011, the Boston Marathon bombings of 2013, and a stream of mass shootings in the United States which miraculously happen at the same time as drills or at locations where drills regularly take place. All those drills were working to the same scenario of what actually happened in the same place at the same time. The police drill based on a bomb going off in Oslo ended just 26 minutes before the real one went off in the same place. And, yes, a drill was happening in Paris on the same day as the 2015 attacks founded on the same scenario of what really happened. The 7/7 London attacks also took place during a G8 summit meeting in Gleneagles, Scotland, so they could be milked to sell the 'solution' and the Paris attacks were on the eve of the G20 summit in Turkey where world leaders were meeting across the border from Syria to discuss their response to Islamic State terrorism. You couldn't make it up – and you don't have to because *they* do. Many other attacks will be planned (another in Britain eventually) to terrify the population into subservience and compliance – we must not fall for it.

The road to World War III

Days after Paris with politicians in meltdown hysteria to expand bombing in Syria and delete freedoms at home came the attack on a Russian fighter jet by Turkey on the ludicrous grounds that it had breached Turkish airspace. Russia said that it did not enter Turkey airspace and for sure the plane came down in Syria. Even the Turkish authorities only claimed that it entered their airspace for *17 seconds*. It is beyond imbecility to suggest that this constituted a threat to Turkey even if that was true (which seems highly unlikely on the evidence); but then the terrorist-supporting President Recep Tayyip Erdogan knew that (Fig 9). Any excuse will do to follow the script and as a member of NATO Turkey was immediately supported by other members of this world-army-in-waiting. 'Turkey has the right to defend itself', said the man-child that is

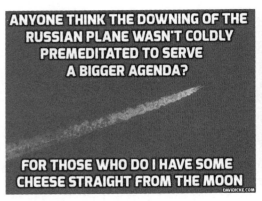

Figure 9: The Turkish attack on the Russian plane.

Figure 10: Turkey's 'elected' dictator.

Obama. The attack was clearly premeditated and triggered by Russian success in pushing back ISIS in Syria – the last thing that Erdogan, Obama and the other NATO psychopaths, liars and hypocrites wanted. ISIS was created by the United States in league with other NATO countries plus Israel, Saudi Arabia and Qatar to (a) remove Assad in Syria and (b) as a manufactured enemy and conduit for terrorism in the West to terrify people into giving their freedoms away. The last thing they wanted was for Putin's Russia to come in and start trying to defeat them when the American-led bombing of ISIS had got nowhere because it wasn't meant to. Turkey has been key to the survival and prosperity of ISIS with weapons and supplies passing across its border to ISIS in Syria and Iraq while oil supplies seized by ISIS came the other way to be sold via Turkey around the world. The Russian government produced evidence in support of this and, together with other reports galore, connected Erdogan and his son, Bilal, to this oil trafficking which is said to constitute some 50 percent of ISIS income. Fighters joining ISIS also reach their destination through Turkey, an allegedly 'democratic' country which Erdogan has turned into his own Islamic fiefdom while destroying any idea of freedom of the press or free political opposition.

The last thing he wants is the end of ISIS and that explains his military attacks on the Kurds and Russians who are both genuinely trying to defeat them (Fig 10). The same is true of the United States which was exposed for dropping leaflets over ISIS territory giving them 45 minutes warning of bombing attacks and where they would be. Russia began to defend its bombers with fighter planes while shipping into Syria state-of-art missile defences and deploying a missile cruiser off the Syria coast with orders to destroy any target posing danger. The potential for Albert Pike's World War III has never been greater and it is happening in the way he described out of the Middle East with the unleashing of his 'Nihilists' – the Western-created Islamic State/ISIS/ISIL. So much has happened in the two weeks between finishing the body of the book and the printing process starting and more is sure to have happened by the time you read this as engineered terrorism and war goes on being used to transform global society in the way I have described. Watch for China being pulled into the picture. Another consequence of the Paris attacks and events in Syria has been to increase calls for a European Union army – long predicted in my books – as another stepping-stone to the world army.

Belgium's Prime Minister, Charles Michel, responded to Paris with a call for the creation of a European CIA: 'We must quickly put in place a European intelligence agency, a European CIA' [to] 'unmask those with hostile intentions.' Try Washington, London, Paris, Ankara, Tel Aviv etc., etc.

Climate Mecca – the believers assemble

As the book goes to press negotiators from 195 countries are attending the latest 'climate change' summit in – yes, Paris – called COP21. Most of them truly believe that they are in a desperate race to save the planet when, in truth, what they think they are 'fighting' doesn't actually exist. They buy the lies through mendacious repetition and/or because of the endless flows of money for those who will promote the fairy tale. Leaders from 147 nations addressed the event and sang from the song sheet. Barack 'I am speaking so it must be bollocks' Obama even had the ludicrous audacity to connect climate change to fighting terrorism using his location as the peg: 'What greater rejection of those who would tear down our world than marshalling our best efforts to save it?' His speech was sickening in both its inversion of truth and its calculated manipulation. The mainstream media repeated unquestioned the unsupported claims and blatant lies about human-caused 'global warming' and protestors who would normally oppose the Establishment turned up to demand that 'global warming' be addressed by transforming the world into the very fascist dictatorship that they, at other times, turn out to protest against. It takes 'being had' into a whole new level of meaning. It is such a head-shaker to watch people demand their own enslavement while having no idea that they are doing so. The aim of COP21, as with all these climate summits, was to secure as many legally-binding agreements as possible between countries to centrally-dictate their domestic policy and so impose the demands of Agenda 21/2030 – the Hunger Games Society. Prominent scientists meeting in Texas before the Paris farce declared that fears about human-caused global warming were 'irrational' and 'based on nonsense' (Fig 11). We were being led down a 'false path' by what they called 'catastrophism'. As one put it: 'Demonisation of CO2 is irrational at best and even modest warming is mostly beneficial.' The latter is confirmed by

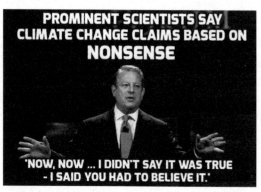

Figure 11: No matter how many climate experts challenge the lies they are ignored because the climate change hoax is vital to the agenda.

Figure 12: US Secretary of State John Kerry said doubters had to be silenced. When you are selling a lie you have to suppress the truth.

historical experience. Greenpeace Co-Founder Dr Patrick Moore said: 'We are dealing with pure political propaganda that has nothing to do with science.' But instead of listening to scientists who produce evidence to expose the said nonsense we have increasing efforts to silence them (Fig 12). US Secretary of State John Kerry said before COP21: 'The science tells us unequivocally [like hell it does] – those who continue to make climate change a political fight put us all at risk and we cannot sit idly by and allow them to do that.' The discredited James Hansen, who has been exposed

Figure 13: The war on truth.

for fixing climate data in support of the lie, called for the prosecution of those who challenge the propaganda for 'high crimes against humanity' while Robert F. Kennedy, Jr., said of those with a mind to call their own: 'This is treason, and we need to start treating them as traitors.' Joe Romm, a former Clinton official now running the *ClimateProgress* website, went further in his warning to non-believers and climate infidels: 'It is not my wrath you need fear [true] when there's an entire generation that will soon be ready to strangle you and your kind while you sleep in your beds.' Oh, really? I'm shaking.

The double-whammy of generating ever more fear through war and terrorist attacks, while silencing those who expose or see the conspiracy, are themes that become more obvious by the day. This includes the leaflet distributed to parents by government 'child protection officials' in Britain warning that opposing government policy and mistrusting the mainstream media are signs that children and young people have been 'radicalised' (Fig 13). Parents were also warned that 'a belief in conspiracy theories' could be a sign of grooming by 'extremists'. See how terrified The System is of the truth when its very existence depends on the lie? I take enormous encouragement from the way far more people are awakening to that truth – or some levels of it, anyway. This can be seen in the increasing distain that people have for the claims of officialdom and indeed the massive surge in the interest in my work during the writing of this book.

The world is indeed mad, but so many more are now becoming sane – becoming conscious.

For daily updates on world events as they really are see davidicke.com/headlines.

Bibliography

Bergrun, Dr Norman: *Ringmakers of Saturn* (Pentland Press, 1986).

Brzezinski, Zbigniew: *Between Two Ages: America's Role in the Technetronic Era* (Greenwood Press; new edition, 1982 – first published 1970).

Brzezinski, Zbigniew: *The Grand Chessboard: American Primacy and Its Geostrategic Imperatives* (Basic Books, 1998).

Carr, Nicholas: *The Shallows: How The Internet Is Changing The Way We Think, Read And Remember* (Atlantic Books, 2011).

Carr, William James Guy: *Satan, Prince of this World* (Dauphin Publications Inc., 2014 – written in 1959).

Castaneda, Carlos: *The Active Side of Infinity* (Harper Collins, 1999).

Deane, Reverend John Bathurst: *The Worship of the Serpent* (BiblioBazaar, 2009, first published 1933).

Greenfield, Susan: *Mind Change* (Rider, 2015).

Hall, Manly P.: *Secret Teachings of All Ages* (Tarcher; new edition, 2004).

Horn, Thomas A.: *Nephilim Stargates* (Anomalos Publishing, 2013).

Huxley, Aldous: *Brave New World* (Vintage Classics, 2007, first published 1932).

Moorjani, Anita: *Dying to be Me* (Hay House, 2014).

Orwell, George: *1984* (Penguin Classics; New Ed edition, 2004, first published 1948)

Purucker, G de: *Occult Glossary* (Theosophical University Press, 1969).

Sagan, Carl: *The Dragons of Eden* (Ballantine Books Inc.; Reprint edition, 1992).

Sand, Shlomo: *The Invention of the Jewish People* (Verso. 2010).

Sheldrake, Rupert: *Science Set Free* (Crown Publishing Group (NY), 2013).

Shine, Betty: *Mind to Mind* (Bantam Press; Reprint edition, 1989).

Talbot, Michael: *The Holographic Universe* (HarperCollins; New Edition, 1996).

Tegmark, Max: *Our Mathematical Universe: My Quest for the Ultimate Nature of Reality* (Penguin, 2015).

Thornhill, Wallace, and Talbott, David: *The Electric Universe* (Mikamar Publishing, 2007).

Thornhill, Wallace, and Talbott, David: *Thunderbolts of the Gods* (Mikamar Publishing, 2005).

Index

Other work by David Icke

The Perception Deception
David's most comprehensive book in which a vast spectrum of subjects are weaved together to present the world in a totally new light. 900 pages copiously illustrated and a colour art gallery by Neil Hague. The Perception Deception is the most detailed dot-connecting book ever written on these subjects.

Remember Who You Are
This book breaks massive new ground and brings a world of apparent complexity, mystery and bewilderment into clarity. The key is in the title. We are enslaved because we identify 'self' with our body and our name when these are only vehicles and symbols for that we really are – Infinite Awareness.

Human Race Get Off Your Knees – The Lion Sleeps No More
A monumental work of more than 650 pages, 355,000 words, 325 images and 32 pages of original artwork by Neil Hague. David's biggest and most comprehensive book introducing the 'Moon Matrix' and providing the fine detail about reality, history and present day events. Highly-acclaimed and a 'must have' for anyone interested in David Icke's work.

The David Icke Guide to the Global Conspiracy (and how to end it)
A masterpiece of dot-connecting that is both extraordinary and unique. There is a 'wow', indeed many of them, on every page as Icke lifts the veil on the unseen world.

Infinite Love is the Only Truth, Everything Else is Illusion
Why the 'world' is a virtual-reality game that only exists because we believe it does. Icke explains how we 'live' in a 'holographic internet' in that our brains are connected to a central 'computer' that feeds us the same collective reality that we decode from waveforms and electrical signals into the holographic 3D 'world' that we all think we see.

Alice in Wonderland and the World Trade Center Disaster – Why the Official Story of 9/11 is a Monumental Lie
A shocking exposé of the Ministries of Mendacity that have told the world the Big Lie about what happened on September 11th, who did it, how and why. This 500 page book reveals the real agenda behind the 9/11 attacks and how they were orchestrated from within the borders of the United States and not from a cave in Afghanistan.

Tales from the Time Loop
In this 500-page, profusely-illustrated book, David Icke explores in detail the multi-levels of the global conspiracy. He exposes the five-sense level and demolishes the official story of the invasions of Iraq and Afghanistan; he explains the inter-dimensional manipulation; and he shows that what we think is the 'physical world' is all an illusion that only exists in our mind. Without this knowledge, the true nature of the conspiracy cannot be understood.

The Biggest Secret
An exposé of how the same interbreeding bloodlines have controlled the planet for thousands of years. It includes the horrific background to the British royal family, the murder of Princess Diana, and the true origins of major religions. A blockbuster.

Children of the Matrix
The companion book of The Biggest Secret that investigates the reptilian and other dimensional connections to the global conspiracy and reveals the world of illusion – the 'Matrix' – that holds the human race in daily slavery.

... And The Truth Shall Set You Free (21st century edition)
Icke exposes in more than 500 pages the interconnecting web that controls the world today. This book focuses on the last 200 years and particularly on what is happening around us today. Another highly acclaimed book, which has been constantly updated. A classic in its field.

I Am Me, I Am Free
Icke's book of solutions. With humour and powerful insight, he shines a light on the mental and emotional prisons we build for ourselves ... prisons that disconnect us from our true and infinite potential to control our own destiny. A getaway car for the human psyche.

Earlier books by David Icke include *The Robots' Rebellion* (Gill & Macmillan), *Truth Vibrations* (Gill & Macmillan), *Heal the World* (Gill & Macmillan), *Days of Decision* (Jon Carpenter) and *It Doesn't Have To Be Like This* (Green Print). The last two books are out of print and no longer available.

David Icke Live At Wembley Arena

Filmed at London's Wembley Arena in 2012 – this is the biggest event of its kind ever staged anywhere in the world. Nearly ten hours of cutting edge information researched, compiled and presented by David Icke that you will hear nowhere else in the world put together in this way.

The Lion Sleeps No More

David Icke marks his 20th year of uncovering astounding secrets and suppressed information with this eight-hour presentation before 2,500 people at London's Brixton Academy in May 2010. David has moved the global cutting edge so many times since his incredible 'awakening' in 1990 and here he does it again – and then some.

Beyond the Cutting Edge – Exposing the Dreamworld We Believe to be Real

Since his extraordinary 'awakening' in 1990 and 1991, David Icke has been on a journey across the world, and within himself, to find the Big answers to the Big questions: Who are we? Where are we? What are we doing here? Who really controls this world and how and why? In this seven-hour presentation to 2,500 people at the Brixton Academy in London, David addresses all these questions and connects the dots between them to reveal a picture of life on earth that is truly beyond the cutting edge.

Freedom or Fascism: the time to choose – 3xDVD set

More than 2,000 people from all over Britain and across the world gather at London's famous Brixton Academy to witness an extraordinary event. David Icke weaves together more than 16 years of painstaking research and determined investigation into the Global Conspiracy and the extraordinary 'sting' being perpetrated on an amnesic human race. Icke is the Dot Connector and he uses hundreds of illustrations to reveal the hidden story behind apparently unconnected world events.

Revelations of a Mother Goddess – DVD

Arizona Wilder was mind-programmed from birth by Josef Mengele, the notorious, 'Angel of Death' in the Nazi concentration camps. In this interview with David Icke, she describes human sacrifice rituals at Glamis Castle and Balmoral in England, in which the Queen, the Queen Mother and other members of the Royal Family sacrificed children in Satanic ceremonies.

The Reptilian Agenda – DVD

In this memorable, almost six hours of interview, contained in parts one and two, Zulu shaman, Credo Mutwa, reveals his incredible wealth of knowledge about the black magicians of the Illuminati and how they use their knowledge of the occult to control the world. Sit back and savour this wonderful man. You are in the presence of a genius and a giant.

Other books available

The Medical Mafia

The superb exposé of the medical system by Canadian doctor, Guylaine Lanctot, who also shows how and why 'alternative' methods are far more effective. Highly recommended.

What The Hell Am I Doing Here Anyway?

A second book by Guylaine Lanctot. We thirst for freedom, yet all the while we are imprisoned by conditioned beliefs.

Trance-Formation Of America

The staggering story of Cathy O'Brien, the mind-controlled slave of the US Government for some 25 years. Read this one sitting down. A stream of the world's most famous political names are revealed as they really are. Written by Cathy O'Brien and Mark Phillips.

Access Denied – For Reasons Of National Security

From the authors of Trance-Formation of America, this is the documented journey through CIA mind-control.

All David Icke books and DVDs, books by other authors, clothing with a message and more are available at the shop at **Davidicke.com.**

DAVID ICKE'S
WORLDWIDE WAKE-UP TOUR
2016/17 – AND BEYOND

David is taking his all-day presentation
all over the world – details at
Davidicke.com

Readings by **Carol Clarke**

Readings are sent via audio file over the internet

*'Carol Clarke is the most consistently accurate psychic
I have come across anywhere in the world and she has
a thirteen year record of remarkable accuracy with me
and many other people that I know.'*
David Icke

To contact Carol for a reading,
email: welshseer15@aol.co.uk

or

email: welshseer@hotmail.co.uk

Right-Brain Thinking In A Left-Brain World

Monnica Sepulveda in California has been a medium for 45 years and specialises in helping people break out of The Program – both their own and that of collective humanity.

Consultations by Skype anywhere in the world.

The RichieAllen Show

Broadcasting The News The Corporate Controlled Mainstream Media Won't Report
Live on DavidIcke.com Mon/Thurs 8pm UK Time
RichieAllen.co.uk Twitter.com/RichieAllenShow Facebook.com/TheRichieAllenShow